Course	Social and Ethical Environment of Business
Course Number	**BA 242**
Professor	Michael E. Brown
	Penn State-Erie

http://create.mcgraw-hill.com

ISBN-10: 1121394914   ISBN-13: 9781121394919

Contents

Credits

Chapter Three

Business Power

James B. Duke and the American Tobacco Company

On December 23, 1856, cries of new life swelled from a North Carolina farmhouse, their source a baby boy named James Buchanan Duke. The lad would have far more impact on the world than the failed president his name honored.

Soon, the Civil War displaced the Duke family from its land. On returning home in 1865 little James's father built a small factory to make a brand of chewing tobacco named Pro Bono Publico (a Latin phrase meaning "for the public good"). James helped. He was a precocious, energetic boy, diligent, gifted at sales and, at the age of 14, an overseer of 20 workers.

By his late teens, James had lost interest in attending college, his love of the business being so great. He had visions of grandeur for the little factory, but the presence of a rival firm, the Bull Durham Co., thwarted them. Its chewing tobacco was so dominant that head-on competition seemed hopeless. Taking a major gamble, he committed the company to a then-novel product—the cigarette. This was a venturesome move, because at the time few people smoked them. Most tobacco users were rural men who associated cigarettes with degenerate dudes and dandies in big cities.

Nonetheless, in 1881 Duke brought 10 Russian immigrant cigarette rollers to his North Carolina factory and set them to work. Each made about 2,000 per day. At first there was no demand. Tobacco shops refused to order his Duke of Durham brand since customers never asked for them. But Duke was a merchandising genius. In Atlanta, he took out a full-page newspaper ad of a famous actress holding Duke cigarettes in her outstretched hand. This use of a woman to advertise cigarettes created a sensation and, along with it, demand. In St. Louis, Duke confronted extreme prejudice against cigarettes. Tobacco shop proprietors simply would not place orders. He had his agents hire a young, redheaded widow to call on the tobacconists, and she got 19 orders on her first day.

By this time a Virginia engineer, James Bonsack, had invented a machine capable of rolling 200 cigarettes per minute. He offered it first to the largest tobacco companies, but they turned him down, believing that smokers would reject newfangled, machine-rolled cigarettes. Duke saw the significance of the technology and jumped at it.[1] In 1883 he negotiated an exclusive agreement to operate the device, and his

---

[1] Patrick G. Porter, "Origins of the American Tobacco Company," *Business History Review,* Spring 1969, pp. 68–69.

Duke lured men to try his new cigarette brands by putting picture cards in packs. The first cards were stage actresses in poses that were provocative for that day. Later card series included Indian chiefs, perilous occupations, ocean and river steamers, coins, musical instruments, flags, fish, ships, and prize fighters. Source: Tobacco Advertising Collection—Database #D0047, D0059, Emergence of Advertising On-Line Project, John W. Hartman Center for Sales, Advertising & Marketing History, Duke University Rare Book, Manuscript, and Special Collections Library. http://library.duke.edu/digitalcollections/eaa/

competitors never recovered. With the new Bonsack machines, Duke simultaneously cut manufacturing costs from $0.80 per thousand to $0.30 and multiplied factory production by many times.[2]

To find new markets for this swollen output, Duke next went to New York City, where he rented a loft and set up a small cigarette factory. Then he moved to create demand. He was tireless, working 12 hours a day in the factory, then making the rounds of tobacco shops at night. He gave secret rebates and cash payments to friendly dealers. He hired people to visit tobacco shops and demand his new machine-rolled Cameo and Cross Cut brands. Immigrants were welcomed with free samples as they emerged from the New York Immigration Station to set foot in America for the first time. Ingeniously, he put numbered cards with glamour photos of actresses in his cigarette packs, encouraging men to complete a collection. Late at night he haunted the streets, picking up crumpled cigarette packs from sidewalks and trash cans, creating a crude sales count.

Overseas, Duke's minions were also at work. One great conquest was China. At the time a few Chinese, mostly older men, smoked a bitter native tobacco in pipes. Cigarettes were unknown. Duke sent experts to Shantung Province with bright leaf

[2] John K. Winkler, *Tobacco Tycoon: The Story of James Buchanan Duke* (New York: Random House, 1942), p. 56.

from North Carolina to cultivate a milder tobacco. His sales force hired "teachers" to walk village streets showing curious Chinese how to light and hold cigarettes. He installed Bonsak machines in four new manufacturing plants that soon ran 24 hours a day. And he unleashed on the Chinese a full range of promotional activities. At one time his cigarette packs contained pictures of seminude American actresses, which were a big hit with Chinese men. In this way, Duke turned China into a nation of smokers.

Back home his tactics wore down competitors. He carefully observed John D. Rockefeller's conquest of the oil industry and saw that Rockefeller's methods could be applied to the tobacco industry. In 1884, at the age of 26, he engineered a combination of his firm and other large firms into a holding company known as the American Tobacco trust. As president, Duke built the trust into a monopoly that controlled 98 percent of the domestic cigarette market by 1892, a year in which 2.9 billion cigarettes were sold.[3] Not content with domination alone, he worked tirelessly to expand the tobacco market. By 1903, more than 10 billion cigarettes were sold in the United States.[4] Over two decades his combination ruthlessly swallowed or bankrupted 250 firms until it dominated the cigar, snuff, and smoking tobacco markets too.

Duke used a simple method to strangle competitors. Instead of selling its output at wholesale prices, Duke's company "consigned" its products to dealers. The dealers had to pay full retail price for tobacco goods sent to them "on consignment" and do so within 10 days of receipt. Three months later, the company paid the dealer a "commission," which was the dealer's profit. Dealers who sold competitors' brands were not eligible to receive this "commission," so they could not make a profit on brands the vast majority of their customers wanted. Duke enforced the scheme using detectives to spy on dealers. Many dealers disliked this arrogant, coercive system, but they had to play along or wither away.

Duke's monopoly lasted until 1911, when the Supreme Court ordered it broken up.[5] Duke himself figured out how to divide the giant firm into four independent companies: Liggett & Myers, P. Lorillard, R. J. Reynolds, and a new American Tobacco Company. After the breakup he retired from the tobacco industry to start an electric utility, Duke Power & Light. He also gave money to a small North Carolina college, which became Duke University. He died of complications from pernicious anemia in 1925.

Duke's career illustrates the power of commerce to shape society. He made the cigarette an acceptable consumer product and spread it around the world. His monopoly destroyed rivals and defined the structure of the tobacco industry. His bribes to legislators blocked antismoking laws and checked the early efforts of antitobacco leagues to publicize health hazards. And, owing largely to Duke's ingenuity, a surging tobacco trade revived the crippled post-Civil War Southern economy. Eventually, he ran into a hard check on power when the Supreme Court dismantled his colossus, but his work endures in the roll call of smokers across 120 years.

[3] "Iron Heel of Monopoly," *The New York Times,* December 28, 1892, p. 10.

[4] "The Caesar of Tobacco," *The Wall Street Journal,* June 27, 1903, p. 6.

[5] *United States v. American Tobacco Company,* 221 U.S. 106 (1911).

THE NATURE OF BUSINESS POWER

Business has tremendous power to change society, and the extent of this power is underappreciated. Companies in ascending industries change societies by altering all three of their primary elements—ideas, institutions, and material things. This effect is visible in the stories of dominant companies such as the American Tobacco Company, the American Fur Company, and the Standard Oil Trust. The cumulative power of all business is a massive, irrepressible shaping force. In this chapter we explain the underlying dynamics of this power to change society. We then discuss its limits.

WHAT IS POWER?

power
The force or strength to act or to compel another entity to act.

Power is the force or strength to act or to compel another entity to act. In human society it is used to organize and control people and materials to achieve individual or collective goals. It exists on a wide spectrum ranging from coercion at one extreme to weak influence at the other. Its use in human society creates change. Although power is sometimes exerted to prevent change, such resistance is itself a force that alters history. The many sources of power include wealth, position, knowledge, law, arms, status, and charisma. Power is unevenly distributed, and all societies have mechanisms to control and channel it for wide or narrow benefit. These mechanisms, which are imperfect, include governments, laws, police, cultural values, and public opinion. Also, multiple, competing formations of power may check and balance each other.

business power
The force behind an act by a company, industry, or sector.

Business power is the force behind an act by a company, industry, or sector. The greater this force, the more the action creates change or influences the actions of other entities in society. Its basic origin is a grant of authority from society to convert resources efficiently into needed goods and services. In return for doing this, society gives corporations the authority to take necessary actions and permits a profit. This agreement derives from the social contract.

legitimacy
The rightful use of power. Its opposite is tyranny, or the exercise of power beyond right.

The social contract legitimizes business power by giving it a moral basis. *Legitimacy* is the rightful use of power. The power of giant corporations is legitimate when it is exercised in keeping with the agreed-upon contract. The philosopher John Locke wrote that for governments the opposite of legitimacy is tyranny, defined as "the exercise of power beyond right."[6] Corporations breach the social contract, exercising "power beyond right," when they violate social values, endanger the public, or act illegally.

Business power is legitimate when it is used for the common good. The grounds of legitimacy vary between societies and over time. Child labor, once widespread in the United States, is no longer permitted, but it exists in other nations. As we will see in subsequent chapters, the definition of the common good that business must serve has expanded throughout American history and is now expanding globally.

[6] John Locke, *The Second Treatise of Government* (New York: Bobbs-Merrill, 1952), p. 112; originally published in 1690.

LEVELS AND SPHERES OF CORPORATE POWER

Business power, like any form of social power, is intangible, its exercise not subject to direct or exact calibrations. Having no physical state to be observed, it is known to be great or small solely by its effects on the world. In this respect, corporate actions have an impact on society at two levels, and on each level they create change.

On the *surface level*, business power is the direct cause of visible, immediate changes, both great and small. Corporations expand and contract, hire and fire; they make and sell products. On a *deep level*, corporate power shapes society over time through the aggregate changes of industrial growth. At this level we encounter an intangible realm of social networks, time, and physical space, a realm crossed by complex chains of cause and effect that converge and interact, shaping and reshaping society. Here the workings of corporate power are unplanned, unpredictable, indirect, and irregular, but they are constant and far more significant. Corporate power "is something more than men," wrote John Steinbeck. "It's the monster. Men made it, but they can't control it."[7] This is a poetic but accurate description of business power at a deep level.

On both the surface and deep levels, business power is exercised in spheres corresponding to the seven business environments set forth in Chapter 2.

- *Economic power* is the ability of the corporation to influence events, activities, and people by virtue of control over resources, particularly property. At the surface level, the operation of a corporation may immediately and visibly affect its stakeholders, for example, by building or closing a factory. At a deeper level, the accumulating impact of corporate economic activity has sweeping effects. For example, over many years corporations have created enough wealth to raise living standards dramatically in industrialized nations.

- *Technological power* is the ability to influence the direction, rate, characteristics, and consequences of physical innovations as they develop. On a surface level, in 1914, assembly lines run by new electric motors allowed Henry Ford to introduce transportation based on the internal combustion engine. Using this method, he turned an expensive luxury of the rich into a mass consumer product. But at a deeper level, as the auto took hold in American society it created unanticipated consequences. One juvenile court judge in the 1920s called the automobile a "house of prostitution on wheels," something that the puritanical Henry Ford doubtless never intended to create.[8]

- *Political power* is the ability to influence governments. On the surface, corporations give money to candidates and lobby legislatures. On a deeper level, around the world industrialization engenders values that radiate freedom and erode authoritarian regimes.

- *Legal power* is the ability to shape the laws of society. On the surface, big corporations have formidable legal resources that intimidate opponents. On a deeper

[7] *The Grapes of Wrath* (New York: Viking Press, 1939), p. 45.

[8] Frederick Lewis Allen, *Only Yesterday: An Informal History of the 1920s* (New York: Harper & Brothers, 1931), p. 100.

American Landscape, a 1930 oil painting, depicts Ford Motor Company's mighty River Rouge plant, which took in raw materials such as sand and iron ore at one end and turned out finished autos at the other. In its day, the plant was regarded as a wonder and people traveled from around the world to see it. Here artist Charles Sheeler evokes the power of business to change and shape society. On the surface, this vista seems to beautify and ennoble the architecture of production, making it seem almost pastoral. Yet on a deeper level the painting provokes anxiety. Factory buildings run nature off the scene, dominating a landscape that is now, but for the sky, entirely artificial. A tiny human figure in the middle ground is overwhelmed and marginalized by the massive complex; its movement limited and regimented by the surrounding industrial structure. Here, then, art reveals emotions and insights about business power. Other Sheeler paintings and photographs are open to the same interpretation. He never revealed his intentions, leaving art critics to debate whether he was, in fact, sanguine or dispirited about how business power was shaping the "American landscape." Source: Digital Image © The Museum of Modern Art/Licensed by SCALA/Art Resource, NY.

level, the laws of the United States—including constitutional, civil, and criminal laws—have been shaped by the consequences of industrial activity.

- *Cultural power* is the ability to influence cultural values, habits, and institutions such as the family. John Wanamaker, founder of a department store chain and a master of advertising, started Mother's Day in the early 1900s. He ran full-page ads in the *Philadelphia Inquirer* about a woman mourning for her mother, creating the sentiment that gratitude for mothers should be expressed by a gift on a special day.[9] At a deeper level, the cumulative impact of ads has altered American society by reinforcing values selectively, for example, materialism over asceticism, individualism over community, or personal appearance over inner character.

- *Environmental power* is the impact of a company on nature. On the surface, a power plant may pollute the air; on a deeper level, since the seventeenth century, emission of gases in the burning of wood, coal, and oil to power industry has altered the chemistry of earth's atmosphere. One study found that since 1882 the Standard Oil Trust and its successor companies have contributed between 4.7 and 5.2 percent of worldwide carbon dioxide emissions.[10]

- *Power over individuals* is exercised over employees, managers, stockholders, consumers, and citizens. On the surface, a corporation may determine the work life and buying habits of individuals. At a deeper level, industrialism sets the pattern of daily life. People are regimented, living by clocks, moving in routes fixed by the model of an industrial city with its streets and sidewalks. Their occupation determines their status and fortune.

Activity in the economic sphere is the primary force for change. From this, change radiates into other spheres. The story of the railroad industry in the United States illustrates how an expanding industry with a radical new technology can change its environments.

THE STORY OF THE RAILROADS

When small railroads sprang up in the 1820s, most passengers and freight moved by horse and over canals. The railroad was a vastly superior conveyance and was bound to revolutionize transportation. Tracks cost less to build than canals and did not freeze in winter. Routes could be more direct. For the first time in history, people and cargo traveled overland faster than the speed of a horse. The trip from New York to Chicago was reduced from three weeks to just three days. And the cost of moving goods and passengers was less; in a day a train could go back and forth many times over the distance that a canal boat or wagon could traverse once.

The initial boom in railroading came at midcentury. In 1850 trains ran on only 9,021 miles of track, but by 1860 30,626 miles had been laid. During that decade, 30 railroad companies completed route systems, which had significant consequences for the financial system. Tracks were expensive, and each of these enterprises was a giant for its day. Many needed $10 million to $35 million in capital, and the smallest at least $2 million. Companies in other industries did not approach this size; only a handful of textile mills and steel plants required capitalization of more than $1 million.[11]

---

[9] Richard Wolkomir and Joyce Wolkomir, "You Are What You Buy," *Smithsonian,* May 2000, p. 107.

[10] Friends of the Earth International, *Exxon's Climate Footprint* (London: FOEI, January 2004), p. 5. See also Richard Heede, *Exxon Mobil Corporation Emissions Inventory:* 1882–2002 (London: Friends of the Earth Trust Ltd., December 17, 2003).

[11] Alfred D. Chandler, Jr., *The Visible Hand: The Managerial Revolution in American Business* (Cambridge, MA: Belknap Press, 1977), pp. 83, 86, and 90.

The call for this much money transformed capital markets. The only place such huge sums could be raised was in large Northeastern cities. Since interest rates were a little higher in Boston at the time, New York became the center of financial activity and has remained so to this day. Railroads sold bonds and offered stocks to raise capital, and a new investment banking industry was created. The New York Stock Exchange went from a sleepy place, where only a few hundred shares might change hands each week, to a roaring market. Speculative techniques such as margin trading, short-selling, and options trading appeared for the first time. Later, the financial mechanisms inspired by railroad construction were in place when other industries needed more capital to grow. This changed American history by accelerating the industrial transformation of the late 1800s. It also put New York bankers such as J. P. Morgan in a position to control access to capital.

At first the railroads ran between existing trade centers, but as time passed and track mileage increased, they linked ever more points. The 30,626 miles of track in 1860 increased to 93,267 miles by 1880 and 167,191 miles by 1890.[12] This required enormous amounts of wood, and whole forests were downed to make ties and stoke fires in early steam locomotives. A deeper consequence of extending the tracks was a society transformed.

Before tracks radiated everywhere, the United States was a nation of farmers and small towns held together by the traditional institutions of family, church, and local government. Since long-distance travel was time-consuming and arduous, these towns often were isolated. Populations were stable. People identified more with local areas than with the nation as a whole. Into this world came the train, a destabilizing technology powered by aggressive market capitalism.

Trains took away young people who might have stayed in rural society but for the lure of wealth in distant cities. In their place came a stream of outsiders who were less under the control of community values. Small-town intimacy declined, and a new phenomenon appeared in American life—the impersonal crowd of strangers. Trains violated established customs. Sunday was a day of rest and worship, so many churchgoers were angered when huffing and whistling trains intruded on services. But new capital accounting methods used by railroad companies dictated using equipment an extra day each week to increase return on investment. This imperative trumped devoutness. In early America, localities set their own time according to the sun's overhead transit, but this resulted in a patchwork of time zones that made scheduling difficult. An editorial in *Railroad Age* argued, "Local time must go."[13] For the convenience of the railroads, a General Time Convention met in 1882 and standardized the time of day, though not without resistance from holdouts who felt that "[s]urely the world ran by higher priorities than railroad scheduling."[14]

---

[12] Bureau of the Census, *Statistical Abstract of the United States,* 77th ed. (Washington, DC: Government Printing Office, 1956), table 683.

[13] Bill Kauffman, "Why Spring Ahead," *The American Enterprise,* April–May 2001, p. 50.

[14] Ibid., p. 50, quoting Michael O'Malley, *Keeping Watch: A History of American Time* (Washington, DC: Smithsonian Institution Press, 1996).

As the railroads grew, they spread impersonality and an ethic of commerce. Towns reoriented themselves around their train stations. Shops and restaurants sprang up nearby so that strangers would spend money before moving on. The railroads gave more frequent service to cities with commercial possibilities and bypassed small towns or let them wither from less frequent service. This speeded urbanization and the centralization of corporate power in cities. Rural areas were redefined. Once the cultural heartland, they now were seen as backward and rustic—places best used for vacations from urban stress.

The railroads also changed American politics. On the surface, their lobbyists could dominate legislatures. On a deeper level, the changes were more profound. Congress had always selected nominees before presidential elections, but now trains brought delegates to national party nominating conventions, changing the way candidates were picked. Trains enabled all sorts of associations to have national meetings, and the rails spread issues that might in an earlier era have remained local. The movement to give women the vote, for example, succeeded after Susan B. Anthony took trains to all parts of the country, spreading her rhetoric and unifying the cause.[15]

At first government encouraged and subsidized railroads. All told, federal and state governments gave them land grants of 164 million acres, an area equal to the size of California and Nevada combined.[16] But later the challenge was to control them. When Congress passed the Interstate Commerce Act in 1887 to regulate railroads, the design of the statute set the example for regulating other industries later.

Many other changes in American society are traceable to the railroads. They were the first businesses to require modern management structures. The need for precise coordination of speeding trains over vast reaches caused railroads to pioneer professional management teams, division structures, and modern cost accounting—all innovations later adopted in other industries.[17] Railroads lay behind Indian wars. For the Plains Indians, tracks that divided old hunting grounds were the main barrier to peace.[18] Thousands of laborers came from China to lay rail, and their descendants live on in communities along the lines. Railroads changed the language. The word *diner,* meaning a place to eat, appeared after the introduction of the Pullman Palace Car Company's first dining car in 1868. The expression "hell on wheels" originally described the raucous body of prostitutes, gambling cars, and saloons that rolled along with construction crews as tracks spread west. The phrase "off again, on again" derives from discussions about train derailments.[19] And social values changed. Big-city commercial values rumbled down the tracks, jolting traditions along rural byways.

---

[15] These and other social and political changes are treated at length in Sarah H. Gordon, *Passage to Union* (Chicago: Ivan R. Dees, 1996).

[16] Page Smith, *The Rise of Industrial America,* vol. 6 (New York: Viking Penguin, 1984), p. 99.

[17] Chandler, *The Visible Hand,* chap. 3.

[18] Smith, *The Rise of Industrial America,* p. 89.

[19] Rudolph Daniels, *Trains across the Continent: North American Railroad History,* 2nd ed. (Bloomington: Indiana University Press, 2000), pp. 53 and 78.

FIGURE 3.1   **Railroad Track Miles in Operation: 1830–2010**

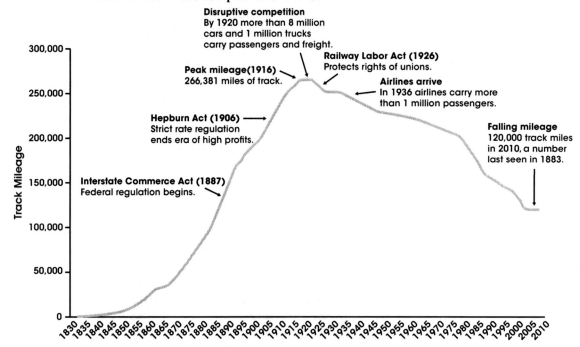

Source: *Statistical Abstract of the United States,* various editions 1878–2010.

As the track system swelled so did the power of railroads to shape the sociopolitical and the physical landscapes. Figure 3.1 shows how track mileage fell after 1916, reflecting a decline in the fortunes of the industry. Government regulation hardened, making rate hikes more difficult and strengthening the hand of unions. In addition, railroads came into competition with new transportation technologies, first autos, buses, and trucks, then aircraft. As the importance of rails receded, these rising technologies hastened to reshape American life, converting the nation from one that ran on steam to one that ran on oil.

TWO PERSPECTIVES ON BUSINESS POWER

dominance theory
The view that business is the most powerful institution in society, because of its control of wealth. This power is inadequately checked and, therefore, excessive.

There is agreement that business has great power. But there is considerable disagreement about whether its power is adequately checked and balanced for the public good. Views about business power cover a wide spectrum, but there are two basic and opposing positions.

On one side is the *dominance theory*, which holds that business is preeminent in American society, primarily because of its control of wealth, and that its power is both excessive and inadequately checked. Corporations can alter their environments in self-interested ways that harm the general welfare. This was the thesis of Karl Marx, who wrote that a ruling capitalist class exploited workers and dominated other classes. The dominance theory is the basis of the dominance model of the business–government–society relationship set forth in Chapter 1.

pluralist theory
The view that business power is exercised in a society where other institutions also have great power. It is counter-balanced and restricted and, therefore, not excessive.

On the other side the *pluralist theory* holds that business power is exercised in a society in which other institutions such as markets, government, labor unions, advocacy groups, and public opinion also have great power. Business power is counterbalanced, restricted, controlled, and subject to defeat. Adam Smith was convinced that largely through market forces, business power could be disciplined to benefit society. The pluralist theory is the basis of the countervailing forces model in Chapter 1.

The Dominance Theory

In industrializing societies, business organizations grow in size and concentrate wealth. According to the dominance theory, business abuses the power its size and wealth confer in a number of ways. The rise of huge corporations creates a business elite that exercises inordinate power over public policy. Asset concentration creates monopoly or oligopoly in markets that reduces competition and harms consumers. Corporations wield financial and organizational resources unmatched by opposing interests. For example, they use campaign contributions to corrupt politicians, hire lobbyists to undermine the independence of elected officials, employ accountants and lawyers to avoid taxes, and run public relations campaigns that shape opinion in their favor.

Moreover, large corporations achieve such importance in a nation's economy that elected officials are forced to adopt probusiness measures or face public wrath. "If enterprises falter for lack of inducement to invest, hire, and produce," writes one advocate of the dominance theory, "members of the political elite are more likely than those of the entrepreneurial elite to lose their positions."[20] We will discuss further the growth in size and wealth of corporations and the presence of elites.

Corporate Asset Concentration

The idea that concentration of economic power results in abuse arose, in part, as an intellectual reaction to the awesome economic growth of the late nineteenth century. Until then, the United States had been primarily an agricultural economy. But between 1860 and 1890, industrial progress transformed the country. Statistics illustrating this are striking. During these 30 years, the number of manufacturing plants more than doubled, growing from 140,433 to 355,415; the value of what they made rose more than 400 percent, from $1.8 billion to $9.3 billion; and the capital invested in them grew 650 percent, from $1 billion to $6.5 billion.[21]

This growth did more than create wealth; it also concentrated it. At the end of the century, between 1895 and 1904, an unprecedented merger wave assembled dominant firms in industry after industry. Since then, there have been other great merger waves, but this was the first. It made a definitive impression on the American mind, and its legacy is an enduring fear of big companies.

[20] Charles E. Lindblom, *The Market System: What It Is, How It Works, and What to Make of It* (New Haven: Yale University Press, 2001), p. 247.

[21] Figures in this paragraph are from Arthur M. Schlesinger, *Political and Social Growth of the United States: 1852–1933* (New York: Macmillan, 1935), pp. 132–44.

Merger waves are caused by changes in the economic environment that create incentives to combine. The main stimulus for the 1895–1904 wave was growth of the transcontinental railroads, which reduced transportation costs, thereby creating new national markets. Companies rushed to transform themselves from regional operations to national ones. Combinations such as James Duke's American Tobacco Company gorged themselves, swallowing competitors, crowding into formerly isolated markets, and wiping out small family businesses. The story was repeated in roughly 300 commodities, including oil, copper, cattle, smelting, and such items as playing cards and tombstones. A 1904 study of the 92 largest firms found that 78 controlled 50 percent of their market, 57 controlled 60 percent or more, and 26 controlled 80 percent or more.[22]

At the time, the public failed to see the growth of huge firms as a natural, inevitable, or desirable response to the new economic incentives. Instead, it saw them as colossal monuments to greed. Companies of this size were something new. They inspired a mixture of awe and fear. In 1904, when the United States Steel Corporation became the first company with more than $1 billion in assets, people were astounded. Previously, such numbers applied in the realm of astronomy, not business.

In the twentieth century, corporations continued to grow in size, but the marked rise in asset concentration slowed and leveled off. By 1929 the 200 largest nonfinancial corporations in the United States (less than 0.7 percent of all nonfinancials) controlled nearly 50 percent of all corporate wealth. But by 1947 the nation's top 200 corporations had only 46 percent of corporate wealth, and this was reduced to 36 percent in 1996.[23] Although no continuing data series exists to provide a current figure, a recent study reveals that asset concentration in the top 200 firms on the Fortune 500 declined by 8 percent between 1995 and 2004.[24]

With economic globalization, the number of multinational firms and the scale of their activity has grown. There are approximately 82,000 multinationals, up from only about 34,000 as recently as 1990. Asset s and sales of the largest of these firms are rising. Between 1990 and 2008, assets of the 100 biggest multinationals increased by 336 percent and sales by 269 percent.[25] Yet even with heightened global merger activity, the largest global firms show no signs of concentrating foreign assets the way that large American firms have concentrated domestic assets. In fact, the foreign assets of the largest 100 multinationals fell from 13 percent of estimated global assets in 1999 to 9 percent in 2008.[26] And these 100 firms are still only a small part of world economic activity. For the decade 1990–2000,

[22] John Moody, *The Truth about Trusts: A Description and Analysis of the American Trust Movement* (New York: Greenwood Press, 1968), p. 487; originally published in 1904.

[23] J. Fred Weston, Kwang S. Chung, and Juan A. Siu, *Takeovers, Restructuring, and Corporate Governance,* 2nd ed. (Upper Saddle River, NJ: Prentice Hall, 1998), p. 116. These figures allow rotation of new firms into the top 200 firms. If the same 200 firms had been followed over the years, asset concentration would have fallen even faster.

[24] Edward Nissan, "Structure of American Business: Goods versus Services," *Southwestern Economic Review* (online), Spring 2006, table 1.

[25] United Nations Conference on Trade and Development (UNCTAD), *World Investment Report 2010* (New York: United Nations, 2010), table I.11; and UNCTAD, *World Investment Report 1993* (New York: United Nations, 1993), table I.11.

[26] UNCTAD, *World Investment Report 2009* (New York: United Nations, 2009), p. xxi.

their output as a share of world GDP grew from 3.5 percent to only 4.3 percent, then fell back to 4 percent by 2008.[27]

Despite this, adherents of the dominance theory believe that the increasing size and financial power of global corporations will be converted into the same old abuses. But the link between market power and abuse remains to be seen. Multinationals with growing assets and sales do not necessarily have increased market power. They face formidable competitors, emerging competition from new industries, geographically enlarged market boundaries, and, in the European Union, more aggressive antitrust enforcement. In the social dimension, these firms face growing global pressures to act responsibly.

Also, no corporation, no matter how large, is assured of prospering. Over time competition, strategic errors, and, most important, technological changes have continuously winnowed the roster of America's biggest companies. Looking back at lists of the top 200 industrial corporations by assets, one study found that of 543 corporations that appeared on the lists between 1900 and 2000 only 28 "persistent giants," or 5 percent of the total number that drifted on and off the list, survived for 100 years.[28] The rest came and went, primarily due to the rise of disruptive technologies. Early in the century railroads and metal companies were dominant, but fell away as new entrants in electrical equipment and chemicals went to the top. By midcentury oil and auto companies appeared, then later, computer-related firms. For the largest companies in each era, economies of scale and oligopoly in markets led to high profits and may have prolonged their dominance, yet these advantages were no shield from the technological changes that dislodged them from the top. Based on this century of evidence, the authors predict that "[t]urbulence is the future, just as it is the past of these giant firms."[29]

Other studies confirm the low survival rate at the top of the asset roster. Of the 100 largest corporations in 1909, only 36 remained on the list until 1948. Between 1948 and 1958, only 65 of the top 100 held their place. Only 116 company names remained on the Fortune 500 list of industrial corporations from its inception in 1955 to 1994 when it was revised to included service industries.[30] Many firms dropped from the list were, of course, acquired by other firms. Among the 100 largest transnational corporations there were 28 American firms in 1990, but that number had declined to 18 by 2008.[31] The lesson in all these numbers is that, with very few exceptions, the power of technology-based market forces exceeds the power of even the largest corporations to maintain their dominance.

---

[27] UNCTAD, *World Investment Report 2002* (New York: United Nations, 2002), box table IV.1.2; and UNCTAD, *World Investment Report 2009* (New York: United Nations, 2009), p. xxi. These figures are based on a value-added calculation (the sum of salaries, pretax profits, and depreciation and amortization) for transnational corporations.

[28] Francisco Louçã and Sandro Mendonça, "Steady Change: The 200 Largest U.S. Manufacturing Firms Throughout the 20th Century," *Industrial and Corporate Change,* August 2002, pp. 818 and 825.

[29] Ibid., p. 840.

[30] Figures in this paragraph are from Neil H. Jacoby, *Corporate Power and Social Responsibility* (New York: Macmillan, 1973), p. 32; John Paul Newport, Jr., "A New Era of Rapid Rise and Ruin," *Fortune,* April 24, 1989, p. 77; and Carol J. Loomis, "Forty Years of the 500," *Fortune,* May 15, 1995, p. 182.

[31] UNCTAD, *World Investment Report 2010,* table I.8.

The Rise and Decline of Corporate Giants

When the New York Stock Exchange was young ordinary investors had trouble making sense of daily trading. Some stocks went up, others went down, and the gyrations hid trends. In 1896 journalist Charles H. Dow created a list of 12 companies as an index of stock market performance. Now investors could see the market's direction by watching a daily sum of these company's share prices. At the time a great merger wave was reshaping the economy by creating giant firms, and Dow filled his index with them. Each was a leader in an important industry and represented its fortunes.

As the years passed America's economy changed, companies came and went; and the index, today called the Dow Jones Industrial Average, grew from 12 to 30 companies by 1928. The most recent additions and deletions were made in 2010.

The leading firms in 1896 reflect a different world. Farming was much more prominent, and four firms dealt in agricultural products. They were James B. Duke's American Tobacco Company, cotton and sugar producers, and a company that made livestock feeds. Two firms represented the centrality of technologies based on iron, lead, and coal. Another, U.S. Leather, made a product in the shadow of imminent obsolescence, leather belts used for power transmission in factories. General Electric, which built electric motors, was the high technology company of that era. Chicago Gas and Laclede Gas Light of St. Louis supplied natural gas for new streetlamps in booming cities. North American operated streetcars.

1896	2010	
American Cotton Oil	3M	Intel
American Sugar Refining	Alcoa	IBM
American Tobacco	American Express	Johnson & Johnson
Chicago Gas	AT&T	JPMorgan Chase
Distilling & Cattle Feeding	Bank of America	Kraft Foods
General Electric	Boeing	McDonald's
Laclede Gas Light	Caterpillar	Merck
National Lead	Chevron	Microsoft
North American	Cisco Systems	Pfizer
Tennessee Coal & Iron	Coca-Cola	Procter & Gamble
U.S. Leather	DuPont	Travelers
U.S. Rubber	Exxon Mobil	United Technologies
	General Electric	Walmart
	Hewlett-Packard	Walt Disney
	Home Depot	

The 2010 list registers the rise of new technologies and of economic sectors providing services and consumer products. General Electric is the only company that was on the 1896 list, and it was removed for nine years between 1898 and 1907. Of the other 11 original firms, 2 (American Tobacco and North American) were broken up by antitrust action, 1 (U.S. Leather) was dissolved, and 8 continue to operate as less important companies or as parts of other firms that acquired their assets.

As a biography of American industry, the index dramatizes the rise and fall of powerful companies and industries. Over more than a century, 100 different firms have been listed. The index teaches that dominance of even the largest firms is transient.

Elite Dominance

Another argument that supports the dominance theory is that there exists a small group of individuals who, by virtue of wealth and position, control the nation. Members of this elite are alleged to act in concert and in undemocratic ways. There is a long history of belief in an economic elite dominating American society. In debates preceding adoption of the Constitution in 1789, some opponents charged that the delegates were wealthy aristocrats designing a government favorable to their businesses. Later, farmers suspected the hand of an economic elite in the probusiness policies of Alexander Hamilton, George Washington's secretary of the treasury, who had many ties to wealth and commercial power. Since the Colonial era, charges of elitism have surfaced repeatedly in popular movements opposed to big business.

The modern impetus for the theory of elite dominance comes from the sociologist C. Wright Mills, who wrote a scholarly book in 1956 describing a "power elite" in American society. "Insofar as national events are decided," wrote Mills, "the power elite are those who decide them."[32] Mills saw American society as a pyramid of power and status. At the top was a tiny elite in command of the economic, political, and military domains. Mills was never specific about its numbers, but said it was small. Just below was a group of lieutenants who carried out the elite's policies. They included professional managers of corporations, politicians beholden to the elite for their election, and bureaucrats appointed by the politicians. The large base of the pyramid was composed of a mass of powerless citizens, including feeble groups and associations with little policy impact. This image of a pyramid corresponds to the dominance model in Chapter 1.

Mills did not see America as a democracy and thought the elite simply used government "as an umbrella under whose authority they do their work."[33] Although he never stated that the economic segment of the elite was dominant over the political and military, he noted, "The key organizations, perhaps, are the major corporations."[34]

power elite
A small group of individuals in control of the economy, government, and military. The theory of its existence is associated with the American sociologist C. Wright Mills.

The Power Elite is a book in which there is more speculation than substantiation. It is based on cursory evidence and included none of the statistical research that would be required to support such sweeping generalizations in a similar work of sociology today. Yet it contained a powerful new explanation of economic power and came out just as many American leftists were becoming disenchanted with Marxism. Mills's vision of a small ruling elite caught on and has been popular with the anticorporate left ever since. Mills would have been pleased. In correspondence, he once expressed indignation about the power of "the sons of bitches who run American Big Business."[35]

Scholars inspired by Mills continue to study elites and are less reluctant to suggest business dominance. One is G. William Domhoff, who, in a series of books extending over 40 years, argues the existence of a cohesive American upper class based on

---

[32] C. Wright Mills, *The Power Elite* (New York: Oxford University Press, 1956), p. 18.

[33] Ibid., p. 287.

[34] Ibid., p. 283.

[35] In a letter to his parents quoted by John B. Judis, "The Spiritual Wobbly," *The New York Times Book Review,* July 9, 2000, p. 9.

wealth, socialization in private schools, membership in exclusive clubs, and occupancy of high positions in business, government, and nonprofit institutions. Within this upper class lies a smaller leadership group, a controlling core of leaders in the corporate community. According to Domhoff, this core is a power elite.

> The power elite is made up of those people who serve as directors or trustees in . . . institutions controlled by the corporate community through stock ownership, financial support, involvement on the board of trustees, or some combination of these factors. [It has] . . . the power to shape the economic and political frameworks within which other groups and classes must operate.[36]

Domhoff does not quantify the power elite. Its power can be measured by the maintenance of a pro-corporate environment. Using foundation money, think tanks, lobbying, and campaign contributions it is consistently able to defeat the policy preferences of liberals and progressives who favor income redistribution and greater equality of opportunities.

In an effort that extended over 25 years, political scientist Thomas R. Dye tried to identify precisely which individuals made up an American elite. Believing that power comes from leadership in organizations, he identified an "institutional elite" of individuals who occupied the top positions in 10 sectors–industrial, banking, insurance, investments, mass media, law, education, foundations, civic and cultural organizations, and government. Applying this method, Dye identified an elite of 5,778 individuals.[37] This is a much larger elite than that suggested by Mills, but it is still only a speck of the population.

Another scholar, David Rothkopf, writes that with globalization, a transnational power elite or "superclass" has emerged, operating across borders through "networks of individuals and organizations."[38] Rothkopf calculates a superclass membership of about 6,000, which is 0.0001 percent of the world population, or a member for each 1 million people. The largest group, 17 percent, is Americans and another third come from European nations. They resemble national power elites in their origins and acculturation. Members attend elite universities. Harvard, Stanford, and the University of Chicago have produced the most. They join exclusive groups such as the Council on Foreign Relations, have memberships on overlapping boards of directors, and meet at events such as the World Economic Forum in Davos, Switzerland. Because multinational corporations, global banks, and hedge funds are "the largest and most significant transnational actors" their leaders dominate, working together "in clusters knit together by business deals, corporate boards, investment flows, old school ties, club memberships, and countless other strands that transform . . . into groups that are proven masters at advancing their aligned self-interests."[39] The new superclass eclipses the power of national elites. According to Rothkopf, it does not rule or conspire,

[36] G. William Domhoff, *Who Rules America?* 6th ed. (New York: McGraw-Hill, 2010), p. 114.

[37] Thomas R. Dye, *Who's Running America? The Bush Restoration,* 7th ed. (Upper Saddle River, NJ: Prentice Hall, 2002), p. 205; emphasis in the original.

[38] David Rothkopf, *Superclass: The Global Power Elite and the World They are Making,* (New York: Farrar, Straus and Giroux, 2008), p. 84.

[39] Ibid., pp. 33 and xvii.

but its dominant business subset, having "vastly more power than any other group on the planet," abets an agenda of oil dependence, free markets, free trade, and military spending.[40]

Elites formed from some combination of wealth, ability, position, and social status are timeless and inevitable. They challenge the logic of democratic ideology because a few citizens, acting in the shadows of electoral mechanisms, pilot a vast majority. Yet elites are not necessarily sinister, oppressive, or conspiratorial. They can be sources of talent, expert leadership, and cultural stability. American and global business elites spring from the pinnacles of corporate, government, religious, and cultural institutions, having arrived at such positions based overwhelmingly on ability.

However, those who move into elites come from a thin range of backgrounds. Every study finds that disproportionately they are male, white, and Christian; come from upper-class families; and attend a short list of prestigious schools. The inclusion of blacks, Latinos, and women is based on their similarity in background and thinking to the existing elite.[41] Rothkopf finds that only 6.3 percent of the global superclass is women.[42] At least in the United States, the idea of a power elite, one perhaps dominated by business interests, troubles citizens with a deep commitment to equality. Yet some argue that its actions are adequately checked and balanced. This view is taken up in the next section.

Pluralist Theory

pluralistic society
A society with multiple groups and institutions through which power is diffused.

A *pluralistic society* is one having multiple groups and institutions through which power is diffused. Within such a society no entity or interest has overriding power, and each may check and balance others. The countervailing forces model in Chapter 1 illustrates how, in such a society, business must interact with constraining forces in its environment. It may have considerable influence over some of them; but over most it has limited influence, and over a few none at all. Several features of American society support this thesis of pluralism.

First, it is infused with democratic values. Unlike many nations, America has no history of feudal or authoritarian rule, so there is no entrenched deference to an aristocracy of wealth. In Colonial days, Americans adopted the then-revolutionary doctrine of natural rights, which held that all persons were created equal and entitled to the same opportunities and protections. The French aristocrat Alexis de Tocqueville, who toured America and wrote an insightful book about American customs in the 1830s, was forcibly struck by the "prodigious influence" of the notion of equality. Belief in equality, he wrote, ran through American society, directing public opinion, informing the law, and defining politics. It was, he wrote, "the fundamental fact from which all others seem to be derived."[43] Thus, in America

---

[40] Ibid., p. xiii.

[41] Richard L. Zweigenhaft and G. William Domhoff, *Diversity in the Power Elite: Have Women and Minorities Reached the Top?* (New Haven: Yale University Press, 1998).

[42] Rothkopf, *Superclass,* p. 290.

[43] Alexis de Tocqueville, *Democracy in America* (New York: New American Library, 1956), p. 26; originally published as two volumes in 1835 and 1850.

J. P. Morgan and the Panic of 1907

In the first decade of the twentieth century, J. P. Morgan (1837–1913), head of J. P. Morgan & Co. in New York, was often called the most powerful man in the country. He specialized in buying competing companies in the same industry and merging them into a single, monopolistic firm. He joined separate railroads into large systems. He combined smaller electrical concerns into General Electric in 1892 and then pulled a collection of manufacturers into the International Harvester Company, which started with 85 percent of the farm machinery market. In 1901 he created the first billion-dollar company when he merged 785 separate firms to form the United States Steel Company with capitalization of 11.4 billion.

Morgan and two of his close associates together held 341 corporate directorships. His power was very independent of government controls since at the time antitrust laws were little enforced, there was no national bank to regulate the money supply, and existing securities and banking laws were rudimentary. One awestruck biographer said that Morgan "was a God" who "ruled for a generation the pitiless, predatory world of cash."[44] His critics were less kind. Senator Robert W. La Follette once called him "a beefy, red-faced, thick-necked financial bully, drunk with wealth and power."[45]

In October 1907 panic swept Wall Street and stocks plummeted as frantic investors sold shares. Soon banks suffered runs of withdrawals and were on the verge of failure. Liquidity, or the free flow of money, was fast vanishing from financial markets, and the nation's banking system teetered on the verge of collapse. So influential was Morgan that he commanded the New York Stock Exchange to stay open all day on October 24 to maintain investor confidence. To support it, he raised $25 million of credit.

[44] John K. Winkler, *Morgan the Magnificent* (New York: Doubleday, 1950), p. 3; originally published in 1930.

[45] Jean Strouse, *Morgan: American Financier* (New York: Random House, 2000), p. x.

The federal government could do little to ease the crisis. President Theodore Roosevelt was off hunting bears in Louisiana, an ironic pursuit in light of the crashing stock market. Without a national bank, the government had no capacity to increase the money supply and restore liquidity. Powerless, Secretary of the Treasury George B. Cortelyou traveled to New York to get Morgan's advice

On the evening of October 24, Morgan gathered members of the New York banking elite at his private library. He played solitaire while in another room the assembled bankers discussed methods for resolving the crisis. Periodically, someone came to him with a proposal, several of which he rejected. Finally, a plan was hatched in which $33 million would be raised to support the stock exchange and failing banks. Where would this money come from? The secretary of the treasury was to supply $10 million in government funds, John D. Rockefeller contributed $10 million, and Morgan the remaining $13 million.

This action stabilized the economy. Perhaps it demonstrates that elite power may be exercised in the common good. It should be noted, however, that the panic of 1907—and other panics of that era—came after Morgan and other titans of finance repeatedly choked the stock exchange with the colossal stock offerings needed to finance their new combinations.

Morgan was widely criticized for his role in ending the panic of 1907. Conspiracy theorists, suspicious of so much power resident in one man, attacked him. Upton Sinclair, for example, accused him of inciting the panic for self-gain, a wildly erroneous accusation. In 1912 Morgan was the focus of congressional hearings which concluded that he led a "money trust" that controlled the nation's finances and that this was bad for the nation. Death claimed him in 1913 just before Congress passed the Federal Reserve Act to set up a central bank and ensure that no private banker would ever again be sole caretaker of the money supply.

laws apply equally to all. All interests have the right to be heard. To be legitimate, power must be exercised for the common good.

Second, America encompasses a large population spread over a wide geography and engaged in diverse occupations. It has a great mixture of interests, more than some other countries. Economic interests, including labor, banking, manufacturing, agriculture, and consumers, are a permanent fixture. A rainbow of voluntary associations (whose size, longevity, and influence vary) compete in governments at all levels.

Third, the Constitution encourages pluralism. Its guarantees of rights protect the freedom of individuals to form associations and freely to express and pursue interests. Thus, business is challenged by human rights, environmental, and other groups. The Constitution diffuses political power through the three branches of the federal government and between the federal and state governments and to the people. This creates a remarkably open political system.

In addition, business is exposed to constraining market pressures that force a stream of resource allocation decisions centered on cost reduction and consumer satisfaction, forces that can fell even the mighty. Henry J. Kaiser seemed unerring in business. The son of German immigrants, he worked his way up from store clerk to owner of 32 companies, including seven shipyards that launched one finished ship a day during most of World War II. When he started an auto company in 1945, nobody thought he could fail. Eager customers put down thousands of deposits before a single car was built.[46] But his cars, the Kaiser and the Frazier, were underpowered and overpriced, and the market eventually rejected them. Kaiser never got costs under control; he had to negotiate the prices of many parts with competing auto companies that made them. Toward the end, he built a model that was sold at Sears as the Allstate. This was a terrible mistake because it gave the car a low-quality image with consumers. The venture failed.

In sum, predictable and strong forces in a pluralistic, free market society limit business power. Wise managers anticipate that, despite having considerable influence on governments, markets, and public opinion, their power can be restricted, challenged, or shared by others. Overall, as illustrated in Figure 3.2, there are four major boundaries on managerial power.

1. *Governments and laws* in all countries regulate business activity. Governments are the ultimate arbiters of legitimate behavior and can act forcefully to blunt the exercise of corporate power that harms the public. Laws channel and regulate operations.

2. *Social interest groups* represent every segment of global society and have many ways to restrict business, including boycotts, lawsuits, picket lines, media campaigns, and lobbying for more regulation. Historically, labor has been the great antagonist and counterweight to business power, but also prominent in recent years are environmental, human rights, religious, and consumer groups. Increasingly, groups form coalitions with other groups, governments, and international institutions.

---

[46] Robert Sobel, "The $150 Million Lemon," *Audacity,* Winter 1997, p. 11.

FIGURE 3.2

Boundaries of Managerial Power

3. *Social values* are transmitted across generations, reflected in public opinion, and embedded in the law. Managers internalize them in schools and churches. Social values include norms of duty, justice, truth, and piety that can direct a manager's behavior as powerfully as laws. For example, in the 1960s shifting generational values gave film studios license to experiment with brazen nudity and violence, but Walt Disney never did. No financial incentive was enough to make him forsake his own values about the importance of morality, family life, and the small-town decency he saw in his Kansas boyhood.[47]

4. *Markets and economic stakeholders* impose strong limits. Stockholders, employees, suppliers, creditors, and competitors influence corporate decisions. The market also registers the great waves of technological change that can sweep away even the largest corporations.

According to the theory of pluralism, these are the boundaries of managerial power. Just as in the solar system the planets move freely within but cannot escape

[47] Richard Schickel, *The Disney Version,* 3rd ed. (Chicago: Ivan R. Dee, 1997), p. 39.

their gravitational fields, so major corporations in American society move within orbits constrained by plural interests.

CONCLUDING OBSERVATIONS

In a recent poll, 87 percent of Americans believed that "big companies . . . have too much . . . power and influence."[48] Are they correct? The answer requires perspective and judgment. In this chapter we break down the idea of corporate power into patterns, categories, and theories to allow critical thinking. We explain how corporate power is a strong force for change and how, at a deep level, economic growth shapes society in sweeping, unplanned ways.

We also set forth two opposing perspectives. The dominance theory holds that inadequately restrained economic power is concentrated in large corporations and in the hands of a wealthy elite. The pluralist theory holds that many restraints in an open society control corporate power. These theories are locked in perpetual conflict. Both are molds into which varieties of evidence must be fitted. Both contain insights, but neither has a lock on accuracy. And both attract adherents based on inner judgments about whether market capitalism moves society in the right direction.

If corporate power remains generally accountable to democratic controls, society will accord it legitimacy. If rule by law and a just economy exist, corporate power will broadly and ultimately be directed toward the public welfare, this despite the habitual breakouts of deviltry that inflame critics.

[48] The Harris Poll, "Business Divides: Big Companies Have Too Much Power and Influence in DC, Small Business Has Too Little," April 1, 2010, table 2, at www.harrisinteractive.com.

John D. Rockefeller and the Standard Oil Trust

This is the story of John D. Rockefeller, founder of the Standard Oil Company. It is the story of a somber, small-town boy who dominated the oil industry with organizational genius, audacity, and ruthless, methodical execution. He became the richest man in America and, for a time, the most hated.

Rockefeller's life spanned nearly 98 years. At his birth Martin Van Buren was president and settlers drove covered wagons over the Oregon Trail. He lived to see Franklin Roosevelt's New Deal, watch the rise of the Nazi party in Germany, and hear Frank Sinatra and *The Lone Ranger* on radio.

The historical backdrop of this lifetime is an economy gripped by the fever of industrial progress. Rockefeller built his fortune in an era that lacked many of today's ethical norms and commercial laws,

an era in which the power of a corporation and its founder could be exercised with fewer restraints.

THE FORMATIVE YEARS

John Davison Rockefeller was born July 8, 1839, in a small village in southern New York. He was the second of six children and the oldest boy. His father, William Rockefeller, was an itinerant quack doctor who sold worthless elixirs. He was jovial, slick, and cunning and made enough money to keep the family in handsome style until he had to flee and live away from home to avoid arrest for raping a local woman. After that, he visited only in the dark of night. But he taught young John D. and his brothers lessons of business conduct, especially that sentimentality should not influence business transactions. "I cheat my boys every chance I get," he once said. "I want to make 'em sharp."[1]

John D.'s mother was a somber, religious woman who gave the children a strict upbringing, emphasizing manners, church attendance, and the work ethic. She preached homilies such as "Willful waste makes woeful want." And she taught charity to the children; from an early age John D. made regular contributions to worthy causes.

Young John D. was not precocious in school. In high school he was an uninspired student, little interested in books and ideas, but willing to work hard. He grew into a somber, intense lad nicknamed "the Deacon" by his classmates because he faithfully attended a Baptist church and memorized hymns. In the summer of 1855 he took a three-month course at a business college in Cleveland, Ohio, and then set out looking for a job. In addition to his formal schooling, he carried the contradictory temperaments of his parents—the wily, self-assured boldness of his father and the exacting, pietistic character of his mother. He internalized both, and the combination was to prove formidable. Here was a man with the precision of an accountant and the cunning of Cesare Borgia.

EARLY BUSINESS CAREER

Rockefeller's first job was as a bookkeeper at a Cleveland firm where he meticulously examined each bill submitted and pounced on errors. He also recorded every cent he earned and spent in a personal ledger. Its pages show that he was parsimonious and saved most of his $25-a-month salary, but that he still gave generously to the Baptist church and the poor.

In 1859 he formed a successful partnership with two others in the produce business in Cleveland and proved himself an intense negotiator, described by an acquaintance as a person "who can walk right up on a man's shirt bosom and sit down."[2] The business boomed from supplying food to the Union army during the Civil War. Although in his early 20s at the time, the steady, unemotional lad was never touched by patriotic fervor. In those days, the law permitted

any man of means to pay someone else to serve in his place, and this he did.

BEGINNINGS OF THE OIL BUSINESS

Profits from the produce business were high, and John D. looked around for a promising new investment. He soon found one—a Cleveland petroleum refinery in which he invested $4,000 in 1863. At the time, petroleum production and refining was an infant industry. A new drilling technology had led to an 1859 oil strike in nearby Pennsylvania, followed by a frenzied boom in drilling and refining.

Soon Rockefeller devoted himself to the oil business, and he began to apply his principles of parsimony. One basic principle was to avoid paying a profit to anyone. For example, instead of buying barrels and paying the cooper $2.50 each, Rockefeller set up his own barrel-making factory and made them for $.96. He purchased a forest to make staves from his own trees. Another basic principle was methodical cost cutting. Lumber for barrel staves was kiln-dried before shipment to the cooperage plant. Water evaporated from the wood, making it lighter and lowering transportation costs.

Though obsessed with details and small economies, Rockefeller also proved aggressive in larger plans. He borrowed heavily from banks to expand the refinery. The risk scared his partners, so he bought them out. In 1865 he borrowed more to build a second refinery. Soon he incorporated an export sales company in New York, making the world his market.

DYNAMICS OF THE OIL INDUSTRY

During this early period, the new industry was in a chaotic state. A basic cause was overproduction in the Pennsylvania oil regions, which were the only source of crude oil. The price of crude fluctuated wildly, but was in long-term decline. Each drop in the price of crude oil encouraged construction of new refineries and by the late 1860s refining capacity was three times greater than oil production. This caused vicious price wars. Some refiners tried to stay in business by selling products at a loss to raise cash for continued debt payments. In doing so, they dragged down profit margins for all refiners.

---

[1] David Freeman Hawke, *John D.: The Founding Father of the Rockefellers* (New York: Harper & Row, 1980), p. 13.

[2] Jules Abels, *The Rockefeller Billions* (New York: Macmillan, 1965), p. 35.

Rockefeller had the insight to invest in large-scale refineries and, because he cut costs relentlessly, his refineries made money. Yet despite disciplined cost control, the market forces of a sick industry ate away at his net earnings. He believed it was time to "rationalize" the entire industry and stop destructive competition.[3] His method for doing this would be monopoly, his tactics hard-nosed.

ROCKEFELLER'S COMPETITIVE STRATEGIES

Rockefeller used a range of competitive strategies. He was a low-cost, high-volume producer. He used debt financing to expand. He attempted to make his refined petroleum products of high and consistent quality, since fly-by-night refiners turned out inferior distillates. Cheap kerosene with a low ignition point had burned many a home down after exploding in a wick lamp. When he incorporated the Standard Oil Company of Ohio in 1870, the name suggested a "standard oil" of uniformly good quality. He engaged in vertical integration by making wooden barrels. As time when on, he also bought pipelines, storage tanks, and railroad tank cars.

Critical to his success, however, was the art of strong-arming the railroads. In this, Rockefeller was the master. Transportation costs paid to railroads were important to refiners, who shipped in crude oil and then shipped out products such as kerosene or lubricating oil. In the 1860s railroads were highly competitive and often altered shipping rates to attract business. No law prohibited this, and published rates were only the starting point of negotiations.

Railroads often granted *rebates* to shippers; that is, they returned part of the freight charge after shipment. These rebates were usually secret and given in return for the guarantee of future business. Large volume shippers, including oil refineries, got the biggest rebates. Standard Oil was no exception.

At this time, Rockefeller has been described by biographers as a prepossessing man with penetrating eyes who drove a hard bargain. He would take the measure of a person with a withering stare, and few were his match. He was formidable in negotiations, being invariably informed in detail about the other's

business. And he was still a pious churchgoer who read the Bible nightly before retiring.

Late in 1870 Rockefeller hatched a brazen plan for stabilizing the oil industry at the refining level. In clandestine meetings, he worked out a rebate scheme between a few major refiners and the three railroads going into the Pennsylvania oil regions. They gave this scheme an innocent-sounding name, the South Improvement Plan. In it, the railroads agreed to increase published rates for hauling oil. Then Rockefeller's Cleveland refineries and a few others would get large rebates on each barrel shipped. For example, the regular rate between the oil regions and Cleveland would be $.80 a barrel and between Cleveland and New York $2.00 a barrel. It would cost a total of $2.80 per barrel for any other refinery in Cleveland to bring in a barrel of crude oil and ship a barrel of refined oil to New York for sale or export. Rockefeller and his accomplices, on the other hand, would be charged $2.80 but then get a rebate of $.90.

In addition, the refineries participating in the South Improvement Plan received *drawbacks* or payments made on the shipment of oil by competitors! Thus, Rockefeller would be paid $.40 on every barrel of crude oil his competitors shipped into Cleveland and $.50 on every barrel of refined oil shipped to New York. Under this venal scheme, the more a competitor shipped, the more Rockefeller's transportation costs were lowered. While competitors were charged $2.80 on the critical route (Pennsylvania oil regions–Cleveland–New York), Rockefeller paid only $1.00. Moreover, the railroads agreed to give the conspirators waybills detailing competitors' shipments; a better espionage system would be hard to find.

Why did the railroads agree to this plot? There were several reasons. First, it removed the uncertainty of cutthroat competition. Oil traffic was guaranteed in large volume. Second, the refiners provided services to the railroads including tank cars, loading facilities, and insurance. And third, railroad executives received stock in the participating refineries, giving them a stake in their success.

The consequences of the South Improvement Plan were predictable. Nonparticipating refiners faced bloated transportation costs and would be uncompetitive. They had two choices. Either they could sell to Rockefeller and his allies, or they could stand on principle and go bankrupt. When they sold, as they must, the flaw in industry structure would be corrected. Rockefeller intended to acquire them, then

[3] Ron Chernow, *Titan: The Life of John D. Rockefeller, Sr.* (New York: Random House, 1998), pp. 130 and 149–52.

close them or limit their capacity. This would give him market power to stabilize the price of both crude oil and refined products. And the rebates would be a formidable barrier to new entrants.

THE CONSPIRACY PLAYS OUT

In February 1872 the new freight rates were announced. Quickly, the full design was revealed, causing widespread, explosive rage in the oil regions. Although it broke no laws, it overstepped prevailing norms. People believed that since railroads got their right-of-ways from the public they had a duty to serve shippers fairly. Volume discounts might be justified, but this shakedown was extortionate. Producers and refiners in the oil regions boycotted the conspirators and the railroads.

Rockefeller, seen as the prime mover behind the South Improvement Plan, was vilified in the industry and the press. His wife feared for his life. Yet he never wavered. "It was right," he said of the plan. "I knew it as a matter of conscience. It was right between me and my God."[4] As journalist Ida Tarbell noted, Rockefeller was not squeamish about such business affairs.

> Mr. Rockefeller was "good." There was no more faithful Baptist in Cleveland than he. Every enterprise of that church he had supported liberally from his youth. He gave to its poor. He visited its sick. He wept with its suffering. Moreover, he gave unostentatiously to many outside charities . . . Yet he was willing to strain every nerve to obtain himself special and unjust privileges from the railroads which were bound to ruin every man in the oil business not sharing them with him.[5]

Within a month, the weight of negative public opinion and loss of revenue caused the railroads to cave in. They rescinded the discriminatory rate structure. All appearances were of a Rockefeller defeat, but appearances deceived. Rockefeller had moved quickly, meeting one by one with rival refiners, explaining the rebate scheme and its salutary effect on the industry, and asking to buy them out. He offered the exact value of the business in cash or, preferably, in Standard Oil Company stock.

By the time the railroads reset their rates, Rockefeller had bought out 21 of his 26 Cleveland competitors. Some acquisitions were simply dismantled to reduce surplus capacity. He now dominated Cleveland, the country's major refining center, and controlled more than a quarter of U.S. capacity. In secrecy, he negotiated a new rebate agreement with the Erie Railroad. Of these actions, Ida Tarbell noted sardonically: "He had a mind which, stopped by a wall, burrows under or creeps around."[6]

Regardless of methods, he had, indeed, corrected structural flaws in the oil industry. It would attract more capital. If any circumstance cast a shadow over this striking victory, it was that public opinion had turned against him. From then on, he was reviled as an unfair competitor, hatred of him growing apace with his burgeoning wealth. He never understood why.

ONWARD THE COURSE OF EMPIRE

Rockefeller, now 33, was wealthy. Yet he drove on, compelled to finish a grand design, to spread his pattern over the industry landscape, to conform it to his vision.

He continued the strategy of horizontal integration at the refinery level by absorbing more and more of his competitors. As the size of Standard Oil increased, Rockefeller gained added leverage over the railroads. Like an orchestra conductor he played them against each other, granting shares of the oil traffic in return for rebates that gave him a decisive advantage.

Some competitors stubbornly clung to their businesses, partly out of hatred for Rockefeller. He made them "sweat" and "feel sick" until they sold.[7] The fleets of tank cars that he leased to railroads were often "unavailable" to ship feedstock and distillates to and from such refiners. Rockefeller concealed many of his acquisitions, disguising the full sweep of his drive to monopoly. These companies were the Trojan horses in his war against rival refiners. They seemed independent but secretly helped to undermine Standard's competitors. Often they were at the center of elaborate pricing conspiracies involving code words in telegrams such as "doubters" for

[4] Peter Collier and David Horowitz, *The Rockefellers: An American Dynasty* (New York: New American Library, 1976), p. 11.

[5] Ida M. Tarbell, *The History of the Standard Oil Company,* vol. 1 (Gloucester, MA: Peter Smith, 1963), p. 43.

[6] Ibid., p. 99.

[7] Abels, *The Rockefeller Billions,* p. 35.

refiners and "mixer" for railroad drawbacks. The phantoms bought some refiners who refused in principle to sell out to Standard Oil. Their existence confronted independents with a dark, mysterious force that could not be brought into the light and fought.

THE STANDARD OIL TRUST

By 1882 Rockefeller's company was capitalized at $70 million and produced 90 percent of the nation's refining output. Its main product, illuminating oil, was changing the way people lived. Before the sale of affordable illuminating oil of good quality, most Americans went to bed with darkness. They could not afford expensive candles or whale oil and feared using the unstable kerosene made by early, small refiners. With the rise of Rockefeller's colossus, they had reliable, inexpensive light and stayed up. Their lives, and the life of the nation, changed.

Rockefeller reorganized Standard Oil as a trust.[8] His purpose was to make state regulation more difficult. Soon other large companies followed his lead, adopting the trust form to avoid government restrictions. Inside Standard Oil, Rockefeller's organizing skills were extraordinary. Working with a loyal inner circle of managers, he directed his far-flung empire from headquarters at 26 Broadway in New York City. As he absorbed his competitors, so had he co-opted the best minds in the industry and much of Standard's success is attributable to this stellar supporting cast. Though dominant, Rockefeller delegated great responsibility to his managers.

High-level committees controlled business operations. He circulated monthly cost statements for each refinery, causing fierce internal competition among their managers that led to high performance. He set up a network of informants around the globe. Critics called them spies, but they functioned as a well-organized information system.

A perfectionist, he insisted on having a statement of the exact net worth of Standard Oil on his desk every morning. Oil prices always were calculated to three decimals. He was so dogged about efficiency and recycling that his Standard Oil plants might win

environmental awards were they operating today. At night he prowled the headquarters turning down wicks in oil lamps.

His management style was one of formal politeness. He never spoke harshly to any employee. Once, when a manager leaked information to the press, Rockefeller said to his secretary: "Suggest to Mr. Blank that he would do admirably as a newspaper man, and that we shall not need his services after the close of this month."[9] Compared with other moguls of that era, he lived simply. He had two large estates, in Cleveland and New York, but neither was too ostentatious. He read the Bible daily, continued regular attendance at a Baptist church, and gave generously to charities.

Rockefeller's organizing skills were critical to his success. Discussions often focus on his ethics, but the key to Standard Oil's long-term domination lay elsewhere. The company was an immense, organized force opposed only by smaller, less united adversaries. Its success came from centralized, coordinated effort. Compromising methods, to the extent they were used, were of far less importance.[10]

EXTENDING DOMINATION

By the 1880s Standard Oil had overwhelming market power. Its embrace of refining activity was virtually complete, and it had moved into drilling, pipelines, storage tanks, transportation, and marketing of finished products. By now the entire world was addicted to kerosene and other petroleum products, and Standard's international sales grew.

Rockefeller's dominating competitive philosophy prevailed. His marketing agents were ordered to destroy independent suppliers. To suppress competition, his employees pioneered fanatical customer service. The intelligence-gathering network paid competitors' employees to pass information to Standard Oil. Railroad agents were bribed to misroute shipments. Standard Oil workers climbed on competitors' tank cars and measured the contents. Price warfare was relentless. A stubborn competitor often

---

[8] A trust is a method of controlling a number of companies in which the voting stock of each company is transferred to a board of trustees. The trustees then have the power to coordinate the operations of all companies in the group. This organizing form is no longer legal in the United States.

[9] Quoted in "A Great Monopoly's Work: An Inner View of the Standard Oil Company," *The New York Times,* February 27, 1883, p. 1.

[10] David M. Chalmers, ed., "Introductory Essay," in Ida M. Tarbell, *The History of the Standard Oil Company, Briefer Version* (Mineola, NY: Dover, 2003), pp. xvii–xviii.

found Standard selling kerosene to its customers at a price substantially below production cost.

Rockefeller himself was never proved to be directly involved in flagrant misconduct. He blamed criminal and unethical actions on overzealous subordinates. His critics thought the strategy of suffocating small rivals and policies such as that requiring regular written intelligence reports encouraged degenerative ethics among his minions.

Rockefeller saw Standard Oil as a stabilizing force in the industry and as a righteous crusade to illuminate the world. How, as a good Christian devoted to the moral injunctions of the Bible, was Rockefeller able to suborn such vicious behavior in commerce? One biographer, Allan Nevins, gives this explanation:

> From a chaotic industry he was building an efficient industrial empire for what seemed to him the good not only of its heads but of the general public. If he relaxed his general methods of warfare . . . a multitude of small competitors would smash his empire and plunge the oil business back to chaos. He always believed in what William McKinley called "benevolent assimilation"; he preferred to buy out rivals on decent terms, and to employ the ablest competitors as helpers. It was when his terms were refused that he ruthlessly crushed the "outsiders." . . . It seemed to him better that a limited number of small businesses should die than that the whole industry should go through a constant process of half-dying, reviving, and again half-dying.[11]

THE STANDARD OIL TRUST UNDER ATTACK

Standard Oil continued to grow, doubling in size before the turn of the century and doubling again by 1905.[12] Eventually its very size brought a flood of criticism that complicated operations. Predatory monopoly was at odds with prevailing beliefs about individual rights and free competition. The states tried to regulate Standard Oil and filed antitrust suits against it. Overwrought muckrakers lashed out at Rockefeller. Because of him, wrote one, "hundreds and thousands of men have been ruined."[13] He was

the personification of greed in political cartoons. Politicians not suborned by his bribery lambasted him.

Rockefeller, by now the richest American, was shaken by public hatred. He hired bodyguards and slept with a revolver. Pinkerton detectives were present at church on Sundays to handle gawkers and shouters. He developed a digestive ailment so severe that he could eat only a few bland foods, and upon his doctor's advice he stopped daily office work. By 1896 he appeared only rarely at 26 Broadway. Soon he was afflicted with a nervous disorder and lost all his hair.

As attacks on Rockefeller grew, the vise of government regulation tightened on his company. A swarm of lawsuits and legislative hearings hung about it. Finally, in 1911, the Supreme Court ordered its breakup under the Sherman Antitrust Act, holding that its monopoly position was an "undue" restraint on trade that violated the "standard of reason."[14] The company was given six months to separate into 39 independent firms. The breakup consisted mainly of moving the desks of managers at 26 Broadway and was a financial windfall for Rockefeller, who received shares of stock in all the companies, the prices of which were driven up by frenzied public buying. Before the breakup kerosene sales had buoyed the company. However, just as electric lightbulbs were replacing oil lamps, the automobile jolted demand for another petroleum distillate—gasoline. Rockefeller, who was 71 at the time of the breakup and would live another 26 years, earned new fortunes simply by maintaining his equity in the separate companies.

Rockefeller remained a source of fascination for the American public. As *The Wall Street Journal* noted, "The richest man in a world where money is power is necessarily a fascinating object of study."[15] This being so, it was his enduring misfortune that muckraking journalist Ida Tarbell turned her gaze on him.

Tarbell wrote two unflattering character studies and a detailed, two-volume biography of Rockefeller, all serialized in the widely read *McClure's Magazine* between 1902 and 1905. Her unsentimental words were no less ruthless than the actions of the old man himself. Although admitting that Rockefeller and Standard Oil

[11] Allan Nevins, *Study in Power: John D. Rockefeller*, vol. 2 (New York: Scribner, 1953), p. 433.

[12] Ibid., app. 3, p. 478.

[13] Henry Demarest Lloyd, "Story of a Great Monopoly," *The Atlantic*, March 1881, p. 320.

[14] *Standard Oil Company of New Jersey v. United States*, 31 U.S. 221. It was an 8–1 decision.

[15] "Incarnate Business," *The Wall Street Journal*, June 26, 1905, p. 1.

had some measure of "legitimate greatness," she was obsessed with his flaws. In one essay she found "something indefinably repulsive" in his appearance, writing that his mouth was "the cruelest feature of his face," and that his nose "rose like a thorn."[16] Such ad hominem attacks lacked merit but, in addition, Tarbell delved deeply into Rockefeller's career, producing narratives of exquisite detail. The thesis she conveyed to the public was that by his singular example, Rockefeller was responsible for debasing the moral tone of American business. She believed his story incited legions of the ambitious to use cold-blooded methods, teaching them that success justifies itself. Like the master, the junior scoundrels often cited biblical verse to support their actions.

Few public figures have a nemesis such as Ida Tarbell. Her relentless pen, along with others, deprived him of some public adulation he may have craved and her scholarship permanently defined him. Her intricate period research cannot be duplicated and subsequent biographers, even more friendly ones, must go to it for insight. Rockefeller may or may not have deserved such a definitive hand. He called her a "poisonous woman."[17]

THE GREAT ALMONER

Since childhood Rockefeller had made charitable donations and, as his fortune accumulated, he increased them. After 1884 the total was never less than $100,000 a year, and after 1892 it was usually over $1 million and sometimes far more. In his mind, these benefactions were linked to his duty as a good Christian to uplift humanity. To a reporter he once said:

> I believe the power to make money is a gift from God—just as are the instincts for art, music, literature, the doctor's talent, yours—to be developed and used to the best of our ability for the good of mankind. Having been endowed with the gift I possess, I believe it is my duty to make money and still more money and to use the money I make for the good of my fellow-man according to the dictates of my conscience.[18]

Over his lifetime, Rockefeller gave gifts of approximately $550 million. He gave, for example, $8.2 million for the construction of Peking Union Medical College in response to the need to educate doctors in China. He gave $50 million to the University of Chicago. He created charitable trusts and endowed them with millions. One such trust was the General Education Board, set up in 1902, which started 1,600 new high schools. Another, the Rockefeller Sanitary Commission, succeeded in eradicating hookworm in the South. The largest was the Rockefeller Foundation, established in 1913 and endowed with $200 million. Its purpose was "to promote the well-being of mankind throughout the world." Rockefeller always said, however, that the greatest philanthropy of all was developing the earth's natural resources and employing people. Critics greeted his gifts with skepticism, thinking them atonement for years of plundering American society.

In his later years, Rockefeller lived a secluded, placid existence on his great Pocantico estate in New York, which had 75 buildings and 70 miles of roads. As years passed, the public grew increasingly fond of him. Memories of his early business career dimmed, and a new generation viewed him in the glow of his

John D. Rockefeller at age 65. This photograph was taken shortly after a disease, generalized alopecia, caused him to lose his hair. Source: The Library of Congress.

[16] Ida Tarbell, "John D. Rockefeller: A Character Study," *McClure's*, August 1905, p. 386.

[17] Chernow, *Titan: The Life of John D. Rockefeller, Sr.*, p. xxii.

[18] Quoted in Abels, *The Rockefeller Billions*, p. 280.

huge charitable contributions. For many years, he carried shiny nickels and dimes in his pockets to give to children and well-wishers.

On his 86th birthday he wrote the following verse.

I was early taught to work as well as play,
My life has been one long, happy holiday;
Full of work and full of play—
I dropped the worry on the way—
And God was good to me every day.

He died in 1937 at the age of 97. His estate was valued at $26,410,837. He had given the rest away.

Questions

1. With reference to the levels and spheres of corporate power discussed in the chapter, how did the power of Standard Oil change society? Was this power exercised in keeping with the social contract of Rockefeller's era?

2. How does the story of Standard Oil illustrate the limits of business power? Does it better illustrate the dominance theory or the pluralist theory discussed in the chapter?

3. Did Rockefeller himself ever act unethically? By the standards of his day? By those of today? How could he simultaneously be a devout Christian and a ruthless monopolist? Is there any contradiction between his personal and business ethics?

4. In the utilitarian sense of accomplishing the greatest good for the greatest number in society, was the Standard Oil Company a net plus or a minus? On balance, did the company meet its responsibilities to society?

5. Did strategies of Standard Oil encourage unethical behavior? Could Rockefeller's vision have been fulfilled using "nicer" tactics?

Chapter Four

Critics of Business

Mary "Mother" Jones

In the early years of the twentieth century Mary Jones (1837–1930), known as Mother Jones, was one of the most notable women in America. Emerging from personal tragedy, she created a singular persona and hurled herself against big corporations and the capitalist system that sustained them. Hers was an era of great change, dissent, and conflict. It was the ideal stage for a defiant performance.

She was born in 1837 as Mary Harris in Cork, Ireland. When she was eight years old, a fungus blighted the nation's potato crop, causing a terrible famine. She emigrated with her family to Toronto and there grew up, graduated from a convent school, and became a schoolteacher. Eventually she moved to Memphis and married an iron molder named George Jones. Between 1862 and 1867 they had four children. She devoted herself to cooking, cleaning, and sewing for the family. Then yellow fever struck.

The deadly epidemic came in the fall of 1867. As mortality rose, rich families left town, leaving those who could not afford travel to become victims. The sounds of death carts taking bodies away filled neighborhoods. Mary Jones describes what happened to her.

> All about my house I could hear weeping and the cries of delirium. One by one, my four little children sickened and died. I washed their little bodies and got them ready for burial. My husband caught the fever and died. I sat alone through nights of grief. No one came to me. No one could.[1]

She nursed the sick until the plague ended, then returned to Chicago to set up a dressmaking business. She often worked for wealthy society matrons.

> I had ample opportunity to observe the luxury and extravagance of their lives. Often while sewing for the lords and barons who lived in magnificence on the Lake Shore Drive, I would look out of the plate glass windows and see the poor, shivering wretches, jobless and hungry, walking along the frozen lake front. The contrast of their condition with that of the tropical comfort of the people for whom I sewed was painful to me. My employers seemed neither to notice nor to care.[2]

[1] Mary Field Parton, ed., *The Autobiography of Mother Jones* (Chicago: C. H. Kerr, 1925), p. 12.
[2] Ibid., chap. 1, p. 13.

Several years passed, then in 1871 the Great Chicago Fire burned her business and left her destitute. After the fire she attended evening meetings of the Knights of Labor, an early union, becoming absorbed in the fight of industrial workers for better wages and conditions. The perspective of class war began to dominate her view of society. She felt that workers were enslaved by corporate employers and by the corrupt politicians and judges who did their bidding. She believed that only by overthrowing capitalism could the laboring class end its bondage and usher in a new day of socialism, so she joined a small socialist political party.

For almost two decades Mary Jones worked in obscurity for labor causes and during this time she created the persona that would make her powerful and famous. Mary Jones became Mother Jones. The loss of her own family had freed her to take on another, to adopt the downtrodden. In an era when women had no vote, held no leadership positions, and received no encouragement to speak up, she would use this metaphor of motherhood to give her power.

She rose to prominence as an organizer for the United Mine Workers. Horrible working conditions prevailed in coal mines. Miners worked 10- and 12-hour days in damp, dusty, cramped, dangerous tunnels. Wages were so low that mining families put their children to work to get by. Boys as young as eight years old toiled six or seven days a week, some spending so many hours in cramped shafts that their bones grew irregularly and they could not stand straight as adults. Textile mills were built near mining towns to employ the miners' wives and daughters. The United Mine Workers wanted to unionize the miners, but the coal companies viciously resisted. Organizers were followed and observed. Miners who shook an organizer's hand were fired. Hired thugs beat up troublemakers. Companies had friendly judges convene lunacy hearings and commit prounion employees to asylums. The miners wanted unions, but they were intimidated.

In the late 1890s Mother Jones arrived in Pennsylvania coal country. At 60 years old she looked like a grandmother. She stood five feet tall with silver hair and sharp blue eyes. With great energy she worked the coal towns. She was an explosive orator with a vocal range from shrill cries to a forceful, low pitch that mesmerized listeners. She knew the miners' language and spoke in colorful terms, calling mine owners "a crew of pirates," "a gang of thieves," and "cowards." She called the men her "boys" and as their "mother" told them to stand up to the companies.

During a bitter strike in 1900 when some miners were losing their nerve, she organized marches of the miners' wives. The women paraded to work sites wearing aprons, waving mops, and banging pans. Laughing company guards saw no danger from the comical processions and let them through, not realizing how Mother Jones had cleverly dramatized the role of aggrieved wives and mothers fighting for the welfare of their families. She scolded the men, telling them they were shamed if their wives stood up to the companies and they did not.

Mother Jones used ironic wit to puncture establishment pretensions. In 1902 she was arrested in West Virginia after the coal companies got an injunction against union organizing. In court, the judge suspended her sentence, but advised her that as a woman it would be "better far for her to follow the lines and paths which the Allwise Being intended her sex should pursue." She appreciated the advice, she said, adding that it was no surprise he was taking the company's side, since

Mary "Mother" Jones. Source: Library of Congress.

experience had taught her that "robbers tend to like each other."[3] When asked by a Princeton professor to address his class, she brought with her a stooped and pale 10-year-old boy. "Here's a textbook on economics," she said. "He gets three dollars a week . . . [working] in a carpet factory ten hours a day while the children of the rich are getting higher education."[4] She had a favorite story for audiences: "I asked a man in prison once how he happened to get there. He had stolen a pair of shoes. I told him that if he had stolen a railroad he could be a United States Senator."[5]

Eventually, Mother Jones fell out with the United Mine Workers because she was more militant than its leadership. She became a lecturer for the Socialist Party, but in time she renounced socialism. She was a doer, not an ideologue, and she lacked patience with hairsplitting doctrinal debates among intellectuals who led comfortable lives. However, in 1905 she helped launch the International Workers of the World (IWW), a radical union dedicated to overthrowing American capitalism. By 1911 she had returned to the front lines in mining regions. Later, she marched with striking

[3] Gene R. Nichol, Jr., "Fighting Poverty with Virtue," *Michigan Law Review,* May 2002, p. 1661.

[4] Quoted in Marilyn Jurich, "The Female Trickster—Known as Trickstar—As Exemplified by Two American Legendary Women, 'Billy' Tipton and Mother Jones," *Journal of American Culture,* Spring 1999, p. 69.

[5] "Mother Jones Speaks to Coney Island Crowd," *The New York Times,* July 27, 1903.

garment and streetcar workers in New York City. In 1916 she started a riot by 200 wives of streetcar workers with an inflammatory speech, telling them: "You ought to be out raising hell."[6]

By the 1920s Mother Jones had grown disillusioned with unions. She quit the IWW saying it was more interested in symbolic displays than in concrete victories. Other unions had grown comfortable with the corporate establishment. She had contempt for union leaders motivated by their own importance and called John L. Lewis, president of the United Mine Workers, a "pie counter hunter."[7] She retired from public life, speaking out now and then, and died in 1930 at the age of 92.

Today Mother Jones is little remembered. Her time passed, and the specific labor abuses that enraged her are mostly ended. Perhaps her invective is unmatched today. She defined "monster capitalism," as a "robber system" supported by the "national gang of burglars of Wall Street." The corporations she attacked had "snake brains" and were run by "idiots" and "commercial pirates." But her ideas live on. Although her life was unique in its tragedy and drama, her attacks were based on enduring values that recycle through time. We may forget Mother Jones, but we hear her in today's business critics. In this chapter we explore the birth and life of these values.

ORIGINS OF CRITICAL ATTITUDES TOWARD BUSINESS

There are two underlying sources of criticism of business, one ancient and the other modern. The first is the belief that people in business place profit before more worthy values such as honesty, truth, justice, love, piety, aesthetics, tranquility, and respect for nature. The second is the strain of economic development. During industrialization and later, when market economies grow large and complex, business has a range of problematic impacts on societies. We will discuss both fundamental sources of criticism. We begin in the ancient Mediterranean world.

The Greeks and Romans

agrarian society
A society with a largely agricultural economy.

The earliest societies were agrarian in nature. An *agrarian society* is a preindustrial society in which economic, political, and cultural values are based on agricultural experience. In these societies, most people worked the land for subsistence. No industrial centers or mass markets existed, so business activity beyond barter and exchange was a tiny part of the economy. The activities of merchants were often thought unprincipled because their sharp trading practices clashed with the traditional, more altruistic values of family and clan relations among farmers. Merchants typically had lower class status than officials, farmers, soldiers, artisans, and teachers.

The extraordinary civilizations of ancient Greece and Rome were based on subsistence agriculture. Economic activity by merchants, bankers, and manufacturers was limited. The largest factory in Athens, for example, employed 120 workers making shields.[8] Commercial activity was greater in Rome, but it was still mainly

---

[6] "Car Riot Started by 'Mother' Jones," *The New York Times,* October 6, 1916, p. 1.

[7] Quoted in Elliot J. Gorn, *Mother Jones: The Most Dangerous Woman in America* (New York: Hill and Wang, 2001), p. 249.

[8] Will Durant, *The Life of Greece* (New York: Simon & Schuster, 1939), p. 272.

an agrarian society. Perhaps because industry was so limited in both societies, inaccurate economic doctrines arose to explain commercial activity.[9] For example, the desire for riches was suspect due to the popular belief that the amount of wealth was fixed. If so, an individual accumulated wealth only by subtracting from the share of others. This is believable logic in an agrarian society because the land on which the economy is based is fixed in amount.

Philosophers moved into this realm of intellectual error, reasoning that profit seeking was an inferior motive and that commercial activity led to excess, corruption, and misery. Their views are of lasting significance because, as with many topics of discourse in Western civilization, they first defined the terms of debate over the ranking of profit relative to other values. In particular, both Plato and Aristotle articulated the fundamental indictment that casts an everlasting shadow over business.

Plato believed that insatiable appetites existed in every person. These could be controlled only by inner virtues painstakingly acquired through character development. The pursuit of money was one such appetite, and Plato thought that when people engaged in trade they inevitably succumbed to the temptation of excess and became grasping. In a society, as with an individual, wealth spawned evils, including inequality, envy, class conflict, and war. "Virtue and wealth," he argued, "are balanced against one another in the scales."[10] Rulers of the utopian society he conceived in *The Republic* were prohibited from owning possessions for fear they would be corrupted and turn into tyrants. So troubled was he about this that they were forbidden even to touch gold or silver.

Aristotle believed there was a benign form of acquisition that consisted of getting the things needed for subsistence. This kind of acquisition was natural and moderate. However, after trading and monetary systems arose, the art of acquisition was no longer practiced this simple way. Instead, merchants studied the techniques of commerce, figuring out how to make the greatest profit, seeking not the necessities, but unlimited pools of money. Aristotle thought this was a lower form of acquisition because it was activity that did not contribute to inner virtue.

For Aristotle, happiness is the ultimate goal of life. It comes to those who develop character virtues such as courage, temperance, justice, and wisdom. He called these virtues "goods of the soul" and held them superior to "external goods," which he defined as possessions and money. Aristotle believed that the amount of happiness a person gained in life was equal to the amount of virtue accumulated in the soul. Since material possessions beyond those needed for subsistence added nothing to the store of virtue in the soul, it followed that they contributed nothing to happiness; thus, it was a waste or "perversion" of any virtue to apply it toward the acquisition of excess. "The proper function of courage, for example, is not to produce money but to give confidence," he wrote.[11]

Thus, both Plato and Aristotle relegated the profit motive to the sphere of lower or base impulses, a place from which it would not escape for centuries and then

---

[9] John Kenneth Galbraith, *Economics in Perspective* (Boston: Houghton Mifflin, 1987), pp. 9–10.

[10] *The Republic,* trans. F. M. Cornford (New York: Oxford University Press, 1945), p. 274.

[11] In *Politics,* trans. Ernest Barker (New York: Oxford University Press, 1962), book I, chap. X, sec. 17. See also book VII, chap. 1, secs. 1–10.

only partially. Soon, Roman law would forbid the senatorial class from making business investments (and the law would be widely circumvented). Likewise, the Stoic philosophers of Rome, including Epictetus and Marcus Aurelius, taught that the truly rich person possessed inner peace rather than capital or property. "Asked, 'Who is the rich man?' Epictetus replied, 'He who is content.'"[12] These sages looked down on merchants of their day as materialists who, in pursuit of wealth, sacrificed character development. Of course, this did not deter the merchants from accumulating fortunes and neglecting the study of ideals. The scornful ethos of the philosophers, though potent enough to endure and to beget perennial hostility, has never had enough power to suppress the tide of commerce.

The Medieval World

During the Middle Ages, the prevailing theology of the Roman Catholic Church was intolerant of profit seeking. As the Christian religion arose, its early practitioners had been persecuted by the wealthy and corrupt ruling class of Rome. The church, then, rejected a focus on wealth and sought special status for the poor. Saint Augustine, the towering figure of early church doctrine, accepted the idea that material wealth was fixed in supply. To become rich, a person necessarily sinned by accumulation that violated the natural equality of creation. Moreover, the love of material things was a snare that pulled the soul away from God.[13]

just price
A price giving a moderate profit; one inspired by fairness, not greed.

The Roman Catholic Church's most definitive theologian, St. Thomas Aquinas, was greatly influenced by the ideas of Aristotle when he set forth church canon about the ethics of profit making and lending money. Merchants were exhorted to charge a *just price* for their wares, a price that incorporated a modest profit just adequate to maintain them in the social station to which they were born. The just price stands in contrast to the modern idea of a *market price* determined by supply and demand without any moral dimension. Today we hear echoes of medieval theology when consumers complain that high prices for a scarce product are unjust. Catholicism also condemned *usury,* or the lending of money for interest. By the twelfth and thirteenth centuries, however, the money supply and economic activity had greatly expanded and interest-bearing loans were common. "Commercial activity," notes historian Will Durant, "proved stronger than fear of prison or hell."[14] In time, the church backed away from the dogma of just price and usury. It was a slow process. Not until 1917 did the Catholic church officially renounce the teaching that lending money for interest was a sin.

market price
A price determined by the interaction of supply and demand.

usury
The lending of money for interest.

The Modern World

As business activity accelerated during the Renaissance, new theories arose to justify previously condemned practices. Two are of great importance. First, is the rise of the *Protestant ethic* in the sixteenth century. The Protestant reformers Martin Luther

Protestant ethic
The belief that hard work and adherence to a set of virtues such as thrift, saving, and sobriety would bring wealth and God's approval.

[12] *The Golden Sayings of Epictetus,* trans. Hastings Crossley, in Charles W. Eliot, ed., *Plato, Epictetus, Marcus Aurelius* (Danbury, CT: Grolier, 1980), p. 179.

[13] Saint Augustine, *The City of God,* trans. Gerald G. Walsh et al. (New York: Image Books, 1958), book XIX, chap. 17. This work was completed in A.D. 426.

[14] *The Age of Faith* (New York: Simon & Schuster, 1950), p. 631.

and John Calvin believed that work was a means of serving God and that if a person earned great wealth through hard work it was a sign of God's approval. This confronted the church's antagonism toward commerce with a new doctrine that removed moral suspicion of wealth. It contradicted the belief that pursuit of money corrupted the soul. Second, in 1776 Adam Smith published his theory of capitalism, writing that free markets harnessed greed for the public good and protected consumers from abuse. This defied the church's insistence on the idea of a just price. Moreover, visible wealth creation in expanding economies forcefully countered the notion that only a more or less fixed amount of wealth existed in a society. These developments ended the domination of doctrines that made business activity seem faintly criminal and released new energies into commerce. But the broom of doctrinal reform failed to make a clean sweep, and many business critics clung to the old approbations of the Greek philosophers and of the Roman Catholic Church.

In addition, just when old strictures were loosening, the Industrial Revolution created new tensions that reinforced critical attitudes about business. These new tensions arose as inventions and industries transformed agrarian societies and challenged traditional values with modern alternatives. During industrialization, rural, slow-paced, stable societies are swiftly and dramatically altered. They become urban and fast-paced. More emphasis is placed on material things and people's values shift. Wealth creation overwhelms self-restraint. Consumption supplants thrift and saving. Conquest of nature replaces awe of nature.

THE AMERICAN CRITIQUE OF BUSINESS

As societies modernize, the antiquarian values of Greece live on in the charges of critics who are troubled by these changes. Always, the fundamental critique is altered to fit current circumstances. We will see how this happened in the United States.

The Colonial Era

The American nation was colonized by corporations. The colonists who landed at Jamestown, Virginia, in 1606 were sponsored by investors in the London Company, who hoped to make a fortune by discovering gold in the New World. Instead, the colonists found a mild strain of native tobacco that caused a sensation in England (and became the basis for the plantation economy that would rise in the South). The Pilgrims who came in the *Mayflower* to Cape Cod, Massachusetts, in 1620 had fled persecution to set up a religious colony. But their voyage was financed by the Plymouth Company, whose backers sought to make a profit. To repay their debt and to buy manufactured goods they exported furs and forest products such as timber, tar, and turpentine. In this way the early colonists became lively traders.

As international trade in coastal regions expanded, settlers moved inland, creating a broad agrarian base for the economy. These frontier farms seethed with profit-oriented activity. Unlike European peasants, American farmers owned their land and this turned them into little capitalists. Most tried to make money by raising crops for market. Some were land speculators. Others built and ran grain mills and in other ways employed their capital like the traders and merchants in towns.

The popular theoretician of the rising capitalist spirit was Benjamin Franklin (1706–1790). Franklin began a business career at the age of 22 by opening a printing shop. He then bought several newspapers and retired rich at the age of 42. During travels in Europe he became acquainted with Adam Smith, who shared parts of the manuscript for *Wealth of Nations* with him. Franklin came to accept Smith's then-radical views on the superiority of laissez-faire markets. Writing prolifically, he gave form to a new American business ethos.

In 1732 Franklin published the first annual *Poor Richard's Almanack,* an eclectic book of facts, information, and self-help advice. Over many years the *Almanack* carried aphorisms and maxims about the road to success in business, a road open to all who practiced virtues such as hard work, thrift, and frugality. "The sleeping Fox catches no Poultry." "Lost Time is never found again." "Diligence is the Mother of Good Luck." "The Art of getting Riches consists very much in Thrift."[15]

Unlike the Old World theologians who taught that commercial success was slightly sinful, Franklin taught that God would approve the pursuit of self-interest and wealth. "God gives all things to Industry."[16] He made business activity synonymous with traditional virtues and released it from moral suspicion. His teaching resonated with the American condition, and he became the prophet of a vibrant economy. Not surprisingly, his *Almanacks* were best sellers.

The Young Nation

The amalgam of a new land, a new people, and a new thinking generated an early emphasis on business activity and material progress. Yet not everyone felt this was either inevitable or proper and dissent soon emerged. After independence in 1783, business interests were important in the new nation but not to the extent that they would be in time. There were few large companies. The economy was 90 percent agricultural, so the interests of farmers and planters dominated those of infant industry. A major debate arose over the direction of the economy, one that would define subsequent debate between business and its critics in America. It was played out in a bitter rivalry between two members of President George Washington's cabinet who differed both in temperament and ideas.

Alexander Hamilton (1755–1804), the first secretary of the treasury, was young, ambitious, brilliant, and inclined to action. He believed that industrial growth would increase national power and designed a grand scheme to promote manufacturing and finance. He was an arrogant, aloof leader who mistrusted the wisdom of common citizens. Having once said "the people is a great beast," he favored rule by an economic elite.[17] Hamilton got Congress to approve his plans for taxation, debt financing, tariffs to protect infant industry, and creation of a national bank, setting a policy of industrialization in motion.

---

[15] Quotations are in *Poor Richard's Almanack,* 1749, and "The Way to Wealth," Preface to *Poor Richard Improved,* 1758, in Nathan G. Goodman, ed., *The Autobiography of Benjamin Franklin and Selections from His Other Writings* (New York: Carlton House, 1932), pp. 198, 206, 207.

[16] Ibid., "The Way to Wealth," p. 207.

[17] Quoted in Vernon Louis Parrington, *Main Currents in American Thought,* vol. 1 (New York: Harcourt, Brace, 1958), p. 300; originally published in 1927.

He was opposed by Secretary of State Thomas Jefferson (1743–1826), one of America's most original and philosophical minds. Jefferson was a shy man who avoided conflict. His thinking achieved great depth, but he was less a man of action than Hamilton. His weakness as a manager is summed up in a revealing statement. "We can only be answerable for the orders we give, and not for their execution."[18] He had grown up in sparsely populated frontier areas of Virginia, never having seen a village of more than 20 houses until he was 18 years old. Awed by the common sense and resourcefulness of the settlers he knew, he formed the opinion that an agrarian economy of landowning farmers was the ideal social order.

Reading books as much as 15 hours a day, he gathered arguments to reinforce his convictions. According to Jefferson, America should aspire to spread farming over its immense, unsettled territory. He wrote that God placed "genuine virtue" in farmers, His chosen people. Manufacturing as an occupation "suffocates the germ of virtue," leads to venality, and corrupts the "manners and principles" of those who work at it.[19] He believed that an agrarian economy would prevent the rise of subservience to the wealthy and bring a state of equality, basic justice, and concern for the common good. Jefferson was well-read in Greek philosophy, and it was no coincidence that he echoed the admonitions against commerce found in Plato and Aristotle. Even as he restated the Greeks, he laid the ground for more than two centuries of American business critics to follow.

Jefferson did not prevail. His agrarian ideal was fated to exist in the shadows of industrial growth. His theory of a nation of small farmers was somewhat nebulous and idealistic. As a policy it was no match for the more concrete design that Hamilton sold to Congress with great energy, a design that was surely more in tune with economic forces afoot in the young nation. With the support of business leaders, Hamilton carried out a bold, visionary program to stimulate the growth of manufacturing. His actions prepared the ground for the unexampled industrial growth that roared through the next century. He so angered Jefferson that the two rarely spoke even as they served together in George Washington's cabinet. Each had many followers and the conflict between their positions created not only the basis for subsequent criticism of business, but the basic cleavage that has prevailed in the American two-party system to the present.

1800–1865

The first half of the nineteenth century saw steady industrial growth. This aroused critics who clung to the values and life of the agrarian society that was fading before their eyes. Early in the century banking and manufacturing expanded. Markets were opened by tens of thousands of miles of new turnpikes. Completion of the 350-mile-long Erie Canal in 1825 inspired another 4,400 miles of canals to transport goods over water.[20] Railroads started to run in the 1830s. Immigrants arrived and cities grew. Business boomed.

[18] Letter to Baron F. W. von Steuben, March 10, 1781, quoted in Stanley Elkins and Eric McKitrick, *The Age of Federalism* (New York: Oxford University Press, 1993), p. 206.

[19] Quotes are from *Notes on Virginia*, in Adrienne Koch and William Peden, *The Life and Selected Writings of Thomas Jefferson* (New York: Random House, 1944), p. 280; first published in 1784.

[20] James Oliver Robertson, *America's Business* (New York: Hill and Wang, 1985), p. 81.

As the force of events put capitalism in control, agrarian romantics were pushed to the side, having only the power to object as cherished values were eroded. "Commerce," complained Ralph Waldo Emerson in 1839, "threatens to upset the balance of man and establish a new, universal Monarchy more tyrannical than Babylon or Rome."[21] Later, his friend Henry David Thoreau wrote to belittle a society in which this commerce smothered the poetry and grace of everyday life.

> This world is a place of business. What an infinite bustle! I am awakened almost every night by the panting of the locomotive. It interrupts my dreams. There is no sabbath. It would be glorious to see mankind at leisure for once. It is nothing but work, work, work. I cannot easily buy a blank-book to write thoughts in; they are commonly ruled for dollars and cents . . . I think that there is nothing, not even crime, more opposed to poetry, to philosophy, ay, to life itself, than this incessant business.[22]

utopia
A socially engineered model community designed to correct faults in the world so its members can find happiness.

Among those who rejected capitalism, some tried to create alternative worlds. Beginning in the 1820s there was a frenzy of *utopia* building. Small bands of people who disdained the values prized in industrial society—materialism, competition, individualism, and tireless labor—built model communities intended to act as beacons for a better way. The largest was New Harmony, Indiana, founded in 1825 by Robert Owen (1771–1858), an English industrialist. Owen ran a large cotton mill in Scotland that had become a model for fair treatment of workers. Yet he believed that human values were corrupted by factory work and life in capitalist societies. He aspired to show that a society based on principles of equality, charity, cooperation, and moderation could flourish. At New Harmony, money was abolished and the residents shared the fruits of communal labor.

Owen called his creation a "socialist" system and in the 1820s the term *socialism* first came into widespread use as a reference to Owen's philosophy. He started several other socialist communities and his ventures inspired others to form utopias based on socialist principles. More than 100 such communities appeared between 1820 and 1850.[23] A few were successful. The Oneida Community in New York lasted 31 years from 1848 to 1879. But most floundered, on average in less than two years.[24]

New Harmony emptied after only four years. Like other utopias it required businesslike activities for subsistence, but it attracted more loafers than skilled farmers and artisans who, in any case, could command higher material rewards in the outside world. After their initial zeal wore off, the sojourners tired of spartan living, regimentation, and rules to enforce cooperation. Most communes had programs to infuse socialist values into human natures tainted by capitalist schooling. Rarely did this work. One indication is that pilfering of supplies from common storehouses was common.

---

[21] Quoted from Emerson's *Journals,* vol. V, pp. 284–86, in Parrington, *Main Currents in American Thought,* vol. I, p. 386.

[22] "Life without Principle," *The Atlantic Monthly,* October 1863, pp. 484–85.

[23] W. Fitzhugh Brundage, *A Socialist Utopia in the New South* (Urbana: University of Illinois Press, 1996), p. 6.

[24] Joshua Muravchik, *Heaven on Earth: The Rise and Fall of Socialism* (San Francisco: Encounter Books, 2002), p. 51.

The agrarian and socialist communes failed utterly as alternatives to the bustling capitalism beyond their margins. Although a few new ones appeared as late as the 1890s, by the 1850s the idea had run its course. It failed in practice because it was based on romantic thinking, not on sustaining social forces. A series of withered utopias and a growing consensus on capitalist values adjourned the experiments. Socialism would return, but it awaited a new day and new ideas.

Populists and Progressives

At the end of the Civil War in 1865, America was still a predominantly rural, agrarian society of small, local businesses. But explosive industrial growth rapidly reshaped it, creating severe social problems in the process. Cities grew as farmers left the land and immigrants swelled slum populations. Corrupt political machines ran cities but failed to improve parlous conditions. Companies merged into huge national monopolies. These changes were the raw material of two movements critical of big business.

populist movement
A political reform movement that arose among farmers in the late 1800s. Populists blamed social problems on industry and sought radical reforms such as government ownership of railroads.

The first was the *populist movement*, a farmers' protest movement that began in the 1870s and led to formation of a national political party, the Populist Party, which assailed business interests until its decisive defeat in the presidential election of 1896. The movement arose soon after the Civil War, when farmers experienced falling crop prices. The declines were due mainly to overproduction by mechanized farm machinery and to competition from foreign farmers exploiting new transport technologies. Farmers overlooked these factors and blamed their distress on railroad companies, the largest businesses of the day, which frequently overcharged for crop hauling, and on "plutocrats" such as J. P. Morgan and other Eastern bankers who controlled the loan companies that foreclosed on their farms.

In a typical tirade, Mary Lease, a populist orator who whipped up crowds of farmers at picnics and fairs, explained:

> Wall Street owns the country. It is no longer a government of the people, by the people and for the people, but a government of Wall Street and for Wall Street. The great common people of this country are slaves, and monopoly is the master. The West and South are bound and prostrate before the manufacturing East.[25]

To solve agrarian ills, the populists advocated government ownership of railroads, telegraph and telephone companies, and banks, a policy dagger that revealed their fundamental rejection of capitalism. They demanded direct election of U.S. senators, who at the time were picked by state legislatures corrupted with money from big business. And to ease credit they sought to abandon the gold standard and expand the money supply.

Historian Louis Galambos believes that despite the populist critique, there existed a great reservoir of respect for and confidence in business until the late 1880s.[26] After that, analysis of newspaper and magazine editorials shows mounting hostility

[25] In John D. Hicks, *The Populist Revolt* (Minneapolis: University of Minnesota Press, 1931), p. 160.

[26] Louis Galambos, *The Public Image of Big Business in America, 1880–1940* (Baltimore: Johns Hopkins University Press, 1975), chap. 3. Galambos examined 8,976 items related to big business that were printed in newspapers and journals between 1879 and 1940, using content analysis to reconstruct rough measures of opinion among certain influential groups.

Was President McKinley the Wizard of Oz?

The Wonderful Wizard of Oz is one of the all-time best-selling children's books.[27] It was written by Lyman Frank Baum (1856–1919), an actor, sales-clerk, and small-town newspaper editor who loved creating stories for children. On the surface, the book is a magical adventure in a fairyland where children are as wise as adults. However, the book has a deeper dimension. It is a parable of populism.[28]

The Wonderful Wizard of Oz satirizes the evils of an industrial society run by a moneyed elite of bankers and industrialists. "Oz" is the abbreviation for ounce, a measure of gold. It and the Yellow Brick Road allude to the hated gold standard. The main characters represent groups in society. Dorothy is the common person. The Scarecrow is the farmer. The Tin Woodsman is industrial labor. His rusted condition symbolizes factory closings in the depression years of the 1890s, and his lack of a heart hints that factories dehumanize workers. The Cowardly Lion is William Jennings Bryan, the defeated Populist Party candidate, whom Baum

regarded as lacking sufficient courage. The Wicked Witch of the East is a parody of the capitalist elite. She kept the munchkins, or "little people," in servitude. At the end of the Yellow Brick Road lay the Emerald City, or Washington, D.C., where on arrival the group was met by the Wizard, representing the president of the United States. At the time Baum wrote the book, William McKinley was president, having defeated Bryan in 1896. Populists reviled McKinley because he had the backing of big trusts and he supported the hated gold standard.

At the conclusion, Dorothy melted the Wicked Witch of the East, the Wizard flew off in a balloon, the Scarecrow became the ruler of Oz, and the Tin Woodsman took charge of the East. This ending is the unrealized populist dream.

Baum's first motive was to be a child's story-teller, not to write political satire for adults. He never stated that the book contained populist themes, leading to debate over whether finding such symbolism is fair. Yet Baum lived in South Dakota while populism was emerging and he marched in Populist Party rallies. *The Wonderful Wizard of Oz* was written in 1898, at the height of ardor for reform. Therefore, it seems reasonable to think that Baum's tale was inspired by the politics of the day.

[27] L. Frank Baum (Chicago: Reilly & Britten, 1915), first published in 1900.

[28] The classic interpretation of symbolism is by Henry W. Littlefield, "The Wizard of Oz: Parable on Populism," *American Quarterly,* Spring 1964.

toward large trusts. Soon the populists succeeded in electing many state and local officials, who enacted laws to regulate the railroads and provided the political groundswell behind creation of the Interstate Commerce Commission in 1887 to regulate railroads.

The populist movement was a diverse, unstable coalition of interests, including farmers, labor, prohibitionists, antimonopolists, silverites, and suffragists. These groups were held together for a time by a common, deep-seated hostility toward big companies. Ultimately, the populists failed to forge an effective political coalition and the movement was moribund after 1900 when William Jennings Bryan, the Populist Party's presidential candidate, was decisively defeated for a second time.

However, the populists refined a logic and lexicon for attacking business. They blamed adverse consequences of industrialization on monopoly, trusts, Wall Street, "silk-hatted Easterners," the soulless "loan sharks" and shameless "bloodhounds of money" who foreclosed on farms, and on corrupt politicians who worked as errand boys for the "moneybags" in a system of "plutocracy" (or rule by the wealthy).

Their criticisms were harsh and colorful. "The James Brothers and the Daltons were limited in their methods," thundered Mary Lease to a cheering crowd. "If they had operated on as large a scale as the millionaires of the country they could have built universities like Rockefeller. . . ."[29] In an essay on the virtues of farming as an occupation, Bryan wrote that for farmers "even the dumb animals are more wholesome companions than the bulls and bears of Wall Street."[30] Thomas Jefferson would likely have applauded.

It was, of course, too late for America to be a nation of farmers. This did not diminish the appeal of the populist message to large segments of the population. On the contrary, continued industrial growth has caused this message to resurface time and again up to the present, each time its vocabulary recycled and its content refined to fit current circumstances.

progressive movement
A turn-of-the-twentieth-century political movement that associated moderate social reform with progress. Progressivism was less radical than populism and had wider appeal.

The second critical movement was the *progressive movement*, a broader reform effort lasting from about 1900 until the end of World War I in 1918. Fueled by wide moral indignation about social problems caused by industry, it had strong support from the urban middle class and professionals. Although a short-lived Progressive Party was formed and unsuccessfully ran Theodore Roosevelt for president in 1912, both the Democratic and Republican parties had powerful progressive wings. Unlike populism, progressivism was a mainstream political doctrine. Like populism, it was at root an effort to cure social ills by using government to control perceived abuses of big business.

Because of broad popular support, Progressives were far more effective than populists in their reform efforts, and during their era a cleansing tide washed over business. "Turn the waters of pure public spirit into the corrupt pools of private interests," wrote Ernest Crosby, editor of *Cosmopolitan* magazine, "and wash the offensive accumulations away."[31] Progressives broke up trusts and monopolies, outlawed corporate campaign contributions, restricted child labor, passed a corporate income tax, and regulated food and drug companies and public utilities. With the Seventeenth Amendment in 1913 requiring direct election of senators they completed part of the Populist agenda.

Socialists

socialism
The doctrine of a classless society in which property is collectively owned and income from labor is equally divided among members. It rejects the values of capitalism.

The full story of the Progressive movement's success lies in the counterpoint it provided to the socialist movement of that era. *Socialism* is a classless social system in which property is collectively owned and income from labor is equally and indiscriminately divided among members. When wealth is shared, want and conflict are eliminated. Socialism poses a revolutionary challenge to capitalist society because it requires a change in property relationships that destroys bedrock arrangements.

Although elements of socialist thinking are ageless, the originator of modern socialist doctrine is Francois-Noël Babeuf (1764–1797), a minor French official and writer who wanted to fulfill the promise of equality for all made during the French

---

[29] Quoted in "Furor over Mary Lease," *The New York Times,* August 11, 1896, p. 3.

[30] "Farming as an Occupation," *Cosmopolitan,* January 1904, p. 371.

[31] Ernest Crosby, "The Man with the Hose," *Cosmopolitan,* August 1906, p. 341.

Art Young, a radical cartoonist of the Progressive era, had an impish ability to highlight the excesses of the industrial age. This cartoon, typical of many then drawn by Young and others, first appeared in 1912. Source: Art Young, *The Best of Art Young*, New York, Vanguard Press, 1936, p. 89)

CAPITALISM

Revolution of 1789. He advocated seizing the possessions of the wealthy and giving them to the masses. Following this seizure, Babeuf envisioned a new communal economy. Private property would be abolished. Citizens would be required to work based on their trade or skill. The government would receive their output and distribute to everyone the basic material necessities of life. To eliminate individual desire for wealth and power, schools would teach egalitarian principles. Babeuf pushed for a violent overthrow of the French regime to achieve his vision and for this he was imprisoned, then beheaded in 1797. But his ideas took hold and circulated throughout Europe. One convert was Robert Owen, who was inspired to set up his tiny utopia in Indiana.

For a half century after Babeuf, socialist thought was splintered and muddied in a ferment of competing schools. Then, in 1848, Karl Marx (1818–1883) and his lifetime collaborator, Friedrich Engels (1820–1895), published *The Communist Manifesto* and put socialism on a new foundation.[32] Marx and Engels argued that the basis for socialism was an inevitable process of class struggle underlying and explaining the history of human society. Under capitalism the working class is exploited by the owners of capital, who pay low wages for dehumanizing work and then usurp for themselves the value of what workers toil to create. Marx often used metaphors in which capitalists became vampires and werewolves, sucking the lifeblood from labor.

Like Babeuf and others, Marx and Engels envisioned an equalitarian society that abolished private ownership of capital and instituted wealth-sharing among all members. Workers would no longer be alienated by miserable, meaningless labor. With class distinctions ended, people would live in harmony, their basic needs fulfilled. While Marx and Engels repeated many of the timeless criticisms of capitalism as characterized by barbaric competition, corruption of values by money, and meaningless work, they made socialism more compelling when they discovered a theory of history to explain it. Class warfare was the underlying dynamic that changed society. Workers in all nations had the duty to rise and overthrow the capitalist class. The last sentence of the *Manifesto* reads: "WORKINGMEN OF ALL COUNTRIES UNITE!"[33]

Meanwhile, in the United States of 1850 to 1900, rapid industrial growth was taking place within a coarse, little-regulated capitalist system that in many ways seemed to bear out the socialist's nightmare of exploitation. Child labor was widespread; factories injured and wore down workers; wealth and power were concentrated in great banks, trusts, and railway systems; inequality between rich and poor seemed obscene; and the masses suffered through financial panics and unemployment. Also, industrial growth was taking people away from agrarian occupations and creating a new class of employed Americans. In 1860 about 1.3 million people worked for the trusts, mines, and railroads, but by 1890 there were 4.3 million so occupied.[34] The rise of this new social class formed the soil in which labor unions could grow, and given widespread labor abuses, these unions might be attracted to socialism. As it turned out, this attraction would be limited.

As unions sprang up employers fought them. Most early unions were tied to single companies or locations. A few were radical and avowedly socialist, especially those with many European immigrants who brought Marxist thinking with them. The first big national union was the Knights of Labor, set up in 1869. Its constitution recognized exploitation of labor by owners of capital, but it called for

---

[32] According to Paul Sweezy, Marx chose to use the word *communist* rather than *socialist* because the meaning of the word *socialist* had become muddled. The term *communist*, in use for centuries to denote pooled property, more clearly conveyed his theory. See *Socialism* (New York: McGraw-Hill, 1949), pp. 8–9.

[33] Karl Marx and Friedrich Engels, *Manifesto of the Communist Party*, in Lewis S. Feuer, ed., *Marx & Engels: Basic Writings on Politics & Philosophy* (New York: Anchor Books, 1959), p. 41.

[34] Arthur M. Schlesinger, *Political and Social Growth of the United States: 1852–1933* (New York: MacMillan, 1935), p. 203.

reforms to protect labor rather than for overthrow of the capitalists. However, the union movement soon struck fear in the capitalist heart.

In the summer of 1877 a wave of violent strikes hit the railroads, then rolled on to other industries as it spread across the nation. Fighting and killing between strikers and the hired armies of employers was widespread. President Rutherford B. Hayes called his cabinet into a continuous session. He was so terrified that the country would fall to a workers' revolution that, rather than using federal troops to restore order in major cities, he gathered them in Washington, D.C., to protect the government. The strikes eventually ran their course, and although there was never again such a violent cluster, from this time until the end of the century the number, size, and violence of strikes only increased.

In this climate of unrest, the socialist movement was surprisingly slow to blossom. The largest union, the American Federation of Labor, formed in 1886, disdained Marxism and elected to work with employers for higher wages and better working conditions. As time passed and the union movement grew, many workers still wanted radical change. They eventually found a home when the Industrial Workers of the World (IWW) was formed in 1905. The IWW proposed to represent all workers of both sexes and all races and in every industry in the fight to overthrow the capitalist system. Its platform was clear.

> We are here to confederate the workers of this country into a working-class movement that shall have for its purpose the emancipation of the working-class from the slave bondage of capitalism. . . . The aims and objects of this organization shall be to put the working-class in possession of the economic power, the means of life, in control of the machinery of production and distribution, without regard to the capitalist masters.[35]

Although the IWW was not as large as other unions, its unmitigated rejection of the system scared mainstream America and it was severely repressed. Laws were passed to prevent IWW members from speaking or assembling and it defied them, sometimes violently.

Working alongside the IWW was a young Socialist Party with growing power. It had been formed in 1901 with the avowed purpose of overthrowing capitalism. At the peak of its popularity in 1912 it had 118,000 members and its presidential candidate, Eugene V. Debs, got 6 percent of the popular vote. More than 1,000 socialists had been elected to state and local office.[36] This moment was the high mark of socialism in the United States. From then on, its appeal rapidly declined and it never recovered meaningful power.

There were four immediate reasons. First, because of its electoral successes the Socialist Party chose to make itself less radical to appeal to more voters. This breached socialist unity by alienating firebrand IWW leaders. Second, moderate reforms of the Progressive movement stole much of the socialists' thunder. Arguably, these reforms came only because the threat of growing socialist popularity put pressure on the capitalist elite. Third, socialist unions made a huge tactical

---

[35] Quoted in Howard Zinn, *A People's History of the United States: 1492–Present,* rev. ed. (New York: HarperCollins, 2003), p. 330.

[36] Irving Howe, *Socialism and America* (New York: Harcourt, Brace, Jovanovich, 1985), p. 3.

mistake (though not a doctrinal error) when they labeled World War I (1914–1918) an imperialist war and said that labor would refuse to shed its blood for wealthy capitalists. In 1917 the government put 101 leaders of the IWW on trial for violating sedition laws and all were convicted. Almost half of them got prison sentences of from 10 to 20 years. Others got shorter terms. This decapitated the IWW and crippled the socialist labor movement going forward. Fourth, as time passed the lot of most workers simply improved. Between 1897 and 1914 real wages rose 37 percent and the average 60-hour workweek declined to 50 hours.[37] Again, the irony is that much of this improvement undoubtedly came out of fear of socialism.

The Great Depression and World War II

With the decline of socialism, capitalism had pushed back its most radical critics. After the triumph of progressive reforms, there was a period of high public confidence in big business during the prosperous, expansive 1920s. This rosy era ended abruptly with the stock market crash of 1929, and business again came under sustained attack. During the 1920s, the idea that American capitalism would bring perpetual prosperity had been widely accepted. The catastrophic Depression of the 1930s disproved this and, in addition, brought to light much ineptness, criminal negligence, and outright fraud by prominent executives. There was a popular feeling that the economic collapse would not have occurred if business leaders had been more honest.

As the Depression deepened, anger at business grew and the old rhetoric of populism reemerged. In the Senate, for example, Huey Long, a colorful populist Democrat from Louisiana who claimed to be the advocate of the poor against the rich, rose to condemn a "ruling plutocratic class."[38]

> The 125 million people of America have seated themselves at the barbecue table to consume the products which have been guaranteed to them by their Lord and Creator. There is provided by the Almighty what it takes for them all to eat: yea, more. . . . But the financial masters of America have taken off the barbecue table 90 percent of the food placed thereon by God, through the labors of mankind, even before the feast begins, and there is left on that table to be eaten by 125 million people less than should be there for 10 million of them.
>
> What has become of the remainder of those things placed on the table by the Lord for the use of us all? They are in the hands of the Morgans, the Rockefellers, the Mellons, the Baruchs, the Bakers, the Astors, and the Vanderbilts—600 families at the most either possessing or controlling the entire 90 percent of all that is in America. . . . I hope none will be horror-stricken when they hear me say that we must limit the size of the big man's fortune in order to guarantee a minimum of fortune, life and comfort to the little man.[39]

These remarks echo the ancient Greek view that wealth in a society is limited and the accumulation of one person is a taking from all others—that great material

---

[37] Louis B. Wright et al., *The Democratic Experience: A Short American History* (Chicago: Scott Foresman, 1963), p. 302.

[38] *Congressional Record,* 73d Cong., 2d sess., 1934, p. 6081, speech of April 5.

[39] Radio speech broadcast March 7, 1935, inserted in the *Congressional Record,* March 12, 1935.

100   Chapter 4   *Critics of Business*

FIGURE 4.1

Production of .30 and .50 Caliber Machine Guns by General Motors: 1941–1944

Source: Based on data in James Truslow Adams, *Big Business in a Democracy* (New York: Scribner's Sons, 1945), p. 251.

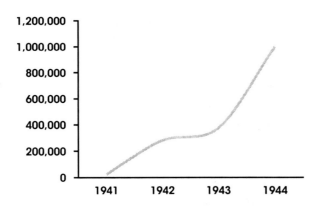

wealth reflects greed. Long used these views to gain moral authority for his radical proposals. In 1934 he introduced a plan to redistribute wealth by collecting annual taxes on corporate assets and large fortunes and then giving every family a $5,000 initial gift followed with a guaranteed annual income of $2,500. In a collapsed economy, this populist-like plan had tremendous appeal, and Long attracted millions of followers. However, he was assassinated before it could be enacted, leaving the milder reforms of President Franklin D. Roosevelt's New Deal to carry the day.

During World War II, support for business rebounded. Industry wrapped itself in patriotism, and its high output proved essential to Allied victory. For example, General Motors converted itself almost entirely to war production. The company made 3,600 war items, including ball bearings, bullets, rifles, torpedoes, trucks, tanks, bombers, and fighter airplanes. In a remarkable effort, it doubled its output of war material between 1942 and 1944. Figure 4.1 shows the production record for one item, machine guns.

Because of similar efforts by many corporations, the war years washed away the populist/socialist/depression era image of the corporation as a bloated plutocracy. It was instead the source of miraculous industrial production. In a radio address President Franklin Roosevelt labeled American business the "arsenal of democracy" that would turn the tide against evil dictatorships that sought to control the world.[40] The wartime performance was spectacular and in a postwar poll, only 10 percent of the population believed that where "big business activity" was concerned "the bad effects outweighed the good."[41] This renascence of respect lasted into the 1960s before the populist seed again sprouted.

The Collapse of Confidence

Strong public support for business collapsed in the mid-1960s. The nation was growing more affluent, but four strong social movements—for civil rights, consumer rights, and the environment and against the Vietnam War—attacked business

[40] Radio address, Washington, D.C., December 29, 1940. U.S. Department of State, *Peace and War: United States Foreign Policy, 1931–1941* (Washington, DC: U.S. Government Printing Office, 1943), pp. 598–607.

[41] Burton R. Fisher and Stephen B. Withey, *Big Business as the People See It* (Ann Arbor: University of Michigan Microfilms, December 1951), p. xiii.

FIGURE 4.2

Percentage of American Public Expressing "A Great Deal of Confidence" in Leaders of Major Companies: 1966–2010

Source: Annual Harris Poll Confidence Index.

for contributing to a range of social ills including racism and sexism, consumer fraud, dangerous and alienating work, political corruption, and war profiteering. These attacks coincided with a negative trend in public opinion toward business. While in 1968, 70 percent of Americans agreed that business tried to strike a fair balance between profits and the public interest, by 1970 the number had declined to 33 percent, and by 1976 to 15 percent. This astonishing drop of 55 points took only eight years.[42]

Scholars who studied the polls theorized that turmoil in American society in the 1960s created a "confidence gap," or a gap between public expectations about how corporations *should* act and public perceptions of how they actually *did* act. Such gaps are perennial. They widened during the populist and Progressive eras and during the Great Depression years. This new gap has now persisted for almost 40 years and continues to define the climate of public opinion.

Figure 4.2 shows the long-term trend for the percentage of Americans expressing "a great deal of confidence" in "people in charge of running major companies." In 1966, 55 percent of the public expressed such confidence, but over the next decade the percentage fell to 16 percent. Since then the confidence trend has bumped along a low road for more than 40 years, recovering to 28 percent in 2000 near the peak of a great bull market, but sinking again to a low of 11 percent in 2009 after banks, insurers, and loan companies led the nation into a financial crisis.[43]

[42] Seymour M. Lipset and William Schneider, "How's Business: What the Public Thinks," *Public Opinion*, July–August 1978.

[43] Figures are based on Harris polls asking this question: "As far as people in charge of running . . . major companies . . . are concerned, would you say you have a great deal of confidence, only some confidence, or hardly any confidence in them?" See Harris Poll, "Virtually No Change in Annual Harris Poll Confidence Index from Last Year," March 9, 2010, table 1, at www.harrisinteractive.com.

The steep fall of public trust after 1966 opened the door for reformers to increase government regulation dramatically. During the late 1960s and early 1970s, liberals in Congress affected a spectacular run of new laws and agencies in defense of nature, consumers, and workers. However, by the mid-1970s business had organized to blunt reform.

Corporations funded conservative think tanks and used advertising to spread the message that excessive regulation imposed unnecessary costs and burdens on companies, reducing American competitiveness in the global economy. Although business was unsuccessful in restoring basic public trust, it did alter key attitudes. With the election of Ronald Reagan in 1980 a tide of Republican conservatism swept through the federal government, frustrating liberal reformers whose ideology of using government to control business was diminished—even discredited.

The New Progressives

old Progressive
Members of a broad political and social reform movement in the early years of the twentieth century.

new Progressive
Members of contemporary left-leaning groups who advocate more radical corporate reform than did old-time Progressives. New Progressives seek to avoid being branded as liberals and try to take advantage of favorable connotations in the word *progressive*.

Out of this liberal defeat rose a new leftist movement with a new ideology. The new movement adopted the label "progressive" after the turn-of-the-twentieth-century movement that sought a broad range of social and political reforms. Both movements have in common the desire to restrain corporate power in the public interest, but major differences exist between them. The *old Progressives* had moderate wings in both the Democratic and Republican parties, so a wide span of politicians, from the left through the middle, often supported reforms. Support for the *new Progressives'* agenda has moved to the left of both the old Progressives and the New Deal liberals.

Unlike the old Progressives and liberals, who wanted to enact reforms through government, the new Progressives have abandoned efforts to build majority coalitions in the mainstream, instead seeking to carry out radical change through direct action. And while the old-timers applied new scientific, legal, and management theories of the day to smooth the harsh edges of capitalism, the obsession of the new Progressives has been attacks on big corporations and the values and laws that support them. Largely blocked from the avenue of reform legislation by conservative, antiregulatory trends that they see as corporate dominance of government, activists confront corporations and industries directly, trying to alter their behavior, even in the absence of laws against what the corporations are doing. Their actions derive from three basic beliefs.

First, corporations have too much power. Free markets do not force them to serve the public interest. Governments cannot control them. They use their wealth to undermine democracy by corrupting politicians. Like entrenched oligarchs, they escape accountability for their self-interested exercise of power.

Second, corporations have inordinate legal rights. In the colonial era the state charters that authorized corporations carefully restricted them to ensure that they acted for the common welfare. For example, they defined the company's business and limited its existence to a fixed number of years. Today, instead of restricting corporations, state charters are very permissive. They allow branching out to new lines of business and grant their creations perpetual life. Over the years legislatures, courts, and trade agreements have regularly added more rights, including the granting of "personhood" to corporate entities, entitling them to many constitutional rights of flesh-and-blood citizens.[44]

Third, corporations are inherently immoral. If often run or staffed by good people, their actions are perverted by an implacable master force, the very logic of the corporation itself. Corporations act to make money. They seek market expansion, sales growth, short-term financial results, and regulatory lenience. They value nature only as a production resource, workers only as costs, and human needs only as demand. Strong corporate cultures inculcate these values, pressuring and ultimately coercing the wills of even the most ethical employees, turning them into witting or unwitting agents of an antisocial institution.

The Progressive network has no single leader, but in the United States a prominent figure and senior diplomat is Ralph Nader. Nader began his activist career more than 30 years ago by writing *Unsafe at Any Speed*, a book that attacked the auto industry for putting styling ahead of safety.[45] The popularity of the book prodded Congress to pass auto safety legislation. Based on this success and his desire to seek change through government, Nader created more than 50 organizations to articulate consumer issues and lobby for protective laws. Over time, his hostility toward corporations deepened and his desire to seek moderate reforms lessened.

Announcing his candidacy for president of the United States in 2000, Nader said he was running to challenge "rampaging corporate titans" and "global corporations . . . astride our planet."[46] He declined to seek nomination as either a Republican or a Democrat because, he explained, both parties "feed at the same corporate trough."[47] Instead, he ran as a candidate for the progressive Green Party. Although he got only 2.7 percent of the popular vote, he prevented Democrat Al Gore from winning the electoral votes of key states, allowing Republican George W. Bush, the more probusiness candidate, to win. This angered many Progressive allies.

GLOBAL CRITICS

Corporate power grows in the world economy. And with it opposition, which is mostly found in an emerging global civic culture shaped by eruptive growth of *nongovernmental organizations* (NGOs), or voluntary, nonprofit organizations that are not part of governments. There are now more than 47,000 NGOs, almost 90 percent of them created since 1970.[48] The variety of NGOs that operate over

nongovernmental organization
A term for voluntary, nonprofit organizations that are not affiliated with governments.

---

[44] For enumeration see Ted Nance, *Gangs of America: The Rise of Corporate Power and the Disabling of Democracy* (San Francisco: Berrett-Koehler, 2003), table 1.1.

[45] Ralph Nader, *Unsafe at Any Speed* (New York: Grossman, 1965).

[46] "Closing the Democracy Gap," *The Progressive Populist,* October 15, 2000, pp. 13 and 14.

[47] Ibid., p. 14.

[48] Michael Edwards, *Civil Society* (Cambridge, England: Polity Press, 2004), p. 23; and World Association of Non-Governmental Organizations, "Worldwide NGO Directory," at www.wango.org, accessed October 30, 2009, showing 47,535 listings.

civil society
A zone of ideas, discourse, and action, dominated by progressive values, that transcends national societies and focuses on global issues.

global justice movement
A coalition of groups united by opposition to economic globalization dominated by corporate capitalism.

neoliberalism
A word denoting both the ideology of using markets to organize society and a set of specific policies to free markets from state intrusion.

liberalism
The philosophy of an open society in which the state does not interfere with rights of individuals.

economic liberalism
The philosophy that social progress comes when individuals freely pursue their self-interests in unregulated markets.

national boundaries encompasses business, cultural, educational, environmental, human rights, social service, health, and religious entities. They animate a global zone of ideas, discourse, and action that has come to be called *civil society*. Although civil society is a vast churning of interests, it is dominated by intellectuals, NGOs, grass roots movements, and institutions with progressive values critical of corporate capitalism. These actors, linked by electronic communications, engage in advocacy and struggle to advance a leftist design that includes global income redistribution, sustainable development, gender equity, and protection of human and labor rights.

In the 1990s a *global justice movement* evolved within civil society. It coalesced around resistance to a global economy directed by markets, corporations, trade agreements, and capitalist-dominated international organizations. It was especially united in rejecting the economic ideology seen as inspiring it all, a doctrine it labeled *neoliberalism*.[49] To understand neoliberalism, it is necessary to know the history of liberalism, an idea that has profoundly shaped Western civilization.

The Story of Liberalism

Liberalism arose in Europe as a social philosophy in the 1500s. It promoted a free and open society in which the power of government to interfere with individual rights such as speech, association, conscience, and occupation was limited. Liberals[50] had great faith in human reason and believed this freedom would lead to social progress. For example, as freedom of speech allowed multiple opinions to be aired, truth would drive out falsehood, allowing progress toward enlightenment. Liberalism proved compelling. It spread over centuries until it came to define the essence of a good society in much of the West.

A natural extension of liberalism was a philosophy of *economic liberalism* that sanctified the pursuit of individual self-interest in markets free from state interferences. According to economic liberals, the market was a natural, self-correcting mechanism. If left alone, free from state interference, forces of supply and demand would maintain a perpetual, automatic, self-correcting balance, continuously elevating material welfare. Adam Smith's vision of *laissez-faire* capitalism defined the essence of economic liberalism.

Economic liberalism seized hold in the West. It was a critical ideology underlying the Industrial Revolution in England. Later, in the United States, it was used to justify the predatory capitalism of the 1800s and early 1900s that so aggravated Mary Lease, Mother Jones, and Huey Long. No matter the market was pitiless to

---

[49] This movement is usually called the "antiglobalism movement" in the press, but its advocates reject that label because it is not opposed to global expansion of economic and political ties, only the current, corporate-dominated expansion suspected of putting profit before human welfare. Some in the movement prefer the name "alter-globalization."

[50] The word *liberal* is used here in its original, classical sense where it refers to freedom from government interference, a *negative freedom*. It should not be confused with the term *liberal* as it is applied in contemporary politics to those who want state power to restrain business, a situation of *positive freedom*, meaning that government acts positively to create a just, free society.

children, miners, farmers, and debtors, it was an inviolate work of nature, a benevolent cosmic design best freed of human meddling.

But classical liberalism perished in the world depression of the 1930s. To end the Depression and make economies perform for the public good, governments began to intervene in markets. A British economist, John Maynard Keynes (1883–1946), argued the then-radical view that, far from being self-correcting, markets could be managed to dampen business cycles and promote full employment. Keynes' ideas, which became known as *Keynesianism*, spread and in the United States and Europe, states dropped the hands-off-the-market philosophy, embracing forms of "mixed economy" to promote stability, full employment, and social welfare. Liberalism changed. Although economic freedoms were important, it was no longer assumed that free markets always produced moral outcomes. They required state supervision. An era of growing market regulation followed.

The Rise of Neoliberalism

Meanwhile, old beliefs about the virtues of laissez-faire hibernated. While Keynes' ideas dominated around the world, in the late 1940s a small, elite group of intellectuals began composing a new free market ideology, readying it for a day when the world would call. They believed that government intrusion in markets menaced human freedom. Left alone, competitive forces and price signals were the most effective way to coordinate individual efforts. And the power of free markets would offset political power. When government regulated markets, it infringed on free choice by individuals and, by intruding, fused economic and political power, removing a counterbalance essential to free society. Such interference was, in the words of the group's founding leader, Austrian philosopher Friedrich Hayek (1899–1992), "the road to serfdom."[51]

Convening just after the end of World War II, the group had before it the terrible specters of fascism in Germany and Stalinism in Russia, both based on state control of the economy, both leading to human misery. What leaped out at them was the importance of the market as a counterbalance to government authority. They would work to promote individual liberty by keeping the state out of markets. In practice, their theories would unchain corporate power.

Another member in the group was Milton Friedman (1912–2006), the leader of free market thinking in the Department of Economics at the University of Chicago. There, he and other like-thinking faculty used statistical models to test free market theories. Like Hayek, Friedman saw markets as bulwarks against tyranny. "Every act of government intervention," he wrote, "limits the area of individual freedom directly."[52] Friedman advocated policies to maximize the market's role, even extending its reach into areas traditionally occupied by government. He wanted to abolish the minimum wage, end Social Security, eliminate tariffs, let for-profit companies compete with the post office, turn America's national parks over to corporations, and end detailed regulation of industries. Friedman, his colleagues,

Keynesianism
An economic philosophy of active state intervention to stabilize the economy and stimulate employment.

[51] Friedrich A. Hayek, *The Road to Serfdom* (Chicago: University of Chicago Press, 1944), see p. 37.
[52] Milton Friedman, *Capitalism and Freedom* (Chicago: University of Chicago Press, 1962), p. 32.

University of Chicago economist Milton Friedman. Source: © Time & Life Pictures/ Getty Images

Chicago School
The name given to a group of economists and to the free market doctrine they taught. It is synonymous with neoliberalism.

and their free market ideas came to be called the *Chicago School*, a shorthand term for a doctrine of privatization, free trade, and deregulation.

In the lore of the global justice movement, the Chicago School, encouraged by funding from corporations, incubated neoliberalism. For decades the doctrine abided within academia as, outside, global prosperity seemed to confirm Keynesian policies. Then, in 1973 it was put into practice in Chile. There, American corporations and the Central Intelligence Agency backed a coup against a democratically elected government with socialist leanings. The economic policies of the new government, which relied on terror to suppress its opponents, were created by graduates of the Chicago School, who opened the country to corporate exploitation by selling state-owned corporations, lowering protective trade barriers, and privatizing social security. Eventually, their efforts led to an economic boom, though it ended abruptly in a 1982 global currency crisis.

Meanwhile, economies in developed countries had become mired in "stagflation," a condition of high unemployment with weak growth. In England, Prime Minister Margaret Thatcher moved in the direction of privatization and deregulation to cure this, as did Ronald Reagan in the United States. The eventual prosperity of these nations led to the further spread of neoliberal ideas. Friedman and his colleagues traversed the globe advising leaders. Graduates of the Chicago School staffed economic ministries, agencies, and international institutions. As economic globalization accelerated in the 1990s neoliberalism was a major force behind it.

Agenda of the Global Justice Movement

Critics in the global justice movement saw neoliberalism as a new doctrine of Western, particularly American, colonialism and imperialism, opening poor nations and indigenous peoples to plunder by corporations advancing on the laissez-faire tide. Exaggerating the movement's anger at what came to pass is hard. One of its leading reporters, Naomi Klein, saw "the rise of disaster capitalism" because neoliberal ideas were frequently imposed after "shocks" such as coups, wars, economic collapse, and natural disasters.[53] In Iraq, for example, the U.S.-dominated coalition in 2003 ordered the government to privatize national companies, allow foreign firms to own Iraqi companies and banks, and eliminate most trade barriers.[54] Another critic calls the process of neoliberal conquest "necrocapitalism," or the creation of death zones that subjugate life to wealth creation, as when nations send their armies to repress indigenous populations on lands being drilled or mined for profit or when poor farmers commit suicide after removal of protective tariffs lowers the price of their crops.[55]

The movement is populated by progressive-leaning actors including labor unions, human rights groups, environmentalists, religious bodies, farmers, socialists, indigenous people's movements, feminists, animal rights activists, Neo-Luddites,[56] and anarchists opposed to any overarching world order. It has little unity. Politely, it is called a movement of movements, more unerringly, "multitudes on the edge of chaos."[57] It first achieved high visibility in 1999 when 50,000 activists gathered to protest World Trade Organization meetings in Seattle and street riots broke out. Two years later at a *Group of Eight* summit in Genoa, Italy, as many as 100,000 came to protest as heads of state from the wealthiest nations met to discuss the global economy. Rioting followed and police killed one activist.

Since then, the movement has created less visible turbulence. Concerns about terrorism made street protests more difficult and protests against trade became awkward after the September 11, 2001, attacks on the World Trade Center, a symbol of free trade. But outside the limelight it has proved durable, growing in numbers and connectivity. With the global economic crisis in 2008 it found vindication. In the words of one adherent, "While eyes were on the absurd charade of the 'threat of Islamist terrorism to western civilization, the real doomsday scenario . . . was gathering pace right next to Ground Zero, in Wall Street."[58]

For now, debate and confrontation often center on the actions of multinational corporations seen as mechanisms of dominance by capital. The struggle against them excites many in the movement. Managers have come to fear clashes between market logic and the moral agenda of civil society. One estimate is that 6,000 of the

Group of Eight
Formerly an annual meeting where eight leaders of large industrial democracies met to discuss economic issues, since replaced by an expanded group of the wealthiest nations called the Group of 20, or G20.

[53] Naomi Klein, *The Shock Doctrine: The Rise of Disaster Capitalism* (New York: Henry Holt, 2007), chap. 2.

[54] David Harvey, *A Brief History of Neoliberalism* (New York: Oxford University Press, 2005), p. 6.

[55] Subhabrata Bobby Banerjee, "Necrocapitalism," *Organization Studies* 29, no. 12 (2008), p. 1542.

[56] The Luddites (1811–1816) were English textile workers who blamed unemployment and low wages on new steam-powered textile machines. The name comes from a mythical figure, Ned Ludd. They wrecked the machines and violently attacked their builders before being suppressed.

[57] Graeme Chesters and Ian Welsh, *Complexity and Social Movements: Multitudes on the Edge of Chaos* (London: Routledge, 2006).

[58] Madeleine Bunting, "Faith. Belief. Trust," *The Guardian,* October 6, 2008, p. 31.

world's NGOs are of the variety that attack corporations.[59] A leading scholar within civil society issues the call to battle.

> [We are in] . . . a struggle between two globalizations grounded in sharply contrasting visions of human possibility—one imperial and the other democratic. It pits an alliance of state and corporate power devoted to a vision of global Empire against an alliance of people power devoted to a vision of Earth Community. Empire holds the edge in institutional power; Earth Community holds the edge in the moral power of the authentic cultural values of a mature consciousness.[60]

Today, the antiglobalism movement remains a cacophony of voices, so ascribing to it a specific goal or platform is difficult. It is broadly against capitalism, corporate power, deregulation, privatization, sweatshops, child labor, trade agreements, consumerism, colonialism, imperialism, racism, sexism, and militarism. Again broadly, it favors *inter alia* popular democracy, horizontalism (the opposite of hierarchical power relationships), subsidiarity (local control of affairs as opposed to control by a centralized power from afar), human rights, sustainability, equality, and, as expressed in one of the movement's catchphrases, "a world in which many worlds fit."

Global Activism

Activists, by definition, take action. Progressive elements have spun unique webs of advocacy to correct perceived problems or abuses. A recent example is the International Campaign to Ban Landmines, composed at its height of 800 groups in 50 countries. Activists from groups such as Human Rights Watch attacked corporations making antipersonnel mines. As a result, Raytheon stopped making the mines, and others, including Motorola, and General Electric, quit selling parts used to make them.[61] Similar advocacy networks have formed to fight sweatshop contracting by clothing makers and environmental abuses by energy and mining companies.

Such efforts are not new. In the early 1800s a remarkably similar advocacy network led the global antislavery campaign.[62] In the 1970s international campaigns forced Nestlé and other infant-formula makers to change the way formula was sold in developing countries. And in the 1980s a fierce human rights coalition pushed foreign corporations out of very profitable markets in apartheid-era South Africa.[63]

---

[59] George Lodge and Craig Wilson, *A Corporate Solution to Global Poverty* (Princeton, NJ: Princeton University Press, 2006), p. 46.

[60] David C. Korten, *The Great Turning: From Empire to Earth Community* (Bloomfield, CT: Kumarian Press, 2006), p. 12.

[61] Christina Del Valle and Monica Larner, "A New Front in the War on Land Mines," *BusinessWeek*, April 28, 1997, p. 43.

[62] Margaret E. Keck and Kathyrn Sikkink, *Activists Beyond Borders* (Ithaca, NY: Cornell University Press, 1998), pp. 8–22.

[63] S. Prakash Sethi and Oliver F. Williams, *Economic Imperatives and Ethical Values in Global Business: The South African Experience and International Codes Today* (South Bend, IN: University of Notre Dame Press, 2001).

Attacks on corporations marshal a range of devices that create pressure. Following is a list, hardly exhaustive, of tactics.

- *Consumer boycotts.* A boycott is a call to pressure a company by not buying its products and services. Perhaps the first global boycott, against white sugar, was called in 1792 by radical groups in England protesting brutal slavery in the British East Indies. It halved sugar sales in England and may have been crucial in ending the slave trade within the British Empire.[61] In recent years, advocacy groups have called hundreds of boycotts. Here are some current examples. Animal Liberation Victoria, an Australian group, is leading a worldwide boycott of Adidas for using the skins of inhumanely killed kangaroos for soccer boots. War on Want, a British group that fights global poverty, has called a boycott of Caterpillar, Volvo, and Daewoo for supplying Israel with the bulldozers used to demolish Palestinian homes. In the effort with perhaps the broadest international base and the most recent success, 115 groups in 20 countries have joined in the Burma Campaign UK boycott of a "Dirty List" of hundreds of companies that do business in Myanmar, thereby supporting a regime accused of flagrant human rights violations.

- *Shareholder attacks.* In European nations and the United States rules permit shareholders of public companies to sponsor resolutions on which all shareholders may vote at annual meetings. Most are on governance issues such as procedures for electing directors, but many are attempts to impose progressive political and social values on corporate action. In this effort, religious organizations take the lead, usually working through the Interfaith Center on Corporate Responsibility in New York, a group that coordinates about 300 religious orders, denominations, and pension funds representing many faiths. Here are examples of some of the 390 resolutions planned through it in 2009. Two orders of nuns, a Catholic hospital, a social responsibility fund, and the United Methodist Church asked Nucor, the nation's second-largest steel company, to stop buying pig iron made with charcoal produced by slaves in Brazil. It got 27 percent of the vote. And seven orders of nuns asked PepsiCo to report to shareholders about the dangers of using genetically engineered corn, rice, and sugar in its products. It got 8.4 percent. Each resolution was opposed by the company. Few such proposals get a majority vote, but they create bad publicity and may damage brand images.

- *Harassment, ridicule, and shaming.* Forms of harassment are limited only by the imagination. Activists bring lawsuits based on clever charges such as racketeering. They disrupt the lives of executives and their families by picketing their homes, protesting at their children's schools, and interrupting services at their churches. They climb corporate buildings to unfurl banners. Some groups hand out mock awards. Corporate Accountability International regularly inducts corporations into its Hall of Shame. Each year on the eve of the World Economic Forum in Davos, a meeting of global corporate and political elites, a progressive jury hands out Public Eye "awards" to corporations nominated by NGOs

[64] "Sick with Excess of Sweetness," *The Economist*, December 23, 2006, p. 93.

around the world for exceptional irresponsibility.[65] Past "winners," including Shell, Walt Disney, Walmart, and Dow Chemical, have declined to send anyone to pick up the statuette that goes with the recognition.

- *Corporate campaigns.* A corporate campaign is a broad, sustained attack, usually by a coalition of groups that mobilizes activists for coordinated warfare and employs a wide range of tactics.[66] The campaign depicts the firm as engaging in antisocial behavior to make a profit while portraying the advocacy groups as moral crusaders for truth and fairness. Multinational corporations have enormous financial resources, strong influence in governments, and trusted brand names. Activists typically have slender financing, little political power, and low name recognition. However, a key source of strength is the public's willingness to see environmental, religious, or human rights groups as selfless and acting for justice. Using this perception, activists seize the ethical high ground and engage the corporation with an assault that might be likened to warfare because the action sometimes stretches or breaks the bonds of civility. A recent example is the campaign of ForestEthics to get Victoria's Secret, a subsidiary of Limited Brands, to stop using pulp from virgin Canadian forests in its catalogs. The company agreed to use recycled paper after enduring two years of a "Victoria's Dirty Secret" campaign that included store picketing by chain-saw-wielding women in lingerie, civil disobedience in shopping malls, and shareholder meetings picketed by hecklers in bear costumes.

The activism of global civil society challenges traditional notions of democracy. Advocacy groups have limited memberships. Unlike representative legislatures, they are not accountable to a broad base of voters even as they claim that their ideas about everything from sustainable forests to healthy diets represent the public interest. They are unwilling to accept corporate behavior guided merely by laws, trade agreements, or the choices of consumers in markets as responsible behavior. Instead, they argue that because corporations have corrupted governments and manipulated consumers, the groups are justified in taking action to impose standards of "responsibility," "justice," "equity," and "rights" as defined by the progressive vision. This vision is not uncontroversial. Once into a campaign, progressive advocates tap the deep cynicism in public opinion to build anger against the corporate target. If the company capitulates and changes its policies, the activists have, in effect, appropriated its power and assets to further their policy agenda.

CONCLUDING OBSERVATIONS

We have narrated a history in which basic criticisms of business are repeated over and over. Each era brings new personalities, new targets, and some new issues, but the fundamental substance endures. The story is one of endless debate between critics and defenders of capitalism. Figure 4.3 shows two timelines that

---

[65] Gustavo Capdevila, "World Economic Forum: Davos Under Fire," Inter Press Service, January 31, 2009, at http://ipsnews.net/news.asp?idnews=45618.

[66] For an extended discussion, see Jarol B. Manheim, *The Death of a Thousand Cuts: Corporate Campaigns and the Attack on Corporations* (Mahwah, NJ: Lawrence Erlbaum, 2001).

FIGURE 4.3   **Timelines of Ideological Conflict in the United States**

	Alexander Hamilton			John D. Rockefeller	J.P. Morgan	Henry Ford		Ronald Reagan	George W. Bush
Capitalists	Federalists	Classical liberalism	Republican party	Laissez-faire		Great Depression		Neoliberalism	

		Robert Owen and New Harmony	Emerson and Thoreau	Mary Lease	Mother Jones	Huey Long	FDR	Ralph Nader	Global Justice Movement
	Thomas Jefferson								
Critics	Antifederalists	Democratic party	Populism	Old Progressives		Radicals		Liberals	New Progressives

| 1790 | 1810 | 1830 | 1850 | 1870 | 1890 | 1910 | 1930 | 1950 | 1970 | 1990 | 2010 |

The two timelines show how a debate between business and its critics moves through American history. Each timeline represents the sweep of people and ideas associated with one side of this enduring debate.

represent this exchange. Imagine a dinner party at which Aristotle, Saint Augustine, Thomas Jefferson, and Ralph Nader sit at one table, while Adam Smith, Benjamin Franklin, Alexander Hamilton, and Ronald Reagan sit at another. Now imagine the harmony among tablemates as contrasted with the gulf between the two groups.

Philosophically, the difference between the two groups is profound. Economic liberals believe that uncontrolled, laissez-faire markets give humans freedom to follow laws of nature leading to the rise of the Good Society. Progressives have a different vision. They believe that people in society should be managed according to a human plan, based on their vision what will create the Good Society. For them, true human liberty is not freedom from government, but the freedom to fulfill human potential in a society unmarked by vices including sexism, racism, homophobia, colonialism, wars, obesity, smoking, and corporate manipulation.

In contrast, the conservative capitalist vision is one of material progress. It sees industrial capitalism as a historical force for continuous, turbulent social change; it is, as the economist Joseph Shumpeter wrote years ago, "a perennial gale of creative destruction" that strains institutions and challenges existing authority.[67] The defense of capitalism is that, for the most part, the changes it brings represent progress, a condition of improvement for humanity. All the while that critics have been objecting, it has steadily improved living standards for billions of people. As against promoting greed, it has promoted positive cultural values such as imagination, innovation, cooperation, hard work, and the interpersonal trust necessary for numberless daily business transactions.

In the end, a broad spectrum of criticism is an important check on power. Legitimate criticism exists and demands attention. If criticism is properly channeled, it can preserve the best of the business institution and bring wide benefit.

[67] *Capitalism, Socialism and Democracy* (New York: Harper & Row, 1976), p. 143; originally published in 1942.

A Campaign against KFC Corporation

Peyton Hull, a 12-year-old middle school student in Pittsburgh, loves animals and hopes to be a veterinarian. One day while volunteering at a shelter she learned that People for the Ethical Treatment of Animals (PETA) was boycotting KFC. Later, at her home computer, she watched actress Pamela Anderson narrate a "Kentucky Fried Cruelty" video showing mangled, abused chickens at facilities supplying KFC.

Peyton organized a dozen friends. Helped by her mother, she stayed up all night with markers and poster paper making signs, and the next day, Saturday, she and her friends stood vigil at a KFC restaurant with their signs. People inside waved their chicken. Some teenagers in the parking lot yelled, "KFC is good. Get a life," and threw chicken at them. However, one older woman approached the girls, talked to them, then decided not to go in. Peyton was pleased and told her mother: "Mom, we saved one person from going to KFC."[1]

The incident is just one skirmish in a larger battle between PETA and KFC. War was declared on January 6, 2003. In a press release, People for the Ethical Treatment of Animals announced the start of a campaign against KFC Corporation, the world's largest chicken restaurant chain. PETA held KFC responsible for "cruel treatment" of poultry raised and slaughtered for its restaurants.[2] It demanded that the company force more humane practices on its suppliers. KFC responded with a statement dismissing such "allegations," saying the birds in its meals were treated humanely.

KFC does not raise any chickens. In the United States it buys them from independent companies in the poultry processing industry, a $40 billion a year business that sells to supermarkets, restaurants, and institutions. Its pieces of fried chicken emerge from a supply chain of hatcheries, feed mills, "grow-out" farms, processing plants, and cold storage buildings. This industry is very competitive. With average net profit after tax a slim 0.8 percent, operations are highly automated and focused on efficiencies that reduce cost.[3]

PETA is angry about how chickens are handled in this supply chain, but the maze of facilities, owned by more than 500 corporations, is out of public view, fragmented, and largely anonymous. In contrast, KFC is vulnerable to PETA's basic strategy of tarnishing a brand by associating it with animal cruelty. By threatening the value of KFC's brand, PETA hopes to make the company use its market power as the world's largest buyer of chickens to force reform on growers and slaughter plants. If this occurs, PETA will have harnessed a reluctant giant to further its agenda.

Going into the chicken war, PETA had a record of success. Its initial effort was a campaign against McDonald's in 1999. After less than a year of exposure to a boycott, restaurant demonstrations, and the group's mccruelty.com Web site the company succumbed, imposing stricter animal welfare standards on its suppliers as a condition for ending the assault. It forced changes on reluctant growers, including roomier cages for hens and surprise slaughterhouse inspections. After McDonald's capitulated, its smaller rivals followed. Burger King adopted animal welfare guidelines after a five-month campaign. Then Wendy's buckled. Safeway lasted only three months. Albertsons and Kroger were subdued by campaigns of only one week each.

INITIAL SKIRMISHES

KFC learned of PETA's intentions in 2001, when Cheryl Bachelder, its president, received a letter from Bruce Friedrich, director of the group's restaurant campaigns. The letter asked why KFC, knowing of PETA's actions against its competitors, was doing "nothing at all" to improve the lives of chickens raised for its restaurants. Friedrich asked what KFC intended to do, offered to put the company in touch with animal welfare experts, and added, "We are looking ahead to our next target."[4]

---

[1] Quotes in this paragraph are from Dev Meyers, "Seventh-Grader Organizes Animal-Rights Protest," *Pittsburgh Post-Gazette*, February 24, 2008, p. W1.

[2] "Company Stonewalls on Animal Welfare Reforms," press release, People for the Ethical Treatment of Animals, January 6, 2003, at www.peta.org.

[3] First Research, "Industry Profile: Poultry Processing, Quarterly Update," October 12, 2009, pp. 2 and 9.

[4] The letter is at www.kfccruelty.com/letter-042501.asp.

Over the next several weeks Friedrich had a series of phone calls and meetings with Bachelder and David Novak, CEO of KFC's parent corporation Yum! Brands. Yum! Brands was created in 1997 when PepsiCo spun off its KFC, Pizza Hut, and Taco Bell chains as a separate corporation. Subsequently, the new firm bought the Long John Silver's and A&W chains. Today, Yum! is the world's largest quick-service restaurant corporation with 36,500 restaurants worldwide. The KFC brand traces its origins to the Kentucky Fried Chicken franchise started by the avuncular Colonel Harlan Sanders in 1952. It has 15,580 restaurants in 109 countries and serves about 12 million customers a day.

The dialogue revealed a wide gulf between the company and its interlocutor. KFC told Friedrich that it included humane treatment guidelines in its poultry supplier contracts. He accused the company of using only inadequate industry standards permitting ghastly treatment of chickens and considering their welfare only at the point where deaths from abuse lowered profits. He stated that the suffering of chickens was an ethical issue going beyond financial considerations.[5] KFC said it would review its guidelines and promised to keep PETA informed.

In the months that followed, KFC took several actions. It convened an Animal Welfare Advisory Council composed of outside academic and industry experts. It began unannounced audits of growers and slaughterhouses. And it worked with industry associations to develop new poultry welfare guidelines. However, its efforts were unsatisfactory to PETA because they did not lead to specific, more radical changes including the following.

- *Gas killing.* KFC chickens are stunned by electrical shock before immersion in scalding water (to loosen feathers) and then exposed to mechanical blades that slit their throats. PETA believes that gas killing is preferable because it ensures that chickens are insensate before these painful procedures, whereas electrical stunning is less reliable.
- *Cameras in slaughterhouses.* Cameras would supplement audits and make oversight more reliable.

- *Mechanized chicken-catching.* Hand-catching crews gather KFC chickens from grower buildings. PETA believes that the crews treat the birds roughly and that mechanical catching systems are less likely to result in bruises and broken bones.
- *New genetic strains of chickens.* The chickens eaten in KFC restaurants, known as "broilers," are bred to gain weight rapidly over their brief lives. However, the "broiler breeders" used to produce the flocks of chickens slaughtered for restaurant meals live longer. They exhibit the rapid weight gain characteristic of all broiler strains, but their skeletons and joints do not grow commensurate with their overall weight and they are prone to painful joint conditions as they age. PETA requested introduction of leaner genetic strains that did not exhibit skeletal deficiencies.
- *Elimination of forced growth.* Broiler strains bred for rapid weight gain under forced growth regimens suffer from metabolic pathologies and excess mortality. Slowing growth means longer upkeep of chickens before slaughter, but it reduces premature deaths.
- *More room for birds to move around.* PETA requests that KFC give its chickens at least two to three times more space per bird and give them sheltered areas and perches in the warehouselike buildings where they are raised.
- *Allowance for instinctive behavior of chickens.* PETA believes that birds raised in captivity suffer from chronic stress and boredom induced by suppression of natural behaviors. Among other measures, it suggests that they get whole green cabbages to peck and eat.[6]

Debate between the antagonists was dysfunctional. PETA addressed the corporation in the tone of a parent scolding an errant child. It was "extremely concerned" that the firm "has no interest in making real progress to stop animal cruelty," adding that "we have pressed you to take action on this issue, yet you have done nothing."[7] KFC, on the other hand, wrote to PETA "[i]n the spirit of open communications," but kept it at arm's length, giving only brief and general information about

---

[5] Letter of May 14, 2001, from Bruce G. Friedrich to Jonathan D. Blum, senior vice president, Tricon Global Restaurants, at www.kfccruelty.com/letter-052401.asp. Yum! Brands was formerly named Tricon Global Restaurants.

[6] Letter of August 6, 2002, from Bruce G. Friedrich to Jonathan D. Blum, at www.kfccruelty.com/letter-080602.asp.
[7] Ibid.

conducting audits, holding meetings, and working on animal welfare standards with industry groups.[8] PETA thought that KFC was dragging its feet.

A LOOK AT PETA

PETA is dominated by its founder, Ingrid Newkirk, who became an animal rights activist after a formative experience. Living in Maryland in 1972, she was training to be a stockbroker. A neighbor moved, abandoning cats that soon bred litters of kittens nearby. She gathered them up and took them to a nearby animal shelter to be cared for. Yet a short time later she learned they had been killed. The episode changed her. With no desire to become a stockbroker remaining, she talked her way into a job at the shelter. Observing brutal treatment of animals, she began to arrive early in the morning to kill them in a humane way before others came. "I must have killed a thousand of them," she says, "sometimes dozens every day."[9]

From the shelter Newkirk moved on to work as a deputy sheriff on animal cruelty investigations, then headed a commission to control animal disease. She was inspired to form PETA after reading a book, *Animal Liberation*, by philosopher Peter Singer.[10]

In the book, Singer argues that animals have moral rights. Moral rights are strong entitlements to dutiful treatment by others—in this case human beings. He asserts that the traditional, absolute dominion of humans over animals is an unfair exploitation. Because animals are living, sentient beings capable of suffering, their interests are entitled to equal consideration with human interests. In his words: "No matter what the nature of the being, the principle of equality requires that its suffering be counted equally with the like suffering . . . of any other being."[11] Thus, he argues, animals have an unalienable right to have their needs accommodated by humans. Denial of this right is speciesism, or the prejudicial favoring of one species over another. Speciesism, according to Singer, is an evil akin to racism and sexism because it restricts moral rights to one species just as racism and sexism have restricted them to one race or sex. The PETA Mission Statement, Exhibit 1, reflects the inspiration Newkirk found in this philosophy.

Newkirk has a combative attitude about animal rights. "The animals are defenseless," she says. "They can't talk back, and they can't fight back. But we can. And no matter what it takes, we always will."[12] After reading about a Palestinian bomb put on a donkey and detonated by remote control she wrote to Yasir Arafat requesting that innocent animals be left out of the Arab–Israeli conflict. Her will stipulates that when she dies the meat on her body is to be cooked for a human barbeque, her skin used to make leather products such as purses, and her feet made into umbrella stands.[13]

PETA is creative. Since most people give no thought to animal rights, its actions are designed to attract attention, even at the cost of offending some. Perhaps the mildest attention-getting tactic is the use of theater. For example, PETA demonstrators have dragged themselves down streets with their feet in leg traps to publicize the evils of fur trapping. Another tactic is that of the outrageous act. To protest pictures of women wearing fur in *Vogue*, activists went to the chic Manhattan restaurant where its editor was having lunch and threw a dead raccoon on her plate. Young ladies at county fairs are crowned as pork queens only to have pies thrown in their faces by PETA activists. The group has asked Wisconsin, the "Dairy State," to change its state beverage from cows' milk to soy milk.

PETA freely uses sexuality to get attention. When the American Meat Institute puts on its Annual Hot Dog Lunches for government officials in Washington, D.C., former *Playboy* Playmates wearing bikinis made of lettuce hand out "veggie dogs" outside. It recruits celebrities to present its message. Fame and glamour attract. Their presence endows a view that might otherwise be disregarded with the celebrity's aura of success and legitimacy. PETA also uses the Internet to get its message out. It has multiple Web sites for issues such as zoos, circuses, and animal testing. The network of sites is easy to navigate, informative in depth, and often entertaining. There are facts, games, pictures,

---

[8] Letter of July 17, 2002, from Jonathan Blum to Bruce G. Friedrich, at www.kfccruelty.com/petakfc.asp.

[9] Quoted in Michael Specter, "The Extremist," *The New Yorker,* April 14, 2003, p. 56.

[10] Peter Singer, *Animal Liberation* (New York: Avon Books, 1975).

[11] Ibid., p. 8.

[12] Quoted in Specter, "The Extremist," p. 54.

[13] Ibid., pp. 57 and 58.

EXHIBIT 1

PETA's Mission Statement

Source: Courtesy of People for the Ethical Treatment of Animals (PETA).

People for the Ethical Treatment of Animals (PETA), with more than 1.2 million members and supporters, is the largest animal rights organization in the world.

PETA focuses its attention on the four areas in which the largest numbers of animals suffer the most intensely for the longest periods of time: on factory farms, in laboratories, in the clothing trade, and in the entertainment industry. We also work on a variety of other issues, including the cruel killing of beavers, birds and other "pests," and the abuse of backyard dogs.

PETA works through public education, cruelty investigations, research, animal rescue, legislation, special events, celebrity involvement, and protest campaigns.

video clips, humor, and celebrities. PETA makes a special effort to influence children. One comic brochure, "Your Mommy Kills Animals" shows a crazed woman wielding a bloody knife over a rabbit. "Ask your mommy," it suggests, "how many animals she killed to make her fur coat."[14]

All these tactics, and more, have been employed in the fight against KFC.

THE CHICKENS

At the center of the conflict are the chickens. Chickens are a species of the order Galliformes, which includes turkeys, pheasants, grouse, and partridges. Galliformes are heavy-bodied, short-duration fliers that feed on insects and seeds, nest on the ground, and hatch precocial (self-caring) young. They are social birds that communicate with each other and establish complex hierarchies in flocks.

The earliest wild chickens, members of the species *Gallus gallus*, inhabited jungles of Southeast Asia. About 4,000 years ago they were domesticated. From Asia the domesticated chicken, *Gallus domesticus*, spread across the globe. In ancient Greece they were valued for the sport of cockfighting, and in imperial Rome prophets read the future in their entrails. Chickens had such a hold on the superstitious Romans that generals kept special flocks in the belief that their behavior could foretell victory or defeat in battle. In the hours before combat, hardened legionnaires crowded around these flocks seeking portents. As the legions marched, they spread *Gallus domesticus* across the empire. Centuries later, the earliest European settlers brought chickens to North America.

In the United States, large-scale chicken production developed slowly. As late as the 1920s chicken

farms had flocks of only about 500 free-ranging birds. Today the industry is highly specialized, with some farms in egg production and others raising broilers (or chickens slaughtered for meat; literally, chickens for broiling—or baking or frying). Flocks are now raised in long, windowless, buildings with automated equipment to maintain as many as 100,000 birds. Consumption of chicken has risen. In 1955 only a little more than 1 billion broilers were raised, or 6.5 chickens for each American; by 2009 there were 9 billion raised, or 30 per American.[15]

Chickens, like other animal species, adapted for survival in an ecological niche. In doing so, certain behaviors became instinctive. They live in flocks of approximately 10 and establish dominance hierarchies called pecking orders. The dominant bird in a flock can peck any other bird, and that bird will yield. Status in the pecking order is conveyed by sounds such as crowing or cackling, aggressive or passive postures, spacing, use of more or less desirable nesting sites, and running at or away from rivals. In mixed-sex flocks there are two pecking orders, one for cocks and one for hens, but the hen hierarchy is subordinate. All hens yield to even the lowest cock. This is a genetically predisposed trait essential for species survival because a cock will not mate with a dominating hen. Pecking orders have survival value. Once dominance is established, fighting ceases and energy is used in socially productive ways.

In nature, chickens are omnivorous, eating plants, insects, and small animals such as lizards. Hens are secretive and build hidden nests, preferably on the ground. During the day chickens spread out to

---

[14] At www.furissdead.com.

[15] Bureau of the Census, *Statistical Abstract of the United States 1956*, 77th ed., tables 1 and 857; and Bureau of the Census, *Statistical Abstract of the United States 2010*, 129th ed., tables 2 and 846.

forage, but at dusk they reduce the spaces between them. At night they often roost in trees. According to PETA, chickens are "inquisitive and interesting animals" and "as intelligent as mammals like cats, dogs, and even primates."[16] In nature, they are individuals with "distinct personalities" that "form friendships and social hierarchies, recognize one another, love their young, and enjoy a full life, dust-bathing, making nests, roosting in trees, and more."[17]

Life in high-density growing environments frustrates these natural behaviors. Cages or crowding prevent division into flocks with established pecking orders. Without a complete pecking order, individuals may not yield to threat displays, and physical attacks occur as birds compete over space, food, and water.[18] Weaker animals have no place to hide and may be assaulted repeatedly until they die. In addition, crowded chickens are unable to engage in a range of ordinary foraging, grooming, nesting, brooding, and roosting behaviors. Critics claim that such deprivation violates the right of an animal to satisfy its needs through natural behaviors.

THE CAMPAIGN

At the start of the campaign, PETA activists descended on KFC outlets worldwide, conducting hundreds of demonstrations in the first months. Members handed out "Buckets of Blood" containing "Psycho Col. Sanders" figures and toy chickens with slit throats. When Yum! Brands CEO David Novak appeared at the opening of a restaurant in Germany, two activists doused him with fake blood and feathers. According to campaign leader Friedrich: "There is so much blood on this chicken-killer's hands, a little more on his business suit won't hurt."[19]

KFC issued a statement calling the attacks "corporate terrorism" that "crossed the line from simply expressing their views to corporate attacks and personal

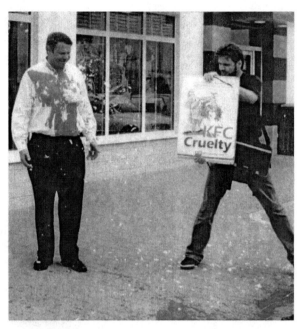

Yum! Brands CEO David Novak after being splattered with fake blood at a PETA demonstration in Hanover, Germany, on June 23, 2003. Source: © AP Photo.

violence."[20] In Paris, Ingrid Newkirk and celebrity musician Chrissie Hynde led activists who stormed into a busy KFC restaurant at the noon hour, smearing the front window with red paint symbolic of chicken blood and lecturing diners until guards threw them out. Outside, the protest blocked traffic on a boulevard for two hours. Back in the United States, PETA put up roadside billboards depicting Col. Sanders hacking a chicken with a bloody knife under the words "Kentucky Fried Cruelty. We do chickens wrong."[21]

Although the main effort was directed toward publicly associating the KFC brand with cruelty to chickens, another focus was on pressuring KFC and Yum! Brands executives at a personal level. Several months into the campaign KFC President Cheryl Bachelder failed to keep what Ingrid Newkirk thought was a commitment to call her. So Newkirk phoned Bachelder at home on a Saturday evening.

[16] "Chickens," at www.peta.org.

[17] "PETA Reveals Shocking Cruelty to Animals at KFC Factory Chicken Farm," press release, October 2, 2003, at www.peta.org.

[18] T. R. O'Keefe et al., "Social Organization in Caged Layers: The Peck Order Revisited," *Poultry Science,* July 1988, p. 1013.

[19] Quoted in Jay Nordlinger, "PETA vs. KFC," *National Review,* December 22, 2003, p. 28.

[20] Cited in "Animal Rights Activists Spray KFC Chief with Fake Blood and Chicken Feathers," The Associated Press State & Local Wire, June 23, 2003.

[21] "Finger-Lickin' Foul," *Houston Press,* December 18, 2003, p. 2.

When Bachelder objected to being called at home, Newkirk responded with a letter that read, in part:

> Of course you would rather not be disturbed in the privacy of your own home, but the animals you torture and slaughter pay for that home with their misery and their very lives yet have nothing remotely like a life or even a nest of any kind. . . . It is merely an accident of birth that you are not one of them.[22]

Newkirk wrote to both Bachelder and CEO Novak at their homes in Louisville, Kentucky, posting the letters with their home addresses on PETA's kentuckyfriedcruelty.com Web site. It enlisted former Beatle Paul McCartney to write to Novak. His letter, which requested an end to "the egregious forms of abuse endured by chickens," ran as a full-page ad in the Louisville *Courier-Journal*. A KFC spokesperson responded that "PETA should follow one of Sir Paul's songs and just 'Let It Be.'"[23] Other celebrities were recruited. The Rev. Al Sharpton asked the black community to boycott KFC. His Holiness the Dalai Lama asked KFC to stop its plans for a restaurant in Tibet.

Taking advantage of Securities and Exchange Commission rules, PETA gained entry to the Yum! Brands 2003 annual shareholders' meeting in Louisville. After activists spoke, CEO Novak called for an end to the campaign saying, "We don't want to be abused, just like you don't want the chickens to be abused." In 2004 PETA qualified a shareholder resolution asking for a company report on actions to reduce cruelty toward chickens. Only 7.6 percent of shareholders voted for it. PETA would go on to introduce similar resolutions each year, getting only single-digit support each time.

A MUTED CORPORATE DEFENSE

Throughout the PETA campaign, KFC and Yum! Brands have maintained a low media profile while working to elevate animal welfare standards. When contacted by reporters a typical response is: "We don't comment on PETA's activities and publicity stunts, which speak for themselves."[24] This reticence is characteristic of the animal agriculture, food, and restaurant industries generally when animal welfare becomes an issue. In mass growing and slaughter, some pain is inevitable. Altering production to address chicken discomfort, injury, and behavior deprivation raises costs.

Most consumers are ignorant of factory farming methods and fail to entertain the link between a KFC meal and the life experience of the creature in it. Despite PETA's efforts, there is no groundswell of demand for more humane treatment of chickens. Reacting to a protest going on outside a restaurant in Israel, a KFC customer said: "There's nothing to do. This is life and it is all part of the food chain. I have to eat."[25]

This vacuum of interest and concern sustains industry calculations balancing poultry welfare against costs. For example, industry guidelines that KFC helped develop and now follows stipulate that corrective action be taken if the number of "DOA" [dead-on-arrival] chickens at a plant exceeds 0.5 percent, if the number of broken or dislocated wings from handling to place chickens on the stun line exceeds 5 percent, and if less than 98 percent of chickens are effectively stunned before having their throats cut by automatic knife.[26] These standards may be defined as humane, but for every 500 chickens they are met if 3 arrive dead, 25 get their wings broken by handlers, and 10 are conscious when plunged into a tank of scalding water to loosen their feathers before further "processing." Magnified to the scale of KFC operations, assuming each of its claimed 720 million annual diners consumes the equivalent of only one-tenth of a chicken, the standard could allow 360,000 dead-on-arrival chickens, 3.6 million broken wings, and 1.4 million live throat cuttings.

Such compromises in chicken welfare to avoid higher costs are tacitly accepted by KFC diners, but difficult to defend in a media debate. PETA's greatest source of power is the desire of average people to see themselves as humane and decent.[27] The impossibility of defending a standard that lets chickens be boiled

[22] Letter of March 24, 2003, from Ingrid E. Newkirk to Cheryl Bachelder, at www.kentuckyfriedcruelty.com/pdfs/letter-032.

[23] Mark Naegele, "McCartney Accuses KFC of Fowl Play," *Columbus Dispatch*, July 25, 2003, p. 2C.

[24] Rick Maynard, manager of public relations at KFC, quoted in Keith Edwards, "These Protesters Aren't Chicken," *Portland Press Herald*, December 17, 2008, p. B1.

[25] Yitchak Mokitada, quoted in Jenny Merkin and Yael Wolynetz, "KFC Diners Remain Unflappable in Face of Chicken Cruelty Protest," *The Jerusalem Post*, July 4, 2006, p. 5.

[26] National Chicken Council, *National Chicken Council Animal Welfare Guidelines and Audit Checklist*, (Washington, DC: National Chicken Council, January 28, 2010), pp. 7–8.

[27] Eric Dezenhall, *Nail 'Em* (Amherst, NY: Prometheus Books, 2003), p. 80.

EXHIBIT 2

Yum! Brands Animal Welfare Guiding Principles

Source: www.yum. com (2004).

Food Safety: Above all else, we are committed to providing our customers with safe, delicious meals and ensuring that our restaurants are maintained and operated under the highest food safety standards. This commitment is at the heart of our entire operations and supply chain management, and is evident in every aspect of our business—from raw material procurement to our restaurant food preparation and delivery.

Animal Treatment: Yum! Brands believes treating animals humanely and with care is a key part of our quality assurance efforts. This means animals should be free from mistreatment at all possible times from how they are raised and cared for to how they are transported and processed. Our goal is to only deal with suppliers who provide an environment that is free from cruelty, abuse and neglect.

Partnership: Yum! Brands partners with experts on our Animal Welfare Advisory Council and our suppliers to implement humane procedures/guidelines and to audit our suppliers to determine whether the adopted guidelines are being met.

Ongoing Training and Education: Yum! Brands recognizes that maintaining high standards of animal welfare is an ongoing process. Training and education has and will continue to play a key role in our efforts. Yum! Brands will continue to work with experts to ensure our quality assurance employees and suppliers have the training and knowledge necessary to further the humane treatment of animals.

Performance Quantification & Follow-up: Yum! Brands' animal welfare guidelines are specific and quantifiable. Yum! Brands measures performance against these guidelines through audits of our suppliers on a consistent basis.

Communication: Yum! Brands will communicate our best practices to counterparts within the industry and work with industry associations such as the National Council of Chain Restaurants and the Food Marketing Institute to implement continuous improvement of industry standards and operations.

alive makes cautious nonconfrontation a better policy than frontal assault on PETA.

Therefore, in response to attacks, the company sidesteps discussing welfare to cost trade-offs and regularly makes four other points. First, it is justified in selling chickens by the morality of the market in which meeting customer demand is a positive duty. Hence, it says, "We support our customers' preference to eat meat—a preference that represents the viewpoint of the majority of Americans."[28] Second, it is the target of false claims by PETA, a "radical organization" that deceptively hides its real goal, the advent of a vegetarian world. Third, it complies with

and usually goes beyond all laws in countries where it has restaurants. And fourth, it is only a purchaser and does not own chicken production facilities where abuses may occur; nevertheless, it accepts that its size as a chicken buyer gives it responsibility and the power to lead in humane treatment of chickens and it is taking a range of actions.

Since 2000 KFC has followed the Yum! Brands set of principles for animal welfare shown in Exhibit 2 and since 2004 it has carried out a more comprehensive set of KFC Poultry Welfare Guidelines covering breeding, growing houses, catching, transport, holding, stunning, and slaughter. KFC calls these guidelines "industry leading" because they exceed standards set by industry groups such as the National Chicken Council, but PETA rejects them because they do not require the changes it demands.

Yum! Brands set up an Animal Welfare Advisory Council of outside experts. When it was set up, PETA recommended people acceptable to it as

[28] KFC, "Animal Welfare Program: Facts," 2009, at www.kfc.com/facts/. A 2007 survey found that 91 percent of respondents had eaten chicken in the past two weeks, averaging 4.5 times combined. Paul Prekopa, "2007 Consumer Chicken Survey," WATT Poultry USA, at www.wattpoultry.com/market_survey2007.aspx.

members and the company appointed four of them. In 2005 three of these panel members submitted a set of recommendations for the welfare of chickens, calling for actions that would have satisfied all of PETA's demands.[29] KFC refused these recommendations and two of the panel members resigned. Currently the advisory group has six members, four academics and two managers from major suppliers, and meets twice a year to "align practices with the latest research and thinking in the field of animal welfare."[30]

KFC ABIDES, PETA IS UNRELENTING

As the campaign moved into its seventh year, KFC stood firm. Although surely it has lost some customers and its executives have been harassed, it has not, on the whole, suffered much from PETA's boycott. Between 2003 and 2010 KFC added more than 4,600 new outlets, an increase of 37 percent, and sales per outlet grew 7 percent despite a severe recession.[31] The performance of its parent, Yum! Brands, has also been strong. Anyone who bought its stock at the beginning of the boycott saw its share price outperform the Dow, the Standard & Poor's 500, and McDonald's since then.

PETA, now joined by more than a dozen other groups, including the Humane Society of the United States, continued its assertive campaign. Demonstrations, of which there have been more than 10,000, remained a staple. A favorite stunt is planting young women in yellow bikinis at KFC outlets where, especially in cold weather, they attract attention. During the winter of 2008–2009 PETA's bikini maidens held signs in below-freezing weather at KFCs in Michigan, Wisconsin, New York, and Maine. Newspapers described scenes where the women trembled uncontrollably as distracted drivers ran their cars over curbs. "It's a little bit chilly," said a protester in 20 degree Kalamazoo weather, "but it's really nothing compared to what the animals go through."[32]

In Louisville PETA set up its KFCruelty campaign headquarters across the street from KFC's flagship restaurant. It continues to visit the neighbors of KFC executives, handing out "bloody" chicken figures, asking them to prevail on their friends to end the cruelty. When Yum! Brands unknowingly tried to buy a building owned by PETA in Norfolk, Virginia, the group offered to give it the property for nothing in return for meeting the campaign's demands.

When KFC gave $3,000 grants of asphalt for cities to fix potholes, PETA offered to double them if it could put chalk marks on the patches reading "KFC Tortures Animals."[33] The offers were rejected. When KFC sponsored an effort at the Talladega Superspeedway to get in the *Guinness Book of World Records* for the most people simultaneously doing the chicken dance, Ingrid Newkirk wrote to Guinness officials, pointing out that records for killing animals are against its rules and asking them to "go a step further" and reject records from companies that subject animals to "needless suffering."[34] The attempt went on, but no record was set.

A PHILOSOPHICAL IMPASSE

Although the campaign against KFC could end if the company adopted specific practices, the plain issue between PETA and the corporation would remain. What is the proper relationship between humans and food animal species? The sides are polarized.

Richard Martin, editor of the industry magazine *Nation's Restaurant News*, says PETA errs in its "rejection of the animal kingdom's remorseless food chain paradigm" and in its "repudiation of the world-wide

[29] "Animal Welfare Recommendations and Proposed Plan of Action for Implementation at KFC Suppliers," memo from Dr. Iam Duncan, Dr. Temple Grandin, and Dr. Mohan Raj to Harvey Brownlee, chief operating officer, KFC, March 11, 2005, at www.kentuckyfriedcruelty.com/pdfs/ March11document.pdf.

[30] KFC, "Animal Welfare Program: Latest News," 2009, at www.kfc.com/about/animalwelfare_news.asp.

[31] Sources of figures are Yum! Brands, Inc., annual reports and Form 10-Ks, various years.

[32] Quoted in "Protester Doesn't Chicken Out," *Kalamazoo Gazette,* January 27, 2009. See also Erin Richards, "PETA Protesters Give Milwaukee KFC the Cold Shoulder," *The Milwaukee Journal Sentinel,* January 24, 2009.

[33] See John Horton, "PETA Asks Cities to Reject KFC Pothole Fix," *Plain Dealer,* April 4, 2009, p. B2; and Cliff Hightower, "PETA Doubles Ante on Pothole Patches," *Chattanooga Times Free Press,* May 1, 2009, p. A9.

[34] Quoted in Dustin Long, "NASCAR, PETA Officials Playing a Game of Chicken," *News & Record,* April 22, 2009, p. C3.

acceptance of meat eating as a proper option for descendants of hunters. . . . "[35]

This position is entirely at odds with the values of animal rights activists, including one who writes, "if we cannot imagine how chickens must feel . . . perhaps we should try to imagine ourselves placed helplessly in the hands of an overpowering extraterrestrial species, to whom our pleas for mercy sound like nothing more than bleats and squeals and clucks—mere 'noise' to the master race in whose 'superior' minds we are 'only animals.'"[36]

Questions

1. Do you support KFC Corporation or People for the Ethical Treatment of Animals in this controversy? Why?

2. What are the basic criticisms that PETA makes of KFC? Are they convincing? Are its criticisms similar to timeless criticisms of business mentioned in the chapter?

3. What methods and arguments has KFC used to support its actions? Is it conducting the best defense?

4. Is the range of PETA's actions acceptable? Why does the group use controversial tactics? What are its sources of power in corporate campaigns?

5. Is it proper for PETA to pressure KFC for change when the company is following the law and public custom? Does PETA represent so compelling a truth or enough people to justify attacks on, and perhaps damage to, major corporations supported by and supporting millions of customers, employees, and stockholders?

6. Do animals have rights? If so, what are they? What duties do human beings have toward animals? Does KFC protect animal welfare at an acceptable level?

[35] Richard Martin, "Game of Chicken: Critics Say Capitulation to PETA Will Worsen Animal Rights Reprisals," *Nation's Restaurant News,* July 28, 2003, p. 31.

[36] Karen Davis, "Animal Suffering Similar to Human Slaves," *Chicago Sun-Times,* September 6, 2005, p. 50.

Chapter Five

Corporate Social Responsibility

Merck & Co., Inc.

Corporate social responsibility takes many forms. The following story stands out as extraordinary.

For ages, river blindness, or onchocerciasis (on-ko-sir-KYE-a-sis), has tortured humanity in tropical regions. Its cause is a parasitic worm that, in its adult form, lives only in humans. People are infected with the worm's tiny, immature larvae when bitten by black flies that swarm near fast-moving rivers and streams. These larvae settle in tissue near the bite and form colonies, often visible lumps, where adults grow up to two feet long. Mature worms live for 7 to 18 years coiled in these internal nodes, mating, and releasing tens of thousands of microscopic new larvae that migrate back to the skin's surface, causing welts, lumps, and discoloration along with a persistent itch that drives some sufferers to suicide. Eventually, the parasites move to the eyes, causing blindness. The cycle of infection is renewed when black flies take a blood meal from an infected person, ingesting tiny larvae, then bite an uninfected person, passing on the parasite.

People suffer in many ways. For Amarech Bitena of Ethiopia, the cost of river blindness is a broken heart. The parasites came in childhood. Now, at 25, her skin is hard and dark, her vision blurred. She has not married. "When I think about the future," she says, "I feel completely hopeless. . . . My vision can't be restored. My skin is destroyed. I would have liked to be a doctor."[1] Almost 18 million people suffer from onchocerciasis in tropical areas of Africa, South America, and Yemen.[2] About 500,000 have impaired vision and 270,000 are blind. It saps economies by enervating workers and driving farmers from fertile, riverside land.

Until recently, no treatment for river blindness existed, and little was done. It is only one of many tropical diseases affecting millions in developing nations. Critics said that big drug companies ignored these epidemics to focus on pills for the diseases of people in rich nations. Years ago the World Health Organization began pesticide spraying to kill the black fly, but it was a frustrating job. Winds carry flies up to

---

[1] Claudia Feldman, "River Blindness: A Forgotten Disease," *The Houston Chronicle,* October 9, 2005, p. 5.
[2] "Fighting River Blindness and Other Ills," *The Lancet* 374, no. 9684 (2009), p. 91.

122   Chapter 5   *Corporate Social Responsibility*

In countries ravaged by river blindness, the blind sometimes hold sticks and follow the lead of children. Merck commissioned this bronze sculpture for the lobby of its New Jersey headquarters, where top executives pass by each day. It symbolizes Merck's commitment to make medicine for the good of humanity. Because of Merck's unprecedented donation of a river blindness drug, such scenes are no longer common. Source: Photo courtesy of Merck & Co., Inc.

100 miles from breeding grounds. And scientists estimate that the breeding cycle must be suppressed for at least 14 years to stop reinfections.

In 1975 scientists at Merck & Co. discovered a compound that killed animal parasites. By 1981 they had synthesized it and marketed it for deworming dogs, cattle, sheep, and pigs. Ivermectin, as it was called, was a blockbuster hit and would be the best-selling veterinary drug worldwide for two decades. Merck's researchers had a strong hunch it also would be effective in humans against *Onchocerca volvulus,* the river blindness parasite.[3]

Merck faced a decision. It would be very expensive to bring a new drug to market and manufacture it. Yet people with the disease were among the world's poorest. Their villages had no doctors to prescribe it, no drugstores to sell it. Should Merck develop a drug that might never be profitable?

George W. Merck, son of the firm's founder and its leader for 32 years, once said: "We try never to forget that medicine is for the people. It is not for the profits. The profits follow, and if we have remembered that, they have never failed to appear."[4] This advice was still respected at Merck; it lived in the corporate culture. Merck's scientists were motivated by humanitarian goals and restraining them was awkward. The decision to go ahead was made. The cost would be $200 million.

Clinical trials of ivermectin confirmed its effectiveness. A single yearly dose of 150 micrograms per kilogram of body weight reduced the burden of tiny worms migrating through the body to near zero and impaired reproduction by adult parasites, alleviating symptoms and preventing blindness.[5]

Eventually, it became clear that neither those in need nor their governments could afford to buy ivermectin. So in 1987 Merck committed itself to manufacture and ship it at no cost to where it was needed for as long as it was needed to control river blindness. The company asked governments and private organizations to help set up distribution.

Since then, Merck has given away more than 2.5 billion tablets in 37 countries at a cost of $3.9 billion. Estimates are that treatment has prevented 40,000 cases of blindness each year; returned to use 62 million acres of farmland, an area the size of Michigan; and added 7.5 million years of adult labor in national workforces.[6] A study

---

[3] David Bollier, *Merck & Company* (Stanford, CA: Business Enterprise Trust, 1991), p. 5.

[4] Roy Vagelos and Louis Galambos, *The Moral Corporation* (New York: Cambridge University Press, 2006), p. 171.

[5] Mohammed A. Aziz, et al., "Efficacy and Tolerance of Ivermectin in Human Onchocerciasis," *The Lancet,* July 24, 1982.

[6] "Merck MECTIZAN® Donation Program: Priorities and Goals," at www.merck.com, accessed December 8, 2009.

of economic effects for two areas in Africa estimated $573 million in net benefits over 40 years.[7]

By 2012 the transmission of onchocerciasis in six Latin American countries is predicted to end. No end is in sight for Africa, but infection rates are falling in the most afflicted areas. In Benin, for example, infection rates in 51 areas ranged from 25 percent to 98 percent in the mid-1990s. Now the highest rate anywhere in the country is 3 percent.[8]

For a drug company to go through the new drug development process and then give the drug away is unprecedented. Merck's management believes that although developing and donating ivermectin has been expensive, humanitarianism and enlightened self-interest vindicate the decision. Few corporations have such singular opportunities to fight evil as did Merck, but every corporation must fulfill a range of obligations to society and many can apply unique commercial competencies to global problems. In this chapter we define the idea of social responsibility and explain how it has expanded in meaning and practice over time. The next chapter explains more about the management methods corporations use to execute social actions.

THE EVOLVING IDEA OF CORPORATE SOCIAL RESPONSIBILITY

corporate social responsibility
The duty of a corporation to create wealth in ways that avoid harm to, protect, or enhance societal assets.

Corporate social responsibility is the duty of a corporation to create wealth in ways that avoid harm to, protect, or enhance societal assets. The term is a modern one. It did not enter common use until the 1960s, when it appeared in academic literature. It often goes by other names, including its abbreviation CSR, corporate citizenship, stakeholder management, sustainability, and, in Japan, *kyosei*, a word that translates as "living and working together for the common good." Whatever it is called, there is no precise, operational meaning. It is primarily a political ideology, because its central purposes are to control and legitimize the exercise of corporate power. As an ideology, it is a worldview of how a corporate should act. In addition, it can be defined more narrowly as a management practice, specifically as the use of special tools and procedures to make a corporation responsible. This practical aspect is the subject of the next chapter.

The fundamental idea is that corporations have duties that go beyond lawful execution of their economic function. Here is the reasoning. The overall performance of a firm must benefit society. Because of market imperfections, the firm will not fulfill all its duties, and may breach some, if it responds only to market forces. Laws and regulations correct some shortcomings, more in developed countries, fewer in less developed. Beyond the law, firms must voluntarily take additional actions to meet their full obligations to society. What additional actions must they take? These have to be defined in practice by negotiation with stakeholders and they change over time.

Advocates of social responsibility, who occupy a very broad middle band of the political spectrum, justify it with three basic arguments. First, it is an ethical duty

[7] H. R. Waters, et al., "Economic Evaluation of Mectizan Distribution," *Tropical Medicine and International Health,* April 2004, p. A16.
[8] "Benin: The End of River Blindness," *Africa News,* May 8, 2008.

FIGURE 5.1   The CSR Spectrum

to promote social justice. A timeless principle is that power should be used fairly. If it harms or fails society, it is badly used. Second, social responsibility is practical. It has concrete benefits. It motivates employees and creates loyal customers. It leads to innovative products and strategies. It strengthens surrounding communities. It protects reputations and avoids regulation. In short, there is a "business case" beyond ethical duty. Third, it is necessary because other forces do not force full responsibility on corporations, particularly multinational corporations that operate across borders in a global arena of weak governance.

Opponents of corporate social responsibility are found toward the left and right edges of the political spectrum shown in Figure 5.1. On the far left, it is seen by radical Progressives as an insufficient doctrine, one that substitutes only poorly for tougher laws and regulations, allowing corporations to form a smoke screen of virtue behind which their "inviolable core" of profit seeking behavior is untouched.[9] On the far right, it is seen as a pernicious doctrine, draining and enervating the strength of the corporate institution. Conservative economists see it as an unwarranted cost. It creates administrative expenses, distracts executives, confuses economic goals with other goals, and subtracts from social welfare when the corporation is less efficient.[10] Corporations are owned by shareholders and the primary responsibility of managers is acting lawfully to maximize profits for them, thereby producing maximum value and surplus wealth for society.

Conservatives see capitalism as a natural, venerable, practical, and beneficent institution that has developed over centuries and led to rising global prosperity. They dislike CSR for thwarting natural market dynamics. They reject the agenda of corporate social responsibility, seeing it as centered in progressive ideology and based, therefore, on the goals of a movement at heart dubious of capitalism. Markets, not politics, should direct corporations. When markets fail, they should be corrected by the policies of representative government, not by unelected executives or activists.

Between these fringes there is wide acceptance of CSR. More moderate progressives are willing to work with responsible corporations. And corporate managers occupy a middle ground. Most now accept the idea as a practical necessity even as they often harbor doctrinal reservations. Years ago, most managers were on the

---

[9] Marjorie Kelly and Allen L. White, "From Corporate Responsibility to Corporate Design," *Journal of Corporate Citizenship,* spring 2009, p. 25. See also Subhabrata Bobby Banerjee, *Corporate Social Responsibility: the Good, the Bad and the Ugly* (Cheltenham: Edward Elgar Publishing, 2007).

[10] See, for example, "The Good Company: A Survey of Corporate Social Responsibility," *The Economist,* January 22, 2005.

right side of this spectrum. Why did they move left? As we will explain, the doctrine of corporate responsibility has evolved over time to require more expansive action by companies largely because stakeholder groups gained more power to impose their agendas, but also because the ethical and legal philosophies underlying it matured to support broader action by managers. In fact, corporate social responsibility is a profoundly durable and successful ideology. All through an era when free market principles were ascendant, it coiled more and more tightly around the corporation to restrain excesses and direct behavior to the public good. The story of corporate social responsibility begins with Adam Smith.

Social Responsibility in Classical Economic Theory

Throughout American history, classical capitalism, which is the basis for the market capitalism model in Chapter 1, has been the basic inspiration for business. In the classical view, a business is socially responsible if it maximizes profits while operating within the law, because an "invisible hand" will direct economic activity to serve the good of the whole.

This ideology, derived from Adam Smith's *Wealth of Nations,* is compelling in its simplicity and its resonance with self-interest. In nineteenth century America, it was elevated to the status of a commandment. However, the idea that markets harness low motives and work them into social progress has always attracted skeptics. Smith himself had a surprising number of reservations about the market's ability to protect human welfare.[11] Today the classical ideology still commands the economic landscape, but, as we will see, ethical theories of broader responsibility have worn down its prominences.

The Early Charitable Impulse

The idea that corporations had social responsibilities awaited the rise of corporations themselves. Meanwhile, the most prominent expression of duty to society was the good deed of charity by business owners.

Most colonial era businesses were very small. Merchants practiced thrift and frugality, which were dominant virtues then, to an extreme. Benjamin Franklin's advice to a business acquaintance reflects the penny-pinching nature of the time: "He that kills a breeding sow, destroys all her offspring to the thousandth generation. He that murders a crown, destroys all that it might have produced, even scores of pounds."[12] Yet charity was a coexisting virtue, and business owners sought respectability by giving to churches, orphanages, and poorhouses. Their actions first illustrate that although American business history can be pictured as a jungle of profit maximization, people in it have always been concerned citizens.[13]

Charity by owners continued in the early nineteenth century and grew as great fortunes were made. Mostly, the new millionaires endowed social causes as

---

[11] Jacob Viner, "Adam Smith and Laissez-Faire," *Journal of Political Economy,* April 1927.

[12] In "Advice to a Young Tradesman [1748]," in *The Autobiography of Benjamin Franklin and Selections from His Other Writings,* ed. Nathan G. Goodman (New York: Carlton House, 1932), p. 210. A crown was a British coin on which appeared the figure of a royal crown.

[13] Mark Sharfman, "The Evolution of Corporate Philanthropy, 1883–1952," *Business & Society,* December 1994.

individuals, not through the companies that were the fountainheads of their wealth.

One of the earliest was Steven Girard, a shipping and banking tycoon. When he died in 1831, the richest person in the nation, he made generous charitable bequests in his will, the largest of which was $6 million for a school to educate orphaned boys from the first grade through high school.[14] This single act changed the climate of education in the United States because it came before free public schooling, when a high school education was still only for children of the wealthy.

Following Girard, others donated generously and did so while still living. John D. Rockefeller systematically gave away $550 million over his lifetime. Andrew Carnegie gave $350 million during his life to social causes, built 2,811 public libraries, and donated 7,689 organs to churches. He wrote a famous article titled "The Disgrace of Dying Rich" and argued that it was the duty of a man of wealth "to consider all surplus revenues . . . as trust funds which he is called upon to administer."[15]

**social
Darwinism**
A philosophy of the late 1800s and early 1900s that used evolution to explain the dynamics of human society and institutions. The idea of "survival of the fittest" in the social realm implied that rich people and dominant companies were morally superior.

However, Carnegie's philosophy of giving was highly paternalistic. He believed that big fortunes should be used for grand purposes such as endowing universities and building concert halls such as Carnegie Hall. They should not be wasted by paying higher wages to workers or giving gifts to poor people; that would dissipate riches on small indulgences and would not, in the end, elevate the culture of a society. Thus, one day when a friend of Carnegie's encountered a beggar and gave him a quarter, Carnegie admonished the friend that it was one of "the very worst actions of his life."[16]

In this remark, Carnegie echoed the doctrine of *social Darwinism*, which held that charity interfered with the natural evolutionary process in which society shed its less fit to make way for the better adapted. Well-meaning people who gave to charity interfered with the natural law of progress by propping up failed examples of the human race. The leading advocate of this astringent doctrine, the English philosopher Herbert Spencer, wrote the following heartless passage in a best-selling 1850 book.

[14] The school became known as Girard College, which one of the authors of this book, George Steiner, attended. It still exists in Philadelphia.

[15] Andrew Carnegie, *The Gospel of Wealth* (Cambridge, MA: Harvard University Press, 1962), p. 25; originally published in 1901.

[16] Quoted in Page Smith, *The Rise of Industrial America,* vol. 6 (New York: Penguin Books, 1984), p. 136.

It seems hard that a laborer incapacitated by sickness from competing with his stronger fellows should have to bear the resulting privations. It seems hard that widows and orphans should be left to struggle for life or death. Nevertheless, when regarded not separately, but in connection with the interests of universal humanity, these harsh fatalities are seen to be full of the highest beneficence—the same beneficence which brings to early graves the children of diseased parents and singles out the low-spirited, the intemperate, and the debilitated as the victims of an epidemic. [17]

Spencer approved of some charity, though only when it raised the character and superiority of the giver. Still, the overall effect of Spencer's arguments was to moderate charity by business leaders and retard the growth of a modern social conscience.

More than just faith in markets and social Darwinism constrained business from undertaking voluntary social action. Charters granted by states when corporations were formed required that profits be disbursed to shareholders. Courts consistently held charitable gifts to be *ultra vires*, that is, "beyond the law," because charters did not expressly permit them. To use company funds for charity or social works took money from the pockets of shareholders and invited lawsuits. Thus, when Rockefeller had the humanitarian impulse to build the first medical school in China, he paid for it out of his own pocket; not a penny came from Standard Oil. Although most companies took a negative view of philanthropy, by the 1880s the railroads were an exception. They sponsored the Young Men's Christian Association (YMCA) movement, which provided rooming and religious indoctrination for rail construction crews. Yet such actions were exceptional.

As the twentieth century approached, classical ideology was still a mountain of resistance to expanding the idea of business social responsibility. A poet of that era, James Russell Lowell, captured the spirit of the day.

> *Not a deed would he do,*
> *Nor a word would he utter*
> *Till he'd weighed its relations*
> *To plain bread and butter.*[18]

Social Responsibility in the Late Nineteenth and Early Twentieth Centuries

Giving, no matter how generous, was a narrow kind of social responsibility often unrelated to a company's impacts on society. By the late 1800s it was growing apparent to the business elite that prevailing doctrines used to legitimize business defined its responsibilities too narrowly. Industrialization had fostered social

---

[17] Herbert Spencer, *Social Statics* (New York: D. Appleton and Company, 1890), p. 354; first published in 1850.
[18] "A Fable for Critics," *The Complete Poetical Works of James Russell Lowell,* Cabinet Edition (Boston: Houghton, Mifflin and Company, 1899), p. 122.

problems and political corruption. Farmers were in revolt. Labor was increasingly violent. Socialism was at high tide. Average Americans began to question unfettered laissez-faire economics and the doctrine of social Darwinism.

As Rockefeller, Carnegie, and other barons of wealth gave away large sums, public doubt about their motives grew. They were accused of cloaking their greed with gifts that confused the eye, diverting it from the coarse origins of their money. As one of Carnegie's workers asked, "What use has a man who works twelve hours a day for a library, anyway?"[19] Thus the criticism that corporate responsibility is a smoke screen first emerged in this bygone era. It has never lost a following.

By now, business feared a growing clamor for more regulation. It was terrified of socialist calls for appropriation of assets. So it sought to blunt the urgency of these appeals by voluntary action.

trustee
An agent of a company whose corporate role puts him or her in a position of power over the fate of not just stockholders, but also of others such as customers, employees, and communities.

During the Progressive era, three interrelated themes of broader responsibility emerged. First, managers were *trustees,* that is, agents whose corporate roles put them in positions of power over the fate of not just stockholders, but also of others such as workers, customers, and communities. This power implied a duty to promote the welfare of each group. Second, managers had an obligation to *balance* these multiple interests. They were, in effect, coordinators who settled competing claims. Third, many managers subscribed to the *service principle,* a near-spiritual belief that individual managers served society by making each business successful; if they all prospered, the aggregate effect would eradicate social injustice, poverty, and other ills. This belief was only a fancy reincarnation of classical ideology. However, many of its adherents conceded that companies were still obligated to undertake social projects that helped, or "served," the public.[20] These three interrelated ideas—trusteeship, balance, and service—expanded the idea of business responsibility beyond simple charity. But the type of responsibility envisioned was still paternalistic, and the actions of big company leaders often showed an underlying Scroogelike mentality.

service principle
A belief that managers served society by making companies profitable and that aggregate success by many managers would resolve major social problems.

One such leader was Henry Ford, who had an aptitude for covering meanness with a shining veneer of citizenship. In the winter of 1914 Ford thrilled the public by announcing the "Five-Dollar Day" for Ford Motor Co. workers. Five dollars was about double the daily pay for manufacturing workers at the time and seemed very generous. In fact, although Ford took credit for being big-hearted, the $5 wage was intended to cool unionizing and was not what it appeared on the surface. The offer attracted hordes of job seekers from around the country to Highland Park, Michigan. One subzero morning in January, there were 2,000 lined up outside the Ford plant by 5:00 a.m.; by dawn there were 10,000. Disorder broke out, and the fire department turned hoses on the freezing men.

The few who were hired had to serve a six-month apprenticeship and comply with the puritanical Ford Motor Co. code of conduct (no drinking, marital discord, or otherwise immoral living) to qualify for the $5 day. Many were fired on pretexts

[19] Quoted in Margaret F. Byington, *Homestead: The Households of a Mill Town* (Philadelphia: William F. Fell Co., 1910), p. 178.

[20] Rolf Lunden, *Business and Religion in the American 1920s* (New York: Greenwood Press, 1988), pp. 147–50.

Inventor and industrialist Henry Ford (1863–1947). The public made him a folk hero and saw him as a generous employer. But he manipulated workers to lower costs. Source: The Library of Congress.

before the six months passed. Thousands of replacements waited outside each day hoping to fill a new vacancy. Inside, Ford speeded up the assembly line. Insecure employees worked faster under the threat of being purged for a younger, stronger, lower-paid new hire. Those who hung on to qualify for the $5 wage had to face greedy merchants and landlords in the surrounding area who raised prices and rents.

Ford was a master of image. In 1926 he announced the first five-day, 40-hour week for workers, but with public accolades still echoing for this "humanitarian" gesture, he speeded up the line still more, cut wages, and announced a program to weed out less-efficient employees. These actions were necessary, he said, to compensate for Saturdays off. Later that year, Ford told the adulatory public that he had started a program to fight juvenile delinquency. He proposed to employ 5,000 boys 16 to 20 years old and pay them "independence wages."[21] This was trumpeted as citizenship, but as the "boys" were hired, older workers were pitted against younger, lower-paid replacements.

A few business leaders, however, acted more consistently with the emerging themes of business responsibility. One was General Robert E. Wood, who led Sears, Roebuck and Company from 1924 to 1954. He believed that a large corporation was more than an economic institution; it was a social and political force as well. In the Sears *Annual Report* for 1936, he outlined the ways in which Sears was discharging its responsibilities to what he said were the chief constituencies of the company—customers, the public, employees, suppliers, and stockholders.[22] Stockholders came last because, according to General Wood, they could not attain their "full measure of reward" unless the other groups were satisfied first. In thought and action, General Wood was far ahead of his time. Nevertheless, in the 1920s and after that, corporations found various ways to support communities. Organized charities were formed, such as the Community Chest, the Red Cross, and the Boy Scouts, to which they contributed. In many cities, companies gave money and expertise to improve schools and public health. In the 1940s corporations began to give cash and stock to tax-exempt foundations set up for philanthropic giving.

1950 to the Present

The contemporary understanding of corporate social responsibility was formed during this period. An early and influential statement of the idea was made in 1954 by Howard R. Bowen in his book *Social Responsibilities of the Businessman*.[23] Bowen said that managers felt strong public expectations to act in ways that went beyond profit-maximizing and were, in fact, meeting those expectations. Then he laid out the basic arguments for social responsibility: (1) managers have an ethical

[21] Keith Sward, *The Legend of Henry Ford* (New York: Rinehart & Company, 1948), p. 176.

[22] James C. Worthy, *Shaping an American Institution: Robert E. Wood and Sears, Roebuck* (Urbana: University of Illinois Press, 1984), p. 173.

[23] Howard Bowen, *Social Responsibilities of the Businessman* (New York: Harper, 1954).

duty to consider the broad social impacts of their decisions; (2) businesses are reservoirs of skill and energy for improving civic life; (3) corporations must use power in keeping with a broad social contract, or lose their legitimacy; (4) it is in the enlightened self-interest of business to improve society; and (5) voluntary action may head off negative public attitudes and unwanted regulations. This book, despite being almost 60 years old, remains an excellent encapsulation of the current ideology of corporate responsibility.[24]

Not everyone accepted Bowen's arguments. The primary dissenters were conservative economists who claimed that business is *most* responsible when it makes money efficiently, not when it misapplies its energy on social projects. The best-known advocate of this view, then and now, is Nobel laureate Milton Friedman.

> There is one and only one social responsibility of business—to use its resources and engage in activities designed to increase its profits so long as it stays within the rules of the game, which is to say, engages in open and free competition, without deception or fraud. . . . Few trends could so thoroughly undermine the very foundations of our free society as the acceptance by corporate officials of social responsibility other than to make as much money for their stockholders as possible. This is a fundamentally subversive doctrine.[25]

Friedman argues that managers are the employees of a corporation's owners and are directly responsible to them. Stockholders want to maximize profits, so the manager's sole objective is to accommodate them. If a manager spends corporate funds on social projects, he or she is diverting shareholders' dollars to programs they may not even favor. Similarly, if the cost of social projects is passed on to consumers in higher prices, the manager is spending their money. This "taxation without representation," says Friedman, is wrong.[26] Furthermore, if the market price of a product does not reflect the true costs of producing it, but includes costs for social programs, then the market's allocation mechanism is distorted.

The opposition of Friedman and other adherents of classical economic doctrine proved to be a principled, rearguard action. In theory the arguments were unerring, but in practice they were inexpedient. When the great tides of consumerism, environmentalism, civil rights, and feminism rose in the 1960s, leftist critics wanted to control rip-offs, pollution, employment discrimination, and other perceived excesses of capitalism with new regulations. In this power struggle Friedman's position seemed cold and indifferent, an abstract calculus aloof from costs in flesh and blood. It incited critics and invited retaliation and more regulation should the business community openly agree. Moreover, the idea that corporations could undertake expanded social responsibility was useful for business. If corporations volunteered to do more it would calm critics, forestall regulation,

---

[24] See, for example, Rosabeth Moss Kanter, *Supercorp* (New York: Crown Business, 2009), the result of three years of research and 350 interviews in 20 countries by the author and her team, leading to the discovery that "vanguard," or socially progressive, companies accept Bowen's basic arguments.

[25] *Capitalism and Freedom* (Chicago: University of Chicago Press, 1962), p. 133.

[26] "The Social Responsibility of Business Is to Increase Its Profits," *The New York Times Magazine,* September 13, 1970, p. 33.

and preserve their legitimacy. Not surprisingly, Friedman's view was decisively rejected by business leaders, who soon articulated a new vision.

In 1971 the Committee for Economic Development, a prestigious voice of business, published a bold statement of the case for expansive social responsibility. Society, it said, has broadened its expectations outward over "three concentric circles of responsibilities."[27]

- An *inner circle* of clear-cut responsibility for efficient execution of the economic function resulting in products, jobs, and economic growth.

- An *intermediate circle* encompassing responsibility to exercise this economic function with a sensitive awareness of changing values and priorities.

- An *outer circle* that outlines newly emerging and still amorphous responsibilities that business should assume to improve the social environment, even if they are not directly related to specific business processes.

Classical ideology focused solely on the first circle. Now business leaders argued that management responsibilities went further. The report was followed in 1981 by a *Statement on Corporate Responsibility* from the Business Roundtable, a group of 200 CEOs of the largest corporations. It said:

> Economic responsibility is by no means incompatible with other corporate responsibilities in society . . . A corporation's responsibilities include how the whole business is conducted every day. It must be a thoughtful institution which rises above the bottom line to consider the impact of its actions on all, from shareholders to the society at large. Its business activities must make social sense.[28]

Friedmanism
The theory that the sole responsibility of a corporation is to optimize profits while obeying the law.

After these statements from top executives appeared, the range of social programs assumed by business expanded rapidly in education, the arts, public health, housing, the environment, literacy, employee relations, and other areas. However, although the business elite formally rejected *Friedmanism*, corporate cultures, which change only at glacial rates, still promoted a single-minded obsession with efficiency and financial results. The belief that a trade-off existed between profits and social responsibility was (and still is) widespread and visible in corporate actions.

BASIC ELEMENTS OF SOCIAL RESPONSIBILITY

The three elements of social responsibility are market actions, externally mandated actions, and voluntary actions. Figure 5.2 illustrates the relative magnitude of each, how that magnitude has changed over historical eras, and how change will progress if the trend toward expansion of the idea of corporate responsibility continues. To be socially responsible, a corporation must fulfill its duties in each area of action.

Market actions are responses to competitive forces in markets. Such actions have always dominated and this will continue. When a corporation responds to

---

[27] Committee for Economic Development, *Social Responsibilities of Business Corporations* (New York: CED, 1971), p. 11.

[28] *Statement on Corporate Responsibility* (New York: Business Roundtable, October 1981), pp. 12 and 14.

FIGURE 5.2

Motives for Social Responsibility and Their Evolving Magnitudes

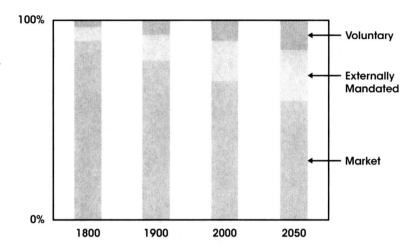

markets, it fulfills its first and most important social responsibility. All else pales before its economic impact. Recently the giant Unilever Group cooperated with Oxfam International, a confederation of progressive NGOs fighting world poverty, to study the overall impact of its branch company in Indonesia. Oxfam is suspicious of corporations and had "ruthlessly challenged" Unilever's profit-seeking actions.[29] Yet the final report detailed a wondrous economic effect in a country where half the population lives below $2 a day.

Unilever Indonesia (UI) is the 13th-largest company in the country. Like its global parent, it sells personal and home products such as Kleenex, Pepsodent, and Lux soap, along with a variety of foods. Over five years ending in 2006, UI made a net profit of $212 million. But the surprise was that its operations created total monetary value of $633 million along its *value chain*. A value chain is the sequence of coordinated actions that add value to a product or service. For Unilever it includes economic actors outside the corporation in both its backward supply chain and forward distribution channels.

Of the $633 million total, only 34 percent was captured by UI; the rest went to others: 4 percent to farmers for their crops, 12 percent to several hundred suppliers, 6 percent to product distributors, and 18 percent to as many as 1.8 million retailers, among them tiny shops and street vendors selling "sachets," or small packets of Unilever products made especially for low-income consumers who could not afford regular sizes. From its share, UI put the majority back into the Indonesian economy, reinvesting 25 percent in its local business, giving 30 percent to the government in taxes, and paying 7 percent in dividends to Indonesian shareholders.[30] Unilever Indonesia employed about 5,000 workers, but the study found that the entire value chain created 300,764 full-time jobs, an important contribution in a nation with more than 9 percent unemployment.

value chain
The sequence of coordinated actions that add value to a product or service.

---

[29] Jason Caly, *Exploring the Links Between International Business and Poverty Reduction: A Case Study of Unilever in Indonesia* (Eynsham, UK: Oxfam GB and Unilever PLC, 2005), p. 10.

[30] The other 38 percent was paid as dividends to overseas shareholders. Figures in this paragraph are from ibid., pp. 14, 82, and 83.

Figures such as these illustrate how the greatest positive impact of a corporation on society is economic and why maximizing that impact is a corporation's greatest social responsibility. From the study, Oxfam concluded that tremendous potential for poverty alleviation existed in UI's routine profit-seeking actions. It absolved Unilever of draining Indonesian society by profiting on the backs of poor people.

Mandated actions are those required either by government regulation or civil regulation. Government, or public, regulation is rooted in the authority of the state and its mandates are enforceable by law. Government mandates have multiplied rapidly in developed countries. *Civil regulation* is regulation by nonstate actors based on social norms or standards enforced by social or market sanctions. Civil regulation, sometimes called private regulation, has many faces. It is imposed when activists, consumers, investors, lenders, shareholders, or employees make demands on a company and failure to comply will lead to reputational or financial damage. Such mandates are enforced by the power of the market, not the power of law.[31] As we will see later in this chapter, mandates based on civil regulation are now expanding rapidly in the global economy.

civil regulation
Regulation by nonstate actors based on social norms or standards enforced by social or market sanctions.

The third element is *voluntary actions* that go beyond those compelled by law or regulation. Some voluntary actions can be called "legal plus" because they exceed required mandates. After the deadly Bhopal, India, gas leak in 1984, the subject of a case study in Chapter 11, the chemical industry introduced plant safety standards that went beyond the requirements of any nation. Other actions are unrelated to mandates, but respond to public consensus. Charitable giving, which is expected of every corporation though not legally required, is an example. Still other actions may be strategic initiatives where the firm seeks to profit from solving a social problem as does GE when it sells energy-saving hybrid locomotives.

GENERAL PRINCIPLES OF CORPORATE SOCIAL RESPONSIBILITY

What must a corporation do to be socially responsible? Many actions are possible. One meticulous study classified CSR into seven main areas with 31 categories containing 147 specific CSR activities.[32] Each company must choose a range of appropriate economic, mandated, and voluntary actions to fulfill its total obligations to society. No precise formula determines these choices. However, the following broad principles are widely accepted.

- *Corporations are economic institutions run for profit.* Their greatest responsibility is to create economic benefits. They should be judged primarily on economic criteria and cannot be expected to meet purely social objectives without financial incentives. Corporations may incur short-run costs on social initiatives that promise long-term benefits. And they should seek ways to solve social problems at a profit.

[31] See David Vogel, "The Private Regulation of Global Corporate Conduct," in Walter Mattli and Ngaire Woods, eds. *The Politics of Global Regulation* (Princeton, NJ: Princeton University Press, 2009).

[32] Ashridge Centre for Business and Society, *A Catalogue of CSR Activities* (Berkhamsted: Ashridge Centre for Business and Society, 2005). The areas are (1) leadership, vision, and values, (2) the marketplace, (3) the workforce, (4) supply chain activities, (5) stakeholder engagement, (6) the community, and (7) the environment.

All firms must follow multiple bodies of law, including (1) corporation laws and chartering provisions, (2) the civil and criminal laws of nations, (3) legislated regulations that protect stakeholders, and (4) international laws, including treaties and trade agreements.

Managers must act ethically. They must respect the law and, in addition, conform their behavior to ethical principles; model ethical values such as integrity, honesty, and justice; and set up codes, policies, and procedures to elevate behavior within the firm.

external cost
A production cost not paid by a firm or its customers, but by members of society.

Corporations have a duty to correct adverse social impacts they cause. They should try to internalize negative *external costs*, or adverse costs of production borne by society. A factory dumping toxic effluent into a stream creates costs such as human and animal disease imposed on innocents, not on the company or its customers. Increasingly, this duty to correct radiates outward to include taking responsibility for adverse impacts along global supply chains.

Social responsibility varies with company characteristics such as size, industry, products, strategies, marketing methods, locations, internal cultures, and external demands. Thus, a global pharmaceutical company such as Merck has a far different impact on society than a local insurance company, so its responsibilities are different and greater.

Managers should try to meet legitimate needs of multiple stakeholders. Although corporations have a fiduciary duty to shareholders, it is not legally required, desirable, or possible, to manage solely in their interest. Consumers, employees, governments, communities, and other groups also have important claims on the firm.

Corporate behavior must comply with an underlying social contract. To understand this contract and how it changes, managers can study the direction of national policies and global norms as evidenced in legislation, regulations, treaties, conventions, trade agreements, and public opinion.

Corporations should be transparent and accountable. They should publicly report on their social performance in addition to their financial performance. This social reporting should cover major social impacts and, like financial reporting, be verifiable; that is, audited and checked by independent parties.

ARE SOCIAL AND FINANCIAL PERFORMANCE RELATED?

Scholars have done at least 127 studies to see if companies that are more socially responsible are also more profitable.[33] Most report a positive correlation between responsibility and profitability. Yet many have mixed, inconclusive, or negative findings. A review of 95 such studies over 30 years found that a majority (53 percent) showed that socially responsible behavior was related to higher profits. However, 24 percent found no relationship, 19 percent a mixed relationship, and 5 percent a negative relationship.[34]

[33] Joshua Daniel Margolis and James Patrick Walsh, *People and Profits: The Search for a Link between a Company's Social and Financial Performance* (Mahwah, NJ: Lawrence Erlbaum, 2001), p. 394.
[34] Ibid., p. 10.

Inconsistent results from study to study are not surprising given the difficult problems of method that researchers face. To begin, if social performance is defined as including economic performance, then any effort to separate the two elements to assess their relationship is doomed. Even if social performance is not defined to include economic performance, profit or loss does not solely depend on virtue, being also determined by market forces oblivious to the grade in a CSR report card. Also, no fixed, neutral definition of social responsibility exists, making it impossible objectively to rank corporations as more or less responsible. Many studies have used corporate responsibility ratings done by progressive analysts who evaluate companies based on whether they fulfill the left's social agenda. Others rely on rankings of reputation made by executives of Fortune 500 companies, who have a more conservative perspective.

As opposed to the subjectivity of a corporation's social performance it might seem that financial performance can be gauged more objectively, but there are many ways to measure profitability. Should researchers use accounting measures such as net income or market measures such as stock price appreciation?

In the above review of 95 studies, the authors report that researchers drew on 27 information sources to rate social performance and used 70 methods to calculate financial performance. This makes it difficult to compare the findings of one study to the findings of others. However, a fresh analysis of 52 studies took advantage of a statistical technique that allows correlations in individual studies to be compared. The authors found that the overall correlation between social and financial performance was "moderately positive," rising to "highly positive" for some combinations of performance measures.[35] Still, confounding results persist. A more recent study looked at companies that made *Business Ethics* magazine's annual list of 100 top corporate citizens four years in a row. It found that most were less profitable than direct competitors in their industries, suggesting to the authors that "higher profitability is associated with less corporate social responsibility."[36]

Overall, the majority of academic studies find that companies rated as notably responsible are at least as profitable, and often more so, than companies rated as less responsible. However, the results are mixed and there are such significant methodological questions that reservations are warranted. The best conclusion is that socially responsible behavior contributes to better financial performance for some companies, but evidence that it does so broadly for most companies is weak. If the evidence were stronger, there would be little need for activists and NGOs to force a CSR agenda on hesitant corporations.

CORPORATE SOCIAL RESPONSIBILITY IN A GLOBAL CONTEXT

In the early twenty-first century the doctrine of corporate responsibility is widely accepted in industrialized nations. Although its early development was strongest in the United States, sometime in the 1990s leadership passed to Europe, where

[35] Marc Orlitzky, Frank L. Schmidt, and Sara L. Rynes, "Corporate Social and Financial Performance: A Meta-Analysis," *Organization Studies* 24, no. 3 (2003).

[36] Arthur B. Laffer, Andrew Coors, and Wayne Winegarden, *Does Corporate Social Responsibility Enhance Business Profitability?* (San Diego: Laffer Associates, 2005), p. 5.

welfare state systems have nurtured some of the most powerful social justice NGOs and consumers are more inclined to purchase goods from companies they see as responsible. Until this time American corporations took the lead in evolving voluntary responses to societal demands because, relative to Europe, American markets were more laissez-faire and government regulation was looser, leaving more of the company's total responsibility in the voluntary category.

In Europe, social welfare states intervened more in markets and mandated extensive protections for workers, consumers, and the natural environment. While American companies volunteered to give health benefits to workers and make recyclable products, for example, their counterparts in the European Union were legally required to do so. So European companies never needed the spectrum of voluntary social actions that American companies did. Then, in the 1990s, Europe reacted to the rise of global competition, engaging with neoliberal ideas, deregulating markets, grinding away protections for workers, and shrinking other legal mandates on companies. In response, leading activist groups pressured firms to engage in more voluntary CSR activity and the stronger social welfare expectations in European nations gave birth to a robust, creative, and expansive design of corporate responsibility that now dominates and defines Western practice.

Corporate responsibility has strong roots elsewhere in both the developed and developing world and, as in Europe, its practice often diverges from the U.S. experience. In Japan, for example, it means paternalism toward workers and there is little tradition of philanthropy. In Australia voluntary CSR is actively encouraged by the government. In India it has risen on the teaching of Mohandas Gandhi that those who accumulate wealth hold it in trust for society.

Global CSR is now defined and dominated by the progressive ideology of Western civil society and the practices of Western multinationals. It has little foundation in some rapidly growing non-Western nations and as their businesses gain power in the world economy the consequences for CSR practice are unknown. The primary mystery is China, where a communist regime plans economic growth as it smothers dissent. Chinese corporations respond to social interests as directed by this unrepresentative, one-party government, and they adopt voluntary codes, standards, and social programs mainly to ease access into Western export markets. Although Confucian ethics teach harmony and reciprocity as central virtues and the basis of Buddhism is the interdependence of a person with the larger community and with nature, the Western idea of stakeholder engagement is lifeless in a Stalinist world.[37]

THE PROBLEM OF CROSS-BORDER CORPORATE POWER

While there is no consensus on the meaning and extent of CSR from nation to nation, the idea has taken on new and novel international dimensions in response to economic globalization. As governments deregulated markets and lowered

---

[37] See, for example, Po Keung Ip, "Is Confucianism Good for Business Ethics in China," *Journal of Business Ethics* 82 (2008); and "From CSR in Asia to Asian CSR," in Jem Bendell, Chew Ng, and Niaz Alam, "World Review," *Journal of Corporate Citizenship,* Spring 2009, pp. 19–22.

trade barriers in the 1980s, cross-border trade and investment began a steep rise. Dominant corporations grew larger and more active. As they did, critics and observers perceived the exercise of too much power and too little restraint, particularly of Western corporations in developing nations.

The perception that transnational corporations elude proper controls is rooted in a group of observations. First, international law, as found in treaties, conventions, and trade agreements, is weak in addressing social impacts of business. It strongly protects commercial rights, but norms protecting labor, human rights, nature, indigenous cultures, and other social resources are far less codified. Second, transnational corporations are subject to uneven regulation in developing nations, where institutions may be rudimentary and enforcement feeble. Some governments have overly bureaucratic agencies riddled with corruption. And some are undemocratic, run by elites that siphon off the economic benefits of foreign investment and neglect public needs. Third, in adapting to global economic growth, corporations use strategies of joint venture, outsourcing, and supply chain extension that create efficiencies, but sometimes also distance them from direct accountability for social harms. And fourth, significantly more government regulation of transnational firms is unlikely. No global government exists and no nation-state has the power (or the wish) to regulate international commerce. Developing nations fear, correctly, that stricter rules will deter foreign investment.

In a world where regulation is uneven, some corporations, such as Merck, have operated with high standards across nations. But others have compromised their standards in permissive host country environments. By the early 1990s, critics of multinational corporations began calling for new standards of responsibility. One by-product of globalization was the growing number, international reach, and networking of nongovernmental organizations (NGOs). Many of these groups developed a close association with the United Nations (UN), which, besides its peacekeeping function, promotes international human rights and interests of poorer, developing nations in the global South. During the 1990s, coalitions of NGOs pushed for a series of conferences sponsored by the UN for member nations. Conferences were held on environmental sustainability (Rio de Janeiro, 1992), population (Cairo, 1993), human rights (Vienna, 1994), social development (Copenhagen, 1995), and gender (Beijing, 1995).

THE RISE OF NEW GLOBAL VALUES

A defining moment came at the Rio conference on sustainability in 1992, when NGOs arrived demanding regulation of corporations. Their agenda failed, in part because the philosophy of economic liberalization driving the world economy was inhospitable to restrictions on business and in part because corporations and business groups that lobbied against regulation promoted an expanded, international doctrine of voluntary corporate responsibility. NGOs, unable to secure the hard regulations they wanted, were forced to work with business groups in developing new, innovative CSR mechanisms.

soft law
Statements of philosophy, policy, and principle found in nonbinding international conventions that, over time, gain legitimacy as guidelines for interpreting the hard law in legally binding agreements.

In hindsight, these conferences led to several important changes in the operating environments of multinational corporations. First, they generated a series of declarations, resolutions, statements of principle, guidelines, and frameworks under UN auspices that shaped international norms for the conduct of both nations and corporations. These documents created what international legal scholars call *soft law*. In the realm of international law, hard law, found mainly in treaties, creates binding rights, prohibitions, and duties. While soft law creates no binding obligations or duties for corporations, if its contents are widely accepted as expressing international norms it can, over time, become the basis for interpreting treaties. Second, the conferences provided occasions for NGOs to interact and develop influence strategies for confronting corporations. And third, they set the stage for further, this time global, expansion of the CSR ideology.

GLOBAL CORPORATE RESPONSIBILITY

The new, global dimension of CSR makes it the duty of a multinational corporation voluntarily to compensate for international and developing country regulatory deficits. It should do this, first, by extending its home country standards outward to its foreign operations and to its supply chain, and, second, by following a growing body of international norms enforced by various mechanisms of civil regulation. This new dimension of CSR flourishes because it has value across much of the CSR political spectrum. It appeals to activists as a substitute for the new laws they would prefer but cannot get and as a way to overcome the failure of weak governments to fight human rights abuses, corruption, ecological insult, and poverty. It also appeals to enlightened corporations as a way to forestall more traditional and formal regulation and to placate belligerent NGOs. As a result, the world seethes with activity pushing the idea along.

Figure 5.3 shows the range of entities and elements in an evolving system of global CSR. This system, solidifying now out of a less mature patchwork, organizes values, principles, rules, institutions, and management tools in support of voluntary corporate actions. Simultaneously, it has grown into a framework of civil regulation that can often command corporate behavior. We illuminate its structure by discussing the elements set forth in Figure 5.3, moving clockwise from the top right. In subsequent chapters we discuss some of them at greater length.

norm
A standard that arises over time and is enforced by social sanction or law.

Development of Norms and Principles

A *norm* is a standard that arises over time and, as agreement on it becomes widespread, is enforced by social sanction or law. It is similar to a *principle*, which is a rule, natural law, or truth used as a standard to guide conduct. The norms and principles that direct global CSR are derived in part from timeless accretions of civilization, but international conventions to codify and interpret them are increasingly influential. The United Nations is a ringleader. An early codification of norms is the *Universal Declaration of Human Rights,* adopted by the UN in 1948,

principle
A rule, natural law, or truth used as a standard to guide conduct.

FIGURE 5.3

**A Global
System of
CSR Activity**

CIVIL SOCIETY
VIGILANCE

DEVELOPMENT
OF NORMS AND
PRINCIPLES

GOVERNMENT
ACTIONS

CODES
OF
CONDUCT

SOCIAL
INVESTMENT
AND LENDING

REPORTING
AND
VERIFICATION
STANDARDS

MANAGEMENT
STANDARDS

CERTIFICATION
AND LABELING
SCHEMES

which spells out a "common standard" of "inalienable rights," that are specified in 30 articles.[38] The rights in this document are now widely accepted and it is the foundation for many of the human rights standards in corporate and NGO conduct codes. It requires, for example, equal rights for men and women, and corporations following such codes must meet this standard, often by imposing it on suppliers in less developed nations where no legislation requires it.

A second milestone in the development of norms is the *Tripartite Declaration of Principles concerning Multinational Enterprises and Social Policy*, adopted by an agency of the UN in 1977. The Tripartite Declaration, so-called because unions, governments, and industry collaborated in its creation, came in response to the rising power of multinational corporations in the 1960s. It sets forth a long list of "guidelines" related to worker rights, for example, that multinational corporations should not offer wages and benefits less than those offered for comparable work elsewhere in a country.[39] Over the years, the *Tripartite Declaration* has been accepted

---

[38] *Universal Declaration of Human Rights,* G.A. res. 217 A (III), UN Doc. A/810, December 10, 1948, Preamble.

[39] *Tripartite Declaration of Principles concerning Multinational Enterprises and Social Policy,* 3rd ed. (Geneva: International Labour Office, 2001), p. v and p. 7, para. 33. First edition published in 1977.

as a foundational statement and it now is the basis for most international labor codes. As new norms solidify, additions are made, most recently a new entry in 2006 suggesting that multinational corporations had a duty to abolish child labor.

At the leading edge of emerging norms is a draft compilation of *Norms on the Responsibilities of Transnational Corporations,* advanced by the UN Human Rights Commission in 2004 and discussed for several years before dying in what has been called a "train wreck" of polarized arguments.[40] The *Norms* would obligate multinational corporations to protect a lengthy list of "universal" rights of peoples, consumers, workers, and the environment. The corporation "shall not use forced or compulsory labour," nor "shall [it] . . . advertise harmful or potentially harmful products" and it "shall generally conduct [its] activities in a manner contributing to the wider goal of sustainable development."[41] It requires transnational corporations to adopt internal rules for compliance, submit to monitoring by the UN in which NGOs would participate, and make "prompt reparation" for injuries due to lack of compliance. Nations would be asked to pass laws to legalize enforcement of the *Norms.*

The draft is an exceptionally aggressive document that advances past the edge of international consensus on corporate responsibility. Nations were skeptical of giving corporations the legal authority to enforce "universal," meaning Western, human rights standards in countries with diverging values. Corporations, with some exceptions, were bitterly hostile to the imposition of new duties and exposure to new liabilities. For now the *Norms* are moribund, but time is their ally.

Landmark statements of norms and principles such as these arise from the steady accretion of innumerable international charters, declarations, conventions, multilateral agency policies, and treaties on labor, human rights, corruption, migratory birds, and other issues that, by their sheer numbers, promote broad acceptance of progressive, developed-country values as universal norms. These norms are the basis for proliferating codes of conduct that target corporate behavior.

Codes of Conduct

Codes of conduct are formal statements of aspirations, principles, guidelines, and rules for corporate behavior. They arise from many sources. Corporations write them. In addition, there are hundreds of codes created by industry associations, NGOs, governments, and international organizations such as the UN. Many codes result from collaborative processes by multiple parties; these are called *multistakeholder initiatives.* Any large multinational corporation will follow more than one code. It will have its own code or codes and, in addition, will be a signatory of multiple codes developed by other actors, likely including an industry code and specialized codes focused on labor, human rights, environmental

codes of conduct
Formal statements of aspirations, principles, guidelines, and rules for corporate behavior.

multistakeholder initiative
A code-based form of civil regulation created by some combination of corporate, government, NGO, or international organization actors.

[40] Spoken remarks of J. Ruggie, the Secretary General's Special Representative on Business and Human Rights, quoted in David Kinley, Justine Nolan, and Natalie Zerial, "The Politics of Corporate Social Responsibility: Reflections on the UN Human Rights Norms for Corporations," *Company and Securities Law Journal* 25, no. 1 (2007), p. 31.

[41] *Norms on the Responsibilities of Transnational Corporations and Other Business Enterprises with Regard to Human Rights,* U.N. Doc. E/CN.4/Sub.2/2003/12/Rev.2 (2003), secs. D(5), F.(13), and G.(14).

protection, corruption, and other matters. Here are examples of codes from different sources.

- Samsung Electronics Company has a *Global Code of Conduct* based on five aspirational principles: legal and ethical behavior, a "clean organization culture" (which means a culture free of discrimination, sexual harassment, insider trading, and similar misbehaviors), respect for stakeholders, care for the environment, and social responsibility. Brief, descriptive statements in each category give more specific guidance to employees.[42]

- The *Electronic Industry Code of Conduct* is intended to protect the safety and rights of workers in overseas plants that do computer assembly and component manufacturing. The 11-page code requires participants, who sign on voluntarily, to "go beyond legal compliance" in enforcing its standards for labor, health and safety, environmental protection, and ethical behavior.[43] It explicitly incorporates standards in the *Universal Declaration of Human Rights* and other codifications of international norms.

- In the 1990s a small band of activists within Amnesty International UK, a human rights NGO, began to work with companies, resulting in a checklist of human rights principles that evolved into a code titled *Human Rights Guidelines for Companies*. Although no companies adopted the Guidelines in their entirety, their appearance altered a widespread belief of executives at that time that only governments, not corporations, had responsibility for human rights. They were the template for a wave of changes written into corporate codes and policies.[44]

- The Ethical Trading Initiative is an alliance of companies, unions, and NGOs based in the United Kingdom. It has a *Base Code* setting standards for working conditions in overseas supplier firms. Its 50 member companies agree to conform their own codes to the *Base Code*, apply the standards across their international supply chains to almost 40,000 contractors with 8.6 million workers, and allow independent monitoring for compliance. Although the entity can discipline and even expel member companies for noncompliance, it does not publicly report such actions or any information about individual companies.

No matter what the source of a code, the target is the corporation. A code's effectiveness depends on how the corporation carries it out. Codes written by corporations themselves often lack rigor. Codes created by other parties usually require companies to sign compliance agreements that require some form of monitoring, and these are more effective, if uneven in result, leading to a growing focus on ways of monitoring corporations to verify code compliance.

---

[42] Samsung Electronics Co., *Global Code of Conduct* (Seoul, Korea: Samsung, 2006).

[43] Electronic Industry Citizenship Coalition, *Electronic Industry Code of Conduct,* v3.0 (2009), p. 1, at www.eicc.info/EICC%20CODE.htm.

[44] Sir Geoffrey Chandler, "The Amnesty International UK Business Group," *The Journal of Corporate Citizenship,* Spring 2009, p. 33.

Reporting and Verification Standards

sustainability reporting

The practice of a corporation publishing information about its economic, social, and environmental performance.

There is growing demand for accurate information about CSR performance. This has led more companies to issue public reports that describe and measure their actions, a practice often called *sustainability reporting*. The reports take many forms. Information may be part of the annual report or appear in separate publications. It is costly to collect data and compile such reports, but they have benefits. They protect corporate reputation and they are a management tool for measuring performance and progress.

Two problems with sustainability reporting are, first, that defining and measuring social performance is difficult and, second, that the reports are not comparable from company to company. But uniformity is growing. In 2000, an organization in the Netherlands, the Global Reporting Initiative (GRI), released a model reporting framework that lists specific performance indicators and methods for doing the reports. Adoption of the GRI format has been so rapid that now 77 percent of the 250 largest global corporations are using it.[45]

Because of deep cynicism about corporate candor, institutions that independently verify reports have arisen. A nonprofit group, AccountAbility, has created a widely used "assurance standard" for independent parties that audit corporate reports for reliability. Reporting is further discussed in Chapter 6.

Certification and Labeling Schemes

Labels are symbols displayed on or with a product to certify that it, or its production process, meets a set of social or environmental criteria. Such schemes try to create a market for social responsibility by influencing consumers to prefer marked products. Criteria for labels are set by the labeling body, which is often a cooperative project of industry, NGOs, unions, and governments. Certified companies must usually allow independent auditors to inspect and monitor their activities. Typically the process is funded with licensing fees paid by producers, importers, and retailers. Here are several examples from dozens of such schemes.

- The *Kimberley Process Certification Scheme* is a device to stop the flow of so-called "blood" diamonds, which are rough diamonds from parts of Africa where sales to exporters fund civil wars and rebellions. Its governing body consists of 74 member nations, including all major diamond producing and importing nations, representatives from the diamond industry, and human rights groups. Each participating country is required to enforce trade rules. Companies export diamonds only in sealed, tamper-proof containers tagged with compliance certificates. Smuggling around the scheme persists, but after its inception in 2003 the share of "blood diamonds" in world markets dropped from 15 percent to 0.1 percent.[46]

- The *Forest Stewardship Council* sets standards to certify that forests are managed sustainably and certifies to mills, wholesalers, and retailers that wood

[45] KPMG, *International Survey of Corporate Responsibility Reporting 2008* (Amstelveen, the Netherlands: KPMG, 2008), p. 35.

[46] These percentages are in Vivienne Walt, "Diamonds Aren't Forever," *Fortune,* December 11, 2006, p. 89; and "Kimberley Process: Frequently Asked Questions," at www.kimberleyprocess.com/faqs/index_en.html, accessed December 5, 2009.

they buy is responsibly grown and harvested. It is an international body with 800 members, including timber companies, foresters, and NGOs ranging from Greenpeace Russia to the East Sepik Council of Women in Papua New Guinea. Members make decisions in a fastidiously democratic assembly where weighted counting gives the global North and South each 50 percent of votes. Because the Council's standards are high, it must compete with rival and less costly forest certification schemes created by industry that confuse consumers who are largely ignorant of differences between standards. The Council certifies only 5 percent of the world's timber harvest.[47]

fair trade
The idea that ethical consumers will pay a premium for commodities from producers in developing nations who use sustainable methods.

- Many certifications promote *fair trade*, or the idea that small, marginal producers in Africa, Asia, and Latin America should be paid a "fair," that is, a stable, guaranteed, and sometimes above-market price for crops so they can make a living and engage in sustainable farming practices. *Transfair USA*, a coalition of religious, human rights, labor, and consumer groups, offers the trademarked *Fair Trade Certified* term and logo on agricultural products such as coffee, tea, cocoa, honey, rice, and flowers exported to the United States. With coffee, for example, it audits sales of beans by farmers to companies. Its black-and-white logo depicting a farmer in front of a globe certifies that coffee farmers were paid a guaranteed minimum price.

Management Standards

management standard
A model of the methods an organization can use to achieve certain goals.

A *management standard* is a model of the methods an organization can use to achieve certain goals. The use of quality standards is widespread. Now, actors in the global CSR network have established standards for social responsibility or elements of social responsibility such as health and safety or environmental protection.

- The *EcoManagement and Audit Scheme* (EMAS) is a standard that rises above legal requirements for environmental performance in European nations that already have some of the world's strictest regulations.[48] Companies that join this voluntary initiative must reduce emissions, energy use, and waste beyond legal requirements. They also agree to publish regular statements of their environmental performance and have them checked for accuracy by outside auditors. More than 4,000 firms participate. They are allowed to use the EMAS logo in ads that make green claims for their products. EMAS is run by representatives of governments, industries, unions, and NGOs.

- The *International Organization for Standardization* (ISO), which has already created widely used standards in other areas, for example, ISO 9000 on quality and *ISO 14000* on the environment, is developing a broad new social responsibility standard named *ISO 2600* intended to set forth underlying principles, core subjects, and methods for integrating social performance in the plans, systems, and processes of organizations. The standard is now in draft form.[49]

[47] Tom Arup, "Timber Standard Pleases Union but Fails to Impress Greens," *Sydney Morning Herald,* November 30, 2009, p. 2.

[48] The standard is set forth in "Regulation (ED) No. 761/2001 of the European Parliament and of the Council of 19 March 2001," *Official Journal of the European Communities,* April 24, 2001, p. L114/1.

[49] International Organization for Standardization, *Draft International Standard ISO/DIS 2600: Guidance on Social Responsibility* (Geneva: ISO, 2009).

Social Investment and Lending

Equity capital and borrowing are critical to corporate financial strategies. Knowing this, actors in the international CSR movement have tried to introduce social criteria into capital markets. Initiatives such as these threaten to raise the cost of capital for corporations that dodge evolving norms.

- Under the auspices of the United Nations, a coalition of institutional investors and civil society groups created a set of voluntary *Principles for Responsible Investment*. Its signatories, about 560 banks, pension funds, hedge funds, and insurers with, collectively, $18 trillion in assets, must consider a company's environmental, social, and governance performance when they evaluate investments.[50] They also must accept a duty to pressure corporations in the direction of responsible behavior.

- The *FTSE4Good Global Index* is intended to set the world standard for those wanting to invest in companies following "good standards of corporate responsibility." The index was started by a British company in 2001. Scanning a universe of about 2,000 companies on 23 world stock exchanges, it first excludes companies producing tobacco, nuclear weapons, nuclear power, and major weapons systems. From what remains, it includes approximately 650 companies that meet somewhat stringent criteria for the practice of CSR. Since its inception it has delisted more than 200 companies for lapses in meeting its standards.

Government Actions

Governments advance corporate responsibility mainly with binding national regulation. Some also promote voluntary actions. European nations lead. The European Commission and European Parliament generate a stream of communications and reports encouraging codes, labels, and forums. The Belgium government set up the *Belgium Social Label,* a brown-and-blue cartoon of a person with arms uplifted in exultation, presumably because the company that made the product saw to it that its entire production chain followed basic International Labor Organization standards. Sweden requires its 55 state-owned companies to produce a yearly sustainability report based on Global Reporting Initiative guidelines. Denmark requires several thousand companies to report annually on their efforts to reduce environmental impacts.

Elsewhere there is also encouragement. The United States does far less than most European governments, but one study found 50 federal activities that could be classified as promoting CSR.[51] However, most were awards or programs with tiny budgets. In Australia the legislature published a study of global CSR initiatives and recommended "greater uptake" of the idea by Australian companies.[52]

---

[50] PRI, "New Data Signals Growing 'Culture Change' Amongst Significant Portion of Global Investors," media release, July 16, 2009, p. 1.

[51] General Accountability Office, *Globalization: Numerous Federal Activities Complement U.S. Business's Global Corporate Social Responsibility Efforts,* GAO-05-744, August 2005.

[52] Parliamentary Joint Committee on Corporations and Financial Sectors, *Corporate Responsibility: Managing Risk and Creating Value* (Canberra: Senate Printing Unit, Parliament House, June 2006).

Although the governments of developing nations where human rights abuses, corruption, and ecosystem destruction are targeted sometimes resist or ignore efforts to impose Western-based schemes of civil regulation, the Chinese commission that manages state-owned firms for the central government recently issued a set of CSR guidelines for the companies it oversees. Calling CSR "an unavoidable pathway" that "has become a key criteria worldwide," these guidelines call on the firms to "develop in a people-centered, scientific way and make profits," and emphasize energy conservation, philanthropy, and jobs creation as core CSR duties.[53] Since the commission appoints, removes, disciplines, and sets the salaries of managers at state-owned firms, the guidelines are unlikely to be ignored. Some companies have already set up internal "CSR work commissions" to implement them.

Civil Society Vigilance

NGOs watch multinational corporations and police actions they see as departing from emerging global norms. A direct action campaign by experienced activists is unpleasant and, if it carries any element of validity, very dangerous to brand reputation. The abiding threat of attack inspires entry into various code, labeling, reporting, and standards schemes.

- The force behind the Electronic Industry Code of Conduct noted earlier is the Catholic Agency for Overseas Development. When the group issued a report on "computer factory sweatshops" and began a "Clean Up Your Computer" campaign, it galvanized Hewlett-Packard, IBM, Dell, and others in the industry to create a protective code of conduct.[54]

- In 2000, the Rainforest Action Network (RAN) began a campaign against Citigroup, alleging that the bank's loans funded socially and environmentally disruptive pipelines, mines, dams, and other projects in developing countries. RAN was the sharp edge of a coalition of more than 100 NGOs opposed to bank lending that failed to take deforestation, pollution, and disruption of indigenous peoples into account. Three years of artful attack on the bank's reputation and harassment of its executives went by until Citigroup tired. Working with other banks it adopted industry lending guidelines based on sustainability guidelines then in use by the World Bank. Today, largely due to pressure by RAN, 69 of the world's largest banks, making 95 percent of the world's private development loans, subscribe to these "voluntary" principles, now called the *Equator Principles*.[55] The *Principles* divide projects into high, medium, and low social and environmental risk and compel borrowers to meet standards for ecological protection and to consult with native peoples. In effect, this is a global environmental regulatory scheme for the banking, mining, forestry, and energy industries.

[53] State-Owned Assets Supervision and Administration Commission, *CSR Guideline for State-Owned Enterprises (SOE)*, January 4, 2008, trans. Guo Peiyuan, 1(a) and 1(d).

[54] CAFOD, *Clean Up Your Computer: Working Conditions in the Electronics Sector* (London: CAFOD, January 2004); and Peter Burrows, "Stalking High-Tech Sweatshops," *BusinessWeek*, June 19, 2006, p. 62.

[55] International Finance Corporation, Treasury Department, *Funding Operations* (Washington, DC: World Bank Group, July 2009), slide 5.

ASSESSING THE EVOLVING GLOBAL CSR SYSTEM

In sum, a perceived shortage of regulation over multinational corporations has been countered mainly by action within civil society to create private regulatory schemes. Elements of civil society, often working through the United Nations, came together on statements and conventions that congealed global norms, raising expectations of corporate behavior and opening miscreants to the reputation risks of activist "name and shame" campaigns. As this dynamic unfolded over 20 years, regulatory leadership flowed from nations to other actors, particularly to multiparty alliances combining NGOs, UN agencies, unions, and corporations. These bodies, novel at first, but now duplicating endlessly, direct corporate adherence to the CSR standards they create using tools such as codes, labels, audits, and certifications. So prolific is the device that one or more standards are now established for almost every industry and commodity.

The growth of civil regulation invites reflection. First, it reveals that for much of civil society constructive engagement with corporations has become more important than hostility and attack. There is a realization that business has unique organizational and financial capacities that can be brought to bear on global problems. Second, the multinational corporation is slowly and reluctantly being redefined as a stakeholder entity. In the new world of international civil regulation it has duties toward the environment, human rights, and social development as real as its duties to shareowners. Third, civil regulation is a pragmatic solution to the regulatory vacuum. It has partially, but not fully, compensated for lack of binding global regulation. Though piecemeal, experimental, partial, and subject to enforcement failures it is a forceful presence.

Finally, because it is an extra-state phenomenon, civil regulation raises issues of representation. Conservatives find the new system undemocratic because it relies heavily for monitoring and compliance on progressive NGOs that are self-constituted communities of belief, unelected and not clearly or formally representative even of their membership rolls, let alone of the people in developing countries affected by transnational corporations.[56] Goals are dominated by the muses/anxieties of Western activists.

CONCLUDING OBSERVATIONS

In this chapter we focused on defining and explaining the idea of corporate social responsibility and its evolution. Figure 5.4 summarizes this evolution.

Historically, corporations have been motivated primarily by profit. However, as they have grown in size and power they have been exhorted and pressured to alter this single-minded focus. This is because (1) the ideology of corporate social responsibility has gradually evolved an expanded ethical duty and (2) the power of stakeholders to enforce this duty has increased.

[56] Larry Cata Backer, 'Multinational Corporations, Transnational Law: The United Nations' Norms on the Responsibilities of Transnational Corporations as a Harbinger of Corporate Social Responsibility in International Law," *Columbia Human Rights Law Review*, Winter 2006, pp. 386–88.

FIGURE 5.4   The Evolution of Corporate Social Responsibility

Although the term corporate social responsibility is of relatively recent use, the idea it represents has been under construction for more than two centuries. These timelines show how its elements have evolved.

Doubts about CSR remain. In the progressive community there is cynicism about its limits. On the conservative side, elaborate CSR schemes might just be abandoned, replaced by nothing, allowing the natural grace of laissez-faire room to work. Debates over its proper nature will continue. Yet no radical changes are likely; the evolved CSR ideology that now exists is entrenched. No corporation of any size can afford to ignore the range of social obligations beyond market activity. In the next chapter, we will discuss specific management practices used to carry out corporate responsibility.

Jack Welch at General Electric

In April 1981 John Francis "Jack" Welch, Jr., became chief executive officer of General Electric. He held the position for 20 years until retiring in September 2001. During that time, he transformed GE, turning a solidly profitable manufacturing company into an exceptionally profitable conglomerate dominated by service businesses. If you had invested $100 in GE stock when Welch took the reins and held it for 20 years, it would have been worth $6,749.

Welch is lauded for his creative management style and became a national business hero. A fawning *BusinessWeek* article called him "America's #1 Manager."[1] *Fortune* magazine gushed that GE under Welch was "the best-managed, best-regarded company in America."[2] Yet the intense, aggressive Welch made fortunes for GE shareholders using methods that had mixed impacts on employees, unions, communities, other companies, and governments. As a result, not everyone sees the GE performance as a

---

[1] John A. Byrne, "Jack: A Close-Up Look at How America's #1 Manager Runs GE," *BusinessWeek*, June 8, 1998, p. 91.

[2] Jerry Useem, "It's All Yours, Jeff. Now What?" *Fortune*, September 17, 2001, p. 64.

model for corporate social responsibility. Upon Welch's retirement, the *Multinational Monitor,* a progressive magazine founded by Ralph Nader, devoted an entire issue to making "The Case Against GE." The lead editorial branded Welch as a corporate titan opposed to rules of society and said his actions were "disastrous" for workers and communities.[3]

Did General Electric under Jack Welch carry out the full range of its duties to society? Did it fall short? Readers are invited to decide.

JACK WELCH RISES

Most top executives come from backgrounds of wealth and privilege. Jack Welch is an exception. He was born in 1935 to working-class Irish parents in a small Massachusetts town. His father was a quiet, passive man who endured as a railroad conductor punching tickets on commuter trains. Welch's mother was a dominating woman who caused her husband to wilt but instilled a powerful drive in her son. Welch was an outstanding student at the University of Massachusetts at Amherst and went on to get a doctorate in chemical engineering at the University of Illinois.

After graduating, he started working at a GE plastics factory in 1960. His tremendous energy and ambition were very apparent. He was so competitive in weekend softball games that his aggressive play alienated co-workers and he stopped going. After one year, he threatened to quit when he got the same $1,000 raise as everyone else. His boss cajoled him into staying and as the years and promotions flashed by he never again wavered.

As he rose, Welch exhibited a fiery temperament and expected those around him to share his intensity. He was blunt, impatient with subordinates, and emotionally volatile. He loved no-holds-barred discussions in meetings but frequently put people on the spot, saying, "My six-year-old kid could do better than that."[4] With every promotion, he sized up his new staff with a cold eye and purged those who failed to impress him. "I'm the first to admit," he says, "I could be impulsive in removing people during those early days."[5]

This was just preparation for the big leagues to come. GE had a polished corporate culture reflecting the Eastern establishment values of its leadership over many decades. Welch did not fit. He was impatient, frustrated by the company's bureaucracy, and lacking in deference. With this mismatch GE might have repulsed Welch at some point, but his performance was outstanding. Several times he got mixed reviews for a promotion, but because of exemplary financial results he was never blocked. In 1981 he took over as CEO of one of America's singular companies.

THE STORY OF GENERAL ELECTRIC

The lineage of General Electric goes back to 1879 when Thomas Alva Edison (1847–1931), with the backing of banker J. P. Morgan, started the Edison Electric Light Company to make lightbulbs and electrical equipment. Although Edison was a great inventor, he was a poor manager and the company lost ground. So in 1892 Morgan took charge, engineering a merger with a competitor and plotting to reduce Edison to a figurehead in the new company.

Morgan disposed of Edison's top managers and dropped the word Edison from its name so that the firm became simply General Electric Company. Morgan sat as a commanding figure on the new company's board. Although Edison was also a director, he attended only the first meeting and never returned.[6]

After the merger, GE built a near-monopoly in the incandescent bulb market. Over the years, great things emerged from the company. Early in the twentieth century, its motors worked the Panama Canal locks, powered battleships, and ran locomotives.[7] GE's research labs bred a profusion of new electrical appliances, including fans, toasters, refrigerators, vacuum cleaners, ranges, garbage disposals, air conditioners, and irons. At first these new inventions were very expensive, but as more people purchased them, production costs fell and they became commodities within the reach of every family. By 1960 GE was credited with a remarkable list of other inventions, including

---

[3] "You Don't Know Jack," *Multinational Monitor,* July–August 2001, p. 5.

[4] Jack Welch, *Jack: Straight from the Gut* (New York: Warner Books, 2001), p. 43.

[5] Ibid., p. 43.

[6] Thomas F. O'Boyle, *At Any Cost: Jack Welch, General Electric, and the Pursuit of Profit* (New York: Knopf, 1998), p. 55.

[7] For more on the early history of GE see John Winthrop Hammond, *Men and Volts: The Story of General Electric* (Philadelphia: J. B. Lippincott, 1948).

the X-ray machine, the motion picture with sound, fluorescent lighting, the diesel-electric locomotive, the jet engine, synthetic diamonds, the hard plastic Lexan, and Silly Putty.[8]

As it added manufacturing capacity to build these inventions, GE grew. By 1981, when Jack Welch took the reins, the company had $27 billion in revenues and 404,000 employees. It was organized into 50 separate businesses reporting to a layer of six sector executives at corporate headquarters in Fairfield, Connecticut, who in turn reported to the CEO. To make it run, a large, almost imperial staff of researchers and planners created detailed annual plans setting forth revenue goals and other objectives for each business.

THE WELCH ERA BEGINS

Welch believes that managers must confront reality and adapt to the world as it is, not as they wish it to be. As he studied GE's situation in the early 1980s, he saw a corporation that needed to change. GE's manufacturing businesses were still profitable, but margins were shrinking. The wages of American workers were rising even as their productivity was declining. International competition was growing, particularly from the Japanese, who had cost advantages because of a weak yen. Although GE seemed healthy at the moment, ominous forces were gathering. In addition, Welch saw GE bloated with layers of bureaucracy that infuriated him by slowing decisions and frustrating change. The company, as currently operated, could not weather the competitive storms ahead. It would have to change.

Welch articulated a simple guiding vision. Every GE business would be the number one or number two player in its industry. If it failed this test it would be fixed, closed, or sold. In addition, Welch said all GE businesses would have to fit into one of three areas—core manufacturing, technology, or services. Any business that fell outside these three hubs was a candidate for sale or closure. This included manufacturing businesses that could not sustain high profit margins.

In the next five years, Welch executed his strategy by closing 73 plants, selling 232 businesses, and eliminating 132,000 workers from GE payrolls.[9] As he conformed GE to his vision, he also bought hundreds of

Jack Welch (1935–). Source: © Bob Daemmrich/CORBIS

other businesses large and small. Within GE businesses he eliminated jobs through attrition, layoffs, and outsourcing. In the largest acquisition of that period, Welch acquired RCA in 1985. RCA was a giant electronics and broadcasting conglomerate with a storied history as the company that had developed radio technology. After paying $6.7 billion for RCA, Welch chopped it up, keeping NBC and selling other businesses one by one, in effect, destroying the giant company as an organizational entity. As jobs vanished, Welch got the nickname "Neutron Jack," comparing him with a neutron bomb that left buildings standing but killed everyone inside.

Welch also attacked the GE bureaucracy. One problem was its size. There were too many vice presidents, too many layers, and too many staffs with authority to review and approve decisions. A second problem was the bureaucratic mentality in which headquarters staff practiced a "superficial congeniality" that Welch interpreted as smiling to your face and getting you behind your back.[10] He demolished the hierarchy by laying

---

[8] Thomas F. O'Boyle, "'At Any Cost' Is Too High," *Multinational Monitor,* July–August 2001, p. 41.

[9] Frank Swoboda, "GE Picks Welch's Successor," *Washington Post,* November 28, 2000, p. E1.

[10] Welch, *Jack,* p. 96.

EXHIBIT 1

The Vitality Curve

Source: *Jack: Straight from the Gut* by Jack Welch with John A. Byrne. Copyright © 2001 by John F. Welch, Jr. Foundation. By permission of Grand Central Publishing. All rights reserved.

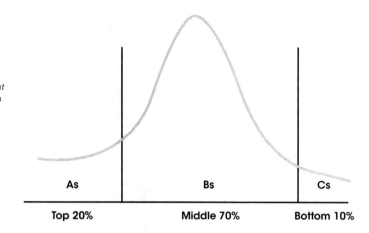

As	Bs	Cs
Top 20%	**Middle 70%**	**Bottom 10%**

off thousands of central staff in strategic planning, personnel, and other areas. Then he set out to change GE's culture by promoting the notion of a "boundary-less" organization, or one in which ideas were freely exchanged so that organizational learning could rapidly occur. Welch compared GE to an old house:

> Floors represent layers and the walls functional barriers. To get the best out of an organization, these floors and walls must be blown away, creating an open space where ideas flow freely, independent of rank or function.[11]

Later, Welch introduced the practice of "workout" sessions in which employees in every GE business had an opportunity to confront their bosses to express frustration with bureaucratic practices and suggest more efficient alternatives. Managers in these sessions sat in front of a room filled with subordinates and had to agree or disagree on the spot to carry out suggestions. Thousands of such sessions were held to drive out the bureaucratic mentality.

Welch also used Crotonville, the company's training center on the Hudson River, to meet with managers and instill his vision. He invited candid discussions, and gradually the company culture became more informal and open.

DIFFERENTIATION

Welch is convinced that having the right people in management positions is the single most important cause of success in a business. Early in his career, he developed a colorful vocabulary to differentiate

between players. Inept managers were "turkeys" and "dinks," standouts were called "all-stars." As CEO he reinforced strategic initiatives with a system of "differentiation" that generously rewarded managers who achieved performance goals and got rid of those who missed them. In this system, every year each GE business was forced to evaluate its managers and rank them on a "vitality curve" that differentiated among As, Bs, and Cs. The As were committed people, filled with passion for their jobs, who took initiative and exceeded performance goals. They had what Welch called "the four Es of GE leadership":

> very high *energy* levels, the ability to *energize* others around common goals, the *edge* to make tough yes-and-no decisions, and finally, the ability to consistently *execute* and deliver on their promises.[12]

The vitality curve was Darwinian. The As were the top 20 percent, Bs were the middle 70 percent, and Cs were the bottom 10 percent (see Exhibit 1). The As received salary increases, promotions, and stock options. Welch followed their careers closely. He kept large loose-leaf notebooks containing evaluations of the top 750 of GE's 4,000 managers. Bs were considered vital to the success of the company and were coached so that some would become As. Cs were not worth wasting time on and were dismissed. The process was repeated annually, and each time the bottom 10 percent had to go. The curve applied to every GE business. No business leader could claim that his or her group was an exception, though some tried. Filling the A, B, and C categories forced difficult decisions. If 20 managers were evaluated, 2 had

[11] Welch, *Jack*, p. 162.

[12] Welch, *Jack*, p. 158.

to be placed at the bottom and their careers at GE ended. After several years of getting rid of low performers, the leaders of GE businesses resisted classifying anyone as a C, but Welch was relentless. If they didn't identify the bottom 10 percent, he refused to carry out stock option and salary recommendations for the entire group until they did. In this way, the bar of performance was continually raised.

Welch compared people to plants. "If they grow, you have a beautiful garden," he said. "If they don't, you cut them out."[13] He disagreed with those who found the system heartless:

> Some think it's cruel or brutal to remove the bottom 10 percent of our people. It isn't. It's just the opposite. What I think is brutal and "false kindness" is keeping people around who aren't going to grow and prosper . . . The characterization of a vitality curve as cruel stems from false logic and is an outgrowth of a culture that practices false kindness.[14]

AN ASSESSMENT OF THE WELCH YEARS

With Jack Welch at the helm GE sustained exceptionally high rates of profitability, and shareholders were enriched. Even with five stock splits, earnings per share rose from $0.46 in 1981 to $1.07 in 2000, his last full year as CEO, and total return on GE shares averaged 21.5 percent.[15] In 2000 GE reported a net operating margin of 19 percent and earned 27 percent on invested capital.[16] These are high figures for a large multinational corporation.

Welch also reshaped GE. He continuously bought and sold businesses both large and small. During his last four years alone he made more than 400 acquisitions. One underlying reason for the increasing profitability of GE is that through this churning of businesses GE's center of gravity shifted from manufacturing to services. The GE he inherited earned 85 percent of its revenues from manufacturing; the GE he created got 70 percent of its revenues from services.[17]

Welch wrung profits from GE by creating a performance culture. Managers were energized. Plants grew more efficient. For instance, when Welch became CEO, GE's locomotive plant in Erie, Pennsylvania, needed 7,500 hourly employees to make 350 locomotives a year. By 2000 productivity had improved so much that only 4,000 workers could make 900 locomotives a year.[18]

The story of the Welch years has the elements of legend. An ambitious son of working-class parents rises through hard work to command a mighty company, inspire managers everywhere, and become rich along with other company shareholders. To reward Welch for the shower of wealth he created, in his last year the GE board awarded him a special bonus bringing his yearly compensation to $174 million.[19] At this time he held more than 22 million shares of GE stock and options worth almost $1 billion, as shown in Exhibit 2. This is astronomical compensation for one person, but his $972 million in stock is only four-hundredths of 1 percent of the $460 billion in equity value created during his tenure.

Exhibit 2 shows how directors shared in the GE equity windfall. When they joined the board, each outside (nonemployee) director was given 5,000 shares of GE stock and a $150,000 life insurance policy. Thereafter, each year directors were given $75,000, $2,000 for each of the 10 meetings they were required to attend, and options on 18,000 more shares of GE stock. If they retired at age 65 with five years of service, they were eligible to receive the $75,000 annual retainer for life. There were other rewards. One GE business sold diamonds and directors could buy them at cost for their personal use or for spouses. The year that Welch retired, the group purchased $975,595 worth of diamonds and must have looked very good at the kinds of parties to which laid-off workers were not invited.[20]

While the board feted Welch, not everyone saw his leadership as something to admire or emulate. Early in his career, he was compared to a speedboat

---

[13] Quoted in Carol Hymowitz and Matt Murray, "Raises and Praise or Out the Door—How GE's Chief Rates and Spurs His Employees," *The Wall Street Journal,* June 21, 1999, p. B1.

[14] Welch, *Jack,* p. 162. See also Jack and Suzy Welch, "The Case for 20-70-10," *BusinessWeek,* October 2, 2006, p. 108.

[15] Swoboda, "GE Picks Welch's Successor," p. E1; Julie Schlosser, "Jack? Jack Who?" *Fortune,* September 17, 2001, p. 52.

[16] General Electric Company, *GE Annual Report 2000* (Fairfield, CT: General Electric Company, 2001), p. 42.

[17] James Flanigan, "New Boss's Challenge: To Keep GE Together," *Los Angeles Times,* August 26, 2001, p. C1.

[18] "Dignity and Defiance: An Interview with John Hovis," *Multinational Monitor,* July–August 2001, p. 35.

[19] *General Electric Company, Notice of 2001 Annual Meeting* and *Proxy Statement,* March 9, 2001, pp. 22 and 27.

[20] Ibid., p. 14.

EXHIBIT 2   **The 2001 GE Board of Directors: Market Value of Total Holdings in GE Stock (shaded entries are inside directors)**

Director	Value	Director	Value
James I. Cash Professor, Harvard Business School	$3,719,059	Sam Nunn Former U.S. Senator from Georgia	$4,516,975
Silas S. Cathcart CEO, Illinois Tool Works(ret.)	$34,601,060	Roger S. Penske Chairman, Penske Corp.	$6,844,896
Paolo Fresco Chairman, Fiat	$111,700,043	Frank H. T. Rhodes President Emeritus, Cornell University	$10,931,672
Ann M Fudge Vice President, Kraft Foods	$1,667,828	Andrew C. Sigler CEO, Champion International (ret.)	$5,820,301
Claudio X. Gonzalez CEO, Kimberly-Clark de Mexico	$9,871,797	Douglas A. Warner Chairman, J. P. Morgan Chase & Co.	$8,323,021
Andrea Jung CEO, Avon Products	$2,733,352	Dennis. D. Dammerman Chairman, GE Capital	$187,238,259
Kenneth G. Langone CEO, Invamed Associates	$14,805,848	Jeffrey R. Immelt President, General Electric	$130,853,846
Rochelle B. Lazarus CEO, Ogilvy & Mather Worldwide	$877,690	John F. Welch, Jr. Chairman and CEO, General Electric	$972,022,731
Scott G. McNealy CEO, Sun Microsystems	$2,089,684	Robert Wright Vice Chairman of GE, President, NBC	$229,777,982
Gertrude Michelson Former Senior V.P., Macy's	$14,381,950		

Source: General Electric Company, *Proxy Statement*, March 9, 2001, p. 12. Total holdings include common stock, option holdings, deferred compensation, restricted stock units, and stock appreciation rights.

going down a narrow canal, leaving considerable turbulence in its wake.[21] His detractors say that once Welch was at the master controls of GE he piloted the mammoth organization through global straits the same way. There is no denying that he created wealth. But what were the costs to people, communities, and society? The flaws in the Welch performance, according to critics, include the following.

Loss of Jobs

Early on, Welch was caricatured as a ruthless job cutter. When he became CEO in 1981, the corporate culture reinforced loyalty. People went to work at GE

directly out of college, stayed for 40 years, retired in communities of GE people, and attended GE alumni clubs until rigor mortis set in.

As Welch remodeled GE there were mass layoffs. Within a few years, one of every four employees was gone. Welch believed that the idea of loyalty in GE's culture retarded change, so he rooted it out. At meetings he told employees it was out of fashion. He instructed staff never to use the word *loyalty* in any company handbook or other document. He wanted all GE managers to prove their value every day and said people who knew they could be fired worked harder.

In the Welch years there was tumultuous change in the workforce. No total number exists for workers who lost jobs. When he took over there were 404,000 GE employees; when he left there were 313,000. In

[21] O'Boyle, *At Any Cost,* p. 59.

between, tens of thousands came and went. Union leaders estimate that in his last 15 years GE eliminated 150,000 jobs in the United States through layoffs, subcontracting, and outsourcing to foreign countries.[22] Welch expressed his feelings about these layoffs in his memoirs:

> Removing people will always be the hardest decision a leader faces. Anyone who "enjoys doing it" shouldn't be on the payroll and neither should anyone who "can't do it." I never underestimated the human cost of those layoffs or the hardship they might cause people and communities.[23]

Welch stressed globalization of production to lower costs. Many jobs still existed, but they left the United States. In 1985 the electrical worker's union had 46,000 members working at GE, but by 2001 the number had declined to 16,000. Ed Fire, the union's president, estimates that two-thirds of the 30,000 lost jobs were simply transferred to low-wage countries.[24] GE eliminated additional jobs in the United States by pressuring suppliers to migrate along with it. After moving production to Mexico, for example, GE Aircraft Engines held a conference for supplier companies and told them to cut costs by moving their facilities (and jobs) to Mexico's low-wage labor market or face inevitable loss of their GE business.[25] Says Fire:

> GE is the quintessential American corporation that has engaged in what has been referred to as the "race to the bottom"—finding the lowest wages, the lowest benefit levels and most intolerant working conditions . . . I don't think they have given enough consideration to the consequences, particularly the human consequences, of the decisions they make. In my opinion, the decisions are designed too much to increase the company's profitability at the expense of the employees.[26]

A Flawed Evaluation System

The vitality curve rating method is controversial. Critics argue that forced ranking hurts the morale of employees who are not placed on top. At first, GE ranked employees in five categories instead of three, but it was soon discovered that everyone who failed to land in the top category was demoralized. Hence, three categories were combined into one to create the "vital" 70 percent of Bs in the middle. Disheartening classifications as 2s, 3s, and 4s were abolished.

The system can also hurt teamwork by pitting people against each other. It may encourage backstabbing behavior. Its inflexibility produces unfair results when high-performing and low-performing units must classify managers the same way. The bottom 10 percent in an outstanding business may be better than middle- or top-ranked managers on a weaker team. If the axing of the bottom 10 percent goes on for many years, people who were once in the middle range may find themselves lopped off. Of course, the curve calls the recruiting system into question if recent hires are lost.

Forced ranking was just one source of pressure on GE managers, who were expected to meet high profit goals and knew that if there were too many mistakes or misjudgments Welch would get rid of them. His confrontational style reduced some to tears. He reportedly believed that overweight people were undisciplined. Some GE businesses hid these people when he visited for fear they would catch Welch's eye and lose their jobs. One large manager trying to save his career had surgery to staple his colon.[27] Working at GE was also hard on marriages because of the long hours required to be a player. Welch himself divorced in 1987 and remarried in 1990.

Because of Welch's status as a management icon, his approach to forced ranking has spread widely, imposing the practice on many managers at other corporations. Even small businesses have picked up the idea. The manager of a Fifth Avenue clothing store once took Welch aside and explained that he had 20 sales workers. "Mr. Welch," he asked, "do I really have to let two go?" "You probably do," replied Welch, "if you want the best sales staff on Fifth Avenue."[28]

[22] "GE Fast Facts," GE Workers United, May 7, 2001, at www.geworkersunited.org/news/fast_facts.asp.

[23] Welch, *Jack,* p. 128.

[24] Ed Fire, president of the International Union of Electronic, Electrical, Salaried, Machine and Furniture Workers–Communications Workers of America, the Industrial Division of CWA, "Resisting the Goliath," *Multinational Monitor,* July–August 2001, p. 31.

[25] Robert Weissman, "Global Management by Stress," *Multinational Monitor,* July–August 2001, p. 20.

[26] Fire, "Resisting the Goliath," pp. 31 and 33.

[27] O'Boyle, *At Any Cost,* p. 76.

[28] Welch, *Jack,* p. 434.

No Diversity at the Top

Using the vitality curve Welch created a high-performance management team, but failed to create diversity. The year before Welch retired *The New York Times* reported that although women and minorities were 40 percent of GE's domestic workforce, white men dominated its top leadership. The paper ran a photo collage of the top 31 executives, including heads of the 20 businesses responsible for 90 percent of corporate earnings. All were male and all but one were white.[29]

Diversity was never a priority for Welch. Later, he would explain why not. "Winning companies are meritocracies . . . [that] practice differentiation" and "this is the most effective way for an organization to field the best team." He argued, "Quotas artificially push some people ahead, independent of qualifications" and that slows the rise of star performers, puts "unprepared people" into important jobs, and "doesn't do much for results."[30] In the subhead for its story *The New York Times* challenged Welch with this question: "Can Only White Men Run a Model Company?"

Pollution in the Hudson River

For 35 years several GE manufacturing plants in New York released polychlorinated biphenyls (PCBs) into the Hudson River. They followed permits that set release levels and stopped in 1977 when PCBs were outlawed because of evidence they were toxic to humans and animals. PCBs cause cancer in test animals and probably cause cancer and other illnesses in humans.

More than 100,000 pounds of PCBs released by GE still lay on the riverbed. Although the biggest deposits were covered by new sediments, slowing their release into the river, the fishing industry had been destroyed, fish were unsafe for children or women of childbearing age to eat, and the chemicals gradually spread downstream from hot spots of contamination, flowing down 200 miles of river to the ocean, from there migrating around the planet.

The Environmental Protection Agency (EPA) studied the river, concluding that dredging the

bottom was necessary to remove the dangerous deposits. This would be expensive, and GE was liable for the cost. Welch objected. During his last year as CEO he ordered an extensive campaign of radio and print ads in the Hudson River region to convince residents that dredging would be an ineffective nuisance. It succeeded in dividing them to such an extent that people began to shop only at stores where the owners supported their position and children teased classmates over their parents' views.[31] GE hired 17 lobbyists, including a former senator and six former House members, to fight an extended political battle against the cleanup.[32] Eventually, the company agreed on a cleanup plan, but only after Welch retired.[33]

The GE Pension Fund

During Welch's tenure the GE pension fund covered approximately 485,000 people, including 195,000 who were retired. As the stock market rose in the 1990s, the fund also rose, and by 2001 it totaled $50 billion. Its liabilities, the future payments it must make to retirees, were only $29 billion, leaving a surplus of $21 billion. GE's retirees and their unions requested increased benefits and cost-of-living increases for pensioners, but the company rejected their demands. By law, it did not have to meet more than the original obligations.

Welch understood that there were several benefits in leaving the pension plan overfunded. First, it generated bottom-line profits. Under accounting rules, a company can put interest earned by the pension fund on the balance sheet as revenue, and during the Welch years these earnings increased GE's net by as much as 13.7 percent.[34] Second, these "vapor profits" increased the income of top GE executives, whose bonuses were tied to corporate profits. And third, the excess funding made it easier for GE

[29] Mary Williams Walsh, "Where G.E. Falls Short: Diversity at the Top," *The New York Times*, September 3, 2000, sec. 3, pp. 1 and 13.

[30] Jack Welch with Suzy Welch, *Winning* (New York: HarperCollins, 2005), p. 346.

[31] John Glionna, "Dredging Up Ill Will on the Hudson," *Los Angeles Times*, October 1, 2001, p. A17.

[32] Charlie Cray, "Toxins on the Hudson," *Multinational Monitor*, July–August 2001.

[33] "GE's New Image: The Company Offers to Cooperate in Dredging the Hudson of PCBs," *The Times Union*, April 11, 2002, p. A12.

[34] Rob Walker, "Overvalued: Why Jack Welch Isn't God," *The New Republic*, June 18, 2001, p. 22. See *GE Annual Report 2000*, Notes to Consolidated Financial Statements, 6, "Pension Benefits."

to acquire companies with underfunded pension plans. This eased deal making, but involved sharing funds set aside for GE workers and retirees with people who got a windfall coming in after careers in other companies.

After being pressured by unions and pensioners, GE announced increases of 15 to 35 percent in 2000. But since 1965 prices had risen by 60 percent, so retirees were still losing ground.[35] Helen Quirini, 81, was part of a group protesting GE's failure to be more generous. After working 39 years at a GE factory, one year less than Welch's 40-year tenure, she retired in 1980 and was receiving $737 a month, or $8,844 a year. She believed that GE management was "out all the time trying to figure out how to screw us" using "accounting gimmicks."[36]

Welch's GE pension is $357,128 a month. Court documents filed in proceedings when Welch divorced his second wife in 2002 revealed that he spent an average of $8,982 a month on food and beverages, slightly more than Helen Quirini's yearly pension income.[37] A 1996 retention agreement between Welch and the GE board also granted him nonmonetary perquisites in retirement. He got lifetime use of a spacious apartment owned by GE at the Trump International Hotel and Tower on Central Park West in New York, including a cook, a housekeeper, and a wait staff plus flowers, laundry, dry cleaning, newspaper and magazine subscriptions, and front-row seats at sporting and entertainment events.[38] He was allowed unlimited use of GE's corporate jets. Criticism of these arrangements arose when they were detailed during the divorce. Although he felt there was nothing improper, he elected to pay GE "between $2 and $2.5 million a year" for continued use of the apartment and the planes.[39]

Criminality at GE

Pressure for performance tempts employees to cut corners. Welch knew this and tried to fuse high performance and integrity in the GE culture.[40] In his own words:

> If there was one thing I preached every day at GE, it was integrity. It was our No. 1 value. Nothing came before it. We never had a corporate meeting where I didn't emphasize integrity in my closing remarks.[41]

Yet during his tenure, GE committed a long string of civil and criminal transgressions. The *Multinational Monitor* compiled a "GE Rap Sheet," listing 39 law violations, court-ordered remedies, and fines in the 1990s alone.[42] Many are for pollution hazards from GE facilities. Others are for consumer fraud, including a $165,000 fine for deceptive advertising of lightbulbs and a $100 million fine on GE Capital for unfair debt-collection practices. Still others are for defense contracting fraud, including a $69 million fine for diverting fighter contract funds to other purposes and other fines for overcharging on contracts.

Since GE is such a large company, technical violations of complex regulations and incidents of wrongdoing by individual managers are inevitable. The *Multinational Monitor* sees "a consistent pattern of violating criminal and civil laws over many years."[43] The key question is whether GE's malfeasance increased because of relentless performance pressure on its managers.

THE WELCH ERA AND WHAT FOLLOWED

General Electric in the Welch era fulfilled its primary economic responsibilities to society. It was remarkably profitable. It paid taxes. Shareholders, including pension and mutual funds, were enriched. Many of its directors and managers became multimillionaires

[35] "GE Pension Fund Story: Workers Pay, GE Benefits," GE Workers United, April 1, 2001, at www.geworkersunited.org/pensions/index.asp?ID_61.

[36] Vincent Lloyd, "Penny Pinching the Retirees at GE," *Multinational Monitor,* July–August 2001, p. 23.

[37] "Here's the Retirement Jack Welch Built: $1.4 Million a Month," *The Wall Street Journal,* October 31, 2002, p. A1.

[38] Geraldine Fabrikant, "G.E. Expenses for Ex-Chief Cited in Filing," *The New York Times,* September 6, 2002, p. C1.

[39] Jack Welch, "My Dilemma and How I Resolved It," *The New York Times,* September 16, 2002, p. A14.

[40] For a description of his efforts see a book by GE's senior vice president for public affairs during the Welch years, Ben W. Heineman, Jr., *High Performance with High Integrity* (Boston: Harvard Business Press, 2008).

[41] Welch, *Jack,* pp. 279–80.

[42] "GE: Decades of Misdeeds and Wrongdoing," *Multinational Monitor,* July–August 2001, p. 26.

[43] Ibid., p. 30.

in GE stock. Welch believed he was acting for the greater good.

> I believe social responsibility begins with a strong, competitive company, only a healthy enterprise can improve and enrich the lives of people and their communities . . . That's why a CEO's primary social responsibility is to assure the financial success of the company. Only a healthy, winning company has the resources and the capability to do the right thing.[44]

In September 2001 Welch was succeeded by a new CEO, Jeffrey Immelt, a carefully groomed Harvard MBA drawn from GE's stable of stars. The new leader proved to have different values. Shortly after taking over he reversed Welch's two decades of opposition to cleaning up the Hudson River and agreed to a cleanup that would cost GE more than $1 billion.[45] He retained the ranking process for managers, but loosened rigid Welch-era guidelines. Now the bottom 10 percent could be 5 percent or 15 percent, but did not have to be exactly 10 percent. He joined the board of directors of Catalyst, a New York organization that promotes progress of women in management through research about sexism. And he appointed a new vice president for corporate citizenship.

But his real love was the environment. In 2002 a Catholic group filed a shareholder's proposal asking the company to measure its global warming gas emissions. It got only 20 percent of the vote at the annual meeting, but Immelt ordered an inventory anyway, then, over objections by subordinates who doubted global warming, pledged to cut GE's emissions. In 2005 Immelt launched GE's "eco-imagination" initiative based on a strategy of profiting from efforts to stop climate change. It focused the corporation on energy-saving, less polluting technologies, moving it into solar panels, wind turbines, coal gasification, recyclable plastics, and hybrid locomotives. Again, some hard-bitten, profit-focused managers resisted, but Immelt pushed on.

Immelt was more visibly alert to GE's social and environmental impacts than Welch. By 2008 the company was the second most socially responsible company among the largest 100 global corporations in one

[44] Welch, *Jack*, pp. 381–82.
[45] See the story of "The Majestic Hudson River," in Chapter 13.

prominent ranking by NGOs.[46] Yet for shareholders, his leadership was bad news.

If you had invested $10,000 in GE on the day Welch retired in 2001, counting dividends your investment shrank to $4,648 at the end of 2010, a loss of 54 percent. It was, of course, a difficult period. Four days after Immelt took over terrorists in jets with GE engines destroyed World Trade Center buildings insured by GE, leading to a global recession. Late in 2008 a global financial crisis caused the stock market to plummet. Nevertheless, over Immelt's tenure, GE underperformed the Dow Jones Industrial Index, a benchmark of large peer corporations. If you had put $10,000 into the Dow the day Welch retired you would have had $11,578 at the end of 2010, even with GE weighing down the index, a meager return for nine years, but 82 percent better than GE's return alone.

Questions

1. Corporate social responsibility is defined in Chapter 5 as the corporate duty to create wealth by using means that avoid harm to, protect, or enhance societal assets. Did GE in the Welch era fulfill this duty? Could it have done better? What should it have done?

2. Does GE under Welch illustrate a narrower view of corporate social responsibility closer to Friedman's view that the only social responsibility is to increase profits while obeying the law?

3. How well did GE conform with the "General Principles of Corporate Social Responsibility" set forth in the section of that title in the chapter?

4. What are the pros and cons of ranking shareholders over employees and other stakeholders? Is it wrong to see employees as costs of production? Should GE have rebalanced its priorities?

5. Was GE a more socially responsible corporation in the Welch era or the Immelt aftermath? In which era did it give the most benefit to society? What lesson(s) can be learned from the differences?

[46] This was the "Accountability Rating 2008: Full G100 Ranking," by the AccountAbility and Two Tomorrows networks, at http://www.accountabilityrating.com/latest_overview.asp. Vodafone was ranked first.

Chapter Six

Implementing Corporate Social Responsibility

The Bill & Melinda Gates Foundation

Growing up in Seattle, William H. Gates III was a slender, intense boy with a messy room and a dazzling mind. At age seven or eight he read the entire *World Book Encyclopedia.* At his family's church the minister challenged young congregants to earn a free dinner by memorizing the Sermon on the Mount, a passage covering Chapters 5, 6, and 7 in the Book of Matthew. At age 11 young Bill became the only one, in 25 years of the minister's experience, ever to recite every word perfectly, never stumbling, never erring.[1] Yet Christianity itself never attracted Gates. Years later he would remark, "There's a lot more I could be doing on a Sunday morning," an incongruous conviction for one who would become devoted to serving the poor.[2] His brilliance, however, was lasting.

At private Lakeside prep school he was a prodigy, often challenging his teachers in class. Obsessed with computers in their then-primitive form, he stayed up all night writing code, a routine that would stay with him. He also read biographies of great historical figures to enter their minds and understand how they succeeded. After high school he attended Harvard University hoping to find an atmosphere of exciting erudition. Instead, he grew bored and left to pursue a fascination with computers. At age 19, Gates founded Microsoft Corporation with his Lakeside School friend Paul Allen. As its leader he was energetic, independent, and confrontational. He developed the reputation of a fanatical competitor willing to appropriate any technology and crush market rivals. He built a dominant business and by 1987, at age 31, he was a billionaire.

Microsoft's stock took flight, making more billions for Gates. However, even as he became the world's richest man he remained absorbed in running the corporation.

[1] James Wallace and Jim Erickson, *Hard Drive: Bill Gates and the Making of the Microsoft Empire* (New York: HarperBusiness, 1992), pp. 6–7.

[2] Garrison Keillor, "Faith at the Speed of Light," *Time,* July 14, 1999, p. 25.

Bill Gates at 31, already a billionaire.
Source: © Ed Kashi/CORBIS.

He put little energy into charity, thinking it could wait until he grew old. But the world expected more. Requests for good deeds and contributions poured in. Gates responded with the help of his father, who worked in a home basement office handling his son's donations.

In 1994, Gates formalized his giving by creating the William H. Gates Foundation and endowing it with $94 million. His father agreed to manage it from the basement. Eventually, this arrangement evolved into the Bill & Melinda Gates Foundation, which included the name of his wife and was run by a professional staff from its new headquarters in Seattle. A foundation is essentially an organization with a pool of money for giving to nonprofit and charitable causes. It is not taxed if it gives out at least 5 percent of its funds each year. Bill Gates gave his foundation $16 billion in Microsoft stock in 2000. Since then he has given more.

Today the Foundation is endowed with $37 billion, making it the world's largest. It has two parts. One part decides what projects to fund. So far, more than $25 billion has been given out. The other part manages the endowment by investing the money to make it grow. The Gateses are deeply involved in the foundation's work, which is based on a pair of "simple values" that inspire them. One is that "all lives—no matter where they are being led—have equal value," and the other is that "to whom much is given, much is expected." Giving is tightly focused on three areas—global health, poverty in developing nations, and U.S. public education.

Because the foundation's endowment is unprecedentedly large, more than the gross domestic products (GDPs) of 107 countries, its goals are ambitious. One is to correct market signals that cause modern medicine to neglect diseases of the poor, thus failing to value all lives equally. Pursuing this goal, the foundation has spent more than $3.8 billion on basic vaccinations for newborns in countries with low GDPs, preventing so far an estimated 3.4 million deaths.[3] It purchases such massive amounts of vaccines that prices fall, allowing doses for millions more children. It spends billions more to create new vaccines for tropical parasitic diseases and to fight a resurgence of polio in Africa.

Bill Gates is characteristically intense, impatient, and direct in the quest to save lives. Learning that the global health staff was paying big travel grants for people to fly to meetings, he issued a curt memo about "rich people flying around to talk to other rich people." He lectured the staff: "Our net effect should be to save years of life for well under $100, so, if we waste even $500,000, we are wasting 5,000 years of life."[4]

[3] Statement of Helen Evans, "State of the World's Vaccines and Immunization Report 2009," GAVI Alliance, October 31, 2009, at www.gavialliance.org.

[4] Quoted in Andrew Jack, "Gates Foundation: Smaller Funds, Hard Decisions," FT.com, September 30, 2009, at www.ft.com.

In 2006 Bill Gates' friend Warren Buffett, chairman of Berkshire Hathaway and, at the time, the world's second-richest man, decided to give most of his wealth away and made a bequest of 10 million shares of Berkshire Hathaway to the Gates Foundation. He believed Bill and Melinda Gates were doing such a superior job he could do no better and, rather than manage billions of dollars of giving on his own, he left his legacy in their hands. At the time, his gift was worth $31 billion, a sum that roughly doubled the Gates endowment. It arrives in annual installments of between $1 billion and $2 billion.

The Gates Foundation confronts enormous social problems. Poverty and disease defy solution. Spending large sums in poor nations is a challenge. Corruption diverts funds. Agencies lack capacity. When infant lives are saved by vaccination, more people live to seek ordinary care. Some nations struggle to provide even the most basic care due to shortages of doctors and nurses. Thus, children are saved from diphtheria only to die in large numbers from common diarrhea.[5] Improving education is another nightmare. After spending $1 billion over six years to make small high schools better, an analysis showed that attendance, graduation rates, and test scores on basic subjects were lower than at similar schools not funded by the Gates Foundation.[6]

Despite its magnificence, the Gates Foundation attracts critics. It is directed by only three trustees–Bill and Melinda Gates and Warren Buffet–putting its multibillion-dollar expenditures in the hands of just two families.[7] It has been called an elitist, antidemocratic institution subsidized by taxpayers (through its tax exemptions) but having no accountability to society.[8] Suspicions are raised that its grants, being so big, shape the world's health agenda and distort research priorities, for example, by over-emphasizing vaccines for tropical diseases as opposed to other forms of treatment.[9]

However, the Gateses and Warren Buffet want to extend the example set by their philanthropy. In 2009 they arranged a series of small, confidential dinners attended by fellow billionaires. Guests were asked to pledge the majority of their wealth to charity, either during their lifetime or at death, each one determining which causes to fund. Over the next year this initiative was formalized in a "Giving Pledge" joined by 40 billionaires.[10] Their pledges are moral commitments; they are not monitored or enforced as legal contracts. The Gateses and Buffet hope to spread the initiative to other nations. Their goal is to divert wealth from the very rich to enlarge the scope of global philanthropy for generations to come.

[5] Laurie Garrett, "The Challenge of Global Health," *Foreign Affairs,* January/February 2007.

[6] The National Institutes of High School Transformation, *Evaluation of the Bill & Melinda Gates Foundation's High School Grants Initiative: 2001–2005 Final Report* (Washington, DC: American Institutes for Research, 2006), pp. 9–10.

[7] Pablo Eisenberg, "The Gates-Buffett Merger Isn't Good for Philanthropy," *Chronicle of Philanthropy,* July 20, 2006, p. 33.

[8] "Philanthropic World Voices Mixed Reaction on Buffett's Gift to Gates Fund," *Chronicle of Philanthropy,* July 20, 2006, p. 12, comment of Rick Cohen.

[9] David McCoy, et al., "The Bill & Melinda Gates Foundation's Grant-Making Programme for Global Health," *The Lancet,* May 9, 2009, p. 1652.

[10] Carol J. Loomis, "The $600 Billion Challenge," *Fortune,* July 5, 2010.

Philanthropy is one method for converting wealth to social value. Bill Gates and Warren Buffet follow a long tradition of rich capitalists who make fortunes, then later in life spend their wealth on works of kindness. In this chapter we will expand on the subject of philanthropy. First, however, we look at how managers implement social responsibility efforts within their firms. Social responsibility, like any other corporate goal, must be systematically planned, organized, and carried out. We will set forth a model of how this can be done.

MANAGING THE RESPONSIVE CORPORATION

Corporations must and do undertake a range of social initiatives. Whatever management's opinion about corporate social responsibility (CSR)—its desirability and its affect on profits—companies must respond to multiple sources of pressure for social actions. There is no alternative. Figure 6.1 shows sources of these pressures on corporations. Each source can generate many demands, some conflicting. We begin here a discussion about how CSR actions may be defined and implemented. First, we look at two elements that can determine the CSR orientation of a firm—its business model and its leadership.

LEADERSHIP AND BUSINESS MODELS

business model
The underlying idea or theory that explains how a business will create value by making and selling products or services in the market.

Founders and top managers set the tone for a company's social response. Their perspective on corporate responsibility is reflected throughout the organization. A *business model* is the underlying idea or theory of how a business will create value by making and selling something in the market. The theory is validated if the business makes a profit. In the universe of business models, there are two distinct types as they relate to corporate responsibility, the progressive model and the traditional model.

A traditional business model is one in which the central strategy for creating value is based on meeting market demands while complying with the law. A progressive business model differs. It creates value by meeting market demands

FIGURE 6.1
Sources of Pressure for Social Responsibility

and, in the process, mitigating social problems or improving society in some way. The value proposition is based on actions that would be considered voluntary responsibilities in more traditional companies. Anita Roddick devised The Body Shop to be a beacon of ethical and social activism in a world darkened with capitalist greed. She saw cosmetics as "an industry dominated by men trying to create needs that don't exist" by selling false, unattainable notions of female beauty. So she devoted herself to "harnessing commercial success to altruistic ideals."[11] Her business model predicted that women would buy from an honest company that used natural ingredients, made realistic product claims, and supported feminist causes. The company's ads encouraged women to accept their natural appearance. One read: "There are 3 billion women who don't look like supermodels and only 8 who do."

Progressive business models are rare, the basis of only a few companies. Other examples include Ben & Jerry's, the ice cream company founded to support Vermont farmers and promote world peace; Patagonia, Inc., a clothing firm that built protection of nature into its strategy; Stonyfield Farm, an organic yogurt maker; and Seventh Generation, which makes nontoxic household cleaning products.[12] The validity of a business model is determined by profit or loss. Each of these businesses has succeeded, at least for an extended time, though each has faced tensions between social visions and market realities. Some have suffered financial difficulties and been absorbed by larger firms run on more traditional business models.

The Body Shop was acquired by L'Oreal, Stonyfield Farm by Groupe Danone, and Ben & Jerry's by Unilever. In each case absorption of the mouse by the elephant has been hard, as the progressive culture clashed with the traditional one. At Unilever, for example, Ben & Jerry's business was subjected to cost-cutting pressures and the social code in its brand was very hard for the big company to decipher, as when it failed to see a problem with using eggs from factory-farmed chickens even as activists were protesting their use.[13]

A rare variant of the progressive model is the large corporation where a founder with noble impulses left a culture inclined to corporate responsibility. The German media conglomerate Bertelsmann was founded in 1835 to publish hymnals by Carl Bertelsmann, a Protestant inspired by the Great Awakening. He believed the primary goal of his company should be to make society better. He shared half the firm's profits with the workers and gave them pensions and other benefits long before other German companies. Bertelsmann has grown into the third-largest global media conglomerate owning, among other brands, BMG Music, Random House, and RCA, but it is still controlled by descendants of the founder. A revealing flash of the old corporate virtue showed when the family fired Bertelsmann's chief

---

[11] Anita Roddick, *Business as Unusual* (London: Thorsons, 2000), pp. 97 and 172.

[12] For other examples see David Y. Choi and Edmund R. Gray, *Values-Centered Entrepreneurs and Their Companies* (New York: Routledge, 2011).

[13] Philip H. Mirvis, "Can You Buy CSR?" *California Management Review*, Fall 2008, p. 114. See also James E. Austin and Herman B. "Dutch" Leonard, "Can the Virtuous Mouse and the Wealthy Elephant Live Happily Ever After?" *California Management Review*, Fall 2008.

executive, in part because he bought Napster, a business they believed was unethical.[14] Another example is Johnson & Johnson, where Robert Wood Johnson, a member of the founding family, wrote "Our Credo" in 1943, just before the company sold stock to the public. Over the years this credo, which required Johnson & Johnson to model a stakeholder firm, became central to the company's culture and helped make major decisions.[15]

Most companies, however, including nearly all of the largest multinationals, begin with no founding impulse for truth, justice, and the stakeholder way. Their social performance is based on responses of their management teams to pressures in the operating environment. Such companies vary in their reaction to these pressures across a spectrum from reluctance to enthusiasm. At the left of this spectrum (see Figure 6.2), companies focus on making a profit and resist demands to go beyond the minimum duty of obeying the law. For them, the extent of citizenship is determined by the power of stakeholders over their behavior. In the middle, companies accept social obligations and may work to mitigate adverse impacts on society before regulations can be passed. And at the right, companies seek to be proactive by anticipating demands and resolving problems before they arise. Companies today are moving to the right, becoming more responsive.

A MODEL OF CSR IMPLEMENTATION

Companies can manage their corporate responsibility efforts by creating an implementation process. Figure 6.3 illustrates a model sequence or method for assessing the societal environment, defining responsibilities, creating a CSR strategy, and

FIGURE 6.2

A Spectrum of Responses to Social Demands

NARROW RESPONSE

EXPANSIVE RESPONSE

| Obey the law, deny further obligations, make a profit. | Obey the law, respond to pressures, accept some added duties. | Anticipate new demands, alter behavior before any pressure, embed management systems and processes to implement CSR. |

[14] Matthew Karnitschnig and Neal E. Boudette, "History Lesson: Battle for the Soul of Bertelsmann Led to CEO Ouster," *The Wall Street Journal,* July 30, 2002, p. A1.

[15] Read "Our Credo" at www.jnj.com/connect/about-jnj/jnj-credo/.

FIGURE 6.3   **A Model Process of CSR Implementation**

| CSR Review | → | CSR Strategy | → | Implementation | → | Reporting and Verification | → |

Revision, Adjustment, Continuous Improvement

taking action. The sequence implied in this basic model is an ideal.[16] It depicts a more systematic approach than likely exists in practice. Beginning at the left with CSR assessment, we discuss each stage and illustrate related company actions.

CSR Review

To begin, a corporation should assess its current situation and activities. No single responsibility formula fits all. Each business must be systematically reviewed to discover its range of societal impacts and the societal expectations that bear on it. Finding these requires looking at factors such as its size, financial structure, products, production processes, employees, culture, geographic location(s), supply chain, and leader's views. The review should be expansive. It can begin with a definition of CSR to focus thinking. Then it might explore legal or regulatory standards, inventory existing CSR projects, and examine competitor's actions. Two other important steps are discovery of core values and engagement of stakeholders.

Discovering Core Values

Core values, the central beliefs that guide decisions, reside deep in the company's culture. Once formed they are very persistent. There are many ways to find them. In 1995 Fujitsu Group, a Japanese information technology corporation, created its "Fujitsu Way," a philosophy of corporate purpose and responsibility, by finding its "corporate DNA" in the speeches of past presidents going back to its origins in the 1930s. Similarly, the origin of a statement of "purpose, values, and principles" that guides social missions at Procter & Gamble was a project by top managers to write down basic beliefs in the company's culture.[17] At other companies, core values are found in existing mission, vision, and values statements, charters, credos, and codes of governance or conduct. Responsibility initiatives taken by a firm should harmonize with core goals and values. If these basic documents do not reference goals and values that facilitate CSR, support for action may be weak.

---

[16] The model is inspired by models and process standards elsewhere, including Business Leaders Initiative on Human Rights, et al., *A Guide for Integrating Human Rights into Business Management* (New York: Global Compact Office, February 2007); International Organization for Standardization, *Draft International Standard ISO/DIS 26000: Guidance on Social Responsibility* (Geneva: ISO, 2009), chap. 7; and Government of Canada, *Corporate Social Responsibility: An Implementation Guide for Canadian Business* (Ottawa: Public Works and Government Services Canada, March 2006).

[17] Rosabeth Moss Kanter, *Supercorp* (New York: Crown Business, 2009), p. 73.

mission statement
A brief statement of the basic purpose of a corporation.

For any corporation a key source of values is the *mission statement,* a document setting forth, with brevity, its basic purpose. The best ones define the business, differentiate it from competitors, explain relationships with stakeholders, and focus energy on critical activities and goals. If social responsibility is central to the company's mission, that should be reflected in its wording. The Ben & Jerry's mission statement sets forth a "social mission," which is "[t]o operate the company in a way that actively recognizes the central role that business plays in society by initiating innovative ways to improve the quality of life locally, nationally & internationally." The idea of "initiating innovative ways" led over the years to specific actions such as planting trees to replace the wood used in popsicle sticks and donating a percentage of Peace Pops sales to fund research on world peace.

In the past, most mission statements centered on profits and products. Many still limit themselves to this narrow focus. AutoNation aspires "[t]o be America's best run, most profitable automotive retailer." AGCO Corporation, a tractor manufacturer, aims for "[p]rofitable growth through superior customer service, innovation, quality, and commitment." National City Corp., a Cleveland bank, plans to "achieve superior levels of financial performance as compared to our peers and provide stockholders with an attractive return on their investment over time." These are firms with traditional business models.

However, many formerly traditional companies have revised their missions to include a social purpose. PepsiCo seeks "to provide financial rewards to investors as we provide opportunities for growth and enrichment to our employees, our business partners and the communities in which we operate." And Pfizer says: "We will become the world's most valued company to patients, customers, colleagues, investors, business partners and the communities where we work and live."

Engaging Stakeholders

Many companies now engage in formal or informal dialogue with a range of stakeholders, those entities that can affect or are affected by their activities. They are driven less by an ethical duty to be open than by a desire to avoid disruption of operations. In the process, they protect their "social license to operate" and can get new ideas. A simple way to identify stakeholders is a *stakeholder map,* a diagram that sketches stakeholders in basic categories and depicts their relationship to the firm. Figure 6.4 shows the basic map of stakeholders used by ArcelorMittal, a global steel manufacturer. Such a map is only the beginning. Figure 6.5 shows how just one category, government and regulators, might be articulated into a more complete picture.

Choosing which stakeholder to engage is an art. In stakeholder theory the corporation has an ethical duty of fairness toward all of them, including, perhaps especially, those it imposes burdens on though they may be powerless. In practice, corporations seriously engage only stakeholders with power to affect operations.

With stakeholders identified, a plan of engagement is constructed. Each company must decide what closeness of engagement, from very structured and frequent to informal and infrequent, is appropriate. Stakeholders can be categorized in many ways, for example, by orientation to the firm (confrontational, neutral, or supportive), by power to affect its business (high, medium, or low influence), or

FIGURE 6.4

**Basic
Stakeholder
Map for
ArcelorMittal**

Adapted from
*Corporate Responsi-
bility Report 2009:
Our Progress towards
Safe Sustainable Steel*
(Luxembourg:
ArcelorMittal,
2010), p. 8.

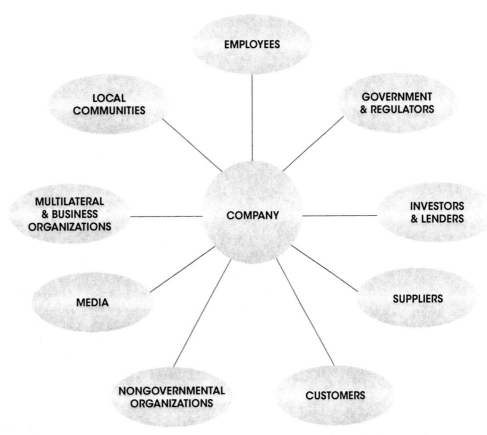

This basic map is used by ArcelorMittal to classify global stakeholders, beginning the company's process of engagement.

FIGURE 6.5

**Stakeholder
Map
Articulated
to Show
Government
Stakeholders**

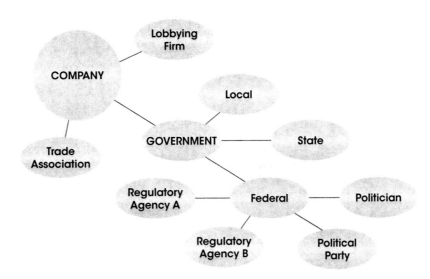

by area of claims (feminists, environmentalists, or investors).[18] These classifications help decide which methods of engagement are best, for example, surveys, private meetings, public hearings, roundtables, advisory panels, focus groups, workshops, or Web-based dialogues.

Here is one story of stakeholder engagement. Newmont Mining Corporation digs for gold around the world. It has large mines in remote parts of Ghana, Indonesia, and Peru that alter life for local villagers, peasants, and indigenous peoples. For every ounce of gold produced, Newmont's mines excavate tons of ore-bearing earth and irrigate it with a cyanide solution, using large volumes of water from local streams and rivers. Natives, as stakeholders, were consulted by Newmont and got relocation allowances, job training, and other assistance, yet enormous tensions lingered. Protests, violence, strikes, and lawsuits hung over the company's most profitable sites. When Indonesian villagers complained of birth defects caused by mining waste, the government arrested Newmont's local manager and held a trial on criminal pollution charges. One of Newmont's lawyers called the villagers "liars" who just wanted money.[19]

By this time an activist coalition of environmental and human rights groups had targeted Newmont with a "No Dirty Gold" campaign and a *New York Times* reporter began a series of critical stories about how its mines hurt remote communities. Some religious investors came to its 2007 annual meeting with a resolution calling for a study of the "pattern of community resistance to the company's operations."[20] Surprisingly, the company endorsed the proposal and began the study and, showing it was learning some lessons, it set up an advisory panel of "independent experts" with a broad mandate to assess the study.

This was a stakeholder panel, but with a very narrow range of stakeholders. Of the seven members, all had roots in progressive activism, and two were former heads of groups in the anti-Newmont advocacy campaign. In the end, this panel, in its own words, "encountered a degree of institutional resistance and defensiveness" in the company as it tried to do its work and suggested that the "root causes" of unrest at the mines lay in "Newmont's corporate culture." But it generally approved of the company's final report, which recommended more active, better managed engagement with villagers.[21] There are innumerable ways to engage stakeholders; this is one example. In its unique way, Newmont co-opted critical stakeholders and made itself a more open, responsible corporation.

---

[18] For some suggested classifications see John F. Preble, "Toward a Comprehensive Model of Stakeholder Engagement," *Business and Society Review* 110, no. 4 (2005); and Patrick Hughes and Kristin Demetrious, "Engaging with Stakeholders or Constructing Them?" *The Journal of Corporate Citizenship,* Autumn 2006.

[19] Palmer Situmorang, quoted in Jane Perlez and Evelyn Rusli, "Spurred by Illness, Indonesians Lash Out at U.S. Mining Giant," *The New York Times*, September 8, 2004, p. 1.

[20] "Proposal No. 4–Stockholder Proposal Requesting a Report Regarding Newmont's Community Policies and Practices," Newmont Mining Corporation, *Notices of 2007 Annual Meeting of Stockholders,* March 5, 2007, pp. 53–54.

[21] Advisory Panel, Newmont Community Relationships Review, *Building Effective Community Relationships: Final Report of the Advisory Panel to Newmont's Community Relationships Review,* February 8, 2009, p. 35.

CSR Strategy

The next stage in Figure 6.3 is the development of an overall strategy for corporate responsibility. A *strategy* is a basic approach, method, or plan for achieving an objective. A company with a strategy is like a traveler with a map showing the city of destination and a plan to reach it by taking the morning train. Like this traveler, a company defining its CSR strategy must first find an objective, or a vision of what it will achieve, then create a method for reaching it.

To establish its CSR objective a company can consider the profile it constructed in the CSR review stage, analyzing it to find strengths and weaknesses in its social response and threats and opportunities in its environment. Then the company can list a range of possible social initiatives. At a minimum, these actions must meet legal requirements. Beyond that, voluntary actions can be listed. Then, a few actions should be given priority. These become the firm's strategic CSR objectives.

For large firms the task of setting priorities is complex. Multiple, even conflicting, stakeholder demands exist. Along the value chain there are potential adverse impacts to correct. More broadly, difficult social problems in the firm's environment may demand attention. To which tasks should the firm assign priority? Companies must respond to some stakeholder demands or risk damage to their reputations and businesses. Ethical duty requires that where the firm has influence it should seek to mitigate value chain activities that damage society. Yet beyond such imperatives there are many options.

Michael Porter and Mark Kramer suggest an "essential test" for the worthiness of any additional social initiative, that is, "whether it presents an opportunity to create shared value—that is, a meaningful benefit for society that is also valuable to the business."[22] According to them, companies should distinguish between a wide range of generic social issues and a much narrower range of social issues that affect their competitive advantage. Generic social issues, such as the need to reduce crime, poverty, and disease, are important in society, but are not affected by and do not affect the company's business. Competitive social issues are those related to factors that influence success in the marketplace. The importance of specific issues to each firm will vary. Greenhouse gas emissions are a generic social issue for Tiffany's, but a competitive factor for General Motors and Toyota, which sell low-emission vehicles. Poverty may be a generic social issue for Lockheed, but a competitive issue for Unilever and Nestlé, which market small, inexpensive, single-use product packages.

An example of how a company can prioritize a social issue to competitive advantage is General Electric's "ecomagination" strategy. Ecomagination is a neologism created to denote concern for the environment and the imagination residing in GE's research labs. As a strategy, it is simultaneously a plan for revenue growth and a social program.

So far, GE has marketed 80 ecomagination products including wind turbines, generators powered by landfill gas, and filters that recycle wastewater without

strategy
A basic approach, method, or plan for achieving an objective.

[22] Michael E. Porter and Mark R. Kramer, "Strategy and Society," *Harvard Business Review,* December 2006, p. 84.

chemicals. To fulfill strategic intent each product must meet a dual test. It has to improve the customer's operating performance measurably. It has to be better for the environment. One example is the Trip Optimizer, a throttle control for freight locomotives. It reads train weight and length, track conditions, elevation, temperature, and engine power, then calculates the most efficient route and throttle movements for on-time arrival with least fuel used, eliminating human variation between locomotive engineers. Depending on terrain, it cuts diesel fuel consumption by 6 to 10 percent and raises the ton-miles-per-gallon ratio railroads use to measure productivity. It also eliminates several hundred tons of polluting emissions per locomotive each year.[23]

Implementation of CSR Strategy

To be carried out, a strategy must be translated into specific goals and performance objectives, embedded in policies and procedures, reinforced with processes, and supported by both the formal structure and the corporate culture. If the structure, culture, and processes of a company are misaligned with its strategic goals, those goals will be slighted. A range of actions that facilitate implementation is discussed.

Organization Structure

An initial step in implementation is to create an effective CSR decision-making structure. Many companies create elements of formal structure at top levels to ensure leadership and overall coordination. Examples of companies with corporate responsibility committees on their boards of directors are Altria, Hasbro, H. J. Heinz, Kellogg, McDonald's, Lockheed Martin, and Occidental Petroleum. Below the board, many companies assign an executive to oversee the action. Companies with staff vice presidents of corporate responsibility include British Petroleum, Chiquita Brands, Campbell Soup, General Electric, Hershey, Nike, Walmart, and Walt Disney.

However, the growing number of board committees and vice presidents implies more centralization than usually exists in practice. At most companies CSR is still supplemental, and largely incidental, to core business strategies. Elements of CSR are isolated in parts of the organization. Charitable giving is in the foundation. Human rights and diversity are managed by the human resources staff. The code of conduct is in the legal department. Environmental impacts are left to operations managers. The CSR agenda is fragmented. To wit:

> Citizenship has many rooms but no home. Rarely is corporate citizenship organized across the business. Many organizational functions touch some piece of the elephant but each unit is generally responsible . . . to a particular part of citizenship. . . . [O]rganizational silos are created and frustrate any overall organization strategy where all units are pulling together around a common vision. . . .[24]

---

[23] "GE's Fuel Autopilot Software Set for 200 Locomotives," *GE Reports*, December 19, 2009, at www.gereports.com.

[24] Bradley K. Googins and Steven Rochlin, "Corporate Citizenship Top to Bottom: Vision, Strategy, and Execution," in Marc J. Epstein and Kirk O. Hanson, eds. *The Accountable Corporation: Corporate Social Responsibility,* vol. 3 (Westport, CT: Praeger, 2006), p. 117.

To centralize oversight, some companies, for example, Coca-Cola, Pfizer, Time Warner, and Vodafone have cross-functional CSR committees made up of managers from different departments or business units. Such organizational forms are still the minority.

Action Planning

When a strategy and decision-making structure are in place, transforming intent into action is still necessary. An action plan sets forth the multitude of tasks that, together, will bring the strategy to fruition. Such tasks include revising or creating policies, budgeting resources, and assigning work.

An illustration of the effectiveness of an action plan is found within Denmark's Novo Nordisk, a pharmaceutical corporation with 24,000 employees in 81 countries. After a CSR review in the late 1990s it decided to focus its corporate responsibility strategy on fighting all forms of discrimination. The strategy turned into three actions. First, employees were trained in national regulations against discrimination. Second, informal barriers to advancement within Novo Nordisk were found and removed. Third, managers were encouraged to turn employee diversity into a business advantage.

Each Novo Nordisk business unit set up its own action plan. In South Africa, where physicians are predominantly white, the company sales representatives were white also, but after a new action plan most of the sales force became black and mixed-race. A strict policy excluded as customers doctors who disliked visits from nonwhite salespersons.

Performance Goals and Timelines

A strong action plan sets performance goals and timelines for their accomplishment. To be effective, goals must be specific and progress toward them should be measurable. Such goals and measures create a common language and focus efforts across organizational units. Examples of time-based, quantitative objectives, desirable for their clarity, are those set by General Electric in 2005 for its ecomagination strategy. By 2008 it would reduce its ratio of greenhouse gas emissions per dollar of revenue by 30 percent. By 2010 it would invest $1.5 billion in ecomagination product research and raise revenues to $25 billion. And by 2012 it would reduce its water use by 20 percent and reduce its absolute emissions of greenhouse gases by 1 percent. It exceeded all but one of its goals by 2009, the exception being revenues from ecomagination products, which were only $18 billion, and set new, more ambitious goals for 2015.[25] Its new revenue goal is to grow ecomagination sales at a rate two times that of sales for the overall company.

One of Procter & Gamble's social strategies is "to improve children's lives." In 2007 it set a goal for 2015 of preventing "160 million days of disease and saving 20,000 lives by delivering 4 billion liters of clean water" to children in areas where diarrheal illness is common. It acts by donating sachets of a product that treats contaminated water, making it drinkable. By 2009 it had delivered 930 million

[25] General Electric Company, *2009 Ecomagination Annual Report* (Fairfield, CT: General Electric Company, 2010), pp. 3–9.

liters of clean water, preventing an estimated 39 million days of disease and 5,200 deaths.[26]

The design of metrics is limited only by the imagination. Many companies use sustainability indicators recommended by an international standard-setting body called the Global Reporting Initiative. We will discuss these later in the chapter. Others design their own. Software vendors sell sustainability software to adapt a company's information system so it collects data on sustainability from dispersed units and even from independent firms in the supply chain.[27] Precise measurement of actions toward goals can be a challenge, but even approximations are helpful since, in the words of one consultant, "ignoring those impacts that are difficult to measure implicitly assigns a value of zero."[28]

Incentives and Accountability

Job descriptions that include sustainability duties encourage accountability. Incentives further encourage meeting goals. Performance evaluations, pay, and promotions are linked to targeted actions. Executive pay is linked to environmental performance at British Petroleum and Dow Chemical. At Alcoa 10 percent of the incentive pay for managers at each business unit is based on achieving diversity.[29] When the board of directors at Johnson & Johnson sets compensation for its top executives, it evaluates whether they modeled core values of responsibility and citizenship in its guiding Credo.[30] But this is exceptional. Formulas for CEO compensation are almost universally focused on attaining specific financial goals.

Business units and facilities can also be rewarded or punished based on sustainable performance. For example, Dow Chemical built a waste landfill in Michigan for its plants to use, but instead of allowing each plant to dump freely, it charged a fee based on how much material was brought for disposal. The fee penalized more polluting plants by, in effect, charging an internal tax on them. To avoid the fee, facilities changed their production processes to reduce waste. Dow now estimates the landfill will last until 2034, instead of filling by 2007 as originally estimated.[31]

Alignment of Strategy and Culture

Corporate culture must be aligned with strategic intent. Where the culture contains deep-seated, informal values that conflict with official CSR policies, those policies are likely to be ignored. If managers who meet financial goals but neglect "soft" sustainability goals are promoted, it indicates that formal policy is inconsistent with underlying beliefs about requirements for career advancement. For example, Timberland Co. executives backed a program allowing

---

[26] Procter & Gamble, *Designed to Matter: 2009 Sustainability Report*, Procter & Gamble 2009, at www.pg.com/en_US/sustainability/reports.shtml.

[27] Chris McClean, "CSR Management Needs Drive Application Revolution," *CRO*, July/August 2008.

[28] Marc J. Epstein, *Making Sustainability Work* (San Francisco: Berrett-Koehler, 2008), p. 256.

[29] Alcoa, *Notice of 2009 Annual Meeting and Proxy Statement*, March 16, 2009, p. 26.

[30] Johnson & Johnson, *Notice of Annual Meeting and Proxy Statement*, March 11, 2009, p. 23.

[31] Epstein, *Making Sustainability Work*, p. 135.

employees to take one week a year at full pay to work at local charities. However, line managers felt pressured to meet production goals and resisted giving workers time off.[32]

Reporting and Verification

transparency
The state in which company social strategies, structures, and processes are visible to external observers.

To complete the cycle of CSR implementation, as shown in Figure 6.3, companies can assess and report information about their social performance. Publishing such reports serves two main purposes. First, by informing stakeholders they create *transparency;* that is, they lift the veil, revealing the internal strategies, structures, and processes that explain social performance. The opposite of transparency is opacity, or an inability to see inside the organization to know how it works and acts. Openness is increasingly necessary to protect a firm's reputation and to establish trust with stakeholders. Second, aggregating data in a report allows both managers and outsiders to appraise the firm's social performance.

sustainability reporting
Documentation and disclosure of how closely corporate operations conform to the goal of sustainable development.

A pioneering fad of social reporting appeared during the 1960s and 1970s in the United States, when a few large firms produced reports called social audits, a term that differentiated them from traditional financial audits. Bank of America, Exxon, and Philip Morris assessed their social impacts, and for a few years in the 1970s Atlantic Richfield Company published an annual social balance sheet that candidly weighed the multiple pluses and minuses of its social performance, an eccentric act of corporate candor that stopped when the company was acquired by British Petroleum. A 1974 survey found that 76 percent of 284 large companies did some form of social auditing.[33]

sustainable development
Economic growth that meets current needs without social and environmental impacts that harm future generations.

Early interest in social audits waned in the 1970s after American companies were hit by a massive increase in environmental and social regulation. The new regulations had strong reporting requirements that were, in effect, government-mandated social reports. However, as time passed and large corporations became more globalized, these requirements were less and less adequate. An information gap between companies and stakeholders opened wide.

triple bottom line
An accounting of a firm's economic, social, and environmental performance.

To fill this gap, the international progressive community created a new reporting format called the Global Reporting Initiative (GRI). The GRI is a set of uniform standards for *sustainability reporting,* or the measurement and disclosure of corporate impacts to inform stakeholders how closely operations conform to the goal of *sustainable development.* Sustainable development is an ideal of economic growth that can "meet the needs of the present without compromising the ability of future generations to meet their own needs."[34] Using GRI guidelines, companies show how closely they conform to this ideal by explaining their performance on a *triple bottom line* of economic, social, and environmental results (see Figure 6.6).

---

[32] Joseph Pereira, "Doing Good and Doing Well at Timberland," *The Wall Street Journal,* September 9, 2003, p. B1.

[33] John J. Corson and George A. Steiner, *Measuring Business's Social Performance: The Corporate Social Audit* (New York: Committee for Economic Development, 1974), pp. 24–25.

[34] Global Reporting Initiative, *Sustainability Reporting Guidelines,* version 3.0 (Amsterdam: GRI, 2000–2006), p. 2, citing World Commission on Environment and Development, *Our Common Future* (Oxford: Oxford University Press, 1987), p. 43.

FIGURE 6.6

**The Prism
of the Triple
Bottom Line**

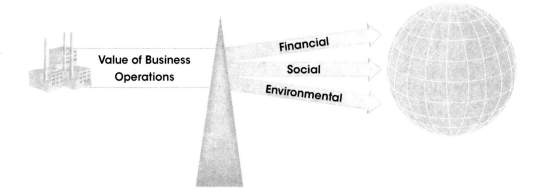

The triple bottom line is an idea attributed to John Elkington, a progressive scholar/activist who first wrote of it in the late 1990s.[35] Its essence is to appraise the total impact of a firm's operations, accounting for the full range of costs and value, by combining nonfinancial measures—social and environmental—with financial ones. It is now the consensus approach to sustainability reporting, not because it is an elegant calculation, but because it indulges a range of demanding stakeholders.

According to GRI guidelines, a good social report also meets certain format criteria. Its content is useful to stakeholders—clear, timely, comparable to past reports, reliable, and verifiable. It should include a statement of management's CSR vision and strategy, an extensive factual profile of the company, a description of its governance structure, policies for matters such as executive pay and stakeholder engagement, and data on a series of 71 performance indicators spanning the triple bottom lines (see the box for a sample). Forty-nine of these are called core indicators because they generally apply to all companies. Another 30 are additional indicators that may or may not be material to every reporter. For instance, additional indicator HR9 (the ninth human rights indicator) requires reporting the "[t]otal number of incidents of violations involving rights of indigenous people," and is only for companies having contacts with such peoples. The indicators span a range of complexity. Many require reporting of multiple measures, so a full report requires expensive data collection.

Additional indicators are set forth in more than a dozen "sector supplements" for specific industries. One of these, for food processing companies, adds eight industry-specific core indicators, for example FPSS4 (the fourth food processing sector supplement indicator) requires reporting the "[p]ercentage of consumer products sold, by product category, that are lowered in saturated fat, trans fats, sodium and added sugars."[36] This is justified, the *Guidelines* state, because the World Health Organization says a global epidemic of obesity exists and companies have a

[35] See John Elkington in *Cannibals with Forks: The Triple Bottom Line of 21st Century Business* (Oxford: Oxford University Press, 1997), chap. 3.

[36] Global Reporting Initiative, *Sustainability Reporting Guidelines & Food Sector Supplement*, version August 24, 2009, p. 46.

A Sample of GRI Core Performance Indicators

Here is a random, illustrative sample of 15 of the total of 49 core performance indicators in the *Global Reporting Guidelines*, five from each of the three "bottom lines."

ENVIRONMENTAL

- Materials used by weight or volume.
- Total water withdrawn by source.
- Description of significant impacts of activities, products, and services on biodiversity in protected areas and areas of high biodiversity value outside protected areas.
- Total direct and indirect greenhouse gas emissions by weight.
- Percentage of products sold and their packaging materials that are reclaimed by category.

SOCIAL

- Total number of incidents of discrimination and actions taken.
- Percentage of employees covered by collective bargaining agreements.
- Ratio of basic salary of men to women by employee category.

- Percentage and total number of business units analyzed for risks of corruption.
- Public policy position and participation in public policy development and lobbying.

ECONOMIC

- Direct economic value generated and distributed, including revenues, operating costs, employee compensation, donations and other community investments, retained earnings, and payments to capital providers and government.
- Financial implications and other risks and opportunities for the organization's activities due to climate change.
- Coverage of the organization's defined benefits plan obligations.
- Significant financial assistance received from government.
- Policy, practices, and proportion of spending on locally-based suppliers of significant locations of operation.

Source: Global Reporting Initiative, *Sustainability Reporting Guidelines*, Version 3.0 (Amsterdam: GRI, 2000–2006).

duty to report whether their products contribute to it. New indicators are frequently added to the *Guidelines.*

assurance
Verification by audit that information in a corporate sustainability report is reliable.

Finally, the GRI strongly suggests providing *assurance*, that is, verification for readers, that a report is reliable. The most effective assurance is provided by independent, outside auditors who assess the reporting process and verify accuracy of information. Only a minority of companies that issue a social report also choose to provide assurance. Of those that do, most hire one of the Big Four accounting and auditing firms that apply a professional assurance standard.[37]

Many of the rest use a standard created by AccountAbility, a civil society entity that provides a free, open-source assurance standard, licensing and training smaller consulting services to evaluate reports based on their inclusiveness, completeness, and transparency.[38] In either case, assurance requires certain steps,

[37] This standard is ISAE (for International Standard on Assurance Engagements) 3000, International Federation of Accountants, *Assurance Engagements Other than Audits or Reviews of Historical Financial Information* (New York: IFA, 2004).

[38] This standard is AA1000AS, AccountAbility, *AA1000 Assurance Standard 2008* (London: AccountAbility, 2008).

including interviews with managers and reviews of policies, processes, documents, and data samples. These audits are expensive, costing $1 million to $2 million for companies in single industries and much more for conglomerates, so some companies provide a more limited assurance by inviting stakeholder panels or academic experts to review their reports and make public statements. Around the world, sustainability reporting is now a mainstream activity.

HOW EFFECTIVELY IS CSR IMPLEMENTED?

In this section we have set forth model process for implementing CSR. If a company navigates this process, it can embed CSR as a countervailing force to the risks of bad behavior in its pursuit of profit. There is a trend, especially among the world's largest corporations, to adopt the elements of this model. A recent survey found that 62 percent of the 250 largest firms in the *Fortune* Global 500 formally engage stakeholders, 73 percent have created a sustainability strategy, 66 percent link performance indicators to strategic objectives, and 60 percent report data for these indicators. Also, 79 percent produce a corporate responsibility report, with 77 percent of these reporters following the Global Reporting Initiative guidelines and 40 percent including third-party assurance statements.[39] These numbers reflect the civil society pressures on the largest, most exposed global firms. Smaller and less-international firms reported far less adoption of model CSR actions in the survey.

A question is whether corporations, especially the largest and most exposed, use mostly ritual, bare compliance with the codes, certifications, and reporting requirements in the new civil regulation to innoculate against activism and more stringent forms of legislated regulation. John Elkington, the early champion of triple-bottom-line reporting, now believes corporations show an "almost willful avoidance of the social dimension."[40] Whatever its advances, social responsibility is still frequently seen as a superfluous activity only indirectly, if that, related to the bottom line, one that costs money, takes time, and reduces efficiency. Within many companies it is still bolted onto, not integrated with, core business strategies, its pieces fragmented in separate departments with no central oversight, and its spirit smothered by cultures of revenue. As one manager notes: "While I may be encouraged to participate in [a CSR event] on the weekend to support the company's CSR initiative, on Monday morning, it is business as usual, and all that really matters is how many cases I've pushed out the door."[41]

---

[39] Survey figures are from KPMG, *KPMG International Survey of Corporate Responsibility Reporting 2008* (Amstelveen: The Netherlands: KPMG Sustainability Services, 2008).

[40] Quoted in Adam Werbach, *Strategy for Sustainability: A Business Manifesto* (Boston: Harvard Business Press, 2009), p. 112.

[41] An anonymous interview subject quoted in Ida P. Berger, Peggy H. Cunningham, and Minette E. Drumwright, "Mainstreaming Corporate Social Responsibility: Developing Markets for Virtue," *California Management Review*, Summer 2007, p. 142. Brackets in the original.

Four Costly Errors of CSR Implementation

In practice, most companies fall short of the model process for CSR action set forth in this section because they make one of these errors.

1. They give no coherent, systematic thought to CSR.
2. They allow CSR strategy to be reactive by not aligning it with major social impacts, core competencies, or business strategies.

3. They fragment responsibility for CSR initiatives by assigning them to separate areas without central oversight.
4. They do not issue credible reports of CSR actions for stakeholders and fail the test of transparency.

CORPORATE PHILANTHROPY

philanthropy
Charitable giving of money, property, or work for the welfare of society.

Philanthropy, meaning literally love of mankind, is charity carried out by business with gifts of money, property, or work given to the needy or for social welfare activities. Large philanthropic contributions by American corporations are relatively recent. Until about 50 years ago courts held that corporate funds belonged to shareholders; therefore, managers had no right to give money away, even for noble motives. This restrictive doctrine made sense in the distant past when businesses were small and charity came mainly from their owners. However, as businesses grew and professional managers took control from their rich founders, the public started to expect giving from corporations, too.

The first major break from legal restrictions on corporate philanthropy was the Revenue Act of 1935, which allowed charitable contributions to be deducted from taxable earnings up to 5 percent of net profits before taxes (raised to 10 percent in 1981). Still, the legality of corporate giving remained doubtful, and managers were tight with charity dollars because they feared stockholder lawsuits. Eventually, the *A. P. Smith* case in 1953 (see the box) cleared away outdated rigidities in the law, freeing companies to be more generous. Now, corporations give $14 billion to $15 billion a year to worthy causes ranging from disaster relief to support for local orchestras. Conservative opponents of corporate social responsibility still argue that such giving is theft, like Robin Hood stealing from stockholders and giving to the poor. However, they no longer receive support from the law.

Patterns of Corporate Giving

Charitable giving is now a traditional dimension of corporate responsibility. Even so, most firms do not give a significant amount compared with their potential. In 2008, for example, corporations gave $14.5 billion, a large sum, but only 0.12 percent of worldwide sales and 1 percent of pretax income. Since the 1950s, overall corporate contributions have been remarkably consistent, hovering around 1 percent of pretax income. This is far less than the 10 percent that is tax deductible. Contributions rise as firms get larger, with the largest firms in one study giving

A. P. Smith Manufacturing Company v. Barlow et al., 13 N.J. 145 (1953)

A. P. Smith was a New Jersey corporation set up in 1896. It made valves and hydrants. In 1951 the firm gave $1,500 to Princeton University's annual fund-raising drive. This was not its first charitable contribution. It gave to a local community chest fund and had donated to other nearby colleges.

These contributions were made in a legal environment clouded by inconsistency. On the one hand was the law of corporate charters. These charters were issued by states, and corporations were not allowed to act beyond the powers expressly granted in them. The assumption in the charters was that the corporation's duty was to maximize profits for shareholders. A. P. Smith's incorporation papers, like those of most firms at the time, did not grant specific authority to make charity gifts. On the other hand was a statute. New Jersey passed a law in 1930 giving its corporations the right to make such donations if they did not exceed 1 percent of capital.

Ruth Barlow and four other angry owners of common and preferred stock thought the company had no right to give away any amount of money, because it was rightfully theirs as share-holders. They sued and in due course a trial was held. Luminaries from the business community appeared as witnesses for A. P. Smith to assert the merits of corporate charity. A Standard Oil of New Jersey executive argued that it was "good business" to show the kind of citizenship the public demanded. A U.S. Steel executive said that maintaining universities was essential to preserving capitalism. Nevertheless, the judge ruled against A. P. Smith, saying that the company had acted beyond its legitimate power.

A. P. Smith appealed. In 1953 the Supreme Court of New Jersey overturned the lower court, holding that rigid interpretation of charters to restrict charitable giving was no longer fitting since, unlike the old days when corporations were small and had limited assets relative to individuals, they now had enormous assets and it was reasonable for the public to expect generosity from them.

The *Smith* case settled the legal question of whether corporations could give to charity. After it, the legal cloud of acting *ultra vires* dissipated, clearing the way for greater corporate giving.

2.38 percent of pretax income. Large drug companies were the most generous, averaging 5.77 percent; aerospace and defense firms gave the least, only 0.45 percent.[42]

Corporate philanthropy is a small part of overall philanthropy in the United States; in 2009 it was only 4.6 percent. Figure 6.7 displays the 10-year trend in giving and segments sources into their relative proportions. During this time total giving rose from $203 billion to a high of $314 billion in 2007, then fell to $304 billion in 2009. As the segmented bars show, individuals gave by far the largest proportion, followed by foundations, charitable bequests, and, finally, corporations (including corporate foundations). In the years shown, corporate giving rose from $10.7 billion to a high of $15.2 billion in 2007, then fell to $14.1 billion in 2009. Corporate giving was consistently about 5 percent of total giving.

Corporations that contribute do so in many ways, including cash, products, services, volunteered employee time, and use of facilities. Cash giving is only about half of all giving. Among the largest corporations, about 42 percent of giving goes to United Way campaigns and grants to health and human service agencies such as the Red Cross and the American Cancer Society. Another 23 percent

[42] Figures in this paragraph are from Carolyn Cavicchio and Judit Torik, *The 2009 Corporate Contributions Report* (New York: The Conference Board, December 2009), pp. 4–10.

FIGURE 6.7

**The Trend
in Private
Philanthropy:
1999–2009**

Source: U.S. Census
Bureau, *Statistical
Abstract of the United
States: 2009*, 129th ed.
(Washington, DC:
U.S. Census Bureau,
2009), table 561; and
Giving USA Foun-
dation, "U.S. Chari-
table Giving Falls
3.6 Percent in 2009,"
news release, June 9,
2010, pp. 2–3.

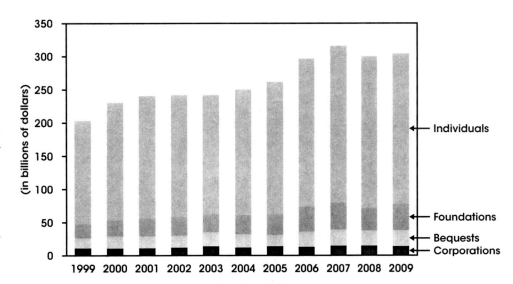

flows to education, about 13 percent goes to civic groups such as YMCA/YWCAs and to local governments, about 6 percent to culture and arts causes, and a tiny amount, less than 3 percent, to environmental groups.[43]

Strategic Philanthropy

With historical roots in religious teachings, the act of philanthropy presumes a selfless motive of giving out of moral duty to benefit the needy or to advance society. Traditionally, corporate philanthropy conformed to such ideals of altruism and magnanimity. Companies and their foundations gave to help the destitute while funding social goods such as education and the arts. Some self-benefit resided in these donations since the elevating deed often raised corporate reputations, created goodwill, or improved the economy by strengthening society.

As corporations gained experience with philanthropy, some concluded that the traditional approach of diffuse giving to myriad worthy causes was noble but flawed. Over time, the number of causes grew. As charity recipients proliferated, the shrinking sums given to each had less and less impact. Executives and their spouses diverted funds into pet artistic and cultural projects unimportant to the firm's main stakeholders. In Detroit, a city hollowed out by race riots and loss of its tax base as whites ran to the suburbs, Ford Motor gave millions of dollars to the Michigan Opera Theater because Jennifer Nasser, the wife of its CEO, was a patron.[44] As vacant downtown buildings sat with broken windows she had Ford employees refurbish the theater. Such an impulsive approach to philanthropy, often called *checkbook philanthropy*, leads to awards, plaques, and honors for executives but lacks an underlying business logic.

Most large corporations still engage in some checkbook philanthropy. How-ever, more and more convert their philosophy of giving from one of pure, if

**checkbook
philanthropy**
A traditional
form of corpo-
rate giving in
which dona-
tions go to mul-
tiple worthy
causes without
any link to busi-
ness strategy.

[43] These figures are from Cavicchio and Torik, *The 2009 Corporate Contributions Report*, p. 49. The 13 percent remainder goes to miscellaneous recipients outside these main categories of giving.

[44] Keith Bradsher, "A Horn of Plenty for Opera in Detroit," *The New York Times*, October 28, 1999, p. E1.

The Secretive Billionaire

George F. Feeney, 79, is one of the greatest living philanthropists. He has given away billions of dollars, much of it anonymously in a style reminiscent of the old television program, *The Millionaire*, where a mysterious benefactor changed the lives of worthy people with anonymous cashier's checks.

Feeney was raised in a working-class New Jersey neighborhood. With partners, he founded the Duty Free Shoppers stores located in airports around the world. He became rich selling cigarettes and luxury goods to travelers and moved among six splendid homes from the French Riviera to Park Avenue in New York. In 1984 he experienced a revelation. "I simply decided I had enough money," he told a reporter.[45]

Without even informing his three partners he set up a foundation in Bermuda. Then he irrevocably transferred his ownership interest in Duty Free Shoppers to it. At the time, this was worth about $500 million. More followed. Over the years, the foundation has given away more than $5 billion.

If Feeney had kept the money he could now be worth as much as $10 billion, but his personal assets may be only about $5 million. He does not own a house and lives in a one-bedroom San Francisco rental. He has no car, preferring to get around by bus. He has no briefcase and brings papers to meetings in a plastic bag. He wears a $15 watch, prefers casual clothes, and doubts the need for more than one pair of shoes.[46] He also has a passion for secrecy coming from a desire to live life without constant importuning from supplicants and from his belief in the teachings of Maimonides, a twelfth century philosopher who counseled that the highest form of giving is anonymous and selfless.

Unsolicited requests for money from the foundation are always rejected. Feeney located his foundation in Bermuda to avoid U.S. disclosure laws and for years forbade its employees to tell anyone where they worked, even their families. Those who got anonymous funding were told that if they revealed the source the funds would stop. Feeney sometimes attends staff meetings with potential recipients, who are not told the identity of the quiet observer.

The existence of the foundation, called Atlantic Philanthropies, became public when Duty Free Shops was sold in 1997. Since then, it has become much more open. It lists its mission as "fostering lasting changes in the lives of disadvantaged and vulnerable people" and to that end it funds projects large and small, from building hospitals in Vietnam to repairing broken windows in South African schools.

Most foundations give away only limited sums each year, allowing them indefinitely to maintain large endowments. But Feeney has instructed Atlantic Philanthropies to exhaust its remaining funds by 2016. He believes his money should start doing good as soon as possible, not in some distant future.

---

strategic philanthropy
A form of corporate philanthropy in which charitable activities reinforce strategic business goals.

scattered and unplanned generosity to one that aligns giving with commercial objectives. This is known as *strategic philanthropy*, or the alignment of charity with business strategy.

General Mills was a pioneer. It has always been a generous company, giving an unusually high 5 percent of its pretax domestic profits to charity. For years it emphasized funding of prestigious cultural and arts programs in its Minneapolis headquarters area. In the late 1990s it began to redirect giving to projects on youth nutrition, schools, and social services in 20 cities where it had facilities. Then it

---

[45] Quoted in Judith Miller, "He Gave Away $600 Million, and No One Knew," *The New York Times*, January 23, 1997, p. A1.

[46] Conor O'Clery, *The Billionaire Who Wasn't* (New York: Perseus Books, 2007), pp. 321–22.

moved to align its brands with philanthropic causes. In its Spoonfuls of Stories campaign it gave millions of dollars to buy new books for children in low-income families and it put children's books in millions of Cheerios boxes. These efforts better matched charity giving with the concerns of average grocery shoppers who buy Cheerios. There are many similar examples.

- Mattel donated $25 million to put its name on the children's hospital at UCLA, now called Mattel Children's Hospital. The company has no role in running the facility, although it gives toys to patients. Adding the company name to the hospital increases brand recognition and contributes to a compassionate corporate image among toy buyers. These benefits reinforce the commercial goals of a toy company while also helping sick children.[47]

- Since 1995 Home Depot has partnered with a nonprofit named KaBOOM! to build playgrounds. The KaBOOM! vision is "a great place to play within walking distance of every child." In 2005 Home Depot gave it $25 million and pledged more support in materials and employee time to build 1,000 playgrounds in 1,000 days. That goal was met and playgrounds are still forthcoming. Home Depot faces strong competitors, including Lowe's and Walmart. It believes that its work on playgrounds, while helping children, differentiates its brand, creates appreciation in local store markets, and underlines the expertise of its staff with building materials.[48]

Cause Marketing

cause marketing
A form of strategic philanthropy in which charitable contributions are based on purchases of a product.

Cause marketing is a variant of strategic philanthropy in which charitable contributions are based on purchases of a product. It links a brand to a social cause so both benefit. Marketers use branding to differentiate products, especially mass-produced products that consumers might see as interchangeable commodities if they lack brand attributes. Companies spend heavily to endow brands with these attributes so they can charge a price premium. Traditional branding creates attributes in two dimensions to influence buying decisions. One is an impression of the product's positive qualities directed to the logical mind. The other is an emotional association with the product that allows consumers to fulfill emotional needs by using it. Marketers have learned that if their brand is connected to a charitable cause a third attribute is created, one that appeals to the consumer's conscience. In cause-related marketing the corporation calculates it will add this benevolent dimension to its brand while also doing a philanthropic good deed.

Cause marketing is a powerful sales tool. In a recent survey 75 percent of consumers said they would try a new brand if it supported a cause and 64 percent said they would be willing to pay more for it if the cause were important to them.[49] In the United Kingdom, for example, Mars Inc. made a donation to animal rescue

[47] Julie Edelson Halpert, "Dr. Pepper Hospital? Perhaps, for a Price," *The New York Times*, February 18, 2001, sec. 3, p. 1.

[48] Sandra O'Loughlin, "Tools for Tots," *Brandweek*, July 10–17, 2006, p. 18.

[49] "Struggling Consumers Say Companies Connect," *Marketing Weekly News*, November 21, 2009, p. 62, citing a 2009 PR Week/Barkley Public Relations Cause Survey.

charities for each of its Pedigree brand dog food products sold. In just three months the campaign raised $778,000 for homeless dogs, increased sales by 6 percent, and led to an 8 percent rise in consumers who identified the brand as having "dogs at its heart."[50] Here are two other examples:

- In the early 1990s restaurant owners felt that American Express card fees were too high. Enough restaurants refused the cards that, rather than face rejection, many cardholders used a competing card instead. To counteract this, American Express started a cause marketing campaign called "Charge Against Hunger" in which it donated 3 cents per transaction to nonprofit anti-hunger groups during the holiday months of November and December each year. The campaign created a clear link between using the card to pay for restaurant meals and fighting hunger. It raised $21 million in four years for donations to 600 anti-hunger groups. It also increased the charge volume by 12 percent and raised the opinion of restaurant owners about the card.[51]

- Avon Products sells more beauty products than any other company. Most of its revenues come from direct sales through 5.4 million part-time, predominantly female sales representatives in 100 countries. In the early 1990s Avon's brand image was deteriorating because its direct-selling strategy carried an old-fashioned, down-market connotation. The company decided to burnish its name using cause-related marketing. The vast majority of Avon's sales are to women. Research showed that fighting breast cancer was important to them, so Avon developed a line of affordable "pink ribbon" products and donated a specified amount from the purchase price to breast cancer research. Its brand has benefited so much that the cause-related "crusade" continues uninterrupted. Since 1992 Avon has collected more than $640 million for breast cancer research, detection, and treatment.[52]

Cause-related marketing raises big sums for worthy causes but, like other forms of strategic philanthropy, its mixture of altruism and self-interest attracts criticism. Skeptics call it "consumption philanthropy" that promotes wasteful materialism and suggest that people simply give directly to causes.[53] They note that companies pick causes based on research into what consumers care about, instead of trying to find the most acute needs. Heart disease is the leading killer of women and the leading fatal cancer in women is lung cancer. However, because the fight against breast cancer resonates more with high-spending female consumers ages 30 to 55, more than 300 companies have copied Avon's marketing innovation. Other causes languish from this convergence.

There is plenty of cynicism about corporate motives. One woman who has had breast cancer complains that "companies are making money off my disease—even

---

[50] "Golden Jubilee Awards 2009: Cause-related Marketing," *Marketing*, June 10, 2009, p. 28.

[51] Shirley Sagawa and Eli Segal, *Common Interest, Common Good* (Boston: Harvard Business School Press, 2000), p. 15.

[52] "Avon Breast Cancer Crusade," at www.avoncompany.com/women/avoncrusade/index.html.

[53] Angela M. Eikenberry, "The Hidden Costs of Cause Marketing," *Stanford Social Innovation Review*, Summer 2009, p. 51.

if they're giving an amount to charity, they're making so much more in profit. . . . [I]t's like getting hit in the face."[54] In current breast cancer campaigns Avon donates $6.24 of the $10 price of its Crusade Tote Bag, and Coach gives $60 for each "awareness watch" it sells. Others are less generous. Duraflame gives 10 cents for each pink color log sold, only 2 percent of the $4.99 price. Yoplait donates 10 cents per yogurt container, but makes customers put their container lids in an envelope and return them by mail before it makes a contribution, imposing the cost of a stamp that exceeds the donation amount on people with fewer than five lids. Corporations, however, do not see commercial interest as an ethically inferior motive and believe that concrete benefits to both companies and causes far outweigh the importance of abstract arguments about base motives.

New Forms of Philanthropy

In traditional philanthropy, foundations and corporations give grants to nonprofit organizations that then spend the money to meet stated goals, for example, increasing literacy or buying medicines for the poor. The donor expects no financial return, in effect losing 100 percent of the capital invested, and may follow up at intervals or at the end of a project to see if objectives were met. Much good has come from this model, including such triumphs as the "green revolution," led by the Rockefeller Foundation's support for research in agriculture that led to new varieties of wheat, maize, and rice, increasing crop yields and saving an estimated 1 billion lives since the 1960s.[55] Nevertheless, it has shortcomings. Large foundation offices and staffs create administrative expenses. Committees slow decisions. Grant officers become conservative, rejecting innovation for fear a mistake will hurt their career. Grant recipients spend much of what they get on overhead, especially the costs of fund-raising necessary to continue their work. Some do not achieve what they promise, and monitoring their performance burdens donors.

Now, another model of philanthropy is emerging based largely, but not entirely, on the philosophies and examples of new billionaires from technology industries. In distinctive ways, new philanthropists such as Bill Gates of Microsoft, Pierre Omidyar and Jeffrey Skoll of eBay, Larry Page and Sergey Brin of Google, and Steve Case of AOL, either themselves or through their companies, apply the business methods that made them rich to the field of philanthropy, blurring the line between charity and business, seeking to harness market forces. This new philanthropy, or *philanthrocapitalism* as it is often called, covers a range of actors and approaches but it is bold, entrepreneurial, results-oriented, closely engaged, and impatient.

Here are some examples of philanthrocapitalism at work, all different, but having in common the use of market incentives.

philanthro-capitalism
An emerging form of philanthropy that relies on market forces to achieve results.

- Before the initial public offering of Google, its founders, Larry Page and Sergey Brin, told investors that 1 percent of equity, 1 percent of annual profits, and 1 percent of employee time would be set aside for "active philanthropy." This

[54] Jeanne Sather, quoted in Kris Frieswick, "Sick of Pink," *The Boston Globe*, October 4, 2009, magazine section.

[55] "A Scholar's Analysis of Grant-Making Successes–and Failures," *Chronicle of Philanthropy*, December 7, 2006, p. 3.

work is done within an entity named Google.org, which is a business unit of the parent company. Within Google.org the company's technologists attack three priority threats—climate change, emerging pandemics, and energy shortages. They bring to bear the engineering skills and information-gathering expertise that are core strengths of Google. One project is an online technology to measure spacial changes in the world's forests. Projects are developed as businesses and any profits accrue to Google.

Around the world 3 billion of the world's poor cook with wood, dung, and coal, filling their dwellings with dangerous smoke causing 1.5 million deaths a year, most of women and children. In the past, aid groups gave away small stoves that reduced indoor pollution, but often they were not used. Many people thought smoke was harmless. Others put no value on what they got free. Some stoves were unsuited for local fuels. The charity model was failing. But this problem fit the mission of the Shell Foundation, set up by the oil company to apply market principles in solving problems of poverty and the environment. It committed $25 million in grants to a small, nonprofit corporation in Colorado named Envirofit that would design, manufacture, and sell stoves in the developing world using a business model. The foundation injected "business DNA" into the company by giving it advice on how to operate as a business. So far, Envirofit has sold more than 120,000 of the small stoves in India.[56] Its vans travel dirt roads in rural areas selling stoves for the equivalent of $17.50 to $55.60 in local currency. They reduce particle emissions by 80 percent, but customers like them because they reduce fuel use by 60 percent and can pay for themselves in months. Envirofit sells stoves as a business, not as a subsidized charity. It reinvests net income to expand the business.

The Robin Hood Foundation was started by billionaire hedge fund manager Paul Tudor to better the lives of the poor in New York City. It funds programs that attack poverty. Of hundreds of such programs offered by agencies and nonprofits in the city, which should it fund to get the most poverty reduction per dollar spent? In a corporation, managers would compare return on capital invested to allocate funds between various business units. Robin Hood uses the same approach, modified to its charitable goals. It calculates a benefit-cost ratio for each grant program by monetizing the results of its work and comparing these with the cost of the grant. If a program has a benefit-cost ratio of 6:1, it creates $6 of benefits to the poor for every $1 of Robin Hood's funds. Measuring benefits requires estimates, for example, that an adolescent's future earnings increase $5,000 a year by avoiding a first arrest.[57] By using this benefit-cost metric Robin Hood disciplines its investment, cutting support for programs with low ratios to move dollars where they purchase more poverty reduction.

The new philanthropy is now small in relation to total philanthropy. Some are skeptical of any impact. Market solutions may be too superficial for bottomless

---

[56] Shell Foundation, *Annual Report and Accounts, 2008,* at www.shellfoundation.org; and Jeffrey Ball, "Small Energy-Saving Steps Can Make Big Strides," *The Wall Street Journal,* November 27, 2009, p. A16.
[57] Michael M. Weinstein, *Measuring Success: How Robin Hood Estimates the Impact of Grants* (New York: Robin Hood Foundation, 2009), p. 34.

social problems such as violence, corruption, bad government, and inequality. Success stories may be limited to initiatives such as indoor stoves, with dimensions that lend themselves to the application of market forces. Also, the pitfall of greed is there. Muhammad Yunus, who won a Nobel Prize for his creative work with *micro-finance,* or small loans to the poor, once criticized Banco Compartamos, a Mexican bank that makes micro-loans, for giving priority to profit over social good. The bank made a 23 percent profit, a fine return for a normal business but, it seems, a questionable one for a social enterprise.[58] According to Yunus, "Social businesses should not make a profit off the poor."[59]

micro-finance
Small loans given to poor people.

CONCLUDING OBSERVATIONS

Good intentions are worth little if not reflected in actions. If a corporation hopes to be socially responsible, it must do the hard work of building its aspirations into its operations. To implement CSR strategies it must use the same methods it uses to implement business strategies. No CSR initiative of any significance will succeed without their application.

Corporate philanthropy is a basic, widely accepted dimension of social responsibility. Traditionally, it was practiced as a form of charity, but today that is changing. Often, corporations align their giving with their profit goals. And both corporations and new billionaires with corporate fortunes are now using business methods to attack social problems. Optimism that capitalist tools can solve social problems as easily as they made people rich is natural, but not yet verified. Still, the new philanthropy in all its variations already shows promise of increasing the power of charity to do good.

[58] Gregory M. Lamb, "Charities Borrow For-Profit Strategies To Do Good," *Christian Science Monitor,* January 5, 2009, p. 14.

[59] Quoted in Steve Hamm, "Capitalism with a Human Face," *BusinessWeek,* December 8, 2008, p. 50.

Marc Kasky versus Nike

Marc Kasky of San Francisco sees his world as a community and has a long history of caring about the others in it. He got early lessons in business ethics from his father, who ran a car repair business.

> The customer would bring his car in and say there's something horribly wrong in my car: I think I need a new transmission. . . . My father would call them back an hour later and say, "Come get your car, there was a loose screw here and there; I fixed it. What does it cost? Nothing." I saw how that affected our family. It impressed me a great deal.[1]

After graduating from Yale University in 1969, he volunteered to work in poor Cleveland neighbor-

hoods. Moving to San Francisco, he headed a nonprofit center for foundations that funded schools. He involved himself in civic and environmental causes. He also became an avid jogger and ran marathons.

Over the years Kasky wore many pairs of Nike shoes and considered them a "good product."[2] But he stopped buying them in the mid-1990s after reading

[1] Quoted in Jim Edwards, "Taking It to the Big Guys," *Brandweek,* August 12, 2002, p. 1.

[2] Steve Rubenstein, "S. F. Man Changes from Customer to Nike Adversary," *San Francisco Chronicle,* May 3, 2002, p. A6. Kasky stated his ownership of Nike shoes in the interview for this article. However, his lawyer told the Supreme Court that he had "never bought any Nikes." *Nike v. Kasky,* No. 02–575, Oral Argument, April 23, 2003 (Washington, DC: Alderson Reporting Company, 2003), p. 30, lines 21 and 22. We give priority to Kasky's story, but this is a remarkable contradiction.

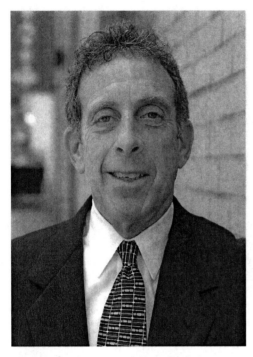

Marc Kasky. Source: © AP Photo/Denis Poroy

NIKE

Nike, Inc., is the world's largest producer of athletic shoes and sports apparel. It grew out of a handshake in 1962 between Bill Bowerman, the track coach at the University of Oregon, and Phil Knight, a runner he had coached in the 1950s. Knight had just received an MBA from Stanford University, where in a term paper he had written about competing against established athletic shoe companies by importing shoes made in low-wage Asian factories. Now he was ready to try it. He and Bowerman each put up $550 and Knight flew to Japan, arranging to import 300 pairs of Onitsuka Tiger shoes.

After seven years, Knight and Bowerman decided to stop selling the Japanese company's brand and create their own. So they designed a shoe and subcontracted its production to a factory in Japan. By now Bowerman and Knight had incorporated, and an employee suggested naming the company Nike, for the Greek goddess of victory. Knight paid a design student at Portland State University $35 to create a logo. She drew a "swoosh." The elements of future market conquest were now in place and the company rapidly grew.

Nike succeeded using two basic strategies. First, its product strategy is to design innovative, fashionable footwear and apparel for affluent markets, then have contractors in low-wage countries manufacture it. This way Nike avoids the cost of building and managing factories. At first, it made most of its shoes in Japan (some were made in the United States until 1980), but as wages rose there it moved contracts to plants in South Korea and Taiwan. When wages rose in these countries, Nike again shifted production, this time to China, Indonesia, and Thailand, and later to Vietnam.

Second, its marketing strategy is to carefully calculated brand images. Advertising associates the Nike brand with a range of ideas. Prominent among them is the idea of sport. Endorsements by professional athletes and college teams endow the swoosh with a high-performance image. Campaigns with the "just do it" slogan add connotations of competition, courage, strength, and winning. Other advertising associates the brand with urban culture to make it "street cool." In this way Nike transforms shoes and T-shirts that would otherwise be low-cost commodities into high-priced, high-fashion items that generate positive emotions when they are worn.

stories about working conditions in overseas factories where they were made. By then Nike, Inc., had become the main focus of the anti-sweatshop cause, accused of exploiting low-wage workers who made its shoes and clothing. The more Kasky read about Nike, the more convinced he was that it was not only victimizing workers, but lying about it too. Kasky sought the help of an old friend, Alan Caplan, an attorney who had achieved fame in progressive circles by bringing the suit that forced R. J. Reynolds to stop using Joe Camel in its ads.

With Caplan's help, Kasky sued Nike in 1998 for false advertising, alleging it had made untrue statements about its labor practices. This was not Kasky's first lawsuit. Previously, he had sued Perrier over its claim to be "spring water" and Pillsbury Co. for labeling Mexican vegetables with the words "San Francisco style." Both suits were settled.[3] Nike sought dismissal of Kasky's suit, arguing that the statements he questioned were part of a public debate about sweatshops and protected by the First Amendment.

[3] Roger Parloff, "Can We Talk?" *Fortune*, September 2, 2002, p. 108.

THE SWEATSHOP LABOR ISSUE

By 1980 when the company went public, it had seized half the world's athletic shoe market. But the outsourcing and advertising strategies that propelled it to the top put it on a collision course with a force in its social environment. This force, the sweatshop issue, would gain power and cause considerable damage.

In 1988 an Indonesian union newspaper published a study of bad working conditions in a plant making Nike footwear.[4] Soon other critical articles appeared in the Indonesian press. The AFL-CIO decided to investigate how workers were being treated in plants that manufactured for American firms and sent an investigator named Jeffrey Ballinger to Indonesia. Ballinger focused on Nike contractors, gathering detailed information.

In 1992 he published a clever indictment of Nike in *Harper's Magazine* by exhibiting the monthly pay stub of an Indonesian woman named Sadisah who made Nike running shoes. Sadisah worked on an assembly line 10-and-a-half hours a day, six days a week, making $1.03 per day or about $0.14 an hour, less than the Indonesian minimum wage. She was paid only $0.02 an hour for 63 hours of overtime during the pay period. Her home was all she could afford, a rented shanty lacking electricity and plumbing. The Nikes she made sold for $80 in the United States, yet the cost of her labor per shoe was only $0.12. If anyone missed the point, Ballinger noted that the year before Nike had made a profit of $287 million and signed Michael Jordan to a $20 million advertising contract, a sum that Sadisah would have had to work 44,492 years to earn.[5]

Ballinger's article appeared with a flurry of other negative stories, but the issue did not immediately heat up. Nevertheless, Nike elected to show more responsibility for the welfare of foreign workers. In 1992 it adopted a "Code of Conduct" requiring its contractors to certify compliance with local minimum wage, child labor, health, safety, workers' compensation, forced labor, environmental, and discrimination laws. In 1994, it hired the accounting firm Ernst & Young to audit code compliance by making spot checks at factories.

These developments suggest that at some point CEO Philip Knight came to believe that even if Nike did not directly employ foreign workers, it benefited from their labor and so had an ethical duty toward their welfare. But Nike would not escape damage from the issue. The code and spot checks were not enough. Negative stories about its contract factories grew more numerous.

Finally, the issue exploded after April 1996 congressional testimony by the leader of a human rights group, who said clothing for Walmart's Kathie Lee apparel line was made at a Honduran factory where children worked 14 hours a day. Daytime television viewers saw talk show host Kathie Lee Gifford reduced to tears as she responded, "You can say I'm ugly, you can say I'm not talented, but when you say that I don't care about children . . . How dare you?"[6] Now the issue had emotional content for American consumers.

Soon after the Gifford spectacle anti-sweatshop activists decided to focus on Nike, and attacks heated up. Nike was an industry leader. If it could be reformed, other clothing companies and retailers would fall into line. It was also vulnerable to a brand name attack. Advocacy groups joined forces to inform the public of what they saw as a gap between the inspiring images in Nike's advertising and the grim reality of its labor practices. This alarmed Nike because bad publicity could rub away the image magic that made its brand cool.

NIKE AT WAR WITH ITS CRITICS

The war over Nike's image would be fought in the media. An early skirmish came when Bob Herbert at *The New York Times* wrote the first of what became a yearlong series of columns berating Nike. After describing a climate of atrocities in Indonesia, including government-condoned killings and torture, he accused Nike of using "the magnificent image of Michael Jordan soaring, twisting, driving, flying" to divert attention from its exploitation of Indonesian workers. "Nike executives know exactly what is going on in Indonesia. They are not bothered by the cries of the oppressed. It suits them. Each cry is a signal that their investment is paying off."[7]

---

[4] Cited in Jeffrey Hollender and Stephen Fenichell, *What Matters Most* (New York: Basic Books, 2004), p. 190.

[5] Jeffrey Ballinger, "The New Free-Trade Heel," *Harper's,* August 1992, pp. 46–47.

[6] Rob Howe et al., "Labor Pains," *People Magazine,* June 10, 1996, p. 58.

[7] Bob Herbert, "Nike's Bad Neighborhood," *The New York Times,* June 14, 1996, p. A29.

EXHIBIT 1

Rise of Negative News Stories about Nike's Labor Practices, 1988–1999

Source: From S. Prakash Sethi, *Setting Global Standards*, 2003. Table 9.2. Reprinted with permission of John Wiley & Sons, Inc.

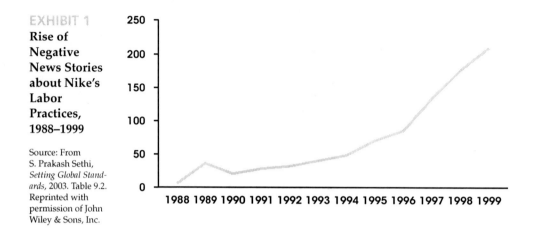

CEO Philip Knight quickly responded with a letter to the editor, citing ways that Nike tried to help workers, and noting that it paid "double the minimum wage" and "had an oversight system that works." He accused Herbert of trying to "sacrifice enlightenment for hype."[8] Herbert's response was a second column rebuking Nike for running theme ads about women's empowerment while most of its shoes were produced "by grossly underpaid women stuck in utterly powerless and often abusive circumstances."[9]

Over the next two years, negative stories about Nike appeared with increasing frequency (see Exhibit 1). An inspection report by the human rights group Vietnam Labor Watch reported that young women working in a Nike factory were paid subminimum wages. A supervisor had forced 56 women to run twice around the 1.2-mile factory boundary under a hot sun for failing to wear regulation shoes. Twelve of them fainted and required hospitalization.[10] Gary Trudeau drew a series of *Doonesbury* cartoons based on these allegations.

Activists urged people to return Nike sneakers during "shoe-ins" at Niketown outlets. A disgruntled Ernst & Young employee leaked a confidential spot inspection report on a Vietnamese shoe factory. It showed violations of Vietnamese labor law and said

that 77 percent of the employees suffered respiratory problems from breathing toxic vapors at levels that violated both Vietnamese and U.S. standards.[11] Another group, the Hong Kong Christian Industrial Committee, released a study of Nike factories in China documenting long workdays, forced overtime, pay below minimum wages, and unsafe levels of airborne dust and toxic chemicals.[12] *The Oregonian*, the paper in Portland where Nike is headquartered, called Nike "an international human rights incident."[13]

Now Nike found itself at the center of a worldwide debate over sweatshops. The company expanded efforts to stop workplace abuses and started a public relations campaign. At great expense it became the only shoe company in the world to eliminate the use of polyvinyl chloride in shoe construction, ending worker exposure to chlorine compounds. It revised its conduct code, expanding protections for workers. It set up a compliance department of more than 50 employees. Its staff members were assigned to specific Asian plants or to a region, where they trained local managers and did audits assessing code compliance.[14]

Working with Kathie Lee Gifford, other apparel companies, human rights and labor groups, and universities that buy school clothing, Nike helped to

---

[8] "Nike Pays Good Wages to Foreign Workers," *The New York Times*, June 21, 1996, p. A26.

[9] "From Sweatshops to Aerobics," *The New York Times*, June 24, 1996, p. A15.

[10] Vietnam Labor Watch, "Nike Labor Practices in Vietnam," March 20, 1997, available at www.saigon.com/~nike/reports/report1.html#summary; and Ellen Neuborne, "Nike to Take a Hit in Labor Report," *USA Today*, March 27, 1997, p. 1A.

[11] Steven Greenhouse, "Nike Shoe Plant in Vietnam Is Called Unsafe for Workers," *The New York Times*, November 8, 1997, p. A1.

[12] *Kasky v. Nike*, 93 Cal. Rptr. 2d 856.

[13] Jeff Manning, "Nike's Global Machine Goes on Trial," *The Oregonian*, November 9, 1997, p. A1.

[14] S. Prakash Sethi, *Setting Global Standards* (New York: John Wiley & Sons, 2003), p. 167.

EXHIBIT 2

**The Nike
Code of
Conduct**

Source: Nike.com.

The Code of Conduct has been revised and articulated since its introduction in 1992. Listed below are its seven "core standards." Another document, the Code Leadership Standards, elaborates 51 specific labor, safety, health, and environmental standards. The Code is translated into local languages and today is posted in more than 900 contract factories making Nike products.

1. **Forced Labor.** The contractor does not use forced labor in any form—prison, indentured, bonded, or otherwise.

2. **Child Labor.** The contractor does not employ any person below the age of 18 to produce footwear. The contractor does not employ any person below the age of 16 to produce apparel, accessories or equipment. If at the time Nike production begins, the contractor employs people of the legal working age who are at least 15, that employment may continue, but the contractor will not hire any person going forward who is younger than the Nike or legal age limit, whichever is higher. To further ensure these age standards are complied with, the contractor does not use any form of homework for Nike production.

3. **Compensation.** The contractor provides each employee at least the minimum wage, or the prevailing industry wage, whichever is higher; provides each employee a clear, written accounting for every pay period; and does not deduct from employee pay for disciplinary infractions.

4. **Benefits.** The contractor provides each employee all legally mandated benefits.

5. **Hours of Work/Overtime.** The contractor complies with legally mandated work hours; uses overtime only when each employee is fully compensated according to local law; informs each employee at the time of hiring if mandatory overtime is a condition of employment; and on a regularly scheduled basis provides one day off in seven, and requires no more than 60 hours of work per week on a regularly scheduled basis, or complies with local limits if they are lower.

6. **Environment, Safety and Health (ES&H).** From suppliers to factories to distributors and to retailers, Nike considers every member of our supply chain as partners in our business. As such, we've worked with our Asian partners to achieve specific environmental, health and safety goals, beginning with a program called MESH (Management of Environment, Safety and Health).

7. **Documentation and Inspection.** The contractor maintains on file all documentation needed to demonstrate compliance with this Code of Conduct and required laws; agrees to make these documents available for Nike or its designated monitor; and agrees to submit to inspections with or without prior notice.

start a voluntary CSR initiative called the Fair Labor Association to enforce a code of conduct and monitoring scheme to end sweatshop labor. It hired Andrew Young, a former U.S. ambassador to the United Nations, to visit Asian plants and write an inspection report. Young toured 12 factories over 15 days and found that conditions "certainly did not appear to be what most Americans would call sweatshops."[15]

[15] Dana Canedy, "Nike's Asian Factories Pass Young's Muster," *The New York Times,* June 25, 1997, p. D2.

Nike purchased full-page editorial advertisements in newspapers to broadcast his generally favorable findings, saying the report showed it was "operating morally" and promising to act on his recommendations for improvement.

Finally, Nike ran a public relations counteroffensive. Unlike some rival firms that lay low, it chose to confront critics. It hired an experienced strategist to manage the campaign. Nike responded to every charge, no matter how small or what the source. Allegations were countered with press releases, letters

At work in a
Vietnam plant
making Nike
footwear.
Source © Steve
Raymer/CORBIS.

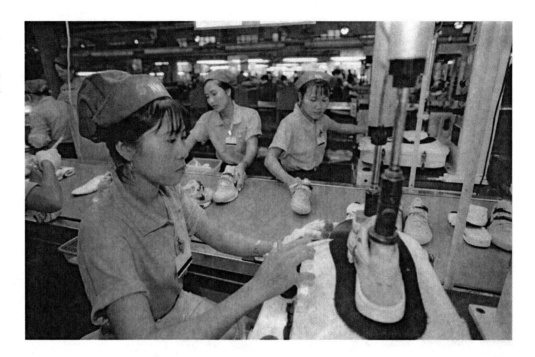

to the editor, and letters to presidents and athletic directors of universities using Nike products. In these communications Nike sought to portray itself as a responsible employer creating opportunity for thousands of workers in emerging economies. CEO Knight expressed the Nike philosophy, saying, "This is going to be a long fight, but I'm confident the truth will win in the end."[16]

THE KASKY LAWSUIT

While Knight thought he was fighting for truth, Marc Kasky perceived something less noble—a fraud conducted to sell shoes and T-shirts. He believed that Nike knowingly deceived consumers, who relied on the company's statements for reassurance that their purchases did not sustain sweatshops. Under an unusual state law, any California citizen can sue a corporation on behalf of the public for an unlawful business practice. Kasky took advantage of this provision, alleging that Nike had engaged in negligent misrepresentation, fraud and deceit, and misleading advertising in violation of the state's commercial code. The code prohibits "any

unlawful, unfair, deceptive, untrue or misleading advertising."[17]

In his complaint, Kasky accused Nike of using a "promotional scheme," including its code of conduct, to create a "carefully cultured image" that was "intended . . . to entice consumers who do not want to purchase products made in sweatshop . . . conditions."[18] He set forth six classes of misleading claims.

* In its Code of Conduct (see Exhibit 2) and in a "Nike Production Primer" pamphlet given to the media, Nike stated that its contracts prevent corporal punishment and sexual harassment at factories making Nike products. But the Vietnam Labor Watch report told of workers forced to kneel in the hot sun and described frequent complaints by female employees against their supervisors.

---

[16] Quoted in Tony Emerson, "Swoosh Wars," *Newsweek*, March 12, 2001, p. 35.

[17] The law is California's Unfair Competition Law, which is codified as §17200 (source of the quotation) and §17500 of the California Business & Professions Code. Kasky also alleged violations of California Civil Code §1572 (which defines fraud) and §1709 and §1710 (which define deceit).

[18] First Amended Complaint of Milberg, Weiss et al., *Kasky v. Nike*, Superior Court, San Francisco County, No. 994446, July 2, 1998, pp. 5, 6, and 10.

* In a range of promotional materials Nike asserted that its products were manufactured in compliance with laws and regulations on wages and overtime. But evidence from a report by the Hong Kong Christian Industrial Committee and the leaked Ernst & Young audit showed that plants in China and Vietnam violated such laws.

* At the Nike annual shareholder meeting in 1997 CEO Knight said that the air in Nike's newest Vietnam shoe factory was less polluted than the air in Los Angeles. But the Ernst & Young report documented exposures to excessive levels of hazardous air pollutants.

* In his letter to the editor of *The New York Times,* Knight stated that Nike paid, on average, double the minimum wage to workers worldwide. But this was contradicted by data from pay stubs in the Vietnam Labor Watch report. He also said that Nike gave workers free meals, but an article in the *Youth Newspaper* of Ho Chi Minh City reported that workers paid for lunches.

* In its paid editorial ads discussing Andrew Young's report on its factories, Nike made the claim that it was "doing a good job" and "operating morally." But the report was deficient because it failed to address central issues such as minimum wage violations.

* In a press release Nike made the claim that it guaranteed a "living wage for all workers." But the director of its own Labor Practices Department had written a letter defining a "living wage" as income sufficient to support a family of four, then stated that the company did not ask contractors to raise wages that high.[19]

Kasky sought no monetary gain for himself. Instead, he asked for an injunction against further deception, a court-approved public information campaign forcing the company to correct misrepresentations, disgorgement of Nike profits from California sales, and payment of his legal expenses.

However, Superior Court Judge David A. Garcia threw the case out. There was no trial to decide whether any of the statements made by Nike were misleading. The judge simply accepted Nike's claim that the statements in question were part of an ongoing public debate and, therefore, entitled to broad protection.

[19] Ibid., pp. 10–25.

COMMERCIAL SPEECH OR PROTECTED EXPRESSION?

Freedom of speech is a central value in American culture. It derives from a long philosophical tradition, exemplified in John Stuart Mill's classic essay *On Liberty.* Mill believed that freedom of opinion and expression were necessary to maintain a free society, the kind of society that could protect liberty and promote happiness. He wrote that a natural tendency existed to silence discomfiting, doubtful, or unorthodox views. But this is wrong, because no person is in possession of unerring truth.

Restricting debate deprives society of the opportunity to find new ideas that are more valid than prevailing ones. Even bizarre or incorrect comments should be valued. The former may contain partial truth and the latter make the truth more compelling because of its contrast to the falsehood. Censorship of any kind is wrong because no person, society, or generation is infallible. It is better to leave open many avenues for expression of views so that error and pretention can be opposed. Truth, said Mill, needs to be "fully, frequently, and fearlessly discussed."[20]

The First Amendment was intended to protect public debate that is critical to the functioning of democracy. It prohibits government from "abridging the freedom of speech, or of the press."[21] A complicating factor is the efforts of courts over many years to distinguish between commercial speech and other speech. Commercial speech, or advertising, receives less protection from restriction by government than speech in the broad marketplace of ideas. Ordinary speech, including political, scientific, and artistic expression, is entitled to strong protection. Laws restricting expression of opinion are regarded as invalid on their face and justified only in extreme circumstances. Commercial speech, however, is often restricted by federal and state laws to prevent consumer deception and fraud.

[20] John Stuart Mill, *On Liberty,* ed. Currin V. Shields (Indianapolis: Bobbs-Merrill, 1956), p. 43. Originally published posthumously in 1907.

[21] The amendment originally applied only to actions by the federal government, but the Supreme Court has held that it also limits state government's infringement on speech.

Over many years, courts have struggled to come up with a clear definition of commercial speech.[22] The Supreme Court has defined it as "speech proposing a commercial transaction," but this still begs clarification.[23] An ad that said "Buy Nike shoes" would be commercial speech under this definition. But what about an ad picturing athletes with the statement "Just Do It," in which there is no literal sales proposal? Elsewhere in the same case, the Supreme Court also defined commercial speech as "expression related solely to the economic interests of the speaker and its audience."[24] Would Nike's statements on sweatshops meet this standard?

The focal point of Kasky's suit would become whether or not Nike's communications were, in fact, commercial speech. At a Superior Court hearing in early 1999, his lawyers argued that they were, therefore, they should be required to meet standards of truth and honesty enforced in California law. They were not entitled to the deference that would be given under the First Amendment to, for example, statements of political candidates or poets. Nike disagreed, saying that its statements about shoe and garment factories were part of a broader public debate and thus were speech entitled to strong First Amendment protection.[25] The judge agreed with Nike and dismissed the case.[26] Kasky appealed, but a year later the appeals court again rejected his argument. Kasky then appealed to the California Supreme Court.

There he won. In a 4–3 decision the California Supreme Court held that Kasky's case should go to trial.[27] In reaching its decision, the majority created a novel, three-part definition of commercial speech and applied it to Nike's messages. For speech to be commercial it had to (1) come from a business, (2) be intended for an audience of consumers, and (3) make representations of facts related to products. Nike's statements fit each requirement. The majority conceded that commercial and noncommercial speech were intermingled in the communications, but argued, "Nike may not 'immunize false or misleading product information from government regulation simply by including references to public issues.'"[28] That put Nike in the position of a used car dealer falsely advertising "none of our cars has ever been in an accident," but evading prosecution for fraud by adding a political opinion such as, "our city should budget more for traffic safety."

Dissenting opinions revealed serious disagreement among the justices. Justice Ming Chin attacked the majority for unfairly tilting the playing field against Nike. "While Nike's critics have taken full advantage of their right to 'uninhibited, robust, and wide-open' debate," he wrote, "the same cannot be said of Nike, the object of their ire. When Nike tries to defend itself from these attacks, the majority denies it the same First Amendment protection Nike's critics enjoy."[29]

A second dissent came from Justice Janice R. Brown, who found Nike's commercial and noncommercial speech inseparable. In her view, "Nike's commercial statements about its labor practices cannot be separated from its noncommercial statements about a public issue, because its labor practices *are* the public issue."[30] She admonished the majority for creating a test of commercial speech that was unconstitutional because it made "the level of protection given to speech dependant on the identity of the speaker—and not just the speech's content."[31]

The consequences of the decision went far beyond Nike. Now any company doing business in California had to be careful about expressions of fact or opinion that reached consumers in the state. The sharpest and most ideological critics of a corporation could take issue with its statements, bring it to court, and force a trial about the accuracy of its claims. The decision was as unwelcome in the business community as it was unexpected. Nike would seek to overturn it.

[22] Samuel A. Terilli, *"Nike v. Kasky* and the Running-But-Going-Nowhere Commercial Speech Debate," *Commercial Law and Policy* 10 (2005).

[23] *Central Hudson Gas & Electric Corp. v. Public Service Commission,* 447 U.S. 562 (1980).

[24] Ibid., at 561.

[25] Nike also asserted speech protections under Article I, section 2(a) of the California Constitution which reads: "Every person may freely speak, write and publish his or her sentiments on all subjects, being responsible for the abuse of that right. A law may not restrain or abridge liberty of speech or press."

[26] *Kasky v. Nike,* 79 Cal. App. 4th 165 (2000).

[27] *Kasky v. Nike,* 27 Cal. 4th 939 (2002).

[28] At 966, quoting *Bolger v. Youngs Drug Prods. Corp.,* 463 U.S. 68 (1983).

[29] At 970–971, quoting *Garrison v. Louisiana* 379 U.S. 75 (1964).

[30] At 980. Emphasis in the original.

[31] At 978.

IN THE UNITED STATES SUPREME COURT

Nike appealed to the United States Supreme Court, which accepted the case. In its brief, Nike asked that the California Supreme Court's definition of commercial speech be struck down to remove its unconstitutional, chilling effect on public debate. Kasky argued once again that statements emanating from Nike's public relation's campaign fell into the category of free speech. He asserted that the First Amendment gave no shelter to false statements by a company about how its products were made.

Strangely, no decision would ever be made. The nine justices heard oral argument in April 2003. Then, late in June, they dismissed their consideration of the case as "improvidently granted."[32] In a brief opinion Justice John Paul Stevens said the Court had erred in accepting it before trial proceedings in California were finished. The Court would wait.

This view was not unanimous. Three justices dissented. They saw no reason to wait and hinted that they were ready to strike down any restriction on Nike's speech.

> In my view . . . the questions presented directly concern the freedom of Americans to speak about public matters in public debate, no jurisdictional rule prevents us from deciding these questions now, and delay itself may inhibit the exercise of constitutionally protected rights of free speech without making the issue significantly easier to decide later on. . . . [A]n action to enforce California's laws—laws that discourage certain kinds of speech—amounts to more than just a genuine, future threat. It is a present reality—one that discourages Nike from engaging in speech. It thereby creates "injury in fact." Further, that injury is directly "traceable" to Kasky's pursuit of this lawsuit. And this Court's decision, if favorable to Nike, can "redress" that injury.[33]

SETTLEMENT AND AFTERMATH

With the Supreme Court dismissal, Kasky's specific charges against Nike could go to trial in California. The company would now be forced to defend the alleged misrepresentations about its labor practices. Its antagonists relished the prospect.

However, late in 2003 Kasky and Nike announced a settlement. In return for Kasky dropping the case, Nike agreed to give $1.5 million to an industry-friendly factory monitoring group. It may have paid Kasky's legal fees. This was not a tough settlement for Nike.

Supporters on both sides were disappointed. Activists lost their grand show trial putting the corporate devil on display. Industry was disappointed that Nike did not stay the course because settlement left standing the California Supreme Court's broad definition of commercial speech. This definition still stands.

NIKE TURNS A NEW LEAF

Meanwhile, Nike was moving through a process of CSR review and implementation. In 2005 it published a *Corporate Responsibility Report* stating three strategic CSR goals.[34] First, it would seek to create industry-wide, systemic change for the better in contractor shoe and apparel factories. Second, it would promote sustainability by eliminating toxic chemicals in shoe-making and using more recycled materials. Third, it would improve society by promoting the idea of sport with its benefits of healthy exercise and keeping young people out of trouble.

Nike learned that its business processes and culture were in tension with the policies in its code for contractors. Many of its own actions triggered violations. For example, it rewarded its buyers for meeting price, quality, and delivery date targets, giving them a financial incentive to push contractors hard. That undermined code policies to limit workweeks and hours in the factories. Nike products were often seasonal and ordered in response to rapidly shifting fashion trends. This led Nike to adopt a low inventory policy, but in consequence the factories it contracted with were often pressured to meet last-minute production goals. Sometimes their managers responded by cheating on labor guidelines. Changing Nike's internal processes to align them with its CSR goals meant slowing its reaction to consumer trends and risking loss of revenue. It also violated the spirit of Nike's

---

[32] *Nike v. Kasky,* 539 U.S. 654 (2003), *per curiam.*

[33] Ibid., at 667, 668. The three dissenters were Anthony Kennedy, Stephen Breyer, and Sandra Day O'Connor.

[34] Nike, Inc., *FY04 Corporate Responsibility Report* (Beaverton, OR: Nike, April 2005).

aggressive procurement culture and met with internal resistance.[35]

Nike's main tactic for improving labor conditions is factory monitoring to check compliance with the Nike Code of Conduct. Its self-run monitoring program has two parts. One is a labor audit of factories requiring inspectors to check off boxes for requirements in areas such as work hours, wages, and grievance systems. The other is an environmental health and safety audit on compliance with rules on chemical management, fire safety, and protective equipment. These audits take 48 working hours to complete and result in letter grades from A to F. Experts say their design is exemplary.[36] Their results are reviewed all the way up to Nike's board of directors. Yet they have failed to end very significant labor problems.

Nike uses about 700 factories in 56 countries employing 800,000 workers. It cannot hope to monitor them all, so it focuses its audits on roughly 20 percent that do most of its production or are high risk, trying to check on them once every three years. For example, in China it has 57 so-called "focus factories," and in 2007 audited 22 of them, handing out five As, six Bs, eight Cs, and three Ds.[37] Other factories are monitored by voluntary responsibility alliances, such as the industry-funded Fair Labor Association. A few pay for their own audits. It is an expansive effort, but bad reports keep coming in.

In Vietnam, 20,000 workers walked off the job for two days at a plant making Nike shoes. They were asking for a 20 percent raise, but received only 10 percent and free lunches. On their return they were in a violent mood and the plant had to be closed for another three days.[38] This was just one of 720 strikes at factories in Vietnam in 2008.[39]

When management at a Nike hat plant in Bangladesh learned that workers had attended a labor rights seminar, the personnel manager interrogated a woman who had attended, threatening to reinjure a hand she had badly injured in the past unless she gave up the names of other attendees. She refused, but management intimidated another person into revealing the names and those named were fired. Nike investigated the situation and got the workers rehired.[40]

An Australian TV reporter posed as a fashion buyer to get inside a Malaysian garment factory making Nike T-shirts where he discovered parlous conditions. It employed immigrant workers who paid large recruiting fees to get their jobs, then had to surrender their passports to plant management, which held them until the recruiting fees were repaid, an unlikely event given the low wages paid. They lived in crowded, malodorous rooms. Nike admitted many code violations, rectified the problems, and called in managers from all of its 37 factories in that country for training.[41]

These are more than isolated episodes. A scholarly analysis of 800 Nike audits concluded that despite years of effort, working conditions at its factories remained highly variable. While conditions improved in some plants, in others they stayed the same, and in many they deteriorated, leaving "little evidence that this system of private voluntary regulation is at all an effective strategy for improving labor standards."[42] And an in-depth report by a global coalition of more than 100 unions and human rights groups concluded this:

> Despite more than 15 years of codes of conduct adopted by major sportswear brands such as Adidas, Nike, New Balance, Puma and Reebok, workers making their products still face extreme pressure to meet production quotas, excessive, undocumented and unpaid overtime, verbal abuse, threats to health and safety related to the high quotas and exposure to toxic chemicals, and a failure to provide legally required health and other insurance programs.[43]

[35] Simon Zadek, "The Path to Corporate Responsibility," *Harvard Business Review,* December 2004, pp. 129–30.

[36] John Ruwitch, "Nike's Chinese Suppliers Defy Labour Laws," *National Post,* March 15, 2008, p. FP16.

[37] Nike, Inc., *Innovate for a Better World: Nike China 2008 Corporate Responsibility Reporting Supplement* (Beaverton, OR: Nike, 2008).

[38] "Nike Strike Ends, Violence Begins," *The Toronto Star,* April 3, 2008, p. B2.

[39] Jeff Ballinger, "Finding an Anti-Sweatshop Strategy that Works," *Dissent,* Summer 2009, p. 6.

[40] Worker Rights Consortium, *Case Summary: Dada Dhaka and Max Embo* (Washington, DC: WRC, November 1, 2008).

[41] Eugenia Levenson, "Citizen Nike," *Fortune,* November 24, 2008, p. 165. The report can be viewed at http://tinyurl.com/63vvpq.

[42] Richard M. Locke and Monica Romis, "The Promise and Perils of Private Voluntary Regulation: Labor Standards and Work Organization in Two Mexican Garment Factories," MIT Sloan School Working Paper 4734–09, January 13, 2009, p. 2. Richard M. Locke, Fei Qin, and Alberto A. Brause, "Does Monitoring Improve Labour Standards? Lessons from Nike," *Industrial & Labour Relations Review,* October 2007.

[43] Play Fair 2008, *Clearing the Hurdles: Steps to Improving Wages and Working Conditions in the Global Sportswear Industry* (Play Fair 2008 Campaign, April 2008), p. 6.

UNDERLYING PROBLEMS

Why do such problems still exist? Nike's 700-factory supply chain is too big to monitor. Its business model invites labor exploitation. When wages rise in one country, it seeks a lower-wage alternative. Factories are still faced with tight deadlines, sudden shifts in orders, and late design changes. They have insufficient power in supply chains to push back against global brands such as Nike. But they often have great power over workers eager for jobs. If timely order fulfillment is threatened, the easiest way to catch up is forced overtime or elimination of days off.[44]

According to Jeffrey Ballinger, monitoring by Nike and groups such as the Fair Labor Association is a prime example of voluntary corporate responsibility being used to avoid real reform.[45] Audits focus on the accuracy of wage slips, worker-to-toilet ratios, and placement of fire extinguishers. They avoid securing core global labor rights such as collective bargaining. Part of the problem is that many nations do not adequately enforce their labor laws.

International Labor Organization Convention No. 81 requires countries to inspect workplaces for compliance, but most countries with low-wage labor markets do not do so, in part because they want to attract foreign investment. They welcome voluntary corporate responsibility inspection regimes that make it look like action is being taken, even if the action is light. Corporations, in turn, prefer voluntary action to strict regulation. So governments and corporations unite in supporting CSR as a cosmetic touch to cover fundamental problems. In nations where labor laws are feebly enforced it is hard for workers to help themselves. They are often uninformed about their rights; they have no examples of successful unionizing before them. Until workers are empowered, forced work in poor conditions will lead to more scandals, violence, and reputation damage for global brands.

Ballinger suggests a solution for Nike.

> My research shows that about 75 cents per pair of shoes to the worker would be needed to fix problems that workers have been complaining about since the 1980s. That is roughly 80 percent more to workers, or $1.80 on a $70 pair of shoes at Foot Locker. If Nike, instead, paid workers that 75 cents more per pair of shoes, the cost to Nike would be $210 million a year. . . .[46]

Questions

1. What responsibility does Nike have for conditions of work at foreign factories making its products?

2. Could Nike have better anticipated and more effectively handled the sweatshop issue? What did it do right? What was ineffective or counterproductive?

3. Has Nike created and implemented an effective approach to social responsibility? Does it address root causes of problems in Nike's supply chain? Should it now do more or do something different?

4. Did the California Supreme Court correctly decide the *Kasky* case? Why or why not?

5. How should the line between commercial and noncommercial speech be drawn?

---

[44] Richard Read, "Nike Gets What It Pays For, Critics Say," *The Oregonian*, August 5, 2008, p. A1.

[45] Jeff Ballinger, "No Sweat? Corporate Social Responsibility and the Dilemma of Anti-Sweatshop Activism," *New Labor Forum*, Spring 2008.

[46] Ibid., pp. 95–96.

Chapter Seven

Business Ethics

Bernard Ebbers

September 27, 2006. At 9:00 a.m. on this Tuesday morning Bernard J. Ebbers, former CEO of WorldCom, pulled away from his home just outside Jackson, Mississippi. At 1:09 p.m. he arrived at a federal prison near Oakdale, Louisiana, drove through the gate, and surrendered himself to begin a 25-year sentence. The trip was 200 miles, far enough to end one life and begin another.

There is no parole for a federal sentence. Time can be reduced up to 15 percent for good behavior, but even with this Ebbers will serve 21 years and 4 months. Since he was 65 when he entered prison, he would be 86 on his projected release date of July 4, 2028. However, he has a serious heart condition. Besides his freedom, Ebbers

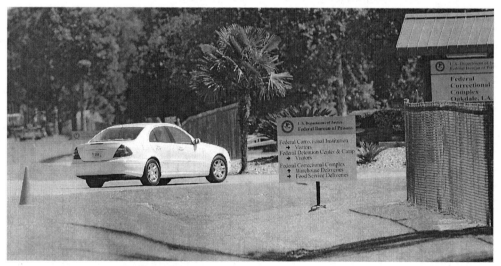

Former WorldCom chief Bernard Ebbers drives through the gates of a federal prison in Oakdale, Louisiana, to begin a 25-year sentence for his role in a massive accounting fraud. Source: © AP Photo/Rogelio V. Solis

also lost his fortune. Once a billionaire, he forfeited all assets except a home and $50,000 to be used by his wife, Kristie.

Ebbers built WorldCom from a small phone company into a global telecommunications giant. His rise began in 1984. After investing in a local long-distance company he was asked to manage it. He made it grow with mergers that were audacious in their reach. Eventually, it became a publicly traded corporation with annual revenues of $39 billion. As WorldCom grew so did Ebbers' wealth, but extravagant spending forced him to use his stock as collateral for loans to pay his debts. If share prices fell too far he would be lost.

Fate is uncaring and about this time the 1990s dot-com investment bubble burst. WorldCom's revenues declined and expenses for its fiber optic network rose more than anticipated. In 2000 the chief financial officer began to report false quarterly revenues, using accounting tricks to disguise rising expenses. The share prices held. However, internal auditors discovered the deceit and reported it to the Securities and Exchange Commission (SEC), which began an investigation.

The revenue manipulations became known to investors, and WorldCom shares lost 90 percent of their value. WorldCom's board of directors forced Ebbers to resign. In 2002 the company set a record in failure, breaking Enron's previous total for the largest bankruptcy in American history. Although it ultimately survived, 17,000 workers lost their jobs and investors lost billions of dollars.

Federal prosecutors charged Ebbers with nine counts of criminal conspiracy, securities fraud, and filing false documents with the SEC.[1] He refused to plead guilty, claiming that his chief financial officer had duped him. At his trial in 2005 he testified that he had no knowledge of the fraud.

Q: Did you ever believe that any of the statements contained in those public filings were not true?
A: No, sir.
Q: Did you ever believe that WorldCom had reported revenue that it was not entitled to report?
A: No, sir. . . .
Q: Did you ever believe that WorldCom was putting out bad numbers in its financial statements in any way at all?
A: No.[2]

Five of Ebbers' subordinates, including the chief financial officer, had pled guilty to related charges and agreed to cooperate with prosecutors. They testified that Ebbers not only knew about the conspiracy, but also actively directed it. A jury convicted him on all counts. It was a big victory for federal prosecutors. "Today's verdict is a triumph of our legal system," declared Attorney General Alberto Gonzalez.[3]

---

[1] *United States v. Bernard J. Ebbers,* Indictment, S3 02 Cr. 1144 (BSJ), 2004.

[2] *United States v. Bernard J. Ebbers,* 458 F.3d 124 (2006).

[3] Department of Justice, *Statement of Attorney General Alberto R. Gonzales on the Bernard Ebbers Conviction,* press release 05–122, March 15, 2005.

Ebbers "wept and sniffled" at his sentencing.[4] Victims of the fraud were invited to speak. One was a former WorldCom sales representative whose retirement money evaporated from a company 401(k) plan. "My life was destroyed by the greed of Bernard Ebbers," he said. "He can't ever repay me or the tens of thousands like me whose lives disintegrated in the blink of an eye."[5]

Federal sentencing guidelines called for a sentence of 30 years based on the presence of certain aggravating factors. Direct losses to investors were estimated to be $2.2 billion, there were thousands of victims, and as a CEO Ebbers had abused a position of public trust. Judge Barbara Jones decided to subtract five years. She was moved by 170 letters from Ebbers' friends and neighbors asking for mercy. That left the sentence at 25 years. Ebbers requested further leniency because he suffers from cardiomyopathy, an inflammation of the heart. The judge rejected the relevance of this condition to sentencing. "Although I recognize . . . this is likely to be a life sentence for Mr. Ebbers," she said, "I find anything else would not reflect the seriousness of the crime."[6]

The judge recommended that Ebbers serve his time in a low-security facility. However, the Federal Bureau of Prisons bases assignments on the length of sentences, assuming that a long sentence signals its bearer is more likely to pose an escape risk and to endanger fellow inmates. Because Ebbers' sentence was 25 years, he was put in a medium-security facility. There, he lives with violence-prone inmates, sleeps in a cell rather than a dormitory, and encounters many locks and fences.

Ebbers' wife, who was making the 400-mile round-trip to visit him on weekends, filed for divorce 19 months into his sentence. Ebbers still maintains his innocence and petitioned President George W. Bush for clemency in 2008. He was denied.

Criminal sentences are intended to punish individuals and deter future crime. Ebbers' sentence inspires rumination. Was it fair retribution for his actions? Was its length necessary to deter more accounting fraud? And how did Ebbers' 25 years compare with the sentences of violent criminals? It exceeded the 20 years given to Salvatore Gravano, a Mafia hit man who confessed to 19 murders.[7] It exceeded the average of 24.4 years served by first-degree murderers in California.[8]

Ebbers is exposed now as unethical, a criminal, and deficient as a leader. In this chapter we add perspective to each of these dimensions. We discuss the sources of ethical values in business, including truth telling, a basic virtue that Ebbers neglected. Then we discuss prosecution of corporate crime. Finally, we look at factors shaping ethical climates in organizations and discuss the managerial tools leaders can use to elevate behavior.

[4] Carrie Johnson, "Ebbers Gets 25-Year Sentence for Role in WorldCom Fraud," *Washington Post,* July 14, 2005, p. A1.

[5] Quoted in Leonard Greene and Richard Wilner, "Bawling Bernie Smacked," *New York Post,* July 14, 2005, p. 3.

[6] Quoted in Johnson, "Ebbers Gets 25-Year Sentence for Role in WorldCom Fraud," p. A1.

[7] Andy Newman, "Mafia Turncoat Gets 20 Years for Running Ecstacy Ring," *The New York Times,* September 7, 2002, p. 3.

[8] Department of Corrections and Rehabilitation, *Time Served on Prison Sentence* (Sacramento, CA: DCR, March 2006), table 1.

WHAT ARE BUSINESS ETHICS?

ethics
The study of good and evil, right and wrong, and just and unjust.

business ethics
The study of good and evil, right and wrong, and just and unjust actions in business.

Ethics is the study of what is good and evil, right and wrong, and just and unjust. *Business ethics,* therefore, is the study of good and evil, right and wrong, and just and unjust actions in business. Ethical managers try to do good and avoid doing evil. A mass of principles, values, norms, and thoughts concerned with what conduct *ought* to be exists to guide them. Yet in this vaporous mass, the outlines of good and evil are at times shadowy. Usually they are distinct enough, but often not. So, using ethical ideas in business is an art, an art requiring judgment about both the motivations behind an act and the act's consequences.

Discussions of business ethics frequently emphasize refractory and unclear situations, perhaps to show drama and novelty. Although all managers face difficult ethical conflicts, applying clear guidelines resolves the vast majority of them. The Eighth Commandment, for example, prohibits stealing and is plainly violated by taking tools home from work or the theft of trade secrets. Lies in advertising violate a general rule of the Western business world that the seller of a product must not purposely deceive a buyer. This general understanding stems from the Mosaic law, the Code of Hammurabi, Roman law, and other sources and is part of a general ethic favoring truth going back at least 3,000 years.

Overall, ethical traditions that apply to business support truth telling, honesty, protection of life, respect for rights, fairness, and obedience to law. Some beliefs in this bundle of traditions go back thousands of years. Others, such as the idea that a corporation is responsible for the long-term health of its workers, have emerged more recently. In keeping with this long and growing ethical heritage, most business actions can be clearly judged ethical or unethical; eliminating unethical behavior such as bribery or embezzlement may be difficult, but knowing the rightness or wrongness of actions is usually easy.

This does not mean that ethical decisions are always clear. Some are troublesome because although basic ethical standards apply, conflicts between them defy resolution.

> In the mid-1970s Lockheed Aircraft Corp. faced default on government loans. It paid $12 million ($48 million today) in bribes to politicians and business executives in Japan, selling 120 warplanes and 21 civilian airliners, protecting its future, and saving thousands of jobs. Making the payments broke no U.S. laws, but they broke a Japanese law. Sixteen people there were convicted of a crime, including a former prime minister and a likely future prime minister. Carl Kotchian, Lockheed's president, had no regrets. Bribes were tangled with foreign sales. "Even when offering a better product," he said, "we would lose out if we did not also make the required payments."[9] Competing in the industry meant slighting ethical norms. When the bribes came out, politicians and publics in both countries went into a dither. Kotchian retired to run an alfalfa farm saying, "I'd do it again."[10]

---

[9] Quoted in Donald E. Fink, "New Lockheed Management Studying Impact of Payments," *Aviation Week & Space Technology,* February 23, 1976, p. 15.

[10] Quoted in Peter Pae, "Ex-Lockheed Chief Told of Paying Bribes," *Los Angeles Times,* December 22, 2008, p. B10.

Daniel Drew
(1797–1879),
speculator in
railroad stocks
and an
exponent of
the theory of
amorality.
Source: © Picture
History/Napoleon
Sarony

Some ethical issues are hidden, at least initially, and hard to recognize.

A. H. Robins Co. began to market its Dalkon Shield intrauterine device through general practitioners while competitors continued selling them only through obstetricians and gynecologists. This strategy was wildly successful in getting market share for Robins and did not, initially, seem to raise ethical issues, but when dangerous side effects with the device appeared, the general practitioners were slower to see than the specialists. Robins' failure to make extra efforts in tracking the safety of the device then emerged as an ethical shortcoming. It cost women their lives.

TWO THEORIES OF BUSINESS ETHICS

In the ageless debate about whether ethics in business may be more permissive than general societal or personal ethics, there are two basic views.

theory of
amorality
The belief that
business should
be conducted
without refer-
ence to the
full range of
ethical stand-
ards, restraints,
and ideals in
society.

The first, the *theory of amorality,* is that business should be amoral, that is, conducted without reference to the full range of ethical standards, restraints, and ideals in society. Managers may use compromising ethics because competition distills their selfish actions into benefits for society. Adam Smith noted that the "invisible hand" of the market assures that "by pursuing his own interest [a merchant] frequently promotes that of the society more effectively than when he really intends to promote it."[11]

The apex of this view came during the latter half of the nineteenth century. It was widely believed that business and personal ethics existed in separate compartments, that business was a special sanctuary in which less idealistic ethics were permissible.[12] Daniel Drew, who made a fortune in the 1860s by manipulating railroad stocks

[11] *The Wealth of Nations,* ed. Edwin Cannan (New York: Modern Library, 1937), p. 423; originally published in 1776. Smith also believed that merchants must abide by prevailing societal ethics.

[12] This was the conviction of social Darwinist Herbert Spencer, who believed in two sets of ethics. *Family ethics* were based on the principle of charity and benefits were apportioned without relation to merit. *State ethics* were based on a competitive justice and benefits were apportioned strictly on merit. Family ethics interjected into business or government by well-meaning people interfered with the laws of nature and would slowly corrupt the workings of Darwinian natural selection. See "The Sins of Legislators," in *The Man versus the State* (London: Watts, 1940); originally published in 1884.

James Cash Penney (1875–1971), son of a Baptist minister and an exemplar of the theory of moral unity. Source: © Oscar White/CORBIS.

without scruple, summed up the nineteenth century compartmentalization of business decisions in these words:

> Sentiment is all right up in the part of the city where your home is. But downtown, no. Down there the dog that snaps the quickest gets the bone. Friendship is very nice for a Sunday afternoon when you're sitting around the dinner table with your relations, talking about the sermon that morning. But nine o'clock Monday morning, notions should be brushed aside like cobwebs from a machine. I never took any stock in a man who mixed up business with anything else. He can go into other things outside of business hours, but when he's in the office, he ought not to have a relation in the world—and least of all a poor relation.[13]

The theory of amorality has far less public acceptance today, but it lives on quietly. Many managers still allow competitive pressures to justify acts that would be wrong in private life. The theory of amorality releases them from feelings of guilt.

The second basic ethical view is the *theory of moral unity*, in which business actions are judged by the general ethical standards in society, not by a special set of more permissive standards. Only one basic ethical standard exists, so business actions are judged by the same principles as actions in other areas of life.

Many managers take this position today, and some did even in the nineteenth century. An example is James Cash Penney. We remember Penney for building a chain of department stores, but his first enterprise was a butcher shop. As a young man, Penney went to Denver, where, finding the shop for sale, he wired his mother for $3,000 to buy it. The departing butcher shop owner warned him that his success depended on orders from a nearby hotel. "To keep the hotel for a customer," the butcher explained, "all you have to do is buy the chef a bottle of whiskey a week." Penney regularly made the gift and business was good, but he soon had second thoughts. Resolving no longer to do business that way, he stopped the bribe, lost the hotel's business, and went broke when the shop failed. He was 23 years old.

Penney later started the Golden Rule Department Store in Denver and always believed that principles of honesty led to its ultimate success. In contrast to the unsentimental lone wolf Daniel Drew, Penney reflects his focus on ethics in this little story.

theory of moral unity
Business actions are judged by the general ethical standards of society, not by a special set of more permissive standards.

---

[13] Bouck White, *The Book of Daniel Drew* (New York: Doubleday, Page & Company, 1910), pp.120-21.

It seems that the manager of a chain store had run out of a certain line of goods and had appealed to the manager of another store in the chain for a share of the supply which this second man had on hand. This man consented—but sent some goods of poor quality which *he* had not been able to sell. He thought he was being very shrewd. But if I had the chance I would fire that man. He was not being square. He hadn't the instinct of fair dealing. You can't build a solid, substantial house with decayed planks, no matter what kind of a veneer is put over their rottenness. That man's action was rotten, even though it was veneered with temporary shrewdness.[14]

To J. C. Penney, and other exemplars of the theory of moral unity, desire to succeed is never an excuse to neglect principled behavior. Actions are not moral just because they make money. Ethical conflicts cannot be avoided simply because they arise in the course of business.

MAJOR SOURCES OF ETHICAL VALUES IN BUSINESS

reciprocity
A form of social behavior in which people behave supportively in the expectation that this behavior will be given in return.

Four great repositories of ethical values influence managers. They are religion, philosophy, cultural experience, and law (see Figure 7.1). A common theme, the idea of *reciprocity*, or mutual help, is found in each of these value systems. This idea reflects the central purpose of ethics, which is to bind individuals into a cooperative social whole. Ethical values are a mechanism that controls behavior in business and in other areas of life. Ethical restraint is more efficient with society's resources than are cruder controls such as police, lawsuits, or economic incentives. Ethical values channel individual energy into pursuits that are benign to others and beneficial to society.

FIGURE 7.1
Major Sources of Ethical Values in Business

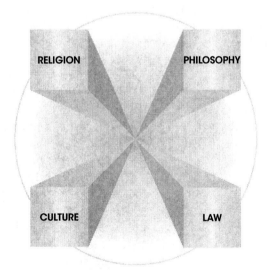

[14] J. C. Penney, "It Is One Thing to Desire—and Another to Determine," in Peter Krass, ed., *The Book of Business Wisdom* (New York: John Wiley & Sons, 1997), p. 89. Reprinted from *American Magazine*, August 1919. Emphasis in the original.

Religion

The great religions, including the Judeo-Christian tradition prominent in American history, converge in the belief that a divine will reveals the nature of right and wrong behavior, including in business. Despite doctrinal differences, major religions agree on ideas forming the basic building blocks of ethics in every society. For example, the principle of reciprocity is found, encapsulated in variations of the Golden Rule, in Buddhism, Confucianism, Hinduism, Islam, Judaism, and Christianity. These religions also converge in emphasizing traits such as promise keeping, honesty, fairness, charity, and responsibility to others.

Christian managers often seek guidance in the Bible. Like the source books and writings of other main religions, the Bible was written in a premodern, agricultural society, and many of its ethical teachings require interpretation before they can be applied to problems in the modern workplace. Much of the ethical teaching in the Bible comes from parables. The parable of the prodigal son (Luke 15:11–32) tells the story of an unconditionally merciful father—an image applicable to ethical conflicts in corporate superior–subordinate relationships. The story of the rich man and Lazarus (Luke 16:19–31) teaches concern for the poor and challenges Christian managers to consider the less privileged, a fitting admonition in a world where billions of people survive on less than $1 a day.[15]

In Islam the Koran is a source of ethical inspiration. The Prophet Muhammad said, "Every one of you is a shepherd and everyone is responsible for what he is shepherd of."[16] In a modern context, the Muslim manager is like a shepherd and the corporation is like a flock. The manager has a duty to rise above self-interest and protect the good of the organization.

In the Jewish tradition, managers can turn to rabbinic moral commentary in the Talmud and the books of Moses in the Torah. Here again, ancient teachings are regarded as analogies. For example, a Talmudic ruling holds that a person who sets a force in motion bears responsibility for any resulting harm, even if natural forces intervene (*Baba Qamma* 60a). This is discussed in the context of an agrarian society in which a person who starts a fire is responsible for damage from flying sparks, even if nature intervenes with high winds. In an industrial context, the ethics lesson is that polluting companies are responsible for problems caused by their waste.[17] Another passage comments on a situation in which laborers are hired to dig in a field, but a nearby river overflows, preventing the work (*Bava Metzia* 76b–77a). The Talmud counsels that if the employer knew the river was likely to overflow then the workers should be paid, but if the flood was unpredictable then the workers should bear the loss. This teaching may inform thinking about modern layoffs. In highly cyclical industries, workers can anticipate

---

[15] See Oliver F. Williams and John W. Houck, *Full Value: Cases in Christian Business Ethics* (New York: Harper & Row, 1978), for discussion of these and other biblical sources of inspiration for managers.

[16] Quoted in Tanri Abeng, "Business Ethics in Islamic Context: Perspectives of a Muslim Business Leader," *Business Ethics Quarterly*, July 1997, p. 52.

[17] Moses L. Pava, *Business Ethics: A Jewish Perspective* (New York: Yeshiva University Press, 1997), pp. 72–73.

the risk of layoffs, but in more stable industries management may bear greater responsibility for job security.[18]

Parables and stories in the literature of ancient worlds can seem so innocent as to have little value for modern managers. However, as one rabbinic scholar notes, "Our world has undergone tremendous technological changes, but the issues stay the same—egotism, jealousy, greed, among others."[19] Thus, the central wisdom remains. When Confucius told Chinese merchants that "He who acts with a constant view to his own advantage (*li*) will be much murmured against," he exposed a speck of truth visible in any era.[20]

Philosophy

A Western manager can look back on more than 2,000 years of philosophical inquiry into ethics. This rich, complex tradition is the source of many notions about what is right or wrong in business. Every age has added new ideas, but it is a mistake to regard the history of ethical philosophy as a single debate that, over centuries, has matured to bear the fruit of growing wisdom and clear, precise standards of conduct. Even after two millennia, there remains considerable dispute among ethical thinkers about the nature of right action. If anything, standards of ethical behavior were arguably clearer in ancient Greek civilization than they are now.

In a brief circuit of milestones in ethical thinking, we turn first to the Greek philosophers. Greek ethics, from Homeric times onward, were embodied in the discharge of duties related to social roles such as shepherd, warrior, merchant, citizen, or king. Expectations of the occupants of these roles were clearer than in contemporary America, where social roles such as those of business manager or employee are more vague, overlapping, and marked by conflict.[21]

Socrates (469–399 BC) asserted that virtue and ethical behavior were associated with wisdom and taught that insight into life would naturally lead to right conduct. He also introduced the idea of a moral law higher than human law, an idea that activists use to demand supralegal behavior from transnational corporations. Plato (428–348 BC), the gifted student of Socrates, carried this doctrine of virtue as knowledge further by elaborating the theory that absolute justice exists independently of individuals and that its nature can be discovered by intellectual effort. In *The Republic*, Plato set up a 50-year program for training rulers to rule in harmony with the ideal of justice.[22] Plato's most apt pupil, Aristotle, spelled out virtues of character in the *Nicomachean Ethics* and advocated a regimen of continuous learning to improve ethical behavior.[23]

[18] See Robert H. Carver, "If the River Stopped: A Talmudic Perspective on Downsizing," *Journal of Business Ethics* 50 (2004), pp. 144–45.

[19] Meir Tamari, quoted in Gail Lichtman, "Ethics Is Their Business," *The Jerusalem Post,* May 25, 2001, p. 13.

[20] *Analects,* book IV, chap. XII. Cited in Stephen B. Young, "The CRT *Principles for Business* as an Expression of Original Confucian Morality," *Caux Roundtable Newsletter,* Fall 2000, p. 9.

[21] Alasdair MacIntyre, *After Virtue: A Study in Moral Theory* (South Bend, IN: University of Notre Dame Press, 1981), p.115.

[22] Plato, *The Republic,* F. M. Cornford, trans. (New York: Oxford University Press, 1945).

[23] *Nicomachean Ethics,* J. A. K. Thomson, trans. (New York: Penguin Books, 1982), p. 51.

The Stoic school of ethics, spanning four centuries from the death of Alexander to the rise of Christianity in Rome, furthered the trend toward character development in Greek ethics. Epictetus (AD 50–100), for instance, taught that virtue was found solely within and should be valued for its own sake, arguing that this inner virtue was a higher reward than external riches or worldly success.

In business, the ethical legacy of the Greeks and Romans lives on in the conviction that virtues such as truth telling, charity, obeying the law, justice, courage, friendship, and the just use of power are important qualities. Today when a manager trades integrity for profit, we condemn this on the basis of the teachings of the ancient Mediterranean world.

Ethical thinking after the rise of Christianity was dominated by the great Catholic theologians St. Augustine (354–430) and St. Thomas Aquinas (1225–1274). Both believed that humanity should follow God's will; correct behavior in business and in all worldly activity was necessary to achieve salvation and life after death. Christianity was the source of many ethical teachings, including specific rules such as the Ten Commandments.

Christian theology created a lasting reservoir of ethical doctrine, but its command of ethical thought weakened during the historical period of intellectual and industrial expansion in Europe called the Enlightenment. Secular philosophers such as Baruch Spinoza (1632–1677) tried to demonstrate ethical principles with logical analysis rather than ordain them by reference to God's will. So also, Immanuel Kant (1724–1804) tried to find universal and objective ethical rules in logic. Kant and Spinoza, and others who followed, created a great estrangement with moral theology by believing that humanity could discover the nature of good behavior without reference to God. To this day, there is a deep divide between Christian managers who look to the Bible for divine guidance and other managers who look to worldly writing for ethical wisdom.

Other milestones of secular thinking followed. Jeremy Bentham (1748–1832) developed the idea of utilitarianism as a guide to ethics. Bentham observed that an ethical action was the one among all alternatives that brought pleasure to the largest number of persons and pain to the fewest. The worldly impact of this ethical philosophy is almost impossible to overestimate, because it validated two dominant ideologies, democracy and industrialism, allowing them first to arise and then to flourish. The legitimacy of majority rule in democratic governments rests in large part on Bentham's theory of utility as later refined by John Stuart Mill (1806–1873). Utilitarianism also sanctified industrial development by legitimizing the notion that economic growth benefits the majority; thus the pain and dislocation it brings to a few may be ethically permitted.

John Locke (1632–1704) developed and refined doctrines of human rights and left an ethical legacy supporting belief in the inalienable rights of human beings, including the right to pursue life, liberty, and happiness, and the right to freedom from tyranny. Our leaders, including business leaders, continue to be restrained by these beliefs.

A *realist school* of ethics also developed alongside the idealistic thinking of philosophers such as Spinoza, Kant, the utilitarians, and Locke. The realists believed that both good and evil were naturally present in human nature; human behavior

realist school
A school of thought that rejects ethical perfection, taking the position that human affairs will be characterized by flawed behavior and ought to be depicted as they are, not as we might wish them to be.

inevitably would reflect this mixture. Since good and evil occurred naturally, it was futile to try to teach ideals. Ideals could never be realized because evil was a permanent human trait. The realist school developed ethical theories that shrugged off the idea of perfect goodness. Niccolò Machiavelli (1469–1527) argued that important ends justified expedient means. Herbert Spencer (1820–1903) wrote prolifically of a harsh ethic that justified vicious competition among companies because it furthered evolution—a process in which humanity improved as the unfit fell down. Friedrich Nietzsche (1844–1900) rejected the ideals of earlier "nice" ethics, saying they were prescriptions of the timid, designed to fetter the actions of great men whose irresistible power and will were regarded as dangerous by the common herd of ordinary mortals.

Nietzsche believed in the existence of a "master morality" in which great men made their own ethical rules according to their convenience and without respect for the general good of average people. In reaction to this master morality, the mass of ordinary people developed a "slave morality" intended to shackle the great men. For example, according to Nietzsche, the mass of ordinary people celebrate the Christian virtue of turning the other cheek because they lack the power to revenge themselves on great men. He felt that prominent ethical ideals of his day were recipes for timidity and once said of utilitarianism that it made him want to vomit.[24] The influence of realists on managers has been strong. Spencer was wildly popular among the business class in the nineteenth century. Machiavelli is still read for inspiration. The lasting influence of realism is that many managers, deep down, do not believe that ideals can be achieved in business life.

Cultural Experience

Every culture transmits between generations a set of traditional values, rules, and standards that define acceptable behavior. In this way, individuals channel their conduct in socially approved directions. Civilization itself is a cumulative cultural experience consisting of three stages; in each, economic and social arrangements have dictated a distinct moral code.[25]

For millions of generations in the *hunting and gathering stage* of human development, ethics were adapted to conditions in which our ancestors had to be ready to fight, face brutal foes, and suffer hostile forces of nature. Under such circumstances, a premium was placed on pugnacity, appetite, greed, and sexual readiness, since it was often the strongest who survived. Trade ethics in early civilizations were probably deceitful and dishonest by our standards, and economic transactions were frequently conducted by brute force and violence.

Civilization passed into an *agricultural stage* approximately 10,000 years ago, beginning a time when industriousness was more important than ferocity, thrift paid greater dividends than violence, monogamy became the prevailing sexual custom because of the relatively equal numbers of the sexes, and peace came to be valued over wars, which destroyed crops and animals. These new values were

---

[24] His exact words were "the general welfare is no ideal, no goal, no remotely intelligible concept, but only an emetic." In *Beyond Good and Evil* (New York: Vintage Books, 1966), p. 157; originally published in 1886.

[25] Will Durant and Ariel Durant, *The Lessons of History* (New York: Simon & Schuster, 1968), pp. 37–42.

codified into ethical systems by philosophers and founders of religions. So the great ethical philosophies and theologies that guide managers today are largely products of the agricultural revolution.

Three centuries ago, society entered an *industrial stage* of cultural experience, and ethical systems began to reflect changed institutions, ideologies, and ecosystems. Powerful forces such as electricity, capitalism, constitutional democracy, population growth, and nuclear weapons have appeared. Industrialism has begun to create a distinct ethic, as its impacts put stress on ethical values that evolved in ancient, agriculture-based worlds, altering people's judgments about good and evil. For example, the copious outpouring of material goods from factories encourages materialism and consumption at the expense of older, scarcity-based virtues such as moderation and thrift. The old truism that nature exists for human exploitation is less compelling when reexamined in a cloud of industrial gases.

Ethical Variation in Cultures

Ethical values differ among nations as historical experiences have interacted with philosophies and religions to create diverging cultural values and laws. Where differences do exist, are some cultures correct about proper business ethics and others wrong? There are two answers to this question.

The school of *ethical universalism* holds that in terms of biological and psychological needs, human nature is everywhere the same. Ethical rules are transcultural because behavior that fulfills basic human needs should be the same everywhere; for example, basic rules of justice must be followed. Basic justice might be achieved, however, by emphasizing group welfare or by emphasizing individual rights, leaving room for cultural variation.

The school of *ethical relativism* holds that, although human biology is everywhere similar, cultural experience creates widely diverging values, including ethical values. Ethical values are subjective. There is no objective way to prove them right or wrong as with scientific facts. Truth is not a property inherent within them. They are ideas that work in their cultural setting. It is wrong, therefore, for one society to claim that its ethics are superior to those of another.

We cannot settle this age-old philosophical debate. However, ethical variation is a practical and urgent issue. Because of globalization, corporations extend their values into foreign markets where they are sometimes inimical. Google is on a mission to make the world's information accessible to everyone across all borders. Its search engine is based on a "democratic" algorithm that registers "votes" on Web pages. Its ethics code is summed in the phrase "Don't be evil." This bundle of values is dear to Google, but alien to the Chinese communist government, which employs Internet police to monitor and suppress dissent. Eventually, Google refused to compromise its strategic and ethical principles by remaining in the Chinese market.

What guidelines exist for companies that want flexibility in their ethical codes? Some scholars argue that at a high level of abstraction, the ethical ideals of all cultures converge to basic sameness. Thomas Donaldson and Thomas W. Dunfee see a deep social contract underlying all human societies. This contract is based on what they call *hypernorms*, or principles at the root of all human ethics. Examples include basic rights such as life, liberty, and the priority of the community over its

ethical universalism
The theory that because human nature is everywhere the same, basic ethical rules are applicable in all cultures. There is some room for variation in the way these rules are followed.

ethical relativism
The theory that ethical values are created by cultural experience. Different cultures may create different values and there is no universal standard by which to judge which values are superior.

hypernorms
Master ethical principles that underlie all other ethical principles. All variations of ethical principle must conform to them.

individual members. These hypernorms validate other ethical norms, which can differ from nation to nation but still be consistent with the hypernorms. For example, many U.S. corporations prohibit people from hiring their relatives. In India, however, tradition places a high value on supporting family and clan members, and some companies promise to hire workers' children when they grow up. Although these practices are inconsistent, neither violates any universal prohibition. They exist in what Donaldson and Dunfee call "moral free space" where inconsistent norms are permitted if they do not violate any hypernorms.[26]

Law

Laws codify, or formalize, ethical expectations. They proliferate over time as emerging regulations, statutes, and court rulings impose new conduct standards. Corporations and their managers face a range of mechanisms set up to deter illegal acts, punish offenses, and rehabilitate offenders. In particular, they face civil actions by regulatory agencies and private parties and criminal prosecution by governments. We will discuss these mechanisms to illustrate how legal controls and sanctions work.

Damages

For seven years Joseph Kelly managed "roll-off" operations in Burlington, Vermont, for Browning-Ferris Industries, a national waste disposal corporation. Roll-off waste is collected in long containers trucked to and from industrial and construction sites. Browning-Ferris had all of the city's roll-off business until Kelly resigned to start a competing company. Soon he had 47 percent of the market and a Browning-Ferris executive in Boston called the local manager, telling him to "[p]ut [Kelly] out of business. Do whatever it takes. Squish him like a bug."[27] The local manager, violating antitrust laws, used predatory pricing, slashing roll-off prices below cost. Even so, Kelly's market share climbed to 56 percent, but he sued Browning-Ferris for antitrust violations anyway.

compensatory damages
Payments awarded to redress actual, concrete losses suffered by injured parties.

A Vermont jury awarded Kelly $51,146 in *compensatory damages*, which are payments to redress actual, concrete losses suffered by injured parties due to wrongful conduct. Then, after Kelly's attorney told the jury Browning-Ferris had a net worth of $1.3 billion, it awarded Kelly an additional $6 million in *punitive damages*, which are payments in excess of a wronged party's actual losses, awarded when corporate conduct is not only damaging, but reprehensible. Punitive damages are intended to punish and deter similar actions in the future.

punitive damages
Payments in excess of a wronged party's actual losses to deter similar actions and punish a corporation that has exhibited reprehensible conduct.

Such awards raise questions of fairness. In this case punitive damages were 115 times greater than compensatory damages. Is it fair to impose such a penalty based on a defendant's status as a large corporation? Is a misdeed to be punished more harshly because the perpetrator is rich? Although Browning-Ferris was guilty, was its conduct so reckless, malicious, and harmful that retribution of $6 million was required?

The company appealed to the Supreme Court, arguing that the $6 million sum violated the Eighth Amendment's prohibition against "cruel and unusual

---

[26] Thomas Donaldson and Thomas W. Dunfee, "When Ethics Travel: The Promise and Peril of Global Business Ethics," *California Management Review,* Summer 1999, p. 61.

[27] *Browning-Ferris Industries v. Kelko Disposal,* 429 U.S. 257 (1989), at 260.

punishment." Although the Court dismissed this appeal on narrow technical grounds, the justices were concerned about capricious punitive damages against large corporations, which were frequent, and in subsequent cases set increasingly strict guidelines. Since the *Browning-Ferris* decision the Court has spent more than 20 years working to limit punitive awards against corporations, not because it considers them too large, but because it believes they can be unpredictable, arbitrary, and disproportionate to the wrongdoing.

It started to rein them in with the case of an Alabama physician, Dr. Ira Gore, Jr., who bought a BMW for $40,751 and drove it for nine months without noticing any problem. After an auto detailer told him that part of the car had been repainted, Gore learned that BMW North America secretly repainted cars with shipping damage and sold them as new. Gore set his damages at $4,000 and sued, charging BMW with malicious fraud. A jury awarded him $4 million in punitive damages—1,000 times his actual loss.

On appeal, the Supreme Court held that such a big award for retouching paint was unconstitutionally excessive.[28] It said punitive damages must be reasonably related to the degree of reprehensibility in the company's conduct and proportionate to the size of actual damages. Thus, the Alabama Supreme Court reconsidered the case and awarded Gore only $50,000.[29]

In a subsequent case, the Court suggested rough guidelines for the ratio of punitive damages to compensatory damages. In it, a jury awarded $1 million in compensatory damages to a Utah couple for emotional distress suffered when State Farm Insurance mishandled their accident claim. Then, believing State Farm had schemed to cheat other customers as well, jurors decided to take away several weeks of its profits with $145 million in punitive damages—a ratio of 145:1. The Supreme Court found this award "neither reasonable nor proportionate to the wrong committed" and suggested that a ratio greater than 4:1 is suspect and a ratio of 10:1 or higher probably could never be justified.[30] The Utah Supreme Court then reduced the award to $9 million, a 9:1 ratio, just below the unjustifiable maximum.[31]

Most recently, the Court dramatically cut the punitive damages award against ExxonMobil for the *Exxon Valdez* oil spill. In 1993 an Alaska jury had given residents near the spill compensatory damages of $500 million, then imposed a $5 billion punitive award on the company. An appeals court subsequently halved this to $2.5 billion. When the Supreme Court got the case it further reduced the award to $500 million, a 1:1 ratio. In its opinion it suggested that the company's actions were not intentionally malicious and, absent extraordinary malice, the 1:1 ratio was sufficient to punish and deter in most cases.[32] Unless the Court backs away from this line of decisions, it is unlikely that corporations will suffer punitive damages exceeding this 1:1 ratio in the future. However, the most important factor in punitive

---

[28] *BMW of North America, Inc., v. Gore,* 116 S.Ct. 1589 (1996). The Court based its decision on the Due Process Clause of the Fourteenth Amendment, which prohibits excessive or arbitrary punishment.

[29] *BMW of North America, Inc. v. Gore,* 701 So. 2d 507 Ala. (1997).

[30] *State Farm Mutual Automobile Insurance Company v. Campbell,* 123 S. Ct. 1513 (2003).

[31] *Campbell v. State Farm Mutual Automobile Insurance Company,* 98 P.3d 409 (Utah, 2004).

[32] *Exxon Shipping Co. v. Baker,* 128 S. Ct. 2605 (2008).

damages continues to be the reprehensibility of corporate behavior and in cases of egregious, willful, or reckless conduct, exceptional awards are still likely.[33]

Criminal Prosecution of Managers and Corporations

Crimes are offenses against the public prosecuted by federal and state governments. Corporate crimes impair lawful competition in markets and harm consumers, investors, and the public. They include managerial wrongdoing that falls in the category of *white-collar crime*, or nonviolent economic offenses involving cheating and deception done for personal or corporate gain in the course of employment. These crimes are often difficult to detect, being hidden or disguised to look like legal activity. Unlike an armed robbery or murder there is no crime scene or body. Evidence may exist only in a perplexing maze of documents and conspiratorial decisions.

white-collar crime
A nonviolent economic offense of cheating and deception done for personal or corporate gain in the course of employment.

Both individuals and corporations are prosecuted for crimes. Both kinds of prosecutions can be complicated, but it is easier to prosecute corporations because criminal law evolved in the twentieth century in ways that make organizations especially vulnerable. Under the doctrine of *respondeat superior*, (rez PON' day aht superior), created by the Supreme Court in 1909, corporations are liable for the actions of employees who commit a crime in the course of their employment when their act is for the benefit of the company.[34]

To establish guilty intent when crimes have occurred, the law assumes that a corporation has the aggregate knowledge of all its employees. Unlike with an individual, prosecutors do not have to prove that a corporation had criminal intent, only that an employee committed a crime intended to benefit it. If so, the corporation is guilty of that crime, even if the employee's action was against company rules and higher management had no knowledge of wrongdoing. And, unlike individuals, corporations are not allowed to invoke the Fifth Amendment right against self-incrimination when prosecutors ask them to turn over documents related to a crime.

Prosecutors find it easier to impose penalties on corporations because they are reluctant to go to trial. Juries are more inclined to convict corporations than individuals. When Royal Caribbean Cruise Lines was indicted for criminal violations of the Clean Water Act it decided to fight and put together an all-star defense team including two former U.S. attorneys general. It still lost the case. For corporations in many industries, criminal prosecution risks catastrophe. A conviction can lead to a drop in share price, higher cost of capital, reputational damage, and loss of federal contracts and licenses. These secondary consequences punish not only the company, but also its employees, pensioners, shareholders, and communities, all innocent of any crime.

Arthur Andersen is a cautionary example. Its auditors failed to deter Enron from stating false earnings. While federal investigators were looking into Enron's books Andersen shredded some germane documents, believing it had the right to do so. Indicted for obstruction of justice, it went to trial, and in 2002 a jury found

---

[33] Note that the Court let pass an $80 million award by an Oregon jury against Philip Morris USA where actual damages were $522,000, a ratio of 153:1. See *Philip Morris USA v. Williams* 129 S. Ct. 1436 (2009), *per curium.*

[34] The Supreme Court established this precedent for liability in *New York Central & Hudson River Railroad Co. v. United States,* 212 U.S. 481 (1909).

Charging Factors

These factors are used by federal prosecutors to decide when a corporation should be charged with a crime. All factors must be weighed, although in some cases, such as the nature of the offense, a single factor could be of overriding importance. Note that the seventh factor requires reflection about consequences for innocent parties, a concern that leads to many deferred and nonprosecution agreements.

1. Nature and seriousness of the offense, including risk of harm to the public.
2. Pervasiveness of wrongdoing within the corporation, including management complicity or involvement.
3. The corporation's history of similar misconduct.
4. The corporation's timely and voluntary disclosure of wrongdoing and its willingness to cooperate in the investigation.

5. Existence and effectiveness of a preexisting compliance program.
6. Remedial actions, including starting or improving a compliance program, replacing management, and disciplining wrongdoers.
7. Consequences for shareholder, pension holders, employees, and other innocent parties as well as the public.
8. Adequacy of prosecuting individuals responsible for the crimes.
9. Adequacy of other remedies such as civil lawsuits or enforcing regulations.

Source: "Principles of Federal Prosecution of Business Organizations," *United States Attorney's Manual,* Title 9 §928.800(B), at 15-16, August 28, 2008 (the Filip Memorandum).

deferred prosecution agreement
An agreement between a prosecutor and a corporation to delay prosecution while the company takes remedial actions.

nonprosecution agreement
An agreement in which U.S. attorneys decline prosecution of a corporation that has taken appropriate steps to report a crime, cooperate, and compensate victims.

it guilty. The judge imposed a $500,000 criminal fine, affordable enough, and put Andersen on five years' probation, but the company was moribund, its clients fleeing from an auditor whose name was now synonymous with scandal. Still, Andersen appealed and three years later a unanimous Supreme Court overturned the conviction, saying flawed jury instructions allowed the guilty verdict.[35] It was too late, Andersen had expired.

The Department of Justice, which controls all criminal prosecutions in which the United States has an interest, weighs nine factors (see the accompanying box) in deciding whether or not to indict a corporation and, depending on the outcome, allows U.S. attorneys to enter *deferred prosecution agreements* (DPAs) and *nonprosecution agreements* (NPAs) in which the government will delay or not prosecute if the corporation takes steps to compensate victims and prevent future wrongdoing. Since 1993 there have been more than 150 DPAs and NPAs, most with well-known companies including Aetna, Boeing, Chevron, Fiat, Monsanto, Pfizer, and Sears.

When a company signs a DPA or NPA it is not indicted. It agrees to a set of terms, typical among them being to set up or improve an internal compliance program, to pay restitution to victims, to forfeit income from criminal activity, to cooperate with an investigation, to fire guilty executives, and to hire a *monitor* who will oversee its compliance with the DPA or NPA and report at intervals to prosecutors. It must fulfill these terms in a specific time, usually three to five years.

[35] *Andersen v. United States,* 544 U.S. 696 (2005).

monitor
A person hired
by a corpora-
tion to oversee
fulfillment of
conditions in
an agreement
to avoid crimi-
nal indictment.

Because corporations are so fearful of indictment, even when they are innocent of wrongdoing or the wrongdoing is confined to a few rogue employees, they are drawn into DPAs and NPAs. Some critics believe the agreements let corporate criminals off too easily. Others think managers of basically innocent companies make rational decisions to avoid trials, but their firms are then unfairly branded as criminals and federal prosecutors gain power to dictate their affairs.

Executives are more often prosecuted than corporations, though harder to convict. Unlike a corporation, where evidence that an employee committed a crime is sufficient for conviction, the government must prove beyond a reasonable doubt that an executive either had specific knowledge of a crime and acted to abet it or realized the probable existence of a crime and consciously avoided inquiring into it. Unlike corporations, executive defendants do not have to produce information, so pretrial investigation can be lengthy and expensive. And cases are complex. At Pfizer the FBI spent four years going through boxes of documents, scanning them into computers, and doing name and keyword searches trying to reveal how a regional sales manager directed kickbacks to doctors who prescribed its drugs.[36] White-collar crimes such as accounting frauds require prosecutors to educate lay juries about intricate financial transactions that even experienced auditors find hard to follow. This was a problem in the trial of Richard Scruchy, former CEO of HealthSouth, who was tried on 36 counts of conspiracy, fraud, and money laundering. After sitting through five months of testimony, fossilized jurors acquitted him of all wrongdoing.

After a cluster of corporate frauds, including the Enron and WorldCom collapses, President George W. Bush set up a Corporate Fraud Task Force to prosecute managers. A separate Enron Task Force was created to concentrate on the labyrinthine Enron fraud. To pierce the veil of culpability, its prosecutors methodically pressured lower-level managers into cooperating as witnesses. In return for guilty pleas and testimony against their former bosses, they received lighter sentences. It was ruthless work. To get the cooperation of former Chief Financial Officer Andrew S. Fastow, prosecutors charged his wife, Lea, a former assistant treasurer at Enron, with defrauding the company for personal enrichment.[37] Both Fastows then agreed to a reduction of charges in return for his testimony. As managers caved in, the task force moved up the chain of responsibility to the very top where former CEOs Kenneth L. Lay and Jeffrey K. Skilling maintained ignorance of any wrongdoing.

Eventually, the task force triumphed in a 17-week trial in which jurors convicted both Lay and Skilling on multiple counts of conspiracy and fraud. After inculpating testimony by almost two dozen former subordinates, jurors simply did not believe that Lay and Skilling lacked knowledge of any schemes.[38] Although Lay died of a heart attack before sentencing, Skilling was sentenced to 24 years and 4 months in prison.[39] Because Andrew Fastow cooperated with the government, his sentence was only six years. Lea Fastow served five months in prison.

[36] Federal Bureau of Investigation, "Pfizer $2.3 Billion Settlement," press release, September 3, 2009.

[37] *United States v. Lea W. Fastow*, Indictment, U.S.D.C., S. Dist. Texas, Cr. No. H-03.

[38] Department of Justice, "Prepared Remarks of Deputy Attorney General Paul J. McNulty at the Corporate Fraud Task Force Fifth Anniversary Event," Washington, DC, July 17, 2007, p. 1.

[39] Skilling has since won an appeal to have his sentence recalculated.

The government's record in prosecuting executives is mixed. The Enron Task Force was disbanded in 2006 after bringing criminal charges against 27 executives and obtaining 20 convictions. The larger Corporate Fraud Task Force investigated more than 400 corporate fraud cases and obtained more than 1,300 convictions, including 350 senior executives, before merging into a 25-agency financial fraud task force in 2009.[40]

Such large conviction numbers are impressive, but most offenders have pleaded guilty. Corporate criminals remain extremely difficult to prosecute. When cases with high-level executives go to trial, prosecutors struggle. A study of 17 major corporate fraud prosecutions over four years, including Enron trials, shows that government prosecutors failed to convict most of the defendants. Of 46 executives, 20 were convicted but 11 were acquitted and juries deadlocked on 15 others.[41]

Sentencing and Fines

In 1991 the U.S. Sentencing Commission, a judicial agency that standardizes penalties for federal crimes, released guidelines for sentencing both managers and corporations. These guidelines are not mandatory, but most judges follow them.[42] When managers are convicted of a crime, their prison sentences are based on a numerical point system. Calculations begin with a base score for the type of offense. Points are then added or subtracted because of enhancing or mitigating factors. A sentence for fraud, for example, begins with a base level of 6, then 15 factors are considered, including the number of victims and their losses. As losses to victims rise on a scale from $5,000 to $400 million or more, between 2 and 30 points are added. As the number of victims rises from 10 to 250 or more, between 2 and 6 points are added.[43] Downward adjustments are made if the manager has no criminal history or cooperated with authorities. The point total is then converted into a prison sentence using a table. Besides prison terms, managers may also be fined, put on probation, given community service, asked to make restitution to injured parties, or banned from working as corporate officers or directors.

Corporations cannot be imprisoned, but they can be fined. Criminal fines are intended to punish, to deter future lawbreaking, to cause disgorgement of wrongful gains, and to remedy harms where possible. As with the prison sentences of managers, judges base their fine calculations on a point system in the federal sentencing guidelines. The calculation begins with a fine range based on the type of offense, then adds or subtracts points based on aggravating or mitigating factors such as top-management involvement and cooperation during the investigation. If, for example, management "willfully obstructed" authorities, three points are added. Up to five points may be subtracted if top managers immediately reported the crime.[44]

[40] Government Accountability Office, *Corporate Crime: DOJ Has Taken Steps to Better Track Its Use of Deferred and Non-Prosecution Agreements, but Should Evaluate Effectiveness,* GAO-10-110, December 2009, p. 36.

[41] Kathleen F. Brickey, "In Enron's Wake: Corporate Executives on Trial," *Journal of Criminal Law & Criminology,* Winter 2006, pp. 401–07. Convictions of K. Lay and J. Skilling are included in the figures.

[42] See *United States v. Booker,* 125 S.Ct. 738 (2005).

[43] United States Sentencing Commission, *Guidelines Manual,* §2B1.1 (November 2009).

[44] Ibid.

A cynical public doubts that fines are large enough to hurt. The Environmental Protection Agency once threatened to impose a $27,500 fine on General Electric each day it failed to clean up toxic waste at a factory. Based on GE's revenues it was the equivalent of trying to intimidate a person making $1 million a year with a fine of three cents a day. Another time, the government fined GE $50 million to settle accounting fraud charges.[45] It was the equivalent of a $2.74 fine for the hypothetical millionaire.

The largest fine ever levied is a $2.5 billion civil penalty by the Securities and Exchange Commission against WorldCom in 2003. The record for a criminal fine is $1.2 billion. It was imposed on Pfizer in 2009 for paying kickbacks to doctors who prescribed its drugs for uses not allowed by the Food and Drug Administration. This was 15 percent of its net income for the year, an amount that affected Pfizer's operations. Corporate fines are frequent. In 2009, for example, 177 companies were sentenced for crimes. Of these 131 were fined. The mean fine was $14,861,234.[46]

FACTORS THAT INFLUENCE MANAGERIAL ETHICS

Strong forces in organizations shape ethical behavior. Depending on how they are managed, these forces elevate or depress standards of conduct. We discuss here four prominent and interrelated forces that shape conduct: leadership, strategies and policies, organization culture, and individual characteristics (see Figure 7.2).

Leadership

The example of company leaders is perhaps the strongest influence on integrity. Not only do leaders set formal rules, but by their example they also reinforce or undermine right behavior. Subordinates are keen observers and quickly notice if

FIGURE 7.2

Four Internal Forces Shaping Corporate Ethics

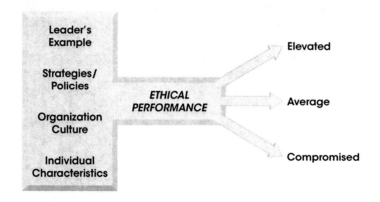

45 Securities and Exchange Commission, "SEC Charges General Electric with Accounting Fraud," *Litigation Release No. 21166,* August 4, 2009.

46 United States Sentencing Commission, *2009 Sourcebook on Federal Sentencing Statistics* (Washington, DC: USSC, 2009), table 52.

standards are, in practice, upheld or evaded. Exemplary behavior is a powerful tool available to all managers. It was well used by this executive.

> When Paul O'Neill arrived as CEO at Alcoa, a secretary put papers in front of him to join an expensive country club. His dues would be paid by the company. He was expected to join because other senior executives could not continue their paid memberships unless the CEO was a member. Before signing, he looked into the club and realized that it had a discriminatory membership policy. He was urged just to go along and join, like others before him. Since he was new, he ought to wait a while before disturbing Alcoa custom. However, he refused to join. His thoughts were: "What excuse am I going to use 6 or 12 months from now? I've just discovered my principles? They were on vacation . . . when I first came?"[47] He then set up a policy against reimbursing executives for dues in discriminatory clubs.

A common failing is for managers to show by their actions that ethical duties may be compromised. For example, when managers give themselves expensive perks, they display an irreverence for the stewardship of money that rightly belongs to investors as owners, not to management. An executive at one large corporation describes how arrogant behavior sends the wrong signals.

> Too often through my career I've been at management dinners—no customers—and I see $600 bottles of wine being ordered. Think about the message that sends out through the whole organization. And don't ever think such attitudes don't spread and infect the whole firm. Leadership, after all, is about communicating values. And deeds trump words any day.
>
> The message in that bottle is this: Some sales representative and a couple of technicians, supported by others, busted their butts to get that $600 to the bottom line. And their work, as evaluated by the guy who bought the wine, was worth a couple of tasty swallows.
>
> If money is the way we keep track of the good things our employees accomplish for our customers, then who do we think we are spilling it?[48]

Many employees are prone to cynicism. Diverting blame for mistakes, breaking small promises, showing favoritism, and diversion of even trivial company resources for personal use are ill-advised—because if the leader does it, an opportunistic employee can rationalize his or her entitlement to do it also. According to Sherron Watkins, a whistle-blower at Enron, Andrew Fastow was such a shrewdly observant subordinate. As Enron's chief financial officer, he created a warren of complex and deceitful investments that not only contributed nonexistent revenue, but also diverted corporate funds into his and his wife's pockets. What inspired Fastow to act as he did? According to Watkins, it may have been the example set by CEO Ken Lay.

---

[47] Quoted in Linda K. Treviño and Katherine A. Nelson, who tell this story in their book, *Managing Business Ethics: Straight Talk about How to Do It Right,* 5th ed. (New York: John Wiley & Sons, 2011), p. 161.

[48] Betsy Bernard, President AT&T, "Seven Golden Rules of Leadership," *Vital Speeches of the Day,* December 15, 2002, p. 155.

Ken Lay had Enron . . . use his sister's travel agency. That gave millions of dollars to that agency and it was a wretched travel agency. The service wasn't even good and I can speak to that because I have some horror stories about their travel scheduling. This went on for years and years and years. Now, if you take someone like Andy Fastow who does not appear to have a good sense of right and wrong, that's telling him that "hey, my partnerships are helping Enron meet their financial statement targets so why shouldn't I carve some out for myself because Ken Lay has been carving some out for his sister?"[49]

He also abused the corporate jet in really onerous ways. He moved a stepdaughter back and forth to France—furniture, not her! . . . [O]nce again that sent a message to executives that when you get to the top, the company is there for you versus you being there to serve the company.[50]

Strategies and Policies

A critical function of managers is to create strong competitive strategies that enable a company to meet strategic goals without encouraging ethical compromise. In companies with deteriorating businesses, managers have great difficulty meeting performance targets and may feel pressure to compromise ethical standards. Even in strong companies, strategies must be executed with policies that reinforce honest achievement. Of special concern are unrealistic performance goals that pressure those who must make them work.

At Lucent Technologies CEO Richard McGinn made the company's shares rocket by promising 20 percent yearly sales growth. Twice he missed quarterly targets and each time the stock plummeted. He could not miss again. Warned by subordinates that fourth quarter sales might fall short, he "went ballistic."[51] Under intense pressure to meet the revenue goal, the sales force reacted. It first offered legitimate discounts to customers, but the goal was still unmet. Other tactics then emerged from the shadows. Customers were given credits toward future purchases and these were booked as revenue in the fourth quarter. Revenues were booked when products were sold to distributors, not final customers, an unoriginal trick known as "channel stuffing." Told again by the head of sales that the revenue target was hopeless, McGinn said he would not take no for an answer. Ultimately, the target was missed. McGinn was fired. Lucent had to report that $679 million in fourth quarter revenue was unallowable. One sales agent lost his job for falsifying sales documents. McGinn later rationalized that he "never asked anyone to do anything untoward."

Reward and compensation systems can also expose employees to ethical compromises.

Ads for the Laser Vision Institute stated a fee of $499 per eye for laser surgery, although small type warned that the "price may vary according to RX and astigmatism." When prospects arrived they did not see physicians at first; instead, they met

---

[49] Sherron S. Watkins, "Ethical Conflicts at Enron: Moral Responsibility in Corporate Capitalism," *California Management Review,* Summer 2003, p. 17.

[50] Sherron Watkins, "Pristine Ethics," *Vital Speeches of the Day,* May 1, 2003, p. 435.

[51] Quotes in this paragraph are from Dennis K. Berman and Rebecca Blumstein, "Behind Lucent's Woes: All-Out Revenue Goal and Pressure to Meet It," *The Wall Street Journal,* March 29, 2001, pp. A1 and A8.

with counselors who decided what type of surgery the person needed and collected a deposit. What patients did not realize was that the counselors worked on an incentive system. They made yearly base salaries of $40,000 but added to their income with bonuses paid when patients were upgraded to more expensive surgeries. For the $499 procedure they got a per-eye bonus of only $1. But the amount rose with the surgery's price—$2 for a $599 surgery, $6 for the $799 procedure, $16 for $999, and so forth, up to $40 for patients paying $1,599. To be eligible for these bonuses the counselors had to have a 75 percent close rate on people who came in. It is no surprise, then, that prospects were subjected to aggressive tactics similar to those faced by car buyers and that, in the end, 88 percent paid more than $499.[52] Eventually, customers sued over "bait and switch" tactics and the Federal Trade Commission ordered the company to stop making false claims.

When companies adopt policies that put employees under pressure, they should build in strong ethical rules too. When the tide of money runs high, shore up the ethical dikes.

Corporate Culture

corporate culture
A set of values, norms, rituals, formal rules, and physical artifacts that exists in a company.

Corporate culture refers to a set of values, norms, rituals, formal rules, and physical artifacts that exists in a company. Corporate cultures are powerful and deep. In the words of one scholar, they are "like water around fish." They evolve as companies cope with recurring stresses in their competitive environments. Over time, attitudes and behaviors that solve problems and bring success are reinforced and become permanent parts of the culture. Often the influence of a founder is important and lasting. Henry Ford's early philosophy of brutal labor policies endured so strongly that more than 50 years after his death Ford Motor had to root out pervasive authoritarianism in its management ranks before it could adapt more flexible manufacturing methods to compete with Japanese rivals.

According to a pioneering researcher, Edgar Schein, a corporate culture can be understood by separating it into three levels and reflecting on their relationship.[53] The first level is one of *artifacts,* which include both physical expressions of culture and visible behaviors. Physical elements include ways of dressing, office layouts, and symbolic displays such as picture walls of former executives. Visible behaviors include patterns of interaction, for example, the use of first or last names as an indication of formality, and the kinds of decisions made.

At the second level are the organization's *espoused values,* that is, formal statements of belief and intention. Espoused values are found in documents such as mission statements, codes of ethics, and employee handbooks. They state what the organization officially stands for. Often, inconsistencies are observed between the physical and behavioral artifacts on the first level and the espoused policies on the second level.

When such inconsistencies arise they are explained by the hidden influence of a third cultural level of *tacit underlying values.* At this level reside the deep, shared assumptions in the organization's culture about how things really work. These are the

---

[52] Marc Borbely, "Lasik Surgery Sales Tactics Raise Eyebrows," *Washington Post,* September 4, 2001, p. A1.
[53] Edgar H. Schein, *The Corporate Culture Survival Guide, rev. ed.* (San Francisco: Jossey-Bass, 2009), pp. 21–27.

unspoken, unwritten beliefs about the nature of the company and what behaviors bring success. Though often unarticulated, these silent assumptions are usually the cause of deviation from nice-sounding espoused values.

A simple example of such an inconsistency is a company with a mission statement that emphasizes teamwork, but in which a visible artifact, a prominently placed employee-of-the-month award plaque, seems to contradict the official emphasis on teamwork. This may indicate that at the level of tacit underlying assumptions employees understand individual achievement as the route to promotion despite the mission statement's endorsement of teamwork.

All corporate cultures have ethical dimensions. When the behavior of employees fails to match the values in a written ethics code, it can be a reflection of silent assumptions lying deep in the culture that confute the code. For example, recent graduates of the Harvard MBA program who were interviewed about the ethical atmosphere in their organizations revealed the strong presence of four informal but powerful "commandments" conveyed to them early in their careers.

> First, performance is what really counts, so make your numbers. Second, be loyal and show us that you're a team player. Third, don't break the law. Fourth, don't overinvest in ethical behavior.[54]

These "commandments" clearly strain the spirit of any strong corporate ethics code. When the contradictions between espoused values and underlying tacit assumptions grow too wide trouble is not far ahead. The story of Fannie Mae illustrates the point.

> Franklin D. Raines was a suave and exceptionally talented manager who became CEO of Fannie Mae, the giant mortgage company. Fannie Mae had a strong Ethical Responsibility Policy that called for "a corporate culture characterized by openness, integrity, responsibility, and accountability."[55] Raines often espoused these values of honesty and openness in talks to employees.
>
> However, in his first few months on the job, he discovered that Fannie Mae would miss earnings per share (EPS) targets that triggered maximum executive bonuses. Raines told the firm's controller to prepare a list of "alternative" accounting methods and in a meeting with senior managers it was agreed to use them to meet the targets. This action overrode the advice of both internal and external auditors and sent the message to the organization that meeting EPS goals was what mattered, not the way they were met.
>
> Next Raines set in motion a five-year plan to double EPS from $3.23 to $6.46 and again tied bonuses to meeting yearly EPS goals. He pushed the plan hard. What happened to the culture is encapsulated in a speech to Fannie Mae's internal auditors by their boss.
>
> "Be objective, be fair but tough . . . [and] never compromise or dilute your conclusions . . . By now every one of you must have 6.46 branded in your brains. You must be able to say it in your sleep, you must be able to recite it forwards and backwards, you must have a raging fire in your belly that burns away all doubts, you

[54] Joseph L. Badaracco, Jr., and Allen P. Webb, "Business Ethics: A View from the Trenches," *California Management Review,* Winter 1995, p. 11.

[55] Warren B. Rudman, ed., *A Report to the Special Review Committee of the Board of Directors of Fannie Mae* (Washington, DC: Paul, Weiss, Rifkind, Wharton & Garrison, February 23, 2006), p. 439.

must live, breath and dream 6.46, you must be obsessed on 6.46 . . . Remember Frank has given us an opportunity to earn not *just* our salaries . . . but substantially over and above if we make 6.46 . . . It is our *moral obligation* to . . . have made tangible contributions to Frank's goals."[56]

The mixed message in this speech typified the pervasive conflict between espoused values of openness and honesty and the tacit underlying assumption that meeting EPS targets in any way possible was the road to success. The result was years of questionable accounting. Eventually, probes by regulators forced Raines and other top executives to resign and the company had to restate $6.3 billion in earnings.[57]

Cultures are resilient. Observers are always puzzled when corporations with strong ethics programs founder. Why after years of formal effort to make Shell Oil a more responsible corporation was the CEO caught leading other executives in a conspiracy to lie about the company's oil reserves? Why was the CEO of Boeing, an experienced executive brought out of retirement to elevate the company's ethics, forced to resign over an affair with a subordinate? Why, after years of effort to elevate its ethics, did Chiquita Brands' top executives and board of directors covertly approve illegal bribes, not once, but many times? One explanation is that these are simply perverse actions by a few bad apples. But a better explanation, insofar as humans can know the source of evils in their nature, likely lies deeper, in the persistence of contradictions in corporate cultures. As the story of Consolidated Edison illustrates, cultures are extremely resistant to change.

> After a steam explosion that killed three people and sprayed asbestos over a Manhattan neighborhood, Consolidated Edison pleaded guilty to four federal environmental crimes. Only two weeks later in a state court it accepted guilt for 319 environmental violations over many years. It entered an agreement for broad reform "from the chairman to the lineman" and the court appointed a monitor to supervise its efforts during three years of probation.[58]
>
> Edison's leadership rolled out a program of environmental responsibility. A new senior vice president for environmental affairs was put in charge. Two high-level environmental committees were formed to review progress. Every employee was made personally responsible for environmental safety and encouraged to raise problems openly. Any worker had the power to stop a job immediately on seeing a problem.
>
> However, violations continued. More than a year later the court-appointed monitor reported that workers who spoke out were being intimidated. When one employee complained about pollutants leaking into the Hudson River, a supervisor called him a "snake" and a "troublemaker."[59] Another was transferred from his job. The monitor believed the company nurtured a "destructive corporate culture" that inhibited environmental responsibility.

---

[56] Quoted in Office of Federal Housing Enterprise Oversight, *Report of the Special Examination of Fannie Mae* (Washington, DC: OFHEO, May 2006), p. 42.

[57] Eric Dash, "Ex-Officers Sued by U.S." *The New York Times*, December 19, 2006, p. 1.

[58] Joe Sexton, "Con Edison Agrees to $9 Million Fine for Contamination," *The New York Times*, November 16, 1994, p. A1.

[59] Dan Van Natta, Jr., "Con Ed Cited in Intimidation of Employees," *The New York Times*, December 19, 1995, p. B1.

This was correct. Although the espoused values of Consolidated Edison had been quickly elevated, tacit underlying assumptions were much slower to change. For decades its workers shared the assumption that keeping power on was the top priority. They went to heroic lengths to fix problems, often ignoring formal procedures to speed the job. The work culture required unquestioned obedience to supervisors. Group loyalty was strong. No one confronted co-workers about environmental hazards and no one ratted outside the group. Anyone who did was ostracized.[60] These underlying values endured, leading to repeated violations of the new environmental policies.

Individual Characteristics

Researchers try to discover what individual qualities are associated with ethical behavior. Demographic factors seem to explain little.[61] Some studies show that women are more ethical than men, but results are mixed.[62] No studies find men to be more ethically sensitive than women, but some show no difference. A few studies suggest that people with more education are more ethical, but others do not. Similarly, some studies find that religious belief leads to more ethical attitudes, but many others fail to discover any relationship.[63] There are indications that higher ethics come with advancing age and longer work experience.[64] Personality traits may be more important, but are less studied in the literature of ethics. The only personality trait extensively studied and correlated with unethical behavior is Machiavellianism, the tendency of an individual to use self-centered, immoral, manipulative behavior in a group. However, the correlations tend to be modest and some studies fail to find a relationship.[65]

Many companies now use integrity tests to predict whether job applicants are inclined to antisocial, counterproductive behaviors such as rule breaking, fraud, cheating, and theft. Over many years these tests have been shown to work well. Some of them simply ask test takers to admit antisocial behaviors such as stealing. They also ask about attitudes toward theft. For example: "When you read about a robbery in the newspaper do you ever hope the thief gets away with it?" or "At your previous job did you think about ways you could have gotten away with stealing if you wanted to?" Using many such questions an integrity test can separate those more inclined to steal from more honest people because thieves think more about stealing and justify it more easily. Other kinds of integrity tests predict a broader range of counterproductive work behaviors by measuring traits such as

---

[60] Schein, *The Corporate Culture Survival Guide,* pp. 153–63.

[61] Liane Young and Rebecca Saxe, "Innocent Intentions: A Correlation Between Forgiveness for Accidental Harm and Neural Activity," *Neuropsychologia* 47 (2009), p. 2070.

[62] See the discussion in Steven Kaplan, Kurt Pany, Janet Samuels, and Jian Zhang, " An Examination of the Association Between Gender and Reporting Intentions for Fraudulent Financial Reporting, *Journal of Business Ethics* 87 (2009), p. 17.

[63] Gary R. Weaver and Bradley R. Agle, "Religiosity and Ethical Behavior in Organizations: A Symbolic Interactionist Perspective," *Academy of Management Review,* January 2002, p. 79.

[64] Terry W. Low, Linda Ferrell, and Phylis Mansfield, "A Review of Empirical Studies Assessing Ethical Decision Making in Business," *Journal of Business Ethics,* June 2000, p. 185.

[65] Kibeom Lee, et al., "Predicting Integrity with the HEXACO Personality Model," *Journal of Occupational and Organizational Psychology* 81 (2008), p. 155.

dependability, conscientiousness, thrill seeking/risk taking, conformity, hostility, response to authority. Although these tests predict integrity, it is not clear exactly what they measure. Experts believe they work by measuring a complex, multilevel hierarchy of personality components that is not fully understood.[66]

While there is limited evidence that fixed traits determine whether a person makes ethical decisions, there is overwhelming evidence that individuals are influenced to be more or less ethical by the situations they are in. Employees, for example, are more ethical when the company has an ethics code. Salespeople are more ethical when the sales manager clearly defines boundaries of ethical behavior.[67] Alternately, in a corporation with a dreary ethical climate, corrupt leaders, or performance pressures, otherwise honest individuals may buckle. This situational variation is due to the work of what sociologist Philip Zimbardo calls "dynamic psychological processes," or innate, predictable, and powerful tendencies in "ordinary" good people. They include obedience to authority, need to belong, desire to conform, self-justification, and rationalization. Consider the Rybergs.

> Nick Ryberg, an ambitious manager, was hired to direct human resources for a large company. He, his wife, Carolyn, and their two daughters moved to the Twin Cities area in Minnesota to begin. They sought status, using material displays to exhibit a lifestyle of success.
>
> Soon, Nick suggested that Carolyn start an executive search firm to find job candidates for his company. It would help the company and bring in a little extra money for their family. In an initial job she submitted some résumés for engineers and billed the company. This was legitimate work, but though legal it was a conflict of interest for Nick. Therefore, he asked her to send the invoice in her maiden name.
>
> Over time the scheme changed. Carolyn started two more companies in her maiden name for invoicing Nick's company.[68] At times Nick and Carolyn worried they had become criminals, but the work was authentic. Gradually, Nick began to submit invoices where little work, then no work, was done. The shadow over their lives darkened.
>
> Besides the human resources department, he also supervised accounting, security, records management, and IT. This was a management mistake. It reduced checks and balances on him. He set the recruiting budget and stayed within it. No one questioned the invoices. The family got luxury cars, expensive vacations, and a $200,000 kitchen remodel. He felt in control. It was hard to stop.
>
> Eventually, they made an error by submitting an invoice with an address that did not match one of Carolyn's companies. An audit led to fraud charges. They pled guilty and agreed to pay $964,265 in restitution. Nick was sentenced to 30 months in federal prison and Carolyn to 24 months.[69] They lost all but 15 boxes of personal belongings. Their high-school-age daughters went to separate homes. Their thoughts turned to shame and remorse. After prison they pursued theology studies and spoke on campuses about the need to avoid ethical traps.

[66] Christopher M. Berry, Paul R. Sackett, and Shelly Wiemann, "A Review of Recent Developments in Integrity Test Research," *Personnel Psychology,* Summer 2007, p. 276.

[67] Jay P. Mulki, Jorge Fernando Jaramillo, and William B. Locander, "Critical Role of Leadership on Ethical Climate and Salesperson Behavior," *Journal of Business Ethics* 86 (2009).

[68] Paul Gallagher, "Lessons from the Dark Side," *Human Resource Executive,* July 2009.

[69] "Two Residents of Minnesota Sentenced for Defrauding Flint Hills Resources," *States News Service,* February 2, 2005.

The story of the Rybergs illustrates many situational dynamics. They started with a small first step, then advanced. They wanted to fit in with an affluent status group. They admit to growing arrogance and sense of entitlement. They rationalized to justify wrongdoing. Also, because of poor management, there was opportunity. According to Zimbardo, situational factors such as these are so powerful, that "any deed, for good or evil, that any human being has ever done, you and I could also do–given the same situational forces."[70]

HOW CORPORATIONS MANAGE ETHICS

ethics and compliance program
A system of structures, policies, procedures, and controls used by corporations to promote ethical behavior and ensure compliance with laws and regulations.

Years ago, little thought was given to formal management of ethics. One pioneer was James Cash Penney, who introduced a company conduct code in 1913. His effort was a lonely one. Until the 1980s, most companies gave more thought to managing petty cash than to elevating ethics. Since then, more and more companies have set up *ethics and compliance programs,* or systems of structures, policies, procedures, and controls designed to prevent lawbreaking and promote ethical behavior. In general, these programs originated in scandal and they continue to grow from it. Although a few companies voluntarily adopted them years ago, more put them in place after being ordered to by courts as part of their restitution for corporate wrongdoing. Now, the vast majority of law-abiding companies use them as protection against criminal indictment.

The wider movement to ethics and compliance programs began in the 1980s. In response to a run of billing frauds and cost overruns, military contractors started the Defense Industry Initiative, a project requiring firms to adopt ethics codes and train employees to obey laws. More scandal-spawned ethics programs came in the mid-1990s, when the federal government cracked down on hospitals and nursing homes for Medicare billing fraud. Corporations in the health care industry rushed to follow the defense industry model.

The need to manage ethics was driven home to other industries in the 1996 *Caremark* case. Caremark International, a health care company, was caught giving kickbacks to physicians who referred patients to its clinics. After being indicted, the company set up a compliance program, but it was too late to prevent a $250 million fine. Angry shareholders sued its directors for breach of duty because they had failed to set up an ethics program earlier and this omission exposed the firm to a big fine. Caremark's directors narrowly escaped paying damages from their own pockets after a settlement. However, the judge who approved this settlement made it plain that if directors fail to set up a compliance program they can be sued for a breach of duty.[71]

Meanwhile, the U.S. Sentencing Commission in 1991 established the first sentencing guidelines. As previously explained, these guidelines set forth imprisonment and fine calculations for managers and corporations, allowing reductions in

---

[70] Philip Zimbardo, *The Lucifer Effect: Understanding How Good People Turn Evil* (New York: Random House, 2007), p. 320.

[71] *In re Caremark International Inc. Derivative Litigation,* 698 A2d 970 (1996).

Seven Steps for an Ethics Program

The U. S. Sentencing Commission sets forth these seven steps as minimally required to prevent criminal behavior and promote an ethical corporate culture. For federal prosecutors and regulators they define an acceptable effort by managers to ensure that companies and their employees follow the law.

1. Establish standards and procedures.
2. Create high-level oversight.
3. Screen out criminals.
4. Communicate standards to all employees.
5. Monitor and set up a hotline.
6. Enforce standards, discipline violators.
7. Assess areas of risk, modify the program.

Source: *Guidelines Manual,* §8B2.1, effective November 1, 2004.

both if companies had ethics and compliance programs. These reductions are a major incentive.

After the turn-of-the-century fraud scandals Congress created requirements for antifraud mechanisms with the Sarbanes-Oxley Act in 2002, including a code of ethics for financial officers, an internal process for reporting illegal behavior, and protection for employees who reveal wrongdoing. The Department of Justice and the Securities and Exchange Commission adopted new guidelines for making the presence of ethics and compliance programs a factor in the decision to prosecute. And both the New York and NASDAQ stock exchanges require that listed companies have in place codes of conduct and procedures to enforce them.[72]

Because of these actions all listed public corporations now have at least some elements of a comprehensive program in place, though the efforts differ in their vigor and their aims. Ethics and compliance programs may combine two distinct approaches to prevent wrongdoing. A *compliance approach* teaches employees to meet legal and regulatory requirements and emphasizes following rules. An *ethics approach* teaches values such as integrity, truth, fairness, and respect for others, preparing workers to separate right from wrong in moral spheres of work life. Most companies focus on compliance, but many put effort into both.

While there is no standard format, the U.S. Sentencing Commission's *Guidelines Manual* sets forth seven minimum steps that define a diligent effort (see the box). Many companies explicitly follow these steps, which have a strong compliance orientation, and others create processes that meet their general requirements in a variety of ways. The seven steps are a convenient framework for explaining the basic elements of programs.

1. *Establish standards and procedures to prevent and detect criminal conduct.* Companies meet this requirement with a variety of written documents. The centerpiece is often a short statement of guidelines at a high level of abstraction. An example

compliance approach
Training employees to follow rules in laws, regulations, and policy.

ethics approach
Training employees to make decisions based on ethical values.

[72] New York Stock Exchange *Listing Manual,* §503 A.10, "Code of Business Conduct and Ethics," amended November 25, 2009; and *NASDAQ Stock Market Listing Rules,* Rule 5610, adopted March 12, 2009.

THE GE Code of Conduct

- Obey the applicable laws and regulations governing our business conduct worldwide.
- Be honest, fair and trustworthy in all your GE activities and relationships.
- Avoid all conflicts of interest between work and personal affairs.
- Foster an atmosphere in which fair employment practices extend to every member of the diverse GE community.

- Strive to create a safe workplace and to protect the environment.
- Through leadership at all levels, sustain a culture where ethical conduct is recognized, valued and exemplified by all employees.

Source: General Electric Company, *Integrity: The Spirit & Letter of Our Commitment,* January 2008, p. 3.

is GE's (see the accompanying box). Most companies also set forth an expanded code of conduct, often in a booklet of 20 to 50 pages with graphic designs and stock photos of well-groomed people at work. Simple writing is used to make the standards clear. Cisco Systems once revised its code to an eighth-grade reading level. Many begin with a list of basic values such as honesty, integrity, fairness, respect for others, and upholding the law and the spirit of the law that should characterize employee behavior. Then they set forth brief guidance in a range of problem areas, including conflict of interest, bribery, gifts, insider trading, antitrust violations, trade secrets, political contributions, and discrimination. These relatively brief treatments are usually backed by separate, detailed compliance policies, so that the complete "code of ethics" of a large company can include dozens of documents running hundreds of pages.

Conduct codes contain typical elements, including introductions by CEOs, ways to report wrongdoing, tips for making ethical decisions, and disciplinary procedures. There is inexhaustible sameness in their content and format. They are saturated with similar principles, cover much the same compliance issues, and contain virtually identical guides for reporting concerns. Creativity comes at the margins. Accenture's graceful *Code of Business Ethics* is filled with photographs of trees and contains simple cases in question-and-answer format. Here is an example from the section titled "Integrity."

> **Q:** My supervisor asked me to prepare a purchase order for services costing $30,000. Her spending authority is only $25,000. Can I break the request into two purchase orders to avoid getting higher level approval? She says that is savvy business practice. What should I do?
>
> **A:** Not getting the proper approvals violates Accenture policy, which is to ensure that adequate internal accounting controls are maintained and operating effectively. If you are uncomfortable telling your supervisor, alert your local Finance lead.[73]

[73] Accenture, *Code of Business Ethics: Our Core Values in Action* (New York: Accenture, August 1, 2007, ver. 4.11), p. 32.

Codes are usually distributed to all employees. Many companies ask them to sign an annual form certifying compliance. Multinational companies translate them into many languages. Dow's booklet is translated into 20, PepsiCo's 30, Abbott Labs' 35, and Merck's 55.

2. *Give oversight of the program to the board of directors and assign responsibility for it to a high-level executive who, in turn, will assign day-to-day responsibility to a specific manager.* The *Guidelines Manual* requires that the board of directors exercise "reasonable oversight" over an ethics and compliance program, that one or more top executives take responsibility for it, and that specific managers be assigned day-to-day supervision. An example of a structure that meets these requirements is the Abbott Laboratories program shown in Figure 7.3. This structure is the result of a strengthened compliance effort coming after the FBI uncovered a 10-year fraud to cheat customers and Abbott paid $614 million in fines.[74]

At Abbott a chief ethics and compliance officer takes day-to-day responsibility for running the program. This ethics chief reports directly to Abbott's top executive, the chairman and CEO, and also reports directly to the board of directors through periodic reports to its Public Policy Committee and annual reports to the full board. This reporting relationship strengthens the ethics effort.[75] In some companies the ethics chief reports to the director of human resources or the legal department, but at Abbott the ethics program is independent and must answer only to the board, which has ultimate responsibility for ethics, and to the CEO, so its actions carry greater credibility. In addition, the ethics officer chairs a Business Conduct Committee that includes the heads of Abbott's business divisions and other top executives.

Below the chief ethics and compliance officer the program structure reaches down into the organization. Each business division has an ethics and compliance officer who reports to a divisional vice president of ethics and compliance, who in turn reports back to the corporate ethics chief. In this way the program parallels Abbott's operating structure. Note how a reporting chain for ethics staff is created separately from the line chain of command all the way up to the board of directors. This separation is an important check and balance. If ethics officers reported only to division managers, without a separate reporting channel, they would have less independence.

3. *Exclude individuals with a history of illegal or unethical conduct from positions of substantial authority.* Criminal background checks are inexpensive. Companies that fail to conduct them can be surprised, as was Smith & Wesson Holding Corp. on discovering that its chairman was the notorious "Shotgun Bandit" who had terrorized victims in a string of armed robberies years before.[76] He resigned.

---

[74] Raymond V. Gilmartin, *Ethics and the Corporate Culture* (Waltham, MA: Bentley College Center for Business Ethics, November 10, 2003), p. 12.

[75] Martin T. Biegelman, *Building a World-Class Compliance Program* (New York: John Wiley & Sons, 2008), pp. 155 and 178; and Michael D. Greenberg, *Perspectives of Chief Ethics and Compliance Officers on the Detection and Prevention of Corporate Misdeeds* (Santa Monica, CA: Rand Corporation, 2009), p. 29.

[76] Vanessa O'Connell, "How Troubled Past Finally Caught Up with James Minder," *The Wall Street Journal,* March 8, 2001, p. A1.

FIGURE 7.3 **Oversight Structure of Abbott Laboratories' Ethics and Compliance Program**

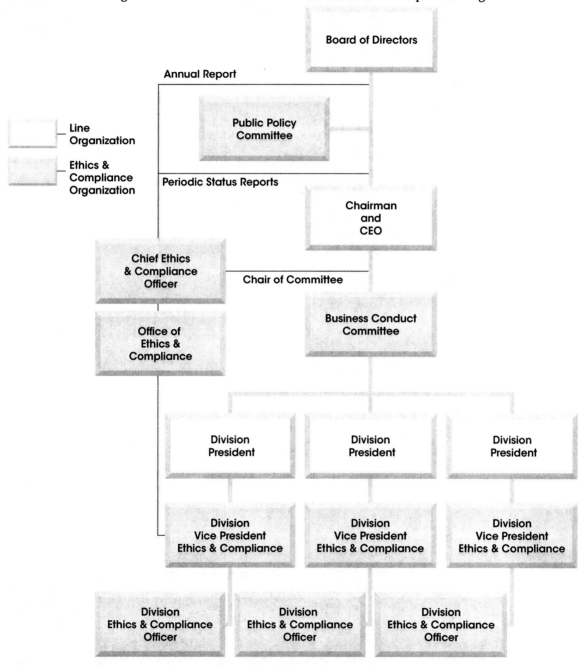

Companies also check for false claims about education and job experience on résumés. Again, failure to check can lead to surprises. In 2006 the chief executive of RadioShack was forced to resign after claiming a bachelor's degree in psychology from a small Baptist college that never offered degrees in that subject.[77] More recently, *The Wall Street Journal* checked the degree claims of 358 senior executives and directors at publicly traded companies and found seven cases of false claims.[78]

Even if an executive candidate's claims are accurate, it is hard to measure their inner character. Some psychologists believe that integrity can be tested in interviews. One expert recommends building rapport with the subject, then eliciting comments on ethical issues late in an interview. He suggests these inquiries. "Give me an example of an ethical decision you have had to make on the job?" "Have you ever had to bend the rules or exaggerate a little bit when trying to make a sale?" and "Tell me about an instance when you've had to go against company guidelines or procedures to get something done."[79]

4. *Periodically communicate standards and procedures to all employees from the lowest up to the board of directors.* Companies reinforce standards using everything from T-shirts to posters to newsletters. At one Kaiser Permanente facility the ethics and compliance staff held a fair with candy, popcorn, and a "Wheel of Compliance" that employees could spin and win prizes if they correctly answered a question about ethical standards.[80] However, training is the key to communicating ethics and compliance knowledge.

Generally, such training is most effective when company managers do it, not outsiders, and when it steers away from abstract philosophy to focus on the work lives of attendees. A few companies offer in-depth seminars lasting one to three days with discussion of policies and case studies. Briefer sessions are more typical. One-to-three-hour yearly sessions in which employees watch a video and discuss cases are common. Most popular are interactive sessions on a company intranet in which employees read short cases and try to pick the correct or most ethical responses from multiple-choice alternatives.

At Lockheed Martin employees attend one- or two-hour training sessions where they discuss incidents enacted on a video. Here are examples.

> On his way to lunch, Charlie cuts his leg on a desk drawer that was not completely closed. Charlie's supervisor has been talking for weeks that the group's injury performance had not been good but one more incident would break the Target Zero goal for the department. Chloe, a co-worker, notices that Charlie hurt himself. Charlie asks her not to say anything.[81]

[77] Gary McWilliams, "RadioShack CEO Agrees to Resign," *The Wall Street Journal,* February 21, 2006, p. A3.

[78] Keith J. Winstein, "Inflated Credentials Surface in Executive Suite," *The Wall Street Journal,* November 13, 2008, p. B1.

[79] William C. Byham, "Can You Interview for Integrity?" *Across the Board,* March/April 2004, pp. 36–37.

[80] Elizabeth Schainbaum, "The Wheel of Compliance," *Compliance Today,* March 2008, p. 31.

[81] Lockheed Martin, *The 2005 Ethics Effect: Leader's Guide* (Marietta, GA: Lockheed Martin, 2005), p. 5.

Vivian, a factory employee, and her supervisor, Rhomeyn, notice that test data is missing from a part already stamped as inspected. Rhomeyn goes to speak with Burt, the employee who stamped the paperwork indicating that the part was inspected. Burt, however, is nowhere to be found. It turns out his co-worker, Chris, has been covering for him. Burt's perception is that he is being harassed. Burt also tells Chris that he didn't do the testing, but it isn't a big deal—he will just do it now.[82]

5. *Monitor the organization for criminal conduct, and set up a system for reporting of suspicious conduct without fear of retaliation.* Monitoring entails collection of data that can indicate suspicious activity. For example, some companies require reports of unusual financial transactions. Ethical audits can also detect problems. HCA Healthcare Corp. conducts two-day ethical compliance audits to reveal strengths and weaknesses at its hospitals. Employees are interviewed randomly as auditors cover a 53-page checklist.

All programs now have 24-hour toll-free telephone and e-mail hotlines for reporting suspected wrongdoing. To protect users' identities, they usually allow anonymous contacts. Whistle-blowers fear revenge, so hotlines must be supported with strong policies against retaliation. On average, between 2 and 4 percent of U. S. employees use hotlines each year.[83]

Hotlines create an enormous amount of work for ethics offices. Many callers seek advice: "Would it be a conflict of interest for me to work in the evening?" Others have trivial complaints, such as "My supervisor came back an hour late from lunch." Allegations must be investigated; for instance, "I think one of my team members gave confidential papers to a client." Although few calls reveal criminal wrongdoing, hotlines open a critical channel of communication. Here is an example of a hotline contact and how it was handled at KPMG.

A hotline report was filed alleging business integrity issues, such as over-stating credentials to a client, about a professional. Additional concerns of unprofessional conduct, such as demeaning team members, were raised by other reporters shortly thereafter. An investigation by the Ethics and Compliance Group substantiated the allegations. Firm and area functional leadership demoted the professional, issued a written reprimand, appointed a coach, and reduced the professional's annual performance rating for the purposes of determining compensation.[84]

6. *Enforce standards by providing both incentives to reward compliance and discipline to deter criminal conduct.* It has been objected that doing the right thing should require no incentive; however, many companies link ethics to performance reviews, promotions, and compensation. This seems like a powerful incentive, but in practice it is difficult and awkward to rate ethical performance. Tenet Healthcare tried to tie the bonuses of its top 800 managers to a numerical ethics score between −5 and +5, with each point changing the bonus by 5 percent. Managers felt

---

[82] Lockheed Martin, *Leader's Guide: A Culture of Trust 2009,* at www.lockheedmartin.com/aboutus/ethics/, p. 12.

[83] Andrew Singer, "Cisco Transmits Ethics to a 'Wired' Work Force," *Ethikos,* September/October 2009, p. 1.

[84] KPMG, *Ethics and Compliance Report 2009* (New York: KPMG LLP, 2009), p. 24.

humiliated, however, when they received negative scores, called "dings" in company slang.[85]

When Boeing made compliance with the company's ethics code part of every employee's evaluation it ran into the same problem. According to a report on Boeing's ethics program, it almost never affected the outcome.

> Managers perceive pressure (often self-imposed) not to rate any employee as below average in ethics. There is also resistance against rating any employee above average, as that implies that other employees are not doing as well with ethical conduct. The strong tendency, therefore, is to award all employees an average score for this component, effectively rendering it meaningless.[86]

Written disciplinary policies are widespread. Discipline is usually based on factors such as seriousness of the violation, the organizational level or leadership role of the violator, extent of cooperation with the investigation, prior misconduct, and willfulness of the action. A progressive range of disciplinary options—counseling, oral reprimand, probation, suspension, salary reduction, termination—can be used as fits the case. Xerox, for example, uses disciplinary guidelines that specify minimum and maximum penalties by type of infraction for first and second offenses but "[t]here are no guidelines for third offenses because there are no options at that point."[87]

7. *If criminal conduct occurs, modify the program to prevent repeat offenses. Periodically assess the risks of criminal conduct and try to reduce them.* Unless lawbreaking is the isolated failure of one person, the program is not working. It should be modified by changing or adding elements, restructuring responsibilities, or reappraising the culture in which it operates.

Some companies use ethical risk assessment to predict areas of ethical and legal risk in their businesses. General Electric, for example, formed a risk committee of top executives that meets quarterly to assess changing global ethical standards. This committee then decides whether GE should alter existing standards or adopt new ones.[88]

ETHICS AND COMPLIANCE PROGRAMS: AN ASSESSMENT

Nearly all large U.S. corporations now have at least some ethics and compliance mechanisms centered on a code of conduct. Fewer have full, comprehensive programs. In a recent survey only 23 percent of human resource managers reported a full range of program elements, comparable to the seven steps discussed above,

---

[85] Andrew W. Singer, "At Tenet Healthcare: Linking Ethics to Compensation," *Ethikos,* January–February 2001, pp. 4–5.

[86] Warren B. Rudman, et al., *A Report to the Chairman and Board of Directors of the Boeing Company Concerning the Company's Ethics Program and Its Rules and Procedures for the Treatment of Competitors' Proprietary Information* (Washington, DC: Paul, Weiss, Rifkind, Wharton & Garrison LLP, November 3, 2003), p. 36.

[87] Xerox, "Overview of Xerox Business Ethics & Compliance Office," at www.xerox.com, accessed February 12, 2010.

[88] Ben W. Heineman, Jr., "Avoiding Integrity Land Mines," *Harvard Business Review,* April 2007, p. 104.

in their organizations. However, 67 percent reported having at least four of these elements.[89]

The main incentive is almost universally the desire to avoid lawbreaking and reduce sanctions for corporations terrified of criminal indictment. One way to look at these programs is that they extend the reach of federal regulators and prosecutors who must police corporations in the public interest. In effect, ethics and compliance programs recruit corporations and their employees to police themselves. Codes of conduct almost always make it the duty of employees to report violations, and some impose discipline for failure to report even suspected illegal behavior, in effect, turning the entire workforce into an army of snitches working for the Department of Justice or, put more politely, "a corporate system of espionage to ferret out wrongdoing."[90]

Do the programs work? Surveys of employees reporting misconduct suggest their effectiveness in reducing unethical or illegal behavior is "modest and/or mixed."[91] Weak effect can result when companies fail to commit resources to the program. Sometimes ethics managers are marginalized in the hierarchy and have inadequate influence. Top executives who fail to lead by example undermine formal efforts. In such cases silent assumptions deep in the corporate culture work to undermine official intentions.

CONCLUDING OBSERVATIONS

Ethics is the study of good and evil. These are understood to be separate due to religious and philosophical teachings at the foundation of social norms and the law. Although it is naively thought that business requires ethical compromise, it does so no more or less than any other part of life. Not everyone can achieve their goals in business because success depends on more than forces the individual can control. It depends also on overcoming competition, economic conditions, and other rudiments of fortune. So there are sometimes strong motives and pressures to reach goals by lying, deceiving, and cheating. But doing evil is never right.

In this chapter we focused on the dynamics of ethics in organizations. The single most important factor in good corporate ethics is the example of leaders, who shape strategies and cultures. In recent years highly standardized ethics and compliance programs have emerged to fight bad conduct in corporations. They still depend heavily on effective leadership to work. Their effectiveness in reducing evil in practice has so far been mixed, but they are promising. In the next chapter we move from a focus on organizations to a focus on individuals and how they make ethical decisions.

[89] Society for Human Resource Management, *The Ethics Landscape in American Business* (Alexandria, VA: SHRM, 2008), p. 10.

[90] Miriam Hechler Baer, "Governing Corporate Compliance," *Boston College Law Review,* September 2009, p. 962.

[91] See Nicole Andreoli and Joel Lefkowitz, "Individual and Organizational Antecedents of Misconduct in Organizations," *Journal of Business Ethics,* 2009, pp. 314–15 and 320–21.

The Trial of Martha Stewart

From indictment to sentencing, the case of Martha Stewart was a matter of intense public interest. Some thought that her misdeeds, if any, were slight. Cynics believed the government was prosecuting a celebrity for a minor infraction to show it was tough on business crime. An indignant *Wall Street Journal* complained that innocent employees and shareholders of Martha Stewart Living Omnimedia were paying the price for the government's zeal.[1] Feminists argued that she was picked on for being a successful woman. "It's hard to imagine a male in precisely this spot," said Mary Becker, a DePaul University law professor. "Targeting a successful woman is very consistent with dominant cultural values."[2]

Others believed that her prosecution was justified. "I don't buy any of it," wrote Scott Turow, a criminal defense lawyer and the author of best-selling legal fiction. "What the jury felt Martha Stewart did—lying about having received inside information before she traded—is wrong, really wrong."[3]

This is the story.

DECEMBER 27

On the morning of Thursday, December 27, 2001, Douglas Faneuil was on duty at the mid-Manhattan office of Merrill Lynch. Faneuil, 24, who had been in his job only six months, assisted a stockbroker named Peter Bacanovic. It was two days after Christmas and Bacanovic was on vacation. Staffing was thin and Faneuil expected a slow day with light trading.

Soon Faneuil took a call from Aliza Waksal. Aliza was the daughter of Samuel Waksal, co-founder of ImClone Systems, a biopharmaceutical company. She wanted to sell her ImClone shares. Faneuil executed the order and by 9:48 a.m. her 39,472 shares had been sold for $2,472,837. Then Faneuil had a call from Samuel Waksal's accountant requesting that another 79,797 shares held in his Merrill Lynch account be transferred to Aliza's account and then

sold. The call was followed by a written direction saying that making the transfer and sale that morning was imperative.

Faneuil sought help on the transfer and called Peter Bacanovic in Florida. Bacanovic, 39, was an old friend of Waksal's. He had worked at ImClone for two years before coming to Merrill Lynch, and he handled the personal accounts of Waksal and his daughter. When Bacanovic learned that the Waksals were selling, he instructed Faneuil immediately to call another of his clients, Martha Stewart, while he remained on the line.

Bacanovic, who was active in New York social life, first met Martha Stewart in the mid-1980s when they were introduced by her daughter Alexis. Stewart was one of his most important clients. He handled her pension and personal accounts. He also handled accounts for her company, Martha Stewart Living Omnimedia, Inc.

At 10:04 a.m. Faneuil dialed Stewart, but reached her administrative assistant Ann Armstrong, who said Stewart was on an airplane. Bacanovic left a brief message, asking Stewart to call back when she became available. In her phone log, Armstrong wrote, "Peter Bacanovic thinks ImClone is going to start trading downward." Bacanovic instructed Faneuil that when Stewart called back he should tell her that the Waksals were selling all their shares. At this time ImClone was priced at $61.53 a share.

This instruction from Bacanovic bothered Faneuil. Merrill Lynch had a written policy (see Exhibit 1) that required its employees to hold client information in strict confidence. But he was very busy and working under a sense of urgency, handling calls from the Waksals, and making calls to Merrill Lynch staff in several offices arranging the transfer of Sam Waksal's shares to his daughter.

Several hours later, Stewart's plane landed in San Antonio to refuel. She went into the airport and on her cell phone called Ann Armstrong to check for messages. At 1:39 p.m. she phoned Merrill Lynch, reaching Faneuil, who told her that Sam Waksal and his daughter had sold all of their shares. She asked for the current price of ImClone. Faneuil quoted approximately $58 a share. Stewart told him to sell all 3,928 shares she owned.

---

[1] "The Trials of Martha," *The Wall Street Journal*, February 13, 2004, p. A12.

[2] Quoted in Jonathan D. Glater, "Stewart's Celebrity Created Magnet for Scrutiny," *The New York Times*, sec. 1, p. 1.

[3] Scott Turow, "Cry No Tears for Martha Stewart," *The New York Times*, May 27, 2004, p. 29.

EXHIBIT 1
**Client
Information
Privacy Policy**

Merrill Lynch protects the confidentiality and security of client information. Employees must understand the need for careful handling of this information. Merrill Lynch's client information privacy policy provides that—

…

- Employees may not discuss the business affairs of any client with any other employee, except on a strict need-to-know basis.
- We do not release client information, except upon a client's authorization or when permitted or required by law.

She hung up and immediately put in a call to Sam Waksal. The two were close friends who had been introduced by Stewart's daughter Alexis in the early 1990s. Unable to reach him, she left a message that his assistant took down as "Martha Stewart something is going on with ImClone and she wants to know what."[4] By 1:52 p.m. Stewart's ImClone shares had been sold at an average price of $58.43, for a total of approximately $228,000.

THE PUZZLE OF THE WAKSAL TRADES

What *was* going on with ImClone? For almost 10 years Waksal had put ImClone's resources into the development of a promising new colon cancer drug named Erbitux. Two months earlier, ImClone had submitted a licensing application for approval of Erbitux to the Food and Drug Administration (FDA). On December 26, Waksal learned from an ImClone executive that, according to a source within the FDA, on December 28 ImClone would receive a letter rejecting the Erbitux application. When the FDA's action was publicly announced ImClone's share price was sure to plummet.

Waksal was in possession of material insider information. It was material because any reasonable investor would find it important in deciding to buy or sell ImClone stock. It was insider information because it was not yet known to the public. Since the FDA application was so critical, ImClone's general counsel had declared a "blackout period" after December 21 when employees should not trade ImClone shares. The purpose of the blackout was to guard against illegal insider trading.

Despite being informed of the blackout and despite possessing knowledge of the law with respect to insider trading, Waksal elected to sell. This was exceptionally foolish. His motive was to escape the unpleasant consequences of debt. He had obligations of $75 million, most of which was margin debt secured by shares he owned in ImClone. Servicing this debt was costing him $800,000 a month. He knew that if ImClone's share price slipped very far, many of his shares would be sold, dramatically lowering his net worth. He also tipped family and friends to sell on December 27. Besides his daughter Aliza, his father sold 135,000 shares, his sister Patti sold 1,336 shares, and another daughter, Elana, sold 4,000 shares. Waksal also tipped an investment adviser who sold all of her 1,178 shares on December 27 and passed the tip to a physician on one of ImClone's advisory boards, who sold more than $5 million in shares—all he owned—on the same day.

On Friday, December 28, the FDA faxed ImClone a "refusal to file" letter at 2:55 p.m. Later in the afternoon, after the market closed with ImClone trading at $55.25 a share, the company issued a press release disclosing the FDA's action. On December 31, the next trading day, ImClone opened at $45.39 a share. If Martha Stewart had waited until then to sell her shares, she would have gotten about $178,292 or $49,708 less than she received by selling on the afternoon of December 27. ImClone closed on December 31 at $46.46. It had dropped about 16 percent on the news of the FDA's action.

AN UNSETTLED AFTERMATH

Four days later a supervisor at Merrill Lynch questioned Faneuil about the ImClone trades. Afterward, Faneuil called Bacanovic, who was still vacationing in Florida. Bacanovic told him that Martha Stewart sold her shares because of a prearranged plan to

---

[4] Complaint, *Securities and Exchange Commission v. Martha Stewart and Peter Bacanovic,* 03CV 4070 (NRB)(S.D.N.Y.), June 4, 2003, p. 7.

reduce her taxes. He told Faneuil about a December 20 telephone call in which he and Stewart had gone down a list of the stock holdings in her account deciding which ones to sell at a loss to balance out capital gains from other sales during 2001.

Soon, however, Faneuil had a call from Eileen DeLuca, Martha Stewart's business manager, who demanded to know why the ImClone shares had been sold, since the sale had resulted in a profit that disrupted her tax-loss selling plan. Again he called Bacanovic. This time, Bacanovic told him that Stewart had sold because they had a preexisting agreement to sell ImClone if the price fell below $60 a share.

Merrill Lynch contacted the Securities and Exchange Commission (SEC) to report suspicions of insider trading in ImClone. On January 3, 2002, SEC attorneys called Faneuil to interview him. Faneuil told them Stewart had sold because the price of ImClone fell below $60 a share. He did not tell them that he had conveyed news about the Waksals' sales to her. On January 7, SEC attorneys interviewed Bacanovic on the telephone. He told them he had spoken to Martha Stewart on the day she traded and recommended that she sell based on their preexisting $60 sell agreement.

On January 16, Martha Stewart and Peter Bacanovic had a breakfast meeting. Their conversation is unrecorded. According to Faneuil, after the meeting Bacanovic told him, "I've spoken to Martha. I've met with her. And everyone's telling the same story . . . This was a $60 stop-loss order. That was the reason for her sale. We're all on the same page, and it's the truth."[5] In at least five subsequent conversations, Bacanovic reassured Faneuil of the need to stick to this story. If he did, Bacanovic promised to give him extra compensation.

On January 30, in response to a request for documents by the SEC, Bacanovic turned over the worksheet that he said was used in his December 20 tax sale conversation with Martha Stewart. It was a single-page printout listing approximately 40 securities in her account and noting the number of shares and the purchase price. The notation "@60" appeared near the entry for ImClone,

On January 31, Martha Stewart had a lengthy conversation with a criminal attorney. Following the conversation she went to her assistant Ann Armstrong

asking to see the telephone log. Sitting at Armstrong's computer, she changed Bacanovic's December 27 phone message from "Peter Bacanovic thinks ImClone is going to start trading downward," to "Peter Bacanovic re imclone."[6] Then, thinking better of it, she told Armstrong to restore the original wording and left.

INTERVIEWS

On February 2, Martha Stewart was interviewed in New York by attorneys from the SEC, the Federal Bureau of Investigation (FBI), and the U.S. Attorney's Office. Asked to explain her ImClone transaction, she said she and Bacanovic had decided to sell if ImClone fell below $60 a share. On December 27 she had spoken to Bacanovic, who told her it had fallen below $60 and inquired if she wished to sell. She had assented, in part, because she was on vacation and did not want to worry about the stock market. She did not recall speaking to Faneuil on that day. She denied knowledge of the December 27 phone message from Bacanovic, even though only two days before she had gone to her assistant's computer to alter its wording. According to one attorney present, at the end of the interview Stewart asked in a "curt, annoyed" tone, "Can I go now? I have a business to run."[7]

On February 13, Bacanovic was subpoenaed by the SEC to testify under oath in New York. He reported a December 20 phone call with Stewart in which he recommended the sale of ImClone if it fell below $60. The worksheet he turned over to the agency had notes of this conversation. He also stated that he had not discussed the ImClone stock sale with Stewart since December 27. Yet records of calls between Bacanovic's and Stewart's cell phones show that by this time they had spoken often, including once on the day of Stewart's interview in New York. The content of their conversations is unrecorded.

On March 7, Douglas Faneuil was interviewed by SEC attorneys. Details of this session have not been made public, but his subsequent indictment alleges that he failed to fully and truthfully disclose all he

---

[5] Brooke A. Masters, "Stewart Ordered Sale, Says Witness," *The Washington Post,* February 5, 2004, p. E1.

[6] Matthew Rose and Kara Scannell, "Dramatic Flourishes at Stewart, Tyco Trials," *The Wall Street Journal,* February 11, 2004, p. C1.

[7] Thomas S. Mulligan, "Jurors Hear of Attempt by Stewart to Alter Phone Log," *Los Angeles Times,* February 11, 2004, p. C7.

knew about the events of December 27.[8] Following the interview, Bacanovic offered Faneuil an extra week of vacation and airfare for a trip as a reward for sticking to Bacanovic's script.[9]

On April 10, Stewart was interviewed again on the telephone by investigators. She told them she had spoken with Bacanovic on December 27, but she could not remember if Bacanovic had mentioned the Waksals. She said again that the two had set up a $60 sell order on ImClone.

TURMOIL

After these interviews, government investigators continued the painstaking work of gathering, verifying, and interpreting details. Meanwhile, the main actors in the ImClone trades struggled in the backwash of their actions. In late May, Samuel Waksal resigned as the CEO of ImClone. In early June, the Associated Press broke the story that Martha Stewart was being investigated, setting off a three-week decline in the share price of Martha Stewart Living Omnimedia. Merrill Lynch suspended Peter Bacanovic without pay.

When Waksal was arrested and charged with criminal insider trading on June 12, shares in Stewart's company fell 5.6 percent. Waksal would eventually plead guilty to insider trading charges, receive a prison sentence of 87 months, and pay a fine of $4 million. The family members were forced to disgorge the profits from their trades, with interest, and the two other tippees—the investment adviser and the physician—paid disgorgement of profits, interest, and civil fines totaling $112,000 and $2.7 million, respectively.

Stewart issued a statement saying she and her broker had agreed on a $60 sell order in October 2001, that he had called her on December 27 and told her ImClone was trading under $60, and that she had told him to sell in line with their prior understanding. She denied having nonpublic information at the time. Later in the month she repeated this story at a conference for securities analysts and investors. Her intent was to halt the decline in her company's shares. At this time she held 61,323,850 shares and had suffered paper losses of more than $462 million over three weeks.

Douglas Faneuil's conscience bothered him. In late June he went to a manager at Merrill Lynch and volunteered what he believed was the complete and accurate story of December 27 and its aftermath. Subsequently, he spoke again to government investigators, who then subpoenaed both Stewart and Bacanovic to testify at an investigative hearing. This time, both declined, invoking their Fifth Amendment privilege against self-incrimination. Faneuil pled guilty to a misdemeanor charge of accepting money from Bacanovic in return for not informing federal investigators of illegal conduct. Merrill Lynch fired Bacanovic.

INDICTMENTS

It took the government a year and a half, but on June 4, 2003, in a "coordinated action," both the U.S. Attorney's Office and the SEC filed indictments against Martha Stewart and Peter Bacanovic.

The U.S. Attorney's Office filed a criminal complaint with multiple counts under the basic charges of, first, conspiracy, and second, obstruction of justice and making false statements.[10] The two were charged with conspiring to conceal evidence that Bacanovic had given nonpublic information about ImClone to Stewart. And they were accused of lying to government attorneys to hamper the investigation. In addition, only Martha Stewart was charged with securities fraud. The charge was that she had made a series of false statements about her innocence to mislead investors and prop up her company's share price. Conviction on all counts could bring a maximum of 30 years in prison and a fine of $2 million. Bacanovic alone was additionally charged with perjury for altering the worksheet that listed Stewart's stocks by adding "@60" near ImClone to fool investigators. He faced a maximum of 25 years in prison and a $1.25 million fine.

In its separate civil action, the SEC charged Stewart and Bacanovic with insider trading.[11] It sought disgorgement of illegal gains and the imposition of a fine. In addition, it sought to bar Stewart from acting as a director or officer of a public company.

---

[8] Misdemeanor Information, *United States v. Faneuil,* 02 Cr. 1287, S.D.N.Y. (2002), pp. 7–8.

[9] Ibid., p. 8.

[10] *United States v. Martha Stewart and Peter Bacanovic,* 03 Cr. 717 (MGC)(S.D.N.Y.), 2003.

[11] *Securities and Exchange Commission v. Martha Stewart and Peter Bacanovic,* 03 CV 4070 (NRB)(S.D.N.Y.), 2003.

Martha Stewart's lawyers immediately issued a statement challenging the government's case. "Martha Stewart has done nothing wrong," they said. They accused the government of making an "unprecedented" interpretation of the securities laws when it charged her with fraudulent manipulation simply because she spoke out publicly to maintain her innocence. And they questioned the government's motive for the other charges, raising themes that would course through the media during the subsequent trial.

> Is it for publicity purposes because Martha Stewart is a celebrity? Is it because she is a woman who has successfully competed in a man's business world by virtue of her talent, hard work and demanding standards? Is it because the government would like to be able to define securities fraud as whatever it wants it to be?[12]

A week later, Martha Stewart went to the FBI's Manhattan office for processing. She was given a mug shot, fingerprinted, and released without bail. She also resigned her positions as director and chief creative officer of Martha Stewart Living Omnimedia, taking on the nonofficer position of founding editorial director. She continued to receive her annual salary of $900,000 and in 2003 she was awarded a $500,000 bonus.

THE TRIAL OPENS

On January 20, 2004, Martha Stewart and Peter Bacanovic appeared in the Manhattan courtroom of the Hon. Miriam Goldman Cedarbaum, a federal district court judge with 18 years' bench experience. They entered pleas of not guilty and jury selection began. Potential jurors were given 35 pages of questions designed to detect biases. One question was, "Have you ever made a project or cooked a recipe from Martha Stewart?"[13] Eight women and four men were picked.

The trial began January 27. The lead prosecutor was Assistant U.S. Attorney Karen Patton Seymour. In her opening argument she told the jury that Martha Stewart sold ImClone after a "secret tip" from Bacanovic that the Waksals were selling. Then, she and Bacanovic tried to cover it up. Stewart's motive, she argued, was a desire to protect her multimillion-dollar business empire. Seymour pointed out that every $1 decline in the stock price of Martha Stewart's company decreased her net worth by $30 million. "Ladies and gentlemen," she said, "lying to federal agents, obstructing justice, committing perjury, fabricating evidence and cheating investors in the stock market—these are serious federal crimes."[14]

In his opening argument Stewart's attorney, Robert G. Morvillo, pronounced her "innocent of all charges" and tried to offer reasonable explanations for her actions. He pointed out that the ImClone shares she sold were less than 1 percent of her net worth. He told the jury that December was a busy month for her and she gets worn out. When she called Faneuil about the trade she was in a noisy airport on her cell phone and thought she was talking to Bacanovic. She had no way of knowing that insider trading was taking place. "How," he asked, "was she supposed to figure out the broker, who has always been honorable, was asking her to commit a crime?" If, indeed, she had been told that Waksal and his daughter were selling, it meant that Merrill Lynch was making the sales, which it would not do if it believed them to be illegal.

Morvillo explained that Stewart and Bacanovic had established a $60 sell agreement the week before her trades. And he called Stewart's alteration of her assistant's entry in the phone log "much ado about nothing." He said that she was changing it "to be consistent with what she recalled," but then quickly realized that her change "might be misconstrued." He concluded his opening statement by asking the jury to "decide the case based upon what is correct and just."[15]

TESTIMONY

Key witnesses for the government were Helen Glotzer, an SEC attorney, and Catherine Farmer, an FBI agent. Both had been present at interviews of Stewart and

---

[12] Robert G. Morvillo and John J. Tigue, "Press Statement," June 4, 2003, at www.marthatalks.com/trial.

[13] Thomas S. Mulligan, "Stewart Case Poses Challenges for All Parties as Trial Begins Today," *Los Angeles Times*, January 20, 2004, p. C1.

[14] Kara Scannel and Matthew Rose, "Early Sparks at the Stewart Trial," *The Wall Street Journal*, January 28, 2004, p. C1.

[15] Quotations of Morvillo are from "Opening Argument on Behalf of Martha Stewart," January 27, 2004, at www.marthatalks.com/trial.

Bacanovic and both testified about apparent false statements, including Stewart's denial that she spoke with Faneuil on December 27 and her denial that she knew that the Waksals were selling.

The government's star witness, however, was Douglas Faneuil. Under questioning by Seymour, Faneuil described his morning phone call to Bacanovic on December 27. On learning that the Waksals were selling Bacanovic said: "Oh my God, you've got to get Martha on the phone!" Faneuil said that he then asked Bacanovic, "Can I tell her about Sam? Am I allowed to?" "Of course," replied Bacanovic, "That's the whole point."[16] When Martha Stewart called in that afternoon, she asked, "What's going on with Sam?" Faneuil said that he told her, "We have no news about the company, but we thought you might like to act on the information that Sam is selling all his shares." He described her end of the conversation as a series of "clipped demands."

Faneuil also recounted how Bacanovic had tried to pull him into a cover-up. He described a scene at a coffee shop near their office in which he told Bacanovic, "I was on the phone. I know what happened." In response Bacanovic put an arm around him and said, "With all due respect, no, you don't."[17]

During cross-examination Bacanovic's attorney, David Apfel, tried to tarnish Faneuil as an unreliable witness. He called Faneuil an admitted liar who had changed his story seeking leniency from prosecutors. He brought out Faneuil's use of recreational drugs. And he introduced e-mail messages by Faneuil to show that he disliked Martha Stewart and might have held a grudge against her. One read: "I just spoke to MARTHA! I have never, ever been treated more rudely by a stranger on the telephone." Another was: "Martha yelled at me again today, but I snapped in her face and she actually backed down! Baby put Ms. Martha in her place!!!"[18] Faneuil also testified about a time when he put Martha Stewart on hold. When he came back on the line she threatened to pull her account from Merrill Lynch unless the hold music was changed. Jurors laughed.

Faneuil's testimony took 13 hours over six days. On his last day he was cross-examined by Stewart's attorney Morvillo, who tried to depict him as overwhelmed by the rush of events on December 27. He pointed out that Faneuil had taken 75 phone calls that day and some e-mails. He questioned why his memory of Stewart's call was sharp, in contrast to some other calls about which he was less clear. He got Faneuil to admit that he suspected the Waksals of insider trading, but said nothing to Bacanovic.

Following Faneuil, Stewart's administrative assistant Ann Armstrong was called to testify about how Stewart altered the message of Bacanovic's call. Taking the stand, she began to sob. After getting a glass of water from the defense table she tried to resume, but could not. Judge Cedarbaum recessed the trial to the next day, when Armstrong recounted how Stewart first altered, then instructed her to restore, the wording of the phone message.

Maria Pasternak was a friend who had been traveling with Martha Stewart on December 27. Pasternak related conversations with Stewart at a resort in Los Cabos over the following days. She said Stewart told her that the Waksals were trying to sell all their shares in ImClone and that she had sold all her shares. She testified that Stewart remarked, "Isn't it nice to have brokers who tell you those things?" But under cross-examination she vacillated about the clarity of her recall. The judge instructed jurors to disregard the remark.

An expert ink analyst with the U.S. Secret Service was called for his analysis of Bacanovic's tax sale worksheet. Larry Stewart, who is not related to Martha Stewart, testified that tests he conducted showed two pens had been used on the worksheet. All the notations on it, except "@60," were made by a "cheap" Paper Mate pen. The "@60" was written with a second, unidentified pen. The second pen did not match any of 8,500 ink samples on record, so he concluded it was either foreign or very rare.[19] This was important evidence for the prosecution, which argued that the "@60" had been added only after December 27, when the defendants constructed a cover-up.

After the prosecution finished its case, Martha Stewart's lawyers elected to use a minimal defense. They called only one witness, a former Stewart lawyer

---

[16] Brooke A. Masters, "Broker's Aide Says He Was Told to Tip Off Stewart," *The Washington Post,* February 3, 2004, p. E1.

[17] Testimony quoted in Constance L. Hays, "Witness Describes Stewart Cover-Up," *The New York Times,* February 5, 2004, p. C4.

[18] Brooke A. Masters, "Broker's Assistant, Stewart Clashed," *The Washington Post,* February 5, 2004, p. E1.

[19] Matthew Rose and Kara Scannell, "Stewart Trial Gets Testimony of a Broker's Tip," *The Wall Street Journal,* February 20, 2004, p. C3.

and note-taker at the February 4 meeting with investigators, who testified for only 15 minutes. There was much speculation about whether Martha Stewart would take the stand in her own defense. If she did, prosecutors would push her, try to trap her in inconsistencies and provoke her temper. If she did not, the intense curiosity of the jurors to learn what she could say to them would be unfulfilled. In the end, she did not take the stand.

Late in the trial Judge Cedarbaum dismissed the government's allegations of securities fraud. This charge had met with wide skepticism from the beginning. How could a defendant exercise her right to speak out in self-defense if doing so could be construed as criminal manipulation of share prices? Cedarbaum held that, given the evidence, no reasonable juror could find her guilty beyond a reasonable doubt.[20]

After the defense called its single witness, there had been 27 witnesses during 19 days of testimony. Closing arguments came on March 2. Prosecutor Michael Schachter told jurors that Stewart and Bacanovic believed they would never be caught. But mistakes they made trying to deceive left a trail of damning inconsistencies. He carefully listed contradictions in their stories. Bacanovic's lawyer gave a closing argument trying once again to undermine the credibility of Douglas Faneuil's testimony.

In his closing argument for Martha Stewart, Morvillo ridiculed the conspiracy charge, saying the events alleged by the government amounted to "a confederation of dunces."[21] Nobody, he argued, "could have done what Peter Bacanovic and Martha Stewart are alleged to have done and done it in a dumber fashion." He asked the jurors to consider that if the two had really conspired they would have been much more consistent in their stories. Their inconsistencies were a sign of innocence. This was a dangerous argument, because it conceded some contradictions in testimony.

Morvillo then made the case for Stewart's innocence. She had no evidence that anything was wrong with the trade. She had no reason to suspect that Waksal would behave so foolishly as to trade during a blackout period. She had a preexisting agreement with her broker to trade ImClone if it fell below $60. She could not hear well enough on the phone to know she was talking to Faneuil, not Bacanovic. The amount of the trade was too small to tempt jeopardizing her future. Her change in Ann Armstrong's telephone log was insignificant. Faneuil was an untrustworthy witness. Finally, he explained that she did not take the stand because she twice testified on the record at investigative hearings two years before and "her recollection [of the events] hasn't gotten any better." He concluded with this.

> This has been a two-year ordeal for this good woman. It's an ordeal based on the fact that she trusted her financial adviser not to put her in a compromising position. It's an ordeal based on the fact that she voluntarily submitted to a government interview. And it's an ordeal that is in the process of wiping out all the good that she has done, all her contributions, all her accomplishments . . . Martha Stewart's life is in your hands . . . I ask you to acquit Martha Stewart. I ask you to let her return to her life of improving the quality of life for all of us. If you do that, it's a good thing.[22]

THE VERDICT

The jury deliberated for 14 hours over three days. On March 5 one female juror wept as the verdicts were announced. Stewart and Bacanovic were each found guilty on four counts of lying and conspiring to lie to conceal the fact that she had been tipped with insider information. However, the jury could not agree that the government had proved beyond a reasonable doubt its allegation that Stewart and Bacanovic fabricated the $60 sale agreement and it acquitted them on those counts.

Jurors described their deliberations as calm. They found Faneuil credible and gave much weight to his testimony. Ann Armstrong was also an important witness because she cried. "We feel that she knew that something was wrong," said the forewoman. Jurors were also suspicious of the January 16 breakfast meeting between Stewart and Bacanovic and they felt cynical about Stewart hiring a criminal defense lawyer even before she was contacted by government investigators. They put little stock in the

[20] *United States v. Martha Stewart and Peter Bacanovic,* 305 F. Supp. 2d 368, February 27, 2004.

[21] "Closing Argument on Behalf of Martha Stewart," March 2, 2004, at www.marthatalks.com/trial, p. 1.

[22] Ibid., p. 10.

236   Chapter 7   *Business Ethics*

Martha Stewart outside the Manhattan courthouse after hearing the verdict. Source: © AP Photo/Julie Jacobson.

"conspiracy of dunces" argument. "We felt that she was a smart lady who made a dumb mistake," said the forewoman.[23]

A juror named Chappell Hartridge characterized the verdict as "a victory for the little guys who lose money in the market because of these kinds of transactions."[24] After looking into Hartridge's background, Stewart's legal team believed he had not been completely honest on his jurors' questionnaire. When asked about contacts with law enforcement, he did not disclose an arrest for assaulting a former girlfriend, and several other problems. Arguing that they would have exercised a challenge to keep Chappell off the jury had they known, her lawyers moved for a new trial. Judge Cedarbaum ruled that the allegations were little more than hearsay and there was no evidence that bias in Chappell affected the verdict.[25]

Meanwhile, prosecutors had filed a criminal complaint against Larry Stewart, the ink expert who testified at the trial. Stewart was accused of perjury for

saying that he had conducted the ink tests after a coworker came forward saying that, in fact, she had done them. Again Stewart's attorneys filed a motion for retrial. Again Cedarbaum denied the motion, because "there was no reasonable likelihood that this perjury could have affected the jury's verdict, and because overwhelming independent evidence supports the verdict . . ."[26] Subsequently, Larry Stewart was tried and, based on evidence that his co-worker had a history of harassment, acquitted of perjury.[27]

SENTENCING

On July 16, 2004, Martha Stewart appeared before Judge Cedarbaum. Addressing the judge, she appealed for leniency, saying, "Today is a shameful day. I ask that in judging me, you remember all the good I've done and the contributions I've made." Prosecutor Seymour countered, arguing that Stewart was "asking for leniency far beyond" that justified for "a serious offense with broad implications" for the justice system. Judge Cedarbaum responded, "I believe that you have suffered, and will continue to suffer, enough."[28] Her sentence was five months' imprisonment followed by five months' of home confinement. She was fined $30,000. This set of penalties was at the light end of what could have been imposed under federal sentencing guidelines and showed that Judge Cedarbaum was using what discretion she had to avoid a harsh sentence.

After the sentencing, Martha Stewart emerged from the courthouse to read a less contrite statement. "I'm just very, very sorry that it's come to this, that a small personal matter has been able to be blown out of all proportion, and with such venom and such gore—I mean, it's just terrible."[29]

At a separate hearing that day, Peter Bacanovic received a nearly identical sentence of five months in prison, five months of home confinement, and a $4,000 fine. A week later Daniel Faneuil appeared before Judge Cedarbaum. Tearfully, he apologized for

[23] Kara Scannell, Matthew Rose, and Laurie P. Cohen, "In Stewart Case, Reluctant Jurors Found Guilt after Skimpy Defense," *The Wall Street Journal,* March 8, 2004, p. A1.

[24] Constance L. Hays, "Martha Stewart Seeks New Trial, Saying a Juror Lied," *The New York Times,* April 1, 2004, p. C3.

[25] *United States v. Martha Stewart and Peter Bacanovic,* 317 F. Supp. 2d 426, May 5, 2004.

[26] *United States v. Martha Stewart and Peter Bacanovic,* 323 F. Supp. 2d 606, July 8, 2004.

[27] "Jurors Acquit Stewart Witness," *Los Angeles Times,* October 6, 2004, p. C3.

[28] Thomas S. Mulligan, "Stewart Gets 5 Months in Prison, Then Delivers a Plug for Her Firm," *Los Angeles Times,* July 17, 2004, p. A4.

[29] Ibid., p. A1.

his actions. His cooperation with federal prosecutors saved him from going to prison. His sentence was a $2,000 fine.

On October 8, Martha Stewart reported to a minimum-security prison camp in West Virginia to begin her incarceration. She had appealed her case, but the appeal was expected to take two years. Therefore, she elected to serve her sentence. Doing so would end much of the speculation and tumult affecting both her and her company.

She served her time. In prison she worked in the garden and cleaned the warden's office for 12 cents an hour. She disliked the food but made some friends among the other women. She gave them yoga lessons and a seminar on entrepreneurship. Her last day of home confinement (extended three weeks due to a violation that was not publicly explained) ended on September 1, 2005. In 2006 a federal appeals court turned down her request to overturn her conviction.[30] Then she settled with the SEC, which had brought a civil case of insider trading against her in 2003. In the settlement, she neither admitted nor denied guilt. She agreed to a five-year ban on serving as an officer or director of her company and a $195,081 fine. In the same settlement,

Bacanovic agreed to a fine of $75,645.[31] Stewart's legal troubles were finally over with the end of court-ordered probation in March 2007.

Questions

1. Did Martha Stewart commit the crime of insider trading when she sold her ImClone shares on December 27, 2001?

2. Did the U.S. attorneys and the Securities and Exchange Commission use good judgment in indicting Martha Stewart? Do you believe that her indictment was based on evidence of a serious crime, or do you believe that prosecutors consciously or unconsciously had additional motives for pursuing the case?

3. Do you agree with the jury that she was guilty beyond a reasonable doubt of the conspiracy and obstruction of justice charges?

4. Was her punishment, including both imprisonment and fines, appropriate? Were the punishments of Peter Bacanovic and Douglas Faneuil appropriate?

---

[30] *U.S. v. Martha Stewart and Peter Bacanovic,* 433F. 3d 273 (2006).

[31] See Securities and Exchange Commission, Litigation Release No. 19794, *SEC v. Martha Stewart and Peter Bacanovic,* 03 Civ. 4070 (RJH) (S.D.N.Y.), August 7, 2006.

Chapter Eight

Making Ethical Decisions in Business

David Geffen

David Geffen entered the world in 1943, the son of poor Russian immigrants. His father, Abe, was without ambition or talent, a passive man, often unemployed, who deferred to life. His mother, Batya, a bustling, pugnacious woman, supported the family making brassieres and corsets in their small apartment. She doted over young David, teaching him worldly lessons as she went about her business. Among them, apparently, was integrity. "She taught me to tell the truth," he would later say.[1]

Batya accepted and praised David even as he turned into a brash young boy. His elementary school teachers found him voluble, impulsive, and hard to discipline. He was also adventurous. At 10 he took trains into Manhattan by himself, getting off at the Times Square station and walking to see Broadway musicals. Show business was another world. It fascinated him. At home he filled out applications in different names for the CBS Record Club, joining it about 50 times to build a collection of show tunes from free sign-up offers. Meanwhile, on Broadway, he bought tickets for shows, then scalped them outside the theaters.[2]

Although Geffen was coming of age as an entrepreneur, he still had to face school. His grades were poor in junior high, and he sometimes forged his parents' signatures on report cards so they would not see. In high school he was enthusiastic about the drama club and involved himself in plays, but in class he rejected authority. An English teacher characterized him this way: "Rather talkative, self-centered, ignores teachers' orders and instructions. Is fresh, at times, and conceited, as well. Is not as good as he thinks he is."[3]

Geffen graduated from high school wanting to get rich in show business. Adversity, its source in his nature, lay ahead. He immediately went to Los Angeles, where he found a menial job and attended night classes at a junior college, telling friends he was going to UCLA. Soon he dropped out of school and returned to New York

---

[1] Quoted in John Duka, "The Ego and the Art of David Geffen," *The New York Times,* October 3, 1982, sec. 3, p. 1.

[2] Tom King, *The Operator* (New York: Random House, 2000), p. 23.

[3] Quoted in King, *The Operator,* p. 32.

because his father was ill. He attended evening classes for a while, then, when his father died, left to attend the University of Texas at Austin. But he was impatient, unsuited for classrooms and libraries, and made little progress before dropping out, abandoning further efforts at formal education, and returning to Los Angeles. This time he found a job in entertainment, working as an usher at CBS Television City. But he was soon fired for trying to hit an audience member. Lacking funds, he went back to New York.

There Geffen got a job with a production company, but he was fired after two weeks. On his untimely departure a casting director suggested a good place to start in the entertainment industry was the mailroom of a talent agency. With résumé in hand, he applied to one agency where his lack of a college degree and irregular job history brought rejection. Geffen learned quickly, just not from textbooks. He telephoned a second agency, the William Morris Agency, saying he was a cousin of famous record producer Phil Spector. This was not true, although he had met Spector. However, the claim got him an interview. He appeared in a suit and tie, his résumé revised to show a theater arts degree from UCLA. He got the job.

In his first week a tremor went through the mailroom. A new trainee had been fired for lying on his application. Now knowing that the agency would check on his degree, Geffen came an hour early every day, going through each mailbag until, after several weeks, he found the letter from UCLA. Conspiring with his brother, a UCLA law school graduate, he counterfeited a confirming letter that saved his job.

From the mailroom a 21-year-old Geffen launched the career that made him "the richest man in Hollywood."[4] He worked harder and faster than others. He read everything that passed through the mailroom to learn how deals were done and even learned to read documents upside down when he stood at agents' desks. He stayed late and skipped vacations. Told that the agency's president, Nat Lefkowitz, worked on Saturdays, he came in too, lingering by the lobby elevators to run into him and impress him on the ride up. Soon Geffen had a mentor and Lefkowitz made him the secretary to an agent, the first step out of the mailroom. But another misadventure lay between Geffen and his destiny.

One day the agent Geffen worked for talked an employee of a rival agency into mailing a list of that agency's clients. This was a precious gem of competitor espionage. When it arrived, Geffen intercepted it in the mail, gave it to Lefkowitz, and took credit for it. The agent, Geffen's boss, was infuriated and fired him.

Geffen ran to Lefkowitz, begging to stay, later telling his brother he had said their mother had cancer and he needed the job to pay for her operation.[5] Geffen not only stayed, but Lefkowitz promoted him to assistant agent.

A lie is a false statement made with intent to deceive. It steals from others the power to make decisions that protect their rights or interests. Lies are condemned by those who believe that ethical rules such as telling the truth must always be followed, that actions are right or wrong in themselves, no matter the consequences. In moral philosophy this position is called *deontological* (dēŏn tĕ logical) *ethics* from the Greek word *deont,* meaning that which is binding.

deontological ethics
The idea that actions are right and wrong in themselves independently of any consequences.

---

[4] Bernard Weinraub, "David Geffen, Still Hungry," *The New York Times Magazine,* May 2, 1993, p. 28.

[5] King, *The Operator,* pp. 56–57.

Irrespective of moral admonitions Geffen was now on his way. His extraordinary qualities—a work ethic, audacity, and shrewdness—prevailed in a business that rewards such traits. He became an agent representing talent such as Janis Joplin and Bob Dylan, started record labels that produced 50 gold and 31 platinum albums, produced Broadway shows, including "Cats" and "Dreamgirls," and co-founded DreamWorks film studios. He would know presidents; own homes in Manhattan, Malibu, and Beverly Hills; fly in his own Gulfstream jet; and sell a painting by Jackson Pollock for more than a painting had ever sold for before. Along the way he joined Henry Ford, Thomas Edison, Steve Jobs, Bill Gates, and others who have prevailed without a college degree. In recent years *Forbes* has listed his wealth at between $4 billion and $5 billion.

In 1980, in an act reflecting ignorance, disregard, or pardon of Geffen's earlier degree claim, Governor Jerry Brown appointed him to the University of California Board of Regents, the governing body that presides over UCLA and the other system campuses. He served for seven years and was subsequently generous with his make-believe alma mater. To support the UCLA theater arts program he donated $5 million for a theater building, which was named the Geffen Playhouse. Later, saying "each of us has a responsibility to give back in some way," he gave $200 million to UCLA's medical school, which was renamed the David Geffen School of Medicine.[6]

consequentialism
The idea that actions are right or wrong, in part or whole, based on their consequences.

Looking back, Geffen's achievements and atonements can be weighed against his early indiscretions. A school of moral philosophy called *consequentialism* holds that actions are right or wrong based on their consequences. This perspective is less majestic than its deontological competitor. It affirms the simple maxim: the greatest good for the greatest number. His career has brought countless hours of entertainment

David Geffen in 1993. Source: Lynn Goldsmith/ CORBIS.

[6] Quoted in Jill Feiwell, "Geffen Gives UCLA $200 Million," *Daily Variety,* May 8, 2002, p. 1.

to millions around the world, employment to tens of thousands, and, through his philanthropic gifts, advances in medicine and the arts.

Geffen's actions challenge moral philosophy. If ethical rules must without exception be followed and doing wrong is never right, his legacy is flawed. If ethical thinking must judge not just the action, but also its consequences for the overall good, if what happens later counts, then the balance tips to a moral outcome.

In this chapter we will discuss a wide range of principles and approaches to making ethical decisions. These include intuitive judgment, principles great and small, procedures that corporations suggest to their employees, and practical tips.

PRINCIPLES OF ETHICAL CONDUCT

We begin with a compendium of ethical principles—some ancient, some modern. There are many such principles in the philosophical and religious traditions of East and West.

From a larger universe, we set forth 14 principles that every manager should know and think about. (See the accompanying box and discussion that follows.) The 14 principles here are fundamental guides or rules for behavior. Each of them has strengths and weaknesses. Some were created to be universal tests of conduct. Others have a more limited reach and apply only in certain spheres of human relations. Some are ideals. Others accommodate balancing of interests where perfection is elusive. A few invite compromise and can be used to rationalize flawed behavior. One principle, might equals right, is a justification for ignoble acts, but we include it here because it has been a basis of ethical reasoning since time immemorial.

These principles distill basic wisdom from 2,000 years of ethical thought. To the extent that they offer ideas for thinking about and resolving ethical dilemmas, they are not vague abstractions but useful, living guides to analysis and conduct.[7] We present them alphabetically.

The Categorical Imperative

categorical imperative
Act only according to that maxim by which you can at the same time will that it should become a universal law.

The *categorical imperative* (meaning, literally, a command that admits no exception) is a guide for ethical behavior set forth by the German philosopher Immanuel Kant in his *Foundations of the Metaphysics of Morals*, a tract published in 1785. In Kant's words: "Act only according to that maxim by which you can at the same time will that it should become a universal law."[8]

In other words, one should not adopt principles of action unless they can, without inconsistency, be adopted by everyone. Lying, stealing, and breaking promises, for example, are ruled out because society would disintegrate if they replaced

[7] T. K. Das asked managers to rank the favorability of these principles for use in business decisions in "How Strong Are the Ethical Preferences of Senior Business Executives," *Journal of Business Ethics,* January 2005. Among the 14 ethical principles discussed in this chapter, they ranked the Golden Rule most favorably and the Conventionalist Ethic least favorably.

[8] Immanuel Kant, *Foundations of the Metaphysics of Morals,* trans. Lewis White Beck (Indianapolis: Bobbs-Merrill, 1969), p. 44; written in 1785.

Fourteen Ethical Principles

The Categorical Imperative   Act only according to that maxim by which you can at the same time will that it should become a universal law.

The Conventionalist Ethic   Business is like a game with permissive ethics and any action that does not violate the law is permitted.

The Disclosure Rule   Test an ethical decision by asking how you would feel explaining it to a wider audience such as newspaper readers, television viewers, or your family.

The Doctrine of the Mean   Virtue is achieved through moderation. Avoid behavior that is excessive or deficient of a virtue.

The Ends–Means Ethic   The end justifies the means.

The Golden Rule   Do unto others what you would have them do unto you.

The Intuition Ethic   What is good or right is understood by an inner moral sense based on character development and felt as intuition.

Might-Equals-Right Ethic   Justice is the interest of the stronger.

The Organization Ethic   Be loyal to the organization.

The Principle of Equal Freedom   A person has the right to freedom of action unless such action deprives another person of a proper freedom.

The Proportionality Ethic   A set of rules for making decisions having both good and evil consequences.

The Rights Ethic   Each person has protections and entitlements that others have a duty to respect.

The Theory of Justice   Each person should act fairly toward others in order to maintain the bonds of community.

The Utilitarian Ethic   The greatest good for the greatest number.

truth telling, property rights, and vow keeping. Using this guideline, a manager faced with a moral choice must act in a way that he or she believes is right and just for any person in a similar situation. Each action should be judged by asking: "Could this act be turned into a universal code of behavior?" This quick *test of universalizability* has achieved great popularity.

test of universalizability
Could this act be turned into a universal code of behavior?

Kant was an extreme perfectionist. He walked the same route each day at the same time, appearing at places along the route so punctually that neighbors set their clocks by him. Before leaving his house he attached strings to the top of his socks and connected them to a spring apparatus held by his belt. As he walked, the contraption would pull the slack out of his socks. To no one's surprise, his ethical philosophies are perfectionist also, and that is their weakness. Kant's categorical imperative is a deontological ethic of the kind discussed in the story about David Geffen. It commands ethical action now; it weighs no future consequences. In this it is dogmatic and inflexible, a general rule that must be applied in every specific situation. There are no exceptions. But real life challenges the simple, single ethical law. If a competitor asks whether your company is planning to sell shirts in Beijing next year, must you answer the question with the truth?

The Conventionalist Ethic

This is the view that business is analogous to a game and special, lower ethics are permissible. In business, people may act to further their self-interest so long as

conven-
tionalist ethic
Business is like
a game with
permissive eth-
ics and actions
that do not
violate the law
are permitted.

they do not violate the law. The *conventionalist ethic*, which has a long history, was popularized some years ago by Albert Z. Carr in *Business as a Game*.[9] "If an executive allows himself to be torn between a decision based on business considerations and one based on his private ethical code," explained Carr, "he exposes himself to a grave psychological strain."[10]

Business may be regarded as a game, such as poker, in which the rules are different from those we adopt in personal life. Assuming game ethics, managers are allowed to bluff (a euphemism for lie) and to take advantage of all legal opportunities and widespread practices or customs. Carr used two examples of situations in which game ethics were permissible. In the first, an out-of-work sales agent with a good employment record feared discrimination because of his age—58. He dyed his hair and stated on his résumé that he was 45. In the second, a job applicant was asked to check off magazines he read, but decided not to check off *Playboy*, *The Nation*, or *The New Republic*. Though he read them, he did not want to be labeled controversial. He checked the *Reader's Digest* instead.[11]

The conventionalist ethic is criticized by those who make no distinction between society's ethics and business ethics. They argue that commerce defines the life chances of millions and is not a game to be taken lightly. As a principle, the conventionalist ethic is a thin justification for deceptive behavior at the office.

The Disclosure Rule

disclosure rule
Test an ethical
decision by
asking how you
would feel ex-
plaining it to a
wider audience
such as news-
paper readers,
television view-
ers, or your
family.

Using the *disclosure rule*, a manager faced with an ethical dilemma asks how it would feel to explain the decision to a wider audience. This simple idea appears in many company ethics codes. Here are two examples.

- Google: When faced with a potential conflict of interest, ask yourself: Would this relationship or situation embarrass me or Google if it showed up on the front page of a local newspaper or the top of a blog?[12]
- Western Union: When faced with a tough situation, ask yourself which course of action . . . [w]ould look better if it were printed in your local newspaper? Would you feel more comfortable explaining to your family? A judge?[13]

The disclosure rule is a mental exercise that invokes the potential for emotional distress. Censure by a community or family members brings shame, humiliation, guilt, and regret. This imaginary test screens out base conduct such as lying and theft, which are unacceptable if disclosed, but it does not always give full guidance for ethical dilemmas in which decent arguments exist for alternative actions. Also, an action that sounds acceptable if disclosed may not, upon reflection, always be the most ethical.

[9] Albert Z. Carr, *Business as a Game* (New York: New American Library, 1968).

[10] "Is Business Bluffing Ethical," *Harvard Business Review*, January–February 1968, p. 149.

[11] Carr, *Business as a Game*, p. 142.

[12] Google, "Google Code of Conduct," April 8, 2009, at http://investor.google.com/conduct.html.

[13] Western Union Company, *Code of Conduct* (Englewood, CO: Western Union Company), 2006, pp. 2–3.

The Doctrine of the Mean

doctrine of the mean
Virtue is achieved through moderation. Avoid behavior that is excessive or deficient of a virtue.

This ethic, set forth by Aristotle in the *Nicomachean Ethics* and sometimes called the *golden mean,* calls for virtue through moderation.[14] Right actions are found in the area between extreme behaviors, which are labeled as excess on the one hand and deficient on the other. Facing an ethical decision, a person first identifies the ethical virtue at its core (such as truthfulness) and then seeks the mean or moderate course of action between an excess of that virtue (boastfulness) and a deficiency of it (understatement).

At ITT, Harold Geneen pushed managers to extraordinary personal sacrifices. Their time, energy, loyalty, and will were bent to corporate purposes. Obsessive work led to remarkable business successes. During his tenure earnings increased for an incredible 58 consecutive quarters. And 130 of the managers he trained went on to take top positions at other companies.[15] Yet, it also led to personal difficulties such as marital problems. While the work of ITT was constructive and ethical, its demands led some to sacrifice a balanced life.[16] To Aristotle, this would have been wrong.

The doctrine of the mean is today little recognized, but the underlying notion of moderation as a virtue lingers in Western societies. The doctrine itself is inexact. To observe it is simply to act conservatively, never in the extreme. The moderate course and specific virtues such as honesty, however, are defined as aspects existing between and defined in relation to polar extremes. What they are is open to wide interpretation.

The Ends–Means Ethic

ends–means ethic
The end justifies the means.

This principle is age-old, appearing as an ancient Roman proverb, *existus acta probat,* or "the result validates the deeds." It is often associated with the Italian philosopher Niccolò Machiavelli. In *The Prince* (1513), Machiavelli argued that worthwhile ends justify efficient means, that when ends are of overriding importance or virtue, unscrupulous means may be employed to reach them.[17] When confronted with a decision involving an ethically questionable act, a person should ask whether some overall good—such as the survival of a country or business— justifies cutting corners.

In the 1980s Oracle Corporation grew rapidly. To get this growth, founder and CEO Lawrence J. Ellison pressed his sales managers to double revenues every year. Methods used by the frenzied sales force were watched less closely than its ability to hit targets. In 1993 the Securities and Exchange Commission fined Oracle for overstating earnings by double-billing customers, invoicing companies for products never sold, and violating accounting standards by recording sales

---

[14] *Nicomachean Ethics,* J. A. K. Thomson, trans. (New York: Penguin Books, 1982), book II, chap. 6.

[15] Alvin Moscow, "Introduction," in Harold Geneen, *Managing* (New York: Avon Books, 1984), pp. 5 and 13.

[16] Manuel Velasquez and Neil Brady, "Catholic Natural Law and Business Ethics," *Business Ethics Quarterly,* March 1997, p. 95.

[17] Niccolò Machiavelli, *The Prince,* trans. T. G. Bergin, ed. (New York: Appleton-Century-Crofts, 1947); written in 1513 and first published in 1532.

revenue before it was received.[18] However, by then Oracle had crushed its early competition in the relational database market. Today Oracle is a $27 billion corporation and Ellison is a billionaire. Oracle employs 105,000 people and has made many of them millionaires. Its software makes governments, businesses, and universities more productive. It pays taxes in 60 countries. It has a wide range of social responsibility programs. Did belief in this end result justify the competitive tactics used to build the company?

Any manager using unscrupulous means concedes the highest virtue and accepts the necessity of ethical compromise. In solving ethical problems, means may be as important, or more so, than ends. In addition, the process of ethical character development can never be furthered by the use of expedient means.

The Golden Rule

Golden Rule
Do unto others as you would have them do unto you.

An ideal found in the great religions and in works of philosophy, the *Golden Rule* has been a popular guide for centuries. Simply put, it is: "Do unto others as you would have them do unto you." It includes not knowingly doing harm to others. A manager trying to solve an ethical problem places him- or herself in the position of another party affected by the decision and tries to figure out what action is most fair from that perspective.

practical imperative
Treat others as ends in themselves, not as means to other goals. This principle prohibits selfish manipulation of other people.

A related principle called the *practical imperative* was set forth by Immanuel Kant. It is: "Act so that you treat humanity, whether in your own person or in that of another, always as an end and never as a means only."[19] This principle admonishes a manager to treat employees as ends in themselves, not to manipulate them simply as factors of production for the self-interested ends of the company.

Around 1900, when E. H. Harriman owned the Southern Pacific railroad, train accidents killed between 5,000 and 6,000 people a year. One day on an inspection tour, his train hit a rough section of track and nearly derailed because a work crew had neglected to post a flagman. Instead of firing the crew chief, Harriman insisted on firing the whole crew. A top executive spoke up, arguing it was cruel to punish them all. "Perhaps," responded Harriman, "but it will probably save a lot of lives. I want every man connected with the operation to feel a sense of responsibility. Now, everybody knew that the man hadn't gone back with the flag."[20] Harriman used this crew of workers to send a message to all other crews. The workers were not treated as individuals; they were punished en masse to signal others in the company.

test of reversibility
Would you be willing to change places with the person or persons affected by your actions?

A manager may comply with both the practical imperative and the Golden Rule by using the *test of reversibility,* that is, by asking if he or she would change places with the person affected by the contemplated action. A problem with the Golden Rule is that people's ethical values differ, and they may mistakenly assume that their preferences are universal. In addition, it is primarily a perfectionist rule for

---

[18] Mike Wilson, *The Difference between God and Larry Ellison* (New York: William Morrow, 1997), p. 239.

[19] Kant, *Foundations of the Metaphysics of Morals,* p. 54.

[20] Quoted in Maury Klein, *The Life & Legend of E. H. Harriman* (Chapel Hill: University of North Carolina Press, 2000), p. 266.

interpersonal relations. So applying it in business life where the interests of individuals are subordinated to the needs of the firm is sometimes hard.

The Intuition Ethic

intuition ethic
What is good or right is understood by an inner moral sense based on character development and felt as intuition.

The *intuition ethic*, as defined by philosophers such as G. E. Moore in his *Principia Ethica*, holds that what is good is simply understood.[21] That is, people are endowed with a moral sense by which they intuitively know the difference between right and wrong. The solution to an ethical problem lies in what you sense or understand to be right or wrong without resort to conscious reasoning.

People facing an ethical decision can experience a rapid, emotional reaction before they make any conscious effort to search for facts, weigh evidence, and reach a conclusion. The situation just bothers them, even if they are not sure why in the instant. Something is wrong. This ethical intuition, according to philosophers, is not simply ungrounded opinion. A person's ethical instincts are the product of socialization, role expectations, education, and experience. Everyone carries a lifetime of moral lessons that can well up in an instant emotional reaction. Though fallible, intuition is usually accurate. As we will see later in this chapter, the idea of an ethical intuition is more than speculative; it has a solid basis in the physiology of the brain.

Many companies recognize the intuition ethic in their conduct codes and offer it as a simple guideline for employees. At Cummins Inc., for example, employees are told to ask, "Do I feel uncomfortable with this particular course of action? If the answer is yes, don't do it."[22] At Dow Chemical Company employees are to ask: "What feels right or wrong about the situation or action?"[23]

Ethical intuition is reliable, but not infallible. Self-interest can be confused with ethical insight. No standard of validation exists outside the individual. It is unpersuasive to others for a manager to say, "It's wrong because I just think so."[24] Also, intuition may fail to give a clear answer when ethical norms are in conflict.

The Might-Equals-Right Ethic

might equals right
Justice is the interest of the stronger.

The classic statement of this ancient ethic is that of Thracymachus (thră-sĭm'-ă-cŭs), an Athenian teacher of rhetoric who argued with Socrates that justice is "nothing but what is the interest of the stronger."[25] No era since has been without both its expression and its practice. In business this thinking is expressed in some competitive strategies and marketing tactics. What is ethical is what a stronger individual or company has the power to impose on a weaker one. When faced with an ethical decision, people should seize what advantage they are strong enough to take, without regard for lofty sentiments.

[21] G. E. Moore, *Principia Ethica* (Cambridge: Cambridge University Press, 1903).

[22] *Cummins Code of Business Conduct* (Columbus, IN: Cummins Inc., undated), p. ii.

[23] Dow Chemical Company, *Code of Business Conduct* (Midland, MI: Dow Chemical Company, September 2006), p. 2.

[24] For an excellent discussion of intuition in managers' decisions, see Joseph L. Badaracco, Jr., *Defining Moments* (Boston: Harvard Business School Press, 1997), chap. 4.

[25] *The Republic*, F. M. Cornford, trans. (New York: Oxford University Press, 1966), p. 18.

In the 1860s Ben Holladay, owner of the Overland Stage Line, perfected a competitive strategy based on overbearing power. He entered new routes with lowball coach fares, subsidizing this service with profits from monopoly routes, waiting until local competitors failed. In 1863 a small stage line between Denver and Central City in Colorado charged $6 per run. Holladay put an elegant new Concord Coach with a leather interior on the line and charged only $2. The competitor soon folded, then Holladay replaced the new stagecoach with a primitive vehicle resembling a freight wagon and raised the fare to $12.

The weakness of the might-equals-right ethic lies in its confusion of ethics with force. Exercising power is different than acting from ethical duty. An ethical principle that can be invalidated by its foundation (e.g., physical force) is not consistent, logical, or valid. Might equals right is not a legitimate approach in civilized settings. It invites retaliation and censure, and it is not conducive to long-term advantage. Seizure by power violates the bedrock ethical duty of reciprocity on which all societies are based.

The Organization Ethic

organization ethic
Be loyal to the organization.

Simply put, this principle is: "Be loyal to the organization." It implies that the wills and needs of individuals are subordinate to the overall welfare of the organization (be it a corporation, government, university, or army). A member should act consistent with the organization's goals. This ethic leads to cooperation and mutual trust.

Many employees have such deep loyalty to an organization that it transcends self-interest. Some Americans jeopardize their health and work excessively long hours without pay out of devotion to the employer. In Asian societies, which have strong collectivist values, identification with and commitment to companies is exceptionally strong. In Japan, workers are so afraid of letting down their work group or employer that they come to work despite broken limbs and serious ailments. This behavior is so common that a word for death from overwork, *karoshi*, has entered the Japanese language.

The ethical limits of obedience are reached when duty to the organization is used to rationalize wrongdoing. The Nuremberg trials, which convicted Nazis of war crimes, taught that Western society expects members of organizations to follow their conscience. Just as no war criminal argued successfully that taking orders in a military chain of command excused his behavior, so no business manager may claim to be the helpless prisoner of corporate loyalties that crush free will and justify wrongdoing.

You are sailing to Rome (you tell me) to obtain the post of Governor of Cnossus. You are not content to stay at home with the honours you had before; you want something on a larger scale, and more conspicuous. But when did you ever undertake a voyage for the purpose of reviewing your own principles and getting rid of any of them that proved unsound?

Source: Epictetus, *The Discourses* (circa. AD 120).

principle of
equal freedom
A person has
the right to
freedom of
action unless
such action de-
prives another
person of a
proper freedom.

The Principle of Equal Freedom

This principle was set forth by the philosopher Herbert Spencer in his 1850 book *Social Statics*. "Everyman may claim the fullest liberty to exercise his faculties," said Spencer, "compatible with the possession of like liberty by every other man."[26] Thus, a person has the right to freedom of action unless such action deprives another person of a proper freedom. Spencer believed this was the first principle of ethical behavior in society because only when individual liberty was protected against infringement by others could human progress occur.

To use the principle, a person asks if an action will restrict others from actions that they have a legitimate right to undertake. Most people know the colloquial version: "Your right to swing your fist ends where my nose begins."

The principle of equal freedom lacks a tiebreaker for situations in which two rights conflict. Such situations require invocation of some additional rule to decide which right or freedom has priority. Ethically permissible management decisions may abridge the rights of some parties for the benefit of others. For example, all employees have broad privacy rights, but management invades them when it hires undercover detectives to investigate theft.

The Proportionality Ethic

propor-
tionality
A set of rules
for making
decisions
having both
good and evil
consequences.

Proportionality, an idea incubated in medieval Catholic theology, applies to decisions having both good and evil consequences. For instance, a maker of small-caliber, short-barreled, handguns that are irreverently called Saturday Night Specials has a dual impact on society. It makes available cheap, easily concealable weapons for criminals. Yet it also creates a supply of affordable self-defense weapons for poor people in crime-ridden areas who cannot afford high-quality handguns costing $1,000 and more. In this and similar cases, where a manager's action has a good effect but also entails a harm, the idea of proportionality fits.

A classic formulation of proportionality into a specific principle is Thomas M. Garrett's *principle of proportionality.* It states that managers are responsible for the consequences when they create situations leading to both good and evil effects. The principle allows them to risk predictable, but unwilled, harms to people (for example, innocent victims being shot by handguns) if they correctly weigh five factors.

principle
of propor-
tionality
Managers can
risk predictable,
but unwilled,
harms to people
after weighing
five factors:
type of good
and evil, proba-
bility, urgency,
intensity of
influence, and
alternatives.

First, managers must assess the *type of good and evil* involved, distinguishing between major and minor forms. Second, they should calculate the *urgency* of the situation. For example, would the firm go out of business unless employees were laid off? Third, they must estimate the *probability* of both good and evil effects. If good effects are certain and risks of serious harm are remote, an action is more favorable. Fourth, the *intensity of influence* over effects must be considered. In considering handgun injuries, for instance, manufacturers might assume that criminal action was an intervening force over which they had no control. Fifth, the existence of *alternatives* must be considered. If, for instance, an advertisement subtly encourages product misuse, the most ethical action might be to change it. Garrett

[26] Herbert Spencer, *Social Statics* (New York: Robert Schalkenbach Foundation, 1970), p. 69; first published in 1850.

principle of double effect
When both good and evil consequences result from a decision, a manager has acted ethically if the good outweighs the evil, if his or her intention is to achieve the good, and if there is no better alternative.

rights ethic
Each person has protections and entitlements that others have a duty to respect.

natural rights
Protections and entitlements that can be inferred by reason from the study of human nature.

legal rights
Protections and entitlements conferred by law.

theory of justice
Each person should act fairly toward others in order to maintain the bonds of community.

believed that taking these five factors into consideration would reveal fully the ethical dimension of a decision.[27]

An alternative formulation of the idea of proportionality is the *principle of double effect,* which is that in a situation from which both good and evil consequences are bound to result, a manager will act ethically if (1) the good effects outweigh the bad, (2) the manager's intention is to achieve the good effects, and (3) there is no better alternative.

These are intricate principles, requiring consideration of many factors. They force a manager to think about and weigh these factors in an organized way.

The Rights Ethic

Rights protect people against abuses and entitle them to important liberties. A strong philosophical movement defining *natural rights,* or rights that can be inferred by reason from the study of human nature, grew in Western Europe during the Enlightenment as a reaction against medieval religious persecutions. Over time, many such rights were given legal status and became *legal rights.*

Basic rights that are now widely accepted and protected in Western nations include the right to life; personal liberties such as expression, conscience, religious worship, and privacy; freedom from arbitrary, unjust police actions or unequal application of laws; and political liberties such as voting and lobbying. In Eastern societies, especially those transfused by the collectivist values of ancient Chinese culture, there is far less recognition of individual rights.

Rights imply duties. Because individuals have rights, many protected by law, other people have clear duties to respect them. For example, management should not permit operation of a dangerous machine because this would deprive workers of the right to a safe workplace. This right is based on the natural right to protection from harm by negligent actions of others and is legally established in common law and the Occupational Safety and Health Act. If some risk in operating a machine is unavoidable, workers have the right to be given an accurate risk assessment.

Theories of rights have great importance in American ethical debates. A problem caused by our reverence for rights is that they are sometimes stretched into selfish demands or entitlements. Rights are not absolute and their limits may be hard to define. For example, every person has a right to life, but industry daily exposes people to risk of death by releasing carcinogens into the environment. An absolute right to life would require cessation of much manufacturing activity (for example, petroleum refining). Rights, such as the right to life, are commonly abridged for compelling reasons of benefit to the public.

The Theory of Justice

A *theory of justice* defines what individuals must do for the common good of society. Maintaining the community is important because natural rights, such as the right to life, are reasonably protected only in a well-kept civil society. A basic principle of justice, then, is to act in such a way that the bonds of community are

---

[27] Thomas M. Garrett, *Business Ethics* (New York: Appleton-Century-Crofts, 1966), p. 8.

maintained. In broad terms, this means acting fairly toward others and establishing institutions in which people are subject to rules of fair treatment. In business life, justice requires fair relationships within the corporate community and using policies that treat its members fairly.

In society, a person's chances for justice are determined by basic economic and political arrangements. The design of institutions such as business corporations and political constitutions has a profound effect on the welfare and life chances of individuals. A contemporary philosopher, John Rawls, has developed an influential set of principles for the design of a just society. Rawls speculates that rational persons situated behind a hypothetical "veil of ignorance" and not knowing their place in a society (i.e., their social status, class position, economic fortune, intelligence, appearance, or the like) but knowing general principles of human society (such as those in political, economic, sociological, and psychological theories) would deliberate and choose two rules to ensure fairness in any society they created. First, "each person is to have an equal right to the most extensive basic liberty compatible with a similar liberty for others," and second, "social and economic inequalities are to be arranged so that they are both (a) reasonably expected to be to everyone's advantage, and (b) attached to positions and offices open to all."[28] In general, inequality would be allowed only if it would make better the lot of the most disadvantaged members of the society.

The impartiality and equal treatment called for in Rawls' principles are resplendent in theory and could even inspire some business decisions, but they are best applied to an analysis of broad societal issues. Acting justly in daily business life, on the other hand, requires the application of maxims that more concretely define justice. Managers can find such guidelines in three basic spheres of justice, as shown in Figure 8.1.

Distributive justice requires that the benefits and burdens of company life be distributed using impartial criteria. Awarding pay raises based on friendship

distributive justice
The benefits and burdens of company life should be distributed using impartial criteria.

FIGURE 8.1
Three Spheres of Justice

Distributive Justice
The distribution of benefits and burdens.

Compensatory Justice
Compensation for victims of injury.

Retributive Justice
Imposition of blame and punishment for wrongdoing.

[28] John Rawls, *A Theory of Justice* (Cambridge, MA: Harvard University Press, 1971), pp. 60–71.

retributive
justice
Punishment
should be
evenhanded
and propor-
tionate to
transgressions.

compensatory
justice
Victims should
receive fair
compensation
for damages.

utilitarian
ethic
The greatest
good for the
greatest number.

rather than performance criteria is unfair. All laws, rules, and procedures should apply equally to each employee. *Retributive justice* requires punishment to be evenhanded and proportionate to transgressions. A cashier should not be fired for stealing $5 if an executive who embezzled $10,000 is allowed to stay on the job and pay it back. And *compensatory justice* requires fair compensation to victims. A corporation that damages nearby property must restore it to its original state; one that hurts a customer must pay damages. The general idea of fairness in such maxims of justice supports orderly communities and organizations in which people secure human rights and meet human needs.

The Utilitarian Ethic

The *utilitarian ethic* was developed between the late eighteenth century and the mid-nineteenth century by a line of English philosophers, including Jeremy Bentham and John Stuart Mill. The principle of utility, on which this ethic is based, is that actions that promote happiness are right and actions that cause unhappiness are wrong. The utilitarians advocated choosing alternatives that led to the greatest sum of happiness or, as we express the thought today, the greatest good for the greatest number.

In making a decision using this principle, one must determine whether the harm in an action is outweighed by the good. If the action maximizes benefit, then it is the optimum choice over other alternatives that provide less benefit. Decision makers should try to maximize pleasure and reduce pain, not simply for themselves but for everyone affected by their decision. Utilitarianism requires comparison of the ethical consequences for each alternative in a decision. It is a popular principle. Cost-benefit studies embody its logic and its spirit.

Utilitarianism illustrates the ethical perspective of consequentialism discussed in the story about David Geffen. It can permit violation of an ethical rule if, in the sequel, that leads to the greatest good. One problem is that in practice it invites self-interested reasoning. Since the exact definition of the "greatest good" is subjective, its calculation has often been a matter of expediency. A second problem is that because decisions are to be made for the greatest good of the community, utilitarian thinking may permit the abridgment of individual or minority group rights. It does not relate individual and community ends in a way that necessarily protects both.[29]

REASONING WITH PRINCIPLES

The use of ethical principles, as opposed to the intuitive use of ethical common sense, may improve reasoning, especially in complex situations. Say a bank teller pockets $20 at the end of the day. The person's supervisor strongly feels that stealing

---

[29] See, for example, Mortimer Adler, *Desires: Right and Wrong* (New York: Macmillan, 1991), p. 61. John Stuart Mill's *Utilitarianism* (London: George Routledge & Sons, 1895) deals directly and brilliantly with these and other criticisms. It was originally published in 1863.

is wrong and fires the teller. Ethical common sense is all that is needed in this situation, but the following situation defies a simple solution.

> I was working as a manager in a division that was going to be closed. The secret clock was ticking away to the surprise mass layoff. Then a co-worker approached. He was thinking of buying a house. Did I think it was a good time to get into real estate?
>
> The man's job was doomed and I knew it. But spilling the secret, I believed, would violate my integrity as a corporate officer and doom the company to a firestorm of fear and rumor. There was no way to win and no way out.
>
> I considered it my fiduciary responsibility to the business to keep my mouth shut, and yet here was this person coming for advice as a friend and a business acquaintance and I had material information that would affect him. For someone with a sense of empathy and sympathy, which I like to think I have some of, it was very, very hard.
>
> In the end I swallowed my anguish and kept silent. The man bought the house and lost his job. The secret held. But now 10 years later I have many times relived the story and second-guessed what I did that day.[30]

This is a vexing situation, and one created by the complexities of modern organizational life. The last paragraph finds the narrator alerted by emotion to the presence of an ethical conflict. Something in the situation causes anguish. In this predicament, however, simple moral homilies such as "tell the truth" or "be fair" are insufficient to resolve conflicts. Let us apply to this case three ethical principles, each of which offers a distinct perspective—utilitarianism, the rights ethic, and the theory of justice.

The *utilitarian* ethic requires the manager to calculate which course of action, among alternatives, will result in the greatest benefit for the company and all workers. A frank response here might disrupt operations. People could resign, take days off, work less efficiently, and engage in sabotage. Keeping the secret will cause hardship for a single employee about to buy a house and perhaps others in a similar situation. On balance, the manager must protect the broader welfare of customers, stockholders, and remaining employees.

From the standpoint of *rights*, the employee is entitled to the truth and the manager has a duty to speak honestly. It would be truthful to say, "As a manager my duty is always to keep such matters confidential," yet this comment veils the full truth. On the other hand, rights are not absolute. The corporation has a competing right to protect its property, and this right must be balanced against the right of an employee to honest treatment. In addition, the manager, in effect, promised to keep the secret and has a duty of promise keeping.

With respect to *justice*, corporations are required to promote fair, evenhanded treatment of employees. Distributive justice demands giving out benefits and burdens impartially. It would be partial to signal the layoff to one worker and not others.

Based on the application of utility, rights, and justice, the manager's decision to remain silent is probably acceptable. Some judgment is required in balancing

---

[30] Paraphrased and quoted from Kirk Johnson, "In the Class of '70, Wounded Winners," *The New York Times,* March 7, 1996, p. A12.

rights, but the combined weight of reasoning with all three principles supports the manager's decision. Yet the manager's moral intuition was not wrongly aroused. The situation offends the rules of deontological ethics. It exacts, by commission or omission, a lie, and it violates the practical imperative by treating the employee as expendable while achieving a corporate goal. Both good and evil result here. In such cases, application of the principle of double effect is appropriate. Here the welfare of the company outweighs the welfare of one employee, the manager's intention is not to hurt the employee but to help the company, and no better alternative presents itself. So the consequentialist principle of double effect confirms the manager's action.

CHARACTER DEVELOPMENT

virtue ethic
Ethical behavior stems from character virtues built up by habit.

Character development is a source of ethical behavior separate from the use of principled reasoning. The idea that character development is the wellspring of ethical behavior is known as the *virtue ethic*. It originated with the Greek philosophers. Aristotle wrote that moral virtue is the result of habit.[31] He believed that by their nature ethical decisions require choice, and we build virtue, or ethical character, by habitually making the right choices. Just as we learn to play the piano through daily practice, so we develop virtues by constant practice, and the more conscientious we are, the more accomplished we become. In a virtuous person ethical behavior comes from inner disposition, not from obeying external rules or applying abstract principles. Plato identified four fundamental traits—justice, temperance, courage, and wisdom—that have come to be called the *cardinal virtues*. Many other virtues have been mentioned over the years, including prudence, reverence, charitableness, hopefulness, and integrity.[32]

cardinal virtues
The four most basic traits of an ethical character—justice, temperance, courage, and wisdom. They were identified by Plato.

The virtue ethic requires conscious effort to develop a good disposition by making right decisions over time. Then acts are generated by inner traits ingrained from repetition and they reflect the disposition of a virtuous character. When Sholom Menora, CEO of Tri-United Technologies, moved out of Chicago, he sent a check for $25 to the city to compensate it for his periodic failure to put coins in parking meters.[33] This act reveals a trait of obsessive integrity, not an exercise of grand principles. However, such flashes of inner virtue are not a rejection of the study and use of philosophical principles, which can still inspire and delight the moral imagination.

THE NEURAL BASIS OF ETHICAL DECISIONS

The traditional view in moral philosophy is that ethical decisions, particularly right ones, come from deliberate reasoning that relies on principles and maxims. However, evidence from study of the brain casts doubt on this assumption. It

---

[31] *Nicomachean Ethics*, p. 91.

[32] Dennis J. Moberg, "The Big Five and Organizational Virtue," *Business Ethics Quarterly,* April 1999, p. 246.

[33] "Chicago Businessman Does Right by Jewish Law," *Ha'aretz,* October 6, 2000.

suggests that a fast, unconscious, and automatic process in neural circuits causes ethical judgments to appear in our awareness without any feeling of having gone through a reasoning process.

There is no specific part of the brain that makes ethical decisions. Rather, imaging shows that ethical problems simultaneously activate arrays or networks of neural circuits in some areas of the brain.[34] These neural circuits operate in parallel, coursing through regions associated with both social emotions and logical thinking, and they compete to dominate without any central control. A judgment is reached when one circuit is amplified over others, causing the decision maker to become conscious of a moral conviction. Although neural circuits involved with both emotions and reasoning are activated when a person considers an ethical dilemma, evidence suggests that emotional circuits tend to dominate the process and that they are needed to reach good moral judgments.

Probing Ethical Decisions

functional magnetic resonance imaging
A method used to map activity in neural networks during ethical decision making.

Researchers use *functional magnetic resonance imaging*, or fMRI, to study the brains of people making ethical judgments. An fMRI test detects and measures changes in blood flow and blood oxygen content related to neural activity. Neurons, the nerve cells in the brain, do not store oxygen, so they require increased blood supply as soon as they activate. An fMRI test measures cognitive function as it arises and spreads in the brain by detecting and mapping these changes in as little as one second after the neurons become active. It works by detecting shifts in magnetic properties of hemoglobin, a protein that carries oxygen in the blood. With a strong enough magnetic field, fMRI can pinpoint neural activity to within 1 millimeter in the brain.

Researchers have asked subjects in fMRI settings to consider ethical dilemmas, for example, these two situations involving trolleys.

> You are standing by a track when you notice a runaway trolley that will kill five workers standing down the track if it continues on its path. If you flip a nearby switch you will divert the trolley to an alternate track, but it will kill one worker on that track. Is it appropriate for you to flip the switch?

> You are standing on a footbridge when you notice a runaway trolley that will kill five workers standing on the track below if it continues on course. You can prevent the trolley from hitting them by pushing an overweight stranger standing next to you down onto the track, killing that person, but stopping the trolley. Is it appropriate for you to push the bystander in front of the trolley?

Both dilemmas could be resolved with utilitarian logic, since in each case the subject can act to save five lives by sacrificing one life. However, they differ in emotional engagement. The first version requires the more remote, impersonal act of flipping a switch. The second version contemplates a hands-on, repugnant, murderous act that will kill an innocent person. Such actions are forbidden in rule-based, deontological thinking. Over many experiments, large majorities of every

---

[34] Chadd M. Funk and Michael S. Gazzaniga, "The Functional Brain Architecture of Human Morality," *Current Opinion in Neurobiology*, December 2009, p. 678.

demographic and cultural background solve the dilemmas in the same way, choosing to flip the switch but refusing to push the bystander.[35] These dilemmas may seem remote from business life, but they allow study of how the brain processes situations in which there is a conflict between deontological rules and utilitarian balances. Business life teems with such situations.

In a defining experiment, brain imaging showed that when subjects made a decision about the more personal footbridge dilemma they engaged four brain regions associated with social emotions. But when deciding about the impersonal track-switching situation they activated three regions associated with working memory (conscious reasoning) and they responded more slowly.[36] Another fMRI study found that subjects with lesions on the ventromedial prefrontal cortex, a brain region needed to produce normal social emotions, were more likely than normal subjects to push the bystander off the footbridge. They lacked neural circuits that generated social emotions such as guilt, shame, and fear of punishment, the feelings that inhibit unimpaired subjects.

The study shows that areas of the brain associated with emotion are necessary to make "normal" distinctions in ethical judgment.[37] All the subjects calculated the 5:1 utilitarian equation correctly, but those with emotional deficits made more cool, calculating decisions. As expected, both the normal and impaired subjects approved of flipping the switch in the first dilemma. However, in the second, those with emotional deficits were far more willing to push the stranger.

Other studies have identified neural circuits activated by different species of ethical decisions. The maxims of retributive justice are one example. Subjects were given multiple scenarios in which a person was more or less blameworthy for a crime. In an fMRI setting they were asked for each scenario, first, to assess the person's blameworthiness, and second, to calculate appropriate levels of punishment. The first decisions, about guilt or innocence, activated neural circuits in the right dorsolateral prefrontal cortex, a region associated with deliberate reasoning. The second decisions, about the level of punishment, activated the amygdala, medial prefrontal cortex, and posterior cingulate cortex, a set of regions linked with unconscious social intuition and emotional processing.[38]

[35] John Mikhail, "Universal Moral Grammar: Theory, Evidence and the Future," *TRENDS in Cognitive Sciences,* April 2007, p. 144. See, for example, Joshua D. Greene, et al., "Cognitive Load Selectively Interferes with Utilitarian Moral Judgment," *Cognition,* June 2008, supplementary materials, pp. 6 and 19, showing that 82 percent would flip the switch and 79 percent would refuse to push a stranger.

[36] Joshua D. Greene, et al., "An fMRI Investigation of Emotional Engagement in Moral Judgment," *Science,* September 14, 2001, fig. 1. Areas associated with emotion were the bilateral medial frontal gyrus, the bilateral posterior cingulate gyrus, the left angular gyrus, and the right angular gyrus. Areas associated with working memory were the right middle frontal gyrus, the left parietal lobe, and the right parietal lobe.

[37] Michael Koenigs, et al., "Damage to the Prefrontal Cortex Increases Utilitarian Moral Judgments," *Nature,* April 19, 2007, p. 908.

[38] Joshua W. Buckholtz, et al., "The Neural Correlates of Third-Party Punishment," *Neuron,* December 2008, pp. 935–36.

Emotions and Intuition

Emotions have a central role in ethical thought because of their importance to adaptive behavior. The extensive cooperation between genetically unrelated individuals that characterizes human society is rare in the rest of the animal kingdom.[39] It is possible only because of strong social norms, including ethical norms. These norms enable cooperation among humans if they are adhered to and if deviation is punished. So the human brain has evolved to generate feelings that motivate fair exchanges with others.

Emotions such as guilt, shame, remorse, contempt, outrage, and disgust are reactions to moral violations. Normal individuals find it emotionally painful to act unethically. A person who creates reproving emotions in others risks punishment, shunning, and loss of relationships, all of which confer disadvantage. So these social emotions enforce and motivate moral conduct, reduce cheating, and promote mutual trust, allowing the large-scale cooperation in human society that confers a survival advantage.[40] Natural selection is the evolutionary basis of ethics.

In sum, evidence suggests that ethical decisions have a basis in brain architecture. They derive from the activation of parallel neural circuits in areas associated with both social emotions and logical reasoning. In the absence of any central control, these parallel circuits compete to lead the decision. Research supports the existence of a moral intuition, driven mainly by rapid activation of neural circuits that process social emotions. This moral intuition creates awareness of a moral judgment without any memory of having gone through a step-by-step reasoning process.[41] Thus, neuroscience provides a basis for the intuition ethic set forth by philosopher G. E. Moore more than a century ago.

Moral intuition is a form of social intuition that is adaptive to the social environment and predominates in individual ethical decisions, more so when they are immediate, personal, and emotional. There is more room for conscious reflection in decisions that are further off, abstract, less emotionally loaded, or amenable to decision regimes such as corporate policies or conduct codes. When subjects in fMRI experiments face more complex dilemmas and engage areas of the brain used for cognitive reasoning they take more time to respond, suggesting reflection beyond simple emotional response.[42]

In addition, although ethical stories and dilemmas activate the same regions of experimental subject's brains, there is considerable individual variation in perceptions of right and wrong. Evidence suggests that the sensitivity of neural pathways is based on social experience and learning. Life experience can bias one circuit over another, leading to a better ethical decision. Young children, for example,

---

[39] Ibid., p. 930.

[40] Bryce Huebner, Susan Dwyer, and Marc Hauser, "The Role of Emotion in Moral Psychology," *Trends in Cognitive Sciences,* December 2008.

[41] James Woodward and John Allman, "Moral Intuition: Its Neural Substrates and Normative Significance," *Journal of Physiology—Paris* 101 (2007), p. 186.

[42] Joshua D. Greene, et al., "The Neural Bases of Cognitive Conflict and Control in Moral Judgment," *Neuron,* October 2004, p. 397.

have a less-developed capacity for empathy and they have difficulty distinguishing between an accident and an intentionally evil action when both have the same outcome.[43]

At first glance, evidence for the importance of unconscious processes seems to reduce the relevance of reasoning with ethical principles. However, that conclusion is incorrect. Brain research discussed here confirms the existence of neural circuits activated by the deontological or consequentialist (utilitarian) approaches found in several principles and by problems of retributive justice. The effectiveness of the disclosure rule—the idea of revealing your action to your family or the world—is shown to rest on emotions such as shame and remorse.

Research into neural sensitivity also affirms the virtue ethic if it is defined as moral intuition enlightened by experience and ethical education. Character development, or the learning of specific virtues such as prudence or honesty, can amplify some neural circuits, biasing the outcome of a competition with other neural circuits in their favor. This explains the rise of a moral habit. Efforts to be more virtuous bias some neural circuits over others.

So neuroscience, as it removes physiological mysteries, reinforces the ethical teachings of centuries. It confirms that principles, at least the noble ones, are still enlightened, practical guides. We follow them unconsciously when we rely on intuition. And, when we have the luxury of reflection, they guide our reason.

PRACTICAL SUGGESTIONS FOR MAKING ETHICAL DECISIONS

Here are practical steps to better define and resolve ethical problems in business.

First, pay attention to your ethical intuition. Ethical intuition is a form of social intuition. Like social intuition it has evolved to protect us by making fast, automatic, unconscious, adaptive judgments in complex situations where risks may be high. Our initial gut reactions are as helpful or more so than judgments we make after lengthy thought. However, it can be wise and reassuring to confirm instant decisions with deliberate.

Second, consider tactics that illuminate alternatives. The philosopher Bertrand Russell advocated imaginary conversations with a hypothetical devil's advocate as an antidote for certitude. Seek out a more experienced, ethically sensitive person in the company as an adviser. This person can be of great value in revealing the ethical climate of a firm or industry. Divide a sheet of paper with columns to enter the pros and cons for various alternatives. Such balance sheets organize information and discipline scattered, agitated thinking. Also, the process of entering all relevant factors sometimes brings hidden considerations to light.

Another tactic is the *critical questions approach.* Ask yourself questions about the ethical implications of an action. This approach is often suggested in corporate

critical questions approach
A method of ethical reasoning in which insight comes from answering a list of questions.

---

[43] Liane Young and Rebecca Saxe, "Innocent Intentions: A Correlation Between Forgiveness for Accidental Harm and Neural Activity," *Neuropsychologia,* August 2009, p. 2071.

conduct codes. At International Paper, employees are given a wallet card with these questions to ask if they are in doubt.

- Are my actions legal?
- Am I being fair and honest?
- Will my action stand the test of time?
- How will I feel about myself afterward?
- How will it look in the newspaper?
- Will I sleep soundly tonight?
- Can I explain my action to the person I admire most?[44]

These critical questions are shorthand for a variety of approaches to ethical reasoning. Some invoke maxims such as "obey the law" and "tell the truth." Others rest on the disclosure ethic and the intuition ethic.

Third, sort out ethical priorities early. Serious ethical dilemmas can generate paralyzing stress. However, clear values reduce stress by reducing temptation and easing conscience as a source of anxiety. For example, when being honest means sacrificing a sale, it helps to clarify in advance that integrity is more important than money. Publicly commit yourself on ethical issues. Tell your co-workers you are opposed to taking office supplies home or price fixing, or any other action that could be an issue. They will now be disinclined to approach you with corrupt intentions, and public commitment forces you to maintain your standards or suffer shame.

Fourth, set an example. This is a basic managerial function. An ethical manager creates a morally uplifting workplace. An unethical manager can make money, but he or she pays the price, and the price is the person's integrity. Employees who see unethical behavior by their supervisor always wonder when that behavior will be directed at them.

Fifth, thoughts must be translated into action, and ethical deeds often require courage. Reaching a judgment is easier than acting. Ethical stands can provoke anger in others, strain relationships, and cost a company business, and there are risks of job loss.

Sixth, cultivate sympathy and charity toward others. The question "What is ethical?" is one on which well-intentioned people may differ. Marcus Aurelius wrote: "When thou art offended by any man's fault, forthwith turn to thyself and reflect in what like manner thou dost err thyself; for example, in thinking that money is a good thing, or pleasure, or a bit of reputation, and the like."[45]

Ethical perfection is illusory. We live in a morally complex civilization with endless rules, norms, obligations, and duties that are like road signs, usually pointing in the same direction but sometimes not. No decision ends conflicts, no principle penetrates unerringly to the good, no manager achieves sainthood.

---

[44] International Paper Company, *Code of Business Ethics,* 3rd ed. (Memphis, TN: International Paper Company, 2008), p. 27.

[45] *The Meditations of Marcus Aurelius Antoninus,* George Long, trans. (Danbury, CT: Grolier, 1980), p. 281; originally written circa AD 180.

Warning Signs

Lockheed Martin gives this list of phrases to all employees, telling them that when they hear one they are "on thin ethical ice."

- "It doesn't matter how it gets done as long as it gets done."
- "No one will ever know."
- "We didn't have this conversation."
- "It sounds too good to be true."
- "Shred that document."
- "I deserve it."

- "It's all for a good cause."
- "Well, maybe just this once."
- "Everyone does it."
- "This will destroy the competition."
- "What's in it for me?"
- "It's okay if I don't gain personally."
- "No one will get hurt."
- "This is a non-meeting."

Source: Lockheed Martin, *Setting the Standard*, October 2008, p. 32.

There is an old story about the inauguration of James Canfield as president of Ohio State University. With him on the inaugural platform was Charles W. Eliot, president of Harvard University for 20 years. After receiving the mace of office, Canfield sat next to Eliot, who leaned over and whispered, "Now, son, you are president, and your faculty will call you a liar." "Surely," said Canfield, "your faculty have not accused you of lying." Replied Eliot, "Not only that son, they've proved it."

CONCLUDING OBSERVATIONS

There are many paths to ethical behavior. Not all managers have studied the repertoire of principles and ideas that exist to resolve ethical problems of business life. One who did was J. C. Penney, who believed they had great value.

> I believe today and shall to the end of my days, that when a man truly works with a principle, such as the golden rule, that principle makes him the representative of a great and positive working force. Then a creative force of the universe is back of him, for the principle is doing the work, while he merely attends to the details.[46]

This is an inspiring quotation. Here Penney offers hope for managers to find a just order in the universe and act with it. Modern science locates this just order not in the universe, but inside each manager, in neural circuits that evolved to facilitate social cooperation. Either way, attending to the details, as Penney puts it, is a difficult art. By reflecting on principles, a person becomes more sensitive to the presence of ethical issues and more resolute in acting with integrity.

[46] J.C. Penney, *Fifty Years with the Golden Rule* (New York: Harper, 1950), p. 78.

Short Incidents for Ethical Reasoning

The following situations contain ethical conflicts. Try to define the ethical problems that exist. Then apply ideas, principles, and methods from the preceding two chapters to resolve them.

A CLOUDED PROMOTION

As chairman of an accounting firm in a large city, you were prepared to promote one of your vice chairmen to the position of managing partner. Your decision was based on a record of outstanding performance by this person over the eight years she has been with the firm. A new personnel director recently insisted on implementing a policy of résumé checks for hirees and current employees receiving promotions who had not been through such checks. Unfortunately, it was discovered that although the vice chairman claimed to have an MBA from the University of Michigan, she dropped out before completing her last 20 units of course work. Would you proceed with the promotion, retain the vice chairman but not promote her, or fire her?

THE ADMIRAL AND THE THIEVES

When Admiral Thomas Westfall took command of the Portsmouth Naval Shipyard, theft of supplies was endemic. It was a standing joke that homes in the area were painted gray with paint stolen from the Navy. Admiral Westfall issued an order that rules related to supply practices and forbidding theft would be strictly enforced. Within a few days, two career petty officers were apprehended carrying a piece of Plexiglas worth $25 out of the base. Westfall immediately fired both of them and also a civilian storeroom clerk with 30 years' service, who lost both his job and his pension. According to Westfall, "The fact that I did it made a lot of honest citizens real quick." Did the admiral act ethically?

SAM, SALLY, AND HECTOR

Sam, Sally, and Hector have been laid off from middle-management positions. Sam and Hector are very upset by their misfortune. They are nervous, inarticulate, and docile at an exit meeting in the personnel department and accept the severance package offered by the company (two weeks' pay plus continuation of health benefits for two weeks) without questioning its provisions. Sally, on the other hand, manifests her anxiety about job loss by becoming angry. In the exit meeting, she complains about the inadequacy of the severance package, threatens a lawsuit, and tries to negotiate more compensation. She receives an extra week of pay that the others did not get. Has the company been fair in its treatment of these employees?

A PERSONALITY TEST

You are asked by a potential employer to take a psychological profile test. A sample segment includes the items shown in Exhibit 1.

Because you have read that it is best to fit into a "normal" range and pattern of behavior, and because it is your hunch that the personnel office will weed out unusual personalities, you try to guess which answers are most appropriate for a conservative or average response and write them in. Is this ethical?

EXHIBIT 1

	Yes	No	Can't Say
It is difficult to sleep at night.			
I worry about sexual matters.			
Sometimes my hands feel disjointed from my body.			
I sometimes smell strange odors.			
I enjoyed dancing classes in junior high school.			
Not all of my friends really like me.			
Work is often a source of stress.			

AL

The CEO of a Midwestern manufacturing company tells the following story.

I was looking over recent performance reviews in the household products division and one thing that struck me was the review of a star sales rep named Al. I know Al because he handles our Walmart account. Al had the highest annual sales for the past five years and last year nearly doubled the next highest rep's total. The sales manager's written evaluation was highly laudatory as expected, but cautioned Al to adhere strictly to discount policy, shipping protocol, and billing protocol. I got curious.

A conversation with the division manager revealed that Al ingratiated himself with workers on the loading dock, socializing with them, sending them birthday cards, and giving them small gifts such as tickets to minor-league ball games. The loading dock supervisor complained that Al was requesting and sometimes getting priority loading of trucks for his customers despite the formal first-in, first-out rules for shipping orders. Second, Al had given several customers slightly deeper discounts than authorized, although the resulting orders were highly profitable for the company. And finally, late in December, Al had informally requested that one big account delay payment on an order by a week so that the commission would be counted in the next year. This would have gotten him off to a running start had not an accountant for the purchaser paid promptly and written to Al's manager in refusing the request.

The division head stuck up for Al. I didn't press or request that any action be taken. Did I do the right thing?

How would you answer the CEO's question?

A TRIP TO SEAWORLD

A sales representative for a large manufacturer of consumer electronics equipment headquartered in Los Angeles, California, has courted a buyer from a nationwide chain of 319 retail stores for more than a year. At company expense the buyer was flown to Los Angeles from Trenton, New Jersey, with his spouse, for a three-day sales presentation. The company is paying all expenses for this trip and for the couple to attend a Los Angeles Dodgers baseball game and dine at fine restaurants.

During the second day of meetings, the buyer discusses a one-year, $40 million order. The chain that the buyer represents has not sold the company's products before, but once it starts, reorders are likely. At dinner that evening, the buyer mentions that he and his wife have always wanted to visit SeaWorld in San Diego. While they are in Southern California and so close, they would like to fly down. It is clear that he expects the company to pay for this trip and that he will delay making a commitment for the $40 million order until he gets a response.

The company has already spent $4,200 for the buyer's trip to Los Angeles. The San Diego excursion would cost about $500. The marketing manager estimates that the company can make a 9 percent gross profit on the sale. The sales representative stands to receive a 0.125 percent commission over base salary.

What should the sales representative do?

MARY AND TOM

Mary P., an aerospace engineer, tells about a difficult career experience in which her friend Tom plays a central role.

My friend Tom and I are employed by Republic Systems Corporation. We started about the same time after graduating from engineering school five years ago. The company does a lot of defense work, mostly for the Air Force, and it's big. Tom and I worked on project teams doing tests to make sure that electronics shipped to customers met specifications. We have very similar backgrounds and job records, and there has always been a little competition between us. But neither one of us pulled ahead of the other on the corporate ladder. That is until last winter.

At that time, we were assigned a special project to modify the testing protocol on certain radar components. The success of the projects was critical; it had to be done before Republic bid for two more years on its big radar systems contract. About 40 percent of our people work radar.

We rolled up our sleeves and put in long hours. After a month, though, Tom volunteered to be on a companywide task force developing a new employee privacy policy. Privacy is a big deal to Al Manchester, our CEO.

Tom continued to work with me, but he gradually put more and more of his energy into the privacy project. I had to start taking up some of the slack. He enjoyed the task force meetings. They met in the dining room at the Kenthill Country Club and he could hobnob with Al and some of the other big shots. He worked overtime to impress them.

We finally finished the testing project and it was a success. But toward the end I did the lion's share of it. One day, Tom made me angry by ending a capacitor test at 94 hours instead of the 100 hours you really have to have for validity. He did it because he was late for a privacy task force meeting. Overall, I guess Tom helped a lot, but he didn't do his share all the way through.

Last month the assistant manager of the radar project left the company and Tom and I both applied for the position. It was a pay raise of several grades and meant getting a lot of recognition. They chose Tom. The announcement in the company newsletter said that he was a "strong team player" and mentioned both the testing project and the privacy task force as major accomplishments.

I don't think it was fair.

Was Tom fair to Mary? Was Tom's promotion fair to Mary? Was the company wrong to promote Tom?

THE HONDA AUCTION

Dave Conant co-owned and managed Norm Reeves Honda in Cerritos, California. Naturally, he worked closely with Honda marketing executives to get cars for his dealership. One day, one of these executives, Dennis Josleyn, the new zone sales manager, approached him, asking him to submit a bid on 64 company cars. These were near-new cars previously driven by corporate executives or used to train mechanics. Company policy called for periodic auctions in which Honda dealers submitted competitive bids, and the high bidder got the cars to sell on its lot. It was Josleyn's job to conduct the auction.

"I want you to submit bids on each car $2,000 below wholesale market value," Joselyn told Dave Conant. Conant dutifully inspected the 64 cars and submitted the asked-for bids. Meanwhile, Josleyn busied himself creating fake auction papers showing that other Honda dealers bid less than Conant. Of course, others bid near the wholesale price, so their bids were higher. Completing the phony auction, Josleyn announced the winner—Conant's dealership. The next day he showed up there and handed Conant an envelope.

"I have a little invoice for you," he said.

Conant went to his office, opened it, and found a bill for $64,000 payable to an ad agency co-owned by Josleyn and his brother. The message was clear. Josleyn wanted a 50–50 split with the dealer on the $2,000 windfall each car would bring, so he was billing

Conant for half the extra $128,000 the entire batch of cars would bring in.

Conant faced a decision. If the invoice was paid, the dealership would make a $64,000 windfall. If he refused to pay, the cars would be rerouted to a dealer who was a "player" and future shipments of new Hondas might be slower. He decided to pay the invoice. In his own words: "I believed I had no choice. If I hadn't paid the amount, I would have incurred the wrath of Dennis Josleyn and possibly some of the other Honda gods, and I believe they would have taken our store down."[1]

Conant was not alone. Honda dealers around the country faced a dilemma. After investing large sums to build new showrooms and facilities and hire employees, they soon found themselves having to choose between two paths. If they gave bribes and kickbacks to Honda executives, they secured a copious flow of cars and made a fortune. On average, a favored dealer made almost $1 million a year in personal income. However, if they stayed clean, no matter how modern their dealership and well trained its sales force; they received fewer cars and less profitable models. If they went bankrupt, and many did, the Honda executives arranged for less scrupulous owners to take over their dealerships.

Many an honest dealer short on cars drove across town to see a rival's lot packed with fast-selling models in popular colors. Over time, it also became clear that the highest Japanese executives at Honda knew what was going on but chose to do nothing.

Did Conant make the right decision? What would you do in his position?

THE TOKYO BAY STEAMSHIP COMPANY

The Tokyo Bay Steamship Company operated a tourist ship between Tokyo and the volcanic island of Oshima 50 miles offshore. It also had a restaurant on the island. It was a modest business until February 1933, when Kiyoko Matsumoto, a 19-year-old college student, committed suicide by jumping into the crater of the volcano, which bubbled with molten lava. Ms. Matsumoto left a poetic suicide note and, through newspaper stories, the Japanese public became obsessed with her story.

[1] Quoted in Steve Lynch, *Arrogance and Accords: The Inside Story of the Honda Scandal* (Dallas: Pecos Press, 1997), p. 106.

Soon other Japanese emulated Ms. Matsumoto. In the next 10 months, 143 people threw themselves into the crater. Many more came to watch. One Sunday in April, for example, 31 people tried to jump; 25 were restrained, but 6 succeeded. People crowded around the edge of the crater waiting for jumpers. Shouts of "Who's next?" and "Step right this way. Lots of room down in front" could be heard.[2]

The Tokyo Bay Steamship Company capitalized on the volcano's popularity. It increased its fleet to 30 ships and added 19 more restaurants. Meanwhile, the Oshima police chief met the boat and tried to weed out potential suicides using a crude behavioral profile (was someone too happy or too sad?). A police officer stood at the rim of the volcano. The Japanese government made purchase of a one-way ticket to Oshima a crime. Many suicides were prevented; others succeeded. Twenty-nine people who were stopped at the volcano killed themselves by jumping into the ocean on the return boat to Tokyo.

In the meantime, Tokyo Bay Steamship Company prospered. Its shares rose on the Tokyo exchange. But did it meet basic standards of ethics?

TIGER WOODS

In the early morning hours of November 26, 2009, golf star Tiger Woods drove from his Florida mansion, hitting a fire hydrant and a tree. The media soon revealed infidelities, destroying his image as a dedicated husband and parent of two small children.

Before this, Woods was one of the world's most popular athletes. Corporations used him as an endorser with global appeal and his income from this was as high as $100 million a year. When the scandal broke, corporate sponsors needed to reassess the relationship.

AT&T, which has a *Code of Ethics* requiring "[e]ach director, officer, and employee . . . to act with integrity . . . including being honest and ethical" was the first to act.[3] It ended an agreement paying Woods to carry its logo on his golf bag.

Two weeks later Accenture, which used Woods in its ads because his golf skills reinforced its slogan, "high performance delivered," chose to end its ties. In its *Code of Business Ethics* the global consulting firm says, "We conduct our personal activities . . . in the same way we conduct our business activities: with the utmost integrity" and it defines integrity as "recognizing right from wrong and understanding the ethical implications of our choices."[4]

Three of Woods' most prominent sponsors, Nike, Gatorade, and Gillette, affirmed their support for him. However, within several months Gatorade, a PepsiCo brand, broke off its sponsorship and the CEO of Procter & Gamble said the company would not use Woods again in its Gillette brand commercials. Nike continued to support Woods. On its Web site Nike says the company was "founded on a handshake" and was "based on trust, teamwork, honesty, and mutual respect." "Our task," it says, "has been to maintain this same ethic across our operations."[5] Nike's code, *Inside the Lines*, sets criteria for employees' behavior.

> Nike's good name and reputation result in large part from our collective actions. That means the work-related actions of every employee must reflect standards of honesty, loyalty, trustworthiness, fairness, concern for others, and accountability. We are expected to be sensitive to any situations that can adversely impact Nike's reputation and are expected to use good judgment and common sense in the way we all conduct business.[6]

Nike was not the only sponsor that stuck with Woods. Electronic Arts continued to feature him on its Web site and in a video game. NetJets, TLC Laser Eye Centers, and Upper Deck made no changes. Tag Heuer reduced, but did not eliminate, his presence in its advertising.

The events here raise many questions, most prominent among them, should corporate sponsors apply their ethics standards to celebrity endorsers?

---

[2] "Profits in Suicide," *Fortune,* May 1935, p. 116.

[3] AT&T Inc., "AT&T Inc. Code of Ethics," at www.att.com/gen/investor-relations?pid=5595, accessed March 6, 2010.

[4] Accenture, *Code of Business Ethics: Our Core Values in Action* (New York: Accenture, August 2007, ver. 4.11), pp. 11 and 12.

[5] "Nike Responsibility Governance" at www.nikebiz.com/responsibility/cr_governance.html, accessed March 6, 2010.

[6] Nike, *Inside the Lines: The Nike Code of Ethics* (Beaverton, OR: Nike, 2008), p. 23.

Tangled Webs

Through the ages philosophers, poets, leaders, teachers, and scholars have spoken on the merits of truth. Yet lying lives on. Here we relate two stories from the business world that, each in a different way, invite discussion of lies.

Years ago philosopher Sissela Bok defined a lie as "an intentionally deceptive message in the form of a *statement*."[1] A lie takes power from others. It allows the person speaking an untruth to manipulate another by withholding information, depriving that person of the ability to make an informed choice.

Lies harm others by causing them to act against their interest. Even small lies can carry a price for the people who tell them. They might pay a conscience penalty. Their resistance to telling other, bigger lies can gradually wear down. They can complicate their lives by having to remember the original lie and cover it with additional lies. And, if found out, they lose the trust of others and have less power in the end.

***

James E. Gansman was an affluent, successful, highly competent, curious, and partly unfulfilled man. In the winter of 2004 he joined Ashley Madison, a social networking site that connects people seeking extramarital affairs. Gansman was a senior partner and an attorney in the New York office of Ernst & Young. His job was to advise client companies about the cost of paying severance and other compensation to executives of firms they targeted for takeovers. However, on Ashley Madison he sought a more gentle form of combination.

***

At Ashley Madison the motto is, "Life is Short, Have an Affair." Users, who must be over 18, go to its Web site, ashleymadison.com, and sign up as members. After that, they create profiles, post photos, and interact with others on the site. Revenue for the company comes when users buy credits needed to initiate chat sessions, post messages, and send virtual gifts. Members can search for amorous contacts by location, age, and descriptive characteristics, compile lists of favorites, and give contacts a special "key" to their personal photo collection.

When members feel comfortable with new acquaintances, they graduate to in-person relationships.

The site provides advice. It recommends safe ways to arrange initial meetings in public locations such as restaurants and coffee shops, and cautions the adventurers to tell friends when they expect to return home. It discusses the risks of sexually transmitted diseases from 20 kinds of sexual activity.

In 2008 Ashley Madison introduced an "Affair Guarantee Program." For $249 a member receives 1,000 credits and a guarantee of finding a willing partner in three months or getting a refund. To qualify, seekers must follow rules that require specific numbers and types of actions on the site.

***

Gansman found a willing companion. She was Donna Murdoch, 40, a consultant, securities broker, and investment adviser living near Philadelphia. The two began to exchange phone calls and text messages and met in luxury hotels in New York and Philadelphia. As the relationship advanced, Gansman tried to impress Murdoch by bragging about his role in a few corporate mergers that appeared in the media.

In time the pair settled into a routine of daily phone calls and started playing a teasing game. With both of them at a computer, looking at the same Yahoo! Finance screens, Gansman would drop clues about deals on which he was working. "The game was," she said, "I wouldn't be looking and he would give me hints: the market cap of $2 billion or market cap of $400 billion and here's what they do, and he'd read it to me, and ultimately make sure I guessed."[2] Eventually, the games stopped and he just told her company names. One day he revealed an upcoming takeover to help one of Murdoch's children with a stock market simulation exercise at school.[3]

These disclosures were indiscreet. Ernst & Young had written confidentiality policies. As an Ernst employee Gansman was "prohibited from disclosing nonpublic information regarding clients or other entities to anyone other than for authorized firm business, or using it for any personal purpose."[4] Each of

[1] Sissela Bok, *Lying: Moral Choice in Public and Private Life* (New York: Vintage Books, 1978), p. 16.

[2] Donna Murdoch, quoted in Dennis K. Berman, "Insider Affair: An SEC Trial of the Heart," *The Wall Street Journal,* July 28, 2009, p. C1.

[3] Ibid., p. C1.

[4] Grand Jury Indictment in *United States v. James Gansman and Donna Murdoch,* U.S.D.C., S.D.N.Y, 1:08-cr-00471, May 27, 2008, pp. 2–3.

the 13 years he had worked for Ernst he also had signed a statement of compliance with a second policy that forbade trading securities based on confidential information. It read, in part:

> It is the firm's longstanding policy that partners . . . may not purchase or sell securities while in possession of material, non-public information and may not disclose such information to anyone except on a strict "need-to-know" basis. Violations of this policy can result in immediate dismissal from the firm.[5]

Gansman's indiscretions were Murdoch's temptations. She and her husband were in debt and struggling to make payments on a $1.45 million home mortgage. Public announcements of big mergers can trigger rapid, large, price movements in the shares of target companies. She began to act on Gansman's tips.

***

Gansman and Murdoch were one of Ashley Madison's success stories. Since its founding in 2000, the site has expanded from North America to Great Britain, Australia, and New Zealand. It claims more than 6 million active members, defined as those who have logged on at least once in the past six months. Among those who sign up, men outnumber women by 7: 3; however, many men are not very active and among those who buy credits women outnumber men by 3:1.[6]

The site grows with amazing rapidity and, unlike most businesses, flourishes during periods of economic hardship when couples face added financial problems and divorce is less of an option. Between 2008 and 2010 its membership rose from 2.2 million to 6 million. At one point in 2008 it got one new member every 20 seconds.[7] In 2010 it opened new sites in Australia and New Zealand. After one month it had 205,224 members in the former and 2,832 in the latter.[8] In Canada its membership rose 79 percent

between 2009 and 2010, from 362,086 to 649,509. The fastest growth, 291 percent, came in "female newlyweds," defined by the site as female members married three years or less.[9]

***

In June 2006 Gansman learned that Blackstone Group, a private equity firm, planned to acquire Freescale, a Texas semiconductor company listed on the New York Stock Exchange. Blackstone wanted the matter treated with utmost confidentiality. "Do not breathe the name of the target outside of [the] team," a colleague told him, "and please advise all others who assist you."[10] Nonetheless, Gansman told Murdoch the news. On July 18 she began trading in Freescale, buying contracts for 50 August $30 call options. The next day she bought 20 more of the same contracts.

Call options allow buyers to speculate on securities they do not own. Each option contract allows the holder to buy 100 shares of a company's stock at a specific price, called the strike price, on the day the option expires. So the 50 contracts she bought on July 18 gave her the right to buy 5,000 shares of Freescale on August 18 at $30 a share. If Freescale were selling below $30 a share she was not obligated to buy the shares. The calls would be worthless because she could buy shares of Freescale on the open market for less than $30. If Freescale were selling above $30 on August 18, for example at $40, she could buy 5,000 shares at $30, taking a profit of $10 a share, or $50,000 (minus the price of the option contracts). Options are priced based on risk. The further they are "out-of-the-money," that is, priced below the current market price of the company's shares, and the closer the expiration date, the lower their price. Buying call options allowed Murdoch to speculate on price movements with less invested than if she had bought common shares of Freescale and paid the full price at the time of purchase.

No matter how adept their calculation, Murdoch's trades violated the written policies of her employer. On her hiring, she received a policy manual and later

[5] Ernst & Young, "Policies Regarding Trading of Securities While in Possession of Confidential or Non-Public Information ("Insider Trading")"; and Grand Jury Indictment in *United States v. James Gansman and Donna Murdoch*, p. 4.

[6] Ashley Madison, "Frequently Asked Questions," at ashleymadison.com, September 1, 2010.

[7] "AshleyMadison.com," *Marketing Weekly News*, November 22, 2008, p. 79.

[8] "Adultery Site Aims to Hook New Zealanders," *The New Zealand Herald*, May 9, 2010.

[9] Shannon Proudfoot, "Adulterous Website Gets More Canadian Hits and More Women," *Nanaimo Daily News*, April 24, 2010, p. C1.

[10] E-mail from an Ernst & Young partner, quoted in Complaint, *Securities and Exchange Commission v. Gansman, Murdoch, and Brodsky*, U.S.D.C., S.D.N.Y., No. 08-cv-4918. May 29, 2008, p. 12.

certified that she had read and understood it. The following two statements were in this manual.

> SEC Rule 10b-5 under the Securities Exchange Act of 1934 generally makes it unlawful for any person to use . . . material inside information that has not been publicly disseminated in connection with the purchase or sale of securities.
>
> It is the policy of [the company] that no personnel . . . may trade . . . any security of any issuer about which the individual possesses material non-public information at or prior to the time such information is publicly disclosed and available in the marketplace.[11]

When Murdoch bought her call options, Freescale shares were selling between $26.09 and $27.89. The options would expire August 18. The discussions between Blackstone and Freescale continued and on August 10 Murdoch sold all of her contracts at a price that allowed her to break even. Late in August, she resumed trading in Freescale options. Between August 30 and September 7, as Freescale's stock hovered between $30.01 and $31.62, she purchased 610 Freescale September $35 call options. She also bought 50 October $30 call options, but suddenly sold them on September 8 and purchased another 80 September $30 contracts.

On the next trading day, Monday, September 11, *The New York Times* reported the possibility that Freescale would be bought and its stock jumped 20 percent, up $6.31 to $37.06. Murdoch sold all her options for a profit of $158,970.

Others also profited. Earlier, Murdoch had met another man through the Ashley Madison site, Richard Hansen, managing director of an investment banking firm near her home. The firm had hired her and was now her current employer. Hansen was her supervisor. She never revealed her relationship with either man to the other. Yet she tipped Hansen. On the same day Murdoch first traded in Freescale, he bought 2,000 shares of the company's common stock in accounts registered to each of his two daughters. On September 11, he sold these shares for a total gain of $45,820.

Murdoch also tipped her father, Gerald L. Brodsky, 73, a man with a past conviction for securities fraud. Years before, as president of a company that sold medical newsletters, he had reported millions of dollars in false income to shareholders. In 1993 he pled guilty to one criminal count of defrauding share-

holders. He was sentenced to a year and a day in prison and had to pay $1,318,864 in restitution.[12] Brodsky was clever in his trading. He asked an old friend to buy 370 September $35 call options. On September 11 he told this friend to sell them, netting a profit of $63,400.

And so it went. For more than a year Murdoch traded in the options of 18 target companies, sometimes tipping others, who traded too. She had made approximately $390,000, but she had been imprudent. Acting with foreknowledge, she at times bought seldom-traded contracts. On some days her trading was all or most of the activity in those contracts. By early 2007 she had appeared on watch lists at the Securities and Exchange Commission (SEC). The SEC monitors trades to identify any that appear suspicious because of their size, their timing, or the individuals who made them. In May an investigator from the agency called her on the telephone. She concealed her actions and denied trading on inside information, then told Gansman about the call. He suggested she get an untraceable cell phone for their calls.[13]

Murdoch continued trading options into November until she learned an SEC investigation was under way. Soon the Department of Justice launched a criminal investigation. Trying to hide her relationship with Gansman, she took her laptop computer to a store and asked a technician to erase the hard drive beyond restoration. The technician accepted the job without question, but did not succeed. Later, when an FBI agent interviewed her, she gave deceptive answers and turned over false documents. Gansman was also named in the investigations. When word of them got to Ernst, it put him on administrative leave. "We are going to jail," he told Murdoch and accused her of ruining his life.[14]

***

Ashley Madison faces continuous criticism. "It's like dumping raw sewage into the culture," states the head of a pro-marriage group.[15] According to Noel

---

[11] Grand Jury indictment, pp. 4–5.

[12] *United States v. Gerald L. Brodsky,* No. 93-cr-10 (E.D. Pa. 1993), judgement entered April 26, 1994: Securities and Exchange Commission, "Gerald Brodsky Enters Guilty Plea," *News Digest,* Issue 93–213, November 4, 1993, pp. 3–4.

[13] Berman, "Insider Affair: An SEC Trial of the Heart," p. C1.

[14] Ibid., p. C1.

[15] Charmaine Yoest, president of Americans United for Life, quoted in Kelly Jane Torrance, *Washington Times,* September 5, 2008, p. B1.

Biderman, 38, the founder of Ashley Madison, such comments are misguided. Biderman is a former sports attorney who shifted his career into online commerce. He married in 2002. He and his wife have two children. He says his marriage is happy and characterized by fidelity. "I do not cheat, no. I've been faithful to date," he says. Once when asked how he would feel if his wife cheated he replied: "I'd be devastated." However, he said, "I wouldn't blame a Web site."[16]

Biderman believes that humans are genetically disposed to philander, that monogamy is unnatural. Equating marriage with monogamy is a "broken paradigm."[17] People naturally stray. Ashley Madison does not persuade anyone to abandon a happy, fulfilling matrimonial bond. Rather, it protects anyone who has already decided to have an extramarital affair.

> [I]f you're predisposed to having an affair, don't have it in the workplace, because someone's going to lose their job. Or don't go on a singles dating site and pretend to be something you're not, because that's unfair to the other person—that's going to end badly for you as well, don't go and break the law and visit an escort.[18]

Dislike of Ashley Madison often manifests itself in resistance to its advertising. "I feel I should have the right, as long as I'm following the regulations, to advertise my product," argues Biderman.[19] Broadcast television networks have rejected its commercials, but it has placed them on CNN, ESPN, Fox News, and MSNBC. In 2009, NBC and the National Football League refused to run its ad during the Super Bowl. A few months later, when it saw a spike in new members from Utah, it placed ads on two Salt Lake City radio stations. However, when the owner of one station heard it on his morning commute, he ordered it stopped.[20] And later in the year the Toronto Transit

Commission turned down $200,000 to put the company's ads in its subways, buses, and streetcars. Biderman disagreed with the commission. "I just think they're mistaken about the average . . . rider's willingness to accept these kind of ads in exchange for cheaper fares," he said.[21]

***

In May 2008 a New York grand jury charged Gansman and Murdoch with 1 count of conspiracy for furthering an insider trading conspiracy and 11 counts of securities fraud based on Murdoch's trades.[22] Murdoch alone faced two additional charges. She was charged with one count of making false statements for lying to the FBI and one count of obstruction of justice for paying an individual to erase evidence from her hard drive. The government collected voluminous evidence of the scheme, about 280,000 pages altogether. A criminal case against the two began. Instead of plotting together, though, their paths would now separate.

The case went to the federal courthouse in Manhattan, where it was assigned to Judge Miriam Goldman Cedarbaum, the same jurist who presided over the trial of Martha Stewart. Gansman pled not guilty. Murdoch initially pled not guilty. Then she decided to change her plea to guilty on all counts and to cooperate with the government for a lighter sentence. At the time she was taking medication for depression. Instead of sticking by her benefactor, she would testify against him.

Before Gansman's trial began, his attorney entered a motion to dismiss the charges. It argued that Gansman never traded on insider knowledge, never knew of Murdoch's trades, and never benefitted financially from her trades. It was correct that Gansman had never traded on confidential information himself. Yet it strained credulity to believe he

---

[16] Quotations are from Zosia Bielski, "His Not-So-Cheatin' Heart," *The Globe and Mail*, November 6, 2009, p. L1.

[17] Noel Biderman, quoted in Proudfoot, "Adulterous Website Gets More Canadian Hits and More Women," p. C1.

[18] Noel Biderman, quoted in Frank Dobrovnik, "2,000 Spouses Looking for Action, Ashley Says," *Sault Star*, April 23, 2010, p. A1.

[19] Ibid.

[20] Sean P. Means, "Infidelity Ad Dumped by Salt Lake City Radio Station," *The Salt Lake Tribune*, April 16, 2009.

[21] Quoted in Don Peat, "Cheating Ad Nixed," *The Toronto Sun*, December 12, 2009, p. 4.

[22] The law prohibits insider trading, defined as buying or selling a security when in possession of significant information not yet available to the public when those purchases or sales violate a duty to keep that information confidential. It also prohibits "tipping," where a person with "material, nonpublic information" breeches a duty of confidence to share that information with a person not covered by such a duty. And if the tipped person buys or sells securities based on the information those transactions also violate the law. See 15 USC §78j and 78ff, 71 CFR §240.10b-5 and 240.10b5-2, and 18 USC §2.

had no knowledge of Murdoch's trades. The government produced records of more than 7,000 phone calls and text messages between the two. Murdoch's testimony also undermined his claim of ignorance. This exchange from the hearing on her plea agreement is an example.

> JUDGE CEDARBAUM: But because of your work you were familiar with the serious consequences of trading on inside material non-public information, isn't that correct?
>
> DONNA MURDOCH: Yes, your honor.
>
> JUDGE CEDARBAUM: All right. What is it that you agreed with Mr. Gansman to do?
>
> DONNA MURDOCH: Well, I knew that he was violating a duty of confidentiality that he owed to these companies and I knew that I was trading based on those terms. I did discuss sometimes with him and sometimes not, not what exactly the specific amounts I was trading, but many times it was discussed with him.[23]

It was also correct that Gansman had received no financial benefit from Murdoch's trades. However, the government argued that the definition of benefit under the law was broader than pecuniary gain. It also included the reputational enhancement to the tipper from benefiting a friend or relative who receives the tip. Still, even with Murdoch's testimony, it proved difficult to pin down Gansman's motive with precision.

> JUDGE CEDARBAUM: Did you [and Gansman] have an agreement of some kind? Did you share money at all?
>
> MS. MURDOCH: Money, no, your honor.
>
> JUDGE CEDARBAUM: Well, did he receive something in exchange for this agreement?
>
> MS. MURDOCH: He received a gift or two. He received—I don't know what he received himself for sharing the information.[24]

Here Murdoch's attorney Paul Schechtman stepped in to offer an explanation.

> MR. SCHECHTMAN: Judge, I think it is fair to say that the arrangement here was . . . an arrangement of a personal nature. I think it is that relationship that Mr. Gansman hoped to foster by giving this information. It was a personal relationship and not a monetary relationship.
>
> JUDGE CEDARBAUM: So in exchange he hoped to gain a closer relationship?
>
> MR. SCHECHTMAN: Or to cement a closer relationship, I think. A close relationship. I think that is right, your Honor.
>
> JUDGE CEDARBAUM: Now [Ms. Murdoch], did you tell Mr. Gansman if he gave you these tips you would give him more affection than you otherwise would?
>
> MS. MURDOCH: Absolutely not, your Honor.
>
> JUDGE CEDARBAUM: It is a puzzling agreement to me.[25]

Murdoch's testimony that Gansman knew about her trades was enough for Judge Cedarbaum to turn down his motion for dismissal. His trial went forward in May 2009. It lasted for eight days and included additional testimony by Murdoch. In the end the jury convicted him of six counts of insider trading.

In February 2010 Judge Cedarbaum sentenced Gansman to one year and one day in federal prison followed by six months of supervised release. In March he was disbarred because of the conviction and no longer can practice law in New York.[26] In August he settled a concurrent civil case brought by the SEC, agreeing to a judgment of $250,000 to disgorge a share of the profits made from Murdoch's trades.[27] In the same settlement Murdoch agreed to a final judgment of $404,054, which was waived based on her inability to pay. Earlier, her father had agreed to a penalty of $265,924, equal to three times his illegal profits plus interest.[28]

Murdoch has yet to be sentenced in the criminal case.

[23] Transcript of Plea Allocution of Donna Murdoch *United States v. Donna Murdoch,* U.S.D.C., S.D.N.Y, 08-cr-471, December 23, 2008, p. 16–17.

[24] Ibid., p. 17.

[25] Ibid., pp. 19–20.

[26] *In the Matter of James E. Gansman,* 898 N.Y.S.2d 18 (2009).

[27] *Securities and Exchange Commission v. Gansman, Murdoch, and Brodsky,* U.S.D.C., S.D.N.Y., No. 08-cv-4918 (2010); Securities and Exchange Commission, litigation release No. 21629, August 18, 2010.

[28] Securities and Exchange Commission, litigation release No. 21059, May 27, 2009.

A Family of Brands

Avid Life Media is the parent company for six brands. Each is a social networking site for a separate niche in the dating universe.

Ashley Madison: A brand described as "the world's leading infidelity service." It targets people who want to break the monotony of their marriage by having an affair.

Hot or Not: A site where "hot singles age 18 to 34" post photographs, rate each other, and contact other members.

Established Men: A site designed to help "rich, successful men and sexy sugar babies" find each other and verify the relationship is what they seek.

Cougar Life: A place for "strong, successful, sexy older women" and "vibrant, ambitious young men" to come together.

Man Crunch: A community for gay men seeking long-lasting relationships. Its motto is: "Putting the MAN back in romance."

Swappernet: A site for "real couples" seeking other couples, singles looking for threesomes, and "wife-swapping adventurers."

Eroticy: An adult personal ad site with erotic photos and videos. It allows members to have "no strings attached fun."

Source: Avid Life Media at www.avidlifemedia.com/brands.html.

Ashley Madison is only one brand in a larger stable. Its parent company is Avid Life Media, headquartered in Ontario, Canada. Avid Life markets six other "targeted niche brands," as shown in the box, each with a Web site of its own. Its mission is: "To hook up like-minded individuals who share the same passions and desires; regardless of their lifestyle preferences."[29] In 2009, the company had earnings of $8 million on sales of $30 million. Ashley Madison accounted for only 15 percent of its sales. The rest came from its other sites.[30]

In 2010 Avid Life proposed a merger with a much larger media advertising firm, Moxey Media, after which the company would make a public stock offering, allowing average investors to buy its shares. The merger made strategic sense. A combination of two profitable firms, one with a network of popular, expanding, recession-proof Web businesses and the other with sophisticated advertising tools, should have charmed investors. It did not. An investment banking firm hired to find partners willing to fund the deal made no progress. Fund managers who might ordinarily have seen an attractive risk showed

no interest. One Canadian billionaire whom they approached as a potential investor had this to say.

> I don't mind investing in liquor because without it, you'd miss something in life. I tell friends to stop smoking, and I still buy tobacco companies. But Ashley Madison shouldn't be a public venture, because it can destroy families. And there is nothing worse than the effect of divorce on children. There are thousands of other stocks to buy, so why bother with this crap?[31]

Eventually, Avid Media's banker ended its efforts, attributing the withdrawal of support to economic conditions. A Canadian magazine reported that the firm backed away when its top executive read this user posting on Ashley Madison.

> To be honest I'm really looking for a sugar daddy, so if that isn't you I wouldn't waste your time replying. I'm looking for a generous man that loves to take care of a younger lady, i am 18 and have just started university and my parents aren't paying a cent for it . . . So if there is a nicer gentlemen on here that really gets off on helping a young woman with some bills, taking stress of her shoulders while receiveing the same back both emotionaly and physically please msg me.[32]

---

[29] www.avidlife.com/about.html.

[30] Andrew Willis and Boyd Erman, "Avid Life IPO Could Be an Affair to Remember," *The Globe and Mail,* January 25, 2010, p. B1.

[31] Stephen Jarislowski, quoted in Thomas Watson, "Abandoned at the Altar," *Canadian Business,* March 2010, p. 47.

[32] Ibid., p. 47.

***

As noted in Chapter 7, otherwise honest individuals can be drawn into evil by circumstances. In this story the Gansman–Murdoch alliance was born in temptation. As time passed James Gansman's early restraint gradually wore away. If, at first, he would not have betrayed his employer, during an interval of growing weakness he gradually abandoned his fidelity and came to lack any limit. Was he simply a fallible man? His attorney seemed to think so. "This is a good person who made a bad decision," he told Judge Cedarbaum just before she sentenced his client.[33]

Donna Murdoch believed she was a good person too. As if in a dream she was granted knowledge of the future that could be turned into gold. At first she resisted temptation, but in the end she went into its snare. Her testimony before Judge Cedarbaum is a window into how she rationalized.

> Your honor, I've, I really have tried to live a good life. I have wonderful children and I've been trying to take care of them, both my husband and my children, and our financial situation was really, really bad, really bleak. I thought I could bail us out. I thought I could keep my kids the way they were, in the schools they were in, and our house from being foreclosed on and whatnot. What I did was wrong. It was wrong. It was wrong. And I'm so sorry, and I wish . . . I could make it disappear.[34]

***

Noel Biderman is comfortable with his labors, which, unlike the actions of Gansman and Murdoch, are legal. "I sleep well at night," he states.[35] His wife Amanda, 34, believes "he's a great husband and father." "Neither of us condones infidelity," she explains, "and we separate our personal beliefs from Noel's business." Yet Amanda Biderman is troubled, saying, "I do feel really bad for the people who are being cheated on as a result of their partners becoming members of the Web site." And she anticipates social opprobrium.

> I'm going to struggle when the children are older. That will be the first major conflict of interest for me. I'm preparing myself for the fact that there are likely to be parents at my children's school and nursery who will point the finger at us if they find out what Noel does.[36]

Questions

1. What lies are present in the "tangled webs" considered here? How were they used? How were they justified by those who executed them? Who was harmed by them? Which lies were most harmful?

2. Were the punishments for James Gansman, Donna Murdoch, and Gerald Brodsky fair?

3. Is Ashley Madison based on an ethical business model?

4. How does Noel Biderman, the founder of Ashley Madison, explain and justify the business? Does he fulfill his ethical duties to all those affected by his actions?

5. What do the events in this story teach us about business ethics? About capitalism?

[33] Barry Bohrer, quoted in Chad Bray, "Gansman Sentenced in Insider Case," *The Wall Street Journal,* February 9, 2010, p. C2.

[34] Waiver of Indictment by Donna Murdoch, *United States v. Donna Murdoch,* U.S.D.C., S.D.N.Y., 08-cr-00471 (December 23, 2008), p. 30.

[35] Quoted in Bielski, "His Not-So-Cheatin' Heart," p. L1.

[36] Quotations of Amanda Biderman are in "I Feel Guilty But He's Just Trying to Help People," *The Express,* April 30, 2010, p. 37.

The Parable of the Sadhu

by Bowen H. McCoy

Harvard Business Review

Reprint 97307

After encountering a dying pilgrim on a climbing trip in the Himalayas, a bus

by Bowen H. McCoy

Last year, as the first participant in the new six-month sabbatical program that Morgan Stanley has adopted, I enjoyed a rare opportunity to collect my thoughts as well as do some traveling. I spent the first three months in Nepal, walking 600 miles through 200 villages in the Himalayas and climbing some 120,000 vertical feet. My sole Western companion on the trip was an anthropologist who shed light on the cultural patterns of the villages that we passed through.

During the Nepal hike, something occurred that has had a powerful impact on my thinking about corporate ethics. Although some might argue that the experience has no relevance to business, it was a situation in which a basic ethical dilemma suddenly intruded into the lives of a group of individuals. How the group responded holds a lesson for all organizations, no matter how defined.

The Sadhu

The Nepal experience was more rugged than I had anticipated. Most commercial treks last two or three weeks and cover a quarter of the distance we traveled.

My friend Stephen, the anthropologist, and I were halfway through the 60-day Himalayan part of the trip when we reached the high point, an 18,000-foot pass over a crest that we'd have to traverse to reach the village of Muklinath, an ancient holy place for pilgrims.

Six years earlier, I had suffered pulmonary edema, an acute form of altitude sickness, at 16,500 feet in the vicinity of Everest base camp–so we were understandably concerned about what would happen at 18,000 feet. Moreover, the Himalayas were having their wettest spring in 20 years; hip-deep powder and ice had already driven us off one ridge. If we failed to cross the pass, I feared that the last half of our once-in-a-lifetime trip would be ruined.

The night before we would try the pass, we camped in a hut at 14,500 feet. In the photos taken at that camp, my face appears wan. The last village we'd passed through was a sturdy two-day walk below us, and I was tired.

Bowen H. McCoy retired from Morgan Stanley in 1990 after 28 years of service. He is now a real estate and business counselor, a teacher, and a philanthropist.

inessman ponders the differences between individual and corporate ethics.

The Parable of the Sadhu

During the late afternoon, four backpackers from New Zealand joined us, and we spent most of the night awake, anticipating the climb. Below, we could see the fires of two other parties, which turned out to be two Swiss couples and a Japanese hiking club.

To get over the steep part of the climb before the sun melted the steps cut in the ice, we departed at 3:30 A.M. The New Zealanders left first, followed by Stephen and myself, our porters and Sherpas, and then the Swiss. The Japanese lingered in their camp. The sky was clear, and we were confident that no spring storm would erupt that day to close the pass.

At 15,500 feet, it looked to me as if Stephen were shuffling and staggering a bit, which are symptoms of altitude sickness. (The initial stage of altitude sickness brings a headache and nausea. As the condition worsens, a climber may encounter difficult breathing, disorientation, aphasia, and paralysis.) I felt strong—my adrenaline was flowing – but I was very concerned about my ultimate ability to get across. A couple of our porters were also suffering from the height, and Pasang, our Sherpa sirdar (leader), was worried.

Just after daybreak, while we rested at 15,500 feet, one of the New Zealanders, who had gone ahead, came staggering down toward us with a body slung across his shoulders. He dumped the almost naked, barefoot body of an Indian holy man – a sadhu – at my feet. He had found the pilgrim lying on the ice, shivering and suffering from hypo-

thermia. I cradled the sadhu's head and laid him out on the rocks. The New Zealander was angry. He wanted to get across the pass before the bright sun melted the snow. He said, "Look, I've done what I can. You have porters and Sherpa guides. You care for him. We're going on!" He turned and went back up the mountain to join his friends.

I took a carotid pulse and found that the sadhu was still alive. We figured he had probably visited the holy shrines at Muklinath and was on his

This article was originally published in the September-October 1983 issue of HBR. For its republication as an HBR Classic, Bowen H. McCoy has written the commentary "When Do We Take a Stand?" to update his observations.

way home. It was fruitless to question why he had chosen this desperately high route instead of the safe, heavily traveled caravan route through the Kali Gandaki gorge. Or why he was shoeless and almost naked, or how long he had been lying in the pass. The answers weren't going to solve our problem.

Stephen and the four Swiss began stripping off their outer clothing and opening their packs. The sadhu was soon clothed from head to foot. He was not able to walk, but he was very much alive. I looked down the mountain and spotted the Japanese climbers, marching up with a horse.

Without a great deal of thought, I told Stephen and Pasang that I was concerned about withstanding the heights to come and wanted to get over the pass. I took off after several of our porters who had gone ahead.

On the steep part of the ascent where, if the ice steps had given way, I would have slid down about 3,000 feet, I felt vertigo. I stopped for a breather, allowing the Swiss to catch up with me. I inquired about the sadhu and Stephen. They said that the sadhu was fine and that Stephen was just behind them. I set off again for the summit.

Stephen arrived at the summit an hour after I did. Still exhilarated by victory, I ran down the slope to congratulate him. He was suffering from altitude sickness – walking 15 steps, then stopping, walking 15 steps, then stopping. Pasang accompanied him

When I reached them, Stephen glared at me and said, "How do you feel about contributing to the death of a fellow man?"

all the way up. When I reached them, Stephen glared at me and said: "How do you feel about contributing to the death of a fellow man?"

I did not completely comprehend what he meant. "Is the sadhu dead?" I inquired.

"No," replied Stephen, "but he surely will be!"

After I had gone, followed not long after by the Swiss, Stephen had remained with the sadhu. When the Japanese had arrived, Stephen had asked to use their horse to transport the sadhu down to the hut. They had refused. He had then asked Pasang to have a group of our porters carry the sadhu. Pasang had resisted the idea, saying that the porters would have to exert all their energy to get themselves over the pass. He believed they could not carry a man down 1,000 feet to the hut, reclimb the slope, and get across safely before the snow melted. Pasang had pressed Stephen not to delay any longer.

The Sherpas had carried the sadhu down to a rock in the sun at about 15,000 feet and pointed out the hut another 500 feet below. The Japanese had given him food and drink. When they had last seen him, he was listlessly throwing rocks at the Japanese party's dog, which had frightened him.

We do not know if the sadhu lived or died.

For many of the following days and evenings, Stephen and I discussed and debated our behavior toward the sadhu. Stephen is a committed Quaker with deep moral vision. He said, "I feel that what happened with the sadhu is a good example of the breakdown between the individual ethic and the corporate ethic. No one person was willing to assume ultimate responsibility for the sadhu. Each was willing to do his bit just so long as it was not too inconvenient. When it got to be a bother, everyone just passed the buck to someone else and took off. Jesus was relevant to a more individualistic stage of society, but how do we interpret his teaching today in a world filled with large, impersonal organizations and groups?"

I defended the larger group, saying, "Look, we all cared. We all gave aid and comfort. Everyone did his bit.

The New Zealander carried him down below the snow line. I took his pulse and suggested we treat him for hypothermia. You and the Swiss gave him clothing and got him warmed up. The Japanese gave him food and

I asked, "Where is the limit of our responsibility in a situation like this?"

water. The Sherpas carried him down to the sun and pointed out the easy trail toward the hut. He was well enough to throw rocks at a dog. What more could we do?"

"You have just described the typical affluent Westerner's response to a problem. Throwing money – in this case, food and sweaters – at it, but not solving the fundamentals!" Stephen retorted.

"What would satisfy you?" I said. "Here we are, a group of New Zealanders, Swiss, Americans, and Japanese who have never met before and who are at the apex of one of the most powerful experiences of our lives. Some years the pass is so bad no one gets over it. What right does an almost naked pilgrim who chooses the wrong trail have to disrupt our lives? Even the Sherpas had no interest in risking the trip to help him beyond a certain point."

Stephen calmly rebutted, "I wonder what the Sherpas would have done if the sadhu had been a well-dressed Nepali, or what the Japanese would have done if the sadhu had been a well-dressed Asian, or what you would have done, Buzz, if the sadhu had been a well-dressed Western woman?"

"Where, in your opinion," I asked, "is the limit of our responsibility in a situation like this? We had our own well-being to worry about. Our Sherpa guides were unwilling to jeopardize us or the porters for the sadhu. No one else on the mountain was willing to commit himself beyond certain self-imposed limits."

Stephen said, "As individual Christians or people with a Western ethical tradition, we can fulfill our obligations in such a situation only if one, the sadhu dies in our care; two, the sadhu demonstrates to us that he can undertake the two-day walk down to the village; or three, we carry the sadhu for two days down to the village and persuade someone there to care for him."

"Leaving the sadhu in the sun with food and clothing – where he demonstrated hand-eye coordination by throwing a rock at a dog – comes close to fulfilling items one and two," I answered. "And it wouldn't have made sense to take him to the village where the people appeared to be far less caring than the Sherpas, so the third condition is impractical. Are you really saying that, no matter what the implications, we should, at the drop of a hat, have changed our entire plan?"

The Individual Versus the Group Ethic

Despite my arguments, I felt and continue to feel guilt about the sadhu. I had literally walked through a classic moral dilemma without fully thinking through the consequences. My excuses for my actions include a high adrenaline flow, a superordinate goal, and a once-in-a-lifetime opportunity – common factors in corporate situations, especially stressful ones.

Real moral dilemmas are ambiguous, and many of us hike right through them, unaware that they exist. When, usually after the fact, someone makes an issue of one, we tend to resent his or her bringing it up. Often, when the full import of what we have done (or not done) hits us, we dig into a defensive position from which it is very difficult to emerge. In rare circumstances, we may contemplate what we have done from inside a prison.

Had we mountaineers been free of stress caused by the effort and the high altitude, we might have treated the sadhu differently. Yet isn't stress the real test of personal and corporate values? The instant decisions that executives make under pressure reveal the most about personal and corporate character.

Among the many questions that occur to me when I ponder my experience with the sadhu are: What are the practical limits of moral imagination and vision? Is there a collective or institutional ethic that differs from the ethics of the individual? At what level of effort or commitment can one discharge one's ethical responsibilities?

Not every ethical dilemma has a right solution. Reasonable people often disagree; otherwise there would be no dilemma. In a business context, however, it is essential that managers agree on a process for dealing with dilemmas.

Our experience with the sadhu offers an interesting parallel to business situations. An immediate response was mandatory. Failure to act was a decision in itself. Up on the mountain we could not resign and submit our résumés to a headhunter. In contrast to philosophy, business involves action and implementation – getting things done. Managers must come up with answers based on what they see and what they allow to influence their decision-making processes. On the mountain, none of us but Stephen realized the true dimensions of the situation we were facing.

One of our problems was that as a group we had no process for developing a consensus. We had no sense of purpose or plan. The difficulties of dealing with the sadhu were so complex that no one person could handle them. Because the group did not have a set of preconditions that could guide its action to an acceptable resolution, we reacted instinctively as individuals. The cross-cultural nature of the group added a further layer of complexity. We had no leader with whom we could all identify and in whose purpose we believed. Only Stephen was willing to take charge, but he could not gain adequate support from the group to care for the sadhu.

Some organizations do have values that transcend the personal values of their managers. Such values, which go beyond profitability, are usually revealed when the organization is under stress. People throughout the organization generally accept its values, which, because they are not presented as a rigid list of commandments, may be somewhat ambiguous. The stories people tell, rather than printed materials, transmit the organization's conceptions of what is proper behavior.

For 20 years, I have been exposed at senior levels to a variety of corporations and organizations. It is amazing how quickly an outsider can sense the tone and style of an organization and, with that, the degree of tolerated openness and freedom to challenge management.

Organizations that do not have a heritage of mutually accepted, shared values tend to become unhinged during stress, with each individual bailing out for himself or herself. In the great takeover battles we have witnessed during past years, companies that had strong cultures drew the wagons around them and fought it out, while other companies saw executives–supported by golden parachutes–bail out of the struggles.

Because corporations and their members are interdependent, for the corporation to be strong the members need to share a preconceived notion of correct behavior, a "business ethic," and think of it as a positive force, not a constraint.

As an investment banker, I am continually warned by well-meaning lawyers, clients, and associates

As a group, we had no process for developing a consensus. We had no sense of purpose or plan.

to be wary of conflicts of interest. Yet if I were to run away from every difficult situation, I wouldn't be an effective investment banker. I have to feel my way through conflicts. An effective manager can't run from risk either; he or she has to confront risk. To feel "safe" in doing that, managers need the guidelines of an agreed-upon process and set of values within the organization.

After my three months in Nepal, I spent three months as an executive-

I wrote about my experiences purposely to present an ambiguous situation. I never found out if the sadhu lived or died. I can attest, though, that the sadhu lives on in his story. He lives in the ethics classes I teach each year at business schools and churches. He lives in the classrooms of numerous business schools, where professors have taught the case to tens of thousands of students. He lives in several casebooks on ethics and on an educational video. And he lives in organizations such as the American Red Cross and AT&T, which use his story in their ethics training.

As I reflect on the sadhu now, 15 years after the fact, I first have to wonder, What actually happened on that Himalayan slope? When I first wrote about the event, I reported the experience in as much detail as I could remember, but I shaped it to the needs of a good classroom discussion. After years of reading my story, viewing it on video, and hearing others discuss it, I'm not sure I myself know what actually occurred on the mountainside that day!

I've also heard a wide variety of responses to the story. The sadhu, for example, may not have wanted our help at all – he may have been intentionally bringing on his own death as a way to holiness. Why had he taken the dangerous way over the pass instead of the caravan route

WHEN DO WE TAKE A STAND?

by Bowen H. McCoy

through the gorge? Hindu businesspeople have told me that in trying to assist the sadhu, we were being typically arrogant Westerners imposing our cultural values on the world.

I've learned that each year along the pass, a few Nepali porters are left to freeze to death outside the tents of the unthinking tourists who hired them. A few years ago, a French group even left one of their own, a young French woman, to die there. The difficult pass seems to demonstrate a perverse version of Gresham's law of currency: The bad practices of previous travelers have driven out the values that new travelers might have followed if they were at home. Perhaps that helps to explain why our porters behaved as they did and why it was so difficult for Stephen or anyone else to establish a different approach on the spot.

Our Sherpa sirdar, Pasang, was focused on his responsibility for bringing us up the mountain safe and sound. (His livelihood and status in the Sherpa ethnic group depended on our safe return.) We were weak, our party was split, the porters were well on their way to the top with all our gear and food, and a storm would have separated us irrevocably from our logistical base.

The fact was, we had no plan for dealing with the contingency of the sadhu. There was nothing we could do to unite our multicultural group in the little time we had. An ethical dilemma had come upon us unexpectedly, an element of drama that may explain why the sadhu's story has continued to attract students.

I am often asked for help in teaching the story. I usually advise keeping the details as ambiguous as possible. A true ethical dilemma requires a decision between two hard choices. In the case of the sadhu, we had to decide how much to sacrifice ourselves to take care of a stranger. And given the constraints of our trek, we had to make a group decision, not an individual one. If a large majority of students in a class ends up thinking I'm a bad person because of my decision on the mountain, the instructor may not have given the case its due. The same is true if the majority sees no problem with the choices we made.

Any class's response depends on its setting, whether it's a business school, a church, or a corporation. I've found that younger students are more likely to see the issue as black-and-white, whereas older ones tend to see shades of gray. Some have seen a conflict between the different ethical approaches that we followed at the time. Stephen felt he had to do everything he could to save the sadhu's life, in accordance with his Christian ethic of compassion. I had a utilitarian response: do the greatest good for the greatest number. Give a burst of aid to minimize the sadhu's exposure, then continue on our way.

The basic question of the case remains, When do we take a stand? When do we allow a "sadhu" to intrude into our daily lives? Few of us can afford the time or effort to take care of every needy person we encounter. How much must we give of ourselves? And how do we prepare our organizations and institutions so they will respond appropriately in a crisis? How do we influence them if we do not agree with their points of view?

We cannot quit our jobs over every ethical dilemma, but if we continually ignore our sense of values, who do we become? As a journalist asked at a recent conference on ethics, "Which ditch are we willing to die in?" For each of us, the answer is a bit different. How we act in response to that question defines better than anything else who we are, just as, in a collective sense, our acts define our institutions. In effect, the sadhu is always there, ready to remind us of the tensions between our own goals and the claims of strangers.

in-residence at both the Stanford Business School and the University of California at Berkeley's Center for Ethics and Social Policy of the Graduate Theological Union. Those six months away from my job gave me time to assimilate 20 years of business experience. My thoughts turned often to the meaning of the leadership role in any large organization. Students at the seminary thought of themselves as antibusiness. But when I questioned them, they agreed that they distrusted all large organizations, including the church. They perceived all large organizations as impersonal and opposed to individual values and needs. Yet we all know of organizations in which people's values and beliefs are respected and their expressions encouraged. What makes the difference? Can we identify the difference and, as a result, manage more effectively?

The word *ethics* turns off many and confuses more. Yet the notions of shared values and an agreed-upon process for dealing with adversity and change – what many people mean when they talk about corporate culture – seem to be at the heart of the ethical issue. People who are in touch with their own core beliefs and the beliefs of others and who are sustained by them can be more comfortable living on the cutting edge. At times, taking a tough line or a decisive stand in a muddle of ambiguity is the only ethical thing to do. If a manager is indecisive about a problem and spends time trying to figure out the "good" thing to do, the enterprise may be lost.

Business ethics, then, has to do with the authenticity and integrity of the enterprise. To be ethical is to follow the business as well as the cultural goals of the corporation, its owners, its employees, and its customers. Those who cannot serve the corporate vision are not authentic businesspeople and, therefore, are not ethical in the business sense.

At this stage of my own business experience, I have a strong interest in organizational behavior. Sociologists are keenly studying what they call corporate stories, legends, and heroes as a way organizations have of transmitting value systems. Corporations such as Arco have even hired consultants to perform an audit of their corporate culture. In a company, a leader is a person who understands, interprets, and manages the corporate value system. Effective managers, therefore, are action-oriented people who resolve conflict, are tolerant of ambiguity, stress, and change, and have a strong sense of purpose for themselves and their organizations.

If all this is true, I wonder about the role of the professional manager who moves from company to company. How can he or she quickly absorb the values and culture of different organizations? Or is there, indeed, an art of management that is totally transportable? Assuming that such fungible managers do exist, is it proper for them to manipulate the values of others?

What would have happened had Stephen and I carried the sadhu for two days back to the village and become involved with the villagers in his care? In four trips to Nepal, my most interesting experience occurred in 1975 when I lived in a Sherpa home in the Khumbu for five days while recovering from altitude sickness. The high point of Stephen's trip was an invitation to participate in a family funeral ceremony in Manang. Neither experience had to do with climbing the high passes of the Himalayas. Why were we so reluctant to try the lower path, the ambiguous trail? Perhaps because we did not have a leader who could reveal the greater purpose of the trip to us.

Why didn't Stephen, with his moral vision, opt to take the sadhu under his personal care? The answer is partly because Stephen was hard-stressed physically himself and partly because, without some support system that encompassed our involuntary and episodic community on the mountain, it was beyond his individual capacity to do so.

I see the current interest in corporate culture and corporate value systems as a positive response to pessimism such as Stephen's about the decline of the role of the individual in large organizations. Individuals who operate from a thoughtful set of personal values provide the foundation for a corporate culture. A corporate tradition that encourages freedom of inquiry, supports personal values, and reinforces a focused sense of direction can fulfill the need to combine individuality with the prosperity and success of the group. Without such corporate support, the individual is lost.

That is the lesson of the sadhu. In a complex corporate situation, the individual requires and deserves the support of the group. When people cannot find such support in their organizations, they don't know how to act. If such support is forthcoming, a person has a stake in the success of the group and can add much to the process of establishing and maintaining a corporate culture. Management's challenge is to be sensitive to individual needs, to shape them, and to direct and focus them for the benefit of the group as a whole.

For each of us the sadhu lives. Should we stop what we are doing and comfort him; or should we keep trudging up toward the high pass? Should I pause to help the derelict I pass on the street each night as I walk by the Yale Club en route to Grand Central Station? Am I his brother? What is the nature of our responsibility if we consider ourselves to be ethical persons? Perhaps it is to change the values of the group so that it can, with all its resources, take the other road.   ▽

Reprint 97307

To place an order, call 1-800-545-7685.

Harvard Business Review

Article Reprints

Many readers have asked for an easy way to order reprints or to obtain permission to copy HBR articles. In response, we have established a Customer Service Team to grant permission, send rush copies in paper form, deliver files in Acrobat (PDF) format electronically, or customize collections. An electronic catalog of all HBR articles is also available.

Please contact the Customer Service Team:

Phone: 617-496-1449
United States and Canada: 800-988-0886
(8 A.M.-6 P.M. weekdays, voice mail after hours)
Fax: 617-496-1029 (24 hours, 7 days a week)
E-mail: custserv@hbsp.harvard.edu
(24 hours, 7 days a week)
Web Site: http://www.hbsp.harvard.edu

Reprint Prices
(Minimum order, $10. Discounts apply to multiple copies of the same article.)

1-9 copies	$5 each
10-99	$4
100-499	$3

For quantity estimates or quotes on customized products, call
Frank Tamoshunas at
617-495-6198

Permissions

For information on permission to quote or translate HBR material, contact:

Customer Service Department
Harvard Business School
 Publishing Corporation
60 Harvard Way
Boston, MA 02163

Phone: 617-496-1449
United States and Canada: 800-988-0886
Fax: 617-495-6985
E-mail: custserv@hbsp.harvard.edu

Subscription Service

United States and Canada
Phone: 800-274-3214
Rates per year: United States, $85;
Canada, U.S.$95

International and Mexico
Phone: 44 1858 435324
Fax: 44 1858 468969
Rates per year: international, $145;
Mexico, $95
Orders, inquiries, and address changes:
Harvard Business Review
Tower House, Sovereign Park
Lathkill Street, Market Harborough
Leicestershire LE16 9EF
England

Payments accepted: Visa, MasterCard, American Express; checks at current exchange rate payable to
Harvard Business Review.
Bills and other receipts may be issued.

Catalogs and Research Tools

Harvard Business School Publishing Electronic Searchable Catalog
Includes abstracts on more than 6,000 articles, cases, collections, books, and videos. The catalog also includes more than 1,000 full text *Harvard Business Review* articles. Now available on CD-ROM (Windows™, Macintosh™, and DOS) and disk (Windows™ and Macintosh™). Network versions also available.

Management Videos from Harvard Business School Publishing
This 28-page, full-color catalog features more than 30 management development video programs.

Harvard Business School Press
This latest full-color catalog features books for the fast-paced business world where you live and work.

Chapter Eleven

Multinational Corporations

The Coca-Cola Company

John S. Pemberton, an Atlanta pharmacist, invented Coca-Cola in 1866. After some experiments to create a headache remedy, he found a formula that pleased him and named it Coca-Cola, after two of its ingredients, namely, "coca," the dried leaf of a South American shrub, and "cola," an extract of the kola nut. It became popular after local druggists began mixing it with soda water at their store fountains. When Pemberton became ill his formula moved into the hands of an Atlanta druggist named Asa Candler. Candler revised the formula, promoted it as a soft drink, and founded The Coca-Cola Company in 1892.[1]

Coca-Cola was the first soft drink to become a national brand. Candler's strategy was to manufacture the syrup, selling it to fountains, and let others add sparkling water and bottle it for the mass market. It made him rich. The company still follows this basic strategy, although its execution has grown far more complex.

The Coca-Cola Company is now an international giant with revenues of $35 billion from more than 200 countries in 2010. Its headquarters are still in Atlanta, but America is no longer its dominant market. It gets 75 percent of its sales in 200 other nations where 86 percent of its 92,800 employees live and work. Its global strategy is to expand by licensing more and more bottlers to make and sell its brands. It produces only about 21 percent of its "unit case volume," the measure it uses to calculate output, in its own syrup manufacturing and bottling plants. The rest comes from licensed bottlers with whom it has a wide range of business relationships. Some, about 23 percent, are from independent bottlers in which Coca-Cola has no ownership. Another 45 percent are bottlers partly owned but not controlled by Coca-Cola, and 11 percent are bottlers it partly owns and controls.[2]

---

[1] The exact nature of the formula is a trade secret. Years ago food and drug regulators accused the company of adulterating its product with a "poisonous" ingredient—caffeine. Coca-Cola denied any health danger and the dispute went to court. When the Supreme Court overturned a lower court ruling in the company's favor, its opinion divulged that Coke syrup contained extracts from coca shrub leaves and cola tree nuts, water (42.63 percent), sugar (52.64 percent), caffeine (1.21 grains per ounce), glycerine, and lime juice. See *United States v. Coca Cola,* 36 S.Ct. 573 (1916), at 574 and 579.

[2] The Coca-Cola Company, *Form 10-K 2010,* February 28, 2011, p. 33.

While some multinational corporations try to project a uniform product and "company way" around the world, Coca-Cola Company adapts to foreign business climates. Its organization structure divides the world into five operating groups—Eurasia and Africa, Europe, Latin America, North America, and the Pacific—reflecting a focus on regional markets. International experience is a key criterion for selecting members of its board of directors. Eight of 14 current directors are noted for strength in this area.

Acting within this structure and through more than 300 bottlers, the company is "a global business that operates on a local scale."[3] Instead of trying to market the same beverages everywhere, it finely adapts its portfolio to local tastes, selling 3,300 products based on 500 brands. It markets Georgia Coffee in Japan, Matte Leao herbal beverages in Brazil, Tian Yu Di (Heaven & Earth) teas in China, Cappy Lemonade in Turkey, and Mazoe peach juice in Ghana. Per capita consumption of its products is highest in Mexico, where the average citizen drinks 665 company beverages a year, far more than the 399 average in the United States.[4]

Around the world 1.6 billion Coca-Cola brand drinks are consumed daily. Yet satisfied customers do not insulate the company from vicious critics. In India, for example, environmental activists released data purporting to show the company's soft drinks harbored pesticides. Although Coca-Cola produced laboratory data certifying the safety of its products, several Indian states prohibited their sale. Indian courts have since reversed these bans.

In Columbia, a widow backed by activist lawyers alleged Coca-Cola was complicit in the murder of her husband, a union leader at a bottling plant. This charge has persisted despite a series of court decisions dismissing the case for lack of evidence that the company had any knowledge of, or control over, events at the independently owned plant.[5] In the United States, legendary labor activist Ray Rogers launched a "Killer Coke" campaign broadening accusations against the company to include condoning torture and kidnapping of union organizers at bottling plants, using child and prison labor, exploiting water resources, and overselling products that cause obesity. At the company's 2010 annual meeting Rogers rose to confront management, charging that the company operated "like a criminal syndicate" and asking the directors to make sure it "reins in its greed [and] cleans up its act."[6] CEO Muhtar Kent dismissed his accusations as having "no merit."[7]

One way Coca-Cola protects its brand is to set rising standards for corporate citizenship. It is spending $6 million to plant 30 million trees in Mexico and $30 million to supply 2 million Africans with clean water. If any of the 60,000 African workers for Coca-Cola and its bottlers or their family members contract HIV/AIDS, the company

[3] The Coca-Cola Company, "The Coca-Cola System," at www.thecoca-colacompany.com, September 19, 2010.

[4] The Coca-Cola Company, "Per Capita Consumption of Company Beverage Products," at www.thecoca-colacompany.com/ourcompany/ar/pdf/2009-per-capita-consumption.pdf, 2010.

[5] See, most recently, *Sinaltrainal v. Coca-Cola,* 578 F.3d 1252 (2009).

[6] Quoted in *Stop Killer Coke Newsletter,* May 6, 2010, at www.killercoke.org/nl100506.htm, at 1.

[7] Quoted in Jeremiah McWilliams, "Mixed Emotions at Coca-Cola Annual Meeting," *Atlanta Journal-Constitution,* April 21, 2010, p. A15.

provides medical coverage. It builds playgrounds in the Ukraine and organized thousands of volunteers to clean parks in Russia. It has global programs to reduce its energy use and replace the water it takes from nature.

Along with other multinational corporations Coca-Cola has embraced schemes of civil regulation that promote responsibility in emerging economies. To protect against accusations of bad behavior it is awash in codes. It has adopted a "Code of Business Conduct," a "Workplace Rights Policy," a "Human Rights Statement," an "Anti-Bribery Policy," and "Supplier Guiding Principles." As a signatory of the United Nations Global Compact it pledges to follow a set of 10 corporate responsibility principles. A statement on its Web site reads: "The Coca-Cola Company and our bottling partners are committed to making a lasting, positive difference in the world."[8]

In this chapter we discuss the nature of multinational corporations, their strategies for internationalization, the impacts of their foreign investment, and their efforts to show responsibility using a range of devices, from voluntary codes of conduct through collaborations with multiple stakeholders. Elements of the Coca-Cola story illustrate all these themes.

THE MULTINATIONAL CORPORATION

multinational corporation
An entity headquartered in one country that does business in one or more foreign countries.

The *multinational corporation* (MNC) is an entity headquartered in one country, its home country, that does at least part of its business in one or more foreign, or host, countries. The universe of MNCs is one of exceptional diversity. Most are private enterprises, but some are cooperatives or state-owned. A few MNCs have the majority of their assets, sales, or employees in foreign countries. Most are primarily domestic businesses with some foreign activity. While some global giants have made a visible impact for good or ill in foreign societies, most MNCs are only medium or small in size and hardly make a ripple. The oldest, largest, and most-powerful ones are based in rich countries. However, those based in China, India, Malaysia, South Africa, and other developing countries now challenge the global leaders, especially in emerging markets.

MNCs also vary widely in their organizational structures and operations. In general, however, there are five tiers of internationalization as shown in Figure 11.1. These tiers are not stages, though they might be for a given company. Rather, they represent options to extend business activity into foreign markets. Each tier is best seen as a theory, model, or ideal. Many of the largest MNCs defy categorization. They have so much structural and strategic variation that they simultaneously use the methods in all five tiers.

1. Export sales to foreign countries.
2. Establish foreign sales offices.
3. License franchises, brands, the use of patents, or technology to foreign firms that make or sell the MNC's products. For example, McDonald's restaurants outside

---

[8] The Coca-Cola Company, *2008/2009 Sustainability Review,* at www.thecoca-colacompany.com/citizenship/index.html, p. ii.

FIGURE 11.1

Five Tiers of Internationalization

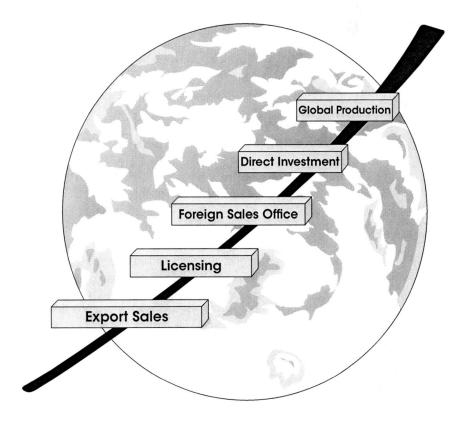

the United States are franchises run by foreign entrepreneurs. Coca-Cola licenses foreign bottlers to make almost all of its beverages in some 200 countries.

4. Buy or create facilities in another country for producing in local markets. Such facilities may become hubs for regional or global sales. The company operates as a group of country-based business units or subsidiaries.

5. Practice global production in which a value chain spans two or more countries. Work on one or more tasks—research, design, manufacturing, logistics, distribution, marketing, sales, or support services—that would be confined to a single country in the fourth-tier model now is done in two or more countries. Organization and control of these cross-border processes are centralized in the parent company's headquarters.

Companies have strategic reasons for moving across these tiers. Through much of the previous century, firms limited themselves to the first four tiers. Before World War II, only a handful of large companies, such as Ford Motor, Singer, and Bayer, had moved into the fourth tier by operating foreign production facilities. Most manufacturers exploited foreign consumer markets through exports and foreign sales offices. The bulk of foreign investment was made in poor countries by multinationals engaged in plantation agriculture, mining, or petroleum extraction.[9]

---

[9] Jeffry A. Frieden, *Global Capitalism* (New York: Norton, 2006), p. 293.

After World War II the situation changed for manufacturers. Strong feelings of nationalism in many countries led to the rise of trade barriers for protecting domestic firms from import competition. Particularly in Europe, rising tariffs made export sales less profitable. Rather than exit large and lucrative domestic markets there, American manufacturers shifted strategies and set up subsidiaries within them. Thus, they moved from one of the first three tiers into the fourth tier. These new foreign subsidiaries often operated very independently of their parent firms, making distinctive products and assuming strong local identities.[10]

liberalization
The economic policy of lowering tariffs and other barriers to encourage trade and investment.

By the end of the century, however, the strategic advantages of this fourth-tier model were less compelling. One reason was the spread of *liberalization*, or the economic policy of lowering tariffs and other barriers to encourage trade and investment. As trade barriers fell it became easier for corporations to move components, products, and services across borders. Also, revolutionary changes in information technology and telecommunications made new forms of global production possible. What ensued was fierce global competition stemming from the adoption of border-spanning production systems. To lower costs and speed output, MNCs created far-reaching networks of suppliers and foreign affiliates. Using new technologies they integrated work across geographic boundaries. As they did, they moved into the fifth tier of internationalization, where their strategic thinking was less influenced by national boundaries.

Today companies with international operations are given many names. They can be called simply international or global. A less preferred name is multidomestic. Usually they are called either multinational or transnational. These names are used loosely, but they occasionally signify diverging beliefs about the nature of these corporations. Sometimes those using the name *multinational* mean to imply that these companies have erased national allegiances, becoming itinerant firms that move investment and activity from nation to nation in search of profits. The name *transnational* is sometimes intended to suggest that rather than becoming stateless entities, large global firms are best understood as invariably and unalterably national companies that have simply extended their reach over borders. The distinction is impractical. There are so many variations of MNCs that either definition fails if applied to the whole universe. Therefore, in this book, we prefer the traditional and long-standing name *multinational* used loosely and interchangeably with transnational, global, and international.

A Statistical Perspective

transnational corporation
As defined by the United Nations, a parent firm that controls the assets of affiliated entities in foreign countries.

Multinational corporations have flourished so spectacularly that if they were a natural species ecologists would inspect their environment for the explanation. One trend is a rapid rise in numbers. The United Nations calculated that in 2008 there were 82,000 *transnational corporations* (TNCs), which it defines as parent firms that control the assets of affiliated entities in foreign countries including branches, subsidiaries, and joint ventures. It estimated that these parent TNCs controlled

[10] Geoffrey G. Jones, "Nationality and Multinationals in Historical Perspective," Working Paper 06-052, Harvard Business School, 2005, p. 23.

FIGURE 11.2

The Dominance of the Largest Transnational Corporations
The United Nations reports there are now 82,000 transnational corporations. Of these, the largest 100 nonfinancial corporations are 12 percent of the number but have a disproportionately great impact on the global economy. All but 10 are from the United States, Europe, and Japan.

Source: Data from United Nations Conference on Trade and Development, *World Investment Report 2009* (New York: United Nations, 2009), p. 17; and United Nations Conference on Trade and Development, *World Investment Report 2010* (New York: United Nations, 2010), annex table 26.

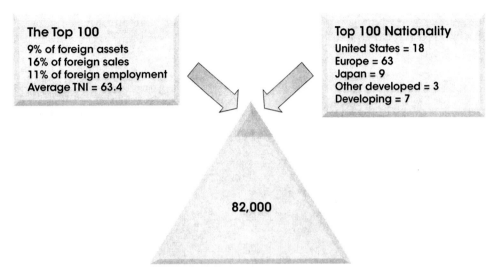

The Top 100
9% of foreign assets
16% of foreign sales
11% of foreign employment
Average TNI = 63.4

Top 100 Nationality
United States = 18
Europe = 63
Japan = 9
Other developed = 3
Developing = 7

82,000

foreign affiliates
Business entities in foreign countries controlled by parent transnational corporations.

807,000 such *foreign affiliates*.[11] This is more than double the 37,000 TNCs in the United Nations' first estimate of their numbers back in 1991 and more than seven times the 10,700 estimated to exist in 1969.[12] The ranks of parent TNCs are dominated by those from developed nations, but the number from developing countries has risen to 28 percent of the total, up from only 8 percent in 1992.[13]

If the largest firms are any indication, transnational firms have also grown in size. In the decade from 1998 to 2008, the assets, sales, and employment of the largest 100 transnational firms increased by 131 percent, 107 percent, and 20 percent, respectively. As they grew, a larger part of their activities became international. During the same decade, the foreign assets, foreign sales, and foreign employment of these top 100 firms grew faster than their overall growth, going up 217 percent, 153 percent, and 35 percent, respectively.[14] On average, each of these big firms operates in 41 countries and 70 percent of their affiliates are in foreign countries.[15]

Figure 11.2 sketches the universe of TNCs and hints at the dominance of the 100 largest firms. Their origins reflect the commanding position in the global economy of the United States, Europe, and Japan, which are home to 90 of the top 100. TNCs

[11] This 2008 estimate is from United Nations Conference on Trade and Development, *World Investment Report 2009* (New York and Geneva: United Nations, 2009), annex table A.I.8.

[12] The 1990 estimate is from United Nations Conference on Trade and Development, *World Investment Report 1993* (New York: United Nations, 1993), table I.6. The 1969 estimate is extrapolated from data in fn. 7 and table I.6.

[13] United Nations Conference on Trade and Development, *World Investment Report,* 2010, p. 17 and figure I.12.

[14] United Nations Conference on Trade and Development, *World Investment Report 2000* (New York: United Nations, 2000), table III.2; and United Nations Conference on Trade and Development, *World Investment Report 2009,* table I.7. Figures are based on an annual list of nonfinancial companies ranked by foreign assets.

[15] United Nations Conference on Trade and Development, "Largest Transnational Corporations Pursued further Expansion Abroad in 2007," press release, September 24, 2008.

TABLE 11.1   Three Top 10 Rankings

Rankings by revenues, foreign assets, and transnationality give three perspectives on transnational corporations. Revenues are for 2009, and foreign assets and transnationality are for 2008.

Source: "Global 500," *Fortune*, July 26, 2010, p. 131; and United Nations Conference on Trade and Development, *World Investment Report 2010* (New York: United Nations, 2010), annex table 26.

Rank	Revenues*		Foreign Assets*		Transnationality	TNI
1	Walmart Stores	$408	General Electric	$401	Xstrata	93.2%
2	Royal Dutch/Shell	285	Royal Dutch/Shell	222	ABB	90.4
3	ExxonMobil	285	Vodafone	202	Nokia	90.3
4	BP	246	BP	189	Pernod Ricard	89.1
5	Toyota Motor	204	Toyota Motor	170	WPP Group	88.9
6	Japan Post Holdings	202	ExxonMobil	161	Vodafone	88.6
7	Sinopec	188	Total	141	Linde	88.3
8	State Grid	185	E.On	141	Anglo American	87.5
9	AXA	175	Electricite De France	134	Nestlé	87.1
10	China National Petroleum	166	ArcelorMittal	127	Air Liquide	86.9

*Revenues and assets are rounded in billions of dollars.

from developing countries occupy only 7 spots in the top 100, but their importance is growing. They account for 28 percent of all TNCs, up from only 8 percent in 1992 and their foreign assets are about 10 percent of all TNC foreign assets.[16] Table 11.1 shows several dimensions of the top 10 firms—their sales, assets, and rank on an index of internationalization to be explained in the next section.

How Transnational Is a Corporation?

One way of gauging the largest TNCs is by measuring the degree to which they have extended critical elements of their operations into foreign countries. Corporations vary in a range of international dimensions. These include the ratio of domestic to foreign operations; the number of foreign countries entered; the size of foreign direct investment; the geographic span of operations; the extent of global integration in the production chain; and the extent of national diversity among shareholders, employees, managers, and directors. Since TNCs differ greatly in these dimensions, no single measure can capture the definitive meaning of "transnational."

Yet measures have been created. The most widely used is the *transnationality index*, or TNI, used by the United Nations to rank corporations based on the relative importance of their domestic and foreign operations. The TNI is calculated as the average of three ratios: (1) foreign assets to total assets, (2) foreign sales to total sales, and (3) foreign employment to total employment. Table 11.2 looks at the TNI index for two of the largest 100 multinational corporations, General Electric, a diversified conglomerate headquartered in the United States, and Philips Electronics of the Netherlands, a global manufacturer of electronic equipment.

transnationality index (TNI)
The average of three ratios: foreign assets to total assets, foreign sales to total sales, and foreign employment to total employment.

[16] UNCTAD, *World Investment Report 2010*, p. 17.

TABLE 11.2   **Calculating the Transnationality Index (TNI) for General Electric and Philips Electronics**

Source: Data from United Nations Conference on Trade and Development, *World Investment Report 2010* (New York: United Nations, 2010), annex table 26. Figures are for 2008.

General Electric		Ratio	Philips Electronics		Ratio
Foreign assets	$401,290		Foreign assets	$ 32,675	
Total assets	797,769	50.3	Total assets	45,986	71.1
Foreign sales	97,214		Foreign sales	37,122	
Total sales	182,515	53.3	Total sales	38,603	96.2
Foreign employees	171,000		Foreign employees	83,946	
Total employees	323,000	52.9	Total employees	121,398	69.2
		TNI = 52.2%			**TNI = 78.8%**

Although GE ranks first in assets among the largest 100 nonfinancial TNCs, it is tied for 80th in its transnationality score. Philips, on the other hand, ranks 65th in assets but 24th in TNI, making it one of the most internationalized of the 100. Although Philips is a much smaller company, its foreign activities are larger in proportion to the whole.

In the eyes of some corporate critics, it is possible for an MNC to become too transnational. Eventually, some MNCs are said to be stateless in a pejorative sense, meaning that not only do foreign operations dominate strategy, but they also structure themselves to elude national controls. This stateless incarnation is more theoretical than operational. The typical MNC remains national rather than international.

Corporations are formed under national incorporation laws. In the United States, for example, each company must be chartered by a state. Most employees at company headquarters are home country nationals. Boards of directors are dominated by home country majorities. It is still rare for top executives to be foreign citizens. Most shareholders are usually in the home country. Record keeping is done in the home country currency. These ties are part of the culture of the company, which is not easily modified. Finally, in many fifth-tier companies there is a strong trend toward more centralized authority rather than more "statelessness."[17] Sprawling global production networks require a strong, controlling hand at headquarters.

For all these reasons, escaping its nationality of origin is awkward for an MNC. Most remain national firms with international operations. Despite these generalizations, a few MNCs find strategic advantage in breaking home country bonds. Consider the odyssey of Weatherford International.

Breaking the Bonds of Country: Weatherford International

Weatherford makes machinery used for oil and natural gas drilling and provides services to energy companies ranging from flushing pipes on drill rigs to cooking meals for crews. It was founded in 1972 in Texas and until the 1990s it operated mostly in the United States. Then it decided to expand into oil fields around the world. It has grown into a company of 53,000 employees with $10 billion in

[17] Geoffrey G. Jones, "The Rise of Corporate Nationality," *Harvard Business Review,* October 2006, p. 21.

360   Chapter 11   *Multinational Corporations*

FIGURE 11.3
Weatherford International: 1972–2002

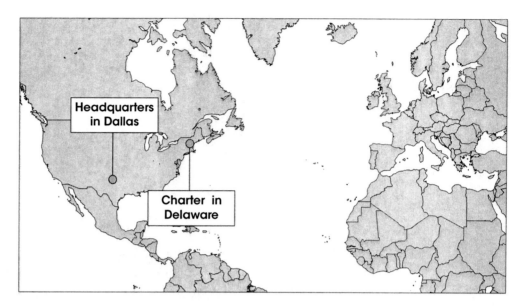

revenues, 62 percent coming from outside the U.S. It operates through about 300 foreign affiliates, including 30 wholly owned subsidiaries and another 250-plus entities in which it has a controlling or noncontrolling interest.

Weatherford was incorporated in Delaware in 1972. Although its headquarters were in Houston, Texas, it could legally charter itself in any state (see Figure 11.3). It picked Delaware because incorporation laws there are business-friendly. In 2002, however, Weatherford decided to restructure and incorporate in Bermuda (see Figure 11.4). It saw several advantages in this. Bermuda law makes it hard for shareholders to sue directors. Hostile takeovers are more difficult. And, most important, corporate taxes are lower because Bermuda has no tax treaty with the United States. By moving there Weatherford could lower its tax rate from 35 percent in the United States, one of the world's highest rates, to about 11 percent.[18] So Weatherford created a new Bermuda corporation, then "reorganized" by making its U.S. corporation a subsidiary of the Bermuda parent. Its headquarters were still in Texas. It remained on the Standard & Poor's 500 index of leading U.S. corporations.

This action irritated some lawmakers. Sen. Max Baucus (D-Montana) was offended that Weatherford and several dozen other U.S. corporations that went to Bermuda were still being run in the United States. "Their executives and employees enjoy all the privileges afforded to honest U.S. taxpayers," he noted.[19] "If companies don't have their hearts in America, they ought to get out," said Sen. Charles Grassley, (R-Iowa)[20] The two senators introduced a tax code amendment to strip Weatherford of its favorable tax treatment.

---

[18] David Cay Johnston, "Tax Treaties with Small Nations Turn into a New Shield for Profits," *The New York Times,* April 16, 2002, p. 1; and Duanjie Chen and Jack Mintz, "U.S. Effective Corporate Tax Rate on New Investments: Highest in the OECD," *Tax & Budget Bulletin,* May 2010, p. 1.

[19] *Congressional Record-Senate,* April 11, 2002, p. S2594.

[20] Ibid., p. S2592.

FIGURE 11.4
Weatherford International: 2002–2009

It did not pass, but after the election of President Barack Obama in 2008, Democratic majorities in Congress targeted corporations moving to tax haven countries. Seeing the danger, Weatherford took itself out of reach again. In 2009 it completed a "redomestication" to Switzerland, another tax-friendly country. It did this by making its Bermuda corporation the subsidiary of a new Swiss parent corporation (see Figure 11.5). Switzerland has a low corporate tax rate and, unlike the United States, does not tax revenue from foreign subsidiaries. By 2009 Weatherford had reduced its tax rate to 6.5 percent.[21]

To put itself out of the reach of Congress, the company relocated its headquarters to Zug, Switzerland, and its top executives moved there. As in the prior Bermuda move, management saw other advantages in Swiss incorporation law. For example, although it allows shareholders to remove directors, it makes the process very complicated. And by holding annual meetings in Switzerland it will be more difficult for its majority of U.S. shareholders to attend. Weatherford will not escape all its U.S. bonds by this reflagging. It still keeps its records in U.S. dollars. Seven of its 10 directors, including Nicholas Brady, a former secretary of the Treasury, are U.S. citizens. Unless directors and executives renounce U.S. citizenship they remain subject to many U.S. laws. An example is the antibribery statute, the Foreign Corrupt Practices Act, which makes it illegal for U.S. citizens anywhere in the world to bribe foreign officials.

Weatherford, now a Swiss corporation run by Americans, continues to expand its international operations. It projects that by 2014 it will get only 20 to 25 percent of its sales in North America.[22] It has been removed from the S&P 500 index.

---

[21] Weatherford International, *2009 Annual Report* (Geneva: Weatherford International, Ltd., 2010), p. AR-25.

[22] Barclays Capital, 2010 CEO Energy-Power Conference, "Weatherford," p. 21, at http://phx.corporate-ir.net/.

FIGURE 11.5

Weatherford International: 2009 to Present

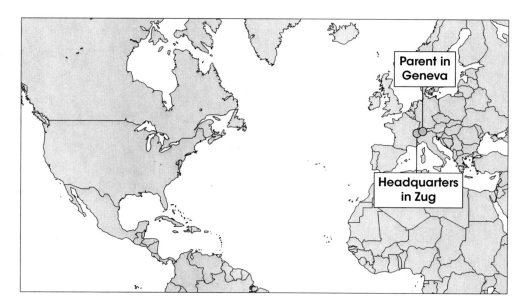

FOREIGN DIRECT INVESTMENT

foreign direct investment
Funds invested by a parent MNC for starting, acquiring, or expanding an affiliate in a foreign nation.

The single measure that best captures the cross-border activity and power of MNCs is how much capital they inject into foreign economies. This capital is called *foreign direct investment,* or FDI, and is measured as the dollar value of funds invested by a parent corporation for starting, acquiring, or expanding an enterprise in a foreign nation. As a form of investment, FDI stands in contrast to *portfolio investment,* or the purchase of stocks and bonds of a foreign company by individuals or equity funds. Compared with FDI, portfolio investment is limited and speculative. Unlike FDI, it does not confer any degree of control over the company and it can be a short-term position sold any time. FDI is the means by which a corporation takes partial or total control of foreign assets with the intention of a long-term presence. Usually, this is defined as an investment of 10 percent or more in a foreign enterprise.

portfolio investment
The limited, speculative purchase of stocks and bonds in a foreign company by individuals or equity funds.

FDI can come through cross-border mergers and acquisitions of existing businesses; through the purchase of property such as factories, mines, or real estate; as earnings reinvested in an affiliate; or from the transfer of funds within a corporation to a foreign affiliate. Almost all FDI comes from multinational corporations. About 1 percent comes from private equity and hedge funds. Tiny fractions of a percent come from individuals and sovereign wealth funds. A *sovereign wealth fund* is a government entity that invests the savings of a nation. FDI by such funds has sometimes raised suspicion because unlike private investors, state-run actors can have geopolitical motives. Although they are emerging as sources of FDI, they so far have little impact. In 2009 they were the source of less than a hundredth of one percent of global FDI.[23]

[23] United Nations Conference on Trade and Investment, *World Investment Report: 2010,* p. 14.

FIGURE 11.6

Where Foreign Direct Investment Flows

Source: UNCTAD, *World Investment Report 2010* (New York: United Nations, 2010), annex table 1.

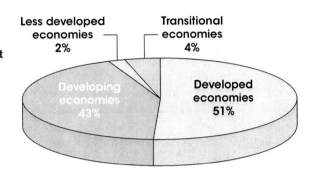

Less developed economies 2%

Transitional economies 4%

Developing economies 43%

Developed economies 51%

sovereign wealth fund

A government entity that invests the savings of a nation. Since it is state-owned, its investment goals may be different from those of private equity funds.

Annual flows of FDI from parent MNCs to foreign affiliates are in a long-term rise, growing from $202 billion in 1990 to $1.1 trillion in 2009, an increase of 537 percent. Over the same period, these annual flows elevated the total assets of foreign affiliates from $6 trillion to $77 trillion, an increase of 1,283 percent.[24]

Corporations make foreign direct investments for many reasons. Three are most common. First, they seek access to new markets. After World War II, for example, European countries had high tariffs on imported goods. American companies jumped over the tariff walls by starting European subsidiaries. Second, companies in nations with small domestic markets enter foreign markets to grow. Nestlé began in the 1860s as a powdered milk company in Switzerland. Now only 1.9 percent of its sales are in the Swiss domestic market. And third, some companies create efficiencies and lower their costs by moving production across borders. By doing so they can use low-wage workers, own sources of critical material, and acquire skills that confer advantages over competitors in, for example, advertising, branding, logistics, or the use of new technologies.

Figure 11.6 shows the distribution of FDI inflows. About half the $1.1 trillion FDI in 2009 moved into 38 developed nations. The United States was the top recipient with $130 billion. European Union countries took in $362 billion collectively. Most of the other half of total FDI, 43 percent, went to 75 developing nations. China took in $95 billion, which was second only to the United States among all nations. Together, China, Brazil, India, and Russia took in 41 percent of developing nation FDI.

Only small portions of FDI entered the world's weakest economies. The 18 transitional economies of South-East Europe and the Commonwealth of Independent States received only 4 percent. A group of 50 least developed countries, the majority in Africa, took in just 2 percent. The $28 billion in FDI entering these poorest of nations was far less than the $51 billion in development aid they received from the world community.[25] Nations with struggling economies are unattractive to investment for a variety of reasons, including weak currencies, political instability, the presence of trade barriers, bad regulatory climates, corruption, unskilled workforces, deficient infrastructure, and tiny domestic markets.

[24] Ibid., table I.5.

[25] Development aid includes both loans and grants from multilateral agencies and donations from donor countries. See World Bank, *World Development Indicators 2010* (Washington, DC: World Bank, April 2010), tables 6.13 and 6.16.

Investment in Developing Economies

Although MNC investment in less developed countries (LDCs) is limited, it can be significant in local economies. MNCs are for-profit entities seeking return on capital invested. In seeking this return they can have many positive effects. They may build or buy facilities, contract with local suppliers, and hire workers. They may bring new management skills and technologies to the region. If conditions are right, FDI can stimulate growth of a local economic "ecosystem." If a local affiliate is integrated into the MNC's international production network, that then links the local economy to foreign markets.

Botswana is an example. On independence from Britain in 1966 it was a poor nation where the average citizen earned $76 a year. The country had little domestic capital to exploit its large deposits of copper, nickel, and diamonds, but foreign mining firms did. The government adopted FDI-friendly policies, giving companies long leases, low tax rates, and freedom to operate. MNCs from England, Australia, Canada, Russia, and South Africa invested in mines and with them roads, airstrips, power stations, waterworks, rail lines, schools, and hospitals. At a time when South African giant De Beers dominated global diamonds, its trading company connected Botswana to world markets, bringing monopoly profits back to the country.

Other MNCs used aerial detectors to chart minute shifts in gravitational fields caused by ore deposits.[26] This technology identified more mineral deposits. Because of foreign investment, Botswana has one of the fastest-growing economies in the world. Per capita annual income rose to $14,100 in 2008. It is now classified as a middle-income country. It is not yet a paradise. It has the highest rate of HIV/ AIDS in the world and more than 30 percent of its people live in poverty. Nevertheless, mining is not the cause of these problems and the country is better off from its receptivity to FDI.

Such stories motivate poor nations to alter their trade and investment policies courting FDI. Other actors in the international community have moved from a hostile attitude toward MNCs to embrace a new pragmatism about the presence of FDI. In the United Nations, international aid groups, and progressive NGOs, long-standing suspicion has been replaced by calculated acceptance of a role for MNCs in development. The United Nations now advises developing nations to set up a "stable and enabling regulatory environment" that indulges the "concern of the business sector for national policies that are enabling but not overly regulating."[27]

Negative effects of FDI are also visible. They are the basis of enduring fear of MNC power. In 1974 two progressive authors of a popular book, *Global Reach*, wrote that "a few hundred" multinational corporations "are making daily business decisions which have more impact than those of most sovereign governments."[28] As trade liberalization produced a more global economy in the 1990s, critics expressed more anxiety over corporate power. One leading progressive, David C. Korten,

---

[26] Keith Jefferis, "The Role of TNCs in the Extractive Industry in Botswana," *Transnational Corporations,* April 2009, p. 63.

[27] United Nations Conference on Trade and Development, *World Investment Report 2010*, p. 117.

[28] Richard J. Barnet and Ronald E. Müller, *Global Reach: The Power of the Multinational Corporations* (New York: Simon and Schuster, 1974), p. 15.

argued that power on earth was being "transferred from national governments . . . to transnational corporations . . . which by their nature serve only the short-term interests of citizens."[29] A subsequent manifesto of progressive theorists said that "several hundred global corporations and banks" held "a concentration of economic and political power that is increasingly unaccountable to governments, people, or the planet."[30] Such statements focused activists on the sins of MNCs, not their promise.

To say that MNCs have so much power is artful. Their economic and social power comes primarily from the impact of FDI. And although FDI has grown, and grown faster than domestic investment, the gross product of all foreign affiliates of all MNCs was only 11 percent of world GDP in 2009.[31] So the economic activity generated by foreign investment is small compared with domestic economic activity. The social impact of this investment, both positive and negative, cannot be measured precisely, but should not be vastly exaggerated. The power of global corporations is closely tied to their foreign investments and cannot too greatly exceed this base. Giant corporations may arguably wield excessive power, but their transnational activities are insufficient in themselves to constitute the excess.

Still, negative economic and social effects of FDI exist. First, we discuss potentially negative economic effects. Although competition from a new foreign affiliate can stimulate local firms, the new entry can also overwhelm them and, in a lax regulatory climate, come to monopolize a domestic market. Governments protect weak or politically powerful industries with patchworks of control. India, for example, forbids foreign investment in retail stores and the manufacture of cigarettes, cheroots, or cigars. It limits investment in FM radio stations to 20 percent of ownership.[32] Russia limits foreign investors to a 10 percent interest in oil, gas, gold, and copper. And China allows officials to reject foreign acquisitions of Chinese companies when "economic security" is threatened.[33]

Multinational corporations are criticized for repatriating profits to home countries, so that local residents get limited benefit from their presence. In Africa, global mining and energy firms own much of the continent's vast stores of oil, natural gas, gold, diamonds, uranium, copper, and platinum. Yet, using intrafirm money transfers, much of the economic value they generate moves out of impoverished nations. Production taxes and royalties paid to African governments are often pocketed by corrupt elites. Critics say this kind of FDI amounts to a "recolonization" that leaves average citizens as poor as they were before its arrival.[34]

[29] David C. Korten, "The Limits of the Earth," *The Nation,* July 15/22, 1996, p. 16. See also Korten's book, *When Corporations Rule the World* (San Francisco: Kumarian Press and Barrett-Koehler, 1995).

[30] The International Forum on Globalization, *Alternatives to Economic Globalization* (San Francisco: Barrett-Koehler, 2002), p. 17.

[31] See United Nations Conference on Trade and Development, *World Investment Report 2010,* table I.5.

[32] Government of India, Ministry of Commerce and Industry, *Consolidated FDI Policy (Effective from October 1, 2010),* Circular 2 (2010), pp. 39 and 54.

[33] Government Accountability Office, *Laws and Policies Regulating Foreign Investment in 10 Countries,* GAO-08-320, February 2008, pp. 10–12.

[34] Jeffrey Gogo, "Vast Mineral Wealth Sparks New 'Scramble for Africa,'" *The Herald* (Zimbabwe), February 27, 2007, p. 1.

Even without making direct investments in a nation, powerful MNCs can shake its economy. For example, about 30 large supermarket and food corporations are now the gatekeepers in global markets for fruits and vegetables. Buyers for Walmart, Carrefour, Royal Ahold, Tesco, and others seek low price, rapid delivery, and uniform quality when they source produce. Their intense pressure pushes low prices all the way back to small farmers growing crops for export. They prefer to contract with a few big export companies rather than with multitudes of small farmers. In the past decade, most of Kenya's small farmers abandoned their livelihoods as more and more produce was purchased from large farms owned by export companies. So, although Walmart and the others made no direct investment in the Kenyan economy, their market power reshaped its agricultural sector.[35]

Social impacts often accompany the economic impacts of multinational corporations. Where the material standard of living is raised, these are positive. But, especially where social regulation is rudimentary, they can be negative. Recurrently there are charges that mining and drilling facilities in remote areas harm the environment and disrupt native peoples. MNCs in manufacturing are accused of exploiting factory workers. And MNCs selling consumer products such as entertainment, fast food, and apparel are suspected of tainting local cultural values with Western indulgence and materialism.

Even as their power builds or distorts, the companies themselves frequently take a beating. Recently, for example, IKEA decided to suspend investment in Russia because of what it called the "unpredictable character of administrative procedures."[36] This was a polite reference to corruption. One problem was a ministry that refused to approve a shopping mall not built to withstand hurricane force winds, though such winds are unknown in the region. Officials hinted the problem would be solved if IKEA hired a certain firm to reinforce the structure. In Thailand, where foreign corporations live with airport closures, mass protests, and threatened military coups, a court suddenly froze $12 billion in foreign investment projects for an unknown time to study its environmental consequences. Ford Motor Company, which exports vehicles from Thailand to 50 other countries, is considering relocation.

A new law in Indonesia shortens the time of exploration licenses for mining MNCs, gives local authorities more power over mining, and prohibits shipping ore away from mines for smelting. Such a law strengthens the hand of towns affected by mines and could lead to smelter investment and employment for Indonesians. However, big miners such as Rio Tinto and BHP Billiton now rate Indonesia's investment climate the worst of any mineral-rich country and may reduce their FDI.[37] In Bolivia the government issued a decree nationalizing four power companies 50 percent-owned by French and British corporations. The next day it took over a metals plant owned by a Swiss company. In nearby Venezuela the president threatened to seize a Toyota Motor assembly plant unless it was converted to

---

[35] United Nations Development Programme, *Human Development Report 2005* (New York: UNDP, 2005), pp. 142–43.

[36] "Courting Disaster," *The Economist,* July 4, 2009, p. 63.

[37] Tom Wright, "Indonesian Mining Law Adds Obstacles for Foreign Investors," *The Wall Street Journal,* December 17, 2008, p. A14.

advanced manufacturing technology and made inexpensive vehicles designed for rough roads.[38]

Nevertheless, fear of MNC power, especially its exercise in LDCs, has led to an international movement promoting responsible behavior. The result is a global web of norms, codes, standards, labels, audits, and certifications already described in Chapter 5. In what follows, we discuss several additional efforts to control MNCs' behavior. We begin with the story of the Sullivan Principles, a pioneering effort that set the stage for further efforts.

INTERNATIONAL CODES OF CONDUCT

international codes of conduct
Voluntary, aspirational statements by MNCs that set forth standards for foreign operations.

International codes of conduct are aspirational statements of principles, policies, and rules for foreign operations that a multinational corporation voluntarily agrees to follow. The first such code to engage a large number of corporations was the *Sullivan Principles.*

In 1977 the Rev. Leon Sullivan, a Baptist minister and civil rights activist who sat on General Motors' board of directors, set forth six broad principles for the conduct of MNCs in South Africa. At the time, South African law decreed an elaborate system of *apartheid,* or separation of the races, in which the civil rights of black, Indian, and mixed-race citizens were restricted by a government of *Afrikaners,* descendants of white Europeans who had settled that part of Africa more than 300 years earlier. Human rights activists charged MNCs that invested in South Africa with complicity in a repressive, racist regime. General Motors, which was the largest employer of black South Africans, sold vehicles to the police and the military. Polaroid, for a time, sold the film used for pictures in official passbooks the government used to classify citizens by race and restrict their movements.

Sullivan Principles
A 1977 code of conduct that required multinational corporations in South Africa to do business in a nondiscriminatory way.

Reverend Sullivan rose to prominence as a civil rights activist and minister at a large Baptist church in Philadelphia. In 1971 General Motors put him on its board of directors, and he became the first black director of a major U.S. corporation. As a director he led GM to hire more black workers and set up more black dealerships. But when he would argue that GM should leave South Africa to protest racism there, other directors were unconvinced. In time, they even began turning in their seats to show him their backs.[39] It was a trip to South Africa, however, that pushed him into more direct action. Years later, he told a reporter what happened.

> When I was getting on the plane to go home, the police took me to a room and told me to remove my clothes. A man with the biggest .45 I'd ever seen said, "We do to you what we have to."
>
> I stood there in my underwear, thinking, "I'm the head of the largest black church in Philadelphia and I'm on the board of directors of General Motors. When I get home, I'll do to you what I have to."[40]

---

[38] Dan Molinski and Norihiko Shirouzu, "Venezuela's President Threatens Toyota, GM," *The Wall Street Journal,* December 26, 2009, p. A1.

[39] Claudia Levy, "Civil Rights Crusader Leon Sullivan Dies," *Washington Post,* April 26, 2001, p. B7.

[40] Quoted in Jan Hoffman, "A Civil Rights Crusader Takes On the World," *The New York Times,* November 3, 1999, p. B2.

The Rev. Leon H. Sullivan (1922–2001). The Sullivan Principles demonstrated that codes of conduct could promote corporate responsibility on a global scale. Source: © Bettmann/ CORBIS.

The Sullivan Principles required MNCs in South Africa to integrate workplaces, provide equal pay, and promote nonwhites to supervisory roles. In effect, they turned foreign corporations into civil disobedients, since these requirements violated South African employment law. This was an early instance when a code called on MNCs to enforce international norms in a host country. Additionally, companies were to improve housing, schools, and health care for nonwhite workers and their families.

The principles remained in place until a change in government ended apartheid in 1994. During this time more than 100 firms became signatories and spent $350 million to carry out their commitments.[41] The results were mixed. The principles helped overcome apartheid, but failed to satisfy global antiapartheid activists whose vicious attacks and domestic boycotts drove many signatory corporations out of South Africa. Coca-Cola, for example, argued that as a signatory it could have a constructive presence in South Africa. However, activists believed that the very presence of Coca-Cola, no matter how principled its operations, gave the regime legitimacy. They called a boycott. As black consumers emptied Coke bottles onto the streets around its Atlanta headquarters, the company sold its facilities to South African entrepreneurs.

The Sullivan Principles inspired more efforts to enumerate and codify international standards of corporate conduct. Code making exploded in the 1990s as a response to expanding FDI. By 2001, one study identified 246 voluntary codes for MNCs, including 118 company codes, 92 from business or industry groups, and

[41] Oliver F. Williams, "Shaping a High-Trust Society: The Crucial Role of Codes of Conduct," *Business Ethics Quarterly* 14, no. 2 (2004), p. 342.

32 from partnerships of stakeholders.[42] Today the global total of conduct codes, sets of principles, and standards of operation for MNCs is doubtless higher. The overall structure of this code-based civil regulation of CSR was discussed in Chapter 5. Here we will take a narrower, case-oriented focus, examining in depth two of the most prominent international schemes to encourage responsible MNC behavior, one a code of conduct backed by governments, the other a set of aspirational principles backed by the United Nations. Neither is, strictly speaking, enforceable. But each, in its own way, has encouraged better MNC citizenship. Then, we discuss an additional element of the global CSR system, the Alien Tort Claims Act.

THE OECD GUIDELINES FOR MULTINATIONAL ENTERPRISES

This is the only comprehensive global code of corporate conduct promoted by governments. The Organisation for Economic Co-operation and Development (OECD) is a group of 33 nations that works to further economic growth by expanding trade. It formed in 1961 as an outgrowth of cooperation to rebuild Europe after World War II. At first it was a select group of advanced economies, including only the United States and 19 European nations. Since then, membership has grown to include Japan, Australia, and some developing countries.

The *OECD Guidelines for Multinational Enterprises* are "recommendations" from OECD governments to multinational corporations that operate within or from their borders. Along with the 33 OECD member nations another 11 nonmember nations now adopt them.[43] The *Guidelines* are an extensive, detailed code of conduct grounded in 11 general policies, as set forth in the accompanying box. These are further articulated in eight chapters of more detailed policies for specific areas—disclosure, employment, environment, bribery, consumers, science and technology, competition, and taxation. Standards in each area are derived from the mesh of hard and *soft law* in international treaties, conventions, covenants, and norms.

soft law
Statements of philosophy, policy, and principle found in nonbinding international agreements that, over time, gain legitimacy as guidelines for interpreting the "hard law" in legally binding agreements.

How the *OECD Guidelines* Work

Observance of the guidelines is voluntary; they are nonbinding. There are no sanctions or penalties for violations. However, a formal process exists to "encourage" observance. Each government that joins in the guidelines sets up an office, called a "national contact point." Any individual or group can file a complaint at one of these offices alleging violations by a corporation. The office then goes through a three-step process. First, it assesses the complaint. Second, if there is merit, it offers to mediate the dispute between the parties. Then, if mediation is rejected or fails, it can issue a "final statement" about the matter, including recommendations to the disputants.

Complaints come primarily from activists and labor unions. In the decade between 2000 and 2010 there were 96 complaints from NGOs and 117 from unions. The complaint process is imperfect. Of 96 complaints from NGOs, for example,

---

[42] Organisation for Economic Co-operation and Development, "Corporate Codes of Conduct: Expanded Review of their Contents," *Working Papers on International Investment,* No. 2001/6, May 2001, p. 31.

[43] These are Argentina, Brazil, Egypt, Estonia, Latvia, Lithuania, Morocco, Peru, and Romania.

The *OECD Guidelines for Multinational Enterprises*

GENERAL POLICIES

Enterprises should take fully into account established policies in the countries in which they operate, and consider the views of other stakeholders. In this regard, enterprises should:

1. Contribute to economic, social and environmental progress with a view to achieving sustainable development.

2. Respect the human rights of those affected by their activities consistent with the host government's international obligations and commitments.

3. Encourage local capacity building through close co-operation with the local community, including business interests, as well as developing the enterprise's activities in domestic and foreign markets, consistent with the need for sound commercial practice.

4. Encourage human capital formation, in particular by creating employment opportunities and facilitating training opportunities for employees.

5. Refrain from seeking or accepting exemptions not contemplated in the statutory or regulatory framework related to environmental, health, safety, labour, taxation, financial incentives, or other issues.

6. Support and uphold good corporate governance principles and develop and apply good corporate governance practices.

7. Develop and apply effective self-regulatory practices and management systems that foster a relationship of confidence and mutual trust between enterprises and the societies in which they operate.

8. Promote employee awareness of, and compliance with, company policies through appropriate dissemination of these policies, including through training programmes.

9. Refrain from discriminatory or disciplinary action against employees who make *bona fide* reports to management or, as appropriate, to the competent public authorities, on practices that contravene the law, the *Guidelines* or the enterprise's policies.

10. Encourage, where practicable, business partners, including suppliers and sub-contractors, to apply principles of corporate conduct compatible with the *Guidelines*.

11. Abstain from any improper involvement in local political activities.

Source: Organisation for Economic Co-operation and Development, *OECD Guidelines for Multinational Enterprises* (Paris, France: OECD, 2008). Reprinted with permission.

only 27 percent were concluded with a settlement or final statement.[44] According to OECD Watch, a network of 80 activist groups that reports on the effectiveness of the *Guidelines,* the code has potential but so far it has "a poor track record in dealing with the social, environmental, and economic problems that matter most."[45] The potential lies in its singular joining of international standards with oversight by governments.

The shortcomings are multiple. Activists lack confidence in favorable outcomes. Doing the research and preparation for filing a complaint is costly. National offices often fail to find merit or decline to pursue the matter. Mediated resolutions are rare. And even when the offices issue final statements, they cannot enforce their

[44] OECD Watch, *10 Years On: Assessing the Contribution of the OECD Guidelines for Multinational Enterprises to Responsible Business Conduct* (Amsterdam: OECD Watch, June 2010), p. 9.

[45] Ibid., p. 8.

FIGURE 11.7

Vedanta
Resources
2010

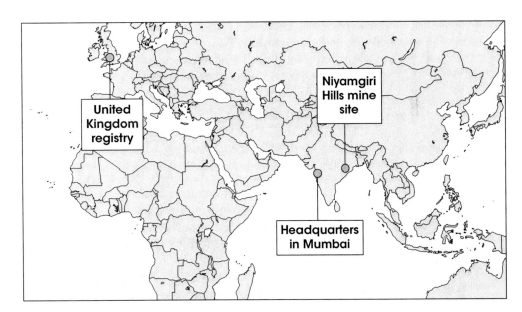

recommendations or apply penalties. They can only ask for follow-up reports from both parties. Lack of cooperation by companies is another obstacle. They often assign junior staff to work with national offices, ignore timetables, and refuse to comply with recommendations.[46] The following story of one complaint shows the *OECD Guidelines for Multinational Enterprises* at work and reveals their strengths and weaknesses.

Vedanta Resources

Vedanta is the largest mining corporation in India. It is officially registered in the United Kingdom so as to be listed on the London Stock Exchange, but it has only an office there. Its headquarters are in Mumbai and it operates through subsidiaries in India, Zambia, and Australia. In 2010 it had 27,000 employees and revenues of almost $8 billion. Most of its assets are in India. Its basic strategy is to "capitalise on attractive growth opportunities arising from India's large mineral reserves."[47]

It seized one such opportunity in 2003, entering an agreement with the State of Orissa to construct a bauxite mine and an aluminum refinery in the Niyamgiri Hills of northeast India (see Figure 11.7). Ore from the mine was to supply the refinery for 25 years. Vedanta first built the refinery, which ran on bauxite ore from other locations. Then it began to secure approvals for the mine, which was to be on top of a nearby mountain. Vedanta claims to be an environmentally responsible company and promises not only to minimize any damage from its projects, but also "to make a net positive impact on the environment."[48] It also promises to work

[46] OECD, *Annual Report on the Guidelines for Multinational Enterprises 2009* (Paris: OECD Publishing, 2010), p. 85.

[47] Vedanta Resources, "About Us," at www.vedantaresources.com/about-us.aspx.

[48] Vedanta Resources, "Mission and Values," at www.vedantaresources.com/mission%20values.aspx.

with local communities, to "create partnerships" and to "actively enter into dialogue and engagement."[49]

For centuries an indigenous people, the Dongria Kondh (DONG-gree-ah cond), have lived near the planned mine site. They speak an ancient language and maintain a unique culture, even as modern life rings them and presses in. They survive by cultivating crops and animals in the area's forest and meadow ecosystem. Their religion holds the land sacred and they believe Niyam Dongar, the mountain where the mine would sit, is a deity. About 8,000 Dongria Kondh live around the god-mountain.

Indian law protects primitive peoples, safeguarding their cultures and lands. Vedanta worked with a consultative body set up by the Orissa government to contact the Dongria Kondh and obtain their consent for clearing three square miles and mining atop the sacred mountain. Eventually, Vedanta claimed to have the Dongria Kondh's approval. In fact, the consultation was deficient. They did not approve.

Now the Dongria Kondh needed a champion. They found one in Survival International, a nonprofit group that defends the rights of indigenous peoples. When the people asked this group for help, it filed a complaint with the United Kingdom OECD office alleging that Vedanta had acted against the OECD *Guidelines*. It said the company had no human rights policy and had barely consulted the Dongria Kondh, citing, for example, the experience of a villager in a group approached by Vedanta's representatives.

> They asked us "do you support Vedanta?" and "Do you want to mine bauxite?" We said no, we do not want to give our mountain.
>
> Then they said everyone from [another village] has agreed to mine bauxite. That's why they have a school, roads, and . . . are getting machines. If you complain to us, then we can't provide anything to you again. You have to say "yes."
>
> . . . Then I said yes! I am really against Vedanta . . . In my heart I have never supported Vedanta. They offered me these temptations, that's why I was tempted. But all our people in the area don't want this company and don't want to mine.[50]

The complaint charged that Vedanta had violated not only the *Guidelines*, but also several international covenants and declarations on which they are based. Even if it created economic growth and jobs, a mine on a sacred mountain operating 24 hours a day, making noise, polluting streams, and scarring a virgin ecosystem intruded too far on the rights of an indigenous people. "The nearest equivalent," said the brief, "might be the demolition of Durham Cathedral to allow access to the rich seam of coal that lies beneath it."[51]

When the UK office received the complaint, it did an initial assessment. Its staff met with members of Survival International. Vedanta did not come to meetings

---

[49] Vedanta Resources plc, *Sustainable Development Report 2008* (London: Vedanta Resources, 2009), p. 40.

[50] Sahadev Kadraka, quoted in Survival International, *Vedenta Resources plc (UK): Complaint to the UK National Contact Point under the Specific Instance Procedure of the OECD Guidelines for Multinational Enterprises,* December 19, 2008, p. 15.

[51] Ibid., p. 20.

but engaged in an exchange of e-mails and letters. Soon, the office offered to mediate the dispute, but Vedanta declined. Thus, the office moved to examine the merits of the complaint, asking both parties for evidence to support their positions. Survival International submitted "a great deal" of material. Vedanta submitted no specific evidence, only a copy of its most recent sustainability development report.

Vedanta claims to be a socially responsible corporation and its sustainability reports seem to confirm this. Its actions fight poverty, disease, and famine. It feeds lunches to 200,000 schoolchildren in poor villages and aspires to feed 1 million. It has built 2,387 public toilets where sanitation is a problem. It plants foliage to protect watersheds. It runs hundreds of health care centers to vaccinate children. It teaches farmers methods that raise crop yields. It funds a charitable cancer hospital.

Yet its benevolence seemed to take a holiday from the mining project. The British OECD office concluded that Vedanta "failed to put in place an adequate and timely consultation mechanism fully to engage the Dongria Kondh."[52] In fact, it verified only three public meetings in six years. Two meetings were attended by 10 people and 30 people, respectively, but there was no evidence of Dongria Kondh in the audience. They might not have known, since the meetings were announced only in English and few know the language. A third meeting was attended by 400 people, but it was unclear if any Dongria Kondh were there and only the aluminum refinery was discussed, not the mine.

The "final statement" of the British office concluded Vedanta had offended three sections of the *Guidelines*.[53] It also stated the company had acted against several international conventions and covenants that define norms for treatment of peoples such as the Dongria Kongh.[54] It made two recommendations to Vedanta. First, it should "immediately and adequately engage with the Dongria Kondh," respecting the outcome of this consultation. Second, it should always analyze the human rights impact when its projects affect an indigenous people. To carry out these recommendations Vedanta was referred to the "Akwe: Kon Guidelines," a set of voluntary principles for studying the social impact of industrial projects on indigenous peoples. These principles issued from the *Convention on Biological Diversity*, a treaty to which India is a signatory. It was also encouraged to develop a human rights policy and referred to a UN Web site on business and human rights for inspiration.

Convention on Biological Diversity
A treaty that requires nations to preserve biological diversity by promoting sustainable economic activity. It emerged from the UN-sponsored Earth Summit in 1992 and has been signed by 163 nations.

---

[52] *Final Statement by the UK National Contact Point for the OECD Guidelines for Multinational Enterprises: Complaint from Survival International against Vedanta Resources plc*, URN: 09/1373 (London: UK National Contact Point, September 25, 2009), p. 1.

[53] These were Chapter V(2)(b) encouraging MNCs to "engage in adequate and timely communication and consultation with the communities directly affected by the environmental, health and safety policies of the enterprise and by their implementation," Chapter II(7) that encourages them to "develop and apply effective self-regulatory practices and management systems that foster a relationship of confidence and mutual trust between enterprises and the societies in which they operate," and Chapter II(2) that encourages them to "respect the human rights of those affected by their activities." See Organisation for Economic Co-operation and Development, *OECD Guidelines for Multinational Enterprises* (Paris: OECD, 2008), pp. 14 and 19.

[54] These included the UN International Covenant on Civil and Political Rights, the UN Convention on the Elimination of All Forms of Racial Discrimination, the Convention on Biological Diversity, the UN Declaration on the Rights of Indigenous People, Convention 138 of the International Labour Organisation, and the UN Convention on the Rights of the Child.

Dongria Kondh tribal women listen to an Indian politician speak about the plan to build a mine on top of their sacred mountain. Source. © AP Photo

Finally, both parties were asked to send the office an update in three months.

To provide this update, Survival International sent a team to the Niyamgiri Hills, but it reported harassment by Vedanta. It believed the company paid some villagers to object to its presence. Someone told local police the group was going to stir up trouble. Its motorcycle was vandalized. However, after interviews with Dongria Kondh in six villages, it found no evidence of systematic consultation on the mine by Vedanta.

The British office's report was quite a load of guilt for any company to bear, but Vedanta stood unbowed. A top executive rejected the authority of the OECD procedure, saying it violated Indian sovereignty.[55] Nonetheless, the company submitted an update to the British office saying construction of the mine was proceeding in accord with applicable laws and regulations in India. It noted an agreement approved by the Indian Supreme Court requiring 5 percent of the mine's profits each year go to improving health services, water quality, and education in the area. It denied hindering the Survival International team.

The final action of the British office was to summarize each side's update. It made no further analysis of claims. It only encouraged the two parties "to engage with each other in order to achieve a mutually satisfactory outcome."[56] This was unlikely, but the *Guidelines* permitted no stronger action. However, the inquiry by the British office prodded the Indian government. One observation in its report was that although India was a signatory to certain relevant treaties and conventions, it was not assuring Vedanta's compliance with them. The report was publicized in India, fueling resistance to the mine.

Subsequently, an Indian ministry sent a team of investigators from New Delhi to examine the Niyamgiri Hills project. The team's report stopped the mine cold. Along with inadequate consultation of the Dongria Kondh, the investigators believed the company had violated Indian laws protecting the environment and indigenous peoples. They also hinted at the presence of corruption or conflict of interest between the company and local officials. Overall, they characterized the mine project as "an act of total contempt for the law on the part of the company and an appalling degree of collusion on the part of the concerned officials."[57]

Late in 2010 the Indian ministry rescinded permits for expansion of the aluminum refinery and construction of the mine. Vedanta's share price fell by 5 percent.

[55] Mukesh Kumar, chief operating officer, quoted in "Vedanta's Orissa Bauxite Mine Plan Under Scrutiny," *Metal Bulletin Weekly,* January 4, 2010, p. 2.

[56] *Follow up to Final Statement by the UK National Contact Point: Complaint from Survival International against Vedanta Resources plc,* URN 10/778 (London: UK National Contact Point, March 12, 2010), p. 1.

[57] N. C. Saxena, et al., *Report of the Four Member Committee for Investigation into the Proposal Submitted by the Orissa Mining Company for Bauxite Mining in Niyamgiri* (New Delhi: Ministry of Environment & Forests, August 16, 2010), p. 14.

It denied breaking any laws and called the accusations against it "lies and hoax."[58] Its chairman argued that the economic benefits of the project far outweighed any harm to the Dongria Kondh or the mountain ecosystem.

The story teaches several lessons. First, multinational corporations can use claims of corporate responsibility as a veneer to disguise corporate cultures that exploit lax regulation in developing economies. Voluntary CSR is not, and can never be, the full corrective for flaws in markets. Second, international codes such as the *Guidelines* effectively wield the soft-law bible to challenge corporations acting outside international norms. Although the *Guidelines* could not be enforced on Vedanta, when its violations came to light they became untenable. Third, although these norms, codes, and agreements are an important force, they have major limitations. Ultimately, only governments can force compliance on defiant MNCs. Vedanta was brought to heel only when the Indian government invoked statute-based regulations.

THE UNITED NATIONS GLOBAL COMPACT

The single most conspicuous effort to promote MNC social responsibility and to harness FDI for economic development is the Global Compact. It started in 2000 when UN Secretary-General Kofi Annan challenged global corporations to collaborate with UN agencies, labor unions, NGOs, and governments in embracing a set of "universal values." He called on MNCs to carry out a set of 10 principles (see the box) in four areas. The Global Compact is not a code of conduct. It does not enforce the principles. Rather, it advances them as an "aspirational" set of "shared values."

The 10 principles condense basic ideas from international declarations and conventions made under UN auspices over the years. They seem simple, broad, and aspirational. However, this rudimentary appearance is deceptive. Their meaning is articulated in voluminous and more specific guidance materials such as reports, handbooks, case studies, best-practice digests, online assessments, and learning tools. And they push boundaries. Principle 6, for example, calls for the "elimination of discrimination," which, as articulated in the Global Compact documents, includes that based on sexual orientation, a protection not found in labor laws of many nations, including the United States. Principle 9 urges a precautionary approach to environmental risks, a philosophy rising from the *Rio Declaration* and accepted by regulators in Europe, but less so in the United States.

Rio Declaration
A set of 27 principles for sustainable development that emerged from the 1992 Earth Summit, a UN Conference of 172 nations and 2,400 NGOs held in Rio de Janeiro.

Other principles are layered on. For example, working with another UN agency, in 2010 the Global Compact launched the Women's Empowerment Principles as a "gender lens" for corporations to use in evaluating their actions (see the box on page 377). In fact, the Global Compact is a fountain of principles. Cooperating with other UN agencies it has developed additional sets of principles for "responsible investment," "responsible management education," and "children's principles" that direct MNCs to support children's rights.

---

[58] Alistair Dawber, "Vedanta's Failure to Speak Out Earlier Could Cost It Dearly," *The Independent,* August 25, 2010, p. 8.

The Global Compact Principles

Human Rights

1. Businesses should support and respect the protection of internationally proclaimed human rights; and

2. Make sure that they are not complicit in human rights abuses.

Labour Standards

3. Businesses should uphold the freedom of association and the effective recognition of the right to collective bargaining;

4. The elimination of all forms of forced and compulsory labour;

5. The effective abolition of child labour; and

6. The elimination of discrimination in respect of employment and occupation.

The Environment

7. Businesses should support a precautionary approach to environmental challenges;

8. Undertake initiatives to promote greater environmental responsibility; and

9. Encourage the development and diffusion of environmentally friendly technologies.

Anti-Corruption

10. Businesses should work against all forms of corruption, including extortion and bribery.

The Global Compact is administered within the United Nations Secretariat. Participation by all parties is voluntary. Its central purposes are to (1) promote responsible corporate behavior that (2) advances central UN goals such as world peace, protection of human rights, poverty reduction, and sustainable markets. Only 47 corporations were aboard when it started in 2000, but by 2010 there were 6,210. This is a large number, and more than any other global corporate responsibility initiative, but less than 8 percent of the total number of MNCs. In addition, about 2,400 NGOs and labor organizations participate.[59]

Companies joining the Global Compact commit themselves to breathe life into the principles, writing them into mission statements, using them to guide strategy, applying them in daily operations, and extending them over their spheres of influence to subsidiaries, partners, and suppliers. There is a modest fee scale for participating; only $10,000 a year for companies with revenues of $1 billion or more. Also, each year, the company must post a progress report on the Global Compact Web site.[60]

communication on progress
The required annual report of a company participating in the Global Compact. It explains how the company is implementing the 10 principles.

These reports, called *communications on progress* in Global Compact jargon, must have three elements. First, the top executive of the company must endorse the Global Compact. Second, the company describes its actions. In the first five years it needs to act on principles in at least two of the four issue areas. After five years it must report action in all four areas. Third, it must measure results using appropriate yardsticks. Companies failing to report are listed as "non-communicating" after the first year. After a second year of silence they are delisted. So far, 1,535 companies,

---

[59] "News & Updates," *UN Global Compact Bulletin,* October 2010, p. 2.

[60] These reports are posted at www.unglobalcompact.org/COP/analyzing_progress.html.

Women's Empowerment Principles

1. Establish high-level corporate leadership for gender equality.
2. Treat all women and men fairly at work—respect and support human rights and nondiscrimination.
3. Ensure the health, safety and well-being of all women and men workers.
4. Promote education, training and professional development for women.
5. Implement enterprise development, supply chain and marketing practices that empower women.
6. Promote equality through community initiatives and advocacy.
7. Measure and publicly report on progress to achieve gender equality.

These principles are the result of collaboration between the United Nations Global Compact and the United Nations Development Fund for Women. Their development included a process of consultation with governments, NGOs, business, and labor groups.

mostly smaller ones, have met this fate. The Global Compact also delists firms that ignore charges of egregious irresponsibility.

The reports reveal a wide range of CSR activity. Since the Global Compact is not a binding code it does not evaluate or judge them. Here is a sampling of actions reported.

- Nikon Corporation joined the Global Compact in 2007. Since then it has written a CSR plan that requires carrying out the 10 principles worldwide. It set up a high-level CSR committee and a department to organize its response. All employees receive training in the 10 principles and take a mandatory online exam about them. The company requires each of its 70 subsidiaries in 23 countries to report on how the principles are carried out. It defines performance indicators, measures outcomes, and reports results for all of the principles.[61]

- In pursuit of Principle 8, which asks companies "to promote greater environmental responsibility," Levi Strauss requires factories in its supply chain to meet a set of "global effluent guidelines."[62] All wastewater from the manufacture of jeans, shirts, zippers, and buttons anywhere in the world must meet standards for 19 measures of water quality and metals residue. In some locations the limits are stricter than local pollution laws. Factories in its supply chain must test discharges and send reports to Levi Strauss.

- As part of the Global Compact companies are asked to promote development in poorer economies. Land in some war-torn nations lies fallow when land mines are not cleared. Komatsu Ltd., a Japanese company that makes construction equipment, built a bulldozer-like machine that removes antipersonnel land

[61] See Nikon Corporation, *CSR Report 2010* (Tokyo: Nikon Corporation, September 2010).
[62] Levi Strauss & Co., *Environment, Health and Safety Handbook,* v. 2.0 (San Francisco: Levi Strauss & Co., April 2007), appendix V.

mines. In Cambodia it donated the machine to clear mines from around a village, allowing the land again to be used for vegetable farming.[63] Then the company improved roads into the village and rebuilt its school, creating a newly vibrant community. Komatsu is now clearing mines in Angola.

- Sexual exploitation of children in tourism is a persistent human rights problem. Tourists from the United States make up 25 percent of customers in a global sex trade involving as many as 2 million children. Carlson Companies, headquartered in Minneapolis, operates hotels and travel services. A centerpiece of its efforts to uphold Principles 1 and 2 is a policy to fight child prostitution. Its Radisson hotels are located in 77 countries, including several—Brazil, Costa Rica, and Thailand—where the child sex trade thrives. Carlson trains hotel staff to observe and report suspicious use of rooms. It acts to discourage demand for sex with children by educating travelers, telling American travelers, for example, that if they have sex with children under age 18 abroad they can be prosecuted under U.S. laws after they return home.

These meritorious examples, taken from hundreds of "noteworthy" reports showcased by the Global Compact, suggest its promise. However, most participating MNCs report less ambitious or less specific accomplishments. A typical communication on progress lists the 10 principles on a chart, with references to pages in a company sustainability report where actions said to be undertaken in support of a particular principle are discussed. It is not clear that the activities referenced were done to further the principles or for unrelated reasons. And many activities, such as setting up a committee to investigate the company's performance with respect to X, Y, or Z responsibility, may or may not have significance.

Criticism of the Global Compact

The Global Compact experiment started slowly. Companies, especially the largest MNCs, were skeptical of the need for another code and feared being sued by NGOs for violating its principles. Cynical NGOs saw it as toothless because the principles were not enforced. To this day, critics believe that MNCs indulge in *bluewashing*, a word that references the color of the UN flag, a worldwide symbol of peace and justice. In bluewashing, the prestige of the United Nations is exploited by insincere corporations that sign onto the principles but fail to fulfill their spirit.

After a decade of the Global Compact, progressives have mixed feelings about its achievements. They see a rapidly growing initiative in which corporations more or less, and sometimes remarkably, act on affirmative principles. A recent survey of CEOs reported that 67 percent believed participation in the Global Compact helped their companies advance CSR performance.[64] The compact is now rapidly evolving and expanding. Its principles contain the potent seed of ideals. An ideal with momentum, which the Global Compact has, generally works to elevate behavior and shame laggards.

bluewashing
The act of a corporation cloaking its lack of social responsibility by insincere membership in the UN Global Compact.

---

[63] "Komatsu Contributing to Safe and Revitalized Communities," *Komatsu Views,* no. 1 (2010), pp. 18–19.

[64] *United Nations Global Compact Annual Review–Anniversary Edition* June 2010, pp. 10 and 16.

However, skeptics think the emphasis is on building the rolls, not on fundamental change, that business is made to feel comfortable, not challenged. Most large MNCs already have broad CSR programs. After joining the Global Compact they simply report what they already do and go on unchanged. Now, say critics, the compact needs to demand more. It must convert itself from a platform for bluewashing to a leadership force that challenges MNCs with a more ambitious agenda.[65] It could, for example, require that top executives link their pay to the achievement of social responsibility goals.[66] Such changes are far in the future, so skepticism about the effort is likely to continue.

A perceived shortcoming of both the *OECD Guidelines* and the Global Compact is the lack of a hard fist behind their normative codes. We turn now to the realm of law for another effort to ensure responsible MNC behavior, one that promises hard sanctions.

THE ALIEN TORT CLAIMS ACT

Alien Tort Claims Act
A 1789 law permitting foreign citizens to litigate, in a federal court, wrongful actions occurring anywhere in the world that violate international law or U.S. treaties.

Critics suspect that in the obscurity of distant places some MNCs behave badly. The docket of cases brought under a singular law, the *Alien Tort Claims Act*, opens a window into some serious allegations. This law allows foreign citizens to sue individuals and corporations of any nation in U.S. courts for wrongful acts committed anywhere in the world violating the law of nations or U.S. treaties. It allows lawsuits against individuals and corporations of any nation.

The original intent of the Alien Tort Claims Act, an old law from 1789, was to protect the rights of ambassadors and to try pirates.[67] Long in disuse, it was rediscovered in the 1990s by progressive and labor lawyers seeking to prosecute MNCs for wrongful actions anywhere in the world. Since then, it has been the basis of more than 125 cases against corporations and their executives for actions occurring in 60 countries. Most cases are eventually dismissed, but they often wind through interminable appeals. Several corporations have tired after more than a decade and settled, while continuing to deny guilt. Only two cases have reached trial and in both federal juries acquitted the corporate defendants.

The initial wave of Alien Tort Claims Act suits alleged human rights abuses by corporations. In one, a group of Indonesian villagers accused ExxonMobil of directing soldiers guarding its natural gas fields to kidnap, rape, and murder villagers who opposed its activities, then providing bulldozers to help the troops dig

---

[65] See, for example, Jem Bendell, "What If We are Failing? Towards a Post-Crisis Compact for Systemic Change," *Journal of Corporate Citizenship,* Summer 2010; and James Epstein-Reeves, "Critics of the UN Global Compact Sound Off," *Citizen Polity,* November 11, 2009; http://citizenpolity.com/2009/11/11/critics-of-the-un-global-compact-sound-off/.

[66] Lifeworth Consulting, "From Global Compact to Global Impact," August 2010, at www.lifeworth.com/consult/2010/08/from-global-compact-to-global-impact/.

[67] The entirety of this statute is a brief clause in the Judiciary Act of 1789 providing that "the district courts shall have original jurisdiction of any civil action by an alien for a tort only, committed in violation of the law of nations or a treaty of the United States."

mass graves.[68] In another, Chevron was charged with helping to repress native activists who opposed oil drilling. It had supplied helicopters to government troops, who flew to a Chevron drilling rig and shot at protesters , killing two and wounding others.[69]

In time, suits appeared based on labor abuses. Relatives of 23 people killed and tortured in Argentina during the years of its military dictatorship have sued Daimler. They accuse its Mercedes-Benz subsidiary of collaborating with the regime by identifying union leaders who were then abducted.[70] Adults and children aged 6 through 16 working at a rubber plantation in Liberia have sued tiremaker Bridgestone Corporation. The workers believe that through unfair labor practices the Japanese company turned them into "modern day slaves, forced to work by the coercion of poverty."[71]

A few suits allege environmental crimes. Residents of New Guinea say that as Rio Tinto worked a gold mine on the island of Bougainville it forced natives to toil in "slavelike" conditions and dumped 200,000 tons of waste rock into waterways each day. The damage caused "environmental devastation" that "undermined the physical and mental health of the island's residents."[72] In another case, DynCorp International was accused of erratic herbicide spraying in Colombia that missed targeted cocaine and heroin fields, hitting a town where it made 89 percent of the people sick and killed four.[73] At the time it was acting as a contractor for the U.S. State Department, which sought to interrupt the flow of illegal narcotics from the country by destroying poppy plantations.

The future of Alien Tort Claims Act cases is uncertain. So far, federal courts have been highly skeptical of legal theories extending an archaic eighteenth century law to the actions of modern corporations.[74] Yet it is an area of law under development as plaintiffs probe with various theories, appealing repeatedly, seeking the key to victory. As the cases go on, opinion about them is divided. Business groups say they victimize the world's poor "by imposing an enormous tax on investment in developing countries at a time the world desperately needs such investment."[75] Progressives believe they bring justice for the oppressed, giving "people in foreign countries comfort that U.S. corporations and officials will abide by international standards and not go to different corners of the globe and exploit the local populations."[76]

[68] *Doe v. ExxonMobil Corporation,* 473 F.3d 345 (2007).

[69] *Bowoto v. Chevron Corp.,* C99-02506 SI, N. Dist. Cal. (2007).

[70] *Bauman v. DaimlerChrysler AG,* 579 F.3d 1088 (2009).

[71] *Roe v. Bridgestone Corporation,* 492 F.Supp. 2d 988 (2007), at 995.

[72] *Sarei v. Rio Tinto Ltd.,* 487 F.3d 1193 (2007), at 1198.

[73] *Arias v. DynCorp.,* 517 F. Supp. 2d 221 (2007).

[74] In *Kiobel v. Royal Dutch Petroleum,* 2010 U.S. App. LEXIS 19382, for example, the Second Circuit held that corporations are not subject to liability under international human rights law. Executives, as individuals, could still be sued.

[75] Curtis A. Bradley and Jack L. Goldsmith, "Rights Case Gone Wrong," *Washington Post,* April 19, 2009, p. A19.

[76] Katherine Gallagher, attorney with the Center for Constitutional Rights, quoted in Nathan Koppel, "Arcane Law Brings Conflicts From Overseas to U.S. Courts," *The Wall Street Journal,* August 27, 2009, p. A11.

FIGURE 11.8
**Drummond
Company
2010**

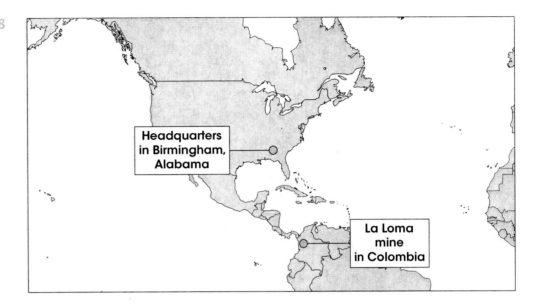

The Drummond Company on Trial

The Drummond Company, a coal mining firm headquartered in Birmingham, Alabama, was the target of the first Alien Tort Claims Act case to go to trial. It was sued by the widows of three murdered union leaders in Colombia. They alleged that the president of its Colombian subsidiary, acting with the knowledge of top U.S. executives, ordered their husbands killed.[77] They requested compensation for these deaths.

Drummond was founded in 1935 to mine coal in Alabama. The company gradually moved across tiers of internationalization. First, it began exporting coal from its Alabama mines to Europe. Then it made its first direct foreign investment by building a mine in northeast Colombia. When it entered Colombia in the late 1980s, it was aware of the country's violence. A shadowy, ongoing civil war persists between the government, Marxist guerillas, and right-wing paramilitary groups. Nevertheless, Drummond put $1 billion into its La Loma mine, a huge facility that ships 25 million tons of coal to Europe and the United States each year (see Figure 11.8). A new subsidiary headquartered in Alabama ran the mine.

In 2001, paramilitaries pulled two La Loma union leaders from a company bus carrying shift workers. Witnesses said the paramilitaries identified the two by name, forced them to show identification, and told both men they "had a problem with Drummond." Outside the bus, in view of its passengers, they shot one victim several times in the head. The other was abducted and found dead several hours later, having been tortured, then shot in the head. Five months later, a third union leader was taken from a public bus on his way home, tortured, and shot twice in the head.

[77] *Complaint, Rodriquez v. Drummond,* CV-02-BE-0665-W, N. D. Ala., March 2002. See also *Rodriquez v. Drummond,* 256 F. Supp. 2d 1250 (2003).

Their widows, using attorneys with the United Steelworkers union in Pittsburgh, filed an Alien Tort Claims Act lawsuit. They sued Drummond in a U.S. district court alleging its managers had committed a wrongful act, aiding and abetting the murders in violation of both "the law of nations," which upholds the fundamental right to associate and organize, and an American law, the Torture Victim Protection Act of 1991, which prohibits extrajudicial killings.[78] The widows were also helped by the International Labor Rights Fund, a Washington, D.C., group that supports Alien Tort Claims Act cases to "address the fundamental human rights abuses that unfettered capitalism leaves in its wake."[79] Its members worked in Colombia, gathering evidence and handing out "Wanted for Murder" posters picturing Drummond's CEO, Garry Drummond.

Drummond "emphatically" denied the allegations and filed slander charges against an individual in Colombia who accused it of ordering the murders. It was "appalled by the vicious, relentless and unfathomable attacks" and refused to settle with the widows.[80] It emphasized its positive impact in Colombia, where it had invested more than $1 billion, employed thousands, created a coal export market, paid the government hundreds of millions of dollars in royalties and taxes, and improved living standards around the mine. Yet for its trade union opponents these benefits meant little.

In 2007 the case came to trial in Alabama. Several witnesses testified that Drummond made covert payments to local paramilitaries for security services and secretly employed their members. Regular Colombian soldiers guarded its property. The Colombian military has a shadowy, cooperative relationship with paramilitaries, and the lawsuit alleged those forces were allowed on the mine property. One former paramilitary said the president of Drummond's Colombia subsidiary met with one of the private army's leaders, paying him $200,000 to "neutralize" the first two union leaders. This and other evidence was hearsay and circumstantial. Much of the testimony came from other paramilitaries who submitted affidavits while in Colombia jails. Drummond questioned the honesty of witnesses with criminal histories. One of its lawyers argued that, "Nobody at Drummond . . . believes that the rules don't apply to them just because they are doing business in Colombia."[81]

---

[78] Specifically, the company's actions violated the "law of nations" found in International Labour Organization Conventions 87 and 98, which protect the right of labor to associate and bargain collectively; Article 8 of the International Covenant on Economic, Social, and Cultural Rights, which protects the right to associate and organize; Article 22 of the International Covenant on Civil and Political Rights, which protects the right to freely associate; the Universal Declaration of Human Rights, which protects *inter alia* rights to associate, organize, and bargain collectively; and the Geneva Conventions, which codify the law of war and prohibit murder by combatants.

[79] International Labor Rights Fund, *Annual Report 2006* (Washington, DC: ILRF, 2006), p. 1.

[80] Drummond Ltd., "Drummond Does Not Negotiate with Illegal Groups," press release, Bogotá, Colombia, March 21, 2007.

[81] William H. Jeffress, quoted in Kyle Whitmire, "Suit in U.S. over Murders in Colombia," *The New York Times,* July 13, 2007, p. A4.

After only a day of deliberation the jury returned a verdict of not guilty, clearing Drummond. Nonetheless, like other Alien Tort Claims Act cases targeting corporations, its backers refuse to let it die, preferring to sink their teeth into the company and hold on. Appeals to reopen the case ended in failure a year later.[82] Then, in 2009, Colombian authorities arrested and convicted the men responsible for the murders. However, the United Steelworkers believed that Drummond executives, the "intellectual authors" of the murders, were still fugitives from justice. It now sued on behalf of the murdered men's children, claiming new evidence that Drummond was involved.[83] When a judge dismissed this case, it sued again on behalf of 252 relatives of 67 union members and farm workers killed by paramilitaries in areas near the Drummond mine, accusing Drummond of paying the paramilitaries to conduct a reign of terror.[84] That case is ongoing. Drummond has announced it will sell its Colombian property and leave the country—if it can find a buyer.

The story of the Drummond litigation illustrates how one law can be used to check, limit, and harass MNCs. To date its main effect has been to harass, but it may develop into a more powerful check with time.

CONCLUDING OBSERVATIONS

Multinational corporations are highly variable entities. They differ in size, strategy, structure, geographic reach, and extent of foreign investment. These variables interact with forces in as many as 200 host economies—poor, developing, and advanced—making generalization about MNC behavior difficult.

It is too great a leap to argue that MNCs dominate and define the global economy. They are better understood as entities reacting to forces of globalization along with governments, NGOs, and international agencies. They can be understood as reacting to change and opportunity with an inner business logic.

While MNCs are widely mistrusted and still act badly at times, the progressive community now has more appreciation of the need to bring them into the fold of cooperation with governments and NGOs to address issues such as poverty, fresh water shortages, and climate warming. In the past two decades a firmament of norms, codes, principles, and citizenship schemes has appeared to guide MNCs. It is too early to say these efforts have caused much increase in MNC responsibility. However, their direction is clear. It is now impossible for the largest, most powerful MNCs to avoid joining at least some collaborative CSR initiatives. Corporate actions are being compared with the principles, reporting standards, and UN-generated "universal" norms that drive arrangements such as the Global Compact. To retain long-term legitimacy, MNCs must show acceptable performance.

---

[82] *Romero v. Drummond*, 552 F.3d 1303 (2008).

[83] *Baloco v. Drummond*, 09-CV-00557, N. D. Ala. (2009).

[84] *Jane Doe v. Drummond*, 09-CV-01041, N. D. Ala. November 9, 2009.

Union Carbide Corporation and Bhopal

On December 3, 1984, tragedy unfolded at the Union Carbide pesticide plant in Bhopal, India. Water entered a large tank where a volatile chemical was stored, starting a violent reaction. Rapidly, a sequence of safety procedures and devices failed. Fugitive vapors sailed over plant boundaries, forming a lethal cloud that moved with the south wind, enveloping slum dwellings, searing lungs and eyes, asphyxiating fated souls, scarring the unlucky.

Bhopal is the worst sudden industrial accident ever in terms of human life lost. Death and injury estimates vary widely. The official death toll set forth by the Indian government for that night is 5,295, with an additional 527,894 serious injuries. Greenpeace has put the death toll at 16,000.[1]

The incredible event galvanized industry critics. "Like Auschwitz and Hiroshima," wrote one, "the catastrophe at Bhopal is a manifestation of something fundamentally wrong in our stewardship of the earth."[2] Union Carbide was debilitated and slowly declined as a company after the incident. The government of India earned mixed reviews for its response. The chemical industry changed, but according to some, not enough. And the gas victims endure a continuing struggle to get compensation and medical care.[3]

UNION CARBIDE IN INDIA

Union Carbide established an Indian subsidiary named Union Carbide India Ltd. (UCIL) in 1934. At first the company owned a 60 percent majority interest, but over the years this was reduced to 50.9 percent. Shares in the ownership of the other 49.1 percent traded on the Bombay Stock Exchange. This ownership scheme was significant because although UCIL operated with a great deal of autonomy, it gave the appearance that Union Carbide was in control of its operations. By itself, UCIL was one of India's largest firms. In 1984, the year of the incident, it

had 14 plants and 9,000 employees, including 500 at Bhopal. Most of its revenues came from selling Eveready batteries.

Union Carbide decided to build a pesticide plant at Bhopal in 1969. The plant formulated pesticides from chemical ingredients imported to the site. At that time, there was a growing demand in India and throughout Asia for pesticides because of the "green revolution," a type of planned agriculture that requires intensive use of pesticides and fertilizers on special strains of food crops such as wheat, rice, and corn. Although pesticides may be misused and pose some risk, they also have great social value. Without pesticides, damage to crops, losses in food storage, and toxic mold growth in food supplies would cause much loss of life from starvation and food poisoning, especially in countries such as India. Exhibit 1 shows a Union Carbide advertisement from the 1960s that describes the company's activities in India.

The Bhopal plant would supply these pesticides and serve a market anticipated to expand rapidly. The plant's location in Bhopal was encouraged by tax incentives from the city and the surrounding state of Madhya Pradesh. After a few years, however, the Indian government pressured UCIL to stop importing chemical ingredients. The company then proposed to manufacture methyl isocyanate (MIC) at the plant rather than ship it in from Carbide facilities outside the country. This was a fateful decision.

Methyl isocyanate, CH_3NCO, is a colorless, odorless liquid. Its presence can be detected by tearing and the burning sensation it causes in the eyes and noses of exposed individuals. At the Bhopal plant it was used as an intermediate chemical in pesticide manufacture. It was not the final product; rather, MIC molecules were created, then pumped into a vessel where they reacted with other chemicals. The reaction created unique molecules with qualities that disrupted insect nervous systems, causing convulsions and death. The plant turned out two similar pesticides marketed under the names Sevin and Temik.

In 1975 UCIL received a permit from the Ministry of Industry in New Delhi to build an MIC production unit at the Bhopal plant. Two months before the

---

[1] "Has the World Forgotten Bhopal?" *The Lancet,* December 2, 2000, p. 1863.

[2] David Weir, *The Bhopal Syndrome* (San Francisco: Sierra Club Books, 1987), p. xii.

[3] Rama Lakshmi, "Justice for Bhopal Victims," *The Economic Times,* February 18, 2011.

EXHIBIT 1
Union Carbide Advertisement This ad appeared in *Fortune* magazine in April 1962.

Source: Courtesy of Union Carbide Corporation.

Science helps build a new India

Oxen working the fields . . . the eternal river Ganges . . . jeweled elephants on parade. Today these symbols of ancient India exist side by side with a new sight—modern industry. India has developed bold new plans to build its economy and bring the promise of a bright future to its more than 400,000,000 people. ▶ But India needs the technical knowledge of the western world. For example, working with Indian engineers and technicians, Union Carbide recently made available its vast scientific resources to help build a major chemicals and plastics plant near Bombay. ▶ Throughout the free world, Union Carbide has been actively engaged in building plants for the manufacture of chemicals, plastics, carbons, gases, and metals. The people of Union Carbide welcome the opportunity to use their knowledge and skills in partnership with the citizens of so many great countries.

A HAND IN THINGS TO COME

UNION CARBIDE

WRITE *for booklet B-3 "The Exciting Universe of Union Carbide", which tells how research in the fields of carbons, chemicals, gases, metals, plastics and nuclear energy keeps bringing new wonders into your life.*
Union Carbide Corporation, 270 Park Avenue, New York 17, N.Y.

issuance of this permit, the city of Bhopal had enacted a development plan requiring dangerous industries to relocate in an industrial zone 15 miles away. Pursuant to the plan, M. N. Buch, the Bhopal city administrator, tried to move the UCIL pesticide plant and convert the site to housing and light commercial use. For reasons that are unclear, his effort failed, and Buch was soon transferred to forestry duties elsewhere.

The MIC unit was based on a process design provided by Union Carbide's engineers in the United States and elaborated by engineers in India.

The design required storage of MIC in big tanks. An alternative used at most other pesticide plants would have been to produce small amounts of MIC only as they were consumed in pesticide production. The decision to use large storage tanks was based on an optimistic projection that pesticide sales would grow dramatically. Since an Indian law, the Foreign Exchange Regulation Act of 1973, requires foreign multinationals to share technology and use Indian resources, detailed design work was done by an Indian subsidiary of a British firm. Local labor using Indian equipment and materials built the unit.

In 1980 the MIC unit began operation under UCIL's management. During the five years of design and construction, densely populated shantytowns sprang up nearby, inhabited mainly by impoverished, unemployed people who had left rural areas seeking their fortunes in the city. A childlike faith that the facility was a benevolent presence turning out miraculous substances to make plants grow was widespread among them.

In fact, when the MIC unit came on line the plant began to pose higher risk to its neighbors; it now made the basic chemicals used in pesticides rather than using shipped-in ingredients. One step in the manufacture of MIC, for example, creates phosgene, the lethal "mustard gas" used in World War I. The benighted crowd by the plant abided unaware.

In 1981 a phosgene leak killed one worker, and a crusading Indian journalist wrote articles about dangers to the population. No one acted. A year later, a second phosgene leak forced temporary evacuation of some surrounding neighborhoods. Worker safety and environmental inspections of the plant were done by the state Department of Labour, an agency with only 15 factory inspectors to cover 8,000 plants and a record of lax enforcement.[4] Oversight was not vigorous.

Meanwhile, the Indian economy had turned down, and stiff competition from other pesticide firms marketing new, less expensive products reduced demand for Sevin and Temik. As revenues fell, so did the plant's budget, and it was necessary to defer some maintenance, lessen the rigor of training, and lay off workers. By the time of the incident, the

MIC unit operated with six workers per shift, half the number anticipated by its designers.

UNION CARBIDE'S RELATIONSHIP WITH THE BHOPAL PLANT

What was the organizational relationship of Union Carbide Corporation in the United States to its subsidiary, Union Carbide India Ltd., and ultimately to the Bhopal plant? How much direction and control did the corporate parent half a world away in Danbury, Connecticut, exercise over the facility?

The Bhopal plant fit into the Union Carbide management hierarchy as shown in the chart in Exhibit 2. Although Carbide employees from the United States managed the plant in its early years, in 1982, under pressure from the government, it was turned over to Indian managers. The experience of colonial rule in India created a strong political need for leaders to put on shows of strength with foreign investors. Indians felt a burning desire to avoid any appearance of subjugation and demanded self-sufficiency. This is what had led to passage of the law requiring foreign investors to use Indian firms and workers in certain ways—and to put pressure on Union Carbide to turn the plant completely over to its Indian subsidiary.

The Bhopal plant was but one of 500 facilities in 34 countries in the Union Carbide Corporation universe. There was no regular or direct reporting relationship between it and Union Carbide's headquarters in Connecticut. At the request of UCIL, employees of Union Carbide had gone to India twice to perform safety inspections on the plant. Other than those occasions, managers in the United States had received information or reporting about the plant only infrequently and irregularly when major changes or capital expenditures were requested. Thus, the Bhopal plant was run with near total independence from the American corporation. In litigation to determine where victims' lawsuits should be tried, a U.S. court described its autonomy in these words:

> [Union Carbide Corporation's] participation [in the design and construction of the plant] was limited and its involvement in plant operations terminated long before the accident . . . [It] was constructed and managed by Indians in India. No Americans were

---

4 Sheila Jasanoff, "Managing India's Environment," *Environment,* October 1986, p. 33.

EXHIBIT 2

**Union
Carbide's
Organization
Structure as
Related to the
Bhopal Plant**

- Board of Directors
- Warren M. Anderson Chairman and CEO
- Alec Flamm President
- Technology, Services & Specialty Products Group — USA
- Union Carbide Agricultural Products Company, Inc. — USA
- Union Carbide Eastern, Inc. — Hong Kong
- Board of Directors
- Union Carbide India Ltd. — Bombay
- Bhopal Pesticide Plant

employed at the plant at the time of the accident. In the five years from 1980 to 1984, although more than 1,000 Indians were employed at the plant, only one American was employed there and he left in 1982. No Americans visited the plant for more than one year prior to the accident, and during the 5-year period before the accident the communications between the plant and the United States were almost nonexistent.[5]

Thus, the Bhopal plant was run by UCIL with near total independence from the American corporation. Despite this, shortly after the gas leak Chairman Warren M. Anderson said that Carbide accepted "moral responsibility" for the tragedy.

[5] *In re Union Carbide Corporation Gas Plant Disaster at Bhopal,* 809 F.2d 195 (1987), at 200.

THE GAS LEAK

On the eve of the disaster, tank 610, one of three storage tanks in the MIC unit, sat filled with 11,290 gallons of MIC. The tank, having a capacity of 15,000 gallons, was a partly buried, stainless-steel, pressurized vessel. Its purpose was to take in MIC made elsewhere in the plant and hold it for some time until it was sent to the pesticide production area through a transfer pipe, there to be converted into Sevin or Temik.

At about 9:30 p.m. a supervisor ordered an operator, R. Khan, to unclog four filter valves near the MIC production area by washing them out with water. Khan connected a water hose to the piping above the clogged valves but neglected to insert a slip blind, a device that seals lines to prevent water leaks into adjacent pipes. Khan's omission, if it occurred, would have violated established procedure.

Because of either this careless washing method or the introduction of water elsewhere, 120 to 240 gallons of water entered tank 610, starting a powerful exothermic (heat building) reaction. At first, operators were unaware of the danger, and for two hours pressure in the tank rose unnoticed. At 10:20 p.m. they logged tank pressure at 2 pounds per square inch (ppsi). At 11:30 p.m. a new operator in the MIC control room noticed that the pressure was 10 ppsi, but he was unconcerned because this was within tolerable limits, gauges were often wrong, and he had not read the log to learn that the pressure was now five times what it had been an hour earlier.

Unfortunately, refrigeration units that cooled the tanks had been shut down for five months to save electricity costs. Had they been running, as the MIC processing manual required, the heat rise from reaction with the water might have taken place over days instead of hours.

As pressure built, leaks developed. Soon workers sensed the presence of MIC. Their eyes watered. At 11:45 p.m. someone spotted a small, yellowish drip from overhead piping. The supervisor suggested fixing the leak after the regular 12:15 a.m. tea break. At 12:40 the tea break ended. By now the control room gauge showed the pressure in tank 610 was 40 ppsi. In a short time it rose to 55 ppsi, the top of the scale. A glance at the tank temperature gauge brought more bad news. The MIC was 77 degrees Fahrenheit, 36 degrees higher than the specified safety limit and hot enough to vaporize. Startled by readings on the gauges, the control room operator ran out to tank 610. He felt radiating heat and heard its concrete cover cracking. Within seconds, a pressure-release valve opened and a white cloud of deadly MIC vapor shot into the atmosphere with a high-decibel screech.

Back in the control room, operators turned a switch to activate the vent gas scrubber, a safety device designed to neutralize escaping toxic gases by circulating them through caustic soda. It was down for maintenance and inoperable. Even if it had been on line, it was too small to handle the explosive volume of MIC shooting from the tank. A flare tower built to burn off toxic gases before they reached the atmosphere was also off line; it had been dismantled for maintenance and an elbow joint was missing. Another emergency measure, transferring MIC from

tank 610 to one of the other storage tanks, was foreclosed because both were too full. This situation also violated the processing manual, which called for leaving one tank empty as a safeguard.

At about 1:00 a.m. an operator triggered an alarm to warn workers of danger. The plant superintendent, entering the control room, ordered a water spraying device be directed on the venting gas, but this last-resort measure had little effect. Now most workers ran in panic, ignoring four emergency buses they were supposed to drive through the surrounding area to evacuate residents. Two intrepid operators stayed at the control panel, sharing the only available oxygen mask when the room filled with MIC vapor. Finally, at 2:30, the pressure in tank 610 dropped, the leaking safety valve resealed, and the venting ceased. Roughly 10,000 gallons of MIC, about 90 percent of the tank's contents, was now settling over the city.

That night the wind was calm, the temperature about 60°, and the dense chemical mist lingered just above the ground. Animals died. The gas attacked people in the streets and seeped into their bedrooms. Those who panicked and ran into the night air suffered higher exposures.

As the poisonous cloud enveloped victims, MIC reacted with water in their eyes. This reaction, like the reaction in tank 610, created heat that burned corneal cells, rendering them opaque. Residents with cloudy, burning eyes staggered about. Many suffered shortness of breath, coughing fits, inflammation of the respiratory tract, and chemical pneumonia. In the lungs, MIC molecules reacted with moisture, causing chemical burns. Fluid oozed from seared tissue and pooled, a condition called pulmonary edema, and its victims literally drowned in their own secretions. Burned lung tissue eventually healed, creating scarred areas that diminished breathing capacity. Because MIC is so reactive with water, simply breathing through a wet cloth would have saved many lives. However, people lacked this simple knowledge.

UNION CARBIDE REACTS

Awakened early in the morning, CEO Warren M. Anderson rushed to Carbide's Danbury, Connecticut, headquarters and learned of the rising death toll. When the extent of the disaster was evident, a senior management committee held an urgent meeting.

It decided to send emergency medical supplies, respirators, oxygen (all Carbide products), and an American doctor with knowledge of MIC to Bhopal.

The next day, Tuesday, December 5, Carbide dispatched a team of technical experts to examine the plant. On Thursday, Anderson himself left for India. However, after arriving in Bhopal, he was charged with criminal negligence, placed under house arrest, and then asked to leave the country.

With worldwide attention focused on Bhopal, Carbide held daily press conferences. Christmas parties were canceled. Flags at Carbide facilities flew at half-staff. All of its nearly 100,000 employees observed a moment of silence for the victims. It gave $1 million to an emergency relief fund and offered to turn its guesthouse in Bhopal into an orphanage.

Months later, the company offered another $5 million, but the money was refused because Indian politicians trembled in fear that they would be seen cooperating with the company. The Indian public reviled anything associated with Carbide. Later, when the state government learned that Carbide had set up a training school for the unemployed in Bhopal, it flattened the facility with bulldozers.

CARBIDE FIGHTS LAWSUITS AND A TAKEOVER BID

No sooner had the mists cleared than American attorneys arrived in Bhopal seeking litigants for damage claims. They walked the streets signing up plaintiffs. Just four days after the gas leak, the first suit was filed in a U.S. court; soon cases seeking $40 billion in damages for 200,000 Indians were filed against Carbide.

However, the Indian Parliament passed a law giving the Indian government an exclusive right to represent victims. Then India sued in the United States. Union Carbide offered $350 million to settle existing claims (an offer rejected by the Indian government) and brought a motion to have the cases heard in India. Both Indian and American lawyers claiming to represent victims opposed the motion, knowing that wrongful death awards in India were small compared with those in the United States. However, in 1986 a federal court ruled that the cases should be heard in India, noting that "to retain the litigation in [the United States] . . . would be yet another example

of imperialism, another situation in which an established sovereign inflicted its rules, its standards and values on a developing nation."[6] This was a victory for Carbide and a defeat for American lawyers, who could not carry their cases to India in defiance of the government.

In late 1986 the Indian government filed a $3.3 billion civil suit against Carbide in an Indian court.[7] The suit alleged that Union Carbide Corporation, in addition to being majority shareholder in Union Carbide India Ltd., had exercised policy control over the establishment and design of the Bhopal plant. The Bhopal plant was defective in design because its safety standards were lower than similar Carbide plants in the United States. Carbide had consciously permitted inadequate safety standards to exist. The suit also alleged that Carbide was conducting an "ultrahazardous activity" at the Bhopal plant and had strict and absolute liability for compensating victims regardless of whether the plant was operating carefully or not.

Carbide countered with the defense that it had a holding company relationship with UCIL and never exercised direct control over the Bhopal plant; it was prohibited from doing so by Indian laws requiring management by Indian nationals. In addition to the civil suit, Carbide's chairman, Warren Anderson, and several UCIL executives were charged with homicide in a Bhopal court. This apparently was a pressure tactic, since no attempt to arrest them was made.

On top of its legal battle, Carbide had to fight for its independence. In December 1985, GAF Corporation, which had been accumulating Carbide's shares, made a takeover bid. After a suspenseful monthlong battle, Carbide fought off GAF, but only at the cost of taking on enormous new debt to buy back 55 percent of its outstanding shares. This huge debt had to be reduced because interest payments were crippling. So in 1986 Carbide sold $3.5 billion of assets, including its most popular consumer brands—Eveready batteries, Glad bags, and Prestone antifreeze. It had sacrificed stable sources of revenue and was now a smaller, weaker company more exposed to cyclical economic trends.

[6] *In re Union Carbide Corporation Gas Plant Disaster,* 634 F. Supp. 867 (S.D.N.Y. 1986).

[7] *Union of India v. Union Carbide Corp. and Union Carbide India Ltd.,* Bhopal District Court, No. 1113 (1986).

INVESTIGATING THE CAUSE OF THE MIC LEAK

In the days following the gas leak, there was worldwide interest in pinning down its precise cause. A team of reporters from *The New York Times* interviewed plant workers in Bhopal. Their six-week investigation concluded that a large volume of water entered tank 610, causing the accident.[8] The *Times* reporters thought that water had entered when R. Khan failed to use a slip blind as he washed out piping. Water from his hose simply backed up and eventually flowed about 400 feet into the tank. Their account was widely circulated and this theory, called the "water washing theory," gained currency. However, it was not to be the only theory of the accident's cause.

Immediately after the disaster, Union Carbide also rushed a team of investigators to Bhopal. But the team got little cooperation from Indian authorities operating in a climate of anti-Carbide popular protest. It was denied access to plant records and workers. Yet the investigators got to look at tank 610 and took core samples from its bottom residue. These samples went back to the United States, where more than 500 experimental chemical reactions were undertaken to explain their chemical composition. In March 1985 Carbide finally released its report. It stated that entry of water into the tank caused the gas release, but it rejected the water washing theory.

Instead, Carbide scientists felt the only way that an amount of water sufficient to cause the observed reaction could have entered the tank was through accidental or deliberate connection of a water hose to piping that led directly into the tank. This was possible because outlets for compressed air, nitrogen, steam, and water were stationed throughout the plant. The investigators rejected the water washing hypothesis for several reasons. The piping system was designed to prevent water contamination even without a slip blind. Valves between the piping being washed and tank 610 were found closed after the

accident. And the volume of water required to create the reaction—1,000 to 2,000 pounds—was far too much to be explained by valve leakage.

The Carbide report gave a plausible alternative to the water washing theory, but within months an investigation by the Indian government rejected it. This study, made by Indian scientists and engineers, confirmed that the entry of water into the MIC tank caused the reaction but concluded that the improper washing procedure was to blame (see Exhibit 3).

There matters stood until late 1985, when the Indian government allowed Carbide more access to plant records and employees. Carbide investigators sought out the plant's employees. More than 70 interviews and careful examination of plant records and physical evidence led them to conclude that the cause of the gas leak was sabotage by a disgruntled employee who intentionally hooked a water hose to the tank.

Here is the sequence of events on the night of December 2–3 that Carbide set forth. At 10:20 p.m. the pressure gauge on tank 610 read 2 ppsi. This meant that no water had yet entered the tank and no reaction had begun. At 10:45 the regular shift change occurred. Shift changes take half an hour, and the MIC storage area would have been deserted. At this time, an operator who had been angry for days about his failure to get a promotion stole into the area. He unscrewed the local pressure indicator gauge on tank 610, hooked up a rubber water hose, and turned the water on. Five minutes would have sufficed to do this.

Carbide claimed to know the name of this person, but it has never been made public. Its investigative team speculated that his intention was simply to ruin the MIC batch in the tank; it is doubtful that this worker realized all that might happen. The interviews revealed that the workers thought of MIC chiefly as a lacrimator, a chemical that causes tearing; they did not regard it as a lethal hazard.

Now the plot thickens. A few minutes after midnight, MIC operators noted the fast pressure rise in tank 610. Walking to the tank, they found the water hose connected and removed it, then informed their supervisors. The supervisors tried to prevent a catastrophic pressure rise by draining water from tank 610. Between 12:15 and 12:30 a.m., just minutes before the explosive release, they transferred about 1 metric ton of the contents from tank 610 to a holding tank. Water is heavier than MIC, and the transfer was made through a drain in the tank's bottom; thus, the

---

[8] The team wrote a series of articles. See Stuart Diamond, "The Bhopal Disaster: How It Happened," *The New York Times*, January 28, 1985; Thomas J. Lueck, "Carbide Says Inquiry Showed Errors but Is Incomplete," *The New York Times*, January 28, 1985; Stuart Diamond, "The Disaster in Bhopal: Workers Recall Horror," *The New York Times*, January 30, 1985; and Robert Reinhold, "Disaster in Bhopal: Where Does Blame Lie?" *The New York Times*, January 31, 1985.

EXHIBIT 3   **Two Theories Clash on Water Entry into MIC Tank**

According to the water washing theory of the Indian government, water was introduced through a hose into bleeder A at filter pressure safety valve lines. As the hose kept running, water proceeded through the leaking valve in that area and rose up into the relief valve vent header line (RVVH). It took a turn at the jumper line, B, and moved into the process vent header line (PVH), filling it in the reverse direction all the way to the slip blind, C. When PVH was completely filled, water rose at line D and proceeded into MIC storage tank 610.

On February 8, 1985, two months after the leak, India's Central Bureau of Investigation drilled a hole in the PVH line at point E to drain any water left in the line. No water emerged. Carbide says this fact alone disproves the water washing theory. The fact that various valves in the pathway to the tank were closed also disproves the theory, according to Carbide.

Carbide espouses an alternative theory: The company says it has proof that water was introduced by a "disgruntled employee" who removed pressure gauge F, attached a hose to the open piping, and ran water into the MIC tank. Gas then escaped through a rupture disk and proceeded through the RVVH and out the vent gas scrubber.

Source: Courtesy of Union Carbide.

supervisors hoped to remove the water. They failed, and within 15 minutes the relief valve blew.

The investigators had physical evidence to support this scenario. After the accident, the local pressure gauge hole on tank 610 was still open and no plug had been inserted, as would have been normal for routine maintenance. When the MIC unit was examined, a crude drawing of the hose connection was found on the back of one page from that night's log book. Also, operators outside the MIC unit told the investigation team that MIC operators had told them about the hose connection that night. In addition, log entries had been falsified, revealing a crude cover-up effort. The major falsification was an attempt to hide the transfer of contents from tank 610.

Why did the supervisors and operators attempt a cover-up? The Carbide investigators gave this explanation.

Not knowing if the attempted transfer had exacerbated the incident, or whether they could have otherwise prevented it, or whether they would be blamed for not having notified plant management earlier, those involved decided on a cover-up. They altered logs that morning to disguise their involvement. As is common in many such incidents, the reflexive tendency to cover up simply took over.[9]

[9] Ashok S. Kalelkar, "Investigation of Large-Magnitude Incidents: Bhopal as a Case Study," paper presented at the Instititution of Chemical Engineers conference on Preventing Major Chemical Accidents, London, England, May 1988, p. 27.

EXHIBIT 4   A Breakdown of the $470 million Settlement

The settlement was based on calculations about the number and size of payments in a range of categories.

Source: Kim Fortun, *Advocacy after Bhopal* (Chicago: University of Chicago Press, 2001), p. 38.

Amount	Medical Categorization
$ 43,500,000	$14,500 payments for 3,000 deaths
50,000,000	$25,000 payments for up to 2,000 victims with injuries of "utmost severity"
156,000,000	$5,200 payments to 30,000 permanently disabled
64,300,000	$3,215 payments to 20,000 temporarily disabled
140,600,000	Amount to cover 150,000 minor injuries, future injuries, property damage, commercial loss, and other claims
15,600,000	Medical treatment and rehabilitation of victims
$470,000,000	Total settlement

A SETTLEMENT IS REACHED

The theory of deliberate sabotage became the centerpiece of Carbide's legal defense. However, the case never came to trial. In 1989 a settlement was reached in which Carbide agreed to pay $470 million to the Indian government, which would distribute the money to victims (see Exhibit 4). In return, India agreed to stop all legal action against Carbide, UCIL, and their executives. India agreed to this settlement, which was far less than the $3.3 billion it was asking for, because a trial and subsequent appeals in the Indian court system would likely have taken 20 years. Carbide paid the settlement using $200 million in insurance and taking a charge of $0.43 per share against 1988 net earnings of $5.31 per share. Victims' groups were upset because they thought the settlement too small, and they challenged it. In 1992 the Indian Supreme Court rejected these appeals but permitted reinstatement of criminal proceedings against Warren Anderson and eight UCIL managers.[10]

In 1993 India issued an arrest warrant for Anderson on charges of "culpable homicide not amounting to murder," but it has never been served. At the trial of the remaining UCIL defendants Indian prosecutors argued the managers were criminally negligent because they knew of lax operating procedures but failed to improve them to avoid costs. After 18 years,

186 witnesses, and various delaying motions, the court convicted seven managers (one had died) of a reduced charge, "causing death by negligence."[11] They were sentenced to two years in prison, and fined the equivalent of $2,100. All appealed and were released on bail. Victims and the Indian public found the punishment outrageously modest.

Meanwhile, the Indian government was slow and inefficient in distributing settlement funds to gas victims. In 1993, 40 special courts began processing claims, but the activity was riddled with corruption. Healthy people bribed physicians for false medical records with which they could get compensation. Twelve court officials were fired for soliciting bribes from gas victims seeking payments. All told, 574,366 claims were paid, including 14,824 death claims, with average compensation about $1,280. Ninety percent of all claims were settled for $550, the minimum allowed.[12]

Because the claims process moved at a glacial pace for years, the settlement money accrued interest and, after all claims were paid, $325 million remained. The government wanted to use the interest

[10] *Union Carbide Corp. v. Union of India,* AIR 1992 (S.C.) 248.

[11] India Central Bureau of Investigation, "Eight Accused Sentenced in Bhopal Gas Tragedy Case," press release, New Delhi, June 7, 2010.

[12] Paul Watson, "Cloud of Despair in Bhopal," *Los Angeles Times,* August 30, 2001, p. A6; and Government of Madhya Pradesh, Bhopal Gas Tragedy Relief and Rehabilitation Department, "Facts and Figures," www.mp.gov.in/bgtrrdmp/facts.htm, accessed June 2010.

to clean up soil contamination at the plant. But in 2004 the Indian Supreme Court ordered it distributed to the victims and families of the dead in amounts proportionate to claims already paid.[13]

AFTERMATH

In the wake of Bhopal, Congress passed legislation requiring chemical companies to disclose the presence of dangerous chemicals to people living near their plants and to create evacuation plans. The chemical industry's trade association adopted a program of more rigorous safety standards that all major firms now follow.

In 1994 Union Carbide sold its 50.9 percent equity in UCIL to the Indian subsidiary of a British company for $90 million. It gave all of this money to the Indian government for a hospital and clinics in Bhopal. After the sale, the company had no presence or current legal obligations in India. Nevertheless, Bhopal had destroyed it. As it exited India, it was a smaller, less resilient company. Forced to sell or spin off its most lucrative businesses, it grew progressively weaker. In 1984, the year of the gas leak, Carbide had 98,400 employees and sales of $9.5 billion; by 2000 it had only 11,000 employees and $5.9 billion in sales. The end came when it merged with Dow Chemical Co. in 2001 and its workforce suffered the bulk of cost-reduction layoffs.[14]

The pesticide plant never reopened. According to a recent visitor, "The old factory grounds, frozen in time, are an overgrown 11-acre forest of corroded tanks and pipes buzzing with cicadas, where cattle graze and women forage for twigs to cook their evening meal."[15] Chemical waste at the site has contaminated the groundwater. In 1998 the state government took over the plant and made cleanup plans, but never carried them out.

In 2004 the United States again denied a request by the Indian government to extradite Warren Anderson. Anderson, who is now 91, has dropped from public view. In the unlikely event of extradition, he would face a long trial. Recently, his wife told a reporter that he had been "haunted for many years" by the accident.[16]

The struggle of gas victims for compensation spawned an activist movement that lives on after more than 25 years. The lead organization is the International Campaign for Justice in Bhopal, a coalition of gas victim groups and charities. Survivors complain of chronic medical conditions including headaches, joint pain, shortness of breath, and psychiatric problems. They believe that gas exposure and toxic wastes from the plant have caused birth defects.

NEW TARGET: DOW CHEMICAL

After Dow Chemical absorbed Union Carbide it became the victims' bull's-eye. Both victims and the Indian government now demand that Dow pay for cleaning up the contaminated plant site and further compensate injured survivors. In 2010 the Indian government filed a petition with the Indian Supreme Court seeking to overturn its 1989 settlement "to cure a miscarriage of justice." The petition, still pending, seeks to force Dow Chemical to pay another $1.1 billion to the victims.[17] This is justified, argues the government, because the full extent of the disaster was unknown in 1989.

Members of the victim's movement have repeatedly sued in U.S. courts seeking to overturn the $470 million settlement, accusing Union Carbide of human rights violations, and trying to hold it responsible for cleaning up groundwater pollution at the plant site. All their efforts have so far failed, although one case still drags on.[18]

Victims otherwise harass the company. They have joined with progressive religious orders and pension funds in the United States to picket its shareholder's meetings while inside, friendly shareholders introduce

[13] "Compensation for Bhopal Victims," *The New York Times*, July 20, 2004, p. A6.

[14] Susan Warren, "Cost-Cutting Effort at Dow Chemical to Take 4,500 Jobs," *The Wall Street Journal*, May 2, 2001, p. A6.

[15] Somini Sengupta, "Decades Later, Toxic Sludge Torments Bhopal," *The New York Times*, July 7, 2008, p. 1.

[16] Celeste Katz, "India Sez Bust Bhopal Yank," *Daily News*, August 2, 2009, p. 26.

[17] Geeta Anand and Arlene Chang, "Dow Chemical Hit Again on Bhopal," *The Wall Street Journal*, December 4–5, 2010, p. B5.

[18] The case is *Janki Bai Sahu, et al. v. Union Carbide Corp.*, No. 04 Civ. 8825, 2010 U.S. Dist. LEXIS 23860, February 11, 2010. Two previous long-running cases are *In re Union Carbide Corp. Gas Plant Disaster at Bhopal*, 634 F. Supp. 842 (S.D.N.Y. 1986) and *Bano v. Union Carbide Corp. and Warren Anderson*, No. 99 Civ. 11329, 2005 U.S. Dist. LEXIS 22871, October 5, 2005).

resolutions asking Dow to acknowledge its responsibilities. All such resolutions have been defeated, garnering only single-digit percentages of the vote. Activists tried to embarrass Dow with a brand of bottled water named B'eau Pal containing groundwater from near the old plant. Children of gas victims once went on a 22-city U.S. tour to promote congressional hearings on Dow's responsibilities. No hearings were held.

Dow never wavers in denying any obligation. "While we have sympathy for this situation," said a company representative recently, "it is not Dow's responsibility, accountability or liability to bear."[19] But the activists are resolute. "I will fight until my last breath against Dow," says one gas survivor. "I will not give up."[20] The fight also has ideological meaning. One movement leader believes that "[u]nless those responsible are punished in an exemplary matter, the message that goes out to the corporate world is that you can kill and maim people and carry on with business as usual."[21]

POSTSCRIPT

Despite the passage of time, Bhopal does not fade away. The library bookshelf on it keeps growing.[22] It has been the subject of at least seven films, including a drama that was a box office hit in India. A tendentious book of reality fiction based on Bhopal became a best seller in Europe.[23] Told as a tragedy, the story stirs basic emotions. A Canadian critic reviewing a play on Bhopal found it badly written and acted, but nevertheless "a touching tale of human suffering" raising "such imposing themes as the relative worth of a human life and the intersection of greed and development in the Third World."[24] Doubtless these themes will keep the story alive.

Questions

1. Who is responsible for the Bhopal accident? How should blame be apportioned among parties involved, including Union Carbide Corporation, UCIL, plant workers, governments in India, or others?

2. What principles of corporate social responsibility and business ethics are applicable to the actions of the parties in question?

3. How well did the legal system work? Do you agree with the decision to try the lawsuits in India? Were victims fairly compensated? Was Union Carbide sufficiently punished?

4. Did Union Carbide handle the crisis well? How would you grade its performance in facing uniquely difficult circumstances?

5. Does Dow Chemical Company have any remaining legal liability, social responsibility, or ethical duty to address unresolved health and environmental claims of Bhopal victims?

6. What lessons can other corporations and countries learn from this story?

[19] Quoted in Brian Bowling, "Group from Bhopal Says Gas Still Kills," *Pittsburgh Tribune Review,* May 1, 2009, p. 1.

[20] Hazara, a one-name activist, quoted in Mark Magnier, "Despair Lingers in Bhopal," *Los Angeles Times,* December 3, 2009, p. 28.

[21] Satinath Sarangi, quoted in Jim Gilchrist, "Bhopal Hero," *The Scotsman,* July 8, 2009, p. 18.

[22] A recent addition is *Surviving Bhopal: Dancing Bodies, Written Texts, and Oral Testimonials of Women in the Wake of an Industrial Disaster* (New York: Palgrave Macmillan, 2010).

[23] Dominique Lapierre and Javier Moro, *Five Past Midnight in Bhopal* (New York: Warner Books, 2002).

[24] Kamal Al-Solaylee, "Bhopal: A Chemical and Theatrical Disaster," *The Globe and Mail,* October 25, 2003, p. R17. The play is Rahul Varma, *Bhopal* (Toronto: Playwrights Canada Press, 2006).

Values in Tension:
Ethics Away from Home

by Thomas Donaldson

 Harvard Business Review

Reprint 96502

Harvard Business Review

HBR Subscriptions

Harvard Business Review
U.S. and Canada
Subscription Service
P.O. Box 52623
Boulder, CO 80322-2623

Outside U.S. and Canada
Tower House
Sovereign Park
Lathkill Street
Market Harborough
Leicestershire LE16 9EF

Telephone: (800) 274-3214
Fax: (617) 496-8145

Telephone: 44-85-846-8888
Fax: 44-85-843-4958

American Express, MasterCard, VISA accepted. Billing available.

HBR Article Reprints
HBR Index and Other Catalogs
HBS Cases
HBS Press Books

Harvard Business School Publishing
Customer Service - Box 230-5
60 Harvard Way
Boston, MA 02163
Telephone: U.S. and Canada (800) 545-7685
Outside U.S. and Canada: (617) 495-6117 or 495-6192
Fax: (617) 495-6985
Internet address: custserv@cchbspub.harvard.edu

HBS Management Productions Videos

Harvard Business School Management Productions videos are produced by award winning documentary filmmakers. You'll find them lively, engaging, and informative.

HBR Custom Reprints

Please inquire about HBR's custom service and quantity discounts. We will print your company's logo on the cover of reprints, collections, or books in black and white, two color, or four color. The process is easy, cost effective, and quick.

Telephone: (617) 495-6198 or Fax: (617) 496-8866

Permissions

For permission to quote or reprint on a one-time basis:
Telephone: (800) 545-7685 or Fax: (617) 495-6985

For permission to re-publish please write or call:

Permissions Editor
Harvard Business School Publishing
Box 230-5
60 Harvard Way
Boston, MA 02163
Telephone: (617) 495-6849

Harvard Business Review

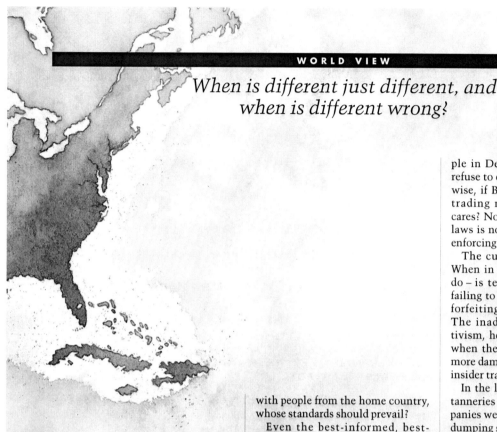

WORLD VIEW

*When is different just different, and
when is different wrong?*

Values in Tension:

by Thomas Donaldson

When we leave home and cross our nation's boundaries, moral clarity often blurs. Without a backdrop of shared attitudes, and without familiar laws and judicial procedures that define standards of ethical conduct, certainty is elusive. Should a company invest in a foreign country where civil and political rights are violated? Should a company go along with a host country's discriminatory employment practices? If companies in developed countries shift facilities to developing nations that lack strict environmental and health regulations, or if those companies choose to fill management and other top-level positions in a host nation

with people from the home country, whose standards should prevail?

Even the best-informed, best-intentioned executives must rethink their assumptions about business practice in foreign settings. What works in a company's home country can fail in a country with different standards of ethical conduct. Such difficulties are unavoidable for businesspeople who live and work abroad.

But how can managers resolve the problems? What are the principles that can help them work through the maze of cultural differences and establish codes of conduct for globally ethical business practice? How can companies answer the toughest question in global business ethics: What happens when a host country's ethical standards seem lower than the home country's?

Competing Answers

One answer is as old as philosophical discourse. According to cultural relativism, no culture's ethics are better than any other's; therefore there are no international rights and wrongs. If the people of Indonesia tolerate the bribery of their public officials, so what? Their attitude is no better or worse than that of peo-

ple in Denmark or Singapore who refuse to offer or accept bribes. Likewise, if Belgians fail to find insider trading morally repugnant, who cares? Not enforcing insider-trading laws is no more or less ethical than enforcing such laws.

The cultural relativist's creed – When in Rome, do as the Romans do – is tempting, especially when failing to do as the locals do means forfeiting business opportunities. The inadequacy of cultural relativism, however, becomes apparent when the practices in question are more damaging than petty bribery or insider trading.

In the late 1980s, some European tanneries and pharmaceutical companies were looking for cheap waste-dumping sites. They approached virtually every country on Africa's west coast from Morocco to the Congo.

Nigeria agreed to take highly toxic polychlorinated biphenyls. Unprotected local workers, wearing thongs and shorts, unloaded barrels of PCBs and placed them near a residential area. Neither the residents nor the workers knew that the barrels contained toxic waste.

We may denounce governments that permit such abuses, but many countries are unable to police transnational corporations adequately even if they want to. And in many countries, the combination of ineffective enforcement and inadequate regulations leads to behavior by unscrupulous companies that is clearly wrong. A few years ago, for example, a group of investors became interested in restoring the SS *United States*, once a luxurious ocean liner. Before the actual restoration could begin, the ship had to be stripped of its asbestos lining. A bid from a U.S. company, based on U.S. standards for asbestos removal, priced the job

DRAWINGS BY MICHAEL REAGAN

at more than $100 million. A company in the Ukranian city of Sevastopol offered to do the work for less than $2 million. In October 1993, the ship was towed to Sevastopol.

A cultural relativist would have no problem with that outcome, but I do. A country has the right to establish its own health and safety regulations, but in the case described above, the standards and the terms of the contract could not possibly have protected workers in Sevastopol from known health risks. Even if the contract met Ukranian standards, ethical businesspeople must object. Cultural relativism is morally blind. There are fundamental values that cross cultures, and companies must uphold them. (For an economic argument against cultural relativism, see the insert "The Culture and Ethics of Software Piracy.")

they had used with U.S. managers: the participants were asked to discuss a case in which a manager makes sexually explicit remarks to a new female employee over drinks in a bar. The instructors failed to consider how the exercise would work in a culture with strict conventions governing relationships between men and women. As a result, the training sessions were ludicrous. They baffled and offended the Saudi participants, and the message to avoid coercion and sexual discrimination was lost.

The theory behind ethical imperialism is absolutism, which is based on three problematic principles. Absolutists believe that there is a single list of truths, that they can be expressed only with one set of concepts, and that they call for exactly the same behavior around the world.

loyalty to their companies, their business networks, and their nation. Americans place a higher value on liberty than on loyalty; the U.S. tradition of rights emphasizes equality, fairness, and individual freedom. It is hard to conclude that truth lies on one side or the other, but an absolutist would have us select just one.

The second problem with absolutism is the presumption that people must express moral truth using only one set of concepts. For instance, some absolutists insist that the language of basic rights provide the framework for any discussion of

Ethics Away from Home

At the other end of the spectrum from cultural relativism is ethical imperialism, which directs people to do everywhere exactly as they do at home. Again, an understandably appealing approach but one that is clearly inadequate. Consider the large U.S. computer-products company that in 1993 introduced a course on sexual harassment in its Saudi Arabian facility. Under the banner of global consistency, instructors used the same approach to train Saudi Arabian managers that

Thomas Donaldson is a professor at the Wharton School of the University of Pennsylvania in Philadelphia, where he teaches business ethics. He wrote The Ethics of International Business *(Oxford University Press, 1989) and is the coauthor, with Thomas W. Dunfee, of* Business Ethics as Social Contracts, *to be published by the Harvard Business School Press in the fall of 1997.*

The first claim clashes with many people's belief that different cultural traditions must be respected. In some cultures, loyalty to a community – family, organization, or society – is the foundation of all ethical behavior. The Japanese, for example, define business ethics in terms of

The Culture and Ethics of Software Piracy

Before jumping on the cultural relativism bandwagon, stop and consider the potential economic consequences of a when-in-Rome attitude toward business ethics. Take a look at the current statistics on software piracy: In the United States, pirated software is estimated to be 35% of the total software market, and industry losses are estimated at $2.3 billion per year. The piracy rate is 57% in Germany and 80% in Italy and Japan; the rates in most Asian countries are estimated to be nearly 100%.

There are similar laws against software piracy in those countries. What, then, accounts for the differences? Although a country's level of economic development plays a large part, culture, including ethical attitudes, may be a more crucial factor. The 1995 annual report of the Software Publishers Association connects software piracy directly to culture and attitude. It describes Italy and Hong Kong as having "'first world' per capita incomes, along with 'third world' rates of piracy." When asked whether one should use software without paying for it, most people, including people in Italy and Hong Kong,

say no. But people in some countries regard the practice as *less* unethical than people in other countries do. Confucian culture, for example, stresses that individuals should share what they create with society. That may be, in part, what prompts the Chinese and other Asians to view the concept of intellectual property as a means for the West to monopolize its technological superiority.

What happens if ethical attitudes around the world permit large-scale software piracy? Software companies won't want to invest as much in developing new products, because they cannot expect any return on their investment in certain parts of the world. When ethics fail to support technological creativity, there are consequences that go beyond statistics – jobs are lost and livelihoods jeopardized.

Companies must do more than lobby foreign governments for tougher enforcement of piracy laws. They must cooperate with other companies and with local organizations to help citizens understand the consequences of piracy and to encourage the evolution of a different ethic toward the practice.

malnourished or starving, a government may be wise to use more fertilizer in order to improve crop yields, even though that means settling for relatively high levels of thermal water pollution.

When cultures have different standards of ethical behavior – and different ways of handling unethical behavior – a company that takes an absolutist approach may find itself making a disastrous mistake. When a manager at a large U.S. specialty-products company in China caught an employee stealing, she followed the company's practice and turned the employee over to the provincial authorities, who executed him. Managers cannot operate in another culture without being aware of that culture's attitudes toward ethics.

If companies can neither adopt a host country's ethics nor extend the home country's standards, what is the answer? Even the traditional litmus test – What would people think of your actions if they were written up on the front page of the newspaper? – is an unreliable guide, for there is no international consensus on standards of business conduct.

Balancing the Extremes: Three Guiding Principles

Companies must help managers distinguish between practices that are merely different and those that are wrong. For relativists, nothing is sacred and nothing is wrong. For absolutists, many things that are different are wrong. Neither extreme illuminates the real world of business decision making. The answer lies somewhere in between.

When it comes to shaping ethical behavior, companies must be guided by three principles.
☐ Respect for core human values, which determine the absolute moral threshold for all business activities.
☐ Respect for local traditions.
☐ The belief that context matters when deciding what is right and what is wrong.

Consider those principles in action. In Japan, people doing business together often exchange gifts – sometimes expensive ones – in keeping with long-standing Japanese tradition. When U.S. and European com-

ethics. That means, though, that entire cultural traditions must be ignored. The notion of a right evolved with the rise of democracy in post-Renaissance Europe and the United States, but the term is not found in either Confucian or Buddhist traditions. We all learn ethics in the context of our particular cultures, and the power in the principles is deeply tied to the way in which they are expressed. Internationally accepted lists of moral principles, such as the United Nations' Universal Declaration of Human Rights, draw on

many cultural and religious traditions. As philosopher Michael Walzer has noted, "There is no Esperanto of global ethics."

The third problem with absolutism is the belief in a global standard of ethical behavior. Context must shape ethical practice. Very low wages, for example, may be considered unethical in rich, advanced countries, but developing nations may be acting ethically if they encourage investment and improve living standards by accepting low wages. Likewise, when people are panies started doing a lot of business in Japan, many Western businesspeople thought that the practice of gift giving might be wrong rather than simply different. To them, accepting a gift felt like accepting a bribe. As Western companies have become more familiar with Japanese traditions, however, most have come to tolerate the practice and to set different limits on gift giving in Japan than they do elsewhere.

Respecting differences is a crucial ethical practice. Research shows that management ethics differ among cultures; respecting those differences means recognizing that some cultures have obvious weaknesses – as well as hidden strengths. Managers in Hong Kong, for example, have a higher tolerance for some forms of bribery than their Western counterparts, but they have a much lower tolerance for the failure to acknowledge a subordinate's work. In some parts of the Far East, stealing credit from a subordinate is nearly an unpardonable sin.

People often equate respect for local traditions with cultural relativism. That is incorrect. Some practices are clearly wrong. Union Carbide's tragic experience in Bhopal, India, provides one example. The company's executives seriously underestimated how much on-site management involvement was needed at the Bhopal plant to compensate for the country's poor infrastructure and regulatory capabilities. In the aftermath of the disastrous gas leak, the lesson is clear: companies using sophisticated technology in a developing country must evaluate that country's ability to oversee its safe use. Since the incident at Bhopal, Union Carbide has become a leader in advising companies on using hazardous technologies safely in developing countries.

Some activities are wrong no matter where they take place. But some practices that are unethical in one setting may be acceptable in another. For instance, the chemical EDB, a soil fungicide, is banned for use in the United States. In hot climates, however, it quickly becomes harmless through exposure to intense solar radiation and high soil temperatures. As long as the chemical is monitored, companies may be able to use EDB ethically in certain parts of the world.

Defining the Ethical Threshold: Core Values

Few ethical questions are easy for managers to answer. But there are some hard truths that must guide managers' actions, a set of what I call *core human values*, which define minimum ethical standards for all companies.[1] The right to good health and the right to economic advancement and an improved standard of living are two core human values. Another is what Westerners call the Golden Rule, which is recognizable in every major religious and ethical tradition around the world. In Book 15 of his *Analects*, for instance, Confucius counsels people to maintain reciprocity, or not to do to others what they do not want done to themselves.

Although no single list would satisfy every scholar, I believe it is possible to articulate three core values that incorporate the work of scores of theologians and philosophers around the world. To be broadly relevant, these values must include elements found in both Western and non-Western cultural and religious traditions. Consider the examples of values in the insert "What Do These Values Have in Common?"

At first glance, the values expressed in the two lists seem quite different. Nonetheless, in the spirit of what philosopher John Rawls calls *overlapping consensus*, one can see that the seemingly divergent values converge at key points. Despite important differences between Western and non-Western cultural and religious traditions, both express shared attitudes about what it means to be human. First, individuals must not treat others simply as tools; in other words, they must recognize a person's value as a human being. Next, individuals and communities must treat people in ways that respect people's basic rights. Finally, members of a community must work together to support and improve the institutions on which the community depends. I call those

What Do These Values Have in Common?

Non-Western	Western
Kyosei (Japanese): Living and working together for the common good.	Individual liberty
Dharma (Hindu): The fulfillment of inherited duty.	Egalitarianism
Santutthi (Buddhist): The importance of limited desires.	Political participation
Zakat (Muslim): The duty to give alms to the Muslim poor.	Human rights

three values *respect for human dignity*, *respect for basic rights*, and *good citizenship*.

Those values must be the starting point for all companies as they formulate and evaluate standards of ethical conduct at home and abroad. But they are only a starting point. Companies need much more specific guidelines, and the first step to developing those is to translate the core human values into core values for business. What does it mean, for example, for a company to respect human dignity? How can a company be a good citizen?

I believe that companies can respect human dignity by creating and sustaining a corporate culture in which employees, customers, and suppliers are treated not as means to an end but as people whose intrinsic value must be acknowledged, and by producing safe products and services in a safe workplace. Companies can respect basic rights by acting in ways that support and protect the individual rights of employees, customers, and surrounding communities, and by avoiding relationships that vio-

late human beings' rights to health, education, safety, and an adequate standard of living. And companies can be good citizens by supporting essential social institutions, such as the economic system and the education system, and by working with host governments and other organizations to protect the environment.

The core values establish a moral compass for business practice. They can help companies identify practices that are acceptable and those that are intolerable – even if the practices are compatible with a host country's norms and laws. Dumping pollutants near people's homes and accepting inadequate standards for handling hazardous materials are two examples of actions that violate core values.

Similarly, if employing children prevents them from receiving a basic education, the practice is intolerable. Lying about product specifications in the act of selling may not

affect human lives directly, but it too is intolerable because it violates the trust that is needed to sustain a corporate culture in which customers are respected.

Sometimes it is not a company's actions but those of a supplier or customer that pose problems. Take

Many companies don't do anything with their codes of conduct; they simply paste them on the wall.

the case of the Tan family, a large supplier for Levi Strauss. The Tans were allegedly forcing 1,200 Chinese and Filipino women to work 74 hours per week in guarded compounds on the Mariana Islands. In 1992, after repeated warnings to the Tans, Levi Strauss broke off business relations with them.

Creating an Ethical Corporate Culture

The core values for business that I have enumerated can help companies begin to exercise ethical judgment and think about how to operate ethically in foreign cultures, but they are not specific enough to guide managers through actual ethical dilemmas. Levi Strauss relied on a written code of conduct when figuring out how to deal with the Tan family. The company's Global Sourcing and Operating Guidelines, formerly called the Business Partner Terms of Engagement, state that Levi Strauss will "seek to identify and utilize business partners who aspire as individuals and in the conduct of all their businesses to a set of ethical standards not incompatible with our own." Whenever intolerable business situations arise, managers should be guided by precise statements that spell out the behavior and operating practices that the company demands.

Ninety percent of all *Fortune* 500 companies have codes of conduct, and 70% have statements of vision and values. In Europe and the Far East, the percentages are lower but are increasing rapidly. Does that mean that most companies have what they need? Hardly. Even though most large U.S. companies have both statements of values and codes of conduct, many might be better off if they didn't. Too many companies don't do anything with the documents; they simply paste them on the wall to impress employees, customers, suppliers, and the public. As a result, the senior managers who drafted the statements lose credibility by proclaiming values and not living up to them. Companies such as Johnson & Johnson, Levi Strauss, Motorola, Texas Instruments, and Lockheed Martin, however, do a great deal to make the words meaningful. Johnson & Johnson, for example, has become well known for its Credo Challenge sessions, in which managers discuss ethics in the context of their current business problems and are invited to criticize the company's credo and make suggestions for changes. The participants' ideas are passed on to the company's senior managers. Lockheed Martin has created an innovative site on the World Wide Web and on its local network that gives employees, customers, and suppliers access to the company's ethical code and the chance to voice complaints.

Codes of conduct must provide clear direction about ethical behavior when the temptation to behave unethically is strongest. The pronouncement in a code of conduct that bribery is unacceptable is useless unless accompanied by guide-

lines for gift giving, payments to get goods through customs, and "requests" from intermediaries who are hired to ask for bribes.

Motorola's values are stated very simply as "How we will always act: [with] constant respect for people [and] uncompromising integrity."

The company's code of conduct, however, is explicit about actual business practice. With respect to bribery, for example, the code states that the "funds and assets of Motorola shall not be used, directly or indirectly, for illegal payments of any kind." It is unambiguous about what sort of payment is illegal: "the payment of a bribe to a public official or the kickback of funds to an employee of a customer...." The code goes on to prescribe specific procedures for handling commissions to intermediaries, issuing sales invoices, and disclosing confidential information in a sales transaction – all situations in which employees might have an opportunity to accept or offer bribes.

Codes of conduct must be explicit to be useful, but they must also leave room for a manager to use his or her judgment in situations requiring cultural sensitivity. Host-country employees shouldn't be forced to adopt all home-country

values and renounce their own. Again, Motorola's code is exemplary. First, it gives clear direction: "Employees of Motorola will respect the laws, customs, and traditions of each country in which they operate, but will, at the same time, engage in no course of conduct which, even if legal, customary, and accepted in any such country, could be deemed to be in violation of the accepted business ethics of Motorola or the laws of the United States relating to business ethics." After laying down such absolutes, Motorola's code then makes clear when individual judgment will be necessary. For example, employees may sometimes accept certain kinds of small gifts "in rare circumstances, where the refusal to accept a gift" would injure Motorola's "legitimate business interests." Under certain circumstances, such gifts "may be accepted so long as the gift inures to the benefit of Motorola" and not "to the benefit of the Motorola employee."

Striking the appropriate balance between providing clear direction and leaving room for individual

Many activities are neither good nor bad but exist in *moral free space.*

judgment makes crafting corporate values statements and ethics codes one of the hardest tasks that executives confront. The words are only a start. A company's leaders need to refer often to their organization's credo and code and must themselves be credible, committed, and consistent. If senior managers act as though ethics don't matter, the rest of the company's employees won't think they do, either.

Conflicts of Development and Conflicts of Tradition

Managers living and working abroad who are not prepared to grapple with moral ambiguity and tension should pack their bags and come home. The view that all business practices can be categorized as either ethical or unethical is too simple. As Einstein is reported to have said, "Things should be as simple as possible – but no simpler." Many business practices that are considered unethical in one setting may be ethical in another. Such activities are neither black nor white but exist in what Thomas Dunfee and I have called *moral free space*.[2] In this gray zone, there are no tight prescriptions for a company's behavior. Managers must chart their own courses – as long as they do not violate core human values.

Consider the following example. Some successful Indian companies offer employees the opportunity for one of their children to gain a job with the company once the child has completed a certain level in school. The companies honor this commitment even when other applicants are more qualified than an employee's child. The perk is extremely valuable in a country where jobs are hard to find, and it reflects the Indian culture's belief that the West has gone too far in allowing economic opportunities to break up families. Not surprisingly, the perk is among the most cherished by employees, but in most Western countries, it would be branded unacceptable nepotism. In the United States, for example, the ethical principle of equal opportunity holds that jobs should go to the applicants with the best qualifications. If a U.S. com-

pany made such promises to its employees, it would violate regulations established by the Equal Employment Opportunity Commission. Given this difference in ethical attitudes, how should U.S. managers react to Indian nepotism? Should they condemn the Indian companies, refusing to accept them as partners or suppliers until they agree to clean up their act?

Despite the obvious tension between nepotism and principles of equal opportunity, I cannot condemn the practice for Indians. In a country, such as India, that emphasizes clan and family relationships and has catastrophic levels of unemployment, the practice must be viewed in moral free space. The decision to allow a special perk for employees and their children is not necessarily wrong – at least for members of that country.

The Problem with Bribery

Bribery is widespread and insidious. Managers in transnational companies routinely confront bribery even though most countries have laws against it. The fact is that officials in many developing countries wink at the practice, and the salaries of local bureaucrats are so low that many consider bribes a form of remuneration. The U.S. Foreign Corrupt Practices Act defines allowable limits on petty bribery in the form of routine payments required to move goods through customs. But demands for bribes often exceed those limits, and there is seldom a good solution.

Bribery disrupts distribution channels when goods languish on docks until local handlers are paid off, and it destroys incentives to compete on quality and cost when purchasing decisions are based on who pays what under the table. Refusing to acquiesce is often tantamount to giving business to unscrupulous companies.

I believe that even routine bribery is intolerable. Bribery undermines market efficiency and predictability, thus ultimately denying people their right to a minimal standard of living. Some degree of ethical commitment – some sense that everyone will play by the rules – is necessary for a sound economy. Without an ability to predict outcomes, who would be willing to invest?

There was a U.S. company whose shipping crates were regularly pilfered by handlers on the docks of Rio de Janeiro. The handlers would take about 10% of the contents of the crates, but the company was never sure which 10% it would be. In a partial solution, the company began sending two crates – the first with 90% of the merchandise, the second with 10%. The handlers learned to take the second crate and leave the first untouched. From the company's perspective, at least knowing which goods it would lose was an improvement.

Bribery does more than destroy predictability; it undermines essential social and economic systems. That truth is not lost on businesspeople in countries where the practice is woven into the social fabric. CEOs in India admit that their companies engage constantly in bribery, and they say that they have considerable disgust for the practice. They blame government policies in part, but Indian executives also know that their country's business practices perpetuate corrupt behavior. Anyone walking the streets of Calcutta, where it is clear that even a dramatic redistribution of wealth would still leave most of India's inhabitants in dire poverty, comes face-to-face with the devastating effects of corruption.

How can managers discover the limits of moral free space? That is, how can they learn to distinguish a value in tension with their own from one that is intolerable? Helping managers develop good ethical judgment requires companies to be clear about their core values and codes of conduct. But even the most explicit set of guidelines cannot always provide answers. That is especially true in the thorniest ethical dilemmas, in which the host country's ethical standards not only are different but also seem lower than the home

If a company declared all gift giving unethical, it wouldn't be able to do business in Japan.

country's. Managers must recognize that when countries have different ethical standards, there are two types of conflict that commonly arise. Each type requires its own line of reasoning.

In the first type of conflict, which I call a *conflict of relative development*, ethical standards conflict because of the countries' different levels of economic development. As mentioned before, developing countries may accept wage rates that seem inhumane to more advanced countries in order to attract investment. As economic conditions in a developing country improve, the incidence of that sort of conflict usually decreases. The second type of conflict is a *conflict of cultural tradition*. For example, Saudi Arabia, unlike most other countries, does not allow women to serve as corporate managers. Instead, women may work in only a few professions, such as education and health care. The prohibition stems from strongly held religious and cultural beliefs; any increase in the country's level of economic development, which is already quite high, is not likely to change the rules.

To resolve a conflict of relative development, a manager must ask the

following question: Would the practice be acceptable at home if my country were in a similar stage of economic development? Consider the difference between wage and safety standards in the United States and in Angola, where citizens accept lower standards on both counts. If a U.S. oil company is hiring Angolans to work on an offshore Angolan oil rig, can the company pay them lower wages than it pays U.S. workers in the Gulf of Mexico? Reasonable people have to answer yes if the alternative for Angola is the loss of both the foreign investment and the jobs.

Consider, too, differences in regulatory environments. In the 1980s, the government of India fought hard to be able to import Ciba-Geigy's Entero Vioform, a drug known to be enormously effective in fighting dysentery but one that had been banned in the United States because some users experienced side effects. Although dysentery was not a big problem in the United States, in India, poor public sanitation was contributing to epidemic levels of the disease. Was it unethical to make the drug available in India after it had been banned in the United States? On the contrary, rational people should consider it unethical not to do so. Apply our test: Would the United States, at an earlier stage of development, have used this drug despite its side effects? The answer is clearly yes.

But there are many instances when the answer to similar questions is no. Sometimes a host country's standards are inadequate at any level of economic development. If a country's pollution standards are so low that working on an oil rig would considerably increase a person's risk of developing cancer, foreign oil companies must refuse to do business there. Likewise, if the dangerous side effects of a drug treatment outweigh its benefits, managers should not accept health standards that ignore the risks.

When relative economic conditions do not drive tensions, there is

a more objective test for resolving ethical problems. Managers should deem a practice permissible only if they can answer no to both of the following questions: Is it possible to conduct business successfully in the host country without undertaking the practice? and Is the practice a violation of a core human value? Japanese gift giving is a perfect example of a conflict of cultural tradition. Most experienced businesspeople, Japanese and non-Japanese alike, would agree that doing business in Japan would be virtually impossible without adopting the practice. Does gift giving violate a core human value? I cannot identify one that it violates. As a result, gift giving may be permissible for foreign companies in Japan even if it conflicts with ethical attitudes at home. In fact, that conclusion is widely accepted, even by companies such as Texas Instruments and IBM, which are outspoken against bribery.

Does it follow that all nonmonetary gifts are acceptable or that bribes are generally acceptable in countries where they are common? Not at all. (See the insert "The Problem with Bribery.") What makes the routine practice of gift giving acceptable in Japan are the limits in its scope and intention. When gift giving moves outside those limits, it soon collides with core human values. For example, when Carl Kotchian, president of Lockheed in the 1970s, carried suitcases full of cash to Japanese politicians, he went beyond the norms established by Japanese tradition. That incident galvanized opinion in the United States Congress and helped lead to passage of the Foreign Corrupt Practices Act. Likewise, Roh Tae Woo went beyond the norms established by Korean cultural tradition when he accepted $635.4 million in bribes as president of the Republic of Korea between 1988 and 1993.

Guidelines for Ethical Leadership

Learning to spot intolerable practices and to exercise good judgment when ethical conflicts arise requires practice. Creating a company culture that rewards ethical behavior is essential. The following guidelines for developing a global ethical perspective among managers can help.

Treat corporate values and formal standards of conduct as absolutes. Whatever ethical standards a company chooses, it cannot waver on its principles either at home or abroad. Consider what has become part of company lore at Motorola. Around 1950, a senior executive was negotiating with officials of a South American government on a $10 million sale that would have increased the company's annual net profits by nearly 25%. As the negotiations neared completion, however, the executive walked away from the deal because the officials were asking for $1 million for "fees." CEO Robert Galvin not only supported the executive's decision but also made it clear that Motorola would neither accept the sale on any terms nor do business with those government officials again. Retold over the decades, this story demonstrating Galvin's resolve has helped cement a culture of ethics for thousands of employees at Motorola.

Design and implement conditions of engagement for suppliers and customers. Will your company do business with any customer or supplier? What if a customer or supplier uses child labor? What if it has strong links with organized crime? What if it pressures your company to break a host country's laws? Such issues are best not left for spur-of-the-moment decisions. Some companies have realized that. Sears, for instance, has developed a policy of not contracting production to companies that use prison labor or infringe on workers' rights to health and safety. And BankAmerica has specified as a condition for many of its loans to developing countries that environmental standards and human rights must be observed.

Allow foreign business units to help formulate ethical standards and interpret ethical issues. The French pharmaceutical company Rhône-

Poulenc Rorer has allowed foreign subsidiaries to augment lists of corporate ethical principles with their own suggestions. Texas Instruments has paid special attention to issues of international business ethics by creating the Global Business Practices Council, which is made up of managers from countries in which the company operates. With the overarching intent to create a "global ethics strategy, locally deployed," the council's mandate is to provide ethics education and create local processes that will help managers in the company's foreign business units resolve ethical conflicts.

In host countries, support efforts to decrease institutional corruption. Individual managers will not be able to wipe out corruption in a host country, no matter how many bribes they turn down. When a host country's tax system, import and export procedures, and procurement practices favor unethical players, companies must take action.

Many companies have begun to participate in reforming host-country institutions. General Electric, for example, has taken a strong stand in India, using the media to make repeated condemnations of bribery in business and government. General Electric and others have found, however, that a single company usually cannot drive out entrenched corruption. Transparency International, an organization based in Germany, has been effective in helping coalitions of companies, government officials, and others work to reform bribery-ridden bureaucracies in Russia, Bangladesh, and elsewhere.

Exercise moral imagination. Using moral imagination means resolving tensions responsibly and creatively. Coca-Cola, for instance, has consistently turned down requests for bribes from Egyptian officials but has managed to gain political support and public trust by sponsoring a project to plant fruit trees. And take the example of Levi Strauss, which discovered in the early 1990s that

two of its suppliers in Bangladesh were employing children under the age of 14—a practice that violated the company's principles but was tolerated in Bangladesh. Forcing the suppliers to fire the children would not have ensured that the children received an education, and it would have caused serious hardship for the families depending on the children's wages. In a creative arrangement, the suppliers agreed to pay the children's regular wages while they attended school and to offer each child a job at age 14. Levi Strauss, in turn, agreed to pay the children's tuition and provide books and uniforms. That arrangement allowed Levi Strauss to uphold its principles and provide long-term benefits to its host country.

Many people think of values as soft; to some they are usually unspoken. A South Seas island society uses the word *mokita*, which means, "the truth that everybody knows but nobody speaks." However difficult they are to articulate, values affect how we all behave. In a global business environment, values in tension are the rule rather than the exception. Without a company's commitment, statements of values and codes of ethics end up as empty platitudes that provide managers with no foundation for behaving ethically. Employees need and deserve more, and responsible members of the global business community can set examples for others to follow. The dark consequences of incidents such as Union Carbide's disaster in Bhopal remind us how high the stakes can be.

1. In other writings, Thomas W. Dunfee and I have used the term *hypernorm* instead of *core human value*.

2. Thomas Donaldson and Thomas W. Dunfee, "Toward a Unified Conception of Business Ethics: Integrative Social Contracts Theory," *Academy of Management Review*, April 1994; and "Integrative Social Contracts Theory: A Communitarian Conception of Economic Ethics," *Economics and Philosophy*, spring 1995.

Reprint 96502

To place an order, call 1-800-545-7685.

Chapter Fifteen

Consumerism

Harvey W. Wiley

On a spring day in 1863 a tall thin lad of 18 left the family farm, walking five miles over dirt roads to a nearby town. There he would be the first in his family to attend college. Like the restless America of his era, he was leaving rural roots behind in a journey of hope and ambition. His name was Harvey Washington Wiley. He would become the first modern consumer crusader.

The example of his parents molded young Harvey's character. His father was a farmer, who through self-learning became an evangelical minister and part-time schoolteacher. A man of Christian virtue, principle, and independent mind, he stood against slavery despite the open anger of neighbors. His mother taught herself to read. Knowledge was so important in the Wiley home that the latest works of science, literature, and commentary were mail-ordered and read aloud to little Harvey.

Harvey got a bachelor's degree from Hanover College, then attended Indiana Medical College, graduating as a physician in 1871. Still hungry for formal education, he enrolled at Harvard and graduated in less than two years with a chemistry degree. He became a professor at the new Purdue University where he was soon absorbed in food chemistry and began working with Indiana state officials to detect adulteration in food products.

With industrialization, the nation's food supply was changing. As people moved from farms to cities they depended on businesses to prepare, can, bottle, package, and distribute edibles. It was a time of major advances in science, and the Victorian era had a childlike faith in the powers of modern chemistry. A large, highly competitive food industry applied new food chemistries using preservatives, colorings, flavorings, texturizers, and other additives. With few laws to police dishonorable operators, dangerous, fraudulent, and cheapened products made their way to market. Canned beef was preserved with formaldehyde. Strawberry jam was made from pulped apple skins, hayseeds, and glucose. Ground pepper was sometimes mostly nutshells.[1]

Working in his campus lab, Wiley pioneered the study of food adulteration. Using new techniques, he detected widespread fraud. His reputation grew and when he was offered the position of chief chemist at the Department of Agriculture in 1883, he accepted.

---

[1] W. E. Mason, "Food Adulteration," *North American Review,* April 1900, pp. 548–53.

Arriving in Washington, D.C., Wiley, now 39, took charge of the Bureau of Chemistry. This small entity had been set up in 1862 to hunt for contaminated agricultural commodities. He worked tirelessly, uncovering danger, dilution, mislabeling, and cheating in the nation's groceries. Yet he lacked the means to protect public health. Fewer than half the states had pure food laws and those were often contradictory—what was banned in one state was legal in another. Worse, no federal law existed to regulate foodstuffs in interstate commerce.

Wiley agitated for a national pure food law. For more than two decades he worked tirelessly, giving speeches, writing reports, convening meetings of scientists and food producers, and lobbying legislators.

As Wiley labored, 190 protective measures were introduced in Congress. None passed. Eventually he departed from the ordinary, staging a melodramatic experiment that captured the country's imagination. He believed that chemical preservatives harmed consumers, but lacked scientific proof, so he designed a series of "hygienic table trials" in which the participants would be fed suspect preservatives and monitored for signs of distress.

Wiley set up a kitchen, dining room, and laboratory in the basement of the Bureau of Chemistry building and advertised for volunteers. A dozen young men, all civil service employees from the Department of Agriculture, signed up. They pledged "on their honor" that while pursuing their regular work and sleep schedules they would take every meal in the basement dining room, eat or drink nothing (except water) that was not given as part of the trial, carry around jars for collection of urine and feces to be submitted for lab analysis, and submit to weekly doctors' exams.

Wiley first fed the men borax, a then-common preservative. He began by adding half a gram a day to their food. Over two years, he gradually added more. The routine was 10 days of healthy food followed by 20 days of food dosed with borax. At a dosage of two grams, appetites dropped off and some subjects had bowel problems. At four grams more serious problems emerged. The men had headaches and abdominal pain. Three took to their beds. Wiley stopped the test, believing he had evidence that borax was a human poison.[2]

A *Washington Post* reporter discovered Wiley's experiment, nicknamed the men the "poison squad," and wrote regularly about them. Whether or not Wiley intended the trials as partly grandstanding, the public was captivated. They inspired considerable levity, becoming the grist for comedians and minstrel shows. Yet they also put growing pressure on Congress to pass Wiley's pure food bill.

For five years Wiley tested other preservatives on new ranks of volunteers. He found signs of ill health caused by salicylic acid, formaldehyde, and copper sulfate, none of which are used as preservatives today. Years later, Wiley believed the experiments had permanently damaged the health of several poison squad members.

In 1906, even as the poison squad continued its work, Congress finally passed the Pure Food and Drug Act "preventing the manufacture, sale, or transportation of adulterated or misbranded or poisonous or deleterious foods, drugs, medicines, and

[2] Harvey W. Wiley, *The History of a Crime Against the Food Law* (Milwaukee: Lee Foundation for Nutritional Research, 1955), chap. II. Originally published in 1929.

Members of the "poison squad" dining in the basement of the old Bureau of Chemistry building. The Civil Service chef hired to cook their meals had once been chef to the Queen of Bavaria. Source: Courtesy of the Food and Drug Administration History Office.

liquors."[3] Opposition by the food industry yielded in the face of acute public indignation about meatpacking plants described in Upton Sinclair's novel *The Jungle*. Wiley's years of hard work and the theater of his poison squad, however, had prepared the ground. Recognizing this, Congress gave Wiley's Bureau of Chemistry the power to examine foods for adulteration or misbranding.

The press called the new law the Wiley Act. Its passage seemed to be the final victory in his crusade for public health. Yet appearance deceived. Wiley attempted vigorous enforcement, but his perfectionist standards often dictated overly strict rules. He was uneasy with compromise. Food makers resisted his severity and outflanked him by appealing to his boss, Secretary of Agriculture James Wilson, and to President Theodore Roosevelt. Both grew exasperated with him. Roosevelt thought him a vexing nag. At one White House meeting with Wiley and food manufacturers on the use of saccharine, the president became furious with the stubborn chemist. Only an idiot, he told Wiley, would be against all use of saccharine in food.

With time, Wiley's authority eroded. Secretary Wilson, with Roosevelt's approval, undermined Wiley's independence. Wilson appointed an assistant to Wiley who reported directly to him, not to Wiley. Then he set up a panel of scientists to look over Wiley's shoulder and review his decisions. Defeated and bitter, the aging warrior resigned his post in 1912. Yet he could not leave the field. He continued lecturing and writing about consumer causes. His new bride, a suffragette whom he had married in 1911 at age 66, was active in women's groups such as the Housekeepers' Alliance

---

[3] Pure Food and Drug Act of 1906, Sec. 1.

Harvey
W. Wiley
(1845–1930).
Source: Redpath
Chautauqua Col-
lection, Special
Collections
Department,
University of
Iowa Libraries
(Iowa City).

that fought for consumer causes. He wrote about food for *Good Housekeeping* magazine and set up the Good Housekeeping Seal of Approval standard. He died in 1930.[4]

Harvey Wiley's campaign for pure food came at the time when small, local markets for goods and services were expanding to national size. It was in this era that the idea of a class of people with a well-defined interest in safe, pure, and honest commodities emerged. This class came to be called consumers. Wiley's distinction is to have been its first national champion.

America's memory of Wiley has dimmed, but his work still touches our lives. The law he fought for is the foundation of modern food and drug regulation. The Bureau of Chemistry, by enforcing its provisions, evolved into the current Food and Drug Administration, a powerful agency that protects public health.

In this chapter we begin by defining and discussing the idea of consumerism. Then we describe the protective shield of statutes, regulations, and consumer law that has risen to protect consumers since Harvey Wiley's era.

CONSUMERISM

consumer
A person who uses products and services in a commercial economy.

A *consumer* is a person who uses products and services in a commercial economy. *Consumerism* is a word with two meanings. In common usage it refers to a movement to promote the rights and powers of consumers in relation to sellers of products and services. It also denotes an exceptionally powerful ideology of pursuit of material goods that shapes social conduct. We will discuss both these themes beginning with the second.

consumerism
A term denoting (1) a movement to promote the rights and powers of consumers in relation to sellers and (2) a powerful ideology in which the pursuit of material goods beyond subsistence shapes social conduct.

Consumerism as an Ideology

In this meaning, consumerism describes a society in which people define their identities by acquiring and displaying material goods beyond what they need for subsistence. Although small pockets of consumerism existed in the distant past, its spread through large populations is relatively recent, happening for the first time in Western Europe only about 300 years ago, then advancing from there.[5] Its appearance and success is explained by the rise of certain conditions.

[4] "Dr. H. W. Wiley Dies; Pure-Food Expert," *The New York Times,* July 1, 1930, p. 24.

[5] Peter N. Stearns, *Consumerism in World History: The Global Transformation of Desire* (London: Routledge, 2001), pp. ix–x.

Economic progress set the stage. By the 1700s, commercial economies based on currency exchange had replaced subsistence and bartering in Western Europe. As economies grew, modest affluence spread in classes below the aristocracy. Expanding overseas trade in colonial empires brought new products, including sugar from the West Indies, porcelain from China, and cotton fabrics from India. Slowly, average people began to spend more for goods and services beyond their basic needs.

As they did, the institutions necessary to support consumerism quickly appeared. Small shops selling goods sprang up in cities. Shopkeepers discovered that their customers' needs were not limited to necessities, but were infinitely expandable. Innovations such as window displays, sale pricing, loss leaders, and print advertising burst forth. Merchants encouraged producers to create a flow of new products, including toys, furniture, books, watches, perfumes, and household decorations.

However, the full bloom of consumerism came only when these economic developments interacted with cultural and social changes. One important change was the declining influence of religion. From the time of its rise in ancient Rome, Christianity sanctified the dignity of the poor and encouraged followers to forsake the life of this world for the goal of otherworldly salvation. This doctrine made no room for any soul living for material pleasure. It would have suffocated rising consumerism. But now this stricture was loosened by the great philosophical current of the *Enlightenment,* a wave of new, challenging ideas that arose early in the 1700s and ran through the century.

A key premise of Enlightenment thinking was that the use of human reason and scientific inquiry should supplant passive acceptance of religious dogma as the basis for understanding the world. This view elevated the importance of human ability, separated humanity from deity in a new way, and led to the rise of *individualism,* or the idea that human beings are ends in themselves. In the social realm it paved the way for consumerism as individual choice gained priority over duty to God and individuals could focus on material pleasures with less guilt.

Then, the Industrial Revolution put societies in flux. This was the final element in the alchemy of consumerism. Populations grew. People left ancestral homes in the country to live beside strangers in cities. New occupations emerged. Some merchants and traders became wealthy. Everywhere centuries-old class and status boundaries wore away. As they faded, people replaced them with displays of material goods intended to establish identity and standing in the social hierarchy. If a man no longer wore the insignia of a trade or guild, he could adorn himself with expensive, brilliantly dyed cotton garments to show that his current occupation made him affluent. A newly rich merchant could emulate the aristocracy by building a manor house of his own. People spent more time "shopping." The acquisition of material objects had a new centrality in their lives.

Enlightenment
A wave of new, challenging ideas based on human reason and scientific inquiry. It swept over Western Europe in the eighteenth century.

individualism
The idea, arising in the Enlightenment, that human beings are ends in themselves.

Consumerism Rises in America

Consumerism dawned in America when social and economic forces akin to those in Europe came into play. It took a century for the process to work. Beginning in the early 1800s, a commercial economy arose. The ascetic Puritan theology that oppressed individualism in the northern colonies was fading. Ambition for riches in the new land leapt the boundaries of the devout, solemn New England towns

517

FIGURE 15.1
Immigrants and others could display and feel a connection with American culture by using consumer products. This collage of tobacco advertising images from the late 1800s and early 1900s illustrates powerful symbolism for the ideals of liberty and freedom in American culture. Liberty Tobacco was an American Tobacco Company brand, George Washington Greatest American Cut Plug was made by R. J. Reynolds Tobacco Co., and Golden Eagle was made by T. C. Williams Co.

Source: Tobacco Collection-Database #D0321, D0347, D0363. Emergence of Advertising On-Line Project, John W. Hartman Center for Sales, Advertising & Marketing History. Duke University Rare Book, Manuscript, and Special Collections Library. http://library.duke.edu/digitalcollections/eaa/.

where it could not flourish. Wealth accumulated from foreign trade, and industrial development spread growing affluence in the last half of the century.

The full emergence of consumerism in America came with changes around the turn of the twentieth century. The railroads had knitted territory together, forming national markets. The great merger wave of 1896–1904 created businesses with the reach to serve them. Machines and assembly lines made possible mass production of consumer goods. Electricity and other new technologies led to a stream of new products, for example, autos, watches, refrigerators, vacuum cleaners, toasters, and radios. Simultaneously, in large numbers, people left cramped small-town societies and moved to cities with more fluid social currents. Waves of immigrants, people newly adrift from their cultural moorings, arrived.

In this open society characterized by loose social ties, high mobility, and cultural variation, people began to express role and status with the products they bought. Immigrants adopted American culture as they brewed Uncle Sam's Coffee, drank Coca-Cola, or ate a Baby Ruth candy bar, the latter named for the widely loved infant daughter of President Grover Cleveland.[6] Their children renounced old-country ways by wearing New World clothing styles. Advertising facilitated this social communication through products. It created new national brands and endowed them with social significance, allowing people to declare their membership in groups, their status, and their values by the goods they displayed (see Figure 15.1). The ads conferred on products meanings that were widely shared and understood, even by strangers, in a large and mobile population.

---

[6] Ruth Cleveland was born in 1891 when Grover Cleveland was out of office between his two nonconsecutive terms. A national mourning took place after her tragic death from diphtheria in 1904. The popular Democrat ran for the presidency three times and was elected in 1884, defeated in 1888, and elected again in 1892. The brand was created by the Curtiss Candy Company to honor the deceased "baby Ruth."

Consumerism in Perspective

Gary Cross, a historian of American commercial culture, defines consumerism as "the belief that goods give meaning to individuals and their roles in society."[7] According to Cross, consumerism, which has never been a formal philosophy, is now the dominant ideology in America. "Americans," says Cross, "define themselves and their relationships with others through the exchange and use of goods."[8] He believes that consumerism expresses a more powerful worldview than political ideologies, religions, or class and ethnic distinctions. If we are unable to appreciate this fully, it is because of its pervasiveness and the lack of a visible alternative.

Acquisitive desire is natural and inevitable in modern society. Purchased objects can fulfill needs beyond subsistence and beyond their practical function. One illustration comes in the story of a home interview conducted by marketers to learn how customers used household insecticides. At one woman's house a roach ran out during the visit. She cursed, sprayed until a puddle formed, then crushed it with the edge of the can, telling her wide-eyed visitors that roaches reminded her of her first husband. It was then, wrote one interviewer, we learned that "even a utilitarian product like bug spray can have deeply emotional, even primal meaning."[9]

Marketing research reveals a widespread, profound effort to find love, status, and self-expression in products. One researcher's studies for large corporations, for example, show evidence for the following conclusions.[10] The basic purpose of shopping is "reconnecting with life"; it is a social experience, not a hunt for necessities. People buy products to fulfill emotional needs rather than practical ones. For Americans, luxury products are like military stripes, a proof of success that confirms the "goodness" of a person. And, not surprisingly, cars are purchased to express identity, distinctiveness, and personality, not as practical conveyances.

These and similar insights invite condemnation by those who reject material possessions as the source of human happiness. *Materialism* is an emphasis on material objects or money that displaces spiritual, aesthetic, or philosophical values. Critics of materialism believe that pursuit of pleasure in external possessions is less worthy than concern for interior virtues, that buying a product creates only false satisfaction. True satisfaction comes from intellectual, artistic, and spiritual attainment. Real wisdom is in the cathedral, museum, or library, not the car lot. Despite lack of any objective evidence as to their inferiority, material values are subject to perennial ridicule and criticism.

One defining rejection of materialism in America came early from Henry David Thoreau. Thoreau was born in 1817 in a small Massachusetts town. As a boy he

materialism
An emphasis on material objects or money that displaces spiritual, aesthetic, or philosophical values.

---

[7] Gary Cross, *An All Consuming Society: Why Commercialism Won in Modern America* (New York: Columbia University Press, 2000), p. 1.

[8] Ibid., p. 4.

[9] Michael J. Silverstein, *Treasure Hunt: Inside the Mind of the New Consumer* (New York: Portfolio, 2006), p. xiv.

[10] Clotaire Rapaille, *The Culture Code: An Ingenious Way to Understand Why People around the World Buy and Live as They Do* (New York: Broadway Books, 2006).

showed a disposition to be an imaginative, independent observer. His mother once asked why he was staying awake long into the night. "Mother," he said, "I have been looking through the stars to see if I couldn't see God behind them."[11] At Harvard College he earned a degree but his real school was Nature. He was briefly a pencil maker, land surveyor, and schoolteacher but he preferred to spend his days in the woods where in idleness he felt freedom. He kept a lifelong journal and published his insights as articles, poems, and books.

In 1845 he built a crude cabin on Walden Pond near Concord, Massachusetts, where for two years he lived in solitude. At this remove from society he composed a shrewd, original critique of material values titled *Walden; or, Life in the Woods*. In nature, he wrote, God gives everyone the "necessaries of life" sufficient to satisfy basic needs for food, shelter, clothing, and fuel. Yet people are not satisfied. They want wealth and material objects. Working to possess these artificial satisfactions they toil away precious days, months, and years. Those who acquired farms, herds, and houses spent most of their hours getting money to pay for them, leaving too little time for the more rewarding tasks of perfecting mind and character. "The mass of men," he wrote, "lead lives of quiet desperation."[12] They are like serfs toiling to push before them loads of houses, barns, boats, and treasures and the endless task smothers their "better part."[13]

Thoreau poked fun at the pretenses of material life. He found one man overly concerned with his house, "how a few sticks are slanted over him or under him, and what colors are daubed upon his box."[14] He called household possessions "trumpery." He saw his neighbor's interest in fine clothes and noted "there is greater anxiety, commonly, to have fashionable, or at least clean and unpatched clothes, than to have a sound conscience."[15] He was particularly skeptical of anyone who wanted to be rich. "Money," he wrote, "is not required to buy one necessary of the soul."[16]

Thoreau was contrary. He was indolent. He did not work. He would not pay taxes. Yet he showed great integrity to the principle of simple living. His example became a beacon for the few in each succeeding generation who reject materialism.

---

[11] Quoted in Edward Waldo Emerson, *Henry Thoreau: As Remembered by a Young Friend* (Boston: Houghton Mifflin Company, 1917), p. 15.

[12] Henry David Thoreau, *Walden; or, Life in the Woods* (New York: Thomas Y. Crowell, 1910), p. 8.

[13] Ibid., p. 4.

[14] Ibid., p. 61.

[15] Ibid., p. 26.

[16] Ibid., p. 434.

But its light has a limited radius. Tourists now drawn to his Walden Pond homesite support three shopping malls within a mile as the crow flies.

A second defining attack on the values underlying consumerism came a half century later. It appeared in the caricature of material society by a maverick economist, Thorstein Veblen. In his 1899 book *The Theory of the Leisure Class,* Veblen challenged conventional economic wisdom that consumers bought goods for their functional utility, seeking the best value for their money. He argued that in the new industrial society people no longer earned their status by conquest in warfare or prowess in hunting. Instead, they acquired property to create what he called "invidious comparison" between themselves and their less successful neighbors.[17] They displayed their status through "conspicuous consumption," or the "unremitting demonstration of the ability to pay."[18]

In one illustration of his thesis, Veblen pointed out that a handcrafted sterling silver spoon does its job no better than a mass-produced base metal spoon of identical design. In fact, since silver requires polishing it is inconvenient and costly to own, making it less utilitarian. The most desirable quality of the silver spoon is its greater cost, which confers status on a display-conscious consumer. When the book appeared, it was received as only a satire, which disappointed Veblen. Now, a century later, this and other core insights are widely accepted.

Thorstein Veblen (1857–1929) wrote a satirical but penetrating account of modern consumer society. He outraged economists of his day with the insight that people bought products not for their utility, but to show off. Source: © Bettmann/ CORBIS

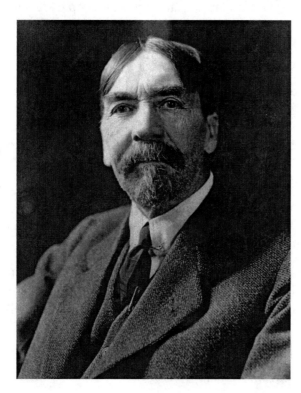

[17] Thorstein Veblen, *The Theory of the Leisure Class* (New York: Penguin Books, 1979), p. 27. Originally published in 1899.
[18] Ibid., p. 87.

Since Veblen, consumerism has been a punching bag for social critics. Here are some general complaints. All are based on the belief that material values undermine other, "higher" values.

- Consumerism leads to commodification of all parts of life. Things are judged for their value on the market rather than by some intrinsic value. People are judged for their external possessions rather than their interior qualities.

- Consumption beyond practical needs for emotional reasons encourages unwise, irrational, and unproductive uses of money. In the 1920s a National Thrift Movement emerged to teach children the thrift ethic. It was inspired by the aphorisms of Benjamin Franklin, who cast industriousness and frugality as central character virtues. The movement had Congress declare that Franklin's birthday in January begin a National Thrift Week and its thrift classes were adopted by thousands of schools. Although its organized influence had withered by 1930, its notion of prudent buying lives on as a second-tier cultural value.

- Heavy consumption is profligate with natural resources and incompatible with sustainability. According to one critic, it even "threatens the collapse of human civilization" from long-term problems such as climate change.[19]

- Consuming beyond necessity, especially by purchasing luxury items, violates "the idea that God's world is already full and complete."[20] Those who consume beyond basic needs are guilty of the sins of gluttony and greed. Heavy consumption of frivolous and luxury goods diverts resources from more noble uses, such as ending world poverty.

- Consumerism distorts our values. It "favors laxity and leisure over discipline and denial," it replaces the work ethic with easy credit and compulsive buying.[21] It converts profligacy into social status. It encourages conspicuous, competitive, and imitative consumption in which people buy material goods to show off, outdo others, or try to fit in with peers. These are inferior motives.

- Consumerism is a pathology of corporate capitalism. Beginning with Lenin, socialists have argued that capitalist economies concentrate production in large firms that seek to expand and control their markets.[22] The continually rising returns necessary to satisfy investors require companies to create powerful marketing methods for manipulating consumers.[23] It is this corporate selling that promotes the false needs, thoughts, and values underlying consumerism.

[19] Erik Assadourian, "The Rise and Fall of Consumer Cultures," in Worldwatch Institute, *2010 State of the World: Transforming Cultures from Consumerism to Sustainability* (New York: W. W. Norton, 2010), p. 3.

[20] James B. Twitchell, *Living It Up: America's Love Affair with Luxury* (New York: Simon & Schuster, 2002), p. 56.

[21] Benjamin R. Barber, "Overselling Capitalism with Consumerism," *The Baltimore Sun,* April 15, 2007, p. A25.

[22] V. I. Lenin, *Imperialism: The Highest Stage of Capitalism* (New York: International Publishers, 1939), originally published in 1917, chap. 1. See also Harry Magdoff and Fred Magdoff, "Approaching Socialism," *Monthly Review,* July–August 2005, who write that consumerism, "the compulsion to purchase more and more, unrelated to basic human needs or happiness," is an "aspect of the culture of capitalism," p. 22.

[23] Michael Dawson, *The Consumer Trap: Big Business Marketing in American Life* (Champaign: University of Illinois Press, 2003).

Criticism of the values in modern consumerism is persistent. Ralph Nader and other leaders of the consumer's movement exhort Americans to be practical in their expenditures, to be vigilant against advertising that tempts them into extravagance, and to put function ahead of excitement in their purchases. From time to time eccentric souls do reject the embrace of consumer culture. A recent book, *Not Buying It: My Year without Shopping,* describes how the author and a companion elected to satisfy their needs without buying new products for a year.[24] In another book, *No Impact Man,* a New York City family tries to live for a year with zero environmental impact.[25] They do not fly, drive, or use taxis. They take stairs to their ninth-floor apartment since elevators use electricity. They live without electric lights or heat. They learn to produce no trash. Such examples come regularly, but they yield few converts. The alternative of simplified, utilitarian living in the mold of the Puritans, Benjamin Franklin, or Henry David Thoreau is now an impractical vision.

Attempts to create sanctuaries from consumerism in American society have also been losing efforts. Blue laws prohibiting stores from opening on Sundays, once pervasive, were an effort to rope off one day of the week and free it of commercialism. Such laws have little coverage now. When radio was new, pioneers of broadcasting such as David Sarnoff at RCA hesitated to air commercials. For the first time, sales pitches came right into the sanctum of the home. Would they offend listeners? Quickly, the answer came. The vast majority felt no affront.

More recently, consumer advocates have tried to fence off childhood from the blandishments of materialism. Battles are fought over ads in schools, school buses, children's television programs, video games, cell phones, and virtual worlds. Although there have been some victories with respect to specific products and locations, it is far too late to sequester children from advertising.

The Global Rise of Consumerism

Among young urban dwellers in Vietnam the "attitude of consumerism is now rampant."[26] In China, where "materialism is the new national ideology,"[27] Prime Minister Wen Jiabao warned that buyers of luxury goods could become "intoxicated with comfort" and sink "into depravity."[28] In Namibia, rising debt, excessive spending at Christmas, and a "growing culture of measuring people's success by material possessions" have caused concern.[29] Crossing the globe, the formula for consumerism is activated by economic growth and social change in one nation after another. The ideology has awakened in Russia, Asia, Latin America, the Middle East, and even sub-Saharan Africa. One historian speculates that it is "the most successful Western influence in world history."[30]

---

[24] Judith Levine, *Not Buying It: My Year without Shopping* (New York: Free Press, 2006).

[25] Colin Beavan, *No Impact Man* (New York: Farrar, Straus and Geroux, 2009).

[26] Roger Mitton, "Young Vietnamese Bitten Hard by Consumer Bug," *The Straits Times,* March 26, 2007.

[27] Noreen O'Leary, "The New Superpower: China's Emerging Middle Class," *Adweek,* January 1, 2007.

[28] Quoted in "If You've Got It, Don't Flaunt It," *The Economist,* June 2, 2007, p. 72.

[29] "Namibia: A Nation in Debt," *Africa News,* January 12, 2007.

[30] Stearns, *Consumerism in World History,* p. 73.

It may, however, be less a Western than a universal phenomenon. Rising like primordial life, it comes when human nature, economic progress, and cultural change interact at a certain moment in a modernizing society. For example, a report by the South African government expressed concern over the growing extent to which consumer goods have become yardsticks for self-identity in that nation. Its explanation is that racial hierarchy determined social status under the old apartheid system. With its end in the early 1990s, people turned to displays of material goods to communicate their social rank.[31]

Once it takes hold, consumerism seems irrepressible, but some resistance continues. Western colonialism in Africa left a persistent disdain for Western values and lifestyles, including consumerism. The presence of an Islamic fundamentalism that rejects Western materialism divides populations in the Middle East. And Catholicism still rejects a material focus. Pope John Paul II called the consumer life "improper" and "damaging" because it promotes "having rather than being" and subordinates "interior and spiritual" dimensions of human life to "material and instinctive dimensions."[32] His successor, Pope Benedict XVI, calls for modern society to switch from lifestyles of consumerism to lifestyles directed by a "quest for truth, beauty, goodness and communion with others for the sake of common growth."[33] Thoreau would have approved.

In Defense of Consumerism

Despite opposition in principle, the ideology of consumerism is triumphant in practice. This is evidence of important virtues. Products and services are designed to fill consumer's needs. Some of these needs are explicit. Others may be latent, waiting to be awakened by marketers. Fulfilling both explicit and latent needs with material objects has emotional benefits. If marketers create an aura of elegance for a brand of perfume, the woman who uses it may feel alluring. Though the chemicals in a $100-an-ounce fragrance may be worth only $0.10, her real purchase is the conviction that she is glamorous.

Successful products either create value for customers or they fail in competitive markets. Intense competition between corporations works to bring consumers more choices, higher quality, and lower prices. Proliferating choices stimulate consumption and economic growth. As prices fall consumer needs at lower income levels are met, in effect raising the standard of living.[34] Some nations adopt conscious policies of stimulating consumerism. After the end of a five-year United Nations embargo in 2003, the Libyan government took measures to reinvigorate its economy, including raising salaries of civil servants by 50 percent. They went shopping. Soon the streets of Tripoli filled with luxury cars going to

[31] Linda Nordling, "Chequered Future: Interview with Deborah Posel," *The Guardian,* May 5, 2009, p. 9.

[32] Ioannes Paulus PP.II, Encyclical Letter, *Centesimus annus* (May 1, 1991), no. 36.

[33] Benedict XVI, Encyclical Letter, *Caritas in veritate* (July 7, 2009), no. 51.

[34] These arguments are in John A. Quelch and Katherine E. Jocz, *Greater Good: How Good Marketing Makes for Better Democracy* (Boston: Harvard Business Press, 2008).

boutiques and malls. "Finally we can shop like everyone else," said one economic patriot.[35]

The most zealous critics of consumerism hold privileged and rare values. They argue that people can and should reject fulfillment in material objects or with money, instead meeting their inner emotional needs by memorizing Shakespeare, showing charity to the poor, communing with nature, or worshiping a deity. However, there is no evidence that happiness derived from a new sports car is less worthy than the joys of the opera.

Consumerism as a Protective Movement

The second basic meaning of consumerism is a movement to promote the rights and interests of consumers in relation to sellers. It arises because fraud, deception, and greed are universal in markets. In the United States, three national movements have sprung up to protect consumers. The first began in the 1870s when Populist farmers attacked railroads for unfair rates and bad service. The second was the Progressive movement. After 1900 both political parties capitalized on the political power of consumers as a class of citizens with similar interests and grievances. This led to passage of early consumer protection laws such as the Food and Drug Act of 1906. Then consumer issues receded until a new era of progressive activism in the 1960s and 1970s prompted a third wave of legislation to protect and expand consumer rights.[36]

There were several triggers for this modern movement. Popular critics accused business of manipulating consumers. In *The Waste Makers*, for example, Vance Packard attacked corporations for everything from using annual model changes to make automobiles obsolete to designing potato peelers that blended in with the peelings and got thrown away, thereby creating a need for another purchase.[37] Ralph Nader aroused the public about automobile safety in his book *Unsafe at Any Speed* and emerged as the leader of a national movement.[38] President John F. Kennedy responded to rising, widespread consumer discontent with a special message to Congress in 1962 in which he said that consumers had basic rights and these rights had been widely abridged.[39] He listed the rights to make intelligent choices among products and services, to have access to accurate information, to register complaints and be heard, to be offered fair prices and acceptable quality, to have safe and healthful products, and to receive adequate service.

Congress responded to President Kennedy's speech, over the next decade passing more than a dozen major consumer protection statutes that expanded the authority of existing agencies and creating four new agencies—the Federal

---

[35] Anonymous, quoted in Imed Lamloum, "Libyans Savour Joys of Consumerism," Agence France Presse, October 1, 2008.

[36] According to Elizabeth Cohen in *A Consumer's Republic* (New York: Knopf, 2003), after the Great Depression, politicians elevated the importance of consumers by defining consumer demand as the key to American prosperity.

[37] Vance Packard, *The Waste Makers* (New York: David McKay, 1960), pp. 40–41.

[38] Ralph Nader, *Unsafe at Any Speed* (New York: Pocket Books, 1966).

[39] See "Text of Kennedy's Message to Congress on Protections for Consumers," *The New York Times*, March 16, 1962.

FIGURE 15.2

Spending on Consumer Health and Safety by Federal Regulatory Agencies: 1960–2010
Figures are in constant (2000) dollars and include spending on a range of consumer protection programs by six departments and agencies. Included are regulation of food and drugs, product safety, and chemical safety. Figures do not include environmental regulation.

Source: Veronique de Rugy and Melinda Warren, *Regulators Budget Report 31* (Arlington, VA, and St. Louis, MO: Mercatus Center and Weidenbaum Center, October 2009), table A-2.

Highway Administration (1966) to set highway safety standards, the Federal Railroad Administration (1966) to regulate rail safety, the National Highway Traffic Safety Administration (1970) to protect the public from unsafe automobiles, and the Consumer Product Safety Commission (1972) to guard against unsafe products.

These legislative successes marked the crest of the modern consumer movement. By the mid-1970s business groups had mobilized to block the great dream of the movement's activists, which was to consolidate enforcement of consumer laws, then scattered among many agencies, into one superagency named the Consumer Protection Agency.

Instead, conservatives and business lobbies won a battle for public opinion, convincing Americans that their government was growing too powerful. They warned a rising tide of regulatory red tape created costs out of all proportion to benefits and handicapped corporations in international competition. In the changed political climate formed by these views, the Consumer Protection Agency bill was decisively defeated in 1976, never to rise again.

Since then, Congress has set up only one new consumer agency, the Bureau of Consumer Financial Protection, which is scheduled to begin its work in 2012. But over the years Congress has passed many new statutes expanding the authority of existing agencies, usually in response to a specific event or concern. The result is continuous growth in consumer regulation. Figure 15.2 shows a rise of spending by 14 consumer protection agencies from $485 million in 1960 to an estimated $5.8 billion in 2010.

The Consumer's Protective Shield

We now turn to the massive statutory shield that protects consumers from abuses, real and imagined. Every state and local government has consumer protection laws, More than 50 federal agencies and bureaus also work to protect consumers. We will focus on the four federal agencies that dominate this area of regulation. A description of their duties reveals the awesome responsibilities Congress has placed on them. While each is flawed, it is astonishing how effective their work is overall despite shifting presidential enforcement philosophies, budget restraints, staff shortages, and power struggles with regulated interests.

The Food and Drug Administration (FDA)

This is a big, complex agency of 11,500 employees in the Department of Health and Human Services. Its administrator reports to the secretary of Health and Human Services, who is a political appointee of the president. Congress created the agency in the Food and Drug Act of 1906. With name changes and relocations it descends from the old Bureau of Chemistry run by Harvey Wiley. The original legislation gave it power to regulate misbranded and adulterated food, beverages, and drugs. Since then, Congress has passed 41 more statutes expanding its responsibilities. Now it has authority to:

- Regulate the quality, safety, and labeling of human food (except poultry, meat, eggs, and alcoholic beverages), pet foods, animal feeds, and food additives.
- Approve human and veterinary drugs and medical devices.
- Set safety and effectiveness standards for over-the-counter drugs.
- Regulate the safety and labeling of cosmetics.
- Regulate the marketing, labeling, and ingredients of tobacco products.
- Set safety standards for radiation-emitting products including microwave ovens, televisions, X-ray machines, lasers, and sunlamps.

The agency's reach extends to economic activity comprising about 25 percent of the nation's GDP. Because its congressionally mandated duties have continuously grown, the FDA traversed the past several decades without suffering the steep declines in staffing and budgets experienced by the other three agencies discussed in this section. Between 1980 and 2010 its budget grew from $608 million to $2.4 billion and the number of employees rose from 8,045 to 11,756.

The FDA's main emphasis in terms of budget and staffing is drug regulation. It requires premarket testing of new prescription drugs to ensure their safety and effectiveness. Each year it approves more than 100 new drug applications. Until the 1990s the approval process was very cautious and took years. Then, AIDS activists challenged its conservatism, demanding fast access to drugs for treating HIV infection. The agency speeded its work and eventually approved the first in a new class of protease inhibitors in just three months. Congress then legislated streamlined procedures and the agency has been faster in recent years, blunting a main criticism against it.

Food regulation overwhelms the agency. One reason is the fundamental change in food markets with globalization. Imports are now 15 percent of America's food supply, including 60 percent of fresh fruits and vegetables and 80 percent of seafood. Each year 20 million shipments of imported food arrive, and the FDA inspects only 1 percent. It has the authority to inspect foreign food factories but the resources to visit only one-tenth of 1 percent of them.[40] Such undercapacity invites

[40] Government Accountability Office, *Food Safety: FDA Could Strengthen Oversight of Imported Food by Improving Enforcement and Seeking Additional Authorities,* GAO-1—669T, May 6, 2010, p. 1.

breaches. In 2007 a contaminated protein from China got into pet foods and cattle feed, causing hundreds of animal deaths and major economic losses from brand recalls and livestock quarantines.

Despite the agency's efforts since the days of Henry Wiley, it is unable to eradicate economically motivated contamination and counterfeiting in the food supply. Recently, it has discovered honey diluted with corn syrup, Mississippi paddlefish labeled as sturgeon caviar, rotten tomatoes sold as high-grade tomato paste, and wine made from a slurry of inexpensive grapes that was sold as pinot noir. One expert estimates that 5 to 7 percent of the food supply is dishonest.[41] Between 2006 and 2009 the agency confronted four outbreaks of salmonella from contaminated peanuts. One company, Peanut Corp. of America, ignored tests that showed contamination and shipped peanuts that killed eight people and sickened 575. More than 2,000 products had to be recalled.[42] When FDA inspectors went to the plant, it was the first visit in eight years. Subsequently, they discovered 20 facilities that, unknown to them, were making food with peanuts. These unregulated plants were found only because they bought peanuts from Peanut Corp.

In 2009 Congress gave the agency power to regulate cigarettes and smokeless tobacco. If cereals or soft drinks were as dangerous as these products, the FDA would prohibit their sale, but the new law forbids banning any tobacco product. It has the power to set nicotine levels but cannot reduce them to zero. It has broader powers over marketing and sales and has already banned the use of the words *light*, *mild*, or *low*, candy-flavored cigarettes, and free cigarette samples. The agency plans to build its tobacco division to 400 employees, making the division almost as large as two of the other agencies discussed in this section.

A federal agency with such importance and scope of responsibility, especially with limited resources, attracts critics. It is under constant pressure to speed its actions and reduce risks to the public. Observers suggest that the FDA needs a radical reorganization. Its jurisdiction comes from piecemeal legislation enacted over many decades. The laws have created internal bureaucratic overlaps and conflict. Repeatedly, however, proposals in Congress to consolidate and clarify FDA authority fail to pass. Some suggest dividing the agency in two, creating separate agencies for drugs and food.[43]

The Federal Trade Commission (FTC)

This venerable regulator was born in the Progressive era, a time of great alarm about the growth of big trusts. In 1914 Congress created it as an independent commission, giving it broad powers to protect the public from unfair competition. The president nominates its five commissioners, including one who is designated

---

[41] John Spink, Michigan State University, cited in Lyndsey Layton, "FDA Pressures to Combat Rising 'Food Fraud,'" *The Washington Post*, March 30, 2010, p. A1.

[42] Thomas H. Maugh II and Mary Engel, "FDA Says Firm Lied About Peanut Butter," *Los Angeles Times*, February 7, 2009, p. A1.

[43] Rob Stein, "Ailing FDA May Need a Major Overhaul," *The Washington Post*, November 26, 2008, p. A2.

chair, who are then approved by the Senate for seven-year terms. No more than three can be of the same political party. Once approved, they act independently of the executive branch. The FTC has broad duties to:

- Protect consumers from any practice that unfairly limits competition, including price-fixing, boycotts, conspiracies, and illegal agreements or combinations.
- Challenge mergers and acquisitions that reduce competition or innovation.
- Prevent false and deceptive advertising.
- Protect the public from fraudulent and deceptive sales practices.
- Prohibit discrimination by lenders based on race, sex, national origin, age, or marital status.

At its birth the agency was a fiery enforcer hurling antitrust actions at surprised cartels and trusts. But by the 1920s laissez-faire doctrines reasserted themselves in national politics, and the FTC lost support in Congress and the courts. It languished for decades until a new consumer movement rose in the 1960s, filling it with idealistic young attorneys who wanted to make markets honest. At its zenith in the 1970s it had a staff of 1,800. However, it was soon undercut again by a conservative philosophy, this time deregulation. Corporations annoyed by its actions got Congress to reduce its authority and cut its funding. By the late 1980s it was a demoralized entity with fewer than 900 employees. Now, 20 years later, the scars of deregulation still show, but it has expanded to 1,100 employees. It pursues two basic missions.

One mission is to promote fair competition in industries by enforcing antitrust laws. It seeks to prevent companies from hurting consumers by illegal actions that allow them to raise prices and stifle innovation. The FTC blocked a merger of Home Depot and Staples that would have created a dominant competitor in office supplies. It allowed Whole Foods Market to purchase its main competitor, Wild Oats Markets, only after Whole Foods sold 13 stores to restore competition in natural foods retailing. Recently it acted to deter collusion between Apple and Google. After an FTC investigation, Eric Schmidt, the CEO of Google, resigned from Apple's board, and Arthur Levinson, a biotechnology executive, resigned from Google's board but remained a director of Apple. Antitrust law prohibits *director interlock,* or the sharing of directors by two or more companies, when those companies compete in the same markets. Although Google is an online search and advertising company and Apple manufactures computers and portable electronics, the commission saw that both companies had some competing businesses. Both made mobile phones and both sold operating systems and browsers for mobile devices. It acted to break the director interlock.

director interlock
A situation arising when an individual sits on the board of directors of two or more corporations. This is illegal under the Clayton Act of 1914 if the corporations compete in the same market(s).

The FTC's second mission is to protect consumers from fraudulent or deceptive advertising and marketing. For example, Kellogg Company advertised that based on "clinical research" eating Frosted Mini-Wheats for breakfast improved the attentiveness of children three hours later by nearly 20 percent over children who ate no breakfast. Not so, said the FTC. In the study only about half the children who ate Frosted Mini-Wheats showed any improvement at all. Only 1 in

7 improved their attentiveness by 18 percent or more, and average improvement was only 10.6 percent.[44] Kellogg withdrew the ad. In another case a religious group called Daniel Chapter One marketed four herbal supplements it said would prevent or cure cancer. When the FTC filed a complaint the group argued the commission had no jurisdiction over a religious ministry and was attempting to censor its speech. The commission prevailed.

As part of its mission to protect consumers from deception the commission also regulates debt collection. After the economic downturn in 2008, Oxford Collection Agency began using illegal practices. Its agents called consumers before 8:00 a.m. and after 9:00 p.m., many times a day, and if they hung up, called back immediately. They used profane language and told employers, co-workers, relatives, and neighbors about the debtor's bills. Eventually, the commission levied a $1,060,000 civil fine against Oxford and four individuals.[45]

These stories only scratch the surface. Among its recent activities the FTC has also fought fraudulent green marketing claims, issued rules to reduce spam, published guidelines for bloggers who endorse products, and studied explicit sexuality and violence in online virtual worlds for children (it found instances of such in 19 of 27 worlds visited).[46] More than 175 million consumers have signed up for its do-not-call registry to stop unwanted telemarketer calls.

The Consumer Product Safety Commission (CPSC)

This agency was created by Congress in 1972. Its mission is "to protect children and families from unreasonable risks of injuries associated with consumer products."[47] It enforces 15 major statutes giving it power to:

* Set mandatory or encourage voluntary safety standards for more than 15,000 consumer products.
* Ban the sale of products that expose consumers to unreasonable risks.
* Require manufacturers to recall dangerous products.
* Investigate the extent and causes of deaths and injuries from consumer products.

The agency was set up at the crest of the third wave of consumer protection. Congress gave it considerable autonomy. It is an independent regulatory commission insulated from presidential control. Its five commissioners have staggered seven-year appointments. Yet from its creation it has faced political adversity. President Nixon, who established the agency, was unenthusiastic about it. President Reagan wanted to abolish it but could not. Instead, his allies in Congress drastically cut its budget and it has never been fully restored. Today it operates

---

[44] Complaint, *In the Matter of Kellogg Company,* Docket No. C-4262, Federal Trade Commission, July 27, 2009, p. 7.

[45] *United States v. Oxford Collection Agency,* CV 09 2467, District Court, E.D.N.Y., June 10, 2009, p. 6.

[46] Federal Trade Commission, *Annual Report: The FTC in 2010* (Washington, DC: FTC, April 2010), p. 45.

[47] Ibid., p. i.

with fewer than 400 employees, down from almost 1,000 in 1980. However, after a national dither over Chinese toys with lead in the paint, Congress in 2008 mandated an increase to 500 by 2013.

Over the years, as the CPSC languished, its regulatory realm dramatically changed. At its inception most consumer products were made in the United States. Now most are imported. Between 1998 and 2007 the value of consumer products entering the country increased by 101 percent to $638 billion. Products from China nearly quadrupled and now account for 43 percent of that total. The agency is required to stop the entry of unsafe consumer products but it is overwhelmed. While there are more than 300 ports of entry, it has only nine inspectors at seven locations. By contrast, the Food and Drug Administration has inspectors at 297 ports of entry.[48]

Despite a shortage of resources, the CPSC faces its massive regulatory task with a certain vigor. It regulates roughly 15,000 types of products, everything except alcohol, tobacco, food, drugs, cosmetics, pesticides, motor vehicles, flotation devices, firearms, and pesticides. It has set 38 mandatory safety standards for products as diverse as matchbooks, bicycles, and bunk beds and it has collaborated with industry to create another 390 voluntary standards. In almost 40 years it has banned only eight products including flammable glues and sharp lawn darts. However, each year it prods companies to carry out between 400 and 600 product recalls.

In one example, it requested that a company recall 1 million folding strollers made in China. It had received 15 reports of children catching fingers in a side hinge. Twelve suffered fingertip amputations.[49] In another case it pushed Mattel to recall 7.3 million Polly Pocket doll sets. Tiny magnets inside the toys could fall out and be swallowed by children. If more than one magnet was ingested, they could come together causing blocked, perforated, or infected intestines. By the time the recall was complete three children with perforated intestines needed surgery. The agency pushes recalls even when dangers seem not so grim. It announced that Ross Stores would recall 1,800 inexpensive plant stands. Two consumers were bruised when the stand's marble tops came loose and fell.[50]

The National Highway Traffic Safety Administration (NHTSA)

This is a small agency of about 550 employees in the Department of Transportation. Its administrator reports to the secretary of Transportation, who is a political

---

[48] Figures in this paragraph are from Government Accountability Office, *Consumer Safety: Better Information and Planning Would Strengthen CPSC's Oversight of Imported Products,* GAO-09-803, August 2009, pp. 1 and 12.

[49] Consumer Product Safety Commission, "Maclaren USA Recalls to Repair Strollers Following Fingertip Amputations," Release No. 10-033, November 9, 2009.

[50] Consumer Product Safety Commission, "Ross Stores Recalls Plant Stands; Marble Top Can Detach and Fall on Consumers," Release No. 09-292.

appointee of the president. Congress created it in 1966, giving it a mission of reducing motor vehicle deaths and injuries. It has authority to:

- Mandate minimum safety standards for automobiles, trucks, and their components, including tires.
- Set fuel economy standards for cars and light-duty trucks.
- Require manufacturers to recall cars and trucks with safety defects.
- Administer grants for states and cities to promote highway safety.

No other agency has such extensive controls over a single product. A short list of past rules just to protect occupants of an automobile includes rules on air bags, brakes, safety belts, energy-absorbing or collapsible steering columns, penetration-resistant windshields, recessed door handles, breakaway rearview mirrors, padded dashboards, collapsible front ends, crush-resistant passenger compartments, and tire standards. Over the years "more than 390 million cars, trucks, buses, recreational vehicles, motorcycles, and mopeds, as well as 46 million tires, 66 million pieces of motor vehicle equipment, and 42 million child safety seats have been recalled to correct safety defects."[51]

Since the agency's creation, highway fatalities per million vehicle miles have fallen from more than 3.5 to 1.4.[52] Although many factors led to this decline, including strict drunk driving laws, a major one is the safety standards NHTSA regulators impose on automakers. Yet critics believe the agency has become lax, slow, meek, ineffectual, even "sleepy."[53] Recently, lobbying by industry led it to relax a roof crush rule and drop a rule strengthening passenger seats. Although power windows have the force to strangle children, it has not required auto reverse features as are mandatory in Europe.

Sudden acceleration incidents in Toyota Motor Company automobiles put a spotlight on the agency in 2010 and it did not fare well. Over the previous decade it had received 3,400 complaints of sudden acceleration in the company's cars.[54] In three investigations the agency simply accepted the company's explanations and required a single recall replacing 55,000 floor mats. Toyota had hired former NHTSA enforcement officials who successfully lobbied the agency to avoid or narrow recall orders. Eventually, the agency ordered recall of 6.1 million Toyota and Lexus automobiles and imposed four fines totaling $49 million on Toyota for failing to notify it promptly of safety defects in brake pedals and floor mats. But by then there were reports of 34 deaths and hundreds of injuries from sudden acceleration crashes, and the agency was criticized for its slow response. The fines were the maximum the agency could give

---

[51] National Highway Traffic Safety Administration, "Motor Vehicle Defects and Recalls Campaigns," www.nhtsa.dot.gov, accessed July 5, 2010.

[52] Government Accountability Office, p. 11.

[53] Ralph Nader, "Toyota's Enablers," *Los Angeles Times,* February 28, 2010, p. A27.

[54] Opening Statement of Chairman Edolphus Towns, hearing on *Toyota Gas Pedals: Is the Public at Risk?* Committee on Oversight and Government Reform, House of Representatives, February 24, 2010, p. 2.

FIGURE 15.3
One Effect of Deregulation on Three Consumer Agencies
Staff reductions at three of the four consumer agencies discussed in this section reflect the philosophy of deregulation that gained strength in the 1970s. These agencies have yet to recover their former staffing levels. The exception is the FDA, which has steadily added employees due to expansion of its regulatory duties.

Source: Veronique de Rugy and Melinda Warren, *Regulators Budget Report 31* (Arlington, VA, and St. Louis, MO: Mercatus Center and Weidenbaum Center, October 2009), table A-3.

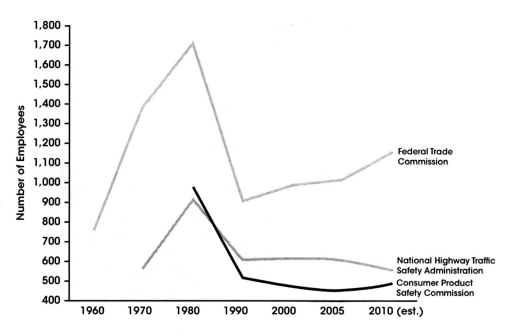

and came over a two-year period during which Toyota took in $452 billion in global revenues.

The Toyota episode bared agency shortcomings. Like other consumer agencies in this section, its staffing has languished with deregulatory trends over two decades (see Figure 15.3). In 2010 it had fewer employees than in 1970. Its enforcement budget is insufficient to conduct investigations, so it relies on manufacturers for information about defects. The product it regulates has changed dramatically. Since the 1960s automobiles have evolved from mechanical to electronic systems, becoming more complex. The agency was willing to accept Toyota's explanation that floor mats caused sudden acceleration because it did not employ a single electrical or software engineer with expertise on computerized acceleration systems.[55] Eventually, it hired outside consultants, including a NASA engineer, to improve its understanding.

Consumer Protection by Other Agencies

Other agencies add to the consumer's protective shield. The Environmental Protection agency defends consumers in many ways, for example, by setting drinking water standards. The Food Safety and Inspection Service in the Department of Agriculture inspects meat, poultry, and eggs. The Equal Employment Opportunity Commission acts against housing and loan discrimination. The Federal Deposit Insurance Corporation insures deposits in 4,900 banks. The new Bureau of Consumer Financial Protection created by Congress in 2010 will oversee all financial

[55] Statement of Joan Claybrook, hearing on *Toyota Gas Pedals: Is the Public at Risk?* Committee on Oversight and Government Reform, House of Representatives, February 24, 2010, p. 6.

FIGURE 15.4   **Federal Agencies Responsible for Ensuring Safe Pizza**

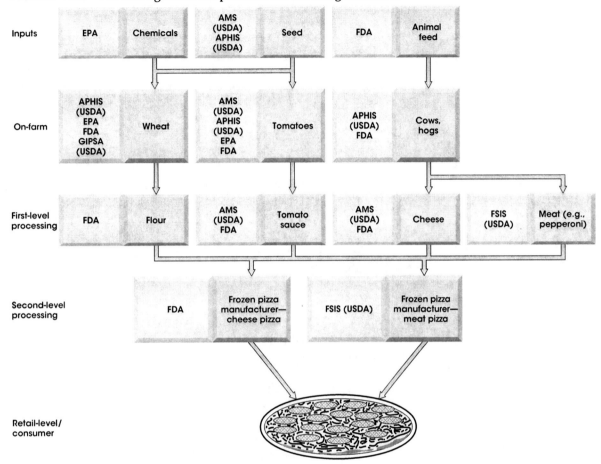

Source: Lawrence J. Dyckman, "Federal Food Safety and Security System," testimony before the Subcommittee on Civil Service and Agency Organization, Committee on Government Reform, House of Representatives, March 30, 2004, p. 5.

Note: AMS—Agriculture Marketing Service
  APHIS—Animal and Plant Health Inspection Service
  GIPSA—Grain Inspection, Packers and Stockyards Administration
  FSIS—Food Safety and Inspection Service

products, protecting consumers from hidden fees, abusive terms, and deceptive practices.

Dozens of other agencies and bureaus have protective duties. In fact, the protective shield, as forged piece by piece over many years, is fragmented, incomplete, and sometimes illogical. The EPA sets drinking water standards, but the FDA regulates bottled water. The FTC has oversight of deceptive marketing, but if the fraud involves a moving van the Federal Motor Carrier Safety Administration takes jurisdiction. And as Figure 15.4 shows, getting a safe pizza to the table is a bureaucratic jubilee. Despite all, consumers receive a great amount of benefit from agencies that struggle to keep up with the flood of work they are given by Congress.

PRODUCT LIABILITY

product liability
A doctrine in the law of torts that covers redress for injuries caused by defective products.

tort
A private wrong committed by one person against another person or her or his property. An injury to a consumer caused by a manufacturer's defective product is one kind of tort.

negligence
An unintentional failure to act as a responsible, prudent person exercising ordinary care.

privity
A relationship giving parties a common interest under the law, as in the relationship between parties to a contract.

Beyond regulation, a major restraint on business is the ability of consumers to file product liability lawsuits when they are harmed. *Product liability* is a doctrine in the body of civil law known as the law of torts. A *tort* is a private wrong committed by one person against another person or her or his property. Under the law of torts, injured persons seek compensation from parties they allege to have caused or contributed to their injury. The tort system is designed to provide compensation to victims and to deter future misconduct. Product liability is the branch of tort law that covers redress for injuries caused by defective products.

Product liability was an obscure backwater of the law until the 1960s, when progressive doctrines of consumer rights energized judges and legislatures to expand it. Earlier, consumers had little recourse when they were injured by defective products. Now product liability law is a powerful tool for gaining compensation. Today, manufacturers or other sellers of products can be held liable for defective products under three fundamental theories, namely, negligence, breach of warranty, and strict liability. In practice, product liability cases are often based on all three theories.[56] We will discuss each one.

Negligence

A tort involves either an intentional or a negligent action that causes injury. Intentional actions by manufacturers to harm consumers are rare. Ordinarily, the claim is that the manufacturer, component manufacturer, wholesaler, or seller of a product exhibited *negligence*. Under this theory, each of these parties has a duty to do what a reasonable, prudent person exercising ordinary care would do under the same circumstances. Thus, any of the parties in the stream of events leading to the final sale can be held liable and must pay damages if their breach of this duty of ordinary care contributed to an injury. The standard seems logical and fair, but early product liability law was not so generous to consumers.

As the United States turned into a consumer society in the late 1800s and early 1900s, manufacturers were well protected from liability suits brought by individuals who were injured by their products. An injured consumer trying to collect damages faced two formidable obstacles in the law.

One was the entrenched principle of *caveat emptor*, a Latin phrase meaning let the buyer beware. It imposed on buyers the responsibility to inspect carefully and skeptically items they purchased. If they failed to see dangerous defects, the legal presumption was that absent any specified remedy in a formal contract they were at fault, not the manufacturer or seller.

The other obstacle was a narrow interpretation of the doctrine of *privity*, which defined the legal relationship between a consumer and other parties to a sale.

---

[56] See, for example, the cases of a farmer who sued a herbicide manufacturer for marketing a chemical that stunted his sunflower crop, *Coleman v. Nufarm Americas*, 693 F. Supp. 2d 1055 (2010); a mother who sued a sperm bank over its product, sperm, that caused her daughter to be born with developmental problems, *Donovan v. Idant Laboratories*, 625 F. Supp. 2d 256 (2009); and a chicken-house worker who sued an equipment manufacturer after he lost a foot in a manure auger, *Vaughn v. Alternative Design Mfg. and Supply*, CV No. 6: 07-429-DCR, U.S.D.C. E.D.K, So. Div (2008).

Courts held that consumers could sue only the party that sold them the product. This restriction was based on English common law and may have been appropriate in an agrarian America where sellers and product makers were in face-to-face contact.[57] As the distribution chain lengthened and grew impersonal in industrial society, that experience became rare. Yet, under the law, injured buyers had no case against a manufacturer. They had to sue the retailer, the party with whom they had a direct relationship. If retailers lost a suit, they could sue the wholesaler, and the wholesaler, in turn, the manufacturer.

This legal wall protecting manufacturers was broken down by the milestone case of *MacPherson v. Buick Motor Co.* in 1916.[58] Donald MacPherson bought a Buick from a Schenectady dealer. While driving it at 8 miles per hour, defective wood spokes on one wheel disintegrated, causing its collapse. MacPherson was thrown out and injured. He sued Buick for negligence because it had sold the automobile without inspecting the spokes. Buick had purchased the wheel from a company that supplied it with 80,000 wheels, none of which had been defective before. Nevertheless, a future U.S. Supreme Court justice, Benjamin Cardozo, then sitting on the New York Supreme Court, affirmed a jury verdict for MacPherson, arguing that, as the manufacturer, Buick "was responsible for the finished product" and could reasonably have been expected to discover the defect by inspection. Furthermore, Buick "owed a duty of care and vigilance" that went beyond the immediate buyer, the dealer, to the driver. Because this extension of the negligence doctrine came in the large marketplace of New York, it spread to other states and became the foundation for a more consumer-friendly modern product liability law.

Over the years since *MacPherson* the negligence doctrine has been continuously stretched to favor consumers. For example, in a 1968 case General Motors made a car that was safe to operate, but was held negligent for not designing it to reduce injury in a collision. Erling Larsen had a head-on collision in a Corvair and suffered severe injuries when the steering wheel was pushed back into his head. He sued, arguing that the steering assembly was defective. Though it had not caused the crash, its design exposed him to greater harm than necessary. General Motors responded that its legal duty was to design a safe car, not a car that protected occupants during head-on collisions. In *Larsen v. General Motors* a federal court held that the design of the steering assembly was negligent because other practical designs could have stopped the wheel from moving back toward the driver after impact and it was foreseeable that there would be collisions.[59] Such expansions in the meaning of negligence have reversed the old *caveat emptor* doctrine. Now, let the manufacturer beware.

Warranty

warranty
A contract in which the seller guarantees the nature of the product. The seller must compensate the buyer if the warranty is not fulfilled.

A *warranty* is a contract in which the seller guarantees the nature of the product. If the product does not conform to the standards in the warranty, the buyer is entitled to compensation for any consequent loss or injury. A manufacturer or seller can be held liable for a breach of one or both of two kinds of warranties, express and implied.

[57] See *Winterbottom v. Wright*, 15 Eng. Rep. 402 (Eng. 1842) 177.
[58] 217 N.Y. 382 (1916).
[59] 391 F.2d 495 (8th Cir. 1968).

express warranty
An explicit claim made by the manufacturer to the buyer.

An *express warranty* is an explicit claim made by the manufacturer to the buyer. It can be a statement that the product will perform in a specified way, a description of the product, or a picture that shows a model product. In the past, manufacturers often put statements in warranties to limit their liability, but the courts have protected consumers by enlarging the idea of an *implied warranty,* or an unwritten, commonsense warranty arising out of reasonable expectations that a product will both fulfill its ordinary purpose and fulfill the particular purpose of the buyer.

implied warranty
An unwritten warranty that a product is adequate to meet a buyer's reasonable expectations that it will fulfill its ordinary purpose and the buyer's particular purpose.

Again, the landmark case involves the automobile industry. Claus Henningsen bought his wife, Helen, a new 1955 Plymouth as a Mother's Day gift. On the back of the purchase order he signed, buried in eight inches of fine print, was a statement that in case of a warranty claim for any defect the buyer must return the parts to Chrysler Corporation, postage paid, and that Chrysler would then decide "to its satisfaction" whether there was a defect. Ten days after getting the car, Mrs. Henningsen was driving about 20 miles per hour when a loud noise came from the front. The car veered at 90 degrees to the side, crashing into a brick wall. The steering mechanism in the front end was crushed, making evaluation of mechanical defects difficult. Both the dealer and Chrysler Corporation denied any obligation to pay for the damaged car and for medical expenses. In *Henningsen v. Bloomfield Motors* the court said the limitation on the express warranty was a "sad commentary" on industry practice and could not override an implied warranty that the car was "reasonably suited for ordinary use" by the purchaser.[60] Chrysler had to pay.

Strict Liability

strict liability
The theory that liability exists, even in the absence of negligence, when an activity or product is inherently dangerous.

The doctrine of *strict liability,* or liability without fault, arose in tort law many years ago in England.[61] There it was established that anyone who engaged in a dangerous activity, such as using explosives or keeping ferocious animals, is liable for damages to others, even if the activity is conducted with utmost care. The key to strict liability is that the injured person need not prove negligence to prevail in court. It is presumed that any person engaged in ultrahazardous activities is automatically liable for adverse consequences to society.

The theory of strict liability was gradually extended to product liability and by the 1960s it was firmly entrenched.[62] This furthered the trend toward expansion of manufacturers' liability because injured consumers no longer had to prove negligence or breach of warranty to prevail in cases where there was some inherent danger in the use of a product. The law transferred much of the risk of using such products from consumers to manufacturers.

A landmark case involved William Greenman, who was turning a piece of wood when it flew off the machine, hitting him in the forehead, and causing serious injury. Greenman found evidence that the machine's design was defective and sued the manufacturer, Yuba Power Products, alleging negligence and breach of warranty. A lower court found no evidence of negligence or breach of express warranty, but a jury awarded Greenman $65,000 for breach of implied warranty. On appeal, the manufac-

---

[60] *Henningsen v. Bloomfield Motors, Inc,* 32 N.J. 358 at 374 and 384.

[61] See *Rylands v. Fletcher,* L.R. 3 H.L. 330 (1868).

[62] See American Law Institute, *Restatement of the Law of Torts,* 2d, ed. vol. 2 (Washington, DC: American Law Institute Publishers, 1965), sec. 402A, pp. 347–48.

turer raised serious issues that might have overturned the verdict, but the California Supreme Court imposed strict liability on the company, holding that all Greenman had to prove was that he was injured by the defective product while using it as it was intended to be used. Proving negligence or breach of warranty was not necessary.[63]

Under strict liability an injured plaintiff must prove only that the manufacturer made a product in a defective condition that made it unreasonably dangerous to the user, that the seller was in the business of selling such products, and that it was unchanged from its manufactured condition when purchased. The "defect" can exist because of poor design, insufficient warning, or even hazards unknown to the manufacturer. It is an inherent danger not anticipated by the buyer and can exist even though the product was carefully made.

This is the legal doctrine that dismantled the asbestos industry. When strict liability was accepted by the courts, sick asbestos workers no longer had to prove that Johns Manville or other companies were negligent because they already knew about asbestos hazards. All they had to prove was that asbestos was "defective," that is, that it contained an inherently dangerous quality. The asbestos companies were then liable to compensate workers having asbestos disease. As the court stated in *Greenman v. Yuba Power Products*, "The purpose of [strict] liability is to insure that the costs of injuries resulting from defective products are borne by the manufacturers that put such products on the market rather than by the injured persons who are powerless to protect themselves."[64] This idea, now embedded in the law, was another big step away from *caveat emptor*.

Costs and Benefits of the Tort System

Product liability suits are filed in every state and in federal courts. There is no central reporting of them. Comprehensive statistics about their number, disposition, and jury awards do not exist. However, they are a significant part of an overall tort system that imposes massive costs on business.

The tort system is designed to compensate injured parties and deter future wrongdoing by imposing the cost of injuries on persons or corporations whose behavior caused harm. A recent estimate is that this system inflicts an annual economic cost of $835 billion on American society, about 2.2 percent of GDP. This is the highest in the world and more than double the 1 percent average of other industrial nations.[65] About a third of this cost is from personal torts, most related to auto accidents; the rest is for commercial torts against businesses including product liability, medical malpractice, and workers compensation.

Much of the cost may be worth it. Because of product liability suits, dangerous products such as asbestos, cigarettes, flammable children's pajamas, and some birth control devices have been either taken off the market, had their sales restricted, or been redesigned. Those injured by them have been compensated. While the public may benefit from such lawsuits, others are more problematic. Lawsuit threats and expensive liability insurance regularly cause companies to

---

[63] *Greenman v. Yuba Power Products, Inc.,* 59 Cal. 2d 57 (1963).

[64] Ibid., at 63.

[65] Lawrence J. McQuillan and Hovannes Abramyan, *U.S. Tort Liability Index: 2010 Report* (San Francisco: Pacific Research Institute, 2010), pp. 17–18.

drop high-risk products such as off-road vehicles, medical implants, football helmets, drugs, and vaccines, some of which are valuable to society. An unknown number of new products and innovations never come to market because their liability potential scares manufacturers. In the pharmaceutical industry, funds that might go into developing new drugs are regularly diverted to litigation expenses. In other cases, liability insurance and litigation costs are simply passed on to consumers—like an extra tax on the products they buy. Sometimes liability costs even have the perverse effect of reducing safety. Extension ladders for home use now carry such a high price premium for product liability costs that many people just go on using deteriorating older ladders.[66]

CONCLUDING OBSERVATIONS

Consumerism is a word with two meanings. It refers both to an ideology and to a protective movement. In this chapter we discuss trends related to both meanings. First, consumerism as a way of life is spreading around the world because the conditions that support it are becoming more common. Where it is already established, it is strengthening its grip. Second, consumers in the United States are now more protected from injury, fraud, and other abuses than in the past because of stronger government regulation and more consumer-friendly common law doctrines.

These trends seem likely to continue. As the ideology of consumerism tightens its hold, responsible governments will expend more resources on issues raised by shopping for, purchasing, using, and displaying material objects. These issues will be more complex as populations grow, product choices expand, new technologies change products, and marketing becomes more amplified and pervasive.

[66] Michael Krauss, "Tort-Eating Contest," *The Wall Street Journal,* May 2, 2007, p. A20.

Alcohol Advertising

Anheuser-Busch had high hopes for Spykes. When the product was introduced in 2005, the giant brewer was losing market share to distilled spirits. In 2001 spirits makers had ended a long-standing voluntary policy against aggressive advertising. Liquor ads filled cable channels, then appeared on network affiliates. At NASCAR races lettering for Jim Beam and Jack Daniels appeared on the cars. More drinkers, notably young adults between 21 and 30 years old, found novelty in new brands, drinks, and mixes marketed by the distillers. Drinking tastes were changing. The trend in bars and clubs was moving away from domestic beers such as Anheuser-Busch's Budweiser.

Chairman August A. Busch III thought the company needed something "fun and new and innovative" to put into the hands of young drinkers.[1] That product was Spykes, a caffeinated malt liquor beverage that was 12 percent alcohol. It came in a 1.7-ounce bottle for $0.75 or a 2-ounce bottle for $1. Spykes included caffeine to capitalize on the popularity of mixing energy drinks with alcohol and it came in multiple flavors—Spicy Lime, Spicy Mango, Hot Melons, and Hot Chocolate. Drinkers could down it as a shot or experiment by mixing the flavors in beer or cocktails.

Anheuser-Busch tried to build the brand slowly through word of mouth at the local level. It set up a

[1] Quoted in Victor Reklaits, "Anheuser-Busch Unveils Product Aimed at 21- to 30-year Olds," *Daily Press-Newport,* December 2, 2005, p. 1.

brightly colored Web site with recipes for Spykes. "Try it as a shot. Spice up your beer. Invent a new cocktail. Mix two or more together for a new flavor."[2] Visitors downloaded music mixes, ringtones, and screen savers. A message board let users interact with the site. One exchange of ideas was, "I wonder if it still tastes good if you heat it up lol," followed by, "I'm gonna try putting one in the microwave . . . lol."[3]

By early 2007 Spykes had been rolled out in 32 states. Then a mighty eruption rose from the precincts of those self-appointed to protect the public from the evils of alcohol. It began with a press release from the Center for Science in the Public Interest, a watchdog group founded by Ralph Nader. In it, George A. Hacker, head of the group's alcohol campaign, unloaded a vicious attack on Spykes, calling it "the latest attempt by Anheuser-Busch to get children interested in alcohol." "This is a shameful ploy to market malt liquor to the Lunchables set," he said. "It's hard to imagine an adult purchasing this beverage, unless they were bringing it for a surprise date with Chris Hansen on Dateline NBC."

The evidence that Spykes targeted underage drinkers included its sweet flavors, the lack of age-verification and "teen-friendly" attractions on its Web site, and its caffeine (because energy drinks are popular with teenagers). Hacker called on the company to "immediately pull Spykes off of shelves, apologize to parents, and hope that in the meantime, no young person wraps his or her car around a tree after being Spyked once too often at the prom."[4]

The Center for Science in the Public Interest is at the forefront in a coalition of antialcohol groups that faults the alcoholic beverage industry for social problems caused by drinking. Others in this coalition piled on. Project Extra Mile, which fights underage drinking, expressed concern that minors could hide small Spykes bottles in pockets and purses.[5] Another

leading antialcohol group, the Marin Institute, called the product "egregious."[6]

Anheuser-Busch was taken by surprise. "Frankly," said a spokeswoman, "we're perplexed at this criticism. These professional critic groups need to stop the fear mongering and focus on reality."[7]

Concern spread. The Michigan State Police put its officers on alert for small bottles of Spykes, especially in women's purses. A county coroner in Illinois warned parents to "check your teen on prom night" because Spykes can "fit easily into a tux jacket pocket or . . . a purse for prom night 'fun.'"[8] The attorneys general of 28 states wrote to Anheuser-Busch expressing "serious concern" about Spykes and its marketing. Soon after receiving this letter, the company gave up. Due to what it called "unfounded criticism" by "perennial anti-alcohol groups" it announced the end for Spykes.

In fact, Spykes was just the opening skirmish in a war over caffeinated alcoholic beverages. It was an important product innovation in a highly competitive industry. Its success had illuminated a lucrative niche market. In fact, Anheuser-Busch had two similar caffeinated brands, Tilt and Bud Extra. MillerCoors was readying a brand named Sparks. And by 2008 more than two dozen smaller companies marketed products with colorful names such as Liquid Charge, Max Fury, Evil Eye, Joose, Four Loco, and Moonshot.

This proliferation was a red flag for antialcohol activists who felt caffeinated alcoholic beverages posed serious risks. These drinks contained less caffeine than a cup of coffee and met federal guidelines of 200 parts per million or less for caffeine in soft drinks. Nonetheless, the critics believed that caffeine stimulated drinkers, leading them to drink more and leaving them less aware they were impaired by alcohol. Studies confirm this. A professor in Florida, for example, found that patrons in a college bar district who consumed alcohol mixed with energy drinks were three times more likely to leave a bar highly

[2] Donna Leinwand, "Beermaker Urged to Pull Spykes," *USA Today,* April 10, 2007, p. A3.

[3] Quoted in Kari Huus, "A Booze Buzz for Teenyboppers?" MSNBC, April 3, 2007 at www.msnbc.msn.com/id/17862137/37273872.

[4] "CSPI Urges Nationwide Recall of Spykes 'Liquid Lunchables,'" Center for Science in the Public Interest, April 4, 2007, at www.cspinet.org.

[5] Jim Osborn, "Tiny Flavored Drink a Worry," *Columbus Telegram,* May 4, 2007, p. 1.

[6] David Lazarus, "Spykes Is No Longer Buzzing," *San Francisco Chronicle,* May 27, 2007, p. G1.

[7] Francine Katz, Anheuser-Busch vice president of communications, quoted in "Anheuser-Busch Product Criticized," *AFX News Limited,* April 6, 2007.

[8] Blog of Dr. Richard Keller, "Live from the Coroner's Office: Spykes, May 4, 2007, at http://coronerlakecountyil.blogspot.com/.

intoxicated and four times more likely to drive home.[9] Critics thought marketing claims duped young drinkers into complacency and they engaged in more risky behavior, from sexual aggression to drunk driving. The products were dangerous, their marketing execrable.

After Spykes, Anheuser-Busch was an easy target. In 2008 it was attacked by 11 state attorneys general who alleged that the labels on Tilt and Bud Extra failed accurately to disclose health risks and that ads for the products illegally targeted minors. The company agreed to reformulate the products, removing caffeine. MillerCoors was next. The attorneys general subpoenaed documents on Sparks, a new caffeinated brand MillerCoors was prepared to market. The Center for Science in the Public Interest sued the company, alleging it used unapproved ingredients that posed health and safety risks for consumers. Eventually MillerCoors gave in and agreed to remove caffeinated ingredients from Sparks.

Next in line was Constellation Brands, which sold a caffeinated schnapps, named Wide Eye. It was advertised with images of a woman boxer. One ad said, "this is your wake-up call." Another stated: "When you party with the world's first caffeinated schnapps it'll seem like the rest of the world is sleepwalking through life."

After receiving complaints from "consumers," the Federal Trade Commission issued a complaint against Constellation Brands, accusing it of saying "expressly or by implication, that consumers who drink Wide Eye will remain alert when consuming alcohol," and charging the statements were "false and misleading."[10] In a settlement the company agreed to stop making misleading claims. In fact, it had already stopped producing the brand.

Late in 2009 the Food and Drug Administration, responding to pressure from activists, sent a letter to 27 companies still making caffeinated alcoholic beverages asking them to explain why they believed caffeine is a safe ingredient. The agency reminded the companies that the Federal Food, Drug, and Cosmetic Act gave it jurisdiction over ingredients added

to drinks and that unless the companies provided data showing caffeine was "generally recognized as safe," it had the power to ban its use.[11]

They failed to do so and a year later the FDA notified them that the caffeine added to their beverages was an "unsafe food additive." The agency cautioned consumers to avoid caffeinated brands. Some of the companies continued to market them anyway, inviting the FDA to proceed toward a ban. If it does, it will write the final chapter in the caffeinated alcoholic brand story.

No matter, the industry and its opponents carry on a ceaseless cat-and-mouse game in which companies find new product and marketing innovations to replace initiatives blunted by critics and regulators. A new fight will emerge.

THE ATTACK ON ALCOHOL MARKETING

In the late 1800s temperance groups launched a noble crusade against the evils of alcohol. Eventually, they dragged the nation into a brief Prohibition era. In 1919 the Eighteenth Amendment banned production and sale of "intoxicating liquors," but the widely evaded ban lasted only until 1933, when the Twenty-First Amendment repealed it. Since then, prohibition attitudes have faded, but not vanished.

Since the end of Prohibition the majority of Americans have been drinkers. In a 1939 Gallup poll 58 percent of adults reported they drank alcohol. The number is a little higher today, 64 percent in a 2010 Gallup poll, and virtually unchanged over a decade.[12] Of the 33 percent who abstain about a third are neoprohibitionists who believe that drinking alcohol "can never be justified."[13]

The alcoholic beverage industry must live with these opponents. Although prohibition is a moribund idea, a strong, well-organized antialcohol movement marches on. Its strength lies in dozens of church,

---

[9] Dennis L. Thombs, et al., "Event-Level Analysis of Energy Drink Consumption and Alcohol Intoxication in Bar Patrons," *Journal of Addictive Behaviors* 11, no. 4 (2009).

[10] Federal Trade Commission, Complaint in the matter of Constellation Brands, Inc., No. C-4266, (2009), pp. 2–3.

[11] See, for example, the letter to City Brewing, undated, at www.fda.gov/Food/FoodIngredientsPackaging/ucm190387.htm.

[12] Gallup Poll, "Alcohol and Drinking," July 8-11, 2010, at http://www.gallup.com/poll/1582/alcohol-drinking.aspx.

[13] Princeton Survey Research Associates International, "Pew Forum 10 Nation Survey of Renewalists," USPSRA, 100506RENEW R29F, November 7, 2006.

health, consumer, and citizens' groups such as Mothers Against Drunk Driving. Its greatest successes have been getting all states to raise the legal drinking age to 21 and establishing a national drunken-driving standard of .08 blood alcohol content. It persists in trying to ban or restrict alcoholic beverage advertising. The movement's indictment against alcohol ads is based on four beliefs.

First, advertising increases consumption. Many ads are designed to attract new drinkers and promote additional drinking. Miller Lite's classic "Tastes Great–Less Filling" spots attempted to reposition beer as a competitor to soft drinks, telling consumers that light beer is a low-calorie drink that can be consumed more often than regular beer. The Michelob beer campaign based on the slogan "Put a little weekend in your week" encouraged weekend social drinkers to think of all days of the week as drinking occasions. And Polygamy Porter states, "Why Have Just One!"

Studies of the effect of advertising on consumption produce mixed evidence. Generally, national studies find no correlation between overall spending for alcohol ads and consumption.[14] The number of drinkers in the United States reached an all-time high of 71 percent in 1976, and per capita consumption reached its all-time high of 28.8 gallons a year in 1981. Although ad spending by the industry has steadily risen since then, the percentage of drinkers and per capita consumption have fallen. Some studies of local areas and small groups show that increased advertising does raise consumption. For example, a study of 139 women in Central Harlem found that alcohol dependence and abuse were associated with the density of outdoor alcohol ads in their neighborhoods.[15] Specific ad campaigns may

[14] See Henry Saffer, "Studying the Effects of Alcohol Advertising on Consumption," *Alcohol Health & Research World* 20, no. 4 (1996); and Hae-Kyong Bang, "Analyzing the Impact of the Liquor Industry's Lifting of the Ban on Broadcast Advertising," *Journal of Public Policy & Marketing,* Spring 1998.

[15] Naa Oyo A. Kwate and Ilan H. Meyer, "Association Between Residential Exposure to Outdoor Alcohol Advertising and Problem Drinking Among African American Women in New York City," *American Journal of Public Health,* February 2009.

also be successful. Recently, Heineken created an online virtual universe named Heineken City. Participants could buy apartments there with awards earned from playing branded games. Apartment owners received "keys" by mail and invitations to special events. They also could send free e-mail through a special domain, @heicity.com. According to the agency behind the campaign, it created 10,000 new Heineken drinkers.[16] Overall, however, no firm conclusion about the effect of advertising on consumption is warranted.

Second, ads encourage underage drinking. Underage alcohol consumption is a serious problem. Survey data show that by the 12th grade 72 percent of students have experimented with alcohol and 55 percent have been drunk at least once. Binge drinking, defined as five or more drinks in a row in the previous week, is reported by 8 percent of 8th graders, 16 percent of 10th graders, and 25 percent of 12th graders. About 40 percent of college students report binge drinking.[17] Overall, youth under 21 years old consume about 20 percent of all alcoholic drinks, forming an $8 billion market for the $40 billion industry.[18]

Each year some 5,000 underage drinkers die of alcohol-related injuries, most in car crashes, homicides, and suicides. Underage drinking is associated with academic failure, risky sexual behavior, and illicit drug use. New evidence shows that alcohol has pernicious effects on the developing adolescent brain.[19]

There is little proof that alcohol advertisers target minors in a calculated way, but there is enough evidence on which to base at least some suspicion. For example, all three segments of the alcohol industry—beer, wine, and distilled spirits—have agreed to voluntary media guidelines that require companies to buy ad placement only when at least 70 percent of the audience is expected to be 21 years of age or older. A study of alcohol ads on television found that companies did an outstanding job following the 70 percent guideline. However, each 1 percent rise in adolescent viewers in the audience was associated with 7 percent more beer ads, 15 percent more spirits ads, and 22 percent more "alcopop" ads, suggesting that some alcohol companies were seeking at least the youngest audiences they could reach while still complying with the media guidelines.[20]

In addition, expenditures for digital marketing are rising. Alcohol companies are putting more alcohol ads on the Internet, a realm heavily trafficked by an underage audience. There are many Internet marketing tactics. Viral marketing has been used for Miller Lite, Bud Light, Absolut, Captain Morgan, Smirnoff, and other brands. A YouTube video titled "Banned Super Bowl 2007 Bud Commercials" had 9 million views.[21] Alcohol advertisers also create sponsored sites and social networking sites with games, applications, widgets, blogs, music, screen savers, drink recipes, and other hooks. Although they often use age verification screens, these are easily bypassed. When viral campaigns work, the online community sends the advertising message. The advertiser is no longer able to screen recipients for age.

Activists claim that companies target underage drinkers not only with advertising but also with products designed to attract youth. These include flavored malt beverages like Spykes, often called "alcopops," single-serving vodka and tequila cocktails with names such as Yellin Melon Balls and Blue-Dacious Kamikaze, and novelty products such as cups of strawberry gelatin containing vodka. Other questionable marketing gimmicks include spring break promotions, brand placements in films seen by children, and brand logos on T-shirts and toys. A recent study showed that elementary school children who played with alcohol-themed toys tended to start drinking earlier.[22]

[16] "Heineken: "Heineken City," *Advertising Age,* September 15, 2008, p. S4.

[17] Figures are from Lloyd D. Johnson, et al., *Monitoring the Future: National Survey Results on Drug Use,* 1975–2008, Vol. II (Bethesda, MD: National Institutes of Health, 2009), pp. 22–23.

[18] Leslie B. Snyder, et al., "Effects of Alcohol Advertising Exposure on Drinking among Youth," *Archives of Pediatric and Adolescent Medicine,* January 2006, p. 18.

[19] Department of Health and Human Services, *The Surgeon General's Call to Action to Prevent and Reduce Underage Drinking: 2007* (Rockville, MD: Office of the Surgeon General, pp. 1–11 and 19–20.

[20] Paul J. Chung, et al., "Association Between Adolescent Viewership and Alcohol Advertising on Cable Television," *American Journal of Public Health,* March 2010, p. 555.

[21] Jeff Chester, Kathryn Montgomery, and Lori Dorfman, *Alcohol Marketing in the Digital Age* (Oakland, CA: Public Health Institute, May 2010), p. 10.

[22] Erica Weintraub Austin, "Why Advertisers and Researchers Should Focus on Media Literacy to Respond to the Effects of Alcohol Advertising on Youth," *International Journal of Advertising* 25, no. 4 (2006), p. 542.

Research about the effect of alcohol advertising on youth points to caution. A review of seven studies following the drinking behavior of 13,000 subjects aged 10 to 26 found that "exposure to alcohol advertising in young people influences their subsequent drinking behavior" and the greater the exposure the greater the frequency of drinking. Yet the study counseled that the effect of advertising was "generally modest."[23] Another study of 200 adolescents found that exposure to advertising influenced subsequent drinking frequency, but very little. It was responsible for only about 1 percent of variation. Peer influence was the strongest factor in drinking behavior, followed by parental influence.[24]

Third, sophisticated lifestyle advertising used by alcohol makers is manipulative because it locks into inner drives. Informational advertising presents details about a product, for example, its price, availability, and quality. In contrast, lifestyle advertising positions a product to fulfill emotional needs. Pictures and copy associate alcohol with fulfillment of desires for popularity, success, sophistication, rebellion, romance, and sexual conquest. The ads endow commodity products such as vodka or lager beer with brand images. Then by drinking that brand, the consumer adopts and projects the brand image. These ads convey little or no objective information about the beverage, only an emotional theme. Sexual images are a stable of alcohol marketing. However, one study of alcohol ads in magazines during a 14-year period found that other appeals predominated over sexual imagery. In *Life,* for example, prestige and social acceptance were more frequent themes.[25] Whatever the image, critics believe that since lifestyle ads play on emotion, they are highly manipulative. Consumers who respond to them are being tricked into fulfilling inner needs by drinking.

Fourth, alcohol advertising is targeted not only at young drinkers but, sometimes inappropriately, at other groups too. Critics object, for example, to endless ads for malt liquors in inner-city black neighborhoods and in black media. Malt liquor has a higher alcohol content than regular beer, and advertisements for it appeal to drinkers seeking inebriation. United States Beverage Company faced this criticism when it introduced a new brand named Phat Boy with graffiti-style ads for a "new malt liquor with an attitude." Phat Boy came in 40-ounce bottles, each having as much alcohol as a six-pack of regular beer. After an outcry by activists, the company dropped the brand. Hispanics are also targets. Perhaps because 40 percent of Hispanics in the United States are under 21 years old, Hispanic neighborhoods are filled with beer billboards. In Chicago, neighborhoods of elementary schools with more than 20 percent Hispanic children have 6.5 times more alcohol advertising than those with lower percentages.[26]

Young women are also targeted. Companies have introduced sweet-flavored drinks appealing to their tastes. Barton Brands sells a brand of vodka martini called Cocktails by Jenn in Blue Lagoon, Lemon Drop, and Appletini flavors. The drinks come in four-packs instead of six packs because they are lighter and easier for women to carry. Around their necks, the bottles have small metal charms such as a high-heeled shoe, diamond ring, or perfume bottle.[27] Only about 25 percent of women drink beer, so they are a huge growth market for brewers, who target them with lighter and flavored malt beverages such as Molson Coors' orange-flavored wheat beer Blue Moon and Anheuser-Busch's blueberry-flavored Wild Blue.

ALCOHOL MARKETERS DEFEND THEIR ADVERTISING

Alcoholic beverages are a mature industry. Due to population aging and health consciousness, per capita consumption is in a slow, long-term decline, dropping by an average 4 percent a year from 1998 to 2008. Still, Americans today drink a lot of alcohol,

[23] Lesley A. Smith and David R. Foxcroft, "The Effect of Alcohol Advertising, Marketing and Portrayal on Drinking Behavior in Young People: Systematic Review of Prospective Cohort Studies," *BMC Public Health,* February 2009, p. 11.

[24] Brian R. Kinard and Cynthia Webster, "The Effects of Advertising, Social Influences, and Self-Efficacy on Adolescent Tobacco Use and Alcohol Consumption," *Journal of Consumer Affairs,* March 2010, p. 39.

[25] Geng Cui, "Advertising of Alcoholic Beverages in African-American and Women's Magazines: Implications for Health Communication," *Howard Journal of Communications,* October 2000, p. 288.

[26] Keryn E. Pasch, et al., "Does Outdoor Alcohol Advertising Around Elementary Schools Vary by the Ethnicity of Students in the School?" *Ethnicity & Health,* April 2009.

[27] "Welcome to the World of Cocktails by Jenn," at www.oropesacreative.com/cbj/cocktails_750_d.htm.

about 26 gallons per capita in recent years, compared with 24 gallons of coffee and 21 gallons of milk.[28] And because the population is growing, industry sales grew from $29 billion in 1998 to $40 billion in 2008, a 39 percent increase.[29]

Amid overall market growth, industry segments compete fiercely for market share. Beer dominates, but since 1998 its sales have dropped from 63 percent of all alcoholic beverages to 49 percent. The wine sector picked up 10 percentage points to 34 percent and distilled spirits added 4 percentage points, rising to 17 percent.[30] Two implications of these figures for advertising are clear. First, if per capita consumption is stagnant but the overall population is growing, ads to recruit new and younger drinkers pay off. Second, if sales of industry segments are in flux, ads that promote brand loyalty can be used to protect or seize market share. Both conclusions lie behind the industry's heavy advertising. It defends its ads against the attacks of critics with these basic arguments.

First, ads are not the cause of alcohol abuse. As noted, studies fail to show that advertising increases consumption. So commercials and billboards cannot be blamed for car accidents, teen suicides, sexual aggression, spousal abuse, binge drinking, and alcoholism. Alcoholism, for example, is a complex disease caused by personality, family, genetic, and physiological factors rather than by viewing ads. Restraints would only deprive moderate drinkers of product information, not relieve social problems. As one advertising executive noted, trying to stop problem drinking with an ad ban "makes as little sense as trying to control the Ku Klux Klan by outlawing bed linens."[31] Ad restrictions would also muzzle a competitive weapon. Without advertising, starting a new national brand would be almost impossible and established brands would have an insurmountable advantage.

Second, antialcohol groups assume the public is too stupid to decide responsibly. The idea of curbing ads is condescending. Consumers are intelligent and skeptical. They are not duped by the association of alcohol with attractive images. Does anyone expect brewers and vintners to associate their products with root canals, traffic congestion, or taxes? The rejection of lifestyle advertising is also condescending. If a marketer positions a brand to satisfy emotional needs for sophistication, popularity, or sexual attractiveness, who is to say the consumer who finds gratification in the brand is wrong? No one would criticize a woman for feeling glamorous while she is wearing perfume, though the perfume is simply a chemical, nonessential to healthy life, and the glamour is created by imagery. Advertising also has the power to endow alcoholic beverages with emotional benefits for drinkers. The critics assume there is no merit to a product beyond its utilitarian qualities. What a dull world it would be if all products were marketed and used on this basis.

Third, the beer, wine, and spirits industries have voluntary codes to regulate advertising behavior. The policies in these codes are extensive and specific. For example, the Beer Institute's Advertising and Marketing Code prohibits depictions of excessive consumption, intoxication, and drinking while driving. Models in beer ads must be over 25 and "reasonably appear" to be over 21 years old. Beer ads should never have "any symbol, language, music, gesture, or cartoon character intended to appeal primarily to persons below the legal purchase age." No depictions of Santa Claus or sexual promiscuity are permitted.[32] The Wine Institute's Code of Advertising Standards has similar guidelines. It also prohibits showing the Easter bunny.[33] The Distilled Spirits Council of the United States' *Code of Good Practice for Distilled Spirits Advertising and Marketing* is similar to the two other codes. It allows advertisers to "depict affection or other amorous gestures," but forbids them to "rely upon sexual prowess or sexual success as a selling point," perhaps a fine distinction.[34]

[28] Department of Agriculture, Economic Research Service, "Data Sets: Beverages," February 1, 2010, at www.ers.usda.gov/Data/FoodConsumption/Spreadsheets/beverage.xls. Figures are for 2008.

[29] Department of Commerce, *Annual Survey of Manufactures, 2002 and 2009* (Washington, DC: Bureau of the Census, 2002 and 2009), sector 31.

[30] Ibid., sector 31.

[31] James Kuras of McCann-Erickson, quoted in Eric Clark, *The Want Makers* (New York: Viking Press, 1988), p. 285.

[32] At www.beerinstitute.org/tier.asp?bid=249, January 2006 edition.

[33] At www.wineinstitute.org/initiatives/issuesandpolicy/adcode, revised September 2005.

[34] At www.discus.org/pdf/61332_DISCUS.pdf, January 2009, p. 8.

DISTINCTIVE SINCE 1953

DISTINCTIVE SINCE 1930

Hef says drink responsibly

www.tanqueray.com

Although the distiller's advertising code warns advertisers not to "rely upon sexual prowess or sexual success as a selling point," this ad links a brand of gin with Hugh Hefner, mastermind of the *Playboy* philosophy. Source: © The Advertising Archives.

All three codes are backed by mechanisms to investigate possible violations. The Distilled Spirits Council, for example, convenes a 10-member Code Review Board to look at complaints. All the board members are industry executives and its rulings can be gentle, but it raps knuckles too. Recently it received a complaint from a company about a vodka print ad run by White Rock Distilleries. The ad depicted a man in a rabbit costume and two women in bikinis around a card table drinking vodka and playing strip poker. As the man smiled one woman removed her top. The complaint alleged that the ad violated the industry code's prohibition against using "sexual prowess or sexual success as a selling point." The board decided the ad violated the code "insofar as the female models are either partially clad or completely unclad in a strip poker game where the male model is fully

clad in a rabbit costume with a lascivious facial expression."[35] White Rock Distilleries stopped running the ad.

Fourth, alcohol makers promote responsible consumption. Companies broadcast public service announcements to preach moderation and safe driving. They sponsor designated-driver programs such as Anheuser-Busch's Alert Cab, which gives free taxi rides to restaurant and bar patrons who have been drinking. The Distilled Spirits Council funds college programs in which students teach other students about moderation. It also trains bartenders to serve drinks responsibly. These efforts, while important, do not get nearly the funding of brand advertising.

[35] Distilled Spirits Council of the United States, *Semiannual Code Report,* 10th ed. (Washington, DC: DISCUS, September 2009), p. 9.

According to one study by an activist organization, responsibility ads are only 2 percent of the alcohol advertising budget and youths see 239 product ads for every message about safe driving.[36]

Finally, targeting respects diverse audiences. The industry agrees that it targets younger drinkers, minorities, women, and other groups with advertising themes. Young adult drinkers find value in advertising that informs them of new products and creates images that fulfill their emotional needs. The puzzle faced by companies is that young adults aged 21 to 25 share many interests and behaviors with those just below the legal drinking age. Some spillover appeal is inevitable. Ads aimed at minorities are also legitimate. Market segmentation and the targeted advertising that makes it work are standard in many industries. When toy companies make black or Latina dolls, social critics applaud, but when alcohol companies make products that appeal to minority communities, critics argue that these consumers are too gullible to withstand manipulation. The implication is that Hispanic or black consumers are not as astute as white consumers. The real problem is that the product is alcohol, not that the ads have ethnic or racial appeal. Finally, there is no evidence that targeting raises consumption. Despite concerns over targeting young women, a large national study found that the percentage of female 12th graders having a drink in the past 30 days declined from 47 percent in 1998 to 41 percent in 2008 and the number of young women aged 19 to 28 who drank a flavored alcohol beverage in the past 30 days declined from 30 percent in 2004 to 27 percent in 2008.[37]

RESTRICTING ALCOHOL ADVERTISING

Alcohol advertising is highly regulated. Companies must navigate a labyrinth of restrictions. Approximately half the states restrict ad placements. Arizona prohibits it on school buses. Ohio bans it near churches, schools, and playgrounds. Many cities also restrict it. San Diego bans billboard ads within 500 feet of playgrounds, child care centers, schools, and libraries. San Jose bans beer and wine ads on fueling islands at gas stations. San Francisco prohibits alcohol ads on public transit.[38]

Three federal agencies have the power to regulate marketing claims. The Food and Drug Administration approves ingredients in alcoholic beverages for safety. The Federal Trade Commission has the authority to stop advertising that is false, deceptive, misleading, or unfair. The Department of Treasury's Alcohol and Tobacco Tax and Trade Bureau enforces labeling requirements and monitors advertising for compliance with certain requirements under a 1935 law. For example, if the words "Scotch whisky" are used, the product must be manufactured in Scotland. Labels cannot resemble a postage stamp. Depictions of the American flag cannot appear on labels or in ads. Advertisers cannot use subliminal means, defined as "any device or technique that is used to convey, or attempts to convey, a message to a person by means of images or sounds of a very brief nature that cannot be perceived at a normal level of awareness."[39]

Originally, the law prohibited statements of alcohol content on labels so that companies could not start strength wars. However, in 1995 the Supreme Court held that censoring this information violated bottlers' speech rights, so alcohol content can now be printed on labels and is required on distilled spirits labels.[40]

Altogether, the body of government regulation covering alcohol advertising imposes significant restraints. But critics want stronger, more uniform measures. In the 1990s several bills were introduced in Congress to limit alcohol ads, for example, by banning them near schools and playgrounds, in publications with large youth readerships, on college campuses, and during prime-time television hours.[41] The prospect for such measures faded after

---

[36] Center on Alcohol Marketing and Youth, *Drowned Out: Alcohol Industry 'Responsibility' Advertising on Television*, 2001–2005 (Washington, DC: CAMY, 2005), p. 1.

[37] Lloyd D. Johnson, et al., *Monitoring the Future: National Survey Results on Drug Use*, 1975–2008, vol. I, table D-70 and vol. II, table 5-3.

[38] Marin Institute, *Out of Home Advertising: A 21st Century Guide to Effective Regulation* (San Rafael, CA: Marin Institute, March 2009), pp. 9–11.

[39] 27 CFR §5.65(h), 2010.

[40] *Rubin v. Coors Brewing Company*, 514 U.S. 618 (1995).

[41] See, for example, the "Voluntary Alcohol Advertising Standards for Children Act," H. R. 1292, 105th Congress, 1st Sess. (1997), introduced by Rep. Joseph P. Kennedy II (D-Massachusetts).

a Supreme Court decision that struck down a federal ban on broadcast ads by casinos.[42]

The court also chipped away at other restrictions. Until 1996 Rhode Island banned price advertising for alcoholic beverages, claiming it was justified in doing so to promote temperance. However, the justices struck the ban down, saying price advertising is protected by the First Amendment's free speech guarantee.[43]

Other initiatives by antialcohol forces have failed. A series of lawsuits sought to regulate the alcohol industry using product liability law. Parents of underage drinkers accused more than 100 companies of defrauding them by attracting their sons and daughters to spend family money illegally on alcohol. The parents alleged injury from a complicated scheme including marketing "alcopops" with themes that appeal to youth, distributing promotional items, using cartoons, sponsoring spring break events, and setting up sham regulatory codes. They sought to recover the money their underage children spent and to stop the ongoing seduction of youth. However, courts dismissed these lawsuits for insufficient evidence that company actions caused underage alcohol abuse.[44]

Some countries go further than the United States in national restrictions. India and Thailand ban all alcohol advertising. Ireland prohibits distilled spirits ads on television and radio and prohibits beer and wine ads before sports events. France bans alcohol ads on television and restricts ad content in other media. Norway, Sweden, Denmark, and Finland prohibit advertising beverages with more than a certain alcohol content ranging from 2.2 to 3.5 percent, less than regular beer or wine. Italy, Spain, and Portugal restrict televised alcohol ads before 8:00, 9:00, and 10:00 p.m., respectively. Greece limits the number of broadcast ads per brand per day. Russia prohibits the appearance of people and animals in television ads. When alcohol companies skirted these rules with off-screen voices and animated bottles, it banned that too. Such restrictions might not work in the United States due to constitutional protections for free speech.

[42] *Greater New Orleans Broadcasting Association, Inc., v. U.S.*, 527 U.S. 173 (1999).

[43] *44 Liquormart v. Rhode Island*, 517 U.S. 484 (1996).

[44] See, for example, *Hakki v. Zima Company*, 03-0009183 (Sup. Ct. Dist. Col., November 14, 2003); and Eisenberg v. Anheuser-Busch, Inc., *1:04 CV 1081* (N.D. Ohio, February 1, 2006).

ARE RESTRICTIONS ON ALCOHOL ADS CONSTITUTIONAL?

Images and statements in advertising are speech. Therefore, proposals for muzzling liquor, beer, and wine companies raise constitutional issues. The First Amendment protects all speech from government curbs, but courts have distinguished *noncommercial* speech from *commercial* speech. The former is speech in the broad marketplace of ideas, encompassing political, scientific, and artistic expression. Such speech is broadly protected. The latter is speech intended to stimulate business transactions, including advertising. This kind of speech receives less protection.

The right of free speech is assumed to be a fundamental barrier against tyranny and is not restricted lightly. Courts will not permit censorship of noncommercial speech unless it poses an imminent threat to public welfare, as it would, for example, if a speaker incited violence or a writer tried to publish military secrets.

With respect to commercial speech, however, various restrictions are allowed. For example, ads for securities offerings can appear only in the austere format of a legal notice and tobacco ads are barred on radio and TV. Would courts approve additional restrictions on alcoholic beverage advertising?

The most important legal guidelines for weighing restraints on commercial speech are those set forth by the Supreme Court in 1980 in the *Central Hudson* case.[45] Here the Court struck down a New York regulation banning advertising by public utilities, a regulation intended to help conserve energy. Justice Lewis Powell, writing for the majority, set forth a four-part test to decide when commercial speech could be restricted.

- The ad in question should promote a lawful product and must be accurate. If an ad is misleading or suggests illegal activity, it does not merit protection.
- The government interest in restricting the particular commercial speech must be substantial, not trivial or unimportant.

[45] *Central Hudson Gas & Electric Corp. v. Public Service Commission*, 447 U.S. 557.

- The advertising restriction must directly further the interest of the government. In other words, it should demonstrably help the government reach its public policy goal.

- The suppression of commercial speech must not be more extensive than is necessary to achieve the government's purpose.

All government actions to ban or restrict alcohol ads could be challenged by industry and would have to pass the four-part *Central Hudson* test to survive.

ALCOHOL ADVERTISING IN PERSPECTIVE

The mainstream antialcohol campaign today is to restrict advertising more. The Prohibition Party argument that alcohol is immoral, sinful, and unhealthy has few advocates now. But those who still believe it have seized on underage drinking as a weapon to attack the alcohol industry. Since underage drinking is a genuine social problem, antialcohol activists find many allies.

Alcohol advertising is creative, witty, and clever. Evidence is strong that children and teenagers are attracted to alcohol ads and increasing exposure is associated with more future drinking. Some of this drinking leads to tragedy for families. Such serious concerns are to be weighed against other factors.

Some studies show the influence of ads is very modest. Most Americans drink alcoholic beverages. Advertising limits would reduce information about products. And the constitution, while permitting restrictions, protects advertisers from needless and sweeping government actions. What dangers of alcohol ads justify what restrictions?

Questions

1. Were Spykes and Wide Eye bad products? Do you think they were marketed in objectionable or misleading ways? Do you think companies should be allowed to market other caffeinated alcoholic beverages?

2. Do alcoholic beverage companies fulfill their ethical duty to be informative and truthful in advertising? Do they generally uphold their ethical duty to minimize potential harm to society from underage drinking?

3. Are some beer, wine, or spirits ads misleading? What examples can you give? What is misleading in them? Do some ads contain images and themes that go too far in appealing to an audience under the legal drinking age? Can you give examples?

4. Do you believe there is a need for more restrictions on alcohol advertising? If so, what limits are needed? Explain how a ban or any restrictions could meet the *Central Hudson* guidelines.

Chapter Eighteen

Corporate Governance

Mark Hurd

Mark Hurd arrived as the chief executive officer at Hewlett-Packard in 2005. The company's board of directors, a body of strong and conflicted personalities, had just fired Carly Fiorina, the first woman ever to lead a corporation as big as HP. Her dual sins were trying to dominate the board and allowing the stock price to languish. Her story is the subject of the case study at the end of this chapter.

Hurd got along with the board and got results. He was diligent and relentless, dictating a regimen of cost-cutting, wringing waste from every department, forcing managers to justify every dollar in their budgets. Soon he eliminated 14,500 jobs, about 10 percent of the company's workforce. His severities were resented by some, but share prices climbed. He also had strategic vision. Major acquisitions moved HP into growing markets. He acquired Electronic Data Systems (EDS), then shed another 24,600 workers in the consolidation. He acquired 3Com, then Palm Inc. In five years he turned HP into the world's largest information technology company. Its share price, shown in Figure 18.1, more than doubled.

Then, on June 29, 2010, Hurd opened a letter from celebrity lawyer Gloria Allred. It accused him of sexually harassing an HP marketing contractor named Jodi Fisher by touching her body suggestively and speaking of intimate personal matters. It also said he had breached his duty of confidentiality in telling her about HP's pending purchase of EDS in 2008. An eight-page chronology of his contacts with Fisher was enclosed. The letter ended with an offer to settle. He immediately gave it to an HP attorney, who forwarded it to the board of directors.[1]

In 2007 Hurd had begun a series of "executive summits" held around the world to meet important customers. An assistant recommended Jodi Fisher as a consultant who could help at the events by briefing him on people, making introductions, and steering him around the room. Her qualifications were elusive. After graduating from Texas Tech University with a political science degree, she moved to Los Angeles seeking her fortune as an actress. Her subsequent portfolio included nude *Playboy* photos, roles in a string of erotic films such as "Intimate Obsession" and "Blood

---

[1] Robert A. Buth, Ben Worthen, and Justin Scheck, "Accuser Said Hurd Leaked an H-P Deal," *The Wall Street Journal,* November 6–7, 2010, p. A1.

FIGURE 18.1

Hewlett-Packard Share Price: 2005–2011

Source: Yahoo! Finance, Historical Prices.

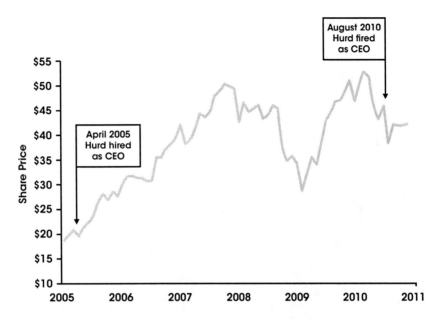

Dolls," and a reality television show appearance. Along the way, she married, divorced, and managed apartments.[2]

Hurd first interviewed Fisher in Los Angeles. Then she was flown to Denver, where they had a three-hour dinner. He hired her and between 2007 and 2009 they worked a dozen meetings together at luxury hotels around the world. Often they dined after the day's event. She was paid between $1,000 and $10,000 each time.

The 10 members of HP's board were concerned about the letter. That weekend they conducted a conference call to talk with him. Hurd said he and Fisher had dined several times but were not closely acquainted. He denied any sexual relationship with her.[3] Later she would say the same. He assured them her accusations were false. Some directors had done searches of her name, discovering her background in adult films. Hurd said he was unaware of this. The board was supportive. It wanted to keep a talented chief executive.

Shortly, Hurd suggested to the board that HP pay to settle the allegations. It did not agree. It also was unsure of its obligation to disclose events to shareholders. If the tale of a CEO and an adult actress came out, tabloid journalism would damage HP's reputation. That could affect the share price. If the claims were groundless, however, was there any duty to reveal them?

The board also hired a law firm to investigate Hurd's actions. That investigation revealed a series of prevarications. While Hurd had denied a close relationship with Fisher, a different picture emerged. The two had often dined together. They met at times when she did not work at an HP event. One night HP flew Fisher to a luxury hotel in Boise, Idaho, where she and Hurd had dinner. They watched a football game

---

[2] Alexandra Berzon, Ellen Byron, and Ben Worthen, "Far From H-P, A Job in Jersey," *The Wall Street Journal,* August 12, 2010, p. B1.

[3] Robert A. Guth, "Former H-P CEO Defends His Acts," *The Wall Street Journal,* October 19, 2010, p. B3.

632   Chapter 18   *Corporate Governance*

Mark Hurd, chief executive officer, chairman of the board, and president of Hewlett-Packard is shown here speaking at a 2010 company event. Source: AP Photo/Danny Johnston.

in the bar, then in his room. The next day Hurd met with some local officials, but Fisher was not present. Hurd told the investigators that he liked to relax with Fisher at the end of the day. She made him feel uplifted. It was, he told investigators, a "very close personal relationship."[4]

Also, study of Hurd's computer revealed he had viewed 30 pornographic Web pages with scenes from her films. An examination of his expense reports found that six times he dined with Fisher but the notations recorded his bodyguard as the dinner companion. Hurd said his assistant filled out the reports and often put the bodyguard's name in when she was unsure who was present.

At this point Hurd's support on the board ebbed. Some directors favored firing him, but at least two holdouts wanted to avoid losing such an effective CEO. If the sexual harassment claims were groundless, the rest was of small concern. The directors scheduled a meeting with Gloria Allred to review the allegations. Hurd offered to repay the company for contested expense claims amounting to about $20,000. This was a minor amount to him and to the company. Since arriving he had received $146 million in compensation.

Other directors were unpersuaded. "He lied to my face and he's lying to you," one said.[5] He had violated HP's conduct code, which requires "uncompromising integrity" from every employee in a "company known for its ethical leadership." Part of the code sets forth a "Headline Test," to distinguish right from wrong by asking how actions would look if they came out in a news story or were reviewed by respected colleagues. It also admonishes employees to "[c]reate business records that accurately reflect the truth."[6] At HP a fabricated expense account was grounds for firing.

Early in August, Hurd reached an undisclosed financial settlement with Fisher that prohibited her from discussing the allegations. She released a statement saying there were many inaccuracies in her letter. Hurd explained he had settled because the amount was small compared with going to court.[7] The board was furious. Now it would have no chance to hear from Fisher and her lawyers. Hurd's remaining supporters gave up and agreed to a unanimous vote calling for his resignation. He complied.

[4] Guth, Worthen, and Scheck, "Accuser Said Hurd Leaked an H-P Deal," p. A10.

[5] Lucille S. Salhany, quoted in ibid., p. A10.

[6] Hewlett-Packard Company, *Our Standards of Business Conduct* (Palo Alto, CA: Hewlett-Packard Company, 2010 revision), front cover and pp. 3, 8, and 11.

[7] Guth, "Former H-P CEO Defends His Acts," p. B3.

His severance package was worth approximately $40 million. HP's share price dropped 14 percent over the next weeks and did not fully recover for six months. Fisher released a statement that she was "saddened" by his downfall.[8]

Not everyone agreed with the decision. A *Wall Street Journal* columnist called Hurd's offenses "piddling."[9] A *Los Angeles Times* business writer suggested "maybe it's the board that should have gone, not Hurd."[10] Larry Ellison, founder and CEO of Oracle Corporation, spoke for many.

> The HP board just made the worst personnel decision since the idiots on the Apple board fired Steve Jobs many years ago . . . In losing Mark Hurd, the HP board failed to act in the best interest of HP's employees, shareholders, customers and partners.[11]

Ellison then hired Hurd as a co-president of Oracle. HP filed a trade secrets lawsuit because Hurd had signed a confidentiality agreement. He was intimately familiar with the pricing details and component costs of HP products in areas where HP and Oracle directly competed. To settle the suit, Hurd waived his rights to $14 million of stock options in his severance package. He stayed at Oracle.

The Mark Hurd story is a story of corporate governance in action. The duty of every company's board is to watch over management in the interest of shareholders. What was the board's duty here, to maximize shareholder wealth or to uphold the integrity of management? In this chapter we define corporate governance and explain how it works. We also discuss its flaws. An unusual part of the Mark Hurd story is that, unlike many corporate boards, this one had the courage to fire a CEO. As we will show, many do not.

WHAT IS CORPORATE GOVERNANCE?

corporate governance
The exercise of authority over members of the corporate community based on formal structures, rules, and procedures.

Corporate governance is the exercise of authority over members of the corporate community based on formal structures, rules, and procedures. This authority is based on a body of rules defining the rights and duties of shareholders, boards of directors, and managers. These parties form a power triangle, shown in Figure 18.2, that controls the corporation. Steady tension exists between them, and the rules are designed to align their interests, distribute power, and settle disputes. The rules come from multiple sources, including state charters, state and federal laws, stock exchange listing standards, and corporate governance policies.

Corporate governance practice has changed dramatically over time. From the rise of market economies in the early 1700s until the mid-1800s most companies were small and run by their owners. However, with industrial capitalism some small companies grew very large and could no longer be capitalized or managed by one or two owner-proprietors. Soon ownership was dispersed in a stockholder

---

[8] Quoted in Ben Worthen and Joann S. Lublin, "Mark Hurd Neglected to Follow H-P Code," *The Wall Street Journal,* August 9, 2010, p. B1.

[9] Holman W. Jenkins, Jr., "The Mark Hurd Show," *The Wall Street Journal,* August 18, 2010, p. A15.

[10] Michael Hiltzik, "Ouster of HP Chief Has Look of Panic," *Los Angeles Times,* August 11, 2010, B6.

[11] Quoted in Ashlee Vance, "Oracle Chief Faults H.P. Board for Forcing Hurd Out," *The New York Times on the Web,* August 10, 2010.

FIGURE 18.2

The Power Triangle
Corporate governance is the exercise of authority over members of the corporate community. It is based on rules that define power relationships between shareholders, boards of directors, and managers.

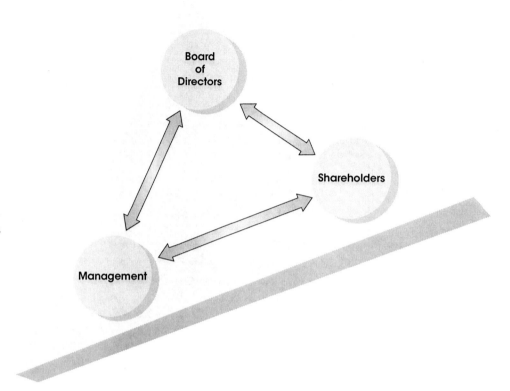

multitude where each person had only a small, fractional investment and most had little knowledge of the business. In this situation, power passed to expert managers who ran companies for the unorganized, inarticulate crowd of owners.

With the transition, boards of directors formed to monitor management for the shareholders. Shareholders were largely unqualified to manage what they owned. Hired managers had the competence to run a complex corporation, but they needed day-to-day freedom from a crowd of meddling owners. Yet they still needed supervision, because as salaried employees they lacked the same incentive to maximize profits as the owners. They might even be tempted to make their continued employment and larger salaries the top priority. It became the board's job to balance, mediate, and reconcile the competing powers and interests of owners and managers. Thus emerged the basic structure of modern corporate governance.

THE CORPORATE CHARTER

corporate charter
A document issued by a state government to create a corporation.

A *corporate charter* is the document that creates a corporation. Charters are also called articles of incorporation. U.S. corporations are chartered by the state in which they incorporate.[12] All 50 states and the District of Colombia charter corporations. When a corporation is formed in a state, it is then governed by that

[12] A few quasi-public enterprises chartered by the federal government, such as the Tennessee Valley Authority, are exceptions.

state's laws. At the Constitutional Convention of 1787, the founders debated a federal chartering power but decided that state controls were appropriate to regulate the more geographically limited corporate activity of that era. Their judgment was eventually outdated. As corporations expanded in size and power, states were unable to control their excesses and, as we will see, the federal government has slowly added layers of corporate law above state laws. However, all corporations are still chartered by a state.

Corporate charters specify the purpose of the corporation, usually "any lawful act for which a corporation may be organized," and specify basic rights and duties of stockholders, directors, and officers. Fundamentally, they lodge control over the enterprise in stockholders who own shares of stock with voting rights in corporate matters. State corporation laws then give directors a *fiduciary responsibility* to shareholders, that is, as the entity entrusted with oversight of the owner's property, they are legally bound to care for that property in the owner's interest. They are responsible for appointing the managers who run the day-to-day affairs of the company.

Charters may also include provisions about numbers of shares and classes of stock authorized, dividends, annual shareholder meetings, the size of boards, and procedures for removing directors. They are brief documents, usually no more than 10 or 20 pages even for the largest companies. They are supplemented with *bylaws,* or rules the company writes to clarify in detail how broad provisions of its charter will work. These bylaws resolve such ordinary matters as who presides over shareholder meetings and whether directors can hold a meeting over the telephone.

States compete to attract the incorporation fees and tax revenues of corporations. For more than a century tiny Delaware has been the victor in this competition. It charters about half of all public corporations in the United States. About 17 percent of its state tax revenues, far more than any other state, come from chartering fees. Although costs of incorporating in Delaware are high, its corporate laws are friendly toward directors and managers. To maintain its addiction to corporate tax revenue the state has repeatedly innovated more flexible and enabling rules. Other states must match or approach its standards to remain competitive.

Delaware refuses to be underregulated. For example, when the personal liability of directors began to expand in the 1980s, several states experimented with tentative limits to such exposure. Delaware reacted by limiting director liability for all but the most witless and negligent acts. Within a year, 35 states matched its leniency.[13] In this race to the bottom "no one in Delaware is willing to play hare while some other state tortoise gains ground."[14] In addition, Delaware also has a special Chancery Court that handles only business cases and is very friendly to boards and managers. It is expensive and difficult for all but the wealthiest shareholders of a Delaware corporation to prevail in a lawsuit against directors or managers.

fiduciary responsibility
The legal duty of a representative to manage property in the interest of the owner.

bylaws
Rules of corporate governance adopted by corporations.

---

[13] Roberta Romano, "The States as a Laboratory: Legal Innovation and State Competition for Corporate Charters," *Yale Journal on Regulation,* Summer 2006, p. 212.

[14] Delaware attorney Lawrence A. Hamermesh, quoted in Mark J. Roe, "Delaware's Shrinking Half-Life," *Stanford Law Review,* December 2009, p. 129.

Shareholder activists, who believe that boards and top executives have too much power in corporate governance, are provoked by Delaware. They lobbied North Dakota to pass a new, model law with provisions that strengthen the powers of stockholders and make boards more independent of management.[15] Corporations such as Whole Foods Markets that emphasize social responsibility in their strategies have been pressured to reincorporate in North Dakota. There has been no rush.

POWER IN CORPORATE GOVERNANCE: THEORY AND REALITY

The legal line of power in state charters and incorporation laws runs from the state, to shareholders, to directors, to managers. However, this legal theory diverges from the reality as widely practiced. The theory is shown on the left side of Figure 18.3. The reality, as shown on the right, is that CEOs often dominate boards of directors and both together dominate shareholders.

Stockholders

Stockholders are said to be owners of corporations. However, rather than owning an identifiable part or fraction of the corporation as property they own only a

FIGURE 18.3   **Flow of Authority in Corporate Governance**

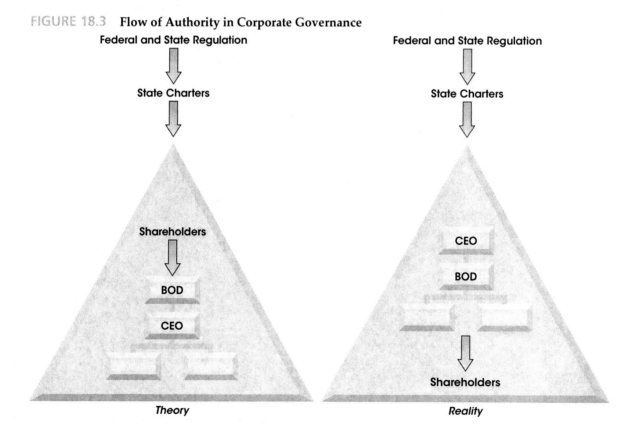

[15] The Publicly Traded Corporations Act (2007).

stock certificate. Owning this certificate gives them certain limited, but important, rights. A basic reason their rights are limited is that under state laws common stockholders are free of liability for the corporation's actions, therefore, their control of those actions is diminished.

Stockholders' rights are given in corporate charters, bylaws, and state and federal laws. Their basic entitlements are to (1) sell their stock, (2) vote to elect directors and on other corporate issues, (3) receive information about the corporation, (4) receive dividends, (5) sue the corporation if directors and officers commit wrongful acts, and (6) acquire residual assets in case of bankruptcy, but only after payment of creditors and bondholders.

If stockholders are dissatisfied with corporate management, they can sell their shares. Otherwise, they influence management by voting in corporate elections. In large public companies stockholders receive notice of elections to be held at annual meetings. Such elections typically ask for a vote on director nominees, management's choice of auditors, charter amendments or changes in bylaws, stock issuances, and nonbinding resolutions. Stockholders are invited to attend an annual meeting and vote their shares. Or, if they do not attend, they can fill out a ballot-like *proxy card* that gives management the authority to cast votes for them as they indicate. The proxy card is accompanied by a *proxy statement* with legally mandated information about the matters up for a vote, including biographies of director nominees and their qualifications, a detailed analysis of executive compensation, and the text of other proposals.

The annual meeting itself is a formal, ritualized event usually held in the spring. Its purpose is to allow voting and interaction between stockholders, directors, and officers. A typical meeting has several parts, a business meeting where agenda items are raised and voting results announced, a presentation by the chief executive about the company's outlook, and a question-and-answer session for stockholders. When the floor is opened for questions at a big company meeting, meaningful exchanges are rare. A few stockholders may praise the CEO for doing a good job. Activists, who have purchased a few shares to gain entry, harangue management for irresponsible behavior. Most are respectful, but some are not. At a recent Chevron Corp. meeting an energy activist started a protest chant and was arrested.[16] Every spring a few others require security escorts to leave. Employees may rise to express grievances. At one FedEx meeting a freight handler stated that while the company was making millions of dollars in profits he and others were not paid enough to "have a decent life."[17]

Shareholder Resolutions

Shareholders, either individuals or funds, can propose resolutions for a vote at the annual meeting. These resolutions are printed in the proxy statement. Securities

---

proxy card
A form stockholders mark giving management the right to vote their shares as indicated. It is also called simply a proxy or a proxy form.

proxy statement
A booklet of information sent to stockholders before annual votes on directors, executive pay, and other matters.

---

[16] John Letzing, "Activist Faces Charges in Chevron Outburst," *The Wall Street Journal,* September 29, 2010, p. B4.

[17] Comments of Ray Mercado, FedEx Corp., *FedEx 2010 Shareowners Meeting Transcript,* September 27, 2010, pp. 10–11.

and Exchange Commission (SEC) regulations set forth the requirements they must meet, including the following.[18]

- Sponsors must own $2,000 or more of the company's shares for at least one year.
- They may not submit more than one resolution a year.
- The resolution cannot exceed 500 words and must be sent to the company for approval at least 120 days before the annual meeting.
- The shareholder must appear at the meeting to present the resolution.
- The resolution must get 3 percent of the vote to be resubmitted the next year, 6 percent to be resubmitted a third year, and 10 percent for the fourth year and after.

Under SEC rules, a company can reject a proposed resolution for any of 13 reasons. For example, it can reject a proposal if it is a personal grievance, contains false or misleading statements, or deals with matters beyond the company's influence. The SEC must approve each rejection. In 2009 a Catholic investor group wanted to introduce a proposal about sensitivity to American Indian peoples at the FedEx annual meeting. The resolution required FedEx to "identify and dissociate with any names, symbols and imagery that disparage American Indian peoples" and to report on whether its diversity training for management was "sensitive to Native American rights, histories and cultures." FedEx contacted the SEC, seeking to omit the proposal because it dealt with "ordinary business operations." Proposals can be excluded under this exception if they constitute shareholder micromanagement of fundamental, day-to-day tasks in running the company. FedEx argued this one sought oversight of advertising and training, both "ordinary" functions that shareholders were unqualified to oversee. The SEC agreed and the proposal was omitted.[19]

Each year hundreds of shareholder resolutions qualify to appear on proxy statements. In 2010, 507 resolutions were voted on. Most, 342, wanted corporate governance reforms such as allowing shareholders to convene special meetings, splitting the chairman and CEO positions, and forcing managers to hold stock awards until two years after their employment ended. Ninety got a majority of votes cast. Another 165 resolutions focused on social issues, including concerns such as political spending, carbon emissions, toxic chemicals, diversity, and animal welfare. There was little support for them. Only two had a majority vote, both requesting the company prepare a report on sustainability.

Almost universally, shareholder proposals are followed by the statement, "The Board of Directors recommends a vote AGAINST this proposal." This is accompanied by an explanation of why the board urges rejection. Its opposition is usually fatal. Even when a proposal receives a majority vote, it is not binding. However, its success puts pressure on the company and often results in change.

---

[18] "Shareholder Proposals," 17 CFR §240.14a-8 (2011).

[19] Securities and Exchange Commission, Office of Chief Counsel, Division of Corporation Finance, FedEx Corporation No Action Letter, July 14, 2009.

Assessing Shareholder Influence

Although in theory shareholders have the voting power to influence or even replace management, they rarely exercise it. First, corporate elections are not fully democratic. They have several elements of democracy. Shareholders are at liberty to vote. Their votes count equally.[20] And the majority rules. However, as in old-style communist elections there is often no contest. Directors usually run unopposed. Stockholders can vote for or against them (or abstain), but they cannot vote for another candidate. Stockholders can submit nominees to board nominating committees, but the directors do not have to pick them. Occasionally a large shareholder tries to challenge the election of one or more directors, but this is hugely expensive and rarely successful.

Management also has other advantages. It is united, while stockholders are fragmented. Among such a large group of passive individuals it is hard for opposition to coalesce. Most shareholders follow management's voting recommendations. And as proxies come in, management can see how the vote is going and, if necessary, call on large shareholders, including brokers or pension funds, to change their votes. In sum, the influence of shareholders is very weak. In 1949 one perceptive investor summed up the contradiction of stockholder power this way. The words are as apt today as then.

> In legal rights and legal machinery . . . stockholders as a class are king. Acting as a majority they can hire and fire managements and bend them completely to their will. Though ownership may be widely scattered, there is no legal obstacle to many stockholders' joining forces so as to create an effective majority voice on any issue that may arise . . .
>
> [I]n practice . . . the stockholders are a complete washout. As a class they show neither intelligence nor alertness. They vote in sheep-like fashion for whatever the management recommends and no matter how poor the management's record of accomplishment may be.[21]

FEDERAL REGULATION OF GOVERNANCE

For more than 150 years state incorporation statutes, laws, and court decisions defined the requirements of corporate governance. At first this worked well. Most corporations were small. Their activities were confined within state boundaries. However, in the late 1800s and early 1900s mergers and firm growth created much larger firms that served national markets. These firms required more capital. Before the 1890s only a small number of very wealthy individuals held stock. But larger firms issued stock freely and their ownership was dispersed among small investors in many states.

---

[20] An exception is when companies have dual classes of stock. An example is Ford Motor Company, where members of the Ford family own Class B shares, which are given greater weight than common shares in company elections.

[21] Benjamin Graham, *The Intelligent Investor* (New York: HarperCollins, 2005), p. 207. Originally published in 1949.

Now both business activity and stock ownership crossed state lines. State corporation laws proved less and less adequate for oversight, especially since corporations sought charters in those states with the most flexible and permissive rules. Perhaps the greatest defect of state governance laws was inability to prevent fraud and manipulation in national capital markets.[22]

This deficiency eventually had catastrophic consequences. Prosperity in the 1920s led to a stock market boom. After 1927, buying in then-unregulated securities markets reached a frenzy. Entrepreneurs set up hollow empires of companies just to issue stock. Brokers allowed investors with very modest incomes to buy shares on margins as low as 10 percent. The buyers often knew little or nothing about the companies behind their shares. When a speculative bubble burst in October 1929, prices collapsed in days of extreme panic. People lost their savings. The nation advanced into depression.

In response to this catastrophe the federal government intervened to protect stockholders and bring integrity to capital markets. Congress passed the Securities Act of 1933 requiring companies to register securities and provide financial statements and other information to buyers before their sale. It then passed the Securities Exchange Act of 1934 giving birth to a regulatory agency, the Securities and Exchange Commission that would police securities markets. The 1934 law also required companies to file periodic reports, including annual reports called 10-Ks, quarterly reports called 10-Qs, and reports known as 8-Ks that quickly update investors on significant events such as votes in annual meetings.

These initial statutes added a layer of governance law above state laws. Since then, this layer has expanded. The Securities and Exchange Commission (SEC) is an independent regulatory commission with five members, one of whom serves as chairman, appointed by the president for five years. Since 1934 Congress has passed 38 more statutes adding to the SEC's powers. It now has a staff of 3,500 and an annual budget of approximately $900 million. Other entities, including the Treasury Department and the Federal Reserve System, also regulate securities markets.

Despite proliferation, federal and state governance laws have not always been a match for situations that arise. The stories of Enron and Lehman Brothers teach how governance reforms still play catch-up with governance abuses.

Enron Corp.

Spectacular business scandals are recurrent in American history. However, not since the epic corporate misdeeds of the 1930s had there been such a wave of business scandals as at the turn of the twenty-first century. Enron's amazing disintegration in 2001 was the supernova in a field of frauds where executives looted shareholder wealth while directors slept. In multiple instances corporate governance failed.

Enron was an energy company headquartered in Houston, Texas, and incorporated in Oregon. Until the 1990s it was a staid natural gas, oil, and electricity

---

[22] Jack B. Jacobs, "The Reach of State Corporate Law Beyond State Borders: Reflections Upon Federalism," *New York University Law Review,* November 2009, pp. 1151–55.

producer. Then it radically changed its business model to become the world's largest online energy trading company. Its apparent success earned the admiration of investors, academics, and the public.

As it grew it created a structural maze of limited partnerships and other financial entities, numbering in the hundreds, to carry out exotic financial transactions. It all seemed to work. Enron's profits went from $1 million in 1996 to $1.1 billion in 2000. Investors, few of whom understood the puzzling structure and hedging activities, romanticized its prospects and drove share prices skyward. They delighted in a 1,415 percent return between 1990 and 2000, a period ending in speculative frenzy as the stock shot from $19.10 in 1999 to a high of $90.80 in 2000.

This bright picture clouded late in 2001 when the company announced a $554 million after-tax charge against revenues. Soon it revised its financial statements from 1997 to 2001, reducing net income more than $1 billion. The reason was it had reported false income from suspicious trading arrangements. Markets turned against Enron. It could not borrow to meet its obligations and late in 2001 it filed for bankruptcy. About $60 billion in market value was wiped out.

Enron had a board of distinguished directors (see the box on the next page). Following the bankruptcy it set up a special committee to investigate its actions. One focus was on a series of off-balance-sheet partnerships created by Andrew S. Fastow, the company's chief financial officer. The board had approved them although they created a conflict of interest.[23] In some partnerships Fastow was both a manager for Enron and an investor in an outside entity that engaged in financial transactions, such as the buying and selling of assets, with Enron. Which interest would be his priority, Enron's or his own? Unfortunately, Fastow was using the partnerships to enrich himself.

Another problem was that the partnerships concealed Enron's true financial state. Accounting rules were that if an outside investor, here Fastow, put in 3 percent or more of the capital in a partnership, the corporation, even if it provided the other 97 percent, did not have to declare it a subsidiary. Therefore, its assets and debt could be withheld from the corporation's balance sheet.[24] Using this loophole, Enron's directors eventually approved removing almost half Enron's assets from its balance sheet, hiding losses and debt totaling hundreds of millions of dollars.

The directors recognized it was a conflict of interest for Fastow to be an outside investor in the partnerships, but rationalized it was a modest risk considering the great possible gain for Enron. They thought it could be handled with controls specified by the board. They were mistaken. Their policy gave a green light to expansion of the partnerships beyond anything they ever envisioned. In fact, this partnership proliferation exposed the company to fatal risks. Simultaneously, Fastow orchestrated side deals netting him more than $30 million as an individual.

---

[23] William C. Powers, Jr., chair; Raymond S. Troubh; and Herbert S. Winokur, Jr., *Report of Investigation by the Special Investigative Committee of the Board of Directors of Enron Corp.*, February 1, 2002. Powers was dean of the University of Texas School of Law. Powers and Troubh were appointed to the board after the committee was formed. Winokur had been a member of the board at the time of bankruptcy.

[24] John R. Emshwiller and Rebecca Smith, "Murky Waters: A Primer on Enron Partnerships," *The Wall Street Journal*, January 21, 2002, p. C14.

Enron's Board of Directors

In 2001, the year that Enron filed for bankruptcy, its board consisted of the 14 members below, including one female, one black, and two Asian directors. Two members, Lay and Skilling, were officers of Enron. The other 12 were nonemployee directors.

ROBERT A. BELFER, 65
Chairman and CEO
Belco Oil & Gas Corp.

NORMAN P. BLAKE, JR., 59
Chairman, President, and CEO
Comdisco, Inc.

RONNIE C. CHAN, 51
Chairman
Hang Lung Group

JOHN H. DUNCAN, 73
Investor

DR. WENDY L. GRAMM, 56
Director, Mercatus Center Regulatory Studies
Program, George Mason University and wife of
U.S. Senator Phil Gramm (R-Texas)

DR. ROBERT K. JAEDICKE, 72
Professor (Emeritus) of Accounting
Stanford University

KENNETH L. LAY, 58
Chairman of the Board

CHARLES A. LeMAISTRE, 77
President (Emeritus)
University of Texas M.D. Anderson Cancer Center

JOHN MENDELSOHN, 64
President
University of Texas M.D. Anderson
Cancer Center

PAULO V. FERRAZ PEREIRA, 46
Executive Vice President
Group Bozano

FRANK SAVAGE, 62
Chairman
Alliance Capital Management International

JEFFREY K. SKILLING, 47
President and CEO
Enron Corporation

JOHN WAKEHAM, 68
United Kingdom Secretary of State (ret.) and
former Member of Parliament

HERBERT S. WINOKUR, JR., 57
Chairman and CEO
Capricorn Holdings, Inc

In the previous year, each nonemployee director received an average cash payment of $79,107, including an annual fee and additional fees for attending meetings or chairing one of the five board committees (executive, audit, finance, compensation, or nominating). In addition, each nonemployee director received grants of Enron stock and stock options valued at $836,517. At the time of the 2001 annual shareholders' meeting the nonemployee directors owned a total of $670 million in Enron shares. The 14 directors also served on the boards of 25 other companies.

Source: Enron Corp., *Proxy Statement*, March 27, 2001, pp. 1–12.

Controls on Fastow were never properly implemented. The board's audit committee was supposed to conduct annual reviews of all partnerships, but it failed to probe deeply into the bizarre transactions being generated. The board also made Enron's chief accounting officer responsible for reviewing and approving all transactions between the company and its partnerships. The review was inadequate because, said the investigating committee, top management was "not watching the store."

Indeed, a fundamental cause of the catastrophe was a change in culture wrought by the two top officers, Chairman of the Board Kenneth L. Lay and CEO Jeffrey K. Skilling. They fostered and permitted a freewheeling climate that tolerated junior officers engaging in illegal activities. Enron became the classic illustration of a Wild West corporate culture characterized by reckless financial deals, avarice, and deceit. It lacked an emphasis on integrity. With Lay as its chairman and Skilling a member, the board failed in its duty to maintain norms of ethics and compliance.

The investigative committee absolved Enron's board of sole blame for the bankruptcy, but accused it of failing to exercise its oversight responsibility. It found that board members "were severely hampered by the fact that significant information was withheld from them," but also that the board "did not fully appreciate the significance of some information that came before it."[25] Partnership arrangements involving substantial sums and risk were presented to the board and it failed to give them the scrutiny they deserved. Some intricate deals received only 10 or 15 minutes of attention. Fastow's first partnership was one of six agenda items in a board meeting that lasted just an hour. One director attended by calling in from a pay phone in Virginia and could not clearly hear the discussion.[26] While the investigating committee felt the board could not be faulted for not acting if it had no or insufficient information, it could be faulted for limited scrutiny and probing.

An investigation by the U.S. Senate was harder on the board. Interviews with board members revealed many conflicts of interest. For example, Enron was paying director John Wakeham $6,000 a month in consulting fees. The current and prior presidents of the M.D. Anderson Cancer Center in Texas were both board members. In the previous five years Enron and Ken Lay had given $600,000 to this institution. Director Wendy Gramm's husband, Senator Phil Gramm, received campaign contributions from Enron.[27] These and several other financial ties undermined the independence of the directors.

The Senate investigation also concluded that the board had authorized excessive compensation of Enron executives. One year the board approved a compensation plan in which executives received $430 million in bonuses when the company's

---

[25] Powers, Troubh, and Winokur, *Report of the Special Investigative Committee of the Board of Directors of Enron Corp.,* pp. 159 and 148.

[26] The director was Wendy Gramm. In John Gillespie and David Zweig, *Money for Nothing* (New York: Free Press, 2010), pp. 67–68.

[27] Report of the Permanent Subcommittee on Investigations, Committee on Governmental Affairs, U.S. Senate, *The Role of the Board of Directors in Enron's Collapse,* 107th Congress, 2nd Session, Report 107-70, July 8, 2002, pp. 54–56.

entire net income was only $975 million. In 2000 Ken Lay earned $140 million. One of his subordinates received $265 million in the same year. The board also approved a line of credit for Lay, who withdrew $77 million in cash from Enron, then replaced it with Enron stock! Overall, concluded the Senate report, "the Enron Board failed to provide the prudent oversight and checks and balances that its fiduciary obligations required and a company like Enron needed."[28]

In 2006, a federal jury found Lay and Skilling guilty of conspiracy and fraud in the Enron collapse. Jurors believed both had lied publicly about the company's financial health while all along profiting from the sale of millions of shares of their Enron stock.[29] Lay's death voided his conviction, but Skilling was sentenced to 24 years and four months in jail. Fastow pleaded guilty to conspiracy and fraud charges. Because of his willingness to testify against former top executives he was given a comparatively light six-year sentence. None of Enron's outside directors faced criminal indictments. However, 10 members of the board agreed to pay $13 million from their own pockets to settle a civil suit by Enron employees charging they had failed in their oversight of company retirement plans.[30]

Other Failures of Governance

The failures of the Enron board were echoed in other fraud scandals at about the same time. Among the most prominent are these.

- At Tyco International the board slumbered while CEO L. Dennis Kozlowski took as much as $125 million in corporate funds for his personal use and conspired with his CFO Mark H. Swartz to misrepresent the company's financial condition and boost its stock price. On conviction for grand larceny, falsifying accounting records, and conspiracy, both received prison sentences of 8 to 25 years. Kozlowski was ordered to pay $97 million in restitution and a $70 million fine. His wife visited him only once in prison, coming to tell him she wanted a divorce.[31] Tyco's directors, who failed to exercise adequate oversight, suffered no formal penalty.

- At Adelphia Communications the directors dozed as founder John J. Rigas and his son Timothy concealed $2.3 billion in off-balance-sheet debt, stole $100 million from the company, and lied to investors about its financial condition. At sentencing, the judge told the elder Rigas that he had "set Adelphia on a track of lying, of cheating, of defrauding," then heard Rigas respond that "in my heart and conscience, I'll go to my grave really and truly believing I did nothing."[32] He was sentenced to 15 years in federal prison, his son Timothy to 20 years, and another son, John, Jr., to 10 months' home confinement. The Adelphia directors were never penalized for their limp oversight.

---

[28] Ibid., p. 59.

[29] *United States v. Jeffrey K. Skilling and Kenneth W. Lay,* Cr. No. H-04-025, S. Dist. Tex. (2006).

[30] *Newby, et al., v. Enron Corp.,* 235 F. Supp. 2d 594 (2002).

[31] Steve Dunleavy, "On Her First Prison Visit, My Wife Told Me, 'I Want a Divorce' Koz," *New York Post,* October 30, 2006, p. 6.

[32] Quotations are in Dean Starkman, "Rigases Given Prison Terms," *The Washington Post,* June 21, 2005, p. D1.

- At WorldCom, in a story told more fully in Chapter 7, the board napped while CEO Bernard J. Ebbers and CFO Scott D. Sullivan concealed falling revenues and rising expenses in an $11 billion accounting fraud. Ebbers was sentenced to 25 years in prison, Sullivan to 5 years. Accused of negligent oversight, 11 WorldCom directors agreed to pay 20 percent of their aggregate net worth, about $20.3 million, in restitution to defrauded investors.[33] As with the Enron directors, this came from their own pockets.

Each of these corporations declared bankruptcy. Jobs and life savings were lost. In each case the directors failed in their duty to protect shareholders from self-interested, predatory managers. Their failure inspired a range of corporate governance reforms aimed at sharpening boardroom vigilance. The centerpiece was the Sarbanes-Oxley Act of 2002.

The Sarbanes-Oxley Act

Sarbanes-Oxley Act of 2002
A statute enacted to prevent financial fraud in corporations. It mandated stricter financial reporting and greater board oversight.

On signing the *Sarbanes-Oxley Act of 2002* into law President George W. Bush said it embodied "the most far-reaching reforms of American business practice since the time of Franklin Delano Roosevelt."[34] There was little disagreement. The law's primary focus is on accounting rules. It also puts devices in place to hold management responsible for accurate financial reports and it increases the oversight responsibilities of boards of directors. Here are its main provisions.

- It creates a Public Company Accounting Oversight Board to oversee accounting firms and improve the accuracy of their audits.
- Audit firms are prohibited from doing consulting work for corporations while also auditing their books. Audit firms must rotate every five years. This broke a long-standing conflict of interest situation where auditors were tempted to please their clients in order to pursue lucrative consulting contracts.
- Companies must tell whether they have a code setting forth "standards of honesty and ethical conduct" for senior financial officers or, if not, why not.
- Every board of directors must create an audit committee to oversee the firm's accounting policies and controls. It must consist of independent directors who do not receive fees from the company other than their director's compensation. One member of this committee must be a "financial expert."
- The CEO and the CFO must sign and certify the accuracy of annual and quarterly financial reports. If the statements are false, they face criminal penalties up to $5 million and 20 years in prison.
- Companies must reveal off-balance-sheet transactions such as those used by Enron.
- Boards of directors are prohibited from approving personal loans for company executives.
- Directors (and managers) are subject to heavy penalties. Civil violations can lead to fines of up to $100,000. Criminal violations can lead to fines of up to $50 million and lengthy prison terms.

[33] Daniel Akst, "Fining the Directors Misses the Mark," *The New York Times,* August 21, 2005, sec. 3, p. 6.
[34] Quoted in Stephen M. Bainbridge, "The Creeping Federalization of Corporation Law," *Regulation,* spring 2003, p. 28.

The business community complained that the law was burdensome. A 2005 survey found the average cost of implementing it in 90 companies ranged from a few hundred thousand dollars for small firms to $7.8 million for the largest.[35] Large corporations now spend millions of dollars a year in complying and complain that its costs may exceed its benefits.[36]

Enron's failure shook up the governance system everywhere. Corporate groups, accountants, credit rating agencies, securities analysts, and stock exchanges all came out with sets of reforms to strengthen boards. The New York Stock Exchange is an example. It maintains rules that all listed companies must follow. Soon after the enactment of Sarbanes-Oxley it revised these rules to conform with and go beyond the new law. It required a majority of independent directors on the boards of all listed companies. In addition, it required every board to have three committees—audit, compensation, and governance (or nominating)—each composed entirely of independent directors.

Did all this rulemaking work to awaken and empower boards? The answer is no. While it may have prevented an unknown number of frauds and scandals, it failed to prevent widespread board somnolence, a curiosity at the center of a near systemwide financial collapse in 2008. The story of Lehman Brothers is exhibit A.

Lehman Brothers

Lehman Brothers Holdings began in 1850 as a cotton broker and grew into the nation's fourth-largest investment bank. Since 1994 it had been run by a CEO named Richard S. Fuld, Jr. Intense, intimidating, and impatient, Fuld had a confrontational manner and, according to one colleague, gave off "little physical cues" hinting any disagreement could turn to physical violence.[37] Once, when a manager asked him to wait, he cleared the person's desk with a sweep of his hand. Fuld referred to Lehman as "the mother ship" and demanded total loyalty. He saw each day, each situation as a battle. You were either on the team or off it. In keeping with this worldview, he made Lehman stock a large part of compensation and required employees to hold it as long as five years before selling. This motivated everyone so long as the stock price rose.

In 2006, Fuld decided that the way to keep share prices rising was to make Lehman grow faster. He introduced an aggressive strategy requiring more risk and increased leverage on capital. Lehman invested its assets in subprime mortgages, commercial real estate, high-yield bonds, leveraged loans, and mortgage-backed securities. This reduced its liquidity and raised firmwide risk. It did grow, to $691 billion in assets by 2007. Its leverage ratio eventually reached 39 to 1, that is, it had borrowed $39 for every dollar in its accounts.

---

[35] Deborah Solomon, "At What Price?" *The Wall Street Journal,* October 17, 2005, p. R3.

[36] One 2007 survey found average annual compliance costs of $5 million and only 31 percent of directors of surveyed firms who thought benefits exceeded costs. Korn/Ferry Institute, *34th Annual Board of Directors Study* (New York: Korn/Ferry International, 2007), p. 16.

[37] Anonymous, quoted in Steve Fishman, "Burning Down His House," *New York Magazine,* December 8, 2008, p. 1.

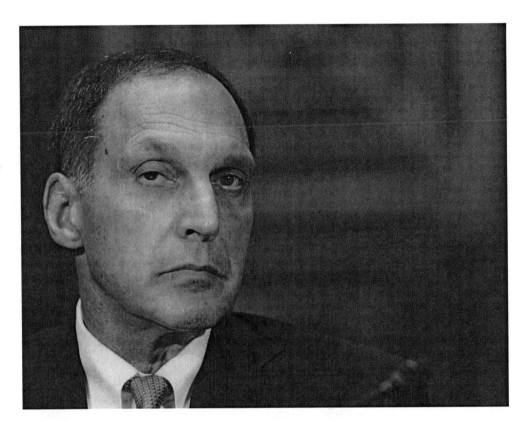

Richard S. Fuld at a 2010 hearing of the Financial Crisis Inquiry Commission where he testified on the bankruptcy of Lehman Brothers. Source: AP Photo/ Carolyn Kaster.

repurchase agreement
A financing transaction in which one firm lends assets to another firm in exchange for cash with a simultaneous agreement to purchase the assets back.

To fund its operations, Lehman depended on borrowing tens of billions of dollars each day in financial markets. Its ability to do so turned on the confidence of others in its liquidity. When the subprime mortgage crisis materialized in 2007, lenders began to lose confidence in Lehman and required more collateral, even for routine financing. To shore up confidence Lehman resorted to an accounting trick its employees called "Repo 105." Ordinarily, Lehman raised cash using *repurchase agreements* in which it sold assets to a counterparty and agreed to repurchase them in the next 24 to 72 hours. During these brief, routine financing transactions the assets stayed on Lehman's balance sheet. But with the Repo 105 technique, Lehman sold assets equal to 105 percent or more of the cash it received, which, under a strained interpretation of accounting rules, allowed it to treat the asset transfer as a sale.

Using Repo 105, Lehman briefly removed up to $50 billion of assets from its balance sheet precisely at the end of the first and second quarters in 2008, allowing it to reduce its net leverage ratio from 13.9 to 12.1. With this sleight of hand Lehman ended reporting periods with a stronger-looking, but misleading, balance sheet. It was not a clear violation of accounting rules, yet Lehman never disclosed its use to lenders, investors, analysts, or its own board of directors. Thus, it concealed the firm's real debt level from interested parties. Not everyone at Lehman accepted the legitimacy of Repo 105. Some of its accountants called it a gimmick. A senior vice president wrote to the firm's controller complaining of "balance sheet manipulation" and reported the use of Repo 105 to Lehman's external auditor Ernst & Young.[38] Nobody acted.

Repo 105 was not enough to save Lehman Brothers. In September 2008, as credit markets began to freeze, another investment bank, Bear Stearns, almost failed and was rescued at the last minute by a government-arranged merger with JP Morgan Chase. Attention then turned to Lehman Brothers, which was viewed as the next most vulnerable investment bank. It faced a run on its assets, was no longer able to borrow, and filed for bankruptcy September 15. It set a new record for the size of a bankruptcy, besting WorldCom and, before it, Enron.

Lehman's bankruptcy caused panic in the markets. That day the Dow Jones average fell 504 points. The next day insurer AIG faced imminent collapse. Prime Fund, a money market fund that held Lehman's notes, was no longer able to maintain its shares at $1 of face value. Both had to be bailed out by an infusion of billions of dollars from the Federal Reserve System. And within a month Congress passed an emergency rescue plan, the $700 billion Toxic Assets Relief Program intended to shore up the nation's "too-big-to-fail" institutions. Fuld would later argue that "Lehman's demise was caused by uncontrollable market forces," but admit that "I, myself, did not see the depth and violence of the crisis. I did not see the contagion. I believe we made poor judgments . . ."[39]

Lehman's shareholders lost almost everything. Its stock fell from a high of $62.19 that January to $3.65 at bankruptcy, a 94 percent decline. Where was the firm's board of directors, the entity charged with monitoring management for them? Lehman had an 11-member board including 10 independent directors and one insider, Richard Fuld, who was both chairman of the board and CEO (see the box). Fuld dominated the selection of directors, and they were a congenial group, unlikely to challenge him. There was little board turnover. And directors were generous in compensating Fuld. Between 2000 and 2008 his average pay was $46 million a year.[40]

Only 1 of the 10 outside directors, Jerry A. Grundhofer, had any recent banking experience and he had served only for five months. Another, 80-year-old Henry Kaufman, had retired from investment banking 20 years earlier. Others included current and retired executives from nonfinancial industries. It was not a group selected for keen insight into financial transactions.

During the year preceding bankruptcy the board met eight times and its members earned between $325,038 and $397,538. The directors were informed that Lehman was taking increased risk to create firm growth. At every board meeting they received a risk report, including a numeric representation of the firm's "risk appetite." Managers told the board they were taking precautions to monitor and limit overall risks. They did not, however, fully inform it about all

---

[38] *Report of Anton R. Valukas, Examiner, In re Lehman Brothers Holdings Inc.,* Chapter 11 Case No. 08-13555, S. Dist. N.Y., March 11, 2010, vol. 1, p. 21.

[39] Testimony of Richard S. Fuld before the Financial Crisis Inquiry Commission hearing on "Too Big to Fail: Expectations and Impact of Extraordinary Government Intervention and the Role of Systemic Risk in the Financial Crisis," Washington, DC, September 1, 2010, p. 203.

[40] Scott Thurm, "Oracle's Ellison: Pay King," *The Wall Street Journal,* July 27, 2010, p. A16.

Lehman Brothers' Board of Directors

These were the 11 members of the Lehman Brothers board of directors in 2008 when the firm filed for bankruptcy. Only Richard S. Fuld was a Lehman Brothers executive. The other 10 were nonemployee directors who qualified as independent under the rules of the New York Stock Exchange.

MICHAEL L. AINSLIE, 64
Private Investor and Former President and
Chief Executive Officer of Sotheby's Holdings

JOHN F. AKERS, 73
Retired Chairman of International Business
Machines Corporation

ROGER S. BERLIND, 77
Theatrical Producer

THOMAS H. CRUIKSHANK, 76
Retired Chairman and Chief Executive Officer of
Halliburton Company

MARSHA JOHNSON EVANS, 60
Rear Admiral, U.S. Navy (Retired)

RICHARD S. FULD, JR., 61
Chairman and Chief Executive Officer,
Lehman Brothers Holdings Inc.

SIR CHRISTOPHER GENT, 59
Non-Executive Chairman of GlaxoSmithKline Plc.

JERRY A. GRUNDHOFER, 63
Chairman Emeritus and Retired Chief Executive
Officer of U.S. Bancorp

ROLAND A. HERNANDEZ, 50
Retired Chairman and Chief Executive Officer of
Telemundo Group, Inc.

HENRY KAUFMAN, 80
President of Henry Kaufman & Company, Inc.

JOHN D. MACOMBER, 80
Principal of JDM Investment Group

In the previous year, each nonexecutive director received an annual cash retainer of $75,000 plus fees for chairing and attending meetings of board committees. Each also received grants of Lehman Brothers stock or stock options valued at $245,038. The 10 nonexecutive directors served on the boards of 16 other companies.

Source: Lehman Brothers Holdings Inc., *Proxy Statement,* March 5, 2008, pp. 6–18.

the dangers. For example, they neglected to mention periodic shortcomings in liquidity tests. And they failed to inform the directors that the firm sometimes exceeded its risk limits. At one board meeting, when the firm had exceeded these limits, the CFO edited a standard chart to remove the risk appetite numbers that ordinarily appeared.[41]

Another time, Lehman's president told a manager not to give the board much detail about risky subprime mortgages because the directors were "not

[41] *Report of Anton R. Valukas, Examiner, In re Lehman Brothers Holdings Inc.,* Chapter 11 Case No. 08-13555, S. Dist. N.Y., March 11, 2010, vol. 1, pp. 21 and 141.

sophisticated."[42] The board did have a risk committee, but it met only twice in the year before Lehman's bankruptcy. It was chaired by the octogenarian Henry Kaufman. Its other members included a retired admiral who had been head of the Girl Scouts, the retired chairman of IBM, a theatrical producer, and the retired chairman of a Spanish-language television company. It was not a group with much background for judging such esoterica as the single tranche collateralized debt obligations that Lehman used to hedge risks.

Lehman's management made serious errors of judgment. Senior officers, including Fuld, certified deceptive financial statements based on accounting tricks. The board failed to detect trouble and rein in extreme risk. Corporate governance let the firm's shareholders down. Although Lehman's headquarters were in New York, it was incorporated in Delaware. A special examiner appointed by the court in Lehman's bankruptcy case found that neither company officers nor directors had breached their fiduciary duty to shareholders under Delaware law. They were protected by its lenient "business judgment" rule, which rejects personal liability absent "reckless indifference," "deliberate disregard," or actions "without the bounds of reason."[43]

Since Lehman had risk policies in place and the directors had discussed risk, their bank accounts were safe from angry shareholders. However, as a group, directors and managers lost considerable wealth. Fuld was Lehman's largest individual shareowner with 12.6 million shares. He held them until the end and, based on price decline from a 2008 high, lost approximately $738 million. The directors held a combined 1.1 million shares that lost about $60 million in value.

The Dodd-Frank Act

Dodd-Frank Act
A statute to reform financial regulation and prevent a recurrence of the 2007–2008 financial crisis.

In the aftermath of Lehman's failure and the financial disaster in its wake, Congress responded with another repair statute, the 849-page *Dodd-Frank Wall Street Reform and Consumer Protection Act of 2010* (the Dodd-Frank Act). At its core it was a huge dose of new financial regulations targeting root causes of the recent crisis. It mandated five new agencies and 330 new rulemakings.[44] There were new powers over banks and financial markets, restraints on risk-taking, limits on hedging and the use of novel financial products, mortgage lending reforms, and strengthened mortgage lending criteria.

While the law's main focus was financial reform, it did not neglect governance failures observed at Lehman and other companies that survived the crisis only with government assistance. The public believed investment bankers were overpaid, and so the Dodd-Frank Act moved to strengthen checks on executive compensation.

- At least once every three years companies have to submit their executive compensation packages to a stockholder vote. The stockholders may approve or disapprove; however, the vote is not binding.

[42] Ibid., p. 90.

[43] Ibid., pp. 47–48 and pp. 54–55.

[44] Curtis W. Copeland, *Rulemaking Requirements and Authorities in the Dodd-Frank Wall Street Reform and Consumer Protection Act,* Congressional Research Service, Report No. R414722, November 3, 2010, p. 8.

- If an executive is entitled to special compensation in case of merger, buyout, or other change of control, the stockholders must have a chance to vote their approval or disapproval. Again, the vote is not binding.
- All members of the board committee that sets executive compensation must be "independent," that is, free of any conflict of interest coming from any paid connection to the company apart from being a director.
- In proxy statements companies must disclose the relationship between executive compensation and their financial performance, including changes in stock values. They must also disclose the ratio of the median pay of all the firm's employees to that of the chief executive.
- If a company issues an accounting restatement, it must recoup any compensation paid to an executive based on financial performance.

It is too early to tell whether and how these requirements will affect executive pay. They attempt to empower stockholders, a notoriously apathetic lot. An additional effort to strengthen stockholders is a requirement that they can submit the names of director nominees and have them included in the proxy materials sent out by companies. This is a big change. In the past shareholders who wanted to run a board candidate had to contact other shareholders at their own very high expense. Now, the company would be forced to put opposition names on its own proxy forms. However, implementation of this procedure is uncertain. When the SEC wrote a new rule giving stockholders who owned 3 percent of the companies' shares access to the proxy, big corporations sued to stop it.[45] They feared that dissident groups, for example, union pension funds or activist coalitions, would be empowered to undermine and distract management by triggering election battles.

BOARDS OF DIRECTORS

The stories of the boards at Enron and Lehman Brothers are singular, but they illustrate widespread tendencies and shortcomings. In fact, the boards of American corporations are marbled with pathologies that enervate them in performance of their watchdog function.

They are often hand-picked by powerful CEOs who fill them with friends and retired CEOs having reputations for congeniality. They depend on management for information and allow management to control agendas. They are unwilling to confront CEOs to whom they owe their selection and compensation. In the harmonious board cultures of most corporations, an abrasive director faces ostracism. Not all directors work hard. Some see their service as largely honorific. Others who are top executives at other companies are preoccupied. A few divide their attention by serving on too many other boards. Many CEOs see their boards as

---

[45] Securities and Exchange Commission, "Facilitating Shareholder Director Nominations; Proposed Rule," 74 FR 29024, June 18, 2009.

unproductive; in a recent survey only 16 percent rated them "highly effective."[46] One described his board as "an aquarium full of dead fish."[47]

Despite pronounced flaws, governance reforms are having an effect. Today boards of directors are in transition, evolving from a collegial, largely honorific group to an assertive watchdog of management. The transition is incomplete, perhaps even preliminary, but that is the direction of change.

Duties of Directors

State incorporation laws require boards of directors. They impose two lofty duties on them, first, to represent the interests of stockholders by conducting a profitable business that enhances share value, and second, to exercise due diligence in supervising management. Directors violate these duties if they put their own self-interest ahead of the shareholders or if they are unreasonably neglectful in their oversight. In practice, directors do not make day-to-day management decisions. Instead, they exercise a very broad oversight, taking responsibility for "the overall picture, not the daily business decisions, the forest, not the trees."[48]

Here is a short list of specific board functions.

* Approve the issuance of securities and the voting rights of their holders.
* Review and approve the corporation's goals and strategies.
* Select the CEO, evaluate his or her performance, and remove that person if necessary.
* Give advice and counsel to management.
* Create governance policies for the firm, including compensation policies.
* Evaluate the performance of individual directors, board committees, and the board as a whole.
* Nominate candidates for election as directors.
* Exercise oversight of ethics and compliance programs.

Board Composition

The average board has 11 members and this has not changed for many years. Most state incorporation laws require a minimum of three, but companies typically have between 7 and 15. The number is often specified as a range in corporate charters. For example, in its Delaware charter Walt Disney Corporation specifies a board of "not less than nine directors or more than twenty-one."[49] Directors are elected by shareholders, usually for terms of one year. Under Delaware law, once

[46] The 2009 National Association of Corporate Directors *Public Company Governance Survey,* cited in Beverly Behan, "Wise Counsel? How to Get Your Board Back on Track," *The Conference Board Review,* Summer 2010, p. 46.

[47] Anonymous, quoted in Ibid., p. 44.

[48] Robert A. G. Monks and Nell Minow, *Corporate Governance,* 3rd ed. (Malden, MA: Blackwell Publishing, 2004), p. 201.

[49] *Restated Certificate of Incorporation of the Walt Disney Company,* Office of the Secretary of State of Delaware, November 17, 1999, Article V(1).

elected they cannot be removed by their fellow directors. Some have terms of two or three years. In such cases only half or a third of the directors are elected each year. Some shareholders dislike such staggered terms, arguing that they insulate directors from frequent accountability.

Directors are most often current or retired executives of other corporations who are sought out for their business acumen. Others include former government officials, politicians, athletes, entertainers, and university presidents or professors. There is growing but limited demographic diversity. In a survey of the largest 100 public corporations 16 percent of directors were female and 15 percent were minorities. Directors are also older; 42 percent were 65 or over.[50] Those who are officers of the company are *inside directors*. They usually come from the ranks of top executives. Those who are not employed by the company are *outside directors*. These directors are also called nonexecutive directors. When outside directors have no important business dealings with the company other than being on its board, they are called *independent directors*.

Standards of independence have tightened. Since recent regulatory and listing rules require a majority of independent directors on the full board and on several committees, they now dominate in numbers. The typical board of 11 has only 1 inside director, the CEO, usually acting as chairman of the board. Overall, outside directors now hold 87 percent of board seats and insiders only 13 percent.[51] The average director serves on only one or two boards; less than 2 percent serve on five or more.[52]

Boards do much of their work in committees. Federal law and stock exchange rules mandate at least three, each composed entirely of independent directors. An *audit* committee oversees auditing and financial reports and assesses financial risks in the company's strategy. A *compensation* committee reviews the performance of top executives and sets their compensation. It also sets the director's pay. The average director of a large public company puts in about 20 hours a month and earns $213,000 a year in retainers and company stock. Shareholders do not approve director's pay packages.[53] And a *nominating* committee identifies candidates for election to the board. Additional committees sometimes found are executive, corporate governance, finance, succession planning, sustainability, science and technology, and investment committees. Board committees usually have three to five members.

Board Dynamics

The average board meets eight times a year, although many meet monthly. In advance, the directors receive "board books" of materials, often voluminous, for their review. Then they travel to corporate headquarters. The day before the meeting is occupied with committee meetings, most of which last two to four hours, followed in the evening by a dinner for directors and company executives.

inside directors
Directors who are employees of the company.

outside directors
Directors who are not company employees.

independent directors
Outside directors of a corporation who, aside from their directors' duties, do not have business dealings with it that would impair their impartiality.

---

[50] Korn/Ferry Institute, *The Korn/Ferry Market Cap 100: Board Leadership at America's Most Valuable Public Companies* (New York: Korn/Ferry, 2010), pp. 10–12.

[51] PwC, *Annual Corporate Directors Survey: The 2010 Results* (New York: PwC, 2010), p. 30.

[52] Ibid., p. 32.

[53] Colin Leinster, "Are Board Members Paid Enough? 'Definitely Not,'" *Corporate Board Member,* Third Quarter 2010, at www.boardmember.com; and Robert C. Pozen, "A New Model for Corporate Boards," *The Wall Street Journal,* December 30, 2010, p. A15.

The full board meets the next day for an average of four to six hours.[54] Agendas include committee reports, mandatory governance matters, and presentations by company executives. Sometimes a favored senior manager comes to give a Power-Point presentation. Much is routine. The agenda is often crowded and rushed, leaving no time for probing discussions of strategy or risks.[55] In a recent survey a majority of directors said they would like "much more" time devoted to these two subjects.[56] Even if there is meaningful dialogue, conflict and discord are rare. For example, Enron directors who had served for many years described an atmosphere of amity and consensus. They recalled only two instances of a dissenting vote.[57]

The chairman of the board presides over meetings. At most companies this title is held by the CEO, giving him or her a dual role. From this position CEOs can dominate their boards by deciding what information to circulate and by fixing agendas. CEO influence often extends to the selection of supportive directors. In the past CEOs simply suggested new names to compliant boards that then approved nominees who were virtually assured of election by shareholders. Stock exchange rules now require that names be approved by nominating committees of independent directors. These committees have the power to hire search firms to find candidates. However, the CEO is still a source of nominations; few boards will act on a nominee over the objection of a CEO, giving the CEO, in effect, a veto power.

In 2003 the New York Stock Exchange modified its listing standards to require that independent directors meet regularly absent members of management. This is intended to allow outside directors to express concerns that might be suppressed for reasons of collegiality or intimidation in the presence of management. Most large company boards elect a *lead director* from the ranks of independent outside directors to create agendas and preside over such sessions. In practice, however, a lead director operating in the shadow of a combined chairman and CEO lacks substantial power to reshape a board.[58]

lead director
An independent director who presides over meetings of nonmanagement directors.

Advocates of greater board independence believe that a better solution for strengthening the board is to split the roles of chairman and CEO. They argue that if the board is supposed to appoint, monitor, evaluate, and compensate the CEO it is a conflict of interest to put the CEO in charge. Having a chairman other than the chief executive would diminish that conflict even if the CEO still sat on the board. Thus, many companies have separated the two roles, appointing a *nonexecutive chairman* to lead their boards. Most still combine the two roles, but the trend is toward a split. After the financial crisis in 2008, given the example of Richard S. Fuld's reign over a

nonexecutive chairman
A chairman of the board who is not an executive of the corporation.

---

[54] Ibid., pp. 8 and 14.

[55] Gillespie and Zweig, *Money for Nothing*, pp. 107–08.

[56] PwC, *Annual Corporate Directors Survey: The 2010 Results*, pp. 8–9.

[57] Report of the Permanent Subcommittee on Investigations, Committee on Governmental Affairs, U.S. Senate, *The Role of the Board of Directors in Enron's Collapse*, p. 8.

[58] Ira M. Millstein and Stephen Davis, eds., *Chairing the Board: The Case for Independent Leadership in Corporate North America*, Policy Briefing No. 4, Millstein Center for Corporate Governance and Performance, Yale School of Management, 2009, p. 20.

weak Lehman Brothers board, Congress stopped short of requiring separation, but the Dodd–Frank Act requires companies to tell their shareholders once a year why they choose to combine or separate the two roles.[59]

Management often opposes separation. One fear is compromising clarity in the chain of command. According to Jack Welch, former chairman and CEO of General Electric, splitting the roles encourages "decision shopping" by managers who seek out the leader most likely to support them. "When there are two bosses," he says, "you can often get two messages, and that's too bad."[60] It can also be harder for the CEO to make quick decisions if the chairman must be consulted. Another fear is that split roles might threaten a collegial board environment by provoking "mindless animosities and ego contests" between the two leaders.[61] To avoid this, advocates of separation advise that the chairman be someone without ambition to run the company, perhaps a retired chief executive. Despite doubts and resistance, the trend is to move to nonexecutive chairmen; about 40 percent of companies on the Standard & Poor's 500 index have done so.[62]

EXECUTIVE COMPENSATION

Top executives are not simply given paychecks. Instead they are compensated using arcane schemes, mysterious in their complexity that can baffle untutored bystanders. When the schemes are well devised, pay follows performance. When poorly devised they result in excessive pay unrelated to performance. In this section we discuss the components, dynamics, and problems of executive compensation.

Components of Executive Compensation

The pay of top corporate officers is set by the board of directors. In keeping with stock exchange rules, each board must have a compensation committee composed entirely of independent directors. Its members, of course, may be cronies of the CEO. Nevertheless, the committee must create a defensible written plan. At most companies the compensation scheme reflects three beliefs. First, to attract and retain managerial talent, compensation must be competitive. Second, it should be based on both individual and company performance. And third, it should align the interests of executives with the interests of shareholders. These goals are typically achieved using some combination of the following elements.

Base Salary

The annual base salary is usually set near the median salary for leaders of similar firms. At Sherwin-Williams, for example, the salaries of the top five executives are based on a survey of the base salaries of executives with similar

[59] Section 972, "Disclosures Regarding Chairman and CEO Structures," 15 USC 78a, sec. 14B.

[60] Jack Welch and Suzy Welch, "A Week of Blows to Business," *BusinessWeek,* May 18, 2009.

[61] Millstein and Davis, *Chairing the Board,* p. 19.

[62] Joann S. Lublin, "Chairman-CEO Split Gains Allies," *The Wall Street Journal,* March 30, 2009, p. B4.

stock option
The right to buy shares of a company's stock at a fixed or *grant price* in the future and under conditions determined by the board of directors.

grant price
The price at which a specified number of shares can be purchased in the future by executives who hold options.

vesting date
The date when stock options can be exercised by purchasing shares at the grant price.

expiration date
A future date, after the vesting date, when shares can no longer be bought at the grant price.

performance shares
Shares of company stock awarded after a fixed period of years if individual and company performance goals are met.

responsibilities at 18 peer companies, all similarly sized industrial firms.[63] Companies use such peer group comparisons as a measure of the market for executive talent. Base salaries for CEOs stay around $1 million, the amount that the Internal Revenue Service allows as tax deductible.[64] At Sherwin-Williams the CEO received $1.3 million in 2009. Its other top executives received between $488,000 and $733,000.

Annual Cash Incentives

Most large companies make an annual bonus part of the compensation package. Criteria for earning the bonus vary. At McGraw-Hill the CEO's incentive pay is based on meeting net income (weighted 75 percent) and revenue (weighted 25 percent) goals.[65] At Abbott Laboratories the CEO's yearly bonus is based on whether the company hits multiple financial goals including profitability, sales, returns, and earnings per share. This resulted in an award of $3.9 million in a recent year.[66] Annual cash incentives are typically based on meeting financial targets. If targets are missed bonuses go down and, when companies do poorly, the bonus columns in compensation tables often contain goose eggs.

Long-Term Stock-Based Incentives

Compensation in stock is designed to align managers' incentives with the interests of stockholders. There are several frequently used types of stock awards.

First, *stock options* give an executive the right to buy the company's stock at a fixed or *grant price* in the future and under conditions determined by the board of directors. Options are usually priced at the closing market price on the day they are granted. The holder of the options then can buy these shares from the company at a specified future date, called the *vesting date*. The holder must buy them before a later *expiration date* when the options can no longer be exercised. At Johnson & Johnson, for example, options vest and can only be exercised (purchased) three years after they are granted and must be exercised within 10 years or they expire.[67] Thus, if Johnson & Johnson grants 1,000 options to an executive at $70 a share and the price rises to $100 after five years, the executive may buy them from the company for $70,000, then sell them for $100,000, making a $30,000 profit (minus taxes and fees). However, if after three years the shares have fallen to $50, they are said to be "under water" and they are worthless. The executive will not exercise the options.

Second, *performance shares* are shares awarded after a fixed period of years only if individual or company performance goals are met. These shares may be awarded in part or not at all depending on how closely performance matches goals. Typically, the time from grant to award is at least three years. General Electric awards its top executives "performance share units" that convert into shares of GE stock after five years. Half the shares are awarded if cash flow from operating activities grows

---

[63] Sherwin-Williams Company, *Proxy Statement,* March 9, 2007, pp. 24–25.

[64] See 26 USC §162(m)(1) 2010.

[65] McGraw-Hill Companies, *Proxy Statement,* March 23, 2010, p. 38.

[66] Abbott Laboratories, *Proxy Statement,* March 15, 2010, pp. 14 and 18.

[67] Johnson & Johnson, *Notice of Annual Meeting and Proxy Statement,* March 17, 2010, p. 29.

an average of 10 percent a year during the interim.[68] The other half of the shares are awarded if total return to shareholders exceeds that of the Standard & Poor's 500 index. If these goals are not met, the "units" are canceled, unlike options that can be exercised any time between vesting and expiration.

restricted stock
A grant of stock with restrictions. It cannot be sold until certain conditions are met, most often the lapse of time or meeting a performance goal.

Third, *restricted stock* is a grant of stock with restrictions on transaction that are removed when a specified condition is met. Usually, the recipient receives dividends and can vote the shares but cannot sell them until the restriction is lifted. Any specified condition can be a restriction. Often, it is tenure at the company. In this way, restricted stock is used to lock in promising talent or key executives. If, for example, the shares vest in 10 years, then the executive must stay on the job that long to realize their value.

IBM uses restricted stock to retain the loyalty of its "senior leadership team" in what it believes is a highly competitive market for executive talent. Awards are typically for five years and are forfeited if the person leaves. In 2010 the top five most compensated executives at IBM held a little more than 14 million restricted stock units worth approximately $2.2 billion.[69] At ExxonMobil 50 to 75 percent of senior executive's pay is in restricted shares. Of these, half are restricted for 5 years and half for 10 years or until the executive retires, whichever is *later*. If the person leaves, the grants are canceled. Its compensation committee argues for such lengthy time restrictions because in the oil and gas industry the wisdom of investments may not be known for many years.[70] Unlike stock options, restricted shares are not worthless if their market price is below the grant price when they vest.[71]

Options, performance shares, and restricted stock are all used to create a long-term performance incentive. They also align manager and shareholder interests by promoting stock ownership of top executives.

Retirement Plans

Companies provide generous pensions for top executives. Each year they credit pension funds with a sum calculated as a percent of the person's salary. This sum is held by the company to cover future pension payments; however, it is reported as part of the executive's total compensation. For large companies with highly paid CEOs the increased value of a pension can be significant. In a recent year it added $1.9 million for Samuel J. Palmisano of IBM, $1.9 million for Jeffrey Immelt of GE, and $4.4 million for Andrew Liveris of Dow Chemical Company.

Perquisites

Acknowledging the needs and lifestyles of top executives, companies often provide extra benefits. Among the most common are annual physical exams, travel on

---

[68] Performance share units granted after 2009 convert if adjusted cumulative industrial cash flow from operating activities is $70 billion or higher. General Electric Company, *Notice of 2010 Annual Meeting and Proxy Statement,* March 9, 2010, p. 24.

[69] IBM *Notice of 2010 Annual Meeting and Proxy Statement,* March 8, 2010, p. 44.

[70] ExxonMobil Corp., *Notice of 2010 Annual Meeting and Proxy Statement,* April 13, 2010, pp. 29–30.

[71] As an example, suppose a manager is awarded both options and restricted stock on a day when shares sell at $20. Five years later, on a day when the price is $18, both the options and the restricted shares vest. The options are worthless, because to exercise them the manager must buy the shares at $20. The restricted stock, on the other hand, is transferred to the manager at its current value. It can be sold immediately for $18 a share.

FIGURE 18.4 **How Emerson Electric Uses Elements of Compensation**

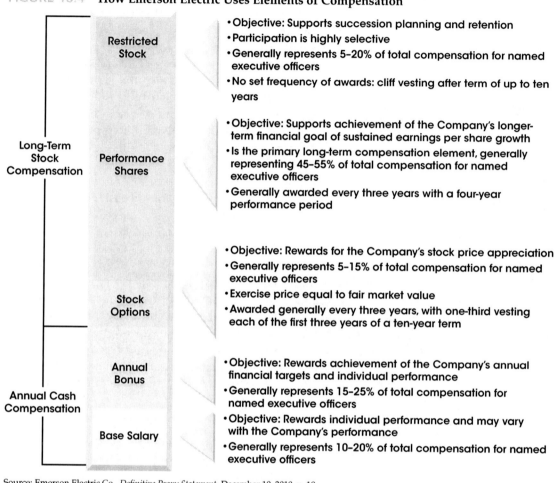

Source: Emerson Electric Co., *Definitive Proxy Statement*, December 10, 2010, p. 18.

company jets, home alarm systems, bodyguards, leased autos, club memberships, personal financial planning, and life and health insurance. SEC rules require that the dollar value of such extras be disclosed to shareholders. A few examples of reported perks are $38,272 in premiums on a medical plan with no deductibles or co-payments for the chief executive at TRW Automotive, $49,440 for a "weekend driver" for Martha Stewart at Martha Stewart Living Omnimedia, $391,000 for personal financial planning for the CEO of Occidental Petroleum, and $3.7 million to a division president at Microsoft for a loss on the sale of his home when he relocated.[72]

At each company, compensation committees choose among these basic elements of executive pay, picking combinations that fit their compensation philosophy. Figure 18.4 shows how Emerson Electric Co. uses a flexible combination of

[72] Joann S. Lublin, "Shareholders Hit the Roof Over Home-Loss Subsidies," *The Wall Street Journal,* October 25, 2010, p. B1; and Daniel Fisher, "The Perk Game," *Forbes,* June 7, 2010, p. 36.

pay elements to reward and retain its top executives. Each executive is compensated based on factors such as level of responsibility, promise, performance, and length of service.

Although the base pay of top executives can be generous, astronomical payouts are usually the fruition of earlier incentive awards. With stock-based awards the bonanza can come as long as 10 years after the shares are awarded, sometimes making it seem that compensation is out of step with current performance.

Problems with CEO Compensation

There are multiple shortcomings of CEO compensation. Here are some of the most important.

First, critics are outraged by extraordinary payouts. The perception of widespread, excessively generous remuneration is an old story. President Franklin D. Roosevelt railed against the "entrenched greed" of executives. Yet pay in his era was modest compared with today. For example, in 1929 Eugene G. Grace, president of Bethlehem Steel, the highest-paid top executive, received a salary of $12,000 and a bonus of $1.6 million. Translated into current dollars this is $20 million. If that sum astonished the nation, it would no longer. The highest paid executive in the decade 2000 to 2010, Larry Ellison, the CEO of Oracle, averaged $184 million a year and took home $700 million in 2001 alone.[73] In 2009 average CEO pay at 456 of the largest companies was $7.23 million and eighteen companies went over the $20 million mark.[74]

The source of outrage about CEO pay is a sense of unfairness. In 2010 the average S&P 500 CEO made 267 times the wages of the least-paid company worker.[75] The CEO is only one person, but hundreds or thousands of employees labored to make the firm profitable. Usually, however, CEO pay is determined by market forces in the competition for managerial talent.[76] And most managers never get the dramatically high salaries that attract criticism. Indeed, some argue that more than a few top executives are underpaid. This is especially true in smaller businesses. However, spectacular excesses define public perception of pay in corporate America.

Second, compensation is not always aligned with performance. While total compensation is higher in larger firms and mostly follows share price performance, there are notable exceptions. Between 2000 and 2009 Barry Diller of IAC/InterActive and Expedia.com received $1.1 billion while the share price declined 12 percent. Over the same years Richard D. Fairbank of Capital One Financial received $569 million while the share price declined 14 percent. From 1999 to 2009 John T. Chambers of Cisco Systems received $393 million while the share price

---

[73] Thurm, "Oracle's Ellison: Pay King," p. A16.

[74] Joann S. Lublin, "Paychecks for CEOs Climb," *The Wall Street Journal,* November 15, 2010, p. A1; and Joann S. Lublin, "A Closer Look at Three Big Paydays," *The Wall Street Journal,* November 15, 2010, p. B5.

[75] Rana Foroohar, "Stuffing Their Pockets," *Newsweek,* September 13, 2010, p. 20.

[76] Steven N. Kaplan, "Are U.S. CEOs Overpaid?" *Academy of Management Executive,* May 2008.

declined 29 percent.[77] Robert Nardelli, who abruptly resigned as CEO of Home Depot in 2007, received exit pay of $210 million on top of his previous year's pay of $33 million. Nardelli, who was reputed to be a despot, failed over six years to raise the company's share price.

Nevertheless, defenders of CEO compensation say many large compensation packages are justified by stockholder gains. This clearly applies to former CEOs Lee Raymond of ExxonMobil and Jack Welch of General Electric. The price of their companies' stock rose significantly over long periods while they were in office. Steven Jobs of Apple received more than $700 million in compensation over the past decade, most in the vesting of restricted shares, but in that time shareholder value increased more than 1,000 percent. Arguably, these executives, and others, devised and executed the strategies responsible for rising equity. Their achievements were rewarded accordingly.

Third, some compensation committees fail to design and execute adequate compensation plans. Such plans are a complex mixture of art and science involving many choices and judgments.[78] Not a few committees choose badly. For example, when they base salaries and bonuses on median levels in a group of peer companies they often choose larger peers. Compensation tends to increase with company size. Since most committees set executive compensation at or above the median in the peer group, choosing larger peer companies increases pay. One study of 429 firms found that more than 96 percent set their CEO's median salary and bonus at or above the peer group benchmark. Because firms chose larger companies in their peer groups, this had the effect of raising chief executive total compensation an average of $1,191,020 over what it would have been if peer groups contained similarly sized companies.[79]

An example is Tootsie Roll Industries, which uses a peer group of 16 companies, all larger than Tootsie Roll, most substantially (see the box). Four have between 20 and 30 times Tootsie Roll's revenues. Using median compensation in the peer group as one element of compensation, Tootsie Roll paid its 90-year-old CEO Melvin Gordon $2.6 million in 2009.[80] Its board has only five directors, including Melvin Gordon and his wife, President Ellen Gordon, who was paid $2.5 million. The remaining three independent directors sit on the compensation committee.

Some compensation committees fall under the spell of a powerful CEO. Imagine a situation in which a committee with a well-constructed compensation plan is approached by such a CEO during a recession. The CEO's pay, which is based on incentives to achieve revenue growth, has fallen. "I'm working harder than ever," argues the CEO. "The economy is beyond my control and I deserve more than the current plan allows." The committee then gives in, making a onetime departure

[77] Thurm, "Oracle's Ellison: Pay King," p. A16.

[78] Robin A. Ferracone, *Fair Pay, Fair Play: Aligning Executive Performance and Pay* (San Francisco: Jossey-Bass, 2010), p. 35.

[79] Michael Faulkender and Jun Yang, "Inside the Black Box: The Role and Composition of Compensation Peer Groups," *Journal of Financial Economics,* May 2010, p. 268.

[80] Tootsie Roll Industries, Inc., *Proxy Statement,* March 26, 2010, pp. 11 and 16.

Tootsie Roll Industries Peer Group

Tootsie Roll Industries uses a study of compensation levels in other companies as a basis for determining the compensation of its top executives. In 2009 it picked these 16 companies as its peers in the snack and confectionary industries. Tootsie Roll had revenues of $496 million.

Peer Company	Annual Revenues (in millions)
Campbell Soup Company	$7,586
Dean Foods Company	$11,158
Del Monte Foods Company	$3,627
Diamond Foods, Inc.	$571
Flowers Foods, Inc.	$2,601
General Mills, Inc.	$14,691
H. J. Heinz Company	$10,148
Hershey Company	$5,299
J&J Snack Foods Corp.	$653
Kellogg Company	$12,587
Lancaster Colony Corp.	$1,051
Lance, Inc.	$918
McCormick & Company, Inc.	$3,192
Ralcorp Holdings, Inc.	$2,892
The J. M. Smucker Company	$3,758
TreeHouse Foods, Inc.	$1,512

Source: Tootsie Roll Industries, *Proxy Statement*, March 26, 2010, p. 11 and Tootsie Roll Industries, *Annual Report*, Form 10-K, March 1, 2010, exhibit 13, p. 2.

from its formal plan, and approves an award of several million stock options, currently of modest value, to the unhappy CEO. Years down the road, when the economy is better, this exception might result in princely sums that are wildly inconsistent with current performance. If pay is to correlate with performance, compensation policies must not only be designed well, but they must be consistently implemented.

Fourth, executives can manipulate their compensation. When annual salary and bonus are based on accounting measures such as net income, the CEO can take actions to maximize short-term profits. When compensation is based on stock options, the CEO can delay taking profits until a future year when options vest. Another problem with options has been *backdating*, or setting the exercise price of options at the price on a date before the date they were granted. As explained, an option gives the owner the right to buy stock in the future at a set price. Normally that price is the closing stock market price on the day of the grant. Backdating occurs when the company, at the time of the grant or retroactively, fixes the grant

backdating

Setting the exercise price of stock options at the price on a date before the date they were granted.

Backdating: A Hypothetical Example

1. On June 1, 2008, a CEO gets an option grant to purchase 1,000 shares of his company's stock which can be exercised in two years. The shares are priced at $30, the closing price on the New York Stock Exchange that day.

2. On June 1, 2010, when the options vest, the stock is selling for $29 a share. At this point the stock option is worthless.

3. The company decides to backdate the options to May 1, 2008, when the shares closed at $22.

4. The executive now decides to exercise the options, buying 1,000 shares from the company at $22 for $22,000, then selling them on the open market for $29 a share or $29,000. This nets a profit before taxes and brokerage fees of $7,000.

5. The value of the options is reported by the corporation as a cost, reducing net income. The lost value, in theory, reduces shareholder value.

date as a past date when the price of the stock was lower. In plain terms, companies search the past for troughs in share prices, then pretend the options were granted at these low points (see the above box).

A statistical analysis of options published in *The Wall Street Journal* found that at some companies they were granted repeatedly on days when share prices hit historic lows.[81] One example was a striking series of favorable coincidences at UnitedHealth Group, where 12 separate option grants went to William W. McGuire, its chairman and chief executive, on days when the stock fell to yearly or quarterly lows. According to the *Journal*, the odds against picking this series of dates by chance were 1 in 200 million, lower than the odds for winning the Powerball lottery. Further investigation found that over time McGuire received 44 million options, most of which were illegally backdated. He was forced to resign and return more than $600 million to the company.[82]

And fifth, disclosures of compensation policy are difficult to understand. Companies must disclose their compensation plans and the annual compensation of the top five executive officers to shareholders. They do this in the proxy statements mailed before annual meetings. The sections on compensation are lengthy. An average "discussion and analysis" is 25 to 30 pages of challenging prose filled with charts, columns of figures, and footnotes that invite a magnifying glass. IBM's most recent compensation discussion covered 53 pages with 30 charts and tables.

These discussions became more complex in 2006 when the SEC imposed more than 100 pages of new rules for their contents.[83] Although the rules were

---

[81] Charles Forcelle and James Bandler, "The Perfect Payday," *The Wall Street Journal,* March 18, 2006, p. A1.

[82] Eric Dash, "Former Chief Will Forfeit $418 Million," *The New York Times,* December 7, 2007, p. C1.

[83] See Securities and Exchange Commission, "Executive Compensation and Related Person Disclosure; Final Rule and Proposed Rule," 71 FR 53158, September 8, 2006; Securities and Exchange Commission, Executive Compensation Disclosure; Interim Final Rule," 71 FR 78338, December 29, 2006; and subsequent conforming amendments, RIN 3235-AI80.

intended to give stockholders more "clear, concise and meaningful information," they may have had a reverse effect.[84] Most companies now design their discussions to satisfy regulators rather than as a communication to the average shareholder, who might be inclined to stop reading after sentences such as the following.

> *United States Steel* The 2006 performance award vested in 2009 at a rate of 53.84 percent of the target based upon U.S. Steel's total shareholder return ranking at nearly the 27th percentile of the peer group for the preceding three-year performance period.[85]

> *Target Corporation* The amounts reported have been adjusted to eliminate service-based forfeiture assumptions and exclude reversals of amounts expensed but not reported in prior years' Summary Compensation Tables, both of which are used for financial reporting purposes.[86]

> *Suncor Energy* Cash payments are provided for annual remuneration during the notice period, for ESP options which, but for the Termination Event, would have become exercisable during the notice period, and for PSUs and RSUs that would pay out during the notice period based on a performance factor calculated at the date of termination, if applicable.[87]

Despite such examples, there is also some clarity in compensation discussions. A required "summary compensation table" gives the sum of annual salaries, bonuses, stock awards, pension value, and perquisites. However, a CEO's true compensation is a stream of value extending into the future that expands or contracts depending on periodic vesting of stock awards, the market value of those shares, incentive payments based on future corporate performance, and unusual events such as hostile mergers, which can trigger special "golden parachutes" for ousted executives. In such a living equation, a precise dollar figure for compensation is an elusive, moving target.

CONCLUDING OBSERVATIONS

In this chapter we discuss how shareholders, boards of directors, and managements interact in an imperfect system of corporate governance. Shareholders have the power to control managers, but they are scattered, passive, and largely absent any influence in practice. Boards of directors exist to monitor management for the shareholders, but they are frequently watchdogs without a bark, content to rubber-stamp the actions of management. Fortunately, most of the time management is trustworthy and proficient, giving stockholders a fair return on their investment.

[84] Securities and Exchange Commission, "Executive Compensation and Related Person Disclosure," 71 FR 53158, September 8, 2006, at 53160.

[85] United States Steel Corporation, *Notice of Annual Meeting of Stockholders and Proxy Statement,* April 27, 2010, p. 57.

[86] Target Corporation, *Proxy Statement,* April 23, 2009, p. 35.

[87] Suncor Energy Inc., *2010 Management Proxy Circular,* p. 29.

Recently, as in the cases of Enron and Lehman Brothers, failures of governance have had awful consequences. As in the past, Congress responded with new rules to strengthen governance by making directors more independent of management and giving shareholders a more powerful voice. So the governance system is evolving. Its formal checks and balances, having been slightly recalibrated, may now better protect corporate stakeholders.

High Noon at Hewlett-Packard

In the beginning there was a garage. As legend has it, this humble structure in Palo Alto, California, gave birth to giant Hewlett-Packard Company. It was there that Bill Hewlett and David Packard, both recent graduates of Stanford University, spent years tinkering before coming up with their first successful product, a precision oscillator. The two partners went public with their company in 1949.

As it grew they ran it using a homegrown philosophy called the HP Way. At its core the HP Way emphasized the worth of each employee. It inspired a nonhierarchical, decentralized, and participative company in which the creativity of each scientist and engineer was freed.

For many years Hewlett-Packard was the bright star in the Silicon Valley firmament. But as the twentieth century approached, it no longer blazed with innovation. Its aging co-founders' hands had lifted from the controls. Despite booming markets, its earnings were lackluster, its share price stagnant. Eventually, its board of directors saw the need for a new CEO.

CARLY FIORINA

The choice was Carleton S. Fiorina, called Carly by friends and associates. Fiorina was the first woman to head a corporation as large as Hewlett-Packard. She came from a position as a group president at Lucent Technologies. Her mandate from the HP board was to shake things up.

Immediately, Fiorina was a celebrity. It frustrated her when the media categorized her as "Carly Fiorina, female CEO" and reporters focused on her as a woman rather than on her mission at HP.[1]

From the first . . . both the language and the intensity of the coverage were different for me than for any other CEO. It was more personal, with much

commentary about my personality and my physical appearance, my dress, my hair or my shoes . . . There was a persistent rumor . . . that I'd built a pink marble bathroom in my office.[2]

She learned that her actions would be interpreted through a gender lens. After taking the helm at HP in 1999 she was called both a "bimbo" and a "bitch" in Silicon Valley chat rooms. When male CEOs fired people, they were called firm and commanding; she was labeled vengeful. Such interpretations made her job "infinitely more difficult."[3]

Fiorina believed that HP had been poorly managed for years. She set to work galvanizing its managers. One problem was that in the HP culture, decisions were decentralized. This was faithful to the HP Way, which taught that employees were the primary source of wisdom. But it slowed operations. Fiorina began to restructure processes so that everything went through her.

The first sign of trouble came in November 2000, when Lewis Platt, the former CEO who continued as chairman of the board, requested that Fiorina leave a board meeting so the other directors could talk.[4] He told them she was moving too fast with her plans for change.

Although the board affirmed its support for her, Fiorina was troubled. She responded by regularly inviting the directors to management meetings and setting up a Web site where they could find any data available to other HP employees. At board meetings she started going around the table asking each director to speak and state what action they would take on important issues. After each meeting she summarized points of agreement and disagreement in writing,

[1] Carly Fiorina, *Tough Choices: A Memoir* (New York: Portfolio, 2006), p. 171.

[2] Ibid., p. 172.

[3] Ibid., p. 173.

[4] Platt's resignation as CEO had been amicable. He would resign as chairman and retire from the company on December 31, 1999. Fiorina was then elected chairman.

EXHIBIT 1

The Hewlett-Packard Board in 1999

When Carly Fiorina arrived at Hewlett-Packard this was the board of directors. There were 13 members, 9 outside directors and, including herself, 4 inside directors. Four of the outside directors were related to the cofounders by birth or marriage. The board had five committees: Audit, Compensation, Executive, Finance and Investment, and Organization Review and Nominating. Each director was paid a $100,000 retainer, of which 75 percent was paid in HP stock. Individual directors were paid $5,000 for serving as committee chairs and a fee of $1,200 for each full board meeting attended.

Philip M. Condit, 57
Chairman and CEO, Boeing Company

Patricia C. Dunn, 46
Chair, Barclays Global Investors

John B. Fery, 69
Retired Chairman and CEO, Boise Cascade

Carleton S. Fiorina, 45
CEO, Hewlett-Packard Company

Jean-Paul G. Gimon, 63
General Representative, Credit Lyonnais and
son-in-law of HP cofounder William R. Hewlett

Sam Ginn, 62
Chairman, Vodafone AirTouch

Richard A. Hackborn, 62
Retired Executive Vice President, Hewlett-Packard

Walter B. Hewlett, 55
Chairman, The William and Flora Hewlett Foundation

George A. Keyworth, 60
Chairman, Progress & Freedom Association

Susan Packard Orr, 53
Chair, The David and Lucile Packard Foundation

David Woodly Packard, 58
Founder, Packard Humanities Institute

Lewis E. Platt, 58 (Chairman)
Former CEO, Hewlett-Packard

Robert P. Wayman, 54
Executive Vice President and Chief Financial Officer, Hewlett-Packard

along with action steps. This detail mentality may have irritated some directors.

TENSION ON THE BOARD

Fiorina had a strong view about the board's role in corporate governance. The directors were there to watch over management. Their duty was to see the big picture and ensure that major strategies were aligned with the stockholders' interests. However, the day-to-day work of running the enterprise was management's job—her job.

> The management team's job is to manage the company and produce results. A board meets six or eight times a year and cannot possibly know enough of the details of a business to manage it. And yet a board must represent the company's owners and this means knowing enough to ask the right questions.[5]

[5] Fiorina, *Tough Choices*, p. 210.

As time went on, she believed that some influential board members failed to draw a line between their broad oversight role and her daily management role. One was Richard Hackborn, a retired HP executive who had worked closely with the co-founders over the years. Another was George Keyworth, a former science adviser to President Ronald Reagan with a doctorate in physics. Both were technologists who, she felt, lacked appreciation for problems of execution. They were filled with suggestions and sometimes wanted to change projects and budgets in midstream. They met with employees. They even suggested that Fiorina fire certain managers.

Among other ideas, they proposed the acquisition of Compaq Computer Corporation. This was an opportunity to expand market share and achieve operating economies, but the combination would be difficult. It would require laying off tens of thousands of people in both companies and blending distinctive cultures.

After considerable debate, the full HP board unanimously agreed to the $22 billion acquisition. Just before the announcement in late 2001, HP's intentions were leaked to the media, obviously by a well-informed insider. Now HP was placed on the defensive. Reaction in the business press and among investors was immediately hostile due to the conventional wisdom that such huge combinations usually failed. HP's share price fell. The identity of the leaker was never discovered.

Then board member Walter Hewlett, the co-founder's son, surprised Fiorina by changing his mind and opposing the acquisition. He was soon joined by David Packard, son of the other co-founder. Together, the two controlled more than 16 percent of HP shares. Both disliked the dilution of their ownership in the company that would come from issuing millions of new shares for the acquisition.

Hewlett stopped attending board meetings and, with Packard, launched a battle to garner enough votes to stop the deal. He persuaded one board member, Sam Ginn, to change his mind. Ginn then came to a board meeting and pressed the other directors to reverse course. They held firm. Finally, after a bitter fight, HP's shareholders approved the acquisition by a slight 3 percent margin.[6] The merger was completed;

Carly Fiorina discusses the plan to buy Compaq at a 2001 news conference. Source: © AP Photo/Paul Sakuma.

however, a consequence of the internecine battle was that investors remained skeptical about it for years.

Fiorina's problems with the board continued. As time passed, expectations from the Compaq merger were far from being met. Earnings targets were missed. HP's share price languished. The board was unhappy. Fiorina continued to believe that the board was intruding on her role as chief executive by nosing into operational details.

A change on the board came when two CEOs, Sam Ginn and Phil Condit, retired in early 2004. That left only two other CEOs with operating experience. These were the kind of board members most valued by Fiorina because she felt that they respected her management prerogatives. It proved difficult to recruit others in their mold, however, because after the passage of the Sarbanes-Oxley Act in 2002 the leaders of large corporations cut back on outside board memberships to focus more on time-consuming governance requirements in their own firms.

Then there was the abrasion of the board's technology committee. It was formed in 2002 at the suggestion

---

[6] A week after the meeting Walter Hewlett filed a lawsuit in the Delaware Chancery Court alleging that HP had bought the vote of Deutsche Bank. In April, the court dismissed the lawsuit and Hewlett did not further contest the vote.

of director Tom Perkins. Perkins had moved to the HP board from the Compaq board in 2001. He was a formidable presence, combining a long history at HP with a keen mind for strategy. He had been hired by Hewlett and Packard in 1957 and ran the company's research labs for more than a decade until they put him in charge of the new computer division. Perkins built the HP computer business, then left in 1972 to co-found what became the nation's leading venture capital firm, Kleiner, Perkins, Caufield & Byers.

This partnership provided seed capital for Silicon Valley start-ups. Its spectacular successes were Genentech, AOL, Netscape, Amazon, and Google. Perkins became a billionaire, soon adopting an extraordinary lifestyle of mansions and fast cars. His sailing ship, the *Maltese Falcon* is, at 289 feet, the longest private yacht in the world. After his first wife died of cancer, he married, then divorced, celebrity romance novelist Danielle Steel. According to Perkins, they remain deeply in love, but they cannot live together because "it would be easier to merge General Motors and General Electric. You know, we lead big, complicated lives."[7]

Perkins was joined on the technology committee by George Keyworth and Dick Hackborn, the inventor of laser printing. All three were fascinated with scientific details and soaring possibilities for new products. All three were dominating directors. Under their lead, the committee began to function as a board-within-a-board. It often met the day before a regular board meeting, and its agenda ranged over all aspects of HP's business. It was a breeding ground for projects and suggestions. Most of them were rejected by Fiorina, who believed that the "disruptive" technologists lacked appreciation for the obstacles to achieving financial results from their ideas. In her view, "They thought because they understood technology, they understood everything."[8] As their suggestions were spurned, the committee members grew restive.

Another conflict also arose. The technologists became impatient with director Patricia Dunn's leadership of the audit committee. Dunn was a determined force. The proof was in her career. She grew up in Las Vegas, where her mother was a model and showgirl and her father booked entertainment at hotels. When she was 11, her father died. When the time for college

HP Director Tom Perkins at the window of his San Francisco office in 2006. Source: © AP Photo/Eric Risberg.

came, she won a scholarship to the University of Oregon, but had to drop out and work as a cook and housekeeper to support herself and her mother. Later she attended the University of California, Berkeley on a scholarship, making a daily three-bus commute and graduating with a journalism degree.[9]

Soon she took a temporary secretarial position at Wells Fargo Bank in San Francisco. After the bank was acquired by Barclays Global Investors, she rose to become that company's CEO from 1995 to 2002. She came to the HP board in 1998. In 2001 she was diagnosed with breast cancer and a year later with melanoma, causing her to step down as CEO. She retained her position as chairman of the board at Barclays.

On the audit committee she focused on governance procedures. She was methodical and organized. Keyworth and others saw an obsession with details that blocked her appreciation of the big picture. Her strength was the minutia of legal compliance, not the spirited, freewheeling strategy debate the technologists thrived on. They worried that the board was moving in the wrong direction. It needed an infusion of imagination.

Perkins felt it had become what he called a "compliance board," or a board focused on obeying laws

[7] "Conversation with Tom Perkins," *The Charlie Rose Show,* December 5, 2007, transcript, p. 12.

[8] Fiorina, *Tough Choices,* p. 280.

[9] George Anders and Alan Murray, "Inside Story of Feud That Plunged HP into Crisis," *The Sunday Times,* October 15, 2006, p. B18.

and rules, where meeting time was consumed with boring hours of reports by lawyers and committees. In contrast, Perkins wanted a "guidance board," or a board of knowledgeable insiders and industry experts that takes an active role in the company, not only reviewing strategy, but becoming deeply involved in its management.[10] A compliance board plodded along checking boxes. A guidance board could better jolt HP from its slumber.

Perkins and his technology committee colleagues wanted to add Silicon Valley friends with scientific and entrepreneurial backgrounds to the board. Fiorina resisted these nominations. She continued to favor candidates with big-company operating experience, ideally, CEOs of other large corporations who were more likely to share her view that the board should stay at arms' length from management. Tension over the role of the board and its composition hung in the air. It did not ease when Tom Perkins retired in 2003 after reaching the mandatory retirement age for HP directors of 72.

Over the next year the directors grew more troubled by Fiorina's performance. Revenues and profits were climbing, largely because the Compaq merger made HP much bigger. However, the merger was not living up to expectations. Fiorina continued to be a media celebrity. She frequently traveled for speeches and appearances. Keyworth, Dunn, and others believed she was distracted from, even unattracted to, the relentless, draining hard work of running a big company. Her subordinates were frustrated. Talented managers were quitting. HP had lost market share in computers to Dell and in network servers to both Dell and IBM. Its profit margins in key business segments were falling. HP's share price was just over $40 when Fiorina was named CEO in 1999. Through 2004 it traded below $20. She had centralized management so that almost every decision went through her, and she resisted efforts by board members to reach into the management process. She failed to communicate with them except at regularly scheduled meetings. They regarded her as imperious.[11]

Late in the year, Keyworth led a movement to bring Perkins back, arguing that the board needed another member with technology expertise. He told Fiorina that Perkins missed being on the board. She countered that his return was a breach of HP's governance policy. In the post-Enron climate of reform, disregard of the retirement rule would look bad. Moreover, what the board really needed was another big-company chief executive with operating expertise. Yet in a momentary lapse of resolve, she agreed to Perkin's return. It was a slip she would regret.

FIORINA'S FALL

Perkins was invited to attend a January 2005 board meeting as a visitor. His official reappointment would take longer to meet the letter of HP's governance policy. However, several members requested that the board vote immediately to appoint him. Fiorina countered that his formal confirmation must wait. He had not studied statements of operating results that needed approval that day. If all voting directors were not well versed on the financials, requirements of the Sarbanes-Oxley Act would be sacrificed. She got her way.

Although not yet officially appointed, Perkins nevertheless stayed in the meeting and was immediately outspoken. He suggested specific actions, including acquisition of another software firm and altering the roles of certain top executives. Fiorina rebuffed the advice, telling Perkins and his allies that it was her prerogative as CEO to make such decisions. According to Perkins, "She made it very clear . . . that our opinions were less than welcome on operational and organizational specifics."[12]

As the meeting wore on, the board proposed a reorganization to delegate some of Fiorina's duties to other executives. She opposed the plan. If the board held her accountable for results, then it should let her make her own decisions about how to achieve them. But by the end of the meeting she had agreed to combine two product groups under a new manager and yielded to ground rules for evaluating other changes over the coming months.

Days later, *The Wall Street Journal* published a front-page story about the meeting quoting "people close to the situation," phrasing that could refer only to two or more directors.[13] According to the article,

---

[10] Tom Perkins, "The 'Compliance' Board," *The Wall Street Journal,* March 2, 2007, p. A11.

[11] Anthony Bianco, *The Big Lie: Spying, Scandal, and Ethical Collapse at Hewlett-Packard* (New York: Public Affairs, 2010), pp. 105–06.

[12] Tom Perkins, *Valley Boy: The Education of Tom Perkins* (New York: Gotham Books, 2007), p. 4.

[13] Pui-Wing Tam, "Hewlett-Packard Board Considers a Reorganization," *The Wall Street Journal,* January 24, 2005, p. A1.

the HP board was still supportive of Fiorina, but very concerned about the company's ragged financial performance, an exodus of managers to competing firms, and weak market performance. Of Fiorina, one source said she "has tremendous abilities," but "she shouldn't be running everything every day. She is very hands on and that slows things down."[14]

"It is hard to convey how violated I felt," said Fiorina.[15] This leak was a profound breach of confidentiality. If directors are to fulfill their oversight role, they must be able to trust the others present. If they fear that remarks will become public they might not engage in the open, honest, and unreserved deliberations that best serve stockholders. She immediately convened a conference call with the entire board. After scolding them for the breach, she asked the board's nominating and governance committee to investigate. It engaged an attorney to interview each board member, not only to ask about the leak, but to solicit their views about the overall effectiveness of the board and how to improve its functioning.

Fiorina was certain that Tom Perkins and his technology committee friend Keyworth were the leakers because they were the ones pushing hardest for the reorganization described in the article.[16] In the investigation, only Perkins admitted speaking to a reporter, insisting that he had not initiated the story, but responded only when he was called to confirm its contents. He claimed he had only tried to ward off some damaging details. No other director admitted involvement. The attorney's report also described the board as "dysfunctional" due to personality conflicts and the tendency of a few dominating members to divert the agenda to long discussions on side topics.

After this, the directors stopped communicating with Fiorina. A special February 8 board meeting was set up in a hotel to keep it out of the media. When Fiorina arrived Patricia Dunn immediately called the group to order, though Fiorina, as chairman of the board, would ordinarily preside. Dunn asked if Fiorina had anything to say. Fiorina read a 30-minute statement defining and defending her role as CEO. It was met with silence. According to Dunn, "The basic message the board took from it was, 'You guys don't

know what you're doing.'"[17] She was asked to leave the room.

After she left, the directors broke into "turbulent" debate, with Perkins and Keyworth pushing hard for her removal.[18] Three hours later, a majority formed behind Fiorina's immediate replacement. She was summoned. On her return, only two board members remained at the conference table, Dunn and Robert Knowling, the retired CEO of Simdesk Technologies. "The Board has decided to make a change," said Knowling. "I'm very sorry, Carly."[19] She left with a bonus package of $21 million, HP shares worth $18.2 million, and a pension of $200,000 a year.[20] Yet in that hour her star fell to earth. She felt devastated.[21]

PATRICIA DUNN ASCENDANT

In the following days, the board named Robert P. Wayman, HP's long-time chief financial officer, to be interim CEO and picked Patricia Dunn to be its non-executive chairman. In this position Dunn would preside at board meetings but would not play an active role in managing the company. Separation of the board chairmanship from the CEO position was Tom Perkins' idea and reflected his belief that a strong board should not be dominated by the same person who is the company's top manager. It also gave the board more power over management.

Dunn's influence had risen during the period when Perkins and Keyworth emerged as the leading antagonists toward Fiorina. At first Dunn was neutral, but at some point she moved over to join the two in their campaign for change.[22] In addition, Dunn had been diagnosed the year before with advanced ovarian cancer and endured surgery and chemotherapy. Both Perkins and Keyworth had lost wives to cancer. They were sympathetic and liked her fortitude. Perkins even proposed that Dunn receive an

---

[14] Ibid., p. 1.

[15] Fiorina, *Tough Choices,* p. 290.

[16] James B. Stewart, "The Kona Files," *The New Yorker,* February 19–26, 2007, p. 155.

[17] Quoted in Bianco, *The Big Lie: Spying, Scandal, and Ethical Collapse at Hewlett-Packard,* p. 120.

[18] Perkins, *Valley Boy,* p. 6.

[19] Fiorina, *Tough Choices,* p. 303.

[20] Pui-Wing Tam and Joann S. Lublin, "H-P Gave Fiorina $1.57 Million in Bonus Payments Last Year," *The Wall Street Journal,* February 14, 2005, p. B2; and Carol J. Loomis, "How the HP Board KO'd Carly," *Fortune,* March 7, 2005, p. 99.

[21] Fiorina, *Tough Choices,* p. 303.

[22] Stewart, "The Kona Files," p. 156.

The Hewlett-Packard Board in Early 2005

This is the board that fired Carly Fiorina on February 8. One director, Sanford Litvak, had abruptly resigned on February 2. He was replaced on February 7 by Tom Perkins. Since 1999 the board had shrunk to nine members due largely to resignations by representatives of the Hewlett and Packard families in protest over the Compaq merger. Finding replacements in the new governance climate created by the Sarbanes-Oxley Act proved difficult. By now each director was paid a $200,000 retainer. The board had voted in 2004 to double its compensation. Directors who chaired committees were paid an additional $10,000.

Lawrence T. Babbio, Jr., 60
Vice Chairman and President, Verizon Communications

Patricia C. Dunn, 51 (Non-executive Chairman)
Chair, Barclays Global Investors

Richard A. Hackborn, 67
Retired Executive Vice President, Hewlett-Packard

George A. Keyworth, 65
Chairman, Progress & Freedom Association

Robert E. Knowling, Jr., 49
Former Chairman and CEO, Simdesk Technologies

Thomas J. Perkins, 73
Partner, Kleiner Perkins Caufield & Byers

Robert L. Ryan, 61
Senior Vice President and CFO, Medtronic

Lucille S. Salhany, 58
President and CEO, JHMedia

Robert P. Wayman, 59
Interim CEO, Hewlett-Packard

additional $100,000 for serving as chairman. She declined to accept it.

The immediate task for the board was to find a new CEO. Dunn, Perkins, and Keyworth headed the search. Within two months they hired Mark Hurd from NCR Corporation. Meanwhile, seven directors had approached Dunn, telling her that identifying the source of leaks and ending them was critical to maintaining trust and integrity on the board. All told, there had been 10 unauthorized leaks. They asked her to make renewed investigation a top priority.[23] She opened a new one and named it Project Kona after a spot in Hawaii where she and her husband own a vacation home.

[23] U.S. House of Representatives, Subcommittee on Oversight and Investigations of the Committee on Energy and Commerce, *Hewlett-Packard's Pretexting Scandal,* 109th Congress, 2d Sess., September 28, 2006, pp. 90, 129.

As the investigation began, other events eroded the comity between Dunn and Perkins. Perkins believed that since he had initiated her elevation to the chairmanship she would be deferential toward him. In this he erred. Early on he came to a board meeting with a sweeping agenda of strategy issues he wanted discussed. Dunn, however, had retreated into her armor of focus on details. She announced her discovery of many inconsistencies between HP's director's handbook and its bylaws. The meeting would be about harmonizing the two. Perkins was taken aback. This button-down approach assaulted his venture capitalist DNA. He had not even read the handbook and had no intention ever of doing so.

Vacancies existed on the board. As chairman of the nominating and governance committee Perkins found nominees, but Dunn was lukewarm. Again a difference of philosophy was the cause. Perkins submitted the names of Silicon Valley comrades who shared his values. Dunn wanted top executives from large, established corporations. When she suggested the president of PepsiCo, Perkins mocked him as "Sugar Daddy."[24]

Other abrasions angered Perkins, including a comment by Dunn in the presence of Hewlett-Packard managers that his new novel, *Sex and the Single Zillionaire,* was not her kind of reading.[25] The two frequently quarreled. However, he thought they had an agreement that if the leak investigation bore fruit, the matter would be handled by the two of them talking privately with the offending director. He wanted to extract an apology and a promise never again to talk with the press, then close the matter and go on. Again, he misjudged.

In the background, the leak investigation continued. One day the head of the Boston security firm told Dunn and HP's general counsel that his investigators had gotten the phone numbers of reporters who had written stories based on leaks. They were now going to obtain phone records using a technique called "pretexting." Investigators would call phone companies, pretending to be the reporters, and ask for records of their calls. Then they would get the directors' phone records the same way and check for calls back and forth. The HP counsel asked if this was legal. The security firm manager said yes. When the phone records were obtained, however, no evidence incriminated any director. The investigation had failed.

Nothing further was done until early in 2006 when another leak appeared. A CNET reporter published a story about the company's annual management retreat in January 2006. In it "a source" was quoted as saying that "[b]y the time the lectures were done at 10 p.m., we were pooped and went to bed."[26] The story also revealed that HP was considering certain kinds of software acquisitions.

Because of this new leak, Dunn launched a second round of investigation labeled Kona II. This time it was run by an HP lawyer with in-house investigators. Again, pretexting was used to obtain the phone records of both reporters and HP directors.

Patricia Dunn at a 2005 news conference. Source: © AP Photo/Paul Sakuma.

Comparing these phone records, they discovered two brief calls between Dawn Kawamoto, the reporter who wrote the January story, and director George Keyworth.

Trying to catch the conspirators in the act, they launched a sting operation. They fabricated a disgruntled HP manager who sent Kawamoto fake e-mails offering to reveal something sensational. A tracking program was embedded, so that if she sought to forward them to Keyworth or another director for confirmation the investigators would know. However, she simply invited the employee to call her. The HP investigators also staked out the homes of Kawamoto and Keyworth. No contact between them was observed.

In weekly meetings the investigative team kept Dunn informed. Questions about the legality of the tactics being used were raised by former police officers in HP's security department, but company attorneys told Dunn that all actions were legal. She said, "Throughout the process I asked and was assured—by both H-P's internal security department and the company's top lawyers, both verbally and in writing—that the work being undertaken to investigate and discover these leaks was legal, proper and consistent with the H-P way of performing investigations."[27]

24 Stewart, "The Kona Files," p. 157.

25 Tom Perkins, *Sex and the Single Zillionaire* (New York: Harper, 2007). Perkins had given Dunn an early draft of the book.

26 Dawn Kawamoto, "HP Outlines Long-Term Strategy," CNET News.com, January 23, 2006.

27 Patricia Dunn, "The H-P Investigation," *The Wall Street Journal,* October 11, 2006, p. A14.

Dunn and Perkins continued to abrade each other. After the regular board meeting in March, Dunn requested that Perkins and two others remain in the meeting room for a moment. The two disagree on what happened next. According to Perkins, Dunn told the others that he was out to get her and burst into tears. Dunn denies the statement, saying she told Perkins that his disruptive outbursts in meetings were counterproductive.[28]

Results of the leak investigation were revealed at the May 18, 2006, board meeting. That morning, just before the board convened, director Robert Ryan, an executive with Medtronic, who was now chair of the audit committee, met with Keyworth. When asked about Kawamoto's CNET article, Keyworth admitted to having lunch with her and discussing the retreat. He considered it a friendly lunch, not a press contact, and said he was surprised by the article. He felt that it was positive and harmless and told Ryan that if anyone had just asked him, he would have divulged the conversation. He was amazed to learn that this piece was the focus of a major investigation.

Meanwhile, Dunn took Perkins aside moments before the meeting and informed him about Keyworth. When she said the matter had to go before the full board, he was startled and irate. In the meeting, Ryan summarized a report from the HP lawyer in charge of the investigation. Keyworth was contrite. "I apologize for any discussion I had with the reporter in question that may have resulted in any of my colleagues on this board losing trust with me."[29] He added, "I would have told you all about this. Why didn't you ask? I thought I was just helping the company through a rough patch with the press. Aren't directors supposed to do that?"[30] He was asked to leave the room.

With Keyworth outside, Perkins spoke up. He argued that his friend's intention was innocent and the leak inconsequential. He believed that once again Dunn was focused on the trivia of process, "the 'sin' of the leak itself," rather than its substance.[31] When a motion was made to ask for Keyworth's resignation, Perkins grew "incandescent," and directed most of his fury at Dunn. After 90 minutes of dispute a vote was taken by secret ballot. The motion passed. At

that, Perkins said simply, "I resign," and walked out.[32] When Keyworth reentered he was asked to resign, but refused, noting that he had been elected by HP share owners and his legal obligation was to serve until they removed him.

THE END OF DUNN

It was Perkins' final meeting as an HP director, but he was not through with the company. He sought to have the minutes of the meeting rewritten to include his remarks that the investigatory tactics were illegal. When he discovered that his home telephone records had been deceitfully obtained, he wrote a letter to the board saying the investigation had violated the law. He demanded that it forward a copy of the letter to the Securities and Exchange Commission. When his demands were rejected, he instructed his lawyer to contact not only the SEC, but U.S. Attorney's offices in Manhattan and San Francisco, the California Attorney General, the Federal Communications Commission, and the Federal Trade Commission. This caused an explosion in the press, removing the cloak from an investigation that could not survive the light.

Within months, Dunn agreed to step down as chairman. Individual board members told her they did not believe she was involved in anything improper or illegal. But she had become a lightning rod for criticism of HP and its board.

CEO Mark Hurd and other directors urged her to remain on the board as a member. Soon, however, it was plain that she would be a major distraction. Finally, the board asked her to resign and she did so on September 22. She was asked not to speak at the press conference where her retirement was announced. Two HP attorneys who played a leading role in the investigations also resigned.

The next week, Dunn testified at a congressional hearing where she was flayed by members of the House Committee on Energy and Commerce. "What were you thinking?" asked Rep. John Dingell (D-Michigan).[33] "[I]s all of this really the HP way?" inquired Rep. Jan Schakowsky (D-Illinois).[34] In her testimony Dunn repeatedly fell back on assurances by

---

[28] Stewart, "The Kona Files," p. 162.

[29] Ibid, p. 163.

[30] Perkins, *Valley Boy,* p. 15.

[31] Ibid., p. 15.

[32] Ibid., p. 16.

[33] U.S. House of Representatives, Subcommittee on Oversight and Investigations of the Committee on Energy and Commerce, *Hewlett-Packard's Pretexting Scandal,* p. 13.

[34] Ibid., p. 96.

HP lawyers and managers that the investigation was legal, at one point saying, "I do not accept personal responsibility for what happened."[35]

On October 4, she was charged by the State of California with four felony counts of wire fraud, identity theft, and conspiracy, charges that carried a potential sentence of 12 years in a state prison. Three investigators were also charged. All pleaded not guilty. Dunn's defense was that she had consistently questioned investigation tactics and been assured that they were legal. Therefore, state prosecutors could not prove she intended to commit a crime, a necessary factor for conviction. Moreover, no federal or state law was specific in making pretexting a crime.[36] Five months later a California Superior Court judge dropped the case against her and agreed to dismiss charges against the others in exchange for 96 hours of community service.[37] Dunn's health was a factor in the judge's decision, but the main reason was the tenuous nature of the charges.

Whether Dunn intended to commit a crime or not, Perkins is convinced that she pursued the investigation on the likelihood that he and Keyworth would be incriminated and forced to resign, thereby removing two of her political enemies. He states that at one point he decided to seek her resignation as chair, but claims he was talked out of it by Keyworth.[38] In the end he brought her down, doing on the outside what he did not do on the inside. His actions put Hewlett-Packard at the center of a scandal, made it the subject of late-night jokes, and ended careers. As a director, he was unruly, challenging, and stubborn. Those who would condemn him, however, should entertain this question. What would happen if he were put in a time machine and returned to the 1990s for service on Enron's board?

Questions

1. Over the time covered here, did Hewlett-Packard's board of directors fulfill its duties to the company's share owners? Explain how it met or did not meet basic duties.

2. What different perspectives on the role of the board are revealed in this story?

3. Was Carly Fiorina treated fairly by the board? Why or why not?

4. Were the leak investigations overseen by Patricia Dunn useful and important? Were they ethical?

5. Should George Keyworth have been asked to resign? Why or why not?

6. How do you appraise the behavior of Tom Perkins? Was he a model director or a renegade?

7. What actions could have been taken to improve the functioning of the HP board?

8. Did gender play any role in the fortunes of Fiorina and Dunn?

[35] Ibid., p. 120.

[36] As a result of the scandal, Congress passed the Telephone Records and Privacy Protection Act of 2006 (P. L. 109-476) to criminalize pretexting. More than a dozen states have passed similar laws.

[37] Matt Richtel, "H.P. Chairwoman and 3 Others Cleared in Spying Case," *The New York Times*, March 15, 2007, p. C1.

[38] Perkins, *Valley Boy,* p. 15.

CPSIA information can be obtained
at www.ICGtesting.com
Printed in the USA
FFOW02n1411220714
6469FF